Senior Editor: David Shafer
Assistant Editor: Lisamarie Brassini
Editor-in-Chief: Natalie Anderson
Editorial Assistant: Christopher Stogdill
Marketing Manager: Tammy Wederbrand
Production Editor: Judith Leale
Managing Editor: Dee Josephson
Manufacturing Buyer: Diane Peirano
Manufacturing Supervisor: Arnold Vila
Manufacturing Manager: Vincent Scelta
Design Manager: Patricia Smythe
Senior Designer: Ann France
Cover Design and Cover Art: Ann France
Back Cover Photo: Courier-Journal (Louisville, KY)

Copyright © 1998, 1995 by Prentice-Hall, Inc.
A Simon & Schuster Company
Upper Saddle River, New Jersey 07458

Earlier editions, entitled *Collective Bargaining and Labor Relations: Cases, Practice, and Law,* copyright © 1991, 1988, 1985.

Library of Congress Cataloging-in-Publication Data
Carrell, Michael R.
    Labor relations and collective bargaining : cases, practice, and
law / Michael R. Carrell and Christina Heavrin.—5th ed.
        p. cm.
    Includes index.
    ISBN 0-13-768607-2
    1. Collective labor agreements—United States. 2. Collective
bargaining—United States. 3. Industrial relations—United States.
I. Heavrin, Christina. II. Title.
KF3408.C37 1997
344.7301′89—DC21   97-24221
                                                    CIP

Prentice-Hall International (UK) Limited, London
Prentice-Hall of Australia Pty. Limited, Sydney
Prentice-Hall Canada, Inc., Toronto
Prentice-Hall Hispanoamericana, S.A., Mexico
Prentice-Hall of India Private Limited, New Delhi
Prentice-Hall of Japan, Inc., Tokyo
Simon & Schuster Asia Pte. Ltd., Singapore
Editora Prentice-Hall do Brasil, Ltda., Rio de Janeiro

Printed in the United States of America

10 9 8 7 6 5 4 3 2 1

For additional information, visit the Web sites of these **labor organizations** featured in this text.

AFL-CIO
http://135.145.28.139:80/

AFSCME (American Federation of State, County, and Municipal Employees)
http://www.afscme.org

American Federation of Teachers
http://www.aft.org//index.htm

American Federation of Television and Radio Artists
http://www.ios.com/~ayfilm/union/aftra.html

American Postal Workers Union
http://www.apwu.org

Communication Workers of America
http://www.3cwa-union.org/home/

International Association of Machinists and Aerospace Workers
http://www.iamaw.org/

International Union of Bricklayers
http://www.bacweb.org

International Brotherhood of Boilermakers
http://www.boilermakers.com

International Brotherhood of Electrical Workers
http://ourworld,compuserv.com/homepages/ibewnet/

International Brotherhood of Teamsters, Chauffeurs, and Warehousemen
http://www.teamster.org

Laborers' International Union of North America
http://www.liuna.org/

Major League Baseball Players Association
http://www.bigleaguers.com/

National Air Traffic Controllers Organization
http://home.natca.org/natca

National Education Association
http://www.nea.org/

Screen Actors Guild
http://sag.com/

Service Employees International Union
http://www.seiu.org

United Auto Workers
http://www.uaw.org/

United Farm Workers of America
http://www.latinoweb.com/ufw/

United Food and Commercial Workers
http://www.ufcw.org

United Mine Workers
http://www.access.digex.net/~miner/

United Paperworkers International Union
http://ourworld.compuserv.com/homepages/dlugdon/

Unit
http://

LABOR RELATIONS AND COLLECTIVE BARGAINING

Cases, Practice, and Law

Michael R. Carrell

Dean, College of Business
Morehead State University

Christina Heavrin, J.D.

Deputy Mayor
City of Louisville, Kentucky

 PRENTICE HALL, Upper Saddle River, New Jersey 07458

This book is dedicated to

Archie Carrell, a distinguished labor negotiator
*   and father*
Myrtle Carrell, a "Top Sergeant"
*   and devoted mother*
*   and*
Colleen Sue, a loving wife and mother, and talented
*   decorator*
Shari Diane, my daughter who has found
*   happiness*
Amber Maureen, my "Master Storyteller"
*   and leaf collection girl*
Alexis Savannah, my "Special Girl" and car show
*   winner*
AnnaBelle Michael, my "Doodle Bug"

**   Michael R. Carrell**

My husband and best friend, Mike Ward,
*   and my sons, Jasper and Kevin,*
*   for giving me the space to complete this book*
*   and*
In loving memory of Alexander Ward

**   Christina Heavrin**

Brief Contents

Contents

PART TWO

Cost of Labor Contracts   228

PART FIVE

Preface

The changing relationships in the workplace have taken their toll on the traditional collective bargaining and labor relations processes. Although the nation's laws still protect collective bargaining as a way to promote commerce, the realities of a changing economy, a decrease in union membership, an increase in government regulations, and a diverse workforce have complicated labor relations.

Drawing upon over 50 years of experience in negotiating, labor law, and teaching, we have developed a text for readers who need a practical working knowledge of labor relations and collective bargaining terms, practices, and law. This text introduces the students to collective bargaining and labor relations with an emphasis on the "real world" situations they will face on the job. Sections of actual labor agreements as well as arbitration cases and decisions of the National Labor Relations Board (NLRB) and the courts illustrate and emphasize contemporary issues of collective bargaining and labor relations. In addition, experts in the fields of labor law and arbitration have contributed "tips" on how the concepts learned can actually be applied.

NEW IN THIS 5TH EDITION

- An experienced, nationally recognized labor arbitrator, Daniel F. Jennings of Texas A&M University, provides a thorough revision of chapter 11 "Grievance and Disciplinary Procedures" and chapter 12 "The Arbitration Process." These revised chapters include recent cases on contemporary labor issues including outsourcing at work, insubordination, absenteeism, and workplace violence.
- Internet support to provide monthly updates on changes in labor news and significant court decisions. At the end of each chapter the following icon refers readers to the Prentice Hall web page:

TAKE IT TO THE NET

We invite you to visit the Carrell/Heavrin page on the Prentice Hall Web site at:

http://www.prenhall.com/carrellr

for this chapter's World Wide Web exercise.

- Coverage of the historic 1996–99 UAW agreements with Ford, GM, and Chrysler that broke new ground in areas such as profit sharing, job security, and outsourcing.
- Thorough coverage of collective bargaining in professional sports including the 1994–95 baseball strike (chapter 3) and the 1996 umpires' union action over the Baltimore Orioles and Sandy Alomar incident (chapter 3).

- A simulation in collective bargaining by Smith, Carrell, and Golden (Prentice Hall, 1996) is referenced at the end of appropriate chapters by the following icon:

If you are using Smith/Carrell/Golden *Collective Bargaining Simulated, 4E,* with this text, please refer to the following:

(Each chapter's icon has different information for cross-referencing to the simulation.)

CONTENT ISSUES

This text begins with a treatment of the historical and legal basis for labor relations and collective bargaining in the United States. An expanded labor history section adds to the students' understanding of the collective bargaining process in the United States by profiling both the people and the events that shaped this process. In addition, the student is exposed to the economic realities in the past, present, and future that have and will affect the workplace. Changes in the application of labor laws due to court decisions, NLRB rulings, and changes in the environment of union and management relations are covered throughout the text and include the latest decisions and rulings, as well as analysis of what these changes might mean in the workplace. The text also includes ways of estimating wage and benefit items and computerized costing methods. It describes negotiating techniques and covers items in depth, giving students direct exposure to how negotiating theory is applied in actual situations. There are detailed explanations of contract enforcement—grievance and arbitration procedures.

PEDAGOGICAL FORMAT

A student-oriented chapter format was designed to integrate theory with the "bread and butter" issues at the core of most actual negotiations. This integration, which includes the following material, provides a sense of how issues in the real world are resolved:

- **Labor News.** These chapter-opening articles summarize current labor-relations activities. The purpose of the articles is to help students relate current events to the day-to-day labor practices discussed in the chapter.
- **Chapter Cases.** Several short cases, which include the decisions of the arbitrator or judge, illustrate those points discussed within each chapter, while bridging the gap between theory and practice.
- **Tips from the Experts.** In chapters 4 to 9, labor lawyers answer questions about the collective bargaining process and point out pitfalls for employers and employees involved in the labor relations field. In chapters 10 to 12, a labor arbitrator gives tips on how employers and employees can avoid labor disputes.
- **Labor Profiles.** In several chapters, a number of profiles of labor leaders or of innovations in the labor relation process help the student understand the concepts in the chapter and the history of labor relations in the United States.

Chapter-end materials include:

- **Case Studies.** Two case studies help students understand both sides of the issues. The case studies describe the facts and lawsuits, but actual decisions are not provided. These cases are taken from court and NLRB decisions and allow students to play the role of the arbitrator or judge in deciding cases.
- **Key Terms and Concepts.** A list of the important terms and concepts discussed in the chapter, including much of the vocabulary unique to labor relations. The student should be able to recognize, define, and discuss the terms after completing the chapter. Key terms appear in **boldface** and are defined in context.
- **Review Questions.** Straightforward questions that focus on the major areas covered. If the review questions present any difficulty, the student should reread the appropriate material.
- **Experiential Exercises.** Two exercises at the end of each chapter: one for individual work and one as a group activity. The exercises require students to apply what they have learned from the chapter to practical and realistic situations. Many of the exercises require the students to go outside the classroom and to visit worksites and/or to contact union and management representatives in the community for information.

A **Glossary** of all key terms presented in the text is included at the end of the book.

Texts of Major Labor Legislation

The text of the National Labor Relations Act and the Labor-Management Relations Act, as amended, is included at the end of this book to provide a ready reference to these important documents.

This text treats comprehensively the environment of labor relations, the activity of collective bargaining, and the need for administrating an agreement after it has been signed. The text also explores some of the labor relations issues in the public sector, the impact diversity in the workplace, and how international labor relations are developing.

COMPRE-HENSIVE COVERAGE

    Part One traces the development of collective bargaining. Chapter 1 focuses on the workforce from the roots of the American labor movement through the predictions of "Workforce 2000." This chapter explores both the causes and the solutions to the challenges unions face in representing workers. Chapter 2 takes the student through the development of the workplace and how that development has affected modern labor relations. Chapter 3, on work rules, discusses the laws that led to and finally established the collective bargaining process. The chapter also covers the structure of labor unions and explores how collective bargaining in major league sports is carried out.

    Part Two examines the collective bargaining process. Chapter 4 discusses provisions of the National Labor Relations Act, how bargaining units are formed and chosen, and the types of units in the workforce. The rights of unions to represent members as well as the obligations of unions to their members is also explored in this chapter. Chapter 5 discusses what conduct is construed as an unfair labor practice. Chapter 6 deals with labor agreements, negotiating techniques, and overcoming an impasse.

Part Three covers the costs of collective bargaining agreements. Chapter 7 deals with wages and the different ways wages are negotiated and paid under collective bargaining agreements. Chapter 8 looks at the benefits negotiated in most contracts, from vacations to health care coverage. Chapter 9 presents issues of job security and employee seniority.

Part Four presents the operational processes involved in enforcing collective bargaining agreements. Chapter 10 explores the basic principles of collective bargaining agreements, methods of enforcement, the NLRB and court intervention, grievance and arbitration procedures, and pressure tactics. Chapter 11 defines individual rights under collective bargaining agreements and presents widely used procedures to resolve grievances between employers and employees. Chapter 12 expands these issues to describe the arbitration process that generally follows an unsuccessful grievance procedure.

Part Five covers some additional issues relating to collective bargaining. Chapter 13 compares how unions with public-sector employees handle procedures for resolving disagreements, settling impasses, and administering contracts in the public sector. Chapter 14 explains civil rights and equal pay legislation and their impact on labor agreements. Expanded sections on minorities, women, and other protected classes give the student a comprehensive review of equal opportunity laws as they affect the collective bargaining process. In Chapter 15 the labor relations practices in other countries are compared and contrasted with those of the United States.

SUPPLEMENTARY MATERIALS

Instructor's Manual

A comprehensive instructor's manual to this text contains chapter lecture outlines and a student-tested test bank of over 600 multiple choice and true-false questions written and tested by the authors. Answers to review questions, discussions of cases, and additional case studies are provided.

Electronic Lecture Outline

An exciting comprehensive set of over 150 PowerPoint® slides on disk provides a broad outline of the material covered in each chapter. A set of these outlines in transparency master format is available only from the authors. Write: Michael R. Carrell, College of Business, Morehead State University, Morehead, KY 40351; or call (606) 783-2174 or (502) 451-3867; or FAX (606) 783-5025.

Windows Custom Test

The extensive test bank found in the Instructor's Manual is available in Windows format. Custom Test allows instructors to prepare examinations and tests consisting of any quantity and combination of questions in the test bank. The instructor also has the option of adding new questions to the test bank or changing existing ones. Specific operating instructions for generating examinations are included.

Simulation

A supplement to this text, *Collective Bargaining Simulated: Computerized and Non-computerized Formats*, 4th edition, by Jerald B. Smith, Michael R. Carrell, and Peggy Golden presents a classroom-tested simulation of a contract negotiation in two parts:

- A costing program shows students how to cost out various wage and benefits proposals.
- A complete negotiation simulation involves students directly in an actual labor contract negotiation.

Students (management) can negotiate directly with the computer (labor) on a wide range of economic and noneconomic items. Students can also negotiate with each other individually or in teams using a computerized costing program as a tool.

World Wide Web Site

Visit the Carrell/Heavrin web site at <**http://www.prenhall.com/carrellr**> for activities and updates specifically designed for this text.

ACKNOWLEDGMENTS

We wish to thank the labor law and arbitration experts who so graciously agreed to answer our questions for inclusion in chapters 4 to 10 of the text. They are: Kay Wolf and Thomas C. Garwood, Jr., of Garwood, McKenna & McKenna, P.A., Orlando, Florida; Nancy E. Hoffman, General Counsel, The Civil Service Employees Association, Inc., Local 1000, AFSCME, AFL-CIO, New York; and Phyllis Florman, Arbitrator, arbitration office of Volz & Florman, Louisville, Kentucky.

For their editorial suggestions on style and content of this text, we wish to thank David L. Leightty, labor attorney; Lucretia B. Ward, author; Marilyn Byrne, author; and T. Christopher Heavrin, attorney. Also for their special contribution, John G. Bishof and William M. Lutes of ARCO Metals Company; Del Melcher and Jim Cain of the Mechanical Contractors Association of Kentucky, Inc.; Dale Detlefs of Mercer-Meidinger, Inc.; John Bruce of the Iron Workers Local No. 70, AFL-CIO; Lynn Hampton, C.P.A., William T. Heavrin, Chair of the Governor's Taskforce on Americans with Disabilities Act, Commonwealth of Kentucky; and Steve Barger of the Kentucky State District Council of Carpenters.

We are grateful to those persons who reviewed prior editions of this text, and to those who gave us their suggestions on how we could improve this Fifth Edition: Professor Steve Briggs, DePaul University, Chicago; Thomas Lloyd, Westmoreland County Community College, Youngwood, Pennsylvania; J. Dane Partridge, Virginia PolyTechnic Institute, Blackburg; Charles Rogiers, University of South Dakota; Ronney Vandeveer, Purdue University; Lane Tracy, Ohio University; and Deborah Kottel, University of Great Falls.

A special thank you to Daniel F. Jennings, labor arbitrator from Texas A&M University who revised chapters 11 and 12.

Michael R. Carrell
Christina Heavrin

Photo Credits

LABOR
RELATIONS
AND
COLLECTIVE
BARGAINING

CHAPTER 1

Collective
Bargaining:
The Workforce

- What Is Collective Bargaining?
- Roots of the American Labor Movement
- Growth of National Unions
- Why Unionize?
- Organizing Challenges for Unions

John L. Lewis, founder of the Congress of Industrial Organizations (CIO).

Union "Summer Camp" for College Students

The "in-your-face" confrontation style of the 1960s is being taught to a new breed of union organizers—college interns. The interns, called *summeristas*, are trained at 34 sites across the United States by the AFL-CIO. They attend a three-week intensive program that includes an overview of union history, current working conditions, and organizing techniques.

One intern, Ron Eldridge, a sophomore at Wichita State University, spent his summer organizing health-care workers in St. Louis. He returned encouraged that "people are beginning to see the light" but surprised at the number of workers who were not receptive to his message, which had focused on the benefits of unionization.

A major goal of the program is to recruit union organizers to be trained at the AFL-CIO's Organizing Institute and return them to the field as full-time organizers. About 20 percent of the interns have signed up in past years. Even those who do not sign up may end up working for unions as lawyers or officers. At least they "won't cross picket lines," and they will "look at power relationships and know that employees don't have real power unless they have their own [union] organization," according to Andrew Levin, a Williams College and Harvard Law School graduate who directed the Summeristas program.

Adapted from Robert Grossman, "AFL-CIO 'Summeristas' Fan Out to Sow Seeds for Unions' Future," *HR News*, September 1996, pp. 1, 10–12.

Two supporters of the International Brotherhood of Electrical Workers (IBEW) hold signs supporting benefits for telephone workers while striking near the NYNEX corporate headquarters in Boston.

Collective bargaining is the process by which union leaders representing groups of employees negotiate specific terms of employment with designated representatives of management. This process has existed in the United States for more than 200 years. It began in 1792 when the Philadelphia Cordwainers (shoemakers) formed a local trade union to bargain for higher wages. Although their action is historically viewed as the beginning of collective bargaining in the United States, current practices were largely formed by federal statutes enacted in the 1930s and 1940s and court decisions interpreting those statutes. Thus, the modern era of collective bargaining is only about 60 years old.

WHAT IS COLLECTIVE BARGAINING?

The term *collective bargaining* originated in the British labor movement. But it was Samuel Gompers, an American labor leader, who developed its common use in this country. The following is a modern-day definition:

> Collective bargaining is defined as the continuous relationship between an employer and a designated labor organization representing a specific unit of employees for the purpose of negotiating written terms of employment.[1]

According to the definition, collective bargaining must be recognized as a *continuous* process, beginning with the negotiation of a contract through the life of the contract with almost daily interpretation and administration of its provisions. In recent years the process has also come to include the handling of employee grievances in most labor agreements and, if necessary, arbitration of such grievances in a final and binding decision.

The *employer* referred to in the definition may be one or more related employers joined together for purposes of collective bargaining. The labor organization bargains on behalf of a specific group of employees recognized by the National Labor Relations Board (NLRB) or by agreement between the employer and employees. Under U.S. law, the labor organization is given the right to represent all employees of the bargaining unit. This right gives the union leadership leverage in negotiation because management cannot seek competing unions to negotiate other agreements.

The **terms of employment** negotiated generally include the price of labor, for example, wages and benefits; work rules, including hours of work, job classifications, effort required, and work practices; individual job rights, such as seniority, discipline procedures, and promotion and layoff procedures; management and union rights; and the methods of enforcement and administration of the contract including grievance resolution.[2]

The American system of collective bargaining and labor relations has often been characterized by confrontation—the "screw the boss" and "keep the union in its place" syndromes.[3] However, most union and management officials view collective bargaining as a rational, democratic, and peaceful way of resolving conflict between labor and management. Of approximately 140,000 collective bargaining agreements negotiated by affiliates of the AFL-CIO before 1987, only 2 percent have resulted in strikes. Ninety-eight percent of all cases involving collective bargaining have ended in successful, peaceful negotiations. This record is the result of years of fine-tuning the collective bargaining process in the United States.[4]

The news media usually report only those cases involving picketing, strike activities, or other work disruptions. Seldom do we see reports on cases such as the Bagdad Copper Mine in Arizona, in which the company has offered guaranteed lifetime employment since 1929 and has never experienced significant labor unrest. In fact, the U.S. Bureau of Labor Statistics reported that in 1991, unions struck less often, and the strikes involved fewer workers, than in any year since 1946.[5]

People sometimes falsely assume that because they are not union members, the activities of labor-management relations do not affect them. In recent years, however, the general public has felt the impact of collective bargaining processes. Millions of travelers missed their scheduled flights because of the 1981 Air Traffic Controllers strike. Sports fans saw the 1994 baseball World Series canceled, and cities lost a great deal of money. Telephone customers had their service disrupted by the 1989 Telecommunications Workers strike. People have suddenly realized that collective bargaining affects everyone in ways never considered before. Indirect effects of collective bargaining might include higher costs for products produced by nonunion labor whose management wishes to remain nonunion.

Collective bargaining can be found in countless meeting rooms countrywide. Representatives of management and labor sit across a bargaining table negotiating a labor contract. Teams of negotiators haggle over appropriate wage levels, hours of work, and other conditions of employment. If the industry is large enough, the public may be aware of the progress of the negotiations. People may be afraid of a breakdown that could result in a strike. The parties could then expect federal mediators to join in the process, hopefully bringing the labor dispute to a successful and peaceful conclusion.

The process of collective bargaining is an accepted part of labor-management relations in this country. Such was not always the case. Employers viewed decisions on wages, hours, and conditions of employment as the inviolate prerogative of management. They did not choose to share decision making with their employees. But the employees would not accept unilateral decisions. They realized that the employers' profit depended on their labor and that employees should not be denied their share of the rewards.

What union in North America has the most members? The Teamsters? The Steelworkers? AFSCME? No! The National Education Association (NEA) is the largest (see Table 1-1). The NEA is largely made up of elementary and secondary school teachers. Although the teachers' union may not be as well-known as some others, it is extremely well organized and consistently keeps its 2.2 million members informed on important issues and political races. In fact, at the 1996 Democratic National Convention in Chicago, roughly 10 percent—more than 400 delegates—were members of the NEA. Indeed, some people believe that the teachers' unions (including the American Federation of Teachers, with 850,000 members) are the core of the Democratic Party. In addition to a sizable budget of over $200 million, the NEA has a strong political asset in its 2.2 million members, most of whom are college-educated and politically aware. Their summer break provides an excellent time to become active in teachers' causes.[6]

Table 1-1 Largest North American Unions

Organization	Number of Active Members
National Education Association	2,200,000
International Brotherhood of Teamsters, Chauffeurs, Warehousemen and Helpers of America	1,300,000
American Federation of State, County, and Municipal Employees	1,200,000
United Food and Commercial Workers International	1,200,000
Service Employees International Union	950,000
American Federation of Teachers	850,000
United Automobile, Aerospace and Agriculture Implement Workers of America	800,000
International Brotherhood of Electrical Workers	750,000
United Steelworkers of America	700,000
Communications Workers of America	700,000
Laborers and International Union of North America	700,000
International Association of Machinists and Aerospace Workers	500,000
Carpenters and Joiners of America	500,000

Source: The World Almanac and Book of Facts 1995. © 1994 by K-III Reference Corporated, Mahwah, NJ.

ROOTS OF THE AMERICAN LABOR MOVEMENT

The roots of the American labor movement can be found in the people of colonial America. Prerevolutionary America was overwhelmingly rural, with upward of 90 percent of the population living in the countryside.[7] A majority of the population earned their living as farm owners, tenants, or hired hands. Supporting these agricultural workers, however, was a workforce of craftspeople and unskilled laborers. Craftspeople included carpenters and masons, shipwrights and sailmakers, tanners, weavers, shoemakers, tailors, smiths, barrel makers, glassmakers, and printers. These artisans at first plied their trades independently, but as demand increased, a master worker would set up a small retail shop and employ journeymen and apprentices in America's original workplace. Prior to permanent trade unions, these workers joined together in combinations of master workers to maintain monopolies.

The original craftspeople came from free laborers, those immigrants who paid their way to the New World and established homes and families and passed on their trade to their children. The increased need for such skilled workers, however, led to the London Company's recruitment of indentured servants for colonial America. Many of these indentured servants were eager to leave England and northern Europe because of the homelessness and unemployment caused by their declining economy. Convicts willing to migrate as an alternative to English prisons also joined the indentured servant pool. Many of these laborers supplemented the craftspeople's workers and learned, by the end of their indentured period, a marketable skill.

Indentured servants, as well as slaves brought from Africa, also supplied the unskilled workforce necessary for farming, the expansion of the colonies into the wilderness, and the distribution of goods. The craftspeople of colonial America supplied some familiar names in the American Revolution: Benjamin Franklin (printer and inventor), Paul Revere (silversmith), and George Washington (surveyor).

After the American Revolution, craftspeople also supplied the first labor unions in America. The Federal Society of Journeymen Cordwainers (shoemakers), formed in 1794, the Journeymen Printers in New York (1794), and New York Cabinetmakers (1796) are prime examples. These "trade societies," as the craftspeople's unions were called, grew of necessity as the volume of goods produced caused a clear separation between worker and employer. Thus, the employers and workers began their struggle for control over the bottom line. The availability of competing craftspeople meant that consumers would no longer pay any price for the crafted goods.

In order to increase profits, the employer needed to decrease cost, and to do that, the employer needed to decrease wages. The organization of skilled craftspeople allowed wage security for the artisans. When all available shoemakers committed to work *only* for the wage they believed fair, the solidarity of the worker, so necessary for success, was born. As the employer moved away from hands-on involvement with the making of the product, the merchant-capitalist emerged. That merchant-capitalist expanded the manufacturing of handicrafts.

These expanded workplaces were the first sites for American unions and consisted primarily of craftspeople who were white males. In the early 1800s, slavery still found African-Americans in servitude, primarily on plantations in the South. Women worked primarily in the home, their own or someone else's. Even though the demographics of the American workforce for the last two centuries has undergone great transition, the profile of American unions has stayed amazingly homogeneous.

As the number of workplaces for skilled laborers increased, so did the need for organizing those workers. During the 1930s, the American factory system was emerging, and the struggle between employer and employee intensified. Factories substituted mechanical power and machinery for muscle power and skills. Industrialization necessitated large capital outlays and a concentration of labor. Mass production for national and even international markets began to develop. By the time the Civil War erupted, the textile, boot and shoe, and iron industries were ready to take the final step to a modern mechanized operation.

In the Northeast, textile mills opened, and in contrast to skilled labor operation, unskilled laborers peopled an American factory in significant numbers. The workers chosen for these factories were often young women recruited from the neighboring rural areas. In the 1840s, these young women found a relatively safe and promising environment in textile mills such as those in Lowell, Massachusetts, and Pawtucket, Rhode Island. Originally, these young women came from the rural New England countryside to work to save enough money for a marriage dowry, to move West, or to preserve the family farm. The work was hard and consumed their days with 11½- to 13-hour schedules. But the time of their lives devoted to this work could be measured in months, not years. The 1850s, though, saw an influx of women immigrants from Ireland and Germany who took these hard, low-paying jobs with little, if any, chance to move on.[8]

The impact of this influx of immigrant labor on American workers between 1846 and the Civil War was not limited to young women in New England. Almost 3 million immigrants entered the country between 1846 and 1855, providing an abundant supply of both skilled and unskilled labor. Workers who had previously protected their wages by agreement not to work for less than their fellow worker were faced with competition from immigrants willing to work for much less. As skilled trades became mechanized, the availability of cheap labor to run that machinery greatly reduced wage rates.

This influx of millions of immigrants over a hundred years ago may be equaled in America today and in the near future. After an initial resistance to these intruders, American labor formed a partnership with some of those immigrant groups.[9] The challenge to today's labor movement may be to repeat that alliance.

After the Civil War, there was another influx of immigrants to the United States. Nearly 5 million immigrants arrived in the last decade of the nineteenth century. These immigrants arriving on the East Coast were, by and large, from southeastern Europe—Italians, Poles, Czechs, Slovaks, Hungarians, Greeks, and Russians. On the West Coast, immigrants from China were welcomed to help build the Transamerican Railroad. During this period the United States grew rapidly, primarily as a result of the creation of national corporations such as E. H. Harriman's railroads, Andrew Carnegie's steel mills, and John D. Rockefeller's oil refineries.

The monopolistic practices of the employer encouraged the employees to unionize.[10] The need for the joint action of laborers in this newly mechanized environment was expressed by Jonathan C. Fincher, an organizer of a union for machinists and blacksmiths.

> In the early days of mechanism in this country but few shops employed many men. Generally the employer was head man; he knew his men personally. . . . If aught went astray, there was no circumlocution office to go through to have an understanding about it. But as the business came to be more fully developed, it was found that more capital must be employed and the authority and supervision of the owner or owners must be delegated to superintendents and under foremen. In this manner men and masters became estranged and the gulf could only be bridged by a strike, when, perhaps, the representatives of the working men might be admitted to the office and allowed to state their case. It was to resist this combination of capital, which had so changed the character of the employers, that led to the formation of the union.[11]

GROWTH OF NATIONAL UNIONS

It was at this point that the unionization of workers left its infancy of informal local communities of like-skilled laborers and tried to find its place in the changing American economy. The idealism of those leaders credited with creating the American labor movement can be seen in the original national unions.

For years, **trade unionists** had tried to develop a national trade union. In 1866, the first National Labor Congress, held in Baltimore, Maryland, was attended by 77 delegates from various local organizations. The Congress resulted in the formation of the **National Labor Union**, which allowed membership for skilled and unskilled workers alike. The National Labor Union saw itself as a political force nationwide and advocated the creation of local unions of workers.

Active at a time when reformists such as Elizabeth Cady Stanton and Susan B. Anthony advocated women's suffrage, a Farmers' Alliance sought government support for farmers' produce, and religious organizations worked in tenements to save lives as well as souls, the National Labor Union advocated reforms to help the workers. It demanded adoption of laws establishing an eight-hour workday and sought restrictions on immigration and the abolition of convict labor. It was the first to ask for the creation of a Department of Labor at the national level. It initially supported women's unions, and it recognized the need to organize African-Americans, although it did not invite them to join the National Labor Union. As the suffragettes' cause gained ground, the willingness to accept women's trade unions in the National Labor Union diminished. And by 1872, most of the women's labor organizations disappeared. The National Labor Union's reluctance to admit African-Americans to full membership led to the creation of the National Colored Labor Union (NCLU). The NCLU hoped to affiliate with the National Labor Union but was refused in the 1870 Congress.[12]

As the National Labor Union's political agenda grew, its effectiveness as a "national union" diminished. When it finally converted to the National Labor Reform Party in 1872 and nominated a candidate for the presidency who withdrew from the election, the National Labor Union ended its days.

Although the National Labor Union could not boast of passing many of the reforms it advocated, it did spur the formation of numerous national trade unions, including spinners, shoemakers, railway conductors, locomotive firemen, and coal miners. When the depression of 1873 hit, these trade unions formed the core of two major national unions and nurtured two legendary labor leaders: Eugene Debs and Samuel Gompers.

The depression of 1873 placed employees at the mercy of their employers and ushered in a violent period for the American labor movement. Following are some examples.

Molly Maguires

In January 1875, miners who were members of the Miners' and Laborers' Benevolent Association went on strike against the anthracite mine owners. Because of hunger, the miners went back to work in June 1875 and took a 20 percent pay cut. The Benevolent Association's leaders were forced to leave the area, and the local miners' unions essentially ceased to function.

After the strike there were a series of murders, assaults, robberies, and acts of arson around the mine fields. Authorities blamed a legendary group of union organizers known as the **Molly Maguires** for the criminal acts. After this group was infiltrated by a Pinkerton private investigator hired by the Philadelphia and Reading Railroad, 24 members of the Molly Maguires were brought to trial. Ten were convicted and executed, the rest sentenced to prison. The fairness of the trial was suspect, but the result was plain. The labor movement was portrayed as a violent and criminal movement.[13] Throughout this period, as seen in Profile 1-1, owners used hired detectives to challenge the labor movement.

Railway Strike of 1877

The treatment of workers by railroad companies is another good example from this period. Railroad companies had, through various capitalization schemes, produced large dividends for wealthy stockholders while consistently losing money. To compensate, the companies increased railway rates and reduced wages. The workers' discontent reached desperation after a 35 percent wage cut in 3 years, irregular employment, increases in railway hotel and transportation costs (use of which was necessitated by work schedules), and a suppression of union activities.

In 1877, numerous eastern lines announced a new 10 percent cut in wages, and the workers in Maryland began a strike. The railway strike spread quickly and violently to West Virginia, Kentucky, Ohio, Pennsylvania, New York, and

"LABOR SPIES"

The use of the **Pinkerton Agency** by employers to infiltrate labor unions in 1875 was just the beginning of more than 65 years of such activities in the United States. Robert Pinkerton, son of Allan Pinkerton, the agency's founder, realized the potential for industrial espionage work and began sending operatives to union meetings.

Between 1890 and 1910, business was so good that he established 15 new offices. The activities of the labor spies included gathering advance warning of strike plans, investigating labor incidents, listing union sympathizers for retaliation purposes, and sowing dissent and unrest within the union's ranks.

The Pinkerton Agency was not alone in this type of work. Between the late 1890s and the early 1940s, various governmental or labor investigatory bodies had documented extensive spy activities. In 1912, the U.S. Commission on Industrial Relations reported approximately 275 detective agencies with active anti-union operatives. And in 1936, a congressional investigative committee headed by Senator Robert M. LaFollette, Jr., uncovered the following costs paid by employers for the detective agency's services:

- General Motors, January 1934–July 1936: $994,000
- Chrysler Motor Company, 1935: $72,000
- Remington Rand Corporation, 1936: $81,000

The committee also reported the income of various agencies:

- Burns Agency, 1934: $580,000
- Pinkerton, 1935: $2,300,000

The LaFollette committee documented the correlation between increased espionage activities and union membership drives. At the end of its investigation, the LaFollette committee proposed sweeping legislation to prohibit employers from using such tactics as violations of the Wagner Act. Although the legislation did not pass, the exposure of the detective agencies' tactics caused many employers to stop using them. Later the National Labor Relations Board cracked down on such tactics as unfair labor practices and, at least publicly, the use of espionage ceased.

Adapted from Robert M. Smith, "Spies against Labor," *Labor's Heritage* 5, no. 2 (Summer 1993), pp. 65–77.

Missouri. State militia dispersed one gathering in Pittsburgh, killing 26 people. Militia were called out in Kentucky, and federal troops fought with workers in Maryland, Ohio, Illinois, and Missouri. The strike lasted less than 20 days, but more than 100 workers were killed and several hundred were badly wounded.[14] For the first time in the history of the U.S. labor movement, a general strike swept the country, and federal troops were called out to suppress it.

The embryonic labor movement realized that the failure of the largely spontaneous strike stemmed from lack of organization. Propertied classes, terrified by the events of 1877, strengthened support of state militia. The construction of armories in major East Coast cities coincides with this period.[15]

The Haymarket Square Riot

The **Haymarket Square Riot** took place in Chicago in 1886. Laborers had called a general strike on May 1, 1886, to demand an eight-hour day. The May 1st day-long strike passed quietly, but a subsequent demonstration on May 3 at the Mc-Cormick Harvester plant in Chicago caused a confrontation with police and resulted in the death of four strikers. A peaceful meeting, held to protest the police

---

shooting, ended when a bomb was thrown into a group of police, killing one policeman and injuring others. The police opened fire and more strikers were killed or injured. Eight so-called anarchists, some of whom had not even been at the meeting, were tried and found guilty, not because of complicity in throwing the bomb but because they held political beliefs that threatened accepted ideas.[16] One account describes the trial as follows:

> Proceedings began before Judge Joseph E. Gary on June 21. The jury, consisting largely of businessmen and their clerks, was a packed one and the trial judge prejudiced.
>
> . . . These witnesses, all of them terrified and some of them paid, testified that the defendants were part of a conspiracy to overthrow the government of the United States by force and violence and that the Haymarket bomb and Degan's murder were the first blow in what was to have been a general assault on all established order. But their testimony was so filled with contradictions that the State was compelled to shift its ground in the midst of a trial. The core of the State's charges then became the allegation that the unknown person who had thrown the bomb was inspired to do so by the words and ideas of the defendants.
>
> Thus, the trial was transformed into a trial of books and the written word, a procedure which was later to be repeated in the United States. Endless editorials by Parsons and Spies were read. Interminable speeches by the defendants were recited to the jury. Excerpts were torn from the context of involved works on the nature and philosophy of politics and described as damning evidence against the conspirators. The political platform of the Working People's Association, its resolutions and statements, were regarded as evidence involving the defendants in the murder of Degan. . . .
>
> The press was there, of course, in all its glory, from every great city of the country. Thousands of words were printed daily in all parts of the country. From these dispatches we learn of the graceful, laughing society people beside Judge Gary on the bench, learn of the wives of the defendants, pale and haggard, their restless, bewildered children clinging to them, as they crowded together in the front row. We are informed that the courtroom was hot and suffocating, that the people packed together had scarcely room enough to wave the fans with which they had supplied themselves, and that the length of trial, dragging on week after week, reflected the justice of American jurisprudence wherein even the guilty get all the impressive forms of the law before hanging. . . .
>
> The verdict was almost a formality, and the trial's big day arrived when the condemned men arose in court to accuse the accuser, to say why death sentence should not be passed upon them by Gary, and why it was not they but society that was guilty. They dominated the courtroom and they dominated the country that day. No newspaper was so conservative that it did not admit that the defendants in defying death and in defending the working class were both dignified and impressive.[17]

Four of the eight defendants were executed, one committed suicide, and the remaining three were sent to prison.[18]

Knights of Labor

Although the **Knights of Labor** (KOL) was formed in 1869, the KOL grew to prominence between the Railway Strike of 1877 and the Haymarket Square Riot of 1886. Once seen as the future of the American labor movement, it sought to promote a national union embracing skilled and unskilled workers in a single labor organization. It recognized that industrial workers, the so-called unskilled workers, would soon outnumber trade unionists. The KOL was begun by trade unionists, who had decided it was safer to keep its membership secret. Members were less likely to be blackballed by anti-union employers. The secrecy of the organization both limited its growth and brought it under suspicion. When it was forced to go public in 1881, it benefited from a rash of labor victories brought about by strikes against Union Pacific Railroad, the Southwest System Railroads, and the Wabash Railroad. The latter resulted in face-to-face negotiations between powerful financier Jay Gould and the KOL: the first instance of bargaining with a specific employer by a nationwide labor organization.

The success of the KOL led to a huge influx of members—so many that the president, Terence V. Powderly, felt overwhelmed.[19] Unfortunately, the KOL began experiencing a number of defeats in 1886 when some 100,000 workers were involved in unsuccessful strikes and lockouts attributed to their organization. The KOL was also blamed for the Haymarket Square Riot, which contributed to its continuing decline. And finally, although the KOL had advocated an eight-hour workday, its leadership refused to support the May 1, 1886, general strike of some 170,000 workers that was called to pressure employers to institute it. Membership in KOL dropped dramatically when trade unionists turned to the American Federation of Labor for a national union and industrial workers simply disbanded the locals they had formed.

Homestead, Pennsylvania, 1892

The Amalgamated Association of Iron and Steel Workers and the Carnegie Steel Company's plant in **Homestead, Pennsylvania**, had enjoyed a relatively friendly relationship while under a three-year agreement that expired in 1892. Andrew Carnegie, while professing satisfaction with the relationship between his plant and the union, turned negotiations over to the local plant manager, Henry Clay Frick. Frick's preparation for negotiations included arranging for both strikebreakers and more than 300 armed guards. With a declared goal of breaking the union, Frick locked the workers out when they refused the wage cuts proposed at the bargaining table and then brought in the armed Pinkerton guards.

The guards and the workers engaged in a gun battle resulting in three dead Pinkerton guards and seven casualties on the workers' side. After an uneasy ceasefire, the governor of Pennsylvania sent 8,000 state militiamen to Homestead and established martial law. The plant, under militia protection, reopened, with strikebreakers replacing the union workers. The union organizers were prosecuted for rioting and murder. The Carnegie Steel Company had successfully crushed the steel workers union, not only at this plant, but in other Pennsylvania mills. In Profile 1-2, the spirit of the labor movement in Homestead, Pennsylvania, is remembered.

Pullman Strike, 1894

Interest was again focused on the railroads when workers in Illinois went on strike in 1894. These workers lived in Pullman's town, where wages were low and rents were high. A group of employees who made the Pullman cars demanded wages be restored to previous levels and rents be lowered. When the demands

"OLD BEESWAX" TAYLOR
(1819–1892)

Thomas W. Taylor, nicknamed Old Beeswax, was a colorful leader of the U.S. labor movement at the height of the power of the Knights of Labor. He was also a founding member of the American Federation of Labor (AFL). In 1892, he was serving as mayor of Homestead, Pennsylvania, one of the nation's pre-eminent labor towns.

In June 1882, 10 years before the Homestead lockout, the Amalgamated Association of Iron and Steel Workers and the Knights of Labor had organized a peaceful "Grand Labor Demonstration" in which 30,000 workers marched and a crowd of 100,000 attended. Old Beeswax rode at the head of the parade. The demonstration, which some call the first Labor Day in the United States, was held to rally support for ironworkers who had recently won a bitter strike with the local mine owners.

Old Beeswax, with many of his contemporaries, believed that the struggle undertaken by labor was one of freedom—a freedom from slavery imposed by the owners. The rally song penned by Old Beeswax and sung on that first Labor Day captured the spirit of the cause.

"STORM THE FORT"

Toiling millions now are walking,
See them marching on,
And the tyrants now are shaking
Ere their power is gone

Chorus:
Storm the fort, ye Knights of Labor,
God, defend our cause;
Equal rights for self and neighbor;
Down with unjust laws,

'Tis labor that sustains the nation,
And 'tis just and fair
That all should help, whate'er
    their station,
To produce their share.

But now the drones steal all the honey,
From industry's hives;
Banks control the nation's money
And control our lives.

In time of war the workmen rally
At their country's call;
From the hilltops and the valley
Come they one and all.

In time of peace the loom and anvil,
Reaper, plow and spade.
Join their chorus with the mandril;
Each man at his trade.

Do not load the workman's shoulder
With an unjust debt;
Do not let the rich bondholder
Live by blood and sweat.

The land and air by God was given,
And they should be free,
For our title came from heaven—
Not by man's decree.

Why should those who fought for
    freedom
Go in bonded chains?
Workingmen no longer need them
When they use their brains.

Adapted from Paul Krause, "The Life and Times of 'Beeswax' Taylor," *Labor History* (New York: Taiment Institute, NYU), pp. 32–54.

were refused, these workers struck. In sympathy, another group of workers refused to switch Pullman cars. When switchers were fired, even more classifications of railway workers went on strike.

This new solidarity among railway workers was the result of the establishment of the **American Railway Union** in 1843 by Eugene V. Debs. His was a new kind of industrial union that placed all workers into one organization, instead of dividing them into hostile craft unions, fulfilling the goal of KOL.

The **Pullman strike** was peaceful and well organized under Debs's leadership. It shut down Illinois Central along with the Southern Pacific and Northern Pacific railroads. The boycott spread from Illinois to Colorado.

With the help of the federal government, railroad owners added mail cars to all trains. The strikers were then charged with interfering with mail delivery. Federal troops were brought in to break the strike. Although violence ensued, the strike continued.

The court ordered the strikers back to work by applying the Sherman Antitrust Act.[20] This 1890 act declared that contracts, combinations, and conspiracies formed in restraint of trade and commerce were illegal. Theoretically directed at business, the court's injunction caused much controversy when applied to labor unions. Yet, along with contempt-of-court sentences and fines, the injunction finally broke the Pullman strike. Debs was sentenced to six months in prison for contempt of court as a result of his participation.

Eugene Debs

Eugene Debs was the son of an immigrant. He left school when he was 14 years old and became a railroad shop worker for 50 cents a day. At age 16 he joined the Brotherhood of Locomotive Firemen and began his work as a union organizer. Although he served as both a city and state elected official, his devotion was to the labor movement. In 1893 he broke away from the Brotherhood and formed the American Railway Union. Frustrated by the inability of the numerous railroad craft unions to maintain solidarity during a strike, Debs hoped this union of employees across craft lines would prove able to sustain a job action.

The resulting success and then failure of the Pullman strike was a watershed for both Debs and the labor movement. The labor movement realized that government involvement in support of employers was their nemesis. At that point the focus of national unions turned to creating a different government agenda.

The six months in prison radicalized Debs. There he read Marx's *Das Kapital* and came to believe that the labor struggle in the United States represented a struggle between the classes. "The issue is Socialism versus Capitalism. I am for Socialism because I am for humanity."[21]

When Debs started out as a labor organizer, he decried strikes and violence. But years of strikebreaking by Pinkerton agents and rival unions, and the futility of intraunion struggles, led to a change of heart. He is quoted as saying, "The strike is the weapon of the oppressed, of men capable of appreciating justice and having the courage to resist wrong and contend for principle."[22]

For the next 30 years, Debs led the democratic socialist movement among the workers of America. He espoused industrial unionism in the economic realm and socialism in the political realm to protect workers from the unbridled capitalism facing the United States in the last decade of the century. As the Socialist Party of America's presidential candidate in 1900, 1904, 1908, 1912, and 1920, he waged a campaign for such "radical" ideas as the abolition of child labor, the right of women to vote, a graduated income tax, the direct election of U.S. senators, an unemployment compensation law, a national Department of Education, and pensions for men and women.

Debs's objection to U.S. entry into World War I was stated frequently in speeches around the nation. In Canton, Ohio, in 1918, his speech pointed out that the burden placed on the workers during a war far exceeded that placed on the business owners. The federal government indicted Debs for that speech under the Espionage Act and convicted him. Debs was again incarcerated and, in fact, was in jail during the 1920 presidential election in which he received a million votes. Although Debs continued to espouse democratic socialism until his death in 1926, he rejected the Communist Party, which had come into power in 1917 in Russia after overthrowing the czar.[23]

American Federation of Labor

The **American Federation of Labor** (AFL) was formed in 1886 under the leadership of Samuel Gompers. Its sole policy was to improve the position of skilled labor. The AFL's program included standard hours and wages, fair working conditions, collective bargaining, and the accumulation of funds for union emergencies. More important, the AFL introduced the concept of business unionism to union management and leadership. A decentralization of authority allowed trade autonomy for national unions, enabling them to make decisions for themselves. A particular craft or trade union had exclusive jurisdiction to ensure protection from competition. The AFL rejected formation of a political labor party, preferring to work as a voting bloc within existing parties. At one of its initial meetings, the AFL prepared the following declaration of principles that embodied the spirit of the national labor movement:

> Whereas, a Struggle is going on in the nations of the civilized world, between the oppressors and the oppressed of all countries, a struggle between capital and labor which must grow in intensity from year to year and work disastrous results to the toiling millions of all nations, if not combined for mutual protection and benefits. The history of the wage workers of all countries is but the history of constant struggle and misery, engendered by ignorance and disunion, whereas the history of the nonproducers of all countries proves that a minority thoroughly organized may work wonders for good or evil. It behooves the representatives of the workers of North America in congress assembled, to adopt such measures and disseminate such principles among the people of our country as will unite them for all time to come, to secure the recognition of the rights to which they are justly entitled. Conforming to the old adage, "In union there is strength," a formation embracing every trade and labor organization in North America, a union founded upon the basis as broad as the land we live in, is our only hope. The past history of trade unions proves that small organizations, well conducted, have accomplished great good, but their efforts have not been of that lasting character which a thorough unification of all the different branches of industrial workers is bound to secure.[24]

It was perhaps ironic that the unification of workers during the Haymarket Square Riot caused the AFL to monopolize the labor scene, overshadowing its predecessors.

Although the Knights of Labor had participated in neither the general strike nor the Haymarket Square incident, their notoriety for other successful strikes led to the assumption that they had engineered the Haymarket upheaval. The public began to associate the Knights of Labor with violence and anarchy. Such criticism caused the Knights to lose support. The AFL began to dominate the labor movement.[25]

With the AFL in a dominant position, labor's goals jelled. Leaders kept labor's ultimate goal—participation in the decision-making process—in sight. This goal meant collective bargaining and an arbitration system to resolve disputes with individual employers. On a national level, labor sought legislative actions to gain an eight-hour day, to prohibit child labor, and to provide for workers' compensation in case of injury on the job.

Thus, the American labor movement was largely based on two competing ideas. One was community: People with common interests can best collectively work to solve their problems—that is, there is strength in numbers. The second idea was individualism: People can become successful through their own hard work and ingenuity. The founders of the AFL were distrustful of the Knights of Labor belief that only the elimination of the wage system could guarantee individual respect within one collectively active political community. The AFL founders believed instead that individual respect and dignity could be achieved through economic rewards for work, and a better life could be achieved through a new class of skilled workers. Thus, through collective action, individuals could achieve better individual rewards such as higher pay, better hours, and better working conditions. The Knights of Labor were pursuing political equality, not individual equality, through collective action.[26]

Samuel Gompers

Samuel Gompers, at age 13, immigrated with his family from England in 1863. His father was a cigarmaker, and Samuel joined his first cigarmakers' union in 1864. Steeped in British trade unionism, Gompers saw the burgeoning labor movement in the United States go from an idealist, reformist cause to a daily bread-and-butter struggle for an improved workplace. It was this focus he brought to the AFL that caused it to survive when the KOL and the Socialist Labor Party lost ground.

Gompers, with two other labor leaders, began the AFL after reorganizing the Cigarmakers International Union in 1875. This reorganized union charged initiation fees and dues to fund sick and death benefits for its members, thus ensuring a stable membership base. Members of the trade locals wanted to copy the revitalization of the Cigarmakers Union, and Gompers supplied the model.

In 1881, the same year the KOL decided to go public with its organization, a meeting of labor leaders from national and international trade unions and the KOL was held in Pittsburgh. Originally, and against Gompers's wishes, the vision for an alliance of unions as a result of this meeting was to include both trade and industrial unions. The resulting Federation of Organized Trades and Labor Unions embraced the idea of the solidarity of all workers and the single-mindedness of the trade unionist who chose a workplace agenda as opposed to a societal overhaul agenda. Although the federation did not survive five years, it was a transition from the KOL's organization to the new unionism espoused by Gompers.

Gompers's AFL placed major emphasis on economic or industrial action as opposed to political action. Although the member trade unions retained their autonomy, the unity of labor was promoted through education and through support of striking locals. Gompers is credited with practically forming the federation by himself. He worked tirelessly, traveled extensively, and devoted his entire life to it for 38 years until his death.

Industrial Workers of the World (IWW)

In contrast to the demise of the trade unionists in the steel mills of Pennsylvania after Homestead, a similar confrontation led to a strengthening of union organizations in the mining country of the West. In 1892, miners in the Coeur d'Alene area of Idaho were locked out when they refused significant wage reductions. The mine owners brought in strikebreakers and armed guards who were confronted and driven out by the miners. Armed federal troops were called in and they restored order, reopened the mines with strikebreakers, and arrested the union men.

The reaction from union members was to form the Western Federation of Miners (WFM) and begin a series of strikes: Cripple Creek, Colorado, 1894; Leadville, Colorado, 1896; Coeur d'Alene, Idaho, 1899; and Telluride, Colorado, 1901. Each strike involved a determined reaction from mine owners, who employed strikebreakers and armed guards and finally the state militia, when necessary, to squelch the strike. The union members were arrested and blacklisted. Nevertheless, the WFM continued to grow. It included in its endeavors the passage of an eight-hour workday for miners. However, even though it succeeded in passing an amendment to the Colorado State Constitution for the eight-hour day, it could not get the legislation passed.

WFM decided, then, to call a strike at a Cripple Creek, Colorado, mill in 1903 to push for the eight-hour day. A sympathetic walkout at neighboring mines caused mine owners to bring in the state militia once again. What followed was a year of pitched battles, arrests, civil disorder, martial law, and a suspension of usual constitutional protections. The strike was crushed in 1904, and the WFM looked as if it would suffer a similar fate. In an attempt for self-preservation, the WFM convened a meeting of activists from both trade and industrial unions as well as representatives of the democratic socialist arm of the labor movement. What emerged from the meeting in 1905 was the Industrial Workers of the World (IWW), whose creed was to organize labor into one great industrial union of the workforce. Like the NLU, the KOL, and the Socialist Labor Party, the IWW embraced both a workplace agenda—to organize all of labor into industrial unions—and a political agenda—to overthrow capitalism for a cooperative society. IWW (members were commonly called **Wobblies**), however, suffered the same fate as its predecessors who had dual agendas when it lost most of its membership within three years.[27] But it did survive long enough for the Wobblies to organize successfully industrial workers in a Lawrence, Massachusetts, textile mill and lead a long and bitter strike there in 1912.

From the turn of the century to the end of World War I, the labor movement struggled through any number of victories and defeats: strikes that broke unions and strikes that solidified union membership, political victories for its reform agenda and a significant split with other reform movements, court injunctions and the passage of protective laws. By the end of the war, the IWW was no longer a leading association, but its stated objective, to organize industrial workers, resulted in the creation of major national industrial unions such as the United Mine Workers, the Ladies Garment Workers, and the Amalgamated Clothing Workers.[28] The tragic turn of many labor struggles can be seen in the life of Fannie Sellins (Profile 1-3).

FANNIE SELLINS (1870–1919)
LABOR'S MARTYR

The story of Fannie Sellins's life is not so different from that of other workers in her time. Sellins was of Irish descent; she lived and worked as a dressmaker in St. Louis at the turn of the century. As recorded in the 1910 census, she was a widow, with three children at home and one already living away from home. She was a union member; in fact, she served as president of the St. Louis Local 67 of the United Garment Workers of America (UGWA). She came to national prominence as a result of a lockout of the members of the UGWA locals by the firm of Marx & Hoas in 1909. Sellins traveled to Chicago to solicit support for the striking union members. Her eloquent and inspirational pleas gained assistance from the Women's Trade Union League, Jane Addams of Hull House, and the United Brotherhood of Carpenters. The striking union was able to stand its ground during the lockout, and in 1911 agreement was reached with the company on union recognition.

Fannie Sellins's leadership in that work stoppage led to her taking a key role in an organizing campaign at the Schwab Clothing Co., also located in St. Louis. Sellins appeared before the twenty-third convention of the United Mine Workers and begged for their assistance—and pledged that the UGWA would never forget their support. The UAW sent money at a critical point in the effort. The boycott of Schwab eventually put the firm out of business.

Fannie Sellins, by this time, had become a full-time labor organizer for the UGWA. While working with garment workers in West Virginia and Pennsylvania, her attention shifted to mine workers. In 1913, she began organizing in the West Virginia and Pennsylvania coal mines. Initially her work focused not on direct organization but on offering support to the families of coal miners. Her presence as a labor leader in the Hutchinson Coal Mine strike resulted in a six-month jail sentence for disobeying a court injunction against union organizing. After being pardoned by President Wilson in 1917, Sellins began again organizing coal miners in earnest.

A 1919 strike of Allegheny Coal & Coke Company miners brought Sellins to the Alle-Kishe region of Pennsylvania. Deputies hired by the coal mine owners to protect company property engaged in a number of confrontations with the striking workers. Sellins witnessed an assault by a deputy of a mine worker and took pictures of it. A melee ensued when Sellins attempted to leave the area with the pictures in order to have the deputy arrested. An investigation of the incident found that Sellins was shot from the back and killed while trying to get away from the deputies. The story the deputies told was that Sellins was shot while attacking the deputies.

Fannie Sellins became a martyr of the labor movement. Pictures of her lifeless body were used as propaganda material in coal fields and steel mills from Gary, Indiana, to West Virginia. She was buried in Union Cemetery, Pennsylvania.

Adapted from John Cassedy, "A Bond of Sympathy," *Labor's Heritage* 4, no. 4 (Winter 1992), pp. 34–47.

John L. Lewis

The 1920s were seen as a crisis period for the labor movement. The postwar posterity, coupled with completing their economic shift to mass production, left U.S. bureaucratic firms in a dominant position. Workplaces with large craft unions became overshadowed by workplaces with unskilled and unorganized industrial workers. The inability of the AFL to change and organize the industrial worker doomed it to lose membership during this decade.

The anti-union position of many employers also crippled attempts of national industrial unions to increase their membership. The United Mine Workers was one such industrial union. Emerging from its leadership in 1924 was John L. Lewis, the next giant in the history of the American labor movement. Poised as a somewhat autocratic leader of the United Mine Workers, Lewis saw the stock market crash of 1929 and the ensuing Great Depression as an opportunity to organize the unorganized workforce. With the passage of the Wagner Act in 1935, which gave government protection to collective bargaining, industrial unionism became possible. John L. Lewis set out to make that possibility a reality.

John L. Lewis was the son of Welsh immigrants. He, along with his father and two brothers, worked in the coal mines of Cleveland, Iowa. He joined the United Mine Workers in 1900. He left mining, and after failed attempts at other careers, ended up as an organizer for the AFL (1910–1916) and then an official of the United Mine Workers (1916–1920).

Congress of Industrial Organizations (CIO)

In 1935, John L. Lewis and leaders of the Ladies Garment Workers and the Clothing Workers set up the **Congress of Industrial Organizations**. Industrial workers, unlike their fellow craft workers, could not rely on the solidarity based on their skill for union strength. Industrial unions had to build such loyalty from the results of their organization.

Reacting to the trade unionization of the AFL, Lewis led the formulation of the Congress of Industrial Organizations. The CIO focused on a workplace agenda, as did the AFL, but unlike AFL, it organized and encouraged industrial unions. Although originally associated with the AFL, by 1938, the CIO was a separate and growing organization. The CIO also differed from the AFL by promoting solidarity with African-American workers and with the women and immigrants in the workforce.

The CIO attracted the auto workers, and in Flint, Michigan, in 1936 the United Auto Workers (UAW) staged the first sit-in strike. The nation watched for weeks as this first display of passive resistance by the union members caused General Motors major problems. When the governor of Michigan was asked to intervene with militia, he instead called for a meeting between General Motors and Lewis, representing the UAW. A compromise was reached, and, although GM did not recognize the UAW as the *exclusive* representative of its employees, it did recognize representation of UAW members to management.

After the auto industry experience, the CIO had similar successes in the steel industry when U.S. Steel recognized the union and signed a contract without the need for a strike. The use of the "sit-down strike" during this brief period forced management to honor the collective bargaining process put into law by the Wagner Act. Most workers identified these successes with the CIO and John L. Lewis. CIO union membership began to increase, but even the AFL membership grew. The competition for union members between the leadership of the CIO and the AFL intensified.

The political activities of the labor movement that resulted in a pro-labor legislation are detailed in chapter 3, as is the evolution of the competing labor organizations. The results of both, however, can be seen in the rise of union membership from the 1930s to its high in the 1950s, when 33 percent of all nonagricultural workers were part of a labor union.

After the mid-1950s, however, there was decreasing interest in unionization. A major reason for the decline of unionization among the U.S. workforce is that the unions have not adapted to the diversity in that workforce. In chapter 2 the workplace changes that caused this decline are examined. In chapter 3, the legal framework that discouraged organizing is described.

WHY UNIONIZE?

Why did workers in many manufacturing industries choose to unionize after the passage of the 1935 Wagner Act? At that time many of the manufacturing plants were oppressive places of employment. Each morning men lined up at the gate. If there was no work, they were sent home; if they were hired, it was for that day only. There was no continuous employment. The men never knew when their workday would end until the whistle blew. One autoworker recalls that some foremen were so intimidating that workers had to do the foremen's yardwork on the weekends and had to bring along their daughters to provide sexual services. The foremen managed by terror and hired prizefighters to keep control. Workers could not talk during lunch and had to raise their hands to go to the bathroom. The bathrooms did not have doors, and foremen followed workers who took a bathroom break to make sure the break was needed. Such indignities, as well as poor wages and unsafe working conditions, made workers ready to join unions.[29]

Today it is unlikely that many managers would consider using the intimidating tactics of the 1930s. In general, however, when workers today choose to unionize, it is for the same frustration with management over issues such as wages, benefits, or fair treatment that caused their grandparents to unionize.

The labor union developed as a means by which individuals could unite and have the collective power to accomplish goals that could not be accomplished alone. Whether that power is used to increase take-home wages, to ensure job protection, to improve working conditions, or simply to sit across the bargaining table as an equal with the employer, members believe that *in union there is strength*.[30]

Unions have been seen as pragmatic organizations seeking to improve the economic and social conditions of their members. The success of their activities can be measured by the improvements in members' work conditions and the perception members have of the union's effectiveness.

Numerous studies have tried to quantify the subjective reasons a worker will vote for union representation. A Lou Harris & Associates poll done on behalf of the AFL-CIO concluded that a decision by a worker to vote for union representation includes the following:

1. A deep dissatisfaction with current job and employment conditions
2. A view that unionization can be helpful or instrumental in improving the job or the employment condition
3. A willingness to overlook the image of unions as "Big Labor" out for themselves and not for the workers
4. Viewing unions as having a significant and substantial role for more altruistic endeavors that improve the lot of members and nonmembers alike by promoting social advances[31]

In a survey of labor leaders around the country, the four most important factors affecting the health of the American labor movement were:

1. Collective bargaining rights
2. Leadership in the labor movement
3. Union member solidarity
4. Action of the National Labor Relations Board

The assessment of these labor leaders certainly coincides with the demands of the workers.[32]

The Lou Harris survey of 1,500 union and nonunion workers went on to answer more basic questions of how members believe they benefit from union representation. The following questions were asked of individuals of both groups: What conditions in the workplace would change if workers lost their unions? Would conditions get better, worse, or stay the same? The results showed a substantial difference between union and nonunion workers. Union workers responded that conditions would get worse in a wide variety of factors. Of the 10 workplace conditions in the survey, they expected the following to worsen: benefits (67 percent of those responding), pay (62 percent), job security (56 percent), treatment by supervisors (46 percent), worker participation in decision making (38 percent), health and safety conditions (38 percent). Nonunion workers, however, predicted that if they became unionized, they would see pay and benefits "get better" (43 percent), but they predicted no change in nonwage conditions. Therefore, workers who are union members believe unions help them improve a variety of important economic and noneconomic conditions, whereas nonunion workers seem unaware of noneconomic benefits of union representation.[33]

Wages

Although economists may debate as to what degree unions cause workers' wages to increase, negotiated agreements do contain significant employment benefits.[34] Some nonwage elements include grievance procedures, seniority rights, and provisions to improve job satisfaction and security. Certainly companies that seek to prevent unionization are advised to approach their employees with similar employment benefits. Nonunion employers may also encourage employees' participation to determine the content of their work, to increase employee job satisfaction, and to decrease the need for a union.[35]

The following describes one employee's view of a union's effectiveness:

> I am a 51-year-old male who has been in the work force for 34 years. I've worked for A&P (Meat Cutters Union), the Louisville Metropolitan Sewer District (nonunion), Wilder Flooring Company (Building Trades Union), Canada Dry Bottling Company (nonunion), Coca-Cola Bottling Company (Teamsters Union), American Synthetic Rubber Company, Olin Matheson (both Chemical and Rubber Workers Union), Murray Asphalt Company (nonunion), J. V. Reed Manufacturing Company (nonunion), General Electric (International Union of Electrical Workers), and for the last 27 years I've worked for the Ford Motor Company (United Automobile, Aerospace, and Agriculture Implement Workers of America [UAW]).
>
> The gut feeling that I and most of my rank-and-file co-workers have is that the leadership of the union on the international level has abrogated its responsibilities towards its members in favor of good public relations activities. The unions have paralleled the degeneration of leadership in the government (federal, state, and municipal), the American churches, the public schools, and the American manufacturing companies. . . .
>
> But, for all the faults that union leadership has today, the unions are still needed (as is, for example, the government), for they are the only protection rank-and-file workers have. Companies, as always, are run by people whose main objective is making as large a profit as possible. Management (no matter what anyone says) is still in the adversary role towards workers. The companies' profits have to be split among stockholders, management bonuses and salaries, building

programs, researching, marketing, advertising, and so forth. The only way the rank-and-file have of getting a fair share of this money is to have a strong, solid union that will affect the running of the companies.

I'm a union member and proud of it![36]

This testimonial reflects the findings of a survey conducted by the U.S. Department of Labor.[37] The survey results showed that workers viewed unions as large and powerful institutions.

> A final question . . . asked the extent to which the respondents saw union leaders as out to do what is best for themselves rather than what is best for their members. . . . Approximately two-thirds of the respondents agreed that unions are more powerful than employers and that leaders are more interested in what benefits themselves than in what benefits union members.[38]

Despite this view, 80 percent of the respondents agreed that unions improved wages and job security for their members and protected them from the unfair labor practices of employers. The survey went on to examine the expectations of union members and how well the unions live up to those expectations. Three of the four main concerns expressed by the respondents reflected strong interest in the governance of the union: improving the handling of grievances, increasing feedback to members, and increasing the influence members have in running the union. The desire for improvements in the traditional bread-and-butter issues of wages, fringe benefits, job security, and safety and health came next in the listing of concerns. Finally, issues covering the quality of work were at the bottom of the respondents' priorities, although they seemed to be looking for an expansion of union activity into these areas.

The primary purpose of unions has also changed. In the years immediately following World War II, the American trade union movement developed a fundamental contradiction of purpose. The 1950s brought a new American dream to union workers—suburban homes, new appliances, two cars, and installment buying. The trade union worker had received ever-increasing paychecks and began seeing unions as a means of satisfying a growing desire for personal material wealth. In other words, union workers had turned from collective to individual orientations.[39]

Job Dissatisfaction

A key element to organizing workers is understanding why workers are dissatisfied with their job conditions. Although a union's collective bargaining success is usually measured by the wage increase it has negotiated, salary levels are not the only reason workers organize.

Management's attitude toward employees, cited as the major factor in employee dissatisfaction, is manifested in the following areas:

1. Disregard for employees when making decisions that affect their jobs
2. No acknowledgment of the seniority of employees in wages, benefits, and layoffs
3. Unfair and inconsistent discipline
4. Beneficial treatment to employees who support management
5. No grievance procedure

6. An unsafe work environment
7. No attempt to regulate production to create job security
8. Inadequate training
9. No consideration of seniority for promotion purposes
10. Lack of communication; failure to listen to employee complaints[40]

Overall, management's failure to include employees as part of the "team," involve them in decision making, or inform them of the business's status motivates employees to organize.

The recent increase of Japanese-owned and -operated businesses in the United States, primarily in the highly unionized automotive industry, has shown a marked contrast in management styles. To increase productivity, Japanese managers cultivate workers' loyalty by shortening or eliminating the distance between them, by giving employees a voice in management, and by minimizing layoffs. Allowing workers to participate in job-related decisions has increased efficiency. Training workers for more than one job cultivates flexibility, job pride, and ultimately more productivity. The relationship at these plants is good between management and employees represented by unions, and at unorganized plants, unions are having difficulties convincing workers that they need a union.[41]

How Management Resists Unions

While unions decry loss of membership and search for new ways to organize and tap nontraditional areas of unionization, managers pursue specific maneuvers to keep unions out of their plants. To discourage organization, management must be willing to address workers' concerns and revamp existing employee relations systems to reflect changes not unlike those sought by unions.[42] Ways to discourage unionization include the following:

1. Instituting valid performance review to ensure employees nonpartial merit raises and promotions and to counter the seniority provisions usually contained in union contracts
2. Improving employee communication so managers sense discontent before it becomes major dissension
3. Establishing fair grievance procedures
4. Creating a pleasant work environment
5. Promoting potential union leaders to management
6. Pursuing a more people-oriented approach to dealing with employees overall[43]

Union Membership

The decline in union membership since the 1940s can be traced to several factors (Table 1-2). The number of new workers included in organizational elections each year has declined significantly, as has the success rate of unions trying to win those new workers in organizational elections. Unions have also lost existing members by losing decertification elections. The 1970s and 1980s were particularly difficult for unions, as membership declined in highly unionized manufacturing industries hard hit by recession and foreign competition. Even if

Table 1-2   Union Membership, 1935–1996

| Year | Total Membership (thousands) | Percentage of Labor Force | |
		Total	Nonagricultural
1935	3,728	6.7%	13.2%
1940	8,944	15.5	26.9
1945	14,796	21.9	35.5
1950	15,000	22.3	31.5
1955	17,749	24.7	33.2
1960	18,177	23.6	31.4
1965	18,519	22.4	28.4
1970	20,751	22.6	27.3
1975	21,090	20.7	25.5
1980	20,100	18.8	23.0
1985	17,400	17.8	19.1
1991	16,568	16.1	17.8
1996	16,400	15.0	16.4

Sources: U.S. Department of Labor, Bureau of Labor Statistics, Bulletin 2070, *Handbook of Labor Statistics* (Washington, DC: GPO, 1980), p. 412. Larry T. Adams, "Changing Employment Patterns of Organized Workers," *Monthly Labor Review* 108, no. 2 (February 1985), pp. 25–31. U.S. Bureau of Census, *Statistical Abstract of the United States: 1996,* 114th ed. (Washington, DC, 1996).

these industries had not lost employment, union membership would have declined because of unions' poor performance in certification and decertification elections.[44]

In the traditional union stronghold—production jobs in metropolitan areas—the proportion of union to nonunion employees declined from 73 percent to 37 percent from 1961 to 1996. The substantial drop in the nation's large cities was not limited to production workers; nonsupervisory office clerical workers in unions also declined. Only part of the decline can be attributed to the employment shift toward service industries because these shifts occurred *within* the union core of manufacturing and related clerical areas. The geographic area of greatest decline was the West, which dropped from 80 percent in 1961 to 48 percent in 1984. All other areas also showed declines: Northeast, 77 percent to 57 percent; South, 48 percent to 32 percent; Midwest, 80 percent to 69 percent. Explanations of the production industry's decline of union membership include the move to less unionized Sunbelt states; the increased number of smaller (and harder to organize) plants; the trend toward building new facilities in rural, less unionized areas; and the dramatic increase in nonunion electronics production facilities as found in Silicon Valley near San Jose, California.[45]

The construction industry, once one of the strongholds of unions in the United States, has had a decline in union membership from about one-half of all construction workers in 1966 to less than one-third 30 years later. The sharpest drops in membership occurred in 1977–1978 and 1981–1985. Possible reasons for the continued decline include (1) the rising number of union members working for nonunion contractors, (2) the gradual narrowing of the union–nonunion wage gap, and (3) the disappearance of the union sector's productivity advantage, which had enabled union contractors to pay higher union salaries and still complete with nonunion contractors. The union productivity advantage had been built on the successful recruitment, screening, and training programs in the construction unions. The perceived lack of a productivity advantage in union workers has given owners and contractors tremendous incentives to switch from union to less costly nonunion labor in the construction industry.[46]

These three factors explain why the construction industry has witnessed a decline in membership since the mid-1960s. Union members, forced to work for nonunion contractors, have realized they can find more work at wage levels that approach union scale and thus realize greater annual income. At the same time, the nonunion contractor can offer the quality workmanship of union labor but underbid union contractors, who must pay union wage scales.

One response to dwindling union membership is the increased merger of labor organizations. Although mergers of labor organizations have always been a part of the labor movement, in the five years between 1979 and 1984 30 mergers took place—35 percent of all mergers since 1955.[47] Since 1984, more than 11 mergers involving 8.7 million members have increased the use of this strategy.

Avoiding unionization has become a major task of human resource managers in such traditional nonunion areas as health care, financial planning, and insurance companies. Although these white-collar workers are obvious targets for organizational campaigns, recent studies confirm the difficulties unions face in organizing these white-collar jobs.[48] The responsibilities and education of these employees cause their expectations of respect and participation at their workplace to be higher than those of assembly-line workers.[49] However, clerical employees, the majority of which are women, are increasingly attracted to organizing, especially when the union organization is a young one geared toward their demographics.[50]

Unions have attempted with limited success to organize in less traditional areas. The affirmative legislative environment of 1935–1947 in the private sector and after the 1962 presidential executive order that allowed collective bargaining in the public sector does not exist today. Certainly the growth of union membership of the 1930s and 1940s cannot be repeated. And even though workers are facing bleak economic prospects, the large number of single people and two-wage families in the workforce lessens the threat of the economic consequences of unemployment.

Salting

As union membership declined in the 1980s, the International Brotherhood of Electrical Workers (IBEW) initiated a program commonly called **salting**. Union members are encouraged to seek employment with target companies that are not unionized. The union members receive permission from the union through "salting resolutions" to work nonunion without being subject to disciplinary action by their union.

There are three types of salting. In cases in which union jobs are not available, the union members are urged to seek employment at nonunion companies and, on their own time, they talk with their fellow workers about the benefits of unionizing. In these cases, the union members are not compensated by the union for their activities. Occasionally, union members seek employment with nonunion companies at the request of the union. Again, on their own time, they promote unionization. As compensation, the union will supplement the regular pay they get from the employer to equal a "union" wage. Often, when union jobs open up or when it is clear that the company will not become unionized, the union encourages these members to move on. Finally, there are instances when regular, full-time employees of a union will seek employment with a nonunion company for the sole reason of organizing the workers. The union makes up the difference between their organizers' pay and what the employer pays the employees of the union while being employed at the nonunion company. The U.S. Supreme Court ruled in a recent case that, regardless of one's relationship with one's union, each employee of the nonunion company has rights under the National Labor Relations Act (NLRA). If the employee is doing the work asked by his or her employer, union activities cannot be used against the employee.[51]

The case, *NLRB v. Town and Country Electric*, was appealed from the 8th U.S. Circuit Court of Appeals in St. Louis. The appeals court had ruled that paid union organizers, or "salts," were not employees in the true meaning of the National Labor Relations Act and thus did not have the right to organize and engage in collective bargaining. The rationale provided by the appeals court was that paid organizers served the union's interests and not the interests of the employer. The U.S. Supreme Court, however, overturned the decision of the appeals court and found that the NLRA guarantees collective bargaining rights to "any employee." Thus, employers cannot discriminate against applicants suspected of being salts or retaliate against them for organizing activities. The central issue in the case and its appeals, then, was whether the practice of salting is a legitimate organizing method, as contended by unions, or, as employers have contended, a violation of an underlying principle of collective bargaining—that employees cannot be loyal to their union and their employer at the same time. A former salt, Scott Lyman, explained how he operated: "I used to get hired at a company to organize and report information back to the union. The big thing you look for is unfair treatment—like a supervisor who's unfair—so you can galvanize the workers together as a group."[52]

ORGANIZING CHALLENGES FOR UNIONS

Organized labor has been unable to reverse the decline in membership that gained momentum in the late 1970s (Table 1-2). In fact, the decline from 1980 to 1991 was 3.5 million members. At its peak in 1945, union membership was 35.5 percent of all nonagricultural workers, yet it was only 16 percent in 1996. The decline in organizing activity is reflected also in the number of union representation elections, which went from nearly 10,000 in 1977 to 2,400 in 1996.

Research in employee elections indicates that union success can be increased by a greater emphasis on grass-roots organization. Narrowing the time to conduct the election will also improve the results for the unions. Union leaders seeking to increase union membership must also keep current members in the fold by discouraging the "current union or no union" employee elections.[53]

Management, in its resistance to unionization, has been very successful in lengthening the time for an election and undermining union organization efforts. Another resistance tactic is giving workers more benefits so that the gains of union representation are minimized. Decertification elections have become more frequent, especially those involving a no-union choice.[54]

Many corporate executives and political leaders are calling for an expansion of cooperative efforts at the workplace, such as quality circles, QWL (quality of working life) programs, and continued moderation in wage demands. At the same time, however, the dominant trend among management is to shift investments and jobs to nonunion employment settings. This trend has been encouraged by Supreme Court decisions that allow plant relocations, liquidations, and partial closings without union input by declaring such practices to be permissive items and not mandatory. It is difficult to see how unions can act cooperatively when management practices undermine their basic existence. If the trend of declining membership continues, unions may face a life-or-death struggle, forcing them into confrontation rather than cooperation. American unions will strive to avoid further membership losses by promoting innovation in the workplace to maintain organizational competitiveness, increasing their influence on strategic business and governmental decisions that affect membership, and pursuing new organizing strategies.

The AFL-CIO voted to put more emphasis on union organizational drives and added a new unit to assist member unions in planning and executing local organized campaigns. Their growth strategy is summarized as follows:

- Make new use of the concept of collective bargaining. Unions should tailor "models to the needs and concerns of different groups that provide greater flexibility in the workplace and greater reliance on mediation and arbitration . . . and address new issues of concern to workers," such as comparable worth and increased worker participation in decision making.
- Set up new membership categories. Although many former union members are now in nonunion positions, they might still be interested in affiliating if costs were not prohibitive and services besides bargaining representation were offered.
- Provide direct services and benefits. The union suggested looking at providing services such as job referrals and supplemental insurance.
- Use corporate campaigns to deflect employer interference with attempts to form unions. Increase nonworkplace pressure—called "corporate" or "coordinated" campaigns—on employers to allow for union development.
- Improve labor communications, including training members to act as representatives to the media to publicize union activity.
- Encourage union mergers.
- Establish organizing committees that would focus attention on a particular industry or region.[55]

To respond to the continued decline in membership, unions have increased their organizing efforts in industries not traditionally unionized. These industries often include a workforce that has also not traditionally supported unions: females, professionals, white-collar, minority, and temporary employees. Union organizers faced with this relatively new situation have altered their organizing strategy accordingly. They believe that house calls during organizing campaigns are more effective than underground campaigns. Organizers also believe that the issues of technical training and work satisfaction appeal more to the nontraditional workforce (especially female workers) than do the issues of job security, participation in decision making, and grievance procedures. In general, however, union organizers still use the traditional issues of pay, benefits, grievance procedures, and security in campaigns while recognizing that other issues and tactics may be more effective in nontraditional industries.[56] Case 1-1 gives an interesting perspective on new issues in the workplace.

One of the brighter aspects of the total membership picture is the potential growth of unionism among professional workers. Professional workers have been turning to unionism as a remedy for their problems. Much of the growth in recent years has resulted from the expansion of collective bargaining in the public sector. In 1993, unions boasted that union membership had in fact increased for the

NEW WORKFORCE ISSUES

Officer Clark Fischer was ordered by his police sergeant to remove an earring (ear stud) from his left ear while on duty. The sergeant's order was upheld by the police chief. Officer Fischer complied with the order but grieved the issue. Officer Fischer alleged there was no written prohibition to the wearing of earrings by police officers in either the contract or the rules by which the force operates. He pointed out, in fact, that the chief himself wore an earring in his off-duty hours.

Anticipating a "safety" argument, Fischer pointed out that officers wear clips, glasses, pins, name tags, and any number of items that present the same kind of risks or more severe risks. The officer also argued that wearing an earring on duty gave him an advantage in his job when dealing with disen-franchised youth naturally hostile to a traditional police officer.

The city, in defending the "no earring" rule, argued that it was a safety issue because in a struggle the earring could pierce the officer's skull, and the city believed an earring would generate more negative than positive reactions from *most* of the people the officer encountered.

Decision

The arbitrator likened police to the military and in doing so pointed out that a "uniform appearance was concomitant with a professional police force." Because an earring was not explicitly *included* in the description of an officer's uniform, it was excluded. Therefore, Officer Fischer's grievance was denied.

Adapted from *Town of Vernon v. International Brotherhood of Police Officers*, 96 LA 736 (March 1, 1991).

first time in 14 years, largely as a result of public sector unions.[57] In the private sector the growth of unionism among professionals may be more prevalent than is generally assumed. The resistance of professional workers to unionism may be weakening, as evidenced by higher union success rates in professional unit elections than in all other units.[58]

Figure 1-1 lists the 10 fastest-growing occupations in the United States, many of which unions have targeted for organizing.

Another challenge facing union organizing is the proliferation of temporary and contract employees in what is called contingent employment. A survey conducted in 1995 showed that 2.2 to 4.9 percent of total employment—between 2.7 million and 6 million workers—were in contingent jobs. In addition, 8.3 million—6.7 percent of the total workforce—were independent contractors, and 3.8 million more—3.2 percent—worked for temporary help agencies, contract firms, or had on-call status. Contingent workers when compared with contingent workers were twice as likely to be young, between the ages of 16 and 24 and slightly more likely to be women and black. About half worked in the service industry, although all fields were covered: construction, professional, administrative, and laborers.[59]

Health-Care Workers

Impressive gains have been scored in adding teachers and government workers to the roles of union employees, but other service workers remain largely unorganized. Among those are most of the country's 6 million hospital, nursing home, and other health-care workers. Today unions represent only 15 percent of these

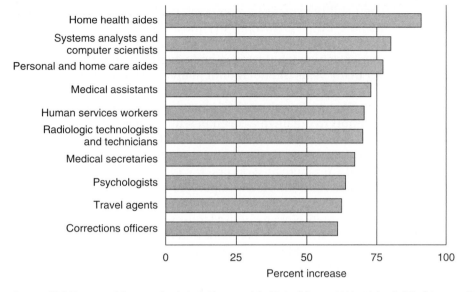

Source: U.S. Bureau of Census, *Statistical Abstract of the United States: 1992* 112th ed. (Washington, DC, 1992), p. 380.

employees. According to one professor of industrial relations, the health-care industry is "one of the key service industries they [unions] need to organize if they're going to adjust to changes in the structure of the economy."[60]

In the past, many health-care employees such as nurses and pharmacists viewed unions as unprofessional and as a potential drawback to achieving quality patient care. A number of unprecedented layoffs and wage and benefit cutbacks, however, have forced many health-care employees to rethink the union issue. Further, unions such as the Hospital and Health-Care Employees Union, the American Federation of State, County, and Municipal Employees, and the Teamsters have become much more sophisticated in their drives to organize health-care workers by hiring professional pollsters to identify workers' problems, producing videotapes to promote the advantages of unionization, and publicizing problems in patient care as well as in the health-care industry.[61]

Because organizing employees hospital by hospital is a slow and often ineffective process, some unions, such as the Service Employees International Union (SEIU), are directing their efforts toward large chains of health-care institutions in hopes that successful organizing drives will add hundreds of thousands to their membership. For example, the SEIU, in concert with another union, planned to spend up to $1 million to organize the employees of Beverly Enterprises, Inc., the nation's largest nursing home chain, employing 60,000 workers. A successful organizing drive at Beverly would likely lead to efforts at other large nonunion hospital and nursing home chains. Consequently, health-care managers have begun to improve the working conditions of their nonunion employees. In addition, organizing efforts were thwarted by a 1994 Supreme Court decision that eliminated nurse supervisors from union representation.[62]

Secretaries and Clerical Workers

The ability of unions to organize clerical workers in the private sector successfully may be critical to their ability to increase membership. Historically, clerical workers have represented one of the growth service industries in which unions have not been able to win new members easily. Possibly because clerical workers are mostly female, experience high job turnover, and usually are not found in large numbers, unions for many years did not mount many organization campaigns in the clerical area.

In 1984, however, Thomas Donahue, then secretary-treasurer of the AFL-CIO, called for a national effort to organize women in white-collar occupations, especially clerical workers. Since that effort by the AFL-CIO began, several national unions including the Teamsters, the Service Employees, the Communication Workers, the Food and Commercial Workers, the Office and Professional Employees, the Auto Workers, and the Hotel Employees have conducted significant organization drives aimed at clerical workers. Successful organizational methods used by unions in clerical units often include a large organizing committee that focuses on small meetings during the lunch hour and avoids after-work meetings that may conflict with responsibilities at home. Flyers and newsletters are carefully prepared with attention given to style, appearance, and grammar.

Private sector clerical workers are not primarily interested in "women's issues" but instead share an interest in the traditional union issues such as wages, benefits, and job security, as well as issues such as satisfying work and career advancement. Clerical workers are more likely to vote in favor of union representation (1) if they are located in a state with a strong union presence, (2) if strike activities are avoided or eliminated, and (3) if employment is increasing in their industry, thus lowering their fear of unemployment. In the past, fears of job loss, strikes, and being ostracized by fellow workers have been the biggest barriers to organizing clerical workers.[63]

According to an official of the SEIU, "With 20 million office workers in the country—90 percent of them unorganized—there is room for all sorts of organizations providing relief from what are most often low-paying, boring, repetitive, dead-end jobs."[64] As a result, the SEIU created District 925 (as in the popular movie *Nine to Five*), whose primary goal is to organize one of the largest and fastest-growing segments of the country's labor force.

But secretaries and clerical workers present a formidable challenge to unions. First, office workers are spread thinly over thousands of employers, making it difficult and time-consuming to organize workers in large numbers. Second, many office employees hold pro-management attitudes and may themselves aspire to management positions.

A great number of secretarial and clerical workers are women, and efforts to organize lower-level administrative employees must be geared toward this group. According to one employee, "Labor has got to go where the workforce is; it has to appeal to the female who's educated and for equal rights."[65] To attract more female employees to organized labor, unions have focused special attention on the working woman by lobbying, for example, for health and safety laws for employees who use computers. Organized labor is also trying hard to destroy the still-popular image of unions as institutions run "for men and by men."

In an attempt to increase the participation of women in the ranks of organized labor, more and more unions are involving women directly in the organizing process. The president of the National Association of Working Women is female, as are the organizing director for the Teamsters and the president of the Association of Flight Attendants.

Although such women may not fit the cigar-smoking, gruff-talking image of the union organizer of generations ago, their philosophies are no different from those of their predecessors. According to the head of the National Association of Working Women, "The key to improving the conditions of working women lies in organizing the private sector."[66] The use of more college-educated female organizers has largely met with success.

Japanese Auto Plants in the United States

The United Auto Workers (UAW) has been considered a powerful force in the labor movement since its formative years in the 1930s. Automation and robots have indirectly taken their toll on the UAW through improved plant productivity, but the most publicized and emotional cause of the declining UAW membership has resulted from the tremendous rise in imported automobiles, notably Japanese-made autos from Honda, Toyota, and Nissan.[67] The crisis intensified in the 1980s as Japanese companies began to build auto plants in the United States, almost all of which were nonunion. "Organizing these plants is as important as it was for us to organize Ford and GM in the 1930s and 1940s," said a UAW official.[68]

The Japanese plants in the United States have used a number of methods to remain union-free. First, they openly oppose the union and make no secret of the fact during interviews with job applicants. Second, many employees feel they will have a job for life and believe a union may interfere with the Japanese philosophy of lifelong employment. Third, the Japanese approach to human relations has apparently won favor among many U.S. workers. At Honda and Nissan plants, hourly workers meet daily with their managers to discuss production problems in a collaborative problem-solving environment. At Nissan, employees are referred to as "production technicians"; at Honda, workers are called "associates." The status differential among managers and hourly workers is also deemphasized by having one dining room and one parking lot for all employees, regardless of position.[69]

Efforts to unionize the Japanese-owned plants have generally been unsuccessful. One Honda employee said, "Why do we need a union? We already get good benefits and good pay. Look at all the companies out of business because of unions."[70] In 1989, Nissan workers gave the UAW a major setback. After a six-year organizing drive, the UAW lost its campaign 1,622 to 711.[71]

Hispanic Workers

By passage of the Immigration Reform and Control Act in 1986, which contained an amnesty provision for undocumented workers, Latino immigrants in California, Texas, Arizona, New Mexico, and Florida gained instant stability in those five labor markets. Such stability allowed these workers to begin organizing with the help of organized labor. The AFL-CIO sent hundreds of thousands of dollars to Los Angeles, for example, to help in union organizing efforts in sweatshop industries.[72]

SUMMARY

The labor union movement in the United States is the history of individuals struggling to survive. As the country grew and developed, the needs of owners and workers intertwined, and the struggle for control caused both strife and cooperation.

Labor unions had to decide whether to follow a social, political, or economic agenda. The emergence of the American Federation of Labor and the Congress of Industrial Organizations, with collective bargaining as their most important goal, meant that labor unions picked an economic agenda.

Today, that economic agenda is still the moving force behind the union movement. The loss of jobs in typically unionized fields and a more diverse workforce threaten the existence of a stronger labor movement in the United States. Unions have to rethink how they are to do their work if they are going to be able to attract new workers into their ranks.

CASE STUDY 1-1

"CRIPPLED OLD LADY"

Facts

The claimant is a 68-year-old woman who suffers from lameness due to polio. She has been a member of an office workers' union for 36 years, and also was employed for 36 years as a clerical worker by another union. She was asked by her boss to change her work schedule on the next work day from 7 A.M.–3 P.M. to 9 A.M.–5 P.M. She told her boss she could not change her schedule because she was needed the next day to accompany her husband, whose elderly mother would be having an operation. The claimant was terminated on the spot and replaced by a 20-year-old woman.

The claimant filed a grievance with her union, alleging that the firing was not based upon her refusal to change her schedule but upon her age and handicap. She cited her boss's alleged reference to her as a "crippled old lady" as proof. Pursuant to the collective bargaining contract under which she worked, her union and her union-employer convened a "Board of Adjustment" consisting of representatives from both unions to attempt to resolve her grievance. When they were unable to do so, they decided to move the case on to arbitration. At no time did her union suggest to her that her claim was weak and should be dropped.

Under the agreement, a move to arbitration set very specific steps and a very short time frame in which to take those steps: Within 24 hours, the panel was to designate one member as a neutral chairperson; if they failed to do that, they were to ask the Federal Mediation and Conciliation Service to do so. When the FMCS came back with names, they had 24 hours to choose the arbitrator.

In this case, however, the two parties—the claimant's union and her union-employer—agreed to waive the 24-hour period for selecting an arbitrator. At this point, the case just stopped. The claimant attempted to get her union to process her grievance or tell her why it would not, but she received no response.

The claimant decided to go around the grievance process and sue her union-employer directly without her own union's help. Her union-employer objected, saying that she had to let the grievance procedure resolve the issue.

Questions

1. It is a union's duty to its members to pursue a legitimate grievance on his or her behalf to a final decision. The claimant felt that her union had breached that duty. Do you agree? Explain your answer.

(continued)

2. As an employee of a union for 36 years and, presumably, a member in good standing of another union for an equal number of years, did the claimant deserve better treatment from both her own union and her union-employer?

3. Does this case lead you to believe that unions can or cannot successfully pursue more-diverse membership to increase their number of minorities, women, disabled, and younger workers?

Adapted from *Herman v. United Brotherhood of Carpenters and Joiners of America, Local Union No. 971, et al.,* 60 F.3d 1375 (9th Cir. 1995).

PROTECTED BEHAVIOR

Facts

Federal labor law protects an employee's right to engage in a union organizing campaign on the employer's property as long as the employee is on his or her own time. Nonemployee union proponents do not enjoy that same right.

Wallace, an employee of Earle Industries, was fired for insubordination because of the following incident. A union organizing campaign was under way at Earle Industries when the Reverend Jesse Jackson came to the plant to address the employees during their lunchtime. He and two union officials, who were not employees at the plant, drove into the plant's parking lot in a flatbed truck and Rev. Jackson spoke from the back of the truck to the luncheon crowd. The union officials refused to leave when told they were trespassing, and they were arrested. Jackson went toward the plant to ask plant officials to have the union representatives released. Wallace was among the crowd accompanying Jackson to the plant. Jackson entered the plant through the Employees Only entrance and was met by a plant manager, who asked him to leave. The manager told him he could reenter the plant through the visitor's entrance. According to the plant manager, Wallace told Jackson that the visitor's

entrance was locked and encouraged him to bypass the manager and to go to the vice president's office. After a few exchanges, Jackson did just that. All of this activity was captured by the news media on film. At the vice president's office, Jackson was again asked to leave and reenter through the Visitor's Entrance, which he finally did. Then the vice president met with him, and eventually the union officials were released.

Wallace was called in by management about a week later and asked to explain her actions. She denied telling Jackson that the Visitor's Entrance was locked, saying she had really been saying "clocked," and was encouraging her fellow workers to make sure they were off of the clock. The company fired her for insubordination and dishonesty, using the tape as evidence. She appealed to the NLRB, and it ruled that the company had fired her in violation of federal law because all of the events complained of were part of an organizing campaign and therefore the employer could not discipline her. The company disagreed and appealed the decision to the U.S. Circuit Court.

Questions

1. Explain why you think confrontations such as the one described in this case still occur in

(continued)

CASE STUDY 1-2 CONT.

the workplace after over a hundred years of union organizing in the United States.

2. Do you think Wallace's behavior toward the plant manager should have resulted in discipline?

3. Could the plant manager have diffused the situation by escorting the Reverend Jackson to the vice president's office and ignoring the entrance violation?

Adapted from Earle Industries v. NLRB, 151 LRRM 2300 (1996).

KEY TERMS AND CONCEPTS

American Federation of Labor (AFL)
American Railway Union (ARU)
Congress of Industrial Organizations (CIO)
Haymarket Square Riot
Homestead strike
Knights of Labor (KOL)
Molly Maguires

National Labor Union (NLU)
Pinkerton Agency
Pullman strike
salting
terms of employment
trade unionists
Wobblies

REVIEW QUESTIONS

1. Why is collective bargaining viewed as a continuous process?
2. What terms of employment are generally negotiated in labor agreements?
3. What factors in the 1800s contributed to the growth of the American labor agreements?
4. Did the Great Depression have any impact on the U.S. labor movement? If so, what?
5. What employment trends should labor leaders study in expanding their membership? What new opportunities for membership would you suggest?
6. What social and economic trends present major hurdles to union organizing during the remainder of this century?
7. What factors are contributing to the decline of union membership?
8. What do union members believe they gain from unionization? What do they lose?
9. How can the use of salts help unions win organizing elections?
10. Why is Fannie Sellins called Labor's Martyr?

TAKE IT TO THE NET

We invite you to visit the Carrell/Heavrin page on the Prentice Hall Web site at:

http://www.prenhall.com/carrellr

for this chapter's World Wide Web exercise.

Labor Heroes and Heroines   EXERCISE 1-1

Purpose:
To make sure students become familiar with leaders of the labor movement.

Task:
Pick one of the people below and write a profile about him or her (similar to the profiles in this chapter) concerning what impact he or she had on the labor movement:

Claude Ramsay	Susan B. Anthony
George Holloway	Frances Perkins
A. Philip Randolph	James Hoffa
Clarence Coe	Lane Kirkland
Cesar Chavez	Walter Reuther
"Mother" Mary Harris Jones	George Meany
Elizabeth Cady Stanton	

Current Labor Issues, Leaders, Facts   EXERCISE 1-2

Purpose:
To acquaint students with the current labor issues, leaders, and facts in their state. (The instructor may assign each student a different state.)

Task:
Use newspaper, library, and electronic references not older than a month to identify: (1) current negotiation, political, or social issues important to labor organizations; (2) the names of top labor or management officials in the news; (3) basic facts about the labor climate.

Labor Issues in the News

1. _____
2. _____
3. _____
4. _____
5. _____

Names of Labor/Management Officials

1. Name _____ Position _____
2. Name _____ Position _____
3. Name _____ Position _____
4. Name _____ Position _____
5. Name _____ Position _____

Labor Climate Facts

1. Percent of workforce that is unionized. _____
2. Right-to-work state. Yes ____ No ____
3. Largest unions in the state: (1) _____ (2) _____ (3) _____
4. Industries with the largest percentage of union membership: (1) _____ (2) _____ (3) _____
5. Recent strike activity: Union _____ Employer _____ Issues _____

CHAPTER 2

Collective Bargaining: The Workplace

- America at Work
- The Challenge of Global Competition
- Technological Change
- Representational Change
- Employee Participation and Teams
- Alternative Work Schedules

Employees at General Electric credit teamwork and better communications for the reduced conflict and increased production at this modernized assembly plant.

TEAM Act Vetoed by Clinton

In 1996, Congress passed the **Teamwork for Employees and Managers (TEAM) Act**, which amended the National Labor Relations Act (NLRA; Wagner Act) to negate the ban on certain types of company-sponsored employee involvement groups. President Clinton vetoed the TEAM Act, stating that he favored labor-management cooperation as is currently allowed under the federal law. In his veto message, he maintained that this change to the NLRA would undermine the collective bargaining process and allow for company-dominated unions.

The TEAM Act would have permitted nonunion employees in team-based workplaces to discuss workplace conditions with management. In the *Electromation* (discussed later) and similar cases, the NLRB has ruled that such teams or committees are illegal "company unions." Supporters of the new act, however, claimed that it reflected the "new economic reality" of the 1990s, which has seen widespread use of employee teams, quality circles, and employee participation committees in American business and thus the law needed to be clarified. They also contended that it was not designed to harm employees' collective bargaining rights.

Adapted from Leon Rubis, "TEAM Act Sent to Clinton," *HR News*, August 1996, pp. 1, 9.

The way the labor movement in the United States began and developed was, obviously, in response to the way the American workplace was structured. In this chapter, the American workplace is examined: its origin, its organization, and the way it is changing. We also look at some options available to unions, which need to change with the times.

AMERICA AT WORK

Historical Perspective

As discussed in chapter 1, to understand the labor-management relationship in today's world one must understand how it developed. The influences of the marketplace in developing the modern workplace cannot be ignored.

Modern history and the modern economy can be traced back to the late 1700s. It was during this period of political revolutions—the American Revolution, the French Revolution, the rise of the English Parliament—that two other revolutions began: the agricultural revolution and the industrial revolution.

During the 1700s a combination of factors caused a population boom in England, Europe, Russia, and China. The decline of diseases such as smallpox, the increase in the use of vaccination, improvements in diet, a younger marriage age for women, who, therefore, produced more children, were all possible causes.[1] People at first feared that the increase in population would strain the resources of the societies they inhabited. The shift of population from farms to urban centers, especially in England and on the continent, increased the need for solutions to this larger population. England led the way and responded in three ways. First, a major emigration occurred. The creation of the British Empire, upon which it was boasted the sun never set, was a creature of necessity. If not for the emigration between 1815 and 1914 of more than 20 million Britons to every corner of the world, the population boom in England would have seriously threatened its existence.

The second response to the needs of an increased population was the agricultural revolution that took place roughly between 1750 and 1880. The agricultural revolution refers to the changes made in farming during that century, including rotation of crops to keep the soil fertile, new breeding techniques of animal stock, and the expansion of farmland—in England both through enclosure of common lands and draining of wetlands and through settlement of England's colonies. Advances in communications and transportation put these new techniques in the reach of farmers throughout Europe and the colonies and put the food they produced on tables around the world.

Finally, the industrial revolution gave England, and then the rest of the developed world, a way to handle the population boom. The substitution of mechanical devices for human skills and of inanimate power for human or animal strength caused a vast leap forward in productivity.

The *new workplace* first benefited the masses in urban centers by providing them with jobs, albeit jobs with meager rewards. But the needs of this newly urbanized workforce were few. Consumer consumption came later and was, in fact, a result of the industrial revolution. High-volume production of affordable goods created a middle class that both produced and consumed those goods.

As modern nations emerged from these political, agricultural, and industrial revolutions, nation-states arose and became identified with the economic needs of their citizens. The growth of materialism in the 1800s was a reflection of the political shift from monarchy to representative government and the creation of a middle class. This middle class depended on partnerships between business and labor, business and capital, and business and government.

The evolution of the relationship between laboring classes and business in the United States is discussed in chapter 1. To review, before the turn of the twentieth century, the United States faced the challenges of converting from an agrarian to an industrial nation and accepting and accommodating more than 26 million immigrants who had come to this country during the half-century after the Civil War.[2] At first these immigrants were primarily of western European origin—Irish, Scandinavian, English, and German. Soon, however, word spread of the opportunities for work and religious freedom, and masses of immigrants came from Italy, Poland, Austria, Hungary, and Russia. From all of these countries groups migrated to escape direct and persistent discrimination in their native lands.[3] This second wave of immigrant workers from southern and eastern Europe also came about because of the need for cheap, plentiful labor to fill the factories and mines that multiplied during the industrial revolution.

Business in the 1890s had to create working environments that would enable people with limited industrial work experience and limited knowledge of English to function in the mines and factories. Frederick Winslow Taylor, author of *Principles of Scientific Management* (1911) and Henry Ford, whose success with the assembly line at the Ford Motor Company in the early decades of the twentieth century is legendary, are credited with establishing in organizations work principles still largely in use in American workplaces today. These principles are:

Fractionalization of work, in which workers could be taught discrete, repetitive tasks regardless of language barriers or educational achievement

"One best way" theory, in which the most efficient way to perform a job is determined by use of a clipboard and a stop watch (see Profile 2-1)

Dividing the workforce, by clearly separating those who are hired to "think" (manage, direct, plan) and those who are hired to "do" (produce, perform)

Protecting the process from the worker, with a system of controls and compliance

These work principles created the "top-down" management organization typical of U.S. corporations. The growth of the labor union movement in response to the industrialized society of early twentieth-century America was one result of this corporate organization.

Business and government joined together to ensure the profitability of the emerging industries by limiting foreign competition through trade tariffs. By keeping cheap foreign products out of the United States, government enabled business to run marginally profitable businesses. But trade tariffs imposed by other countries in response to the U.S. tariffs kept U.S.-manufactured goods out of the international market. So, to ensure that profits were sufficient to keep production going, business and capital entered into a partnership.

The partnership of business and capital was reflected in the creation of national corporations. They were created to reduce domestic competition and thereby keep profits high enough to keep businesses operating. The so-called **robber barons** who built the railroads, produced steel, and mined minerals became the focus of both admiration and contempt.

"ONE BEST WAY" THEORY

Frederick Winslow Taylor, in his work *Principles of Scientific Management,* proffered his theory that there is "one best way" to perform a job and that it is determined by using a clipboard and a stop watch. Taylor's theory did not go unchallenged even in his own time. Labor unions criticized Taylor's attitude that systems should drive the work rather than people. They complained that scientific management ignored workers' skills and know-how, that it failed to address the motivation of workers, and that the monotonous jobs were detrimental to workers' performance. At that same time, Frank and Lillian Gilbreth, credited with being the first "efficiency experts," were leading scientific management into a far more humanistic era.

Frank Gilbreth was an apprentice bricklayer who rose through the ranks to become a successful owner of a construction company. His observations of the varied ways in which construction workers performed their tasks convinced him that by observation and by addressing what motivates employees, he could arrive at a better system for construction.

Lillian Gilbreth, as a student of industrial psychology, brought an academic's discipline and scientific protocol to her husband's practical knowledge. Between 1912 and 1924, the Gilbreths advised man-

ufacturing companies on improving their work processes. Their approach, unlike Taylor's, included sensitivity to the concerns of the workers.

One noted innovation they used to study the workplace was micromotion, utilizing the new motion picture camera. The Gilbreths refined the technique by using cyclegraphs in which workers had small lights attached to hands, feet, and head and photos were taken of them with long-exposure techniques. This innovation enabled the Gilbreths to analyze the motions for wasted, strained, or duplicative efforts. These studies led to suggestions of changes in processes, such as where to place key equipment used in production, as well as to improve worker stations, for example by raising or lowering benches or using chairs on springs to reduce vibration. The Gilbreths' work led to their theory of the "one best way" based upon the 17 "pure motions" recorded by their cameras and which they believed any job included.

The growth of labor unions before and immediately after World War I, which coincided with Taylor's and the Gilbreths' work, caused many industrialists to start internal industrial relations departments and company unions. Personnel management began to decrease the use of scientific management, at least by that name.

Adapted from Peter Liebhold, "Seeking 'The One Best Way,'" *Labor's Heritage* 7, no. 2 (Fall 1995), p. 18.

The United States had always suspected monopolies, having suffered in colonial days from the abuse of royally protected monopolies such as the East India Company.[4] The Sherman Antitrust Act of 1890 prohibited price fixing by American firms. But in effect the act promoted the acquisition of smaller companies by large conglomerates because when U.S. Steel, for example, had to pay more for domestic than foreign iron and coal, it simply bought the companies that produced iron and coal domestically.

The laborers who organized to counter the power of the Carnegies, Rockefellers, and Goulds had little success until the passage of the Wagner Act. By forcing big business to sit down at a bargaining table with representatives of the workers, government was able to create more-equal partners where previously only inequality had existed.

This protection by, and promotion of, unions by government led to the heyday of union organizing. By 1945, 35 percent of the nonagricultural workers in the

Wagner's Act

United States were represented by unions. The ability of labor to organize and support strikes before, during, and after World War II caused business to seek restraints on labor's legal protection. When the Taft-Hartley Act was passed in 1947 to curb unions' right to strike, organized labor was not able to prevent its passage or to effect its repeal.[5]

Decline and Rebirth of Manufacturing

In the 1950s the United States was at its peak as the mass producer of goods for a global consumer market. The reason was clear. Except for the bombing of Pearl Harbor, World War II had not taken place on U.S. soil. Unlike Europe and Japan, the United States emerged from World War II with its industrial base intact. Its production system was geared to turn out standard, assembly-line products in high volume. For the United States, a buyer's market existed worldwide. Plenty of customers, domestic and international, were ready to absorb its goods while other industrial nations sought to rebuild from the war.

If one imagines national production as the progress of a locomotive, the United States stayed on track through the war and was still moving forward after the war. Other nations had been derailed by the war, and it would take years for them to rebuild. However, while the United States forged ahead using prewar techniques, those other countries were rebuilding by moving into advanced technology. This buildup of industry using the latest technology, especially during the last quarter of this century, now places the United States at a competitive disadvantage. Figure 2-1 and Table 2-1 show a declining growth rate for domestic products in the United States and a reduced output as compared with Japan and the European countries in the 1970s and 1980s. The United States has rebounded in the 1990s as U.S. manufacturing has instituted "lean and mean" management and new technology.

Rates of Growth of U.S. Domestic Product (annual average)   **Figure 2-1**

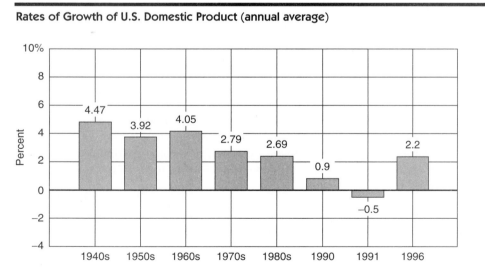

Source: Reprinted with permission of Paul Kennedy, *Preparing for the Twenty-First Century* (New York: Random House, 1993), p. 295 and the U.S. Federal Reserve Bank, St. Louis, 1996.

Table 2-1	U.S. Output as a Percentage of Selected Nations' Output for Five Selected Years				
	1970	1975	1980	1987	1996
Japan	495%	317%	254%	188%	256%
Germany	547	371	330	401	363
France	706	462	409	507	466
United Kingdom	820	673	502	649	740
European Economic Community	158	113	93	104	156

Source: Reprinted with permission of Paul Kennedy, *Preparing for the Twenty-First Century* (New York: Random House, 1993), p. 295 and the U.S. Federal Reserve Bank, St. Louis, 1996.

THE CHALLENGE OF GLOBAL COMPETITION

As the American marketplace expanded in the 1950s and 1960s, it shared its knowledge with the recovering industries in Japan and, to a lesser extent, Germany. The current global marketplace consists of both consumers and industries competing with U.S. industries.

The United States is being challenged to compete in the global marketplace because of the changes in the way the world does business. Specifically these changes were caused by the creation of worldwide consumer demands and quality standards, by changes in the doctrine of comparative advantage, and by a revolution in how manufacturing is done.[6]

What's in a Name?

Everyone in the world is a potential consumer. Advertising agencies and marketing research groups spend millions of dollars each year to discover what sells. The United States has long been a country of name brands. Now we can point to a worldwide consumer market that demands the elegance of a Gucci shoe, the consistency of a McDonald's hamburger, and the practicality of disposable diapers from Proctor & Gamble. This name brand market grew up in the world's richest countries and has spread to every corner of the globe.

A worldwide standard of performance associated with a name brand is created by active marketing. In addition, the product presented in the marketplace as the *best* has had to perform that way in order to maintain the demand. A company must be big enough, and profitable enough, to invest in the research and development necessary to maintain a quality product. Unless companies are in the worldwide marketplace, they do not have enough capital to keep up with their competitors. In addition to the need for capital, businesses must go international to take advantage of the rapid development of technology. Companies have to form alliances to secure access to new technologies and to share in the risk of capital investments.[7]

Changes in Comparative Advantage

In the past, economists explained the international competition of nations in trade through the doctrine of **comparative advantage**. The doctrine is simple enough: Nations concentrated their efforts in the area in which they had a competitive advantage. In Florida, for example, farmers grew grapefruit and oranges because of the soil and weather. In Iowa they grew potatoes. Michigan produced cars and trucks because of the nearby steel industry and energy resources. In South Carolina, the garment industry took hold because of cheap labor.

Before the availability of labor, energy, and raw materials became global, this doctrine worked well and defined free trade among nations. Now, few resources are so static as to preclude their availability elsewhere. Labor is mobile, energy is plentiful, and raw materials are transportable. Companies must seek their competitive advantage separate from their nation's historical competitive advantage. To capture the market, companies must not only create the best so that consumers demand their products but must also produce them at a price consumers can pay. To drive down the price and maintain the quality, companies must produce products in bulk, thereby realizing savings by economies of scale.

Manufacturing Revolution

From Henry Ford's creation of the assembly line in the 'teens to its heyday in the 1950s, manufacturing in the United States defined efficiency. Planned obsolescence of manufactured products ensured a continuous market. Uniformity of costs in major U.S. companies were arrived at through nationwide union agreements that controlled wages and by domestic suppliers that controlled availability of raw materials. Competition was not an all-or-nothing situation. Market shares were traded among the big players, depending on who could offer the latest new and improved model.

External competition developed in the 1970s when Japanese-made products exceeded U.S.-made products in quality at lower prices.[8] The Japanese had discovered quality control and converted their straight-line assembly plants into team assembly plants. The workers in the teams worked on and saw the finished products instead of seeing only their discrete part of a long assembly process. It became clear to workers how important their part was to the whole. Quality control became the responsibility of each worker.

The Japanese manufacturers had also learned the value of automation in quality control. Automation gave Japan a competitive advantage not because it reduced labor costs but because it increased both the quality and efficiency of the manufacturing process. Workers on the assembly line might allow an irregular or damaged piece of goods to get by them; an automated system did not. In addition, an automated system coupled with a just-in-time inventory system forced the reduction of inefficiencies because in order for it to work, it had to run perfectly. (A just-in-time [JIT] inventory system delivers parts to a production area when needed. The timing forces the process to be precise.)

In response to the loss of U.S. superiority in the worldwide consumer market, American companies tried a number of avenues. First, they pushed for protection from the importation of foreign manufactured products. The success of such embargoes was short-lived. External competitors simply circumvented the bans or imported the discrete pieces of a product and assembled them on U.S. soil. Second, U.S. companies tried to beat the price of competitor goods by cutting costs to the bone. They closed inefficient plants and laid off workers. They moved operations to the very countries their competitors came from and set up "cheaper" plants. But they still could not beat the price of their foreign competitors. Third, U.S. companies embarked in the 1960s and 1970s on transforming themselves into financial holding companies: buying and selling corporate assets, engaging in unfriendly takeovers and leveraged buyouts. Such transactions changed the bottom-line numbers for a given year but did nothing to restore the health of the operation.[9]

As we head for the year 2000, American industry has found new ways to compete successfully in the global economy. Thus, U.S. companies must operate in a new manner. The competitive standards at play in the global market are productivity, quality, variety, customization, timeliness, and convenience. Linking all of these standards is the need to be flexible.[10]

Flexible Productivity in Manufacturing.   Flexible productivity in manufacturing is seen as a need for the future. As manufacturers regroup, retrain, and retool to manufacture in a more efficient and effective way, something more will be needed to pull away from the pack. Being able to produce unique products for different demands at the same manufacturing plant will give companies that competitive edge. Using automation, robots, and computerization, an assembly operation can change and adopt products for isolated consumer markets with ease and at low cost. U.S. manufacturing has been designed to produce homogeneous products to satisfy an upwardly mobile population. The use of automation and unskilled work was productive for that type of product. But to become the producer of many unique products of high quality for a worldwide market of eager consumers willing to pay for customized goods demands flexible and skilled employees. New technology can be used to tailor products to unique needs.

Flexible Productivity in Services.   Flexibility is not limited to the manufacturing of goods. Leading-edge companies will be relying on customized *knowledge* and *service* as well as customized products for sale in the marketplace. Such businesses will be peopled by problem solvers, problem identifiers, and strategic brokers. *Problem solvers* must be able to change constantly and adapt a product to the customer's needs; *problem identifiers* will need to be able to identify customers' needs and show how customized goods fill those needs; and *strategic brokers* must put the problem solvers and problem identifiers together.[11]

A business with these groups of people will naturally shed the pyramid bureaucracy of the past to enable these three groups to interrelate properly. In addition, a network that includes suppliers, customers, regulators, and financiers will be established to enable the business to beat its competition. In an "out-of-the-box thinking" exercise, 15 executives from leading U.S. companies designed just such a theoretical network and demonstrated that such an operation could produce a custom-made, defect-free automobile in three days.[12]

The valuable asset of these enterprises will be its employees. Workers for these businesses will no longer be interchangeable. The days of cheap labor will be over. Education, experience, and inventiveness will be required. Competition for good employees will be fierce.

William B. Johnston, author of "Global Workforce 2000," studied world workforce trends and concluded that companies prepared to operate globally and compete for human resources on a worldwide basis can develop a competitive advantage. The willingness to tap worldwide labor sources, however, will mean that changes will have to be made. Johnston suggests that the flow of skilled and unskilled labor from the developing world to the well-paid jobs in cities of the industrial world will cause nations to reconsider their immigration policies. It will become cost-effective for U.S. companies to locate in countries such as Cuba,

Poland, and Hungary, which are economically underdeveloped but with a well-educated workforce. It will also lead to standardized labor practices.[13] Table 2-2 gives a brief overview of workforce growth in selected countries.

Flexible Productivity in Ideas.   The third and final area of flexibility for U.S. companies to adopt from international companies is to be alert to new opportunities and make change happen. Companies that have been bested by their competitors have learned to change the rules. When 3M introduced the photocopier, it thought it stood alone and apart from its competitors. But three years later Xerox had left 3M behind by supplying the photocopier market with rentals instead of sales. At that time, this marketing approach was quite revolutionary. Hitachi overtook Caterpillar in the marketing of heavy machinery by leasing the heavy equipment through Hertz Rent-a-Car locations. And, of course, the Japanese-devised Toyota Production System is pointed to as the most significant factor for quality improvement in Japanese products since World War II.[14]

Flexibility in organizations will enable them to compete in timeliness. There is a rush to develop new products and then a rush to produce them and put them in the consumer's hand. There continues to be a need to improve the product before the competitor does and then to use what has been learned to develop the *next* new product.[15]

The effect on the American workforce of these major changes in the way business is done has been predictable. Layoffs, subcontracting, and relocations have hit every manufacturing industry. Because union jobs had been concentrated within trades and manufacturing industries, unions have lost members and influence. Case 2-1 is an example of how unions lose jobs through **outsourcing** of the work to subcontractors. Unions however, have tried to address the changes happening in the workplace in a number of ways.

Perhaps the most important contribution to the dramatic improvement in U.S. manufacturing and overall business activity has been the use of **international alliances**. In the 1980s alone, U.S. companies formed more than 2,000 alliances in Europe as the markets of former communist countries opened up. U.S.

World Workforce Growth (in millions)				Table 2-2
Country/ Region	Labor Force, 1970	Labor Force, 1985	Labor Force, 2000	Labor Force Annual Growth Rate, 1985–2000
United States	84.9	122.1	141.1	1.0
Japan	51.5	59.6	64.3	0.5
Germany	35.5	38.9	37.2	−0.3
France	21.4	23.9	25.8	0.5
Canada	8.5	12.7	14.6	0.9
China	428.3	617.9	761.2	1.4
Indonesia	45.6	63.4	87.7	2.2
Mexico	14.5	26.1	40.6	3.0
Turkey	16.1	21.4	28.8	2.0
Philippines	13.7	19.9	28.6	2.4

Source: Adapted from William B. Johnston, "Global Work Force 2000: The New World Labor Market," *Harvard Business Review* (March–April 1991), p. 117.

OUTSOURCING

The company allowed a nonbargaining unit employee to repair an electrical relay on the plant's security system, and the union filed a grievance.

The union contended that the contract was violated because it prohibits supervisors from performing the work normally performed by members of the bargaining unit except in emergencies, for training purposes, or to check equipment.

The company's position was that maintenance of the plant's security system is work not normally performed by the union members but contracted out to an outside contractor. Therefore, the repair is not within the scope of the contract.

The union acknowledged that the normal maintenance is done by an outside contractor but contended that those contracts were entered into pursuant to provisions of the collective bargaining agreement that stated that prior to outside contracting, the company and union would agree on the scope of the contract. The scope of this contract did not allow supervisors to perform the work. It was the union's position that it agreed to have an outside contractor maintain the security system but not to allow supervisors to make repairs on the system. The union believed it has some control on the scope of outside contracts but none on work assigned to supervisors.

Decision

The arbitrator decided this grievance on the past practice of the parties. The security system had never been maintained by union members. Because it had not, it was not work normally done by the unit members; therefore, the section prohibiting supervisors from performing the work did not apply. The union's point on agreeing to the scope of an outside contract only was simply dismissed as irrelevant to this case.

Adapted from *Pennsylvania Power Co. v. International Brotherhood of Electrical Workers Local 272*, 85 LA 797 (1985).

---

companies, now multinational companies, have formed partnerships, joint business ventures, and licensing arrangements with companies from other countries to enable them to effectively compete in the world economy.[16]

The North American Free Trade Agreement (NAFTA) between the United States, Mexico, and Canada, signed in 1993, and the General Agreement on Tariffs and Trade (GATT) in 1994, which reduced tariffs worldwide and created protection for intellectual property rights among 124 nations also provided substantial boosts to U.S. global activities. In the first year alone under NAFTA U.S. exports rose 22 percent.[17]

NUMMI: Apex of Labor-Management Cooperation

In 1962, General Motors built a new Chevrolet plant in Fremont, California. By 1982, the plant's constant labor problems were blamed for poor quality, low productivity, high absenteeism, and GM's decision to close the plant. But the plant reopened in 1983 as New United Motor Manufacturing Inc. (NUMMI), a unique international joint effort between GM and Toyota. It was the United States' first taste of the Japanese-style team management. Over the next several years the new Japanese management combined with United Auto Workers (UAW) members to make U.S. labor history. For years, GM had complained that the UAW was the cause of its problems at the Fremont plant. But 85 percent of the NUMMI workers were those same union workers, who when combined with Japanese management, produced high-quality Toyota Corollas and Chevrolet Novas (now GEO Prizm). The NUMMI plant convinced many Americans that the old problems were with American *management* not with American *labor*. GM, however, did learn a great deal about Japanese management and manufacturing methods. Many of the NUMMI techniques, especially employee involvement teams, were incorporated into GM's highly regarded Saturn plant in Tennessee.

Exactly how did the new Japanese management change one of the least productive U.S. auto plants into one of the finest? Several factors combined may provide the answer:

- *Cooperation*. The most significant change was the spirit of cooperation that began with the UAW/NUMMI "letter of intent" including these broad guidelines:

  1. Management and labor should work together as a team.
  2. Management and labor should build the highest-quality automobile at the lowest cost.
  3. Management should provide workers a voice in decision making.
  4. Management and labor should constantly seek quality improvement.
  5. Management should maintain a profitable business and provide fair wages and benefits, job security, and opportunity for advancement.

- *Training*. The initial 240 NUMMI production workers were sent to Japan for three weeks of training on a Toyota production line and in the classroom. Subjects included:

  1. *Kaizen* (continuous improvement)
  2. *Jidoka* (the pursuit of superior quality)
  3. Just-in-time inventory
  4. Teamwork
  5. Union-management relations

- *Fewer job classifications*. In the old GM plant there were 95 job classifications that generally produced routine, boring jobs. NUMMI has four classifications—one unskilled and three skilled.
- *Fewer supervisors*. With teams performing routine management functions and a focus on *building* quality (rather than *inspecting* for it), fewer supervisors and inspectors were needed.
- *Work teams*. The 2,400 hourly employees were organized into teams of five to ten members who rotate among as many as 15 tasks.

The NUMMI plant has been so successful that in 1991 Toyota opened a new $350 million compact-truck line on the same site.[18]

Historically, union leaders have been skeptical of some so-called technological change programs initiated by management. Labor's past resistance is especially deep-rooted in the manufacturing sector, where changes have robbed workers of their special skills. Computer-controlled equipment not only replaced many jobs

TECHNO-LOGICAL CHANGE

but also replaced the skills required to do them, undermining labor's traditional position. The unskilled or semiskilled workers following in the wake of these changes can be quickly and easily trained on jobs and do not have the bargaining power of their forerunners, who took years to develop the necessary experience and skills.[19]

Another deep-rooted resistance to technological change may have resulted from labor's negative experience with past management plans that were sometimes thinly veiled methods of reducing the workforce or pay levels rather than implementing true technological change. Management programs disguised as reorganization attempts, introduction of more efficient equipment, or job enrichment programs have not always been in good faith and resulted in arousing the suspicions of union officials.

In recent years, labor leaders have been particularly skeptical of job enrichment programs. Because employees take on additional responsibilities, determining whether a program will result in increased job autonomy or simply increased workloads is difficult at best. William Winpisinger, president of the International Association of Machinists, stated what many of his labor colleagues believe to be true:

> Studies tend to prove that workers' dissatisfaction diminishes with age. That's because older workers have accrued more of the kinds of job enrichment that unions have fought for—better wages, shorter hours, vested pensions, a right to have a say in the working conditions, a right to be promoted on the basis of seniority and all the rest. That's the kind of enrichment that unions believe in.[20]

Technological change programs that attempted to reorganize or redesign jobs to reduce the number of union employees or affect pay scales left hard feelings.

Unions have utilized collective bargaining to protect their members against technological changes leading to layoffs, demotions, or the expansion of unskilled versus skilled positions. Many labor agreements contain clauses requiring the retraining of workers displaced by automation, forbidding layoffs due to technological changes, and providing expensive severance pay plans. Such actions tend to reduce cost-effectiveness of proposed technological advances.

Today, however, many union leaders agree that collective bargaining practices that require that work be performed by obsolete, low-productivity methods are self-destructive. It has taken years for some leaders to develop this attitude, but they realize that a company cannot stay competitive within the marketplace using outdated manufacturing methods. Therefore, labor does not always resist technological change and instead allows management a free hand in the collective bargaining agreement when profits can be shared. For example, in the Scanlon plan (see chapter 7), productivity and profit sharing are related, and increased earnings are shared. A fair way of dividing up productivity and profits has been agreed upon by labor and management in advance. As the profits grow because of increased productivity, everyone gets a larger total share.

With strict agreed-upon means of measuring productivity and profit sharing, the exact wages and benefits due labor are not set forth in the collective bargaining agreement but rather are negotiated with stated productivity and profit-sharing formulas to determine what labor will get at the end of a predetermined period of time. This flexibility enables management to pay increases only when they are earned, and thus the company is able to pay them, and jobs may be saved because fewer layoffs are needed during hard times.

Retraining Rights

Because the need to stay competitive with nonunion and foreign businesses has caused union leaders to accept technology changes as necessary and normal conditions of work today rather than oppose technological change, negotiators anticipate it and bargain for advance notice, retraining rights, and outplacement assistance for affected workers.

A total systematic approach to **technological change** and **worker retraining** was developed by the Ford Motor Company and the United Auto Workers (UAW) in 1982. The decision to close the San Jose, California, plant was announced along with a labor-management initiative to provide assistance to displaced workers. The total program included the following agenda:

- *Orientation and benefits.* All workers were included in meetings that provided information about available services, company benefits, and "personalized" information about specific benefits at the time of shutdown.
- *Assessment and testing.* More than 1,600 workers participated in retraining programs after taking a skills test administered by the California Employment Department.
- *Basic education and vocational courses.* In-plant courses in basic math, reading, and English enabled 183 workers to pass the general equivalency diploma (GED) examination. In addition, Ford personnel taught courses in computers, welding, statistical quality control, auto mechanics, metal repair, electronics, and so on. More than 2,100 workers participated.
- *Seminars and programs.* Additional in-plant seminars were offered in small business, real estate, armed security, and more.
- *Target vocational retraining.* Local technical training institutions taught more than 30 courses in areas such as microwave and machine tool technology and auto service. The courses were paid for by the 1982 Ford-UAW "Nickel Fund" for training, Job Training Partnership Act (JTPA) of 1982, and the state of California.
- *Job search and placement.* Two-day job search workshops were conducted by California Employment Development Department staff workers.
- *Ford plant relocation.* Under the 1982 agreement, 117 San Jose hourly workers chose to relocate to other Ford plants in the United States.[21]

As a result of the program, more than 83 percent of those employees who reentered the labor market secured employment, and 21 percent chose retirement under the agreement's benefit plan. Both labor and management consider the program a model worker-retraining program, a workable approach to the challenge of technological change.

Robotics

Because one of the most dramatic areas of technological development has been in the science of robotics it is important to understand it. Industrial robots are often divided into two classes: anthropomorphic robots, which approximate the appearance and functions of humans; and nonanthropomorphic robots, which are very machinelike and have limited functions.[22]

During the 1950s and 1960s, robots could not compete with human dexterity and ability to make instant or complicated decisions. Although computerized automation was desirable, automated machinery could not be easily adapted to various production functions.

In the 1970s, the development of the *microprocessor,* which automates production functions, and the *silicon chip,* a miniaturized system of integrated circuits about the size of a quarter, gave robots greater capabilities than previously envisioned. The silicon chip can perform millions of multiplications per second. It has been estimated that a calculation costing 80 cents with 1950s computer technology now costs less than one cent after adjusting for inflation.[23]

The first generation of robots of the 1950s performed simple jobs and had limited capabilities. The second generation of robots, which are predominant today, have the senses of vision and touch, making them more anthropomorphic in their complex capabilities and more adaptable to production needs. Carl Remick, a General Motors official, believes that second-generation robots also have decision-making capabilities, enabling them to react to their environment much as humans do.[24]

Second-generation robots are particularly desirable for hazardous and dangerous jobs. A study conducted at Carnegie-Mellon University estimates that it will become technically feasible to replace *all* manufacturing operations in the automotive, electrical equipment, machinery, and fabricated metals industries with robots in the future.[25]

The economics of robotics is quite simple. Robots, as compared with human labor, can provide lower cost, higher reliability, and fewer errors. For example, the average labor cost in the United States has increased to about $20 per hour, while the average cost of robot use is less than $5 per hour. Even more dramatic is the fact that inflation will increase human labor costs, but additional technological advances will most likely reduce the costs of robotics.[26] General Motors, for example, recognizes that it can use robots at an average cost of $6 per hour for many functions previously performed by skilled workers at $27 per hour.[27]

The increased use of robotics is supported by both labor and management because of their growing concern for quality control and competitiveness in international markets. Union leaders, anticipating the robotics revolution, have recently bargained for advance notice of the implementation of robots and for retraining rights so members have new skills for long-term employment.

In general, then, unions have not been opposed to robots *if* the affected workers are provided with the training necessary for the new jobs created by technological change. Although unions realize that robotics will cut into their membership, it is preferable to losing all jobs to foreign competition.[28]

REPRESEN- TATIONAL CHANGE

As the United States struggles to remain competitive in international markets and to respond to changing domestic needs, the process of collective bargaining will need to undergo substantial changes. From the early 1800s, management fought labor unions as being illegal combinations in restraint of trade and used many techniques to combat unions' existence. The passage of the National Labor Relations Act in the 1930s and the subsequent Taft-Hartley amendments put into law the requirement to bargain collectively. But because the process was imposed by law, a general adversarial relationship developed and has remained.[29]

A Harris poll reported that a majority of the general public believes that unions contribute significantly less than they once did to the growth and efficiency of business.[30] Although a majority of union leaders surveyed disagreed with that judgment, the Harris poll reflected a change of attitude toward unions. Many people do not feel that unions aid in the process of making organizations more efficient and productive. Following are some attempts by labor and business to change.

Win-Win Strategy

Can labor and management change from an adversarial relationship to a problem-solving one? Such a change should, of course, benefit both management and employees. At least one successful example occurred in a large, modern manufacturing plant that was plagued by union-management conflict. Union and management were dependent on each other for their existence, and they had a long history of bitter hostility. The plant had suffered two major strikes within a few years, and a third strike because of upcoming negotiations seemed inevitable. The employee relations manager, realizing that both sides had more to lose than to gain in an increasingly competitive marketplace, proposed a development seminar to improve relations. Both sides reluctantly agreed to participate rather than to suffer through a third strike. External labor consultants, using conflict resolution techniques, set four primary goals for the seminar: (1) Establish a basis for a problem-solving relationship; (2) develop concrete plans for moving away from an adversarial relationship toward one of mutual trust; (3) create task forces to solve identified problems; (4) plan follow-up and reevaluation programs.

After a considerable amount of antagonism and disagreement, each side conceded major changes in policy that indicated its willingness to cooperate. Both groups saw the real need to pursue a superordinate goal of keeping the plant productive and competitive if there were to be a prosperous future for the company. Once both groups adopted a positive attitude, they were able to develop specific means of improving labor-management relations.

Toward the end of the seminar, the plant manager admitted that management had painted itself into a corner by its labor relations policy. Management then issued a summary statement to the union describing its thoughts and feelings:

1. We recognize we have a deep win-lose orientation toward the union.
2. We want to change!
3. Barriers to overcome: Convince the union we want to change; convince ourselves we have the patience, skill, and convictions to change.
4. We're responsible to bring the rest [of the management team] on board.
5. We recognize the risk but want to resist the temptation to revert to win-lose when it gets tough.[31]

Before the use of conflict resolution, the plant ranked last in economic performance among 11 similar companies; five years later, it was number one. While this experience may not be the solution for all companies and unions, it might be one to consider when faced with the economic consequences of a shutdown. Some proponents of new approaches to labor-management relations believe that allowing diverse types of representational forms—alternatives to unions—is necessary.[32]

Saturn Agreement

An excellent example of what is sometimes called "the new industrial relations" in the United States is the agreement for the Saturn plant. In 1983, General Motors and the UAW began jointly planning to build a new competitive small car. By 1985, they had signed a Memorandum of Agreement that included many innovative joint labor-management methods. This agreement was accomplished several years before the Saturn plant in Tennessee would produce a single automobile. Some of the innovative provisions of the **Saturn agreement** include:[33]

1. **Single-union recognition**. The UAW is given exclusive representation rights for bargaining unit employees and union shop security and checkoff clauses.
2. **Single status**. "Saturn and the Union will strive to achieve positive symbols that minimize the differentiation between people in the elements of a successful organization, such as methods of pay, purchase of GM products, common cafeterias, parking identification, entrances, lack of time clocks, etc."
3. **Labor flexibility**. The Saturn mission is to achieve the highest possible operational efficiency through effective integration of human, technological, and business systems by means of broader job classifications, continuous employee education and training, and qualified permanent job security.
4. **Advisory/negotiation board(s)**. The Saturn decision-making process emphasizes information sharing, consultation, decentralization of authority and responsibility, and consensus building. UAW representatives play key roles at several structural levels: a UAW counselor elected by work unit members to lead them; a UAW business unit adviser elected at-large to help coordinate interrelated work units and work unit modules representing common work areas; a UAW manufacturing advisory committee adviser elected at-large as the plant agreement administrator; and a UAW strategic advisory committee adviser selected by the International UAW to participate in long-term company planning.
5. **No-strike clause**. The agreement states that unauthorized strikes, lockouts, restriction of output, slowdowns, and the like are inconsistent with the Saturn philosophy, mission, and culture. None of these actions shall be taken until all the requirements of the procedure to modify the agreement are fulfilled. The parties may then exercise their right to strike or lockout.

The GM-UAW Saturn agreement is only one example of the fundamental changes in collective bargaining relationships that are becoming more common each year. Although none of the individual elements of the Saturn agreement is entirely new, taken together they can be considered a substantial departure from the traditional adversarial approach to one of mutual interests.[34]

Associated Unionism

Another alternative representation system being promoted by advocates of unionization is **associated unionism**. It combines the employee association, thought of as a bar to unionism, and the traditional union.

Employee associations grew up in occupations that traditionally either rejected the idea of unions, bargaining, and strikes, such as engineers and nurses, or among groups barred from such activities by law, such as teachers and other public employees. Such associations gave these professionals a support system and a way to push for improvements for their profession in lobbying for legislative protections or by continuing education programs.

Today, unions are borrowing from this tradition and approaching those who are, perhaps, anti-union and offering them associate memberships. Such associations have lower dues and do not engage in collective bargaining but do give individuals helpful services. They educate people as to their job rights; they offer affordable health care; and they help with job training and career planning.[35] Like the workplace itself, where flexibility and response to unique demands have become necessities, unions have had to become flexible and responsive to individual worker demands. See Case 2-2, for example, for how maternity leave issues affect unions.

Thus, the challenge for unions in the future might be to combine the flexibility and responsiveness of associations with the discipline and solidarity of unions in order to provide the workforce with an effective representative to the employer. In addition, such new associational unions must avoid the dichotomy of pushing for social reforms at the expense of workplace representatives, which doomed the early workers' unions.

If the association and the union are to mesh, five issues need to be understood:

1. **Focus on principles**. The new workplace demands more of the workforce. Individuals must make decisions. Certainly that is true in professional and white-collar jobs, but more and more it is a part of the way line employees are asked to work also. Teamwork, as described later in this chapter, is not a theory but an actual workplace necessity. Therefore, the group representing employees to the employer must be able to articulate more than the financial needs of the workplace.
2. **Internal communication**. Just as top-down management is being compressed in today's workplace, top-down unionism must change. Today's workers demand participation in the union's decision making. "Big labor" has begun to realize it must establish a two-way communication network.
3. **More services**. Workers' needs are more than just representation during contract negotiations. Unions need to participate in the changes taking place in the workplace, such as teamwork issues and quality circles issues. Unions, like associations, need to offer direct services, such as insurance, and job training.
4. **New tactics**. Alternatives to strikes as a power tactic must be developed. With the increased use of replacement workers during strikes, this "right" has lost much of its effectiveness. Unions are turning to public relations as a tool of choice in disagreement with an employer. In addition, employee-owned companies are becoming more prevalent.
5. **New alliances**. Unions must broaden their appeal. They have to begin to see allies outside of their own space. For example, when locked in a strike with Eastern Airlines, the union was able to join with bankers interested in preserving their investments to force a settlement. Unions must begin to see where their interest coincides with others—investors, the public, other nonunion workers, or indeed the target employer—to forge alliances to further their objectives.[36]

MATERNITY LEAVE

A member of the bargaining unit represented by the union adopted a baby girl. She delayed the adoption for three weeks to avoid missing work because it was a busy time for her employer. When she finally adopted the baby, she took a two-week vacation then applied for a six-month unpaid maternity leave pursuant to the contract, which read in part:

ARTICLE X
Leaves of Absence
Section 4
Unpaid Leaves

Reasonable Purpose

1. Leaves of absence for a limited period without pay—not to exceed 90 days—shall be granted for any reasonable purpose. Extension to be granted with approval of Borough Council.
2. Reasonable purpose in each case shall be agreed upon by the Union and the Borough.

Maternity

1. Maternity Leaves—not to exceed six months—shall be granted at the request of an employee. Maternity leaves shall, upon the request of the employee, be extended or renewed for a period not to exceed six months.

The employer denied her maternity leave request but offered her a first and second 90-day leave for "reasonable purpose." The employee filed a grievance.

The employer contended that the employee is not entitled to maternity leave because she did not conceive and bear the child. The term *maternity* modifies *leaves* and as such is an adjective defined by *Webster's Dictionary* to refer to "women during pregnancy and confinement." Other collective bargaining agreements correctly refer to the leave as *childbirth leave* and this is obviously the purpose. The employer offered the grievant a *reasonable-purpose leave* she refused to take, which would have been the same six months off.

The grievant contended that the term *maternity leaves* in the contract is a noun defined by *Webster's Dictionary* to refer to "the quality or state of being a mother." Maternity leaves are to provide both for the physical health and recovery of the mother and for the child rearing after birth. The length of time, an initial six months, and the ability to request another six months would not have been provided if it were for the purpose of physical recovery *alone*. Obviously, the maternal relationship during the first months of life is important to an infant's development, whether the infant is adopted or natural.

Decision

The arbitrator found no basis for the employer's contention that the leave was limited to childbirth leave. Other contracts that mean childbirth leave use that term. This contract said *maternity leaves* and the arbitrator agreed that maternity included acting as mother after the child is born. The six-month leave was granted.

Adapted from *Ambridge Borough v. American Federation of State, County, and Municipal Employees*, Local 1051-A, 81 LA 915 (1983).

In addition to the kinds of technological and representational changes taking place in the workplace, changes in response to workers' desires can be seen in some of the ways work is accomplished—by empowered employees, sometimes working in teams or groups.

Quality of Working Life (QWL)

Many different programs, often referred to as **quality of working life (QWL)**, are designed and implemented to increase employees' satisfaction with their work environment along with their productivity. *Quality of working life* is a catchall phrase characterizing the process by which management, union, and employees determine together what action, changes, and improvements can better the quality of life at work for all members of the organization and the effectiveness of both the company and the union.[37] QWL programs attempt to establish practical relationships outside the traditional union-management means of negotiations, grievance handling, and joint committees.

QWL programs, some workers and employers believe, have significantly altered the conduct of labor relations. Unlike past efforts, QWL programs try to establish direct channels of communication between workers and their supervisors and give workers a greater voice in decision making. One of the most widely heralded QWL programs was introduced by General Motors and the United Auto Workers. This program was adopted by 18 similar GM plants and was subjected to careful empirical review. It was designed to enrich jobs by removing the most boring, repetitive tasks and by increasing employee autonomy. Results of plant-level data from 10 years showed that more intensive QWL programs were associated with product quality and lower grievance and absentee rates. It was then concluded that QWL efforts represent one possible strategy for breaking the traditional union-management cycle of high conflict and low trust.

Such change might be evident in a displacement of resources and energies from dealing with conflicts to concentrating on work problems; increased worker motivation because of greater participation in job-related decision making; and greater flexibility in human resource management resulting from less reliance on strict work rules and assignments. Although the GM experience with QWL programs has been quite positive, such efforts will not likely produce an end to all labor-management differences, as is sometimes predicted.[38]

Quality Circles

One employee participation technique that quickly became popular is **quality circles (QC)**. William Ouchi, author of *Theory Z*, correctly predicted that quality circles would become the "management fad of the eighties." He further stated that QC success would be longer lived than management by objectives (MBO) or zero-based budgeting.[39]

The QC concept is generally one of "people building" rather than "people using." Usually five to ten employees with common work interests meet voluntarily in groups once a week. The purpose of their meeting is to identify, analyze, and develop solutions to work problems. Solutions are presented to management for final approval. There is no reward for the circle members other than the recognition and satisfaction they receive from helping to increase the efficiency of the organization. QC programs generally start with only two to three circles and add circles as more employees become interested. Circles are independent; they are not part of the organizational chart, members volunteer to participate, and they choose what problems to address and how to analyze them.

Quality circles began in Japan in the 1960s as a major effort for Japan to overcome its image as a producer of cheap, inferior goods. By the 1980s, there was no question that Sony, Panasonic, Toyota, and others had built a reputation for excellence. It has been estimated that 80 percent of Japanese production workers belong to quality circles.

The most obvious advantage to quality circles is that they produce solutions to work-related problems and thus increase quality and efficiency. However, managers and employees have been amazed at the intrinsic rewards—personal satisfaction and peer recognition—that also result.

Thus far, unions in the United States have adopted a neutral attitude toward the QC concept. They probably recognize that circles do increase efficiency, helping the job security of their members. However, they also are aware that employees do not directly share in the reduced costs. As the QC concept grows, union leaders may wish to take a closer look at their operation and resulting savings.

Workplace Violence

One aspect of change in the workplace is the growth of violence—often directed at coworkers or managers. Union and management leaders have a common goal—to avoid workplace violence and respond properly when it occurs.

Employers and employees are aware of some negative changes in the workplace. Extreme incidents of workplace violence are highlighted in national news stories: A disgruntled employee comes to the workplace with a semi-automatic weapon and kills or wounds fellow employees; an ex-spouse or lover hunts down his partner in the workplace and kills her and himself; employees of a government building become victims of an antigovernment terrorist attack. Fortunately, such instances are still rare, but less extreme instances of injury happen in many workplaces on a regular basis. Incidents of assault and battery or threatening behavior can cause major disruption for employers and employees.

The following guidelines have been developed for avoiding workplace violence.[40]

1. Develop a management-labor team that includes a human resource manager, a labor leader, a security officer, a psychologist, and a public relations manager. The team should be responsible for responding to a crisis or incident involving violence.
2. Develop a written, negotiated policy that prohibits threats and intimidating actions and provides for appropriate disciplinary action. Make certain that *each* such incident results in disciplinary action so that employees have no doubts about the employer's resolve.
3. Train managers and union leaders to recognize employee behavior that could foreshadow violence and train them in conflict resolution techniques.
4. Educate employees about how to respond to violence or a sudden emergency in the workplace.
5. Confirm that physical security measures are appropriate for the workplace and all security procedures are being followed, such as requiring company IDs or sign-in after hours.

6. Work with local law enforcement agencies and take proactive measures to preserve peace in the workplace.
7. Respond immediately to any incident of violence. Conduct a thorough and confidential investigation. Ensure the security of any person being threatened. If the employee causing the incident is to be removed from the workplace, take caution in how that is done.

Working in Teams

A large portion of the work within most organizations occurs within groups. Most jobs do not exist in isolation but instead involve both formal work groups (departments, sections, and so forth) and informal groups of employees whose strong friendships affect their working relationships. The effectiveness of these employee groups or teams can be critical to the success of the entire organization.

A major reason for the frequent utilization of groups is *synergy;* the production of the whole (group) is greater than the sum of the parts (individuals). When people work together in a group, they exchange ideas, learn from each other, and motivate each other to achieve more than they typically achieve when working in isolation. The heart of this interaction is the social mingling of the group. Employees build strong friendships with each other; in fact, often their best friends are their coworkers. Thus, when a group develops a successful working interaction, synergy occurs, and more can be achieved as a group than the members could achieve working individually. This enhanced productivity occurs in three primary areas:[41]

1. **Decision making**. Without a designated leader who is looked to for most decisions, groups often make better decisions than the member would if acting alone.
2. **Problem solving**. Through the exchange of ideas and sharing of information, groups usually solve common problems better than individuals who are limited to their own knowledge and experience.
3. **Creativity**. Groups are more willing to make innovative or creative changes in their tasks because they have the support of members.

In many organizations, formal groups of employees responsible for an identifiable work process, a specific project, or solving a problem are called employee teams or committees. These groups have been called the productivity breakthrough of the 1990s, even though the first ones—such as those at General Foods in Topeka, Kansas—have been in existence for more than 20 years.[42] A *Chicago Tribune* survey of the 500 largest companies in the United States found that about 80 percent utilize some form of committees, employee involvement groups, or employee teams.[43] We refer to all of these groups as teams.

Types of Teams

Formal employee teams can generally be divided into three categories: special project teams, problem-solving teams, and self-managed teams (Table 2-3). Self-managed teams are characterized as permanent groups of employees who perform all tasks required of one general activity and perform the supervisory duties related to their work. Special project teams are usually formed by combining

| Table 2-3 | What Is a Team? |

Problem Solving	Special Project	Self-Managed
Usually 5 to 12 volunteers who meet a few hours a week to discuss ways of improving quality, efficiency, and work environment.	Usually 10 to 15 people from different functional areas. May design and introduce work reforms or new technology or meet with suppliers and customers. In union shops, labor and management collaborate at all levels.	From 5 to 15 workers who learn all production tasks and rotate from job to job. Teams do managerial duties such as schedule work and order materials.

Source: Aaron Bernstein, "Putting a Damper on That Old Team Spirit," *Business Week*, May 4, 1992, p. 60.

people from different functions to design, develop, and produce new products or services. Problem-solving teams usually meet on a regular basis to analyze, recommend, and implement solutions to selected problems.

In the 1980s, a handful of U.S. companies began using a new approach to new product development—special project teams. They most often consist of 10 to 15 people from different functions, such as research and development, engineering, manufacturing, and marketing, brought together to design and develop a new product quickly and successfully. The project team is viewed as an autonomous group operating independently within the organization. Some of the early project teams' successes include the IBM Personal Computer, 3M's Post-It™, and Jell-O's Pudding Snacks.[44]

Several factors have caused a growing number of employers to turn to project teams:

1. Rising global competition has greatly increased the need to reduce the time required to put a new product on the market successfully.
2. Employees today expect and are able to provide greater meaningful input for the development of new products.
3. The past successes of project teams as well as other employee teams have convinced more managers to relinquish their authority to project teams.
4. The synergy factor is believed to be a significant force that drives team members to be more creative, work harder, and achieve greater productivity than they would if they were given only a limited view of the project.

Problem-solving teams have increased in popularity but are generally used less than special projects teams are. They can, however, be highly successful. Many problem-solving teams have their roots in quality circles and may be characterized as mature, fully empowered quality circles. The creation of permanent problem-solving teams should not be surprising; an American Society for Training and Development survey of organizations with employee teams found that the most common objective of the teams was problem solving (72 percent of those responding listed as an objective), team building was second (61 percent), and improving quality was third (58 percent).[45] Thus, many organizations with positive experiences with quality circles and with problem solving as an ongoing concern allowed the evolution of quality circles or similar groups into permanent problem-solving teams.

Self-managed employee teams (also called employee or worker involvement groups, autonomous work groups, or self-directed teams) have become commonplace in many American organizations. Special project teams and self-managed teams are the most common and, perhaps, best publicized types of employee teams. They have even been called "the new American industrial weapon" in cover stories in *Business Week*, *Fortune*, and other business publications.[46]

Exactly what are self-managed employee teams? Although no universal definition exists, the following is accurate:[47]

> A *self-managed team* is a small group of employees responsible for an entire work process or segment. Team members work together to improve their operation or product, plan their work, resolve day-to-day problems, and manage themselves.

Thus, self-directed teams are groups of employees who normally work together on a daily basis. They are not groups formed to design and develop special projects or new products or to analyze and solve problems as discussed previously. Their members have not been selected from functional areas to work together as a team. Instead, these teams are permanent components within the organization that "get the work out" on a daily basis. The key difference is that their work is assigned to a team, whereas in traditional organizations it would be assigned to a department with a supervisor or head who then assigns portions of the work to individuals within the department.

Common characteristics of self-managed teams include the following:[48]

- They plan, control, and make decisions about their work (they self-manage!).
- Within limits, they set their own productivity goals and evaluate their own work.
- They set their own work schedules.
- Members select, appraise, and discipline each other.
- They are responsible for the quality of their work.

Organizations that have chosen to organize work to be performed by self-managed teams may be quite different from traditional organizations with highly specialized jobs. They often have far fewer levels of management. For example, the Nucor Corporation (a highly successful steel manufacturer), which extensively uses teams, has only four levels of management compared with an average of 10 in the steel industry. The teams may perform many of the functions normally performed by the additional layers of management—assign work, check to see that it is done properly, discipline people when necessary, hire employees, appraise performance, and so forth. Thus, a large amount of savings often occurs for the reduction in the number of supervisors and managers eliminated by self-managed teams.[49] Another difference is that all members of the teams must learn all the tasks and jobs not just a single job as they would in a traditional organization. The key differences between traditionally designed organizations and self-directed team organization are summarized in Table 2-4.

The successful creation and utilization of self-directed teams (both union and nonunion) has been reported by a large number of U.S. companies including Ford Motor Company, Procter & Gamble, Digital Equipment, IDS, Honeywell,

| Table 2-4 | Key Differences between Self-Directed Team Organizations and Traditional Organizations |

Element	Traditional Organizations	Self-Directed Teams
Organizational structure	Layered/individual	Flat/team
Job design	Narrow single-task	Whole process/ multiple-task
Management role	Direct/control	Coach/facilitate
Leadership	Top-down	Shared with team
Information flow	Controlled/limited	Open/shared
Rewards	Individual/seniority	Team-based/skills-based
Job process	Managers plan, control, improve	Teams plan, control, improve

Source: Richard S. Wellins, William C. Byham, and Jeanne M. Wilson, *Empowered Teams* (San Francisco: Jossey-Bass, 1991), p. 6. Used by permission.

Cummins Engine, General Electric, Boeing, and LTV Steel. In general, these companies all report many positive benefits from their experience with self-directed teams, including higher productivity, improved quality (usually the major goal), improved employee morale, better attendance, and lower turnover.[50] A survey of top managers of these and other companies using self-directed teams asked why these organizations should consider developing teams. The major reasons cited were:[51]

- **Improved quality, productivity, and service**. To stay competitive, most organizations must continually improve quality, service, costs, and speed. The day-to-day attention of all employees is required. The Japanese call this principle *kaizen*—continuous improvement. The sense of ownership that members of a team develop makes continuous improvement possible.
- **Greater flexibility**. Organizations must be able to respond constantly to changing customer needs. Work teams communicate better, identify new opportunities faster, and implement needed changes more quickly because they do not need to wait for approval from a traditional hierarchy. The team members are more alert to customer needs and are proactive because they realize they can make the difference between success and failure.
- **Reduced operating costs**. Self-directed teams enable organizations to reduce costs by eliminating layers of middle management. The teams make the decisions, plan the work, and solve problems that are "passed up" the organization in traditional companies.
- **Faster response to technological change**. New technologies demand greater skills, communication among workers, and coordination among work activities. Thus, workers who previously worked alone must work more closely together. Teams provide a natural environment for such coordination.
- **Fewer job classifications**. Increased technology demands multiskilled employees with greater flexibility to perform many related job functions. Traditional organizations often have many job classifications, each with one or two employees. Self-directed teams train their members to perform all tasks. Thus,

each work team has only one job classification. In addition, the reduced number of management layers, as previously discussed, also reduces the number of classifications. The Toyota plant in Georgetown, Kentucky, for example, has only three job classifications, compared with an average of 150 in most U.S. plants.

- **Ability to attract and retain good people**. Employees in today's workforce want greater autonomy, challenge, and responsibility in their jobs. Teams offer the type of jobs desired by the most creative and talented members of the workforce.

Another survey of the American Society of Training and Development of companies that use self-directed teams indicated that the following factors had "improved" or "significantly improved":[52]

- Productivity (77 percent of the firms)
- Quality (72 percent)
- Job satisfaction (65 percent)
- Customer service (57 percent)
- Waste reduction (55 percent)

Employees with higher levels of job satisfaction, as reported in the survey, are naturally going to increase productivity, quality, and customer service. Debra Boggan, Northern Telecom's plant manager, explains: "The status quo wasn't going to cut it. . . . In the 1990s the companies that will succeed are the ones that put innovation and team spirit back into the workplace." Northern Telecom experienced a 63 percent increase in revenues; productivity per employee increased by 60 percent; earnings increased by 46 percent; and, with 40 percent *fewer* quality inspectors, quality increased by 50 percent![53]

A few examples of firms' experiences with self-managed teams include:[54]

- *Westinghouse Furniture Systems*. Increased productivity by 74 percent in three years.
- *Federal Express Corporation*. Reduced service errors (from an industry-leading low) by 13 percent.
- *Carrier*, the heating/air division of United Technologies Corp. Reduced average turnaround (completion) time by 20 percent.
- *General Electric*'s Salisbury, North Carolina, plant. Increased productivity by 250 percent compared with other GE plants producing the same products.
- *Corning Glass*. Decreased defect rates from 1,800 parts per million to 9 parts per million at its work team ceramics plant.
- *General Mills* food-processing plants that use teams. Averaged 40 percent higher productivity than the traditional plants.

Jack Bergman, a 38-year General Electric employee, explained the remarkable 250 percent increase in production at the Salisbury plant: "Team direction is one of the best techniques for realizing a payback in quality and customer service. It's the ultimate productivity tool." GE has continued to expand the team concept since the success of the Salisbury plant. Rob Birch, vice president of operations, Steelcase, Ltd., agreed with Bergman. At Steelcase he led the effort to establish the first work teams because, "We recognized that our people were underutilized. They weren't being challenged." Birch saw the expansion of teams at Steelcase reach over 80 percent of the workforce.[55]

Problems with Teams

Some analysts have called self-managed teams the key to management success for the 1990s, but others have warned that they are not always successful. Dick Richardson, IBM's Teams Practice Leader, chronicled five factors that have led to the failure of self-managed teams in U.S. organizations:[56]

1. *Solitary work.* When the nature of the work requires little or no interdependence of employees, forcing them into teams can result in unneeded time spent in meetings. As one salesman at an electronics firm said, "It doesn't take 10 people to make a sale; it takes one."
2. *Fixed-speed equipment.* Teams in a diode manufacturing plant became frustrated when they could not increase production because the work was driven by the speed of the equipment, which was fixed and could not be altered. New equipment was far too expensive.
3. *Culture.* The Sealed Air Corporation in Grand Prairie, Texas, tried to change to self-managed teams because teams had been successful in a northern Sealed Air plant. But in Texas, where most employees were immigrants from Latin America and Asia and placed a high value on authority, the employees found teams to be disrespectful of managers. They would not participate in team decision making.
4. *Stable membership.* Real teams take time to mature. The constant change in team membership that occurs in companies with a high percentage of temporary employees keeps teams from succeeding.
5. *Managers.* The Rockwell International plant in Coralville, Iowa, tried team-based operating for nine years. From the beginning, the members had good training and coaching. Some flourished, others did not. Why? The managers "just weren't ready for the new way of managing." The plant returned to a traditional hierarchy.

Union Response to Teams

Union leaders and members have varied greatly in their responses to the creation of self-directed employee teams. At a Ford Motor Co. assembly plant, the creation of self-directed teams has made the facility "a much better place to work," according to J. R. "Buddy" Hoskinson, union co-chairman of the UAW–Ford Education Development and Training Programs. "In the old days we punched a time card and had no say in what was going on. . . . We'd just do what we had to to get by." But today Hoskinson credits the self-directed teams, which have no direct supervision and devise their own work schedules, with creating a "new sense of pride. . . . We know we're doing the best we can do."

The feeling is similar on a project team at the Ford assembly plant. It consists of 10 hourly union workers who implemented the plant manager's idea of modifying the Ford Explorer sport utility vehicle for export. Ralph Wiseman, a project team member, noted that in the past the modification would have been done by an outside firm (a nonunion one most likely). For the project, the 10 members received special training that was unheard of for hourly workers in the past. Wiseman, who bid for a place on the project team, said, "I've never worked so hard, or had a job I liked so much." He emphatically explained his interest in the project: "Our jobs depend on it."[57]

Many other unions, however, view teams as a threat to union strength. They see employee involvement groups and teams as a bridge between management and employees, and once the gap has been bridged, the obvious question may become, "Why do we need a union?" Lewis Maltby, director of the Workplace Task Force of the American Civil Liberties Union, claims union concerns are justified and that employee teams or involvement groups have no place in a union setting because, "Employees have already chosen a union to speak for them." Citing this concern over duplication of interest, the United Transportation Union decided its 8,000 Union Pacific members would not participate in quality improvement teams.[58]

The National Labor Relations Board and the courts have generally agreed with Lewis Maltby and others who have considered employee involvement programs and self-directed work teams as potentially unlawful under Section 8(a)(2) of the Wagner Act. In general, for a violation to occur it must be shown that (1) the entity created by the program is a "labor organization" and (2) the employer dominates or interferes with the formation or administration of that labor organization, or contributes support to it. A committee or group is generally considered a "labor organization" if employees participate in it and at least one purpose is to "deal with" the employer on issues of grievances, labor disputes, wages, work rules, or hours of employment. The "dealing" must involve give and take—as in collective bargaining. If the employer simply says yes or no to employee proposals (often the case with committee quality circles), or if an employee group can decide such issues by itself (often the case with self-directed teams), then the element of dealing is missing and the group is probably not a labor organization.

With regard to the second criterion for violation—employer domination or interference—Section 8(c) of the Wagner Act allows an employer to voice an opinion on labor-management issues but not to create or initiate a labor organization. Thus, an employer can suggest the idea of committees or work teams, but employees must be free to adopt or reject the concept (as did the Union Pacific workers). In cases involving employers' suggesting the creation of employee teams, motive may be considered a factor, although Section 8(a)(2) of the Wagner Act does not require the presence of an anti-union motive; it condemns any interference or domination.[59] Some "employee-management" teams have been in existence for years and avoid any criticism, how? See Profile 2-2!

The National Labor Relations Board (NLRB) in two historic decisions has limited the creation of employee committees or teams by its strict interpretation of the Wagner Act as just described. In the *Electromation*[60] case, the board found that the company illegally created and dominated a labor organization. The case involved the Electromation Company of Elkhart, Indiana, a nonunion electrical parts manufacturer. The employer crafted six "action committees" to deal with the employees on various issues. The committees contained members of both management and hourly workers and were charged with developing proposals for management's consideration. Issues considered by the action committees included pay, absenteeism, and attendance bonus programs. The Teamsters Union had begun an organizing drive at the company about the time the committees were created. The NLRB ruled that the company clearly violated Section 8(a)(2) of

LABOR-MANAGEMENT TRUST FUNDS

The Laborers' International Union of North America (LIUNA) has, since its creation in 1903, prided itself on policies and programs it provided for its members above and beyond workplace representation. Formed as a haven for unskilled construction workers who had been excluded from craft unions, LIUNA, as early as 1906, established a Death Benefit Plan so that members could be buried with dignity and not in paupers' graves.

Today the union boasts of three innovative trust funds created in partnership with construction company owners. These trusts were created to support their members' needs, attract workers to their union, and increase the opportunities for jobs for both its members and the construction companies.

Laborers-AGC Education and Training Fund. Established in 1969, this training fund receives money from general contractors and federal grants. It is jointly administered by the union and the Association of General Contractors and has offered courses in basic construction skills as well as in asbestos abatement, hazardous waste cleanup, and lead abatement. Environmental cleanup has become a conscious focus of the union as an expanding opportunity for its members.

The National Health and Safety Fund. This fund was started in the late 1980s to research and reshape the construction workplace and to address its extreme occupational hazards.

Cooperation Trust. Created in 1989, this trust is to generate work for union contractors and safe, secure jobs for LIUNA members. By combining labor, management, and government, the Cooperation Trust gives a unique opportunity to promote new markets for its members. The major area of growth is in hazardous waste cleanup. The Cooperation Trust helps contractors get insurance, bonds, and bidding information and fosters research, communications, and beneficial legislation for its members.

These union-owner trust funds were created under authority granted to unions and employers under the Taft-Hartley Law. Such trusts escape the problem created by "employee-management" teams because the cooperation is outside of any particular workplace and works for the betterment of an entire industry.

Adapted from John F. Goodman, *Working at the Calling* (Hopkinton, MA: New England Laborers' Labor-Management Cooperation Trust, 1991).

the National Labor Relations Act by creating the action committees. The board decided that the committees had been formed for the purpose, at least in part, of "dealing with" the employer over conditions of employment.

In the 1993 landmark *duPont* case,[61] the NLRB ordered the company to dismantle seven committees of labor and management representatives that had been established to work on safety and recreation issues at the Deepwater, New Jersey, plant. The board ruled that the company had illegally bypassed the plant's union by setting up the committees and thus violated the Wagner Act. This was the board's first ruling on labor-management committees in a unionized plant. The board did note that "brainstorming" sessions may be held if decisions are made by a majority vote and management representatives are in the minority.

From these cases and others it can be concluded, in general, that employee teams having the authority to make decisions and act without obtaining employer approval are not illegal labor organizations.[62] If joint labor-management teams or committees are created to consider employment issues, and a union represents the employees, the union must be involved in the creation of the groups. If such groups are created, they should be voluntary and should contain more union members than management.

After the Electromation and duPont decisions, an attempt was made to amend the NLRA to allow for employee work teams. The Teamwork for Employees and Managers (TEAM) Act passed Congress in 1996 but was vetoed by President Clinton. If adopted, the act would have allowed an employer to establish or participate in any organization in which employees participate to address matters of mutual interest, so long as the organization does not seek to be the exclusive bargaining representative of the employees.

ALTERNATIVE WORK SCHEDULES

Increasing numbers of workers in the United States are desiring more diversity in their work schedules. The American workplace has experienced substantial erosion of the standard workweek. The increased desire for leisure time and the need to care for children and elderly relatives resulted in more than 40 percent of all work schedules including compressed workweeks, part-time work, or long-hour schemes (common in 24-hour organizations such as hospitals and chemical processing plants). Among alternative schedules, the compressed workweek and flexible hours are the most common.

About 18 percent of all workers have flexible schedules, and it is fairly certain that more workers will desire alternative work schedules.[63] Most important, it is one area in which both labor and management can realize real advantages to a negotiated change and can look to several successful examples when developing a new proposal. There is little doubt that the traditional work schedule no longer meets the needs of today's families—perhaps because the "traditional American family" accounts for less than 7 percent of all American families. Single working parents, both parents working, or one working a second job are more common. These arrangements put greater demands on employees' time—to take kids to day care, attend after-school events, attend exercise classes, care for elderly relatives, and run errands.[64] Unions and employers have found that alternative work schedules can enable employees to more easily meet family and work demands, decrease stress, and increase their workplace motivation.

Alternative work schedules allow employees to change the standard five eight-hour-day workweek established after passage of the Fair Labor Standards Act of 1938. This act provided mandatory overtime pay for more than 40 hours of work a week. Unlike many QWL programs, alternative work schedule programs change neither the nature nor the type of work performed but only the scheduling to provide motivation and other benefits to employees. Common forms of alternative work schedules have included the four-day workweek, flextime, and part-time work. Successful alternative work schedule techniques generally fall into one of three categories, outlined in Table 2-5.

Alternative Work Schedules   **Table 2-5**

Compressed Workweek	Discretionary Workweek	Part-Time
4/40	Flextime	Job sharing
4/48 + 3/36	Staggered start	Job splitting
4½/40 or 4½/36	Variable hours	Permanent part-time
	Telecommuting	Work sharing

Compressed Workweek

One of the first forms of alternative work schedules was the **compressed workweek**, usually implemented as the four-day week. Successfully utilized by manufacturing organizations, the four-day week provides employees with three-day weekends as well as a weekday to take care of personal business. Management generally reports substantial savings by reducing startup time and decreasing energy consumption, as well as the savings typically gained from increased employee morale and productivity. The usual four-day workweek is four 10-hour days. Sixty percent of all compressed workweeks fall within this 4/40 category.

Another compressed workweek schedule, 4/48 and 3/36, was negotiated by the union and management of Monsanto Company. The program allows three- and four-day workweek schedules that rotate a four-day shift with a three-day shift. In this technique, employees who work four 12-hour days are off three days and then follow with three 12-hour days and four days off. For example, one crew of employees may work from 9 P.M. to 9 A.M. and a second crew from 9 A.M. to 9 P.M. In total, then, four shifts of employees are used. The Monsanto example produced considerable savings due to fewer shift changes and a substantial increase in employee morale as well as a substantial decrease in turnover and absenteeism. Fatigue, often a factor in compressed workweeks, was surprisingly absent with the 12-hour workdays.[65]

Still another form of the compressed workweek is to provide for a half-day on Friday, giving employees time to go to the grocery store or the bank or to perform other personal business, yet still providing the organization with a five-day production schedule and allowing the business to be open for the convenience of customers.

Discretionary Workweek

Discretionary workweek examples of alternative work schedules provide employees with greater freedom in regulating their work schedules within certain guidelines. **Flextime**, the most liberal of discretionary workweek schedules, allows employees to determine their beginning and ending time each day as long as they work a specified core of hours and a certain total number of hours per day or week. Flextime, developed in Europe in the 1960s, is often mistakenly used to define other types of alternative work scheduling techniques.

The flextime discretionary workweek is often used by both union and nonunion organizations (see Case 2-3). At the heart of its popularity is the employees' actual control of their working hours and greater sense of independence and self-worth.

The importance of the feeling of control has been directly linked to critical motivation and behavior of employees. Employees become motivated to achieve higher levels of productivity because of their perception of increased autonomy and personal control over their work environment. In comparison, employees who perceive that they have no control over their work environment are likely to merely "go through the motions," with little commitment to and involvement in the organization.[66] The substantial increase in personal satisfaction with the work schedule and environment that employees typically report from flextime programs may also carry over to their family and friends because employees report

FLEXTIME

In 1977, the company (Food and Drug Administration, a federal agency) instituted a flextime plan after negotiations between the company and the union. The plan allowed employees, within certain boundaries, to choose their own starting and quitting times. One provision allowed either party to cancel the plan at any time. The plan could be modified by the company after negotiations with the union.

In 1980, the company and the union entered into a new contract. The new contract referenced the flextime plan in the following section:

ARTICLE 20
Hours of Work and Tour of Duty

1. The District agrees to consult with the Union regarding any changes in the Flextime Plan currently in force in the Chicago District. The District agrees to negotiate with the Union on the impact and implementation of any changes in the Plan.

The contract also included the following definitions:

Consultations. Verbal or written discussion between representatives of the District and representatives of the Union for the purpose of obtaining or exchanging viewpoints on any aspect of working conditions, and on new or changed policies or programs that affect the morale and general working conditions of employees in the bargaining unit. It is not mandatory that the end result of consultation be agreement between the parties.

Negotiation. Joint discussions by representatives of the District and the Union on subjects appropriate for negotiations as set forth in the Civil Service Reform Act of 1978 to include policies affecting personnel and practices, and matters affecting working conditions, which are under control of the District Director. Negotiation should result in execution of agreement, including amendments or supplements thereto, or a memorandum of understanding.

In 1983 the company sent the union major modifications to the flextime plan and notified the union that it would meet to negotiate the "impact and implementation" of those changes as required by the contract. The union protested that the company was required to negotiate the substance of the modifications to the plan as well as the impact and implementation, and a grievance was filed.

The union's position was that "hours of work" is a mandatory bargaining subject, and any change during the term of the contract must be negotiated.

The company agreed with this basic premise but pointed out that the union waived its right to bargain under Article 20 of the contract. In the company's opinion the language of Article 20 clearly delineates the responsibilities vis-à-vis the flextime plan. The company must "consult" on changes and "negotiate" on impact and implementation. Article I includes definitions for *consultation* and *negotiation*, which clearly provide that consulting is an exchange of ideas with no agreement necessary and negotiating is discussions that result in an agreement.

The union pointed out that a waiver must be clear and unequivocal and disagreed with the company's interpretation of these sections. It stated that Article 20 is vague as to what the difference between "changes" and "impact and implementation" might be, and therefore, the vagueness precludes any waiver of rights by the union.

The company acknowledged that *changes* and *impact and implementation* are not defined

(continued)

in this collective bargaining agreement but averred that those terms are clearly defined in the federal statute that created the bargaining obligation on federal agencies.

1. Nothing in the Section shall preclude any agency and any labor organization from negotiating—
2. procedures that management officials of the agency will observe in exercising any authority under this Section; or
3. appropriate arrangements for employees adversely affected by the exercise of any authority under this Section by such management officials.

Even if the contract looks like a waiver, using bargaining history and past practice the union believed it could show it did not intend to waive its rights. Article 20 was added to the 1980 contract to counteract the provision of the flextime plan that allows either party to cancel it at any time. Obviously, the union wanted its rights preserved. Also it pointed out that changes made in the plan from 1980 to 1983 were minor, and the parties may have negotiated only the impact of those changes.

Decision

The arbitrator agreed with the company that the language of the contract was clearly and unequivocally a waiver.

Adapted from *U.S. Department of Health & Human Services v. American Federation of Government Employees Local 112*, 83 LA 883 (1984).

increased satisfaction with their personal lives. Increased quality of customer service is another advantage in flextime implementations.[67]

Flextime was initially resented by union leaders, who contended that it increased employees' productivity but did not affect their weekly wage. Employees working flexible hours often decide to stay to finish a job and involuntarily offset these hours by taking time off during a slack period of the day. Thus, the company's overtime costs are significantly reduced because the total hours worked per week do not exceed 40. In recent years, however, union resistance has somewhat diminished because of employees' increased demand for flextime. Union leaders will likely be more interested in negotiating guarantees for flextime as well as increased wages when merited by increased productivity.

The staggered start system of discretionary workweek allows employees to choose one of several starting times and work an eight-hour day. Management determines how many employees will be needed at different hours and defines the different options. Thus, management still has greater control over the workplace than do the employees. Similarly, the variable hours system allows employees to contract with their supervisors to work for a specified time each day or week, with the possibility of varying schedules on a daily basis whenever agreeable to both parties. Again, management maintains greater control.

In Europe, some German companies negotiated flexyear schedules. In one such experiment, a trade company of 850 employees negotiated a working-year contract system that, within parameters, allowed employees to choose how many hours they would work in a month. Through the careful use of core time, management was able to guarantee it would have adequate labor to meet production demand while giving employees a maximum of flexibility with a monthly system.[68]

New technological opportunities such as electronic mail and bulk data transmission have created a new alternative in work scheduling called **telecommuting**. Telecommuting allows employees to complete some or all of their work at home. For example, computerized clerical work and computer programming can be accomplished at home because those jobs do not require constant supervision or contact with customers or coworkers. Estimates of the number of Americans who will use home offices by the year 2000 range as high as 22 percent of all jobs.

A company allows employees to work outside of direct supervision because of cost savings. For example, less expensive office space is required. Employees enjoy flexibility in their work schedules, cost savings because they eat lunch at home and do not commute, and the opportunity to stay with their families. But there are disadvantages to telecommuting. Employees miss the social contacts at work that are important for personal and professional needs. Also, they are not privy to the office grapevine or social network.

Federal and state laws such as those for safe working conditions, equipment, and employment status do not apply to telecommuters, full- or part-time.[69] In fact, the 1938 Fair Labor Standards Act contains a "no home-working" provision that was upheld by a U.S. Appeals Court in 1984. The case involved the International Ladies Garment Workers Union, which objected to allowing retired women and housewives to knit at home because the union could not prevent "sweatshop" conditions.[70] Unions in general are likely to be concerned about an increase in telecommuters, who are difficult to organize.

Part-Time Work

The Bureau of Labor Statistics defines *part-time workers* as those who work less than 35 hours a week and divides them into three groups: (1) those who voluntarily work part-time (students, retirees, second-income households), (2) those working part-time for economic reasons (their hours have been reduced by employers), and (3) those who usually work full-time (but worked less than 35 hours in a week because of vacation, illness, etc.). Younger (ages 16 to 24) and older (65 and older) workers account for a much higher proportion of the part-time workforce than of the full-time employed.[71]

Part-time work has become an alternative scheduling system that has recently increased in usage. Part-time techniques include permanent part-time work as traditionally used by organizations; job splitting, whereby a single job is divided into two or more part-time positions; and job sharing, involving two individuals' handling one full-time position. With job splitting, the two people perform the same work but at different set schedules. They often have no direct contact. In job sharing, the two people decide who does what, when, and how for the single full-time position.

There is little doubt that part-time jobs will be increased in the future. Union negotiators, because of hard economic times, have sometimes favored increased part-time work to provide their members with at least some income as opposed to total unemployment. As the number of two-income families increases, union members will also demand more part-time jobs because of childrearing or other pursuits. Benefits will continue to be provided by the full-time family member.

Some unions, however, have opposed part-time work because it has sometimes been forced on members who desire full-time employment.

Work sharing reduces the number of employees who are laid off by asking all employees to work fewer hours. For example, Motorola, Inc., used work sharing in 1983 by offering to keep those workers who were scheduled for layoff employed if all employees would work four hours a day instead of five. Employees included in the plan would receive only 80 percent of their normal wages. Motorola had helped pass a 1981 Arizona state law that allowed workers to collect unemployment compensation for the time not worked during work sharing. One employee, for example, received $12 in state unemployment because of a $40 cut in wages as a result of the work-sharing program. Only a few states, however, have enacted similar laws.[72]

Many employees avoided economic hardship with this system. In addition, work sharing improved labor-management relations because everyone was pulling together during hard times. Although Motorola continued to pay benefits to employees who would otherwise have been laid off, management believed that higher productivity from thankful employees made up for the increased cost. Unions favor work sharing because they do not lose members during recessions. Perhaps the greatest advantage of work sharing is that employees and their families are not subjected to the destructive psychological and financial stresses of a layoff, which sometimes leave lifelong scars.

SUMMARY

The U.S. workplace was designed for and supported the industrial revolution. In that context, a labor union organized and represented workers to make sure they shared in the profits of those industries. The roles of owner and worker were clearly defined.

As the twenty-first century approaches, the United States is in the throes of the technological revolution and new global competition. Union leaders realize the need to be flexible to survive in the new workplace.

Participatory management, alternative work schedules, and creative representation have changed the historical role of workers, and therefore unions, in the workplace. Instead, employee teams, quality circles, and QWL programs are enabling employees to increase their workplace contributions.

DISCIPLINARY ACTION

Facts

The employee, a union shop steward, was on her regularly scheduled day off at home. She was called by her supervisor and told to talk to three union members and instruct them to attend a work function called a "Quest for Quality Interaction Committee" meeting. The Quest for Quality program was a high priority with the employer for improving patient care at the facility and was part of a corporate program. The union had objected to the implementation of the Quest for Quality program and had taken a position that employees could attend the program if their jobs were threatened, but they should do so under protest and then file a grievance afterward.

On the day in question, the union shop steward, in a three-way conversation with the three employees, told them that she would not order them to attend the Quest for Quality meeting, although she had been asked by her supervisor to instruct them to go to the meeting. The supervisor who had called the union shop steward had herself refused to order the employees to attend the meeting but relied on the union shop steward to issue the order to the employees. When the union shop steward failed to order the employees to attend the meeting, the employer suspended the union shop steward for two weeks. The steward grieved the two-week suspension.

The union position was that the company had no authority to discipline the union shop steward on her day off for failure to give what it termed a management direction to perform the specific job function of attending a mandatory corporate meeting. The union pointed out that it was unfair that the employer refused to order the employees directly to attend the meeting but then expected the union shop steward to do so. The union argued that, although it is not unusual to call upon a union shop steward for assistance in problem solving, the company has no right to demand that he or she replace supervisors or management in giving orders and then discipline the union official for refusing to do so.

The company position was that the opposition of the union to the Quest for Quality meetings put the employees in a position of being unable to attend the meetings without direction from the union shop steward; that the union shop steward was given a job assignment of directing the employees to attend the meeting; and that failure to follow that job assignment was insubordination and just cause for her suspension.

Nonetheless, the union contended that the arbitrator must examine the nature of the order when deciding whether the insubordination was grounds for discipline. As to the nature of the order in this case, the employer had to demonstrate that the order was directly related to the job classification and work assignment of the employee disciplined. The refusal to obey such an order must be shown to pose a real challenge to supervisory authority. The employee did not dispute the fact that she failed to follow the orders given to her by her supervisor but pointed out that she was not on duty at the time and that the task being given to her was not because of her job with the company but because of her status as a union shop steward.

Questions

1. As the arbitrator, do you think the employer had just cause to discipline the employee?
2. If the union's opposition to the Quest for Quality program encouraged the employees not to participate, why shouldn't the union be held responsible for directing the employees to attend?
3. Did the employee's action really justify the penalty imposed by the company?

Adapted from *Cheltenham Nursing and Rehabilitation Center*, 89 LA 361 (1987).

CASE STUDY 2-2

COMPANY UNIONS

Facts

In January 1991, the company was not unionized but had established a "Plant Council," which consisted of three managers and five employees elected by the plant's workers. The council was created and designed by the employer to offer recommendations to management about proposed changes in working conditions. The employer had agreed to consider those recommendations, recognizing that if the managers and employees on the council reached a consensus then that idea would likely be acceptable to both management and employees. In February 1991, the union began an organizing campaign to try to establish a collective bargaining unit for the company. During the campaign, the employer emphasized the role of the Plant Council when urging employees to vote against the union. In addition, the employer told employees that their vote was a choice between an "employee involvement process" and selecting a union as a representative. After the union lost the election, it filed an unfair labor charge against the employer for interfering with the election and for creating a "company union" in violation of the National Labor Relations Act.

Questions

1. Do you think the union should or should not have challenged the election? Why?
2. One of the techniques used by companies in the late 1800s to discourage union organizing was to create company unions as discussed briefly in chapter 1. This case would seem to suggest that nothing about the workplace had changed in over 100 years. What decision do you think the judge made in this 1991 case and why?
3. The employer obviously wanted the employees to participate in the decisions in the workplace because such buy-in would result in better decisions. Why then did the employer prefer the council to the union?

Adapted from *Webcor Packaging, Inc.*, 151 LRRM 1221 (1995).

KEY TERMS AND CONCEPTS

alternative work schedules
associated unionism
comparative advantage
compressed workweek
discretionary workweek
flextime
international alliances
outsourcing
quality circle (QC)
quality of working life (QWL)
retraining rights

robber barons
Saturn agreement
self-managed teams
Teamwork for Employees and Managers (TEAM) Act
technological change
telecommuting
worker retraining
workplace violence
work sharing

REVIEW QUESTIONS

1. What are some of the reasons behind union mistrust of technological change? How might this mistrust be remedied?
2. How did the organization of work in the late 1800s contribute to the way unions organized?
3. What changes have caused the global marketplace to expand?

4. How have U.S. businesses changed to compete in the global marketplace? How have unions changed?
5. How have the central issues of collective bargaining changed since the 1930s? Which issues are still critical today?
6. How do quality of working life (QWL) programs differ from past union-management communications?
7. Which alternative work schedule techniques are most used? What new alternatives might develop?
8. Why is outsourcing a critical workplace issue?
9. How will the emergence of associational unions affect the labor market?
10. Why has the use of "employee teams" been called the productivity breakthrough of the 1990s?

TAKE IT TO THE NET

We invite you to visit the Carrell/Heavrin page on the Prentice Hall Web site at:

http://www.prenhall.com/carrellr

for this chapter's World Wide Web exercise.

Today's Labor Leaders | EXERCISE 2-1

Purpose:
To understand the leadership of today's labor movement.
Task:
Research and profile the current leadership, nationally or locally, in one of the following labor organizations:

AFL-CIO
United Mine Workers of America
United Auto Workers
International Brotherhood of Teamsters, Chauffeurs, Warehousemen and Helpers of America
United Steelworkers of America
American Federation of State, County and Municipal Employees (AFSCME)
Communication Workers of America
International Association of Machinists & Aerospace Workers (IAM)

Attitudes toward Unions | EXERCISE 2-2

Purpose:
To examine your general attitude toward unions and discuss the possible causes for any positive or negative feelings.

Task:

Divide into small groups. Complete the following survey. The statements in this survey are listed in pairs. Put an X next to the statement that you agree with more firmly. If you *strongly* agree with the statement, put two Xs next to it. You may not entirely agree with either of them, but be sure to mark one of the statements. *Do not omit any item.* When you have completed the survey, add the "a" Xs and the "b" Xs and compare.

After the completion of the survey, your instructor will ask a group with more "a" answers and a group with more "b" answers to lead a discussion of attitudes toward unions and labor-management relations.

1. a. Unions are an important, positive force in our society.
   b. The country would be much better off without unions.
2. a. Without unions, the state of personnel management would be set back a hundred years.
   b. Management is largely responsible for introducing humanistic programs and practices in organizations today.
3. a. Unions help organizations become more productive.
   b. Unions make it difficult for management to produce a product or service efficiently.
4. a. Today's standard of living is largely due to the efforts of the labor movement.
   b. The wealth that people are able to enjoy today is largely the result of creativity, ingenuity, and risk taking by management decision makers.
5. a. Most unions are moral and ethical institutions.
   b. Most unions are as corrupt as the Mafia.
6. a. Unions afford the worker protection against arbitrary and unjust management practices.
   b. Managers will treat their employees fairly regardless of whether a union exists.
7. a. Unions want their members to be hardworking productive employees.
   b. Unions promote job security rather than worker productivity.
8. a. Unions promote liberty and freedom for the individual employee.
   b. With the union, employees lose their individual freedoms.
9. a. Section 14(b) of the Taft-Hartley Act (which allows individual states to pass right-to-work laws) should be repealed.
   b. Congress should pass federal right-to-work legislation.
10. a. Unions are instrumental in implementing new, efficient work methods and techniques.
    b. Unions resist management efforts to adopt new, labor-saving technology.
11. a. Without unions, employees would not have a voice with management.
    b. Labor-management communication is strengthened with the absence of a union.
12. a. Unions make sure that decisions about pay increases and promotions are fair.
    b. Union politics often play a role in deciding which union employee gets a raise or is promoted.
13. a. The monetary benefits that unions bargain for are far greater than the dues the member must pay to the union.

b. Union dues are usually too high for what the members get through collective bargaining.
14. a. Employee discipline is administered fairly if the organization is unionized.
    b. Union procedures generally make the disciplinary process slow, cumbersome, and costly.
15. a. Without the union, the employee would have no one with whom to discuss work-related problems.
    b. The best and most accessible person for the employee to discuss work-related problems with is the immediate supervisor.
16. a. Union officers at all levels carry out their jobs in a competent and professional manner.
    b. Union officers are basically political figures who are primarily interested in their own welfare.
17. a. Most unions seek change through peaceful means.
    b. Most unions are prone to use violence to get what they want.
18. a. Unions are truly domestic institutions with full participation of the rank and file.
    b. Unions are controlled by the top leadership rather than by the rank and file.
19. a. Union members do the real work in our society and form the backbone of our country.
    b. Union employees are basically manual laborers who would flounder without management's direction and guidance.
20. a. Unions are necessary to balance the power and authority of management.
    b. The power and authority of management, guaranteed by the Constitution and the right to own private property, are severely eroded by the union.

Collective

Bargaining:

Work Rules

Young Houston Astros fans express their feelings about the looming 1994 strike by the Major League Baseball Players Association. The strike began on August 12, and caused the World Series to be canceled for the first time in history.

Job Security and Cooperation: Negotiation Philosophy in 1996

For a period of about 50 years from World War II to the 1990s, the U.S. automobile industry was subjected to strikes and hard times each time labor agreements with the United Auto Workers Union (UAW) expired. From the 1950s to the 1980s, especially, the UAW announced which auto maker was the "strike target." In most cases, it was the most profitable of the "Big 3" (GM, Ford, Chrysler). After the agreement expired, a costly strike would idle hundreds of thousands of workers and disrupt production. Then, once a new agreement had been reached, the UAW would demand similar agreements from the other auto makers—to follow the "pattern" set by the first. The year 1996, however, proved to be a historic turning point in UAW–auto maker negotiations. In that year, a "no-strike" philosophy was followed in several related industries.

Ford Motor Company was chosen as the "negotiation target"—not the *strike* target. The UAW wanted it to be clearly known that no strikes were planned. Instead, a historic agreement with Ford was reached in record time. The agreement provided the UAW with its top priority: *95 percent* of the 105,025 UAW-Ford jobs were *guaranteed* to be maintained, with no layoffs or downsizing or shutdowns during the three-year agreement. Another historic precedent in the Ford-UAW agreement was the wage package: 3 percent raises in years 2 and 3 with a $2,000 *lump-sum* payment in the first year, thus no first-year wage-rate hike. Chrysler Corporation followed the Ford pattern within weeks. Chrysler Chairman Robert Eaton noted the historic changes in the negotiations: "These negotiations were very different. . . . We never faced a strike deadline. . . . They produced very, very good results for both sides. It was very professional on both sides."

Adapted from "Chrysler, UAW Forge Agreement," Associated Press as reported in the *Omaha World-Herald*, September 30, 1996, p. 12.

The preceding two chapters gave a historical overview of the people and the type of work that gave rise to the labor movement in the United States. In addition, they explored the changing workforce and workplace that challenge unions and management today. The legal framework for labor-management relations must also be viewed within its historical context and examined in light of the many changes in work rules confronting labor and management today.

EARLY JUDICIAL REGULATION

As previously discussed, prerevolutionary America saw little division between the employers and employees. The economy of the colonies was primarily agricultural, with some handicraft trade. Basic goods were supplied by skilled laborers: shoemakers, tailors, carpenters, printers, smiths, and mechanics. The growth of the economy benefited these laborers, who, because their skills were scarce, could enjoy relatively high wages and job security. They were largely self-employed and dealt with consumers on an equal footing.

After the American Revolution, some of these skilled workers became shop owners employing others to fill orders that became more frequent as the economy began to build. Their need to produce goods in an increasingly competitive market demanded cheaper production costs and lower wages. Thus, a clearer distinction between employer and employee began. Skilled workers of a single craft formed associations and societies to protect their handiwork and their livelihood. Their method of action was to agree on a wage scale and then pledge to work only for an employer who would pay those wages. The response from the employer to this erosion of management rights was swift and decisive. Using a very supportive court system, those workers were charged with criminal conspiracy in a series of cases known as the Cordwainers conspiracy cases.[1]

The Cordwainers Conspiracy Cases

In the **Cordwainers conspiracy cases**, the state courts stated that the common law of criminal conspiracy was the law of the United States. In other words, if two or more people conspired to commit an illegal act, they were then guilty of conspiracy whether or not they ever completed the particular illegal act. Early American labor law was interpreted by judges and based on English common law. Whereas English judges had relied largely on statutes to find criminal conspiracy in labor cases, U.S. judges, who often shared a common background with employers, chose to find legal precedents in the common law for protecting the employer's property rights over the employee's job rights.[2]

In the 1806 Philadelphia Cordwainers case, the court considered the mere "combination" of workers to raise wages an illegal act. The court felt that such combinations were formed to benefit the workers and to injure nonparticipants. Public outcry over judicial interpretation of combinations led later courts to find other grounds for declaring them illegal.

In a New York Cordwainers case three years later (*People v. Melvin*), the court dismissed the idea that it was illegal merely to combine. But it denounced using a combination of workers to strike because it deprived others, primarily the employers, of their rights and property. Further, in an 1815 Pittsburgh case, the court clearly characterized the offense involved in organizing workers as conspiracy to impoverish a third person, be it the employer or another worker willing to work against the combination's rules.

The threat of criminal conspiracy charges and the depression following the War of 1812 practically destroyed the fledgling labor movement. When prosperity returned, the demand for skilled labor put the employees in a better bargaining position, and combinations of skilled laborers began again.

Employers responded to this attempt by labor to enter again the decision-making process by taking employee combinations to court. Conspiracy cases against the New York Hatters (1823), Philadelphia Tailors (1827), and Philadelphia Spinners (1829) questioned the legality of the means used to force the employer to meet labor's demands—picketing, circulation of scab lists, and the sympathetic strike. Before labor could rally from such attacks by the courts, another depression weakened the demand for labor, and the combinations lost their bargaining power.

As seen in earlier chapters, the development of the American factory system and the monopolies created by the robber barons in the later part of the nineteenth century softened public opinion for a while; to some extent there was sympathy to the needs of the worker. Because of this need for the worker to meet the employer as an equal, the courts began to move away from finding workers guilty of criminal conspiracy.

The conspiracy doctrine was further narrowed during *Commonwealth v. Hunt 1842*, which involved a stubborn journeyman who worked for less than union scale and repeatedly broke other union rules.[3] Union members caused his dismissal by refusing to work with him, and his complaint led to the criminal conspiracy charge. The court found that criminal conspiracy required either an illegal purpose or a resort to illegal means. In this instance, the purpose was to induce workers to become union members and abide by union rules; hence, it was not illegal. Also the means, refusing to work with a worker who did not comply, was not unlawful because no contract was breached. The court upheld the workers' right to organize and to compel all workers to comply with the union scale.

Use of Labor Injunctions

Abandonment of the criminal conspiracy doctrine by the courts did not signal judicial acceptance of unions, however, nor did it enhance the employers' relationships with unions. Indeed, judicial and business attitudes toward union activities became even more hostile as viable union organizations sought to use economic measures to regulate the terms and conditions of worker employment.

The labor incidents cited in chapter 1 coincided with the growth and development of national labor organizations. Employers' use of court **injunctions** to stop these acts, supported by court reaction to these incidents, took on national importance and to a large extent created the need for a national labor policy.

The ability of railway workers to cripple the national railroads during the Pullman strike caused alarm in the government and among employers. A state court invoked the Sherman Antitrust Act, which declared monopolies illegal, against the striking workers.

The lower court's application of the Sherman Antitrust Act to the Pullman strike was later confirmed by the U.S. Supreme Court during another strike, known as the Danbury Hatter's case.[4] The Supreme Court stated that the act was designed to prevent conspiracies in restraint of interstate commerce and that a boycott was a form of this interference and therefore prohibited.

The Erdman Act

A key by-product of the Pullman strike was the passage of the Erdman Act of 1898.[5] President Grover Cleveland had formed the United States Strike Commission to investigate the cause and results of the Pullman strike. The commission recommended a permanent federal commission to conciliate and, if necessary, decide railway labor disputes. Congress used this recommendation as its basis for passage of the Erdman Act. This act gave certain employment protections to union members and offered facilities for mediation and conciliation of railway labor disputes. Although the legislation was limited to employees operating interstate trains, its mere passage suggested that federal regulation of the employer-employee relationship might be necessary to ensure peace in interstate industries.

Unions Gain a Foothold

The courts continued to use the injunction as a way to regulate union activity. As Case 3-1 demonstrates, an attempt to unionize mine workers resulted in a court-ordered injunction.

But not all court actions against organized labor were successful in discouraging union actions. In 1902, the United Mine Workers organized a strike of anthracite coal miners, demanding an increase in wages and union recognition. With the widespread support of boycotts and money for the workers, the United Mine Workers withstood federal troops and antitrust lawsuits. President Theodore Roosevelt stepped in and offered to establish a president's commission to arbitrate. The offer was accepted by the workers almost immediately, but the mine owners balked. Threatening to seize the mines unless the coal operators accepted a plan of arbitration, the president gained acceptance of his offer.[6] The commission's recommendation included wage increases but fell short of union recognition.

Another successful strike during this period was conducted by textile workers in Lawrence, Massachusetts, in 1912. Again the strikers were supported by contributions from around the country. After nine and one-half weeks, mill owners capitulated and met most of the workers' demands.

A 1913 strike by mine workers in Ludlow, Colorado, spurred the start of company unions. The mine owner, John D. Rockefeller Jr., realized the inevitability of such workers' organizations. By instituting his own recognized employee organization and initiating reforms such as health funds and better living conditions, Rockefeller sought to eliminate the need for union recognition. Such company unions created the illusion of participation but lacked the essential element whereby labor and the employer meet as equals at a bargaining table.

INJUNCTION

The Hitchman Coal and Coke Company had reluctantly accepted unionization in 1903. For the next three years it was plagued with strikes over mine workers' pay scales, causing considerable losses to the company. A two-month strike in 1906 prompted a self-appointed committee of employees to inform the company that they could not afford to stay off the job, and they asked the company upon what terms they could return to work. The company said they could come back—but without the union. The employees agreed and returned to work.

Prospective employees were told that, although the company paid the same wages demanded by the union, the mine was nonunion and would remain so; that the company would not recognize the United Mine Workers of America; and that the company would fire any worker who joined. Each worker employed assented to those conditions.

The United Mine Workers of America wanted to expand union mines in the area because nonunion mines tended to keep the cost of production low. Union mines could not compete and still grant workers the pay increases they demanded.

Union organizers repeatedly declared the need to organize the nonunion mines by means of strikes. They were determined to protect themselves from the unorganized mines. A plan was devised whereby the unionized mines would stay open while the nonunion mines would strike. The working miners would provide strike benefits for the strikers to ensure their cooperation.

When the Hitchman Company was approached by union officials requesting recognition, the company refused and informed the union of the employment agreements not to unionize.

Representatives of the union began organizing the miners with the express intent of shutting down the mine until the company recognized the union. Their organizational means were limited to orderly and peaceful talks with individual workers and a few unobtrusive public meetings. The company sought and received an injunction against the union's activities.

Decision

The injunction was upheld on appeal. The U.S. Supreme Court reasoned that the company was within its rights in excluding union workers from its employ and that even though the union was within its rights in asking workers to join, it could not injure the company when exercising that right. The court found that the express intent of the union—to organize the workers to strike for recognition—would injure the company in two ways. It would interfere with the employer-employee relationships, and it would cause a loss of profits.

Because the union's goals were illegal, the union's activities could be enjoined.

Adapted from *Hitchman Coal & Coke Co. v. Mitchell*, 62 L.Ed. 260 (1917).

These successes increased the resolve of organized labor to establish viable collective bargaining relationships with employers. But the employers were not ready to yield control to their employees. When faced with an employee strike, employers resisted, seeking and often receiving support from the courts in the form of labor injunctions. Figure 3-1 recaps the era of strong union opposition.

| Figure 3-1 | Era of Union Opposition |

1790	*New York Printers strike.* First strike by employees.
1790s	*First unions.* Craft workers formed first known unions, including printers, shoemakers, tailors, carpenters, and bakers.
1806	*Philadelphia Cordwainers case.* Court found combination of employees illegal.
1837	*Severe depression.* Mass unemployment reduced union membership.
1842	*Commonwealth v. Hunt.* The conspiracy doctrine greatly narrowed.
1860s	*Civil War.* Buildup of coal, steel, and other war-related industries.
1866	*National Labor Union.* Advocated consumer cooperatives, immigration restrictions; disbanded in 1872.
1869	*Knights of Labor.* National social union formed to organize farmers and skilled and unskilled workers.
1875	*Molly Maguires.* After a strike by coal miners, union organizers were tried and executed for strike-related violence.
1877	*Railway strike.* More than 100 workers were killed, and several hundred were wounded in the first national strike.
1886	*American Federation of Labor (AFL).* Samuel Gompers led the first national trade union to advocate collective bargaining, trade autonomy, exclusive jurisdiction, standard hours, and better wages and working conditions.
	Haymarket Square riot. Several workers were killed; others were found guilty of anarchism. The Knights of Labor suffered the blame for the riot, shifting much of their support to the AFL.
1890	*Sherman Antitrust Act.* Designed to break up corporate monopolies.
1892	*Homestead, Pennsylvania.* A strike by steel workers against Carnegie Steel Company ended with the town's being placed under martial law.
1894	*Pullman strike.* Rail workers demanded higher wages and lower rents. The strike was ended by court orders under the Sherman Act. The strike led to passage of the 1898 Erdman Act giving railroad employees employment protection.
1905	*Industrial Workers of the World (IWW).* The "Wobblies" were organized in response to the strong opposition to the labor movement. They advocated including all workers in one union and the end of capitalism.
1913	*Colorado Mine Workers strike.* The strike spurred the start of company unions by John D. Rockefeller Jr.

PRO-LABOR LEGISLATION

The Clayton Act

Public criticism of the use of the injunction against labor unions caused Congress to pass the **Clayton Act** in 1914.[7] This act sought to limit the court's injunctive powers against labor organizations. The Clayton Act stated that labor was not a commodity; that the existence and operation of labor organizations were not prohibited by antitrust; and that individual members of unions were not restrained from lawful activities. The act provided that neither the labor organization nor its members were considered illegal combinations or conspiracies in restraint of trade.

Still, courts continued to apply the Sherman Antitrust Act after passage of the Clayton Act by narrowly interpreting its provisions. The courts felt that secondary strikes, boycotts, and picketing were not covered by the Clayton Act because of the employee-employer language and because legitimate objects of labor would not include strikes and activities if their purpose or effect was the unreasonable restraint of trade.

Though the Clayton Act was practically ineffective, its passage signaled a hopeful period for labor organizations. With other political victories behind them, such as child labor laws, workers' compensation, and some limitations on working hours, members of the labor movement believed that a new era was upon them.

The National War Labor Board

During World War I, President Woodrow Wilson formed the **National War Labor Board** to prevent labor disputes from disrupting the war effort. Formed to provide a means of settlement by mediation or conciliation of labor controversies in necessary war industries, it adopted self-organization and collective bargaining as its basic policy.[8] Federal recognition of labor rights continued and expanded when the federal government began to operate the railroads. After World War I, the National War Labor Board was abolished, and railroads were returned to their owners. Despite the economic sense of avoiding labor disputes through cooperation, collective bargaining was no longer protected by the federal government.

The labor movement sustained losses in the early 1920s. Another postwar depression and labor's alleged association with American sympathizers for Russian communism eroded public support. Even though the Clayton Act supposedly exempted labor unions from injunctions, the courts interpreted the Clayton Act as granting immunity only if an injunction was not necessary to prevent irreparable injury to property or its rights. In the broadest sense, any labor action could injure property or property rights.[9]

Trade union leadership and the rank and file turned to political action and industrial unionism to counteract their losses. They allied with the progressive movement, a loose coalition of farmers, socialists, and reformers who represented a populist view. Many people, fearing that the use of militia, federal troops, and court injunctions against unions represented a threat to the democratic process, adopted the progressive doctrine. That doctrine espoused the control of the political activities of corporations, graduated income and inheritance taxes, stringent conservation measures, federal regulations of the labor of women and children, and workers' compensation laws. The movement, although not widely embraced, successfully supported the passage of the Railway Labor Act.

The Railway Labor Act

In an effort to avoid the interruption of commerce, the Railway Labor Act passed in 1926 with the support of both labor and management.[10] It required railroad employers to negotiate with their employees' duly elected representatives. It provided for amicable adjustment of labor disputes and for voluntary submissions to arbitration.

As a result of the Railway Labor Act, Congress again fostered peaceful settlement of labor disputes through negotiation and mediation. The Supreme Court case upholding that act removed major judicial obstacles by supporting a national labor policy based on the affirmative legal protection of labor organizations.[11] Under the umbrella of the commerce clause of the United States, the Court said Congress could facilitate settlements of disputes and that:

> The legality of collective action on the part of employees in order to safeguard their proper interests is not to be disputed. . . . Congress . . . could safeguard it and seek to make their appropriate collective action an instrument of peace rather than of strife.[12]

In 1929 the stock market crashed and the United States plunged into a major depression. The impact of the Great Depression on the workers was devastating. One-third of the country's workforce was unemployed. Hoover's programs to combat unemployment served mainly to highlight the deprivation. The labor movement made more emphatic efforts to organize and demand recognition and became more politically active. The severity of conditions led to public sympathy for workers' problems.

For years this nation struggled over the right of workers to organize and to negotiate collectively with employers. Judicial solutions to the struggle were ineffective. Court decisions, by their nature, were confined to particular parties, to narrow situations, and to fixed time frames. Such decisions could not give national guidance. The judicial process was also time-consuming; neither labor nor management wanted disputes to drag on while the wheels of justice ground to a decision.

State legislation was also ineffectual because organized labor transcended state boundaries. With few exceptions, the disruption of an industry in any one state affected industries throughout the country.

The Norris–La Guardia Act

Congress recognized the need for a national labor policy. The Erdman Act and the Clayton Act were the first steps in ensuring industrial peace based on the balanced bargaining relationship of worker to owner.

The Davis-Bacon Act, passed in 1931, was another attempt to support the fledgling union movement. The Davis-Bacon Act put into place a requirement that companies using federal dollars for construction projects use the "prevailing wage rate" of the area as the minimum wage rate on their construction project. Because the trades needed for construction—carpenters, plumbers, and electricians—were generally organized, the prevailing wage rate would most often be the union wage rate. Companies are selected to do federally funded jobs through a competitive bidding process. The Davis-Bacon Act meant that companies who use union labor did not lose their competitive advantage when bidding on federal jobs by paying their workers union wages.[13]

The **Norris–La Guardia Act** (1932) was the next step in formulating a comprehensive national labor policy.[14] This act, like the Clayton Act, sought to restrict federal judicial intervention in labor disputes, thereby giving the unions an opportunity to grow. Courts could not enjoin strikes without actual violence, nor could they restrict the formation of a union or associated activities. The act also made illegal "yellow-dog" contracts, in which employees pledged to refrain from union membership. These protections were extended to secondary boycotts and strikes by expanding the employer-employee language of the Clayton Act.

The National Labor Relations Act (The Wagner Act)

The Great Depression and the selection of Franklin D. Roosevelt with strong labor support set the stage for passage of national legislation. Roosevelt quickly proved his interest in the plight of the worker. The National Industrial Recovery Act (1933) recognized workers' rights in selecting their own representatives.[15] Well intentioned but poorly constructed, the National Recovery Administration had no power to enforce the act, and industry largely ignored it. Within two years the National Industrial Recovery Act was declared unconstitutional.[16]

Relief of the unemployment problem continued by creation of such New Deal programs as the Civilian Conservation Corps (CCC), unemployment insurance, the Social Security program, and the Works Progress Administration (WPA). But these measures alone were not enough.

> By 1935, the judiciary policy toward labor was one of selective suppression of organized labor's activities whenever they trenched too heavily upon the interest of any other segment of society. Commercial interests must not be injured by disruption of the interstate flow of goods; consumers and unorganized laborers must not be injured by wage standardization; employees and the public at large must not be injured by expansion of labor disputes through secondary boycotts.[17]

Senator Robert Wagner, a champion for labor, proposed an act that recognized employee rights to organize and bargain collectively. A quasi-judicial tribunal with the power and authority to enforce its own orders would be created. Although the act was purported to protect the public from the disruption of interstate commerce resulting from labor disputes, Senator Wagner stated that the act would also give the employee freedom and dignity.[18]

The **National Labor Relations Act** (also known as the **Wagner Act**) gave most private sector employees the right to organize.[19] It required employers to meet with accredited representatives of a majority of their employees and to make an honest effort to reach agreement on issues raised. Employees now had the right to strike, and the employer's retaliatory powers were limited under the act's unfair labor practice provisions. The National Labor Relations Board (NLRB) was created to enforce provisions of the act. Case 3-2, decided only three years after passage of the act, gives an interesting interpretation of the NLRB's powers.

By legislating the recognition of employee representatives and protecting the right to strike, Congress forced the employer to share the decision-making power with employees. Labor no longer depended on work stoppages to get to the bargaining table or on economic factors to determine its equality.

The entire thrust of the Wagner Act was to protect employees from employers and to establish a balance of bargaining power between the two. Later it was criticized for its one-sided nature, but at the time it was passed organized labor had no leverage to pose a threat to management; thus, equal protection for management seemed unnecessary.

Critics claimed that the act was unconstitutional because, although it was based on the commerce clause, the latter did not specifically allow Congress to dictate the relationship between employers and employees. The National Labor Relations Board was careful in its activities, delaying adjudication on the constitutionality question until the Supreme Court upheld the act in a 1937 case, *Jones and Laughlin Steel Corporation*.[20] Labor-management relations improved somewhat under the Wagner Act but still remained uneasy. Figure 3-2 outlines the major provisions of the Wagner Act.

The creation of a national labor policy dominated the labor scene in 1935, but the character of the national labor union was also undergoing changes. The American Federation of Labor (AFL), a confederation of craft unions, had been the principal union model for half a century. However, in 1935 the Committee of Industrial Organizations, later called the Congress of Industrial Organizations (CIO), challenged the leadership of the AFL by successfully supporting industrial unions. Membership in industrial unions was based on employment in a particular industry, such as automobile, steel, or clothing, rather than on a particular skill.

THE NATIONAL LABOR RELATIONS ACT

The corporation manufactures and sells products made from rare metals and is clearly subject to the commerce definition of the National Labor Relations Act.

A group of employees organized a union that the corporation refused to recognize. The union organized a sit-down strike in which about 95 employees occupied two key buildings of the corporation's facility. All work stopped.

The corporation asked the employees to leave and, when they refused, fired them. It obtained an injunction, which the employees ignored; law enforcement officials forcibly ousted and arrested them.

Production resumed, and some of the strikers were hired back. Others, however, refused to return unless their union was recognized. The corporation had supported the organization of another independent union the National Labor Relations Board found to be a company union in violation of the act.

In light of that finding, the NLRB ordered the corporation to stop interfering with the rights of employees to organize and to select their own bargaining representatives; not to dominate their labor organization; and to stop refusing to bargain with the employees' union.

The NLRB went one step further to effectuate its policies by ordering the corporation to reinstate all the striking employees with back pay, even if it involved discharging people hired since the strike. The corporation appealed the NLRB order.

Decision

The U.S. Supreme Court upheld the finding of an employer unfair labor practice for refusing to bargain with the union. It also pointed out that the employer's discharge of the employees was proper because the employees illegally took and held possession of the employer's property while engaging in the strike.

The Court was left to examine the authority of the NLRB to order the reinstatement of the strikers. The NLRB's reasoning was that, since the strike was in response to an unfair labor practice, the act provided that the employees retained their status despite discharge for illegal conduct or, that as an alternative, the NLRB's authority was broad enough to order reinstatement to effectuate the purposes of the act.

The Court found that the National Labor Relations Act's protection of employee activity is limited to lawful conduct. A lawful strike, the exercise of the right to quit work, is protected, and the employees retain their employment status. But an illegal strike, one that includes the seizure of buildings to prevent their use by the employer, is outside the scope of the act.

The Court found that the NLRB's authority under the act was broad but not unlimited. The NLRB's authority to order affirmative action is limited to orders that will in fact restrain unfair labor practices; it does not extend to punishing an employer for past practices. Therefore, an affirmative order requiring the employer to recognize and bargain with the union was within its authority because of the impact on the employer's future actions. But reinstatement of certain strikers who participated in an illegal act would not effectuate the purposes of the National Labor Relations Act to encourage peaceful resolution of labor disputes.

Adapted from *National Labor Relations Board v. Fanstead Metallurgical Corporation*, 83 L.Ed. 627 (1938).

Figure 3-2

Findings and Policy

- Denial by employers of employee collective bargaining leads to strikes, industrial unrest, and obstruction of commerce
- Inequality of bargaining power between employees and employers affects the flow of commerce and aggravates recurrent business depressions

- Protection of the right of employees to organize and bargain collectively safeguards commerce
- Policy of the United States to encourage practice and procedure of collective bargaining and the exercise of employees of their right to organize and negotiate

Rights of Employees

- To organize into unions of their own choosing
- To assist such labor unions
- To bargain collectively with their employer through representatives of their own choosing

- To strike or take other similar concerted action

Employer Unfair Labor Practices (illegal)

- Interfering with employee rights guaranteed by the act
- Refusal to bargain in good faith with employee representatives

- Discrimination against union members or employees pursuing their rights under the act
- Any attempt to dominate or interfere with employee unions

Representatives and Elections

- Employee representatives shall be exclusive representatives of the appropriate unit
- NLRB decides appropriateness of unit for bargaining purposes

- NLRB shall conduct secret ballot elections to determine employee representatives

National Labor Relations Board

- Members appointed by president of the United States
- Conducts elections to determine employee representatives of appropriate unit

- Exclusive power to prevent employer unfair labor practice

The CIO grew to 5 million members in less than 20 years under the leadership of John L. Lewis. This growth was attributed to the passage of the Wagner Act, the increased shift of the American economy from agriculture to manufacturing, and the heightened economic activity of World War II and the Korean War.

The Fair Labor Standards Act

The National Labor Relations Act was followed by the passage of the Walsh-Healey Act and the Fair Labor Standards Act (FLSA). The Walsh-Healey Act, passed in 1936, foreshadowed the passage of the FLSA. It again imposed rules on employers who received federal dollars. It required those employers with federal contracts to pay time and one-half to any employee working more than eight hours per day.[21]

The Fair Labor Standards Act, passed in 1938, applied primarily to employees engaged in interstate commerce and provided a federal minimum wage and a 44-hour week to be reduced to 40 hours in three years.[22] Passage of the act secured three main objectives of the labor movement: wages adequate to maintain a decent standard of living, shorter hours, and the abolition of labor by children under the age of 16.

World War II and the war effort resulted in a shortage of labor and more labor demands. Strikes brought charges that labor unions were unpatriotic. Congress, reacting to pressure, passed the Smith-Connally Act to control strikes injurious to the war effort.[23] Passage of this act showed a shift in political forces against strong federal support of union activities.

The Wagner Act, however, was still in place at the end of the war, and labor entered the postwar economic slump with considerable legal protection. The collective bargaining rights mandated by the act forced business to deal with labor on an equal footing. Supported by two Supreme Court decisions in the early 1940s, labor unions were allowed the use of peaceful picketing to inform the public of their alleged grievances and to elicit support for their cause.[24]

Widespread strikes during 1945–1946 and wage drives in 1946–1947 caused critics of the Wagner Act to increase the political pressure for amendment. The amendment's stated goal was to equalize its impact on employers. The relentless campaigning of the Chamber of Commerce and the National Association of Manufacturers, resentment over wartime strikes, and internal union irregularities began to turn the tide against organized labor.

Numerous bills were introduced to change the Wagner Act, to weaken the powers of the National Labor Relations Board, to redefine appropriate bargaining units, to outlaw a closed union shop, to subject unions to unfair labor practices charges, and to limit strikes and other concerted activities. Although these bills did not pass, they laid a foundation for the passage of the **Taft-Hartley Amendments** in 1947. Figure 3-3 gives a brief chronology of the era of strong union support in the United States.

The Fair Labor Standards Act has been amended several times since 1938. The minimum wage has been raised several times, most recently to $4.75 per hour on October 1, 1996, and $5.15 on September 1, 1997.[25] In 1989, a "subminimum," or "training," wage was created as a concession to employers. It had primarily allowed teenagers to be paid 64 cents per hour less than minimum wage during training, to make up to employers for the imposition of a higher minimum wage.[26] In a 1993 about-face, as a concession to unions, the subminimum wage was abolished.

The Labor-Management Relations Act (Taft-Hartley Amendments)

For 12 years the Wagner Act gave unions the time and ability to grow strong. From 1935 to 1947 union membership went from 3 million to 15 million, with some industries having 80 percent of their employees under collective bargaining agreements.[27] The image of organized labor in Congress was one of power—power to stop coal production during World War II and to shut down steel mills, seaports, and automobile assembly plants after the war.

Figure 3-3

1914	*Clayton Act.* Congress attempted to limit use of court injunction. First national pro-union legislation.
1914–1918	*World War I.* President Wilson created the National War Labor Board to mediate labor disputes. The board also recognized employee collective bargaining rights during the war.
1926	*Railway Labor Act.* Railroad employees were given collective bargaining rights and the right to use voluntary arbitration.
1929	*Stock market crash.* Beginning of Great Depression and 33 percent national unemployment.
1931	*Davis-Bacon Act.* Required federal contractors to pay "prevailing wages," which are usually union wages.
1932	*Norris–LaGuardia Act.* Limited use of court injunction, made yellow-dog contracts unenforceable.
1935	*Wagner Act.* The Magna Carta of U.S. labor history. Within 12 years, union membership tripled in the United States. Upheld by the Supreme Court in 1937. Created the NLRB.
1935	*Committee for Industrial Organizations.* John L. Lewis led industrial unions to split with the AFL.
1936	*Flint, Michigan.* The UAW staged the first "sit-in" strike, occupying the GM auto plant. *Walsh-Healey Act.* Required federal contractors to pay time and one-half for overtime, over an eight-hour day.
1938	*Fair Labor Standards Act.* Provided minimum wage, 40-hour week, overtime pay, and the abolition of child labor.
1941–1945	*World War II.* Widespread labor strikes during and after the war harmed the war effort and caused strong antilabor public sympathy.

A Republican Congress in 1946 introduced 200 bills on labor relations during its first week, and President Harry Truman proposed some revision of the nation's labor laws in his State of the Union Address. After extensive hearings by both the House and Senate, the 1947 Labor-Management Relations Act (known as the Taft-Hartley Amendments) was passed.[28] Although President Truman vetoed it, Congress overrode his veto and the bill became law on August 22, 1947.

Management saw the Taft-Hartley Amendments as a shift to a more balanced approach to labor relations. Labor unions were subjected to many of the same duties as employers. Whereas the Wagner Act gave employees the right to organize, the Taft-Hartley Amendments recognized their right not to organize. Under the Wagner Act employers were required to bargain in good faith; under Taft-Hartley, that duty was extended to unions. The unfair labor practices section protected employees and employers from labor unions' unfair labor practices. The Wagner Act had protected employees from being fired for joining a union; the Taft-Hartley Amendments protected employees from losing their jobs for *not* joining a union. The 1947 amendments recognized and gave preference to state right-to-work laws over bargained-for provisions in collective bargaining agreements that required union membership as a condition of employment. Figure 3-4 outlines the major provisions of the Taft-Hartley Amendments.

Organized labor immediately began to work for the repeal of Taft-Hartley. Labor had, by opposing any change to the Wagner Act, shut itself out of congressional decision making and demanded that Taft-Hartley be repealed before even

Figure 3-4   Major Provisions of the Taft-Hartley Amendments

Findings and Policy

- Certain practices of labor organizations, such as secondary strikes, burden and obstruct the free flow of commerce

- Elimination of such practices is necessary to guarantee rights of act

Rights of Employees

- To refrain from any and all union activities except union shop provision in valid collective bargaining agreements

Union Unfair Labor Practices

- Restraint or coercion of employees in exercise of their rights
- Refusal to bargain in good faith with employer

- Discrimination against employee for not engaging in union activities

Restrictions on Strike Activities

- No secondary strikes and boycotts
- Prohibits strikes conducted by one labor union to dislodge another labor union
- Outlaws strikes to force employers to make work for union members

- Prohibits strikes during the term of a valid collective bargaining agreement unless employees give 60 days notice to employer and 30 days notice to the Federal Mediation and Conciliation Service (FMCS)

Right-to-Work Laws

- Give states the right to outlaw union shop requirements in collective bargaining agreements so employees can refrain from joining the union representing them at the bargaining table

---

discussing possible changes in the Wagner Act. This all-or-nothing approach backfired, and Taft-Hartley was left unchanged. Labor legislation did not receive national attention again until 1957.

Certainly one response of the labor community to the passage of the Taft-Hartley Amendments was a reemergence of the "in union there is strength" approach to organized labor. The AFL-CIO merger in 1955 ended a 20-year separation of the two dominant national labor organizations and enabled the united group to claim a total membership of 16.1 million workers: 10.9 million members from 108 AFL unions and 5.2 million members from 30 CIO unions.

Besides fear of anti-union sentiment represented by the Taft-Hartley Amendments, the merger was prompted by a desire to end union raiding, in which one union pirated members from another. A change in leadership in both, as well as internal housecleaning by the CIO to rid itself of 11 communist front unions and by the AFL to expel the racket-ridden International Longshoremen's Union, created the mutual respect necessary to overcome past differences.

The Labor-Management Reporting and Disclosure Act of 1959

The famed McClellan hearings in 1957 set the stage for the second major change to the national labor policy since the Wagner Act. Initiated to investigate wrongdoings in the labor-management field, the Senate committee soon unearthed corruption in some major unions. Charges of racketeering centered on threats that strikes would be called against employers and on incidents in which union officials sold out the interests of union members for cash.[29] The public outcry for labor legislation to protect the internal operations of unions was noticed by political leaders, and congressional bills offering sweeping reforms were introduced. Labor supported reforms as long as amendments to Taft-Hartley were included. Management also supported them as long as *their* amendments to Taft-Hartley were included. The mood created by the McClellan hearings was in management's favor, and the **Labor-Management Reporting and Disclosure Act of 1959** (known as the **Landrum-Griffin Act**) was passed.[30]

The Landrum-Griffin Act provisions amending the Wagner and Taft-Hartley Acts further eroded the power of labor unions by limiting such economic activities as boycotts and picketing. In regulating the internal operation of labor unions, the Landrum-Griffin Act introduced controls on internal handling of union funds. It established safeguards for union elections and in certain cases gave members the right to bring suit against the union. Under the act, unions were required to have a constitution and bylaws and to file these and other disclosure documents with the secretary of labor. It also established due process rules for disciplining members. For example, in 1995 a union member was expelled from his union after working to remove his union and put another in its place. After he was expelled from the union, he stopped paying dues. The union notified him that under the collective bargaining agreement they would have him terminated for failure to pay dues. He appealed, and the NLRB upheld the union.[31]

The Labor-Management Reporting and Disclosure (Landrum-Griffin) Act of 1959 protects the democratic nature of unions. The act assures full and active participation by the rank and file in the affairs of the union. It accords protection of union members' right to participate in the election process. It requires high standards of responsibility and ethical conduct by union officials and protects members from the arbitrary and capricious whims of union leaders.

The Bill of Rights of Members of Labor Organizations established the machinery necessary to enforce this act. The rights under this Title I section include the right to nominate candidates and to vote in union elections, to attend membership meetings, and to participate in the deliberation of those meetings. Freedom to speak about union affairs and to assemble with union members was also reaffirmed. Title I protects union members from excessive charges because dues, fees, and assessments are decided by a majority vote of the membership. Members are given the right to sue the union and are assured due process protections in the union's disciplinary actions.

Under subsequent titles of the Landrum-Griffin Act, union members gained access to union financial reports; local unions received protection from their national organization in the assertion of trustee rights; the fair and democratic conduct of union elections was assured; and the fiduciary duty of union officials to their members was clearly outlined.

With passage of the Landrum-Griffin Act the legislation that established the national labor policy—a policy characterized by strong support of collective bargaining as a means of ending industrial strife—was in place. Successive chapters will discuss how that bargaining process is to be carried out under the provisions of the act.

UNION STRUCTURE

The structure of labor unions reflects the reasons they were formed and the influences of the times in which they grew. Unions seek to secure a better living standard for their members through higher wages and fringe benefits and to enhance job security through tenure, layoff provisions, and seniority rights. In addition, labor organizations have broadened their interests to seek legislative protections for workers such as occupational health and safety laws, workers' compensation, and unemployment insurance. To advance the welfare of all workers, unions also support social legislation such as Social Security, funding for public education, and environmental laws. To meet the unions' objectives, a two-tiered labor organizational structure has evolved. On the local level, job-oriented units form the basis for bargaining with employers. On the national level, a network or federation of unions pursues broader goals. Figure 3-5 shows AFL-CIO–affiliated union memberships.

Types of Unions

Craft Unions.   The U.S. labor movement began when associations and combinations of skilled workers joined together for short periods of time to confront an employer on a specific job action. These associations were the bases of the **craft unions**.

Craft unions are made up of workers who have been organized in accordance with their craft or skill. "*One craft, one union*" is their slogan. For example, in the building construction industry, skilled workers include electricians, carpenters, bricklayers, and iron workers; in the printing industry, printers, typesetters, and engravers; in the service industry, barbers, cooks, and telephone workers; and in the manufacturing industry, millwrights, machinists, and tool-and-die makers.

The craft union, as an organization of skilled workers, is able to approach an employer on a much different footing than the industrial union. A craft union local typically seeks to organize all practitioners of its trade employed by a certain employer or within a specific geographic area. By doing so successfully, the craft union creates a union shop. Employers who need the services of a skilled laborer must employ a union member. Craft unions also seek to restrict the supply of skilled laborers so they can demand higher wages. Stringent apprenticeship programs consisting of several years of classroom instruction and on-the-job training limit craft union membership. State or local licensing boards composed of members of the trade union can often restrict the number of licenses issued.

Union members enter the craft union after an apprenticeship of several years. Craft unionists remain members for their working lifetimes, moving from job to job as required but always remaining a part of their craft union. Even after retirement, their contact with the union remains as a tribute to their craft.

Labor agreements entered into by craft unions usually cover a geographic region rather than one employer. Union members may work for more than one employer within a year and still be covered by that same agreement. This practice is common when the building trade unions have negotiated a labor agreement with all the major construction companies in the area. Electricians, plumbers, drywallers, and other trades can go from job to job under the same agreement.

[**In thousands.** Figures represent the labor organizations as constituted in 1989 and reflect past merger activity. Membership figures based on average per capita paid membership to the AFL-CIO for the two-year period ending in June of the year shown and reflect only actively employed members. Labor unions shown had a membership of 50,000 or more in 1991.]

Labor Organization	1979	1985	1989	1991
Total[1]	13,621	13,109	14,100	13,933
Actors and Artistes	75	100	97	99
Allied Industrial Workers	92	63	60	53
Automobile, Aerospace and Agriculture (UAW)	X	974	917	840
Bakery, Confectionery and Tobacco	131	115	103	101
Boiler Makers, Iron Shipbuilders[2,3]	129	110	75	66
Bricklayers	106	95	84	84
Carpenters[2]	626	616	613	494
Clothing and Textile Workers (ACTWU)[2]	308	228	180	154
Communication Workers (CWA)	485	524	492	492
Electrical Workers (IBEW)	825	791	744	730
Electronic, Electrical and Salaried[2,4]	243	198	171	160
Operating Engineers	313	330	330	330
FireFighters	150	142	142	151
Food and Commercial Workers (UFCW)[2]	1,123	989	999	997
Garment Workers (ILGWU)	314	210	153	143
Glass, Molders, Pottery, and Plastics[2]	50	104	86	80
Government, American Federation (AFGE)	236	199	156	151
Graphic Communications[2]	171	141	124	113
Hotel Employees and Restaurant Employees	373	327	278	269
Ironworkers	146	140	111	101
Laborers	475	383	406	406
Letter Carriers (NALC)	151	186	201	210
Longshoreman's Association	63	65	62	60
Machinists and Aerospace (IAM)[2]	688	537	517	534
Marine Engineers Beneficial Assn	23	22	48	53
Mine Workers	X	X	X	82
Office and Professional Employees	83	90	84	89
Oil, Chemical, Atomic Workers (OCAW)	146	108	71	90
Painters	160	133	128	124
Paperworkers Int'l	262	232	210	202
Plumbing and Pipefitting	228	226	220	220
Postal Workers	245	232	213	228
Retail, Wholesale Department Store	122	106	137	128
Rubber, Cork, Linoleum, Plastic	158	106	92	89
Seafarers	84	80	80	80
Service Employees (SEIU)[2,5]	537	688	762	881
Sheet Metal Workers	120	108	108	108
Stage Employees, Moving Picture Machine Operators	50	50	50	50
State, County, Municipal (AFSCME)[5]	889	997	1,090	1,191
Steelworkers	964	572	481	459
Teachers (AFT)	423	470	544	573
Teamsters[6]	X	X	1,161	1,379
Transit Union	94	94	96	98

(continued)

Figure 3-5

U.S. Membership in AFL-CIO–Affiliated Unions, by Selected Union (continued)

Labor Organization	1979	1985	1989	1991
Transport Workers	85	85	85	85
Transportation/Communications International	127	102	86	73
Transportation Union, United	121	88	X	64
Utility Workers	53	52	51	55

Note: X, Not applicable. [1]Includes other AFL-CIO–affiliated unions, not shown separately. [2]Figures reflect mergers with one or more unions since 1979. For details see source. [3]Includes Blacksmiths, Forgers and Helpers. [4]Includes Machine and Furniture Workers. [5]Excludes Hospital and Health Care Employees, which merged into both unions on June 1, 1989 (membership of 23,000 in 1985; 60,000 in 1987; and 58,000 in 1989). [6]Includes Chauffeurs, Warehousemen, and Helpers.

Source: American Federation of Labor and Congress of Industrial Organizations, Washington, DC, *Report of the AFL-CIO Executive Council*, biannual.

The **business agent** of the craft union is usually a full-time administrator paid by the union to handle negotiation and administration of the union contracts as well as the day-to-day operation of the union hiring hall. On the job, one union member performs the role of **steward**; he or she may be the first person hired for that construction project, the most senior member of the construction crew, or a person chosen by the business agent. Stewards are the eyes and ears of the business agent. The steward's job is to make sure the contractor lives up to the agreement and to report to the business agent if he or she does not. This arrangement assures the business agent an active contact at each job site at which the craft union is supplying laborers. There is, however, no continuing role for any particular steward in the craft union local. The steward's authority is limited to the job site, and when that job is finished, the steward returns to regular union membership.

Industrial Unions. Whereas craft unions can be traced to the earliest days of this country, **industrial unions** have a wider and stronger base of mostly unskilled laborers. The slogan *"One shop, one union"* typifies the industrial union seeking to organize workers at one workplace with the same employer regardless of their jobs. The industrial union seeks to increase membership to ensure its influence.

Typical industrial unions include organizations of autoworkers, rubber workers, textile workers, commercial workers, steelworkers, miners, and truck drivers. Increasingly, government employees such as firefighters, police, and hospital workers are organizing industrial-type unions.

The local union most often is affiliated with a national or international union. Some national unions will negotiate **master agreements**, which are regional or national labor agreements covering wages, transfers, pensions, layoffs, and other benefits. The **local agreement** must be negotiated separately to cover matters of specific concern to the local union and the plant. An example of such a two-tiered agreement is the labor agreement between the United Auto Workers and Ford Motor Company. The table of contents in this particular master agreement includes the following:

Article I   Recognition
Article II   Union Shop
Article III   Dues and Assessments
Article IV   Company Responsibilities

The local agreement negotiated by Local 862, UAW Unit No. 2, includes the following:

Day-off program	Other miscellaneous agreements
Employee information	Overtime agreement
Job-posting agreement	Paid holidays
Letters of understanding	Seniority agreement
Line spacing	Shift preference agreement
Manning of medical facility	Shift starting time
Miscellaneous agreement	

Members of an industrial union often join the union *after* being hired simply because of a union shop provision in the contract. Members regard their union as their voice with the employer, and when employment ends, their membership usually ends as well.

The work of local industrial unions is typically administered by elected officials who are also full-time employees at the workplace. Their duties include negotiation and administration of the local union contract, normally with the assistance of a representative of the national or international union. This work is aided by elected shop stewards who form a permanent tier in the local industrial union hierarchy. At the departmental, shift, or line level, the shop stewards are the eyes and ears, voice, and strong right arm of the union. Their position enables them to communicate members' desires and complaints to union officials and to relay information back to the membership. Stewards participate in grievance adjustment and, through steward councils, assist in contract negotiations.

Levels of Unions

The four levels of unions are local unions, national (or international) unions, intermediate unions, and the federation of unions.

Local Unions. Unionized workers are members of a **local union**, which is the organizational component of the labor union. It handles the day-to-day operations of the collective bargaining agreement, disposes of most grievances, manages strikes, and disciplines members. A local union may fill a social role in the lives of its members, sponsoring dances, festivals, and other functions. It may be the focal point of the political organization and activity of its members.

A local union usually meets once a month to conduct business. At such meetings, annual elections are held, union issues are discussed, and activities are organized. Although this level is the most important to its members, attendance at the union meetings varies and is highest at times of crisis. Unlike paid business agents for craft unions, elected officials of local industrial unions are compensated by being given time off the job when conducting union business.

National (or International) Unions.   Typically, but not always, the local union is affiliated with a **national** or **international union**. Craft and industrial unions organize on a national basis and designate local unions by region. The national union serves as the local's parent, having created it. But a local union is considered a separate and distinct voluntary association owing its existence to the will of its members.

The relationship between a national union and its subordinate local unions is determined by the union's constitution, bylaws, and charter. The *charter* is a contract between the national and local organization and its members. The *constitution* and *bylaws* authorize the national union to function but also to protect individual rights.

Constitutions are adopted or changed at conventions of representatives of member locals. Officers and executive boards are elected to take action consistent with policies established by the convention. Most national unions allow their elected officials to hire and organize the union's administrative staff. Most unions have the following operational departments: executive and administrative, made up of president, vice president, secretary-treasurer, and assistant; financial and auditing; organizational and service (to serve local unions); and the technical staff, which gives expert assistance in arbitration, labor laws, and data research.

The national union provides services to the locals, and the fundamental relationship is based on the services rendered. Services include organizing the nonunion workers within the jurisdiction of the local union. In appropriate circumstances, the national negotiates master agreements with nationwide employers and assists the local union in its local agreement. Even if no national contract is entered into, the national union assists the local unions in their contract negotiations through its research and educational services and may provide an expert negotiator. A national helps with grievance and arbitration administration and provides support in strike activities. National unions play an important political and representative role on behalf of their locals in national and statewide political action. Local unions support the national unions with dues and fees.

Intermediate Organizational Units.   **Intermediate organizational units** consisting of regional or district officers, trade councils, conference boards, and joint councils lie between national and local unions. For industrial unions, the intermediate office serves to bring the national office closer to the local unions to provide better services. For craft unions, joint councils often bring the various crafts together to give them better negotiating power with local construction employers, to coordinate their activities, and to assist in resolving jurisdictional disputes between craft unions.

Federation of Unions.   Perhaps the most familiar level of unions is the **federation of unions**, specifically the only U.S. federation of unions, the American Federation of Labor and Congress of Industrial Organizations (AFL-CIO). Composed of approximately 95 national and international unions, the AFL-CIO has 45,000 local unions and 13.6 million members. Figure 3-6 illustrates its structure.

Federations were formed to increase union power. Although the AFL-CIO is itself not a union, it represents U.S. labor in world affairs and coordinates union activities such as lobbying, voter registration, and political education. The federation also helps to coordinate activities aimed at organizing nonmember workers.

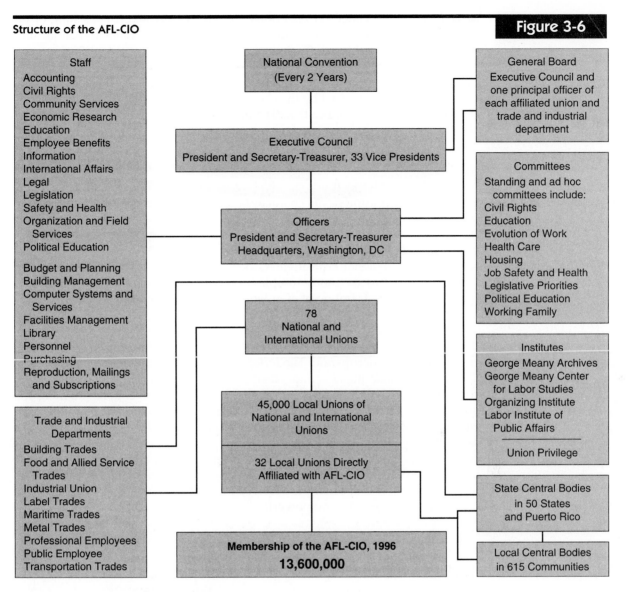

Staff
Accounting
Civil Rights
Community Services
Economic Research
Education
Employee Benefits
Information
International Affairs
Legal
Legislation
Safety and Health
Organization and Field
    Services
Political Education

Budget and Planning
Building Management
Computer Systems and
    Services
Facilities Management
Library
Personnel
Purchasing
Reproduction, Mailings
    and Subscriptions

**Trade and Industrial
Departments**
Building Trades
Food and Allied Service
    Trades
Industrial Union
Label Trades
Maritime Trades
Metal Trades
Professional Employees
Public Employee
Transportation Trades

National Convention
(Every 2 Years)

Executive Council
President and Secretary-Treasurer, 33 Vice Presidents

Officers
President and Secretary-Treasurer
Headquarters, Washington, DC

78
National and
International Unions

45,000 Local Unions of
National and International
Unions

32 Local Unions Directly
Affiliated with AFL-CIO

Membership of the AFL-CIO, 1996
13,600,000

General Board
Executive Council and
one principal officer of
each affiliated union and
trade and industrial
department

Committees
Standing and ad hoc
    committees include:
Civil Rights
Education
Evolution of Work
Health Care
Housing
Job Safety and Health
Legislative Priorities
Political Education
Working Family

Institutes
George Meany Archives
George Meany Center
    for Labor Studies
Organizing Institute
Labor Institute of
    Public Affairs

Union Privilege

State Central Bodies
in 50 States
and Puerto Rico

Local Central Bodies
in 615 Communities

Source: Labor Net, AFL-CIO Home Page, 1996.

The AFL-CIO assists in mediation and resolution of disputes between national unions that might otherwise result in work stoppages.

In 1987, the AFL-CIO ended one of the deepest rifts in the labor movement when the executive council unanimously voted to allow the International Brotherhood of Teamsters to rejoin the federation. After 30 years of "exile" over a 1957 ethics dispute, one of the nation's largest national unions asked to rejoin the AFL-CIO at a time when many of its leaders were under federal investigation for alleged criminal activities. The Teamsters brought 1.6 million members and their dues to the AFL-CIO.

As with national unions, the officers, policies, activities, and business of the AFL-CIO are voted on at periodic conventions, to which each national union sends delegates. Between conventions, the executive council, consisting of the president, secretary-treasurer, and 33 vice presidents, convenes to handle such items as union corruption, charters of new internationals, and judicial appeals from member unions. The general board is composed of the executive council plus the chief executive officer (CEO) of each affiliated union. The general board rules on questions referred by the executive council and includes items deemed to be politically sensitive and those requiring council action by the AFL-CIO Constitution.

Independent Unions.   As stated earlier, not all local unions are affiliated with a national or international union, which in turn is a part of the AFL-CIO. These local independent unions are characterized by smaller memberships, more limited funds, and a lower profile. They are, however, growing. One major reason for their growth is that these independent unions find their membership primarily among government and white-collar workers. The American Nurses Association, the National Education Association, and the National Federation of Federal Employees are good examples of independent unions. Table 3-1 reflects the growth and distribution of of independent unions by industry between 1967 and 1991.

Indepenent unions are generally not designed along either the craft or the industrial unit model, preferring to open their membership to employees of a specific professional occupation. The independent unions resemble other unions in that they do target membership, albeit often a wider target. They hold national conventions and elect national officers, although the conventions are more frequently and seemingly more democratic among the independent unions. The election of their national officers reflects the smaller size of these unions in that the membership often elects the national officers themselves not the delegates to the conventions. In union disciplinary procedures, the independent unions are more likely to invoke outside arbitrators or hearing panels than are the traditional affiliated unions. This approach to union self-regulation keeps union officials from becoming too autocratic and powerful.[32]

Table 3-1	Distribution of Independent Unions by Industry		
		1967	1991
	Manufacturing	24	15
	Skilled trades	15	12
	Federal government	12	10
	Police and security	10	12
	Utilities	5	6
	Other professionals	5	11
	Service employees	2	6
	Health-care providers	0	6
	Education	0	6
	Other	27	16

Source: James W. Robinson, "Structural Characteristics of the Independent Union in America Revisited," *Labor Law Journal* (September 1992), p. 596. Published and copyrighted 1992 by CCH Inc., 4025 Peterson Avenue, Chicago, IL 60646. All rights reserved.

The Wagner Act gave most private employees the right to collective bargaining. In January 1962, President John F. Kennedy signed **Executive Order (E.O.) 10988** extending that right to most federal government employees. That executive order was subsequently amended by President Richard Nixon in **E.O. 11491**, which attempted to parallel private employee rights with one major exception: public employees were denied the right to strike.

In 1978, Title VII of the **Civil Service Reform Act** replaced the executive orders as the legal protection for federal employee collective bargaining rights. Although similar in most respects to the Wagner Act, the Civil Service Reform Act also prohibits employee strikes and mandates that all contracts contain a grievance procedure with binding arbitration as the final step. Chapter 13 explores that act and how public employee unions function under the act.

PUBLIC SECTOR COLLECTIVE BARGAINING

As the numbers of jobs in traditionally unionized industries continue to drop, a generation of Americans learn about collective bargaining through the news media instead of around the dinner table. Students may better relate to the following look at unions in the sports world.

Collective bargaining and unions have had a substantial impact on professional sports in the United States. Through contract negotiations players in recent years have received an increasing share of gate receipts and television revenues. Some sports fans may complain that the days when athletes "played because of their love for the game" are gone forever; however, others recognize that today's players are able to make a career out of their profession and are sharing in the wealth they generate through their accomplishments. Still other sports fans blame the high players' salaries (see Figure 3-7) for the high stadium prices, and they miss the days when players stayed with one team for their entire careers. In addition, collective bargaining has resulted in long strikes and lockouts and has disrupted several seasons.

COLLECTIVE BARGAINING IN SPORTS

How Does Your Salary Compare?   **Figure 3-7**

In their 1993 collective bargaining negotiations, major league baseball players complained that they received an average salary increase of *only* 7.6 percent, the smallest negotiated increase in 13 years. In the previous 12 years the average player had received an average increase of 17.83 percent. Many working men and women could have trouble sympathizing with the players since the average player's salary is 34 times that of the average man and 40 times that of the average woman! How does your salary compare with these national averages?

Occupation	1997 Average Salary
U.S. worker	$ 28,038
Baseball player	1,156,666
Football player (NFL)	599,863
Basketball player (NBA)	1,935,308
Hockey player (NHL)	809,834

Source: U.S. Department of Labor, Major-League Baseball Players Assn., National Football League Players Assn., National Basketball Players Assn., National Hockey League Players Assn.

In general, the sports industry can be viewed as a part of the larger entertainment industry, which enthralls the American public. In this respect, star athletes are similar to musicians, stage bands, actors, and other performers. The principal common features among these professionals are technology, media, market constraints, and societal power. The televising of sporting events, including cable and satellite distribution, has become the largest source of revenue for professional sport franchises. Schedules, locations, and times of games are quickly changed to meet the needs of the television industry.

Similar influences can be found in other entertainment fields. Both sports and other professional entertainment areas are highly subject to the "star system," in which a few stars command a substantial influence on their professions and derive substantial income from outside sources such as product endorsements. Like the older unions in entertainment—the Screen Actors Guild, National Association of Broadcast Engineers and Technicians, and American Federation of Television and Radio Artists—sports unions are concerned about the welfare of the other players (nonsuperstars), who are more subject to the desires of management.[33]

The key elements of labor relations in professional sports are shown in Figure 3-8. The three principal participants are management (leagues and team owners), labor (players and unions), and government. The federal government performs the regulatory function under the National Labor Relations Act in the same capacity that it oversees all private commerce. A body of National Labor Relations Board and court decisions unique to collective bargaining in professional sports has been compiled since 1935. In this respect, the sports industry is similar to many other American industries—steel, auto, service, clothing—in that it falls under the NLRB, but it contains past practices, unions, and historical events unique to the industry.

Management in the sports industry operates through league structures. The leagues negotiate collective bargaining agreements, set rules for drafting players, determine management rights, and negotiate national television agreements. Thus, club owners yield a great deal of the traditional management authority to the leagues. They do, however, retain decision making over front office personnel, local television contracts, and stadium management, and they negotiate individual player contracts.

Labor unions in the sports industry operate much as other unions do. They organize the players for the purpose of collective bargaining, promote solidarity, negotiate contracts, utilize power tactics such as strikes and picketing if necessary, file and administer grievances, collect dues, and lobby for the interests of their members. The roles of the commissioners and agents are unique to the sports industry. In general, commissioners serve both management and labor and act as the public spokespeople for the league. Because they are hired and paid by management, however, they tend to be viewed as part of the management structure.

Agents serve as representatives of individual players and negotiate their contracts with individual team owners. Some agents also manage the assets of their players and negotiate their outside contracts. Many observers believe that agents have become a destructive force in the sports industry and have caused the colossal salaries of some players, while the unions have concentrated on increasing the salary, benefits, and working conditions of all players. Unless the unions take over the role of negotiating individual contracts, a change that superstar players are unlikely to support, the influence of players' agents is likely to continue to grow. The other major participants are the mediators and arbitrators. The common

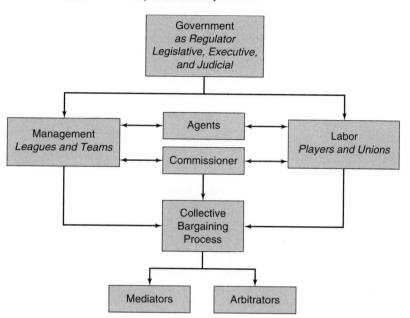

Source: Paul D. Staudohar, *The Sports Industry and Collective Bargaining* (New York: ICR Press, 1986), p. 8.

use of individual player salary arbitration in the sports industry has had a significant influence on player salaries and has developed a highly specialized field of collective bargaining.[34]

Baseball

The National and American Leagues of Professional Baseball Clubs represent management for purposes of collective bargaining. The union is the Major League Baseball Players Association (MLBPA), formed in 1952 and using collective bargaining since 1966. Professional baseball, owing to a 1922 U.S. Supreme Court decision (upheld in the 1972 Curt Flood decision), is not covered by federal antitrust laws. The Court cited baseball's unique needs as an industry and its place in U.S. history.[35] For many years agreements covered limited areas including salary, insurance, and pensions. Then in 1970 a new provision provided for a tripartite grievance arbitration panel to replace the commissioner as the last step in resolving disputes.

The "modern era" of professional sports and collective bargaining began in the mid-1970s. Arbitration of salary disputes in baseball (after three years of service) was first provided in the 1973 agreement. The arbitrator, however, must choose the final salary offer of either the player or the team without any compromise. The 1976 baseball agreement first allowed players to become free agents (after six years of service) and thus limited to newer players the **"reserve clause"** status under which teams reserve the sole right to negotiate a contract with the player. The reserve clause is a most unusual labor-management principle in that it takes from players a basic right enjoyed by other American workers—to sell

Table 3-2   Major League Baseball Salaries 1970–1996

Year	Average Salary
1970	$ 29,303
1975	44,676
1980	143,756
1985	371,157
1990	597,537
1996	1,156,666

Source: Major League Baseball Players Association.

their services to any employer. The NBA limited its reserve clause contract language in 1980, the NFL in 1993. As a free agent, the player can sign with the highest bidder or whomever he chooses. These major changes in the 1970s began what is called the "modern era" of professional sports as other sports unions followed the lead of baseball.[36]

The effect of free agency and salary arbitration on average players' salaries can be seen in Table 3-2. In recent years, rising salaries, combined with declining stadium attendance in many parks, declining revenues from television contracts, and a skeptical public, has caused many industry specialists to worry. In 1992, 18 of the 26 major league baseball teams reported losses.[37]

Peter Magowan, part owner of the San Francisco Giants, warned: "Baseball is going through a really serious economic crisis. The player compensation system and distribution of revenue among the clubs must be changed if baseball is going to compete effectively for the entertainment dollar." CBS Inc. estimated that from 1990 to 1993 it lost $170 million on its four-year baseball broadcasting agreement, and thus future agreements will provide much less revenue to the owners, leagues, and players. Will high salaries and overpriced contracts kill baseball? "I don't know where it is going to stop except at the end," said baseball legend Yogi Berra.[38]

Baseball Strikes.   The first major league strike that affected season play occurred in 1972. The MLBPA struck over a pension issue, and 86 games were canceled. The first costly and most significant strike in professional sports, however, occurred in baseball in 1981. The issue was players' free agency rights, with owners demanding a replacement player for teams that lost a player because of free agency as a means to reduce the use of the free agency process. The players' union held fast to protect the free agency process, which had significantly increased players' salaries. At the last minute, the NLRB petitioned the U.S. district court for any injunction, but the court refused, and on June 12 a 50-day strike began.

No major league sport had ever witnessed a sustained strike, and the financial and emotional effects on the industry were unexpected and shocking. In total, 713 games were canceled, costing players, owners, television networks, ballparks, and cities millions of dollars in related revenues. Most surprising was the loss of fan support: Once the strike was settled (resulting in a split season with division winners for each half), fans both at the ballparks and in front of their televisions showed a loss of interest. By the end of the season, it was clear that a strike in professional sports has far greater effects on all business related to the sport, as well as on cities with major league teams, than those involved had predicted.

In 1985 another baseball strike occurred, but it lasted for only two days. The strike occurred within two months of the end of the season and centered on the owners' contribution to the players' benefit plan and the system for salary arbitration. Players wanted the owners to continue to put one-third of their national television revenues into the players' benefit plans. Revenues from 1985 would have put such contributions into the $60 million range, an increase of $45 million a year. Owners felt that such contributions were excessive. Also, the owners felt that the previous awards from arbitrators had resulted in inflated salaries, which they could no longer afford to pay. They proposed salary caps, which the players rejected.

The strike was settled within 27 hours of its beginning. The agreement was praised for its reasonableness. Rather than paying one-third of the television revenues, the owners' contribution to the players' benefit plans increased from $17.2 million to $32.7 million a year. The owners gave up on the proposed salary cap, but the players agreed to increase the time of employment from two to three years before salary arbitration. The parties credited the quick settlement to both the memory of the 50-day strike in 1981 and the owners' decision to allow the players access to their financial records. With information to support the owners' position that some teams were in serious trouble, the players' representatives were better able to sell compromise to their members.

The 1994 Baseball Strike: No World Series!   In 1994, for the first time in history, the World Series was canceled! A union-called strike did what two world wars, a depression, and an earthquake (1989, in San Francisco), could not—cancel the World Series. It was the eighth work stoppage since 1972, and by far the most damaging to the game, its players, and its owners. The strike began on August 12, 1994, and eventually caused the World Series to be canceled. By spring of 1995, the owners had assembled teams of replacement players, but at the last minute the Major League Players Association agreed to let its players on the field without a new contract and thus kept out the replacement-player games. The 1994 issues all centered on money—or greed, as outlined in Figure 3-9.

The owners contended that several small-market major-league teams had lost money for years and could not survive without a total salary cap. They proposed a revenue-sharing plan (50 percent) similar to that of the NFL (64 percent) and NBA (53 percent). But the players' union rejected that proposal. The biggest losers may have been San Francisco's Matt Williams, who with 50 home runs had over a month to beat the Roger Maris season record of 61, and Tony Gwynn, who was batting .399 with a real shot of breaking Ted Williams's modern season record of .406.[39] A federal court injunction in March 1995 brought the players back to the field without a contract.

On November 26, 1996, more than two years since the devastating strike of 1994 began, the owners, by a vote of 26 to 4, accepted the union's last offer, and a new contract was signed. Neither side claimed victory. The new agreement provided for revenue sharing to benefit smaller-market teams as requested by the owners; a historic first-interleague play; no salary cap as the union demanded; and a four-year agreement. The 235-day strike and negotiations that had started almost two years earlier produced a new era in major league baseball—with a three-division format and expansion to 30 teams. Was the strike really necessary? Experts and fans could not agree.

WHAT THE PLAYERS ASSOCIATION WANTED

Free agency. Eliminate the restriction on repeat free agency within a five-year span if a player's club offers salary arbitration at the end of his contract

Salary arbitration. Reduce the threshold to two years of major league service, its level from 1974 to 1986; it was three years

Minimum salary. Increase from $109,000 to $175,000–$200,000

WHAT THE OWNERS WANTED

Revenue. A 50-50 revenue split with players, with a $1 billion total guaranteed over seven years

Salary cap. After a four-year phase-in period in the seven-year agreement, clubs could not have payrolls more than 110 percent of the average or less than 84 percent of the average

Arbitration. Salary arbitration eliminated

Minimum salary. Escalating scale of minimum salaries for players with less than four years' major league service, but they would be allowed to sign for more than the minimum

The National Football League

Although the National Football League (NFL) shares some cost and revenue factors with major league baseball, there are several important differences. On the cost side, the NFL does not maintain an expensive farm system of minor league teams. However, each NFL team has 45 players and the NFL has about 1,500 players compared with only 600 major league baseball players. On the revenue side, each NFL team plays only 20 regular-season and preseason games, compared with 162 for each major league baseball team. The NFL, however, has built a strong television audience. Of all professional sports, only the NFL has been able to command network contracts for all its televised games. Baseball, basketball, and hockey, for example, have most of their games televised on free local television or cable.

The National Football League Players Association (NFLPA) is the union that represents professional football players. It was first registered with the U.S. Department of Labor in 1968. The players, in selecting the NFLPA also rejected the Teamsters Union, which tried to organize them. In 1974 the NFLPA became the first sports union to receive a charter from the AFL-CIO. The union, however, had difficulty negotiating with the NFL. One major break occurred when the NLRB ruled that playing on artificial turf was a mandatory subject for collective bargaining.

A major difference between football and baseball players is one of team emphasis versus individual players. Football is a team game that requires a highly coordinated team effort. Few players actually touch the ball, and individuality is not encouraged. The focus on the organization in football also carries over to negotiations, which have been less turbulent than baseball negotiations. For example, until 1993, far fewer football players played out their option and signed with a new team as a free agent. Another unique aspect of football is the annual NFL player draft of college players. It provides a more equal distribution of talent among teams because teams pick in reverse order of their last league standing. However, players contend that the draft keeps the most talented players from going to the top teams and enables owners to restrain salaries by forcing new players to negotiate with one team. Only the NFL limits its draft of new players to college seniors; baseball and basketball permit signing after high school, and hockey at age 18.[40]

In 1993 the NFL and the union signed a historic contract that ended five years of negotiations and a landmark court decision, *McNeil et al. v. The National Football League*. The primary issue was the owners' reserve clause and the players' free agency rights. In the new agreement, players will receive true free agency status after six years of service, and thus owners lose their reserve clause that binds players to one team. In return the owners received the first salary cap in football that limits total players' pay to 67 percent of designated gross revenues (61 percent after three years). In the first NFL "free agency derby," 120 players changed teams, and a new era in NFL collective bargaining had begun.[41] Whether the new free agency provision will drive up NFL salaries to equal those in baseball and basketball is a question only time can answer.

In 1996, the U.S. Supreme Court, in *Brown v. Pro Football*, made it clear that the National Football League was a legitimate multiemployer bargaining group under labor law statutes and that negotiations by the League were not in violation of the Sherman Antitrust Act.[42]

The 1982 NFL Strike.   In 1982 the first major strike in professional football was called by the NFLPA. Negotiations focused on how money from football revenues should be paid. The unions began by demanding a 55 percent share of the National Football League's gross revenues but compromised with a request for $1.6 million over four years. The union proposal included a demand for distribution of the dollars by an established wage scale with incentives and performance bonuses. Management position was that any percentage of the gross was unacceptable but that it could offer $1.6 billion over five years. The parties also differed on wage scales, with management preferring that each team decide its own salaries.

Negotiations dragged on for several weeks. They were marked by name calling, extensive analysis of which side was losing the most, and hostile feelings by loyal fans, who saw their season delayed and cut in half. When a settlement was finally reached, neither side could boast of major gains.

The National Basketball Association

In a process similar to baseball, professional basketball players have a union, the National Basketball Players Association (NBPA), which negotiates a general contract with the league—the National Basketball Association (NBA). Also as in baseball, outside agents negotiate individual player contracts with the team owners. Compared with baseball and football, basketball has the unique advantage of requiring only 12 players per team. This factor, combined with an 82-game season, has resulted in the teams' profitability largely depending on home-game attendance. Perhaps because of the competition from college games, however, professional basketball has consistently ranked a distant third behind baseball and football in television ratings. Overall, however, the combination of a relatively small number of players (300) in a game that has many individual stars and far more home games than football has enabled NBA players to negotiate high salaries. In fact, in the 1980s the NBA average player's salary surpassed that of players in all other professional sports.

Other major factors that have escalated NBA salaries include competition from other leagues (starting with the old American Basketball Association) and the NBA 1981 contract that provided players with free agency status. The NBA was the first sport to adopt the "hardship rule," which allowed young players to be drafted before their college senior year if they could prove financial need.

The most important labor relations case in NBA history is *Robertson v. NBA*.[43] The players involved, led by Oscar Robertson, filed suit against the NBA, contending that the draft, uniform contract, and reserve clause together were a violation of the Sherman Antitrust Act because they eliminated competition among the teams for the individual players. A final settlement of all issues was reached through collective bargaining between the NBA and NBPA in 1976. The historic contract provided a first right of refusal for players with expired contracts (the original team can keep the player if it matches the offer of another team), and the college draft was amended to allow a player who chooses not to sign with his drafting team the right to be selected by any team in the following year's draft.[44]

The issue of antitrust violations in professional basketball was litigated again in 1995. In *Caldwell v. NBA, Inc.*, Caldwell, a professional basketball player, charged the National Basketball Association with an antitrust violation for failure to play him. He alleged that they failed to play him because of his activities as president of the NBPA. The Court dismissed his case, saying that the Association's activities were exempted from the Sherman Antitrust Act because they fell under the NLRA.[45]

NBA Decertification Defeated. In 1995 several of the NBA's biggest stars, including Michael Jordan and Patrick Ewing, mounted a decertification drive to oust the union. By a vote of 226 to 134, the players voted to keep the union. The owners supported the union and even threatened to end the season if the union was ousted and the new six-year agreement not approved. They feared even higher payrolls without the agreement. Many players, according to Charles Smith of the New York Knicks, did not want to "do what baseball did" and believed that the owners would have followed through with their threat. The dissident players thought that they, as individuals, could negotiate a better deal with owners.[46]

The David Stern Era. In 1984, David Stern became commissioner for the NBA, and a new era in the economics of professional basketball began. Stern inherited a league in which 18 of 23 teams were losing money and arenas were averaging less than 50 percent attendance. Through shrewd marketing techniques Stern increased average attendance by 70 percent in 10 years and negotiated lucrative new television contracts. He also negotiated a new collective bargaining agreement that established a salary cap—the maximum a team could pay its players. The contract also contained a tough antidrug policy.

Stern convinced the NBPA that the salary cap and antidrug policy were good for the game's image and would enable the owners to climb out of debt. The NBA made concessions as well—including sharing 53 percent of the league's revenue with the players. This unique "revenue-sharing" clause began a new concept in sports collective bargaining. It provides that the league distributes certain revenues equally among all teams and it created a fixed pool of revenue for players' salaries. These major changes in the NBA transformed it from a league on the verge of bankruptcy to one of fixed soundness (and the highest players' salaries) in less than 10 years.[47]

The National Hockey League

The National Hockey League (NHL) for many years was the least economically successful of the four major professional sports because it had limited television contracts and small arena seating capacities (average about 15,000) for the 80-game season. Cooperation between the NHL and the National Hockey League Players Association (NHLPA) has historically been good, and thus the difficult task of requiring joint U.S.-Canadian collective bargaining laws for professional hockey has been limited. The NHL drafts new players from amateur hockey leagues in a process similar to the NFL draft, except that the players gain experience in minor leagues instead of college.

Collective bargaining in hockey is unique in that negotiations begin spontaneously as new issues arise, resulting in modifications to long-term agreements. As in other sports, agents negotiate individual contracts with team owners, and salary arbitration is utilized if either side requests it. However, the practice is used far less often than it is in baseball. Contractual grievances also go to arbitration in hockey if unresolved in earlier steps. Hockey players have gained free agency rights, with teams retaining the right of first refusal on those who might leave.[48]

The 1990s have witnessed a substantial rise in the fortunes of professional hockey. Under NHL Commissioner Gary Bettman, the league has enjoyed greater revenues through new television contracts and two new expansion teams—the Mighty Ducks of Anaheim and the Florida Panthers. Bettman has also helped improve the sport's image by reducing violence in the game by negotiating strict penalties for unnecessary violence.[49]

SUMMARY

In 1935, Congress articulated a national labor policy with the passage of the Wagner Act. That act was the culmination of more than 100 years of organized labor's efforts to recognize the employee's right to bargain collectively. During that struggle, the labor movement faced hostile court decisions, economic depressions, and internal power struggles. The disruptive nature of work stoppages caused political leaders to seek a national solution to labor's problems. Under the Wagner Act, employees were free to organize and were given the right to strike, and employers were required to bargain with employee representatives.

The Great Depression and the New Deal set the stage for Congress to pass legislation that not only protected organized labor but promoted its growth. Although the Taft-Hartley Amendments and the Landrum-Griffin Act modified the Wagner Act, its support of collective bargaining was not changed. A summary of the events and legislative actions that have shaped the modern era of the U.S. labor movement is found in Figure 3-10.

Professional sports operate under unique collective bargaining work rules that have led to multimillion dollar individual salaries and the highest paid union workers in the world.

Figure 3-10   Modern Era of Unionization

1947	*Taft-Hartley Amendments.* Amended Wagner Act to equalize the balance between labor and management. Also created the Federal Mediation and Conciliation Service (FMCS) and right-to-work states.
1952	*No-raiding pact.* After 17 years of bitter fighting, new labor chiefs in the AFL and CIO signed a no-raiding pact.
1955	*AFL-CIO merge.* New unity spurred labor hopes for membership gains, which failed to materialize (25 percent of labor force in 1955, 18 percent in 1988).
1959	*Landrum-Griffin Act.* U.S. Senate hearing on labor corruption led Congress to establish stricter controls on union operations.
1962	*Kennedy's Executive Order 10988.* Gave federal employees the right to organize but not to strike.
1974	*Health-care amendments.* Wagner Act was extended to include private, nonprofit hospital employees.
1977	*Foiled Labor Law Reform Bill.* Supported by President Carter and organized labor, a major revision of the NLRA passed the House but failed in the Senate.
1983	*NUMMI.* A General Motors-Toyota joint venture is the first U.S. attempt at team management.
1987	*Longest steel strike in U.S. history.* Ended after six months, signaling the demise of the once-proud industry (over 200,000 jobs lost in 10 years). *Teamsters Union.* Rejoins AFL-CIO after 30 years of separation. Many other unions merge in the 1980s to increase their strength.
1993	*Family and Medical Leave Act of 1993.* Allows job-protected leave for family or health emergencies.
1994–1996	*The Major League Players Association Strike.* Cancels the 1994 World Series and lasts for 235 days.
1996	*Teamwork for Employees and Managers Act.* Vetoed by President Clinton.

CASE STUDY 3-1

EMPLOYER DOMINATION

Facts

The company operates about 700 convenience stores.

A sales assistant at one of the company's stores was murdered while on duty. The murder was widely publicized, and employees complained of inadequate security measures.

As a result of the murder, 15 sales assistants telephoned the union requesting a union organization effort. The union sent representatives to 60 stores in the area where the murder had occurred and left union authorization cards. Two days later the company notified the union that an injunction had been issued during a prior union campaign prohibiting solicitation on company property.

(continued)

The next workday, the company had a meeting with the store managers in the area and talked about the need to improve security. The company officials also discussed the union's organization activities and reminded the managers of the "no solicitation" policy and stated that a union would not necessarily do the employees any good.

Later that week, the company had an unprecedented meeting for all sales assistants. Approximately 200 sales assistants attended and were paid for their time. The company officials told the employees that they did not need a union and that the employees from the union could retrieve their authorization cards. The employees were asked their complaints, and the employees listed the following: getting less than 40 hours work per week; not having breaks; not being paid for overtime work; working alone at night; and poor lighting at the stores.

The next day the company sent a memorandum to all regional personnel directing that sales assistants should work a 40-hour workweek; canopy lights were installed at all the stores; a policy was adopted that no one would be required to work alone at night; and sales assistants began receiving wages for after-hours overtime work. The company posted "no solicitation" signs in all stores and directed that those signs be enforced; if the employees did not enforce the signs, they would lose their jobs.

Later that month the company held further meetings with sales assistants, who again were paid for their time. They were asked to select committee representatives to meet with management to discuss their complaints. Management officials left the room while the employees selected their representatives. The company made a list of the 10 most frequently mentioned items from the employees' recommended subjects for the committee to discuss.

Meanwhile, the union filed a representation petition with the NLRB seeking an election in a unit of all Summit, Ohio, sales assistants. The company president told the managers to tell the sales assistants that if they joined the union, the company would close those stores. The first meeting of the Employee Management Committee was held, and the 10 priority items were listed, granting employees a new vacation policy, improved health-care benefits, sick days, change in holiday hours for pay, recognition of seniority ranks, and improved security systems. Not long after that, the company sent an additional memo around announcing other improvements in life, major medical, and accident insurance plans, in addition to death and family benefits and a revised disciplinary appeal system.

The union charged the company with unfair labor practice for granting benefits to prevent a fair election and for creating an employer-dominated labor union. The company denied that the motivation for the benefits to the employees was to prevent a union; furthermore, the company denied that the employee organization was a "labor organization" under the National Labor Relations Act. But even if it was a labor organization, the company denied that it was a company-dominated organization.

Questions

1. Did the company's actions in forming an Employee Management Committee interfere with the union's organizational efforts? Explain your answer.
2. Should a company be prevented from instituting necessary employee benefits because of union organizing?
3. Explain why the Employee Management Committee could be considered a "company union."

Adapted from *The Lawson Company*, 118 LRRM 2505 (1985).

UNION DISCIPLINE

Facts

Local 100 of the CL & G Union represented employees at the Kaiser Cement Corporation. The CL & G merged with the International Brotherhood of Boilermakers, and the Local became Local D-100 of the Boilermakers. The local president both before and after the merger and three other union members had not favored the merger. They were also angered by how the Boilermakers had treated some long-term local union representatives. The four union members began actively opposing the Boilermakers. They met with management and proposed that 37 or 38 jobs covered by the contract be changed to nonunion positions; they began the process for a decertification election; and they presented management's proposals on eliminating union positions to the employees.

A union member filed charges against the four with the Boilermakers and the union found them guilty. The discipline imposed was to suspend them from holding any local union office; bar them from holding office in the future; and prohibit them from attending union meetings, except when a vote on a contract was to be held. The four informed the union that since they had been "suspended" from the union they would no longer pay union dues.

The union warned them that if they failed to pay union dues the union would ask the employer to discharge them. Under the collective bargaining agreement, a "union security" clause required employees to be members of the union in order to stay employed. However, under the NLRA, paying dues directly related to the collective bargaining activity is the only obligation a union can impose on the workers subject to such a union security clause.

The four disciplined union members filed a grievance charging that the union had violated the Labor Management Relations Act (LMRA). The LMRA gave employees the right not to be discriminated against if they choose *not* to engage in union activities. Both the discipline and the threat of being discharged amounted to discrimination, they contended.

The union's position was that their discipline was an internal union matter protected under the Labor-Management Reporting and Disclosure Act of 1959 and that the LMRA allows for union security clauses in collective bargaining agreements so long as the employee is required to pay only those union dues that actually reflect the collective bargaining service provided by the union.

Questions

1. As the judge in this case, would you agree with the four disciplined union members or with the union? Why?
2. The efforts of the four union members to either switch union positions to nonunion positions or vote the new union out were not supported by the employees. Do you think the union should have ignored the four rather than disciplining them?
3. Do you think it is right for a union and an employer to agree in a collective bargaining agreement that all of the workers subject to the collective bargaining agreement have to join the union in order to keep their jobs?

Adapted from *Boilermakers*, 144 LRRM 1121 (1993).

KEY TERMS AND CONCEPTS	business agent Civil Service Reform Act of 1978 Clayton Act company unions Cordwainers conspiracy cases	craft union Executive Order (E.O.) 10988 E.O. 11491 federation of unions industrial union

intermediate organizational units
labor injunctions
Labor-Management Reporting and Disclosure Act of 1959 (Landrum-Griffin Act)
local union
master agreement
National Labor Relations Act (Wagner Act)

national (or international) union
National War Labor Board
Norris–La Guardia Act
reserve clause
steward
Taft-Hartley Amendments

REVIEW QUESTIONS

1. Describe the federal and court actions against union workers in the 1800s.
2. Did the Great Depression have any impact on the U.S. labor movement? If so, what?
3. Why did the Wagner Act have a major impact on employees' rights?
4. What is generally included in the "duty to bargain in good faith" as imposed by the National Labor Relations Act (Wagner Act)?
5. What is the general role of the NLRB? How and when was the NLRB created?
6. What circumstances prompted Congress to pass the Taft-Hartley Amendents? The Landrum-Griffin Act? What are the key provisions of these acts?
7. How are craft and industrial unions different in their origins and basic concepts?
8. What are the basic objectives of each of the levels of unions, and how do they work together?
9. Why do many people believe that unions must be democratic?
10. Describe the parties and their interests in a major sports collective bargaining situation.

TAKE IT TO THE NET

We invite you to visit the Carrell/Heavrin page on the Prentice Hall Web site at:

http://www.prenhall.com/carrellr

for this chapter's World Wide Web exercise.

Sources of Labor Relations Information   **EXERCISE 3-1**

Purpose:
For the student to gain practice in the library research of labor relations topics.
Task:
Choose a labor relations topic of interest to you (or you may be assigned one by your instructor) from the list on the following page. After choosing a topic, complete the following steps:

1. Find at least six recent references (or more, depending on your instructor's wishes) that pertain to your topic. Do not use a reference (e.g., *Monthly Labor Review*) more than once.
2. For each reference, indicate the title of the book, journal, and so on; the title of the journal article (if applicable); the author's name; the publisher and the publication date. In addition, indicate how you located each reference (e.g., *Business Periodicals Index*).
3. Write a one-paragraph abstract for each source. (If your source is a book, review at least one important chapter and write the abstract for that chapter.)

Topics

- AFL-CIO
- Benefit "givebacks"
- Cost-of-living adjustments
- Craft unions/industrial unions
- Drug testing
- Duty of fair representation
- Employee assistance programs (EAPs)
- Greyhound strike
- Grievance arbitration
- Health-care cost containment
- Just cause
- Mediation
- NLRB certification/decertification elections
- Outsourcing
- Professional Air Traffic Controllers Organization (PATCO) strike
- "Payback" agreements
- Pay for time not worked
- Plant closing
- Profit-sharing plans
- Public sector unions
- Recent strikes
- Right-to-know laws
- Right-to-work states
- Seniority systems
- Sick leave provisions
- Subcontracting
- Successorship
- Termination at will
- Trends in union membership
- Two-tier wage contracts

| EXERCISE 3-2 | Baseball Umpires Strike, 1996 |

Purpose:
For students to gain an appreciation of the dynamics of a work stoppage through role playing.

Task:

The instructor will assign to five people the roles of (1) Roberto Alomar of the Baltimore Orioles; (2) Baseball Commissioner Bud Selig; (3) Umpires Union President Richie Phillips; (4) American League President Gene Budig; and (5) Baltimore Oriole CEO Peter Angelos. Each student should then study the following fact situation and assume the identity of his or her assigned role. In a round-table discussion format the instructor will ask each student to respond to the three questions at the end.

Facts:

On September 30, 1996, the Major League Baseball Umpires unanimously voted to begin an unprecedented strike the next day—the first day of the playoffs. The strike vote was a response to the decision by American League President Gene Budig. The disputed decision was to allow Baltimore Oriole second baseman Roberto Alomar to play in postseason games. Alomar had been given a five-game suspension by Budig only days earlier for intentionally spitting in the face of umpire John Hirschbeck, who had ejected him from the game for arguing a called third strike. Alomar later apologized to Hirschbeck publicly and donated $50,000 to a medical charity. Alomar served two days of the suspension but then appealed the decision, and Budig allowed the final three days of the suspension to be the first three days of the 1997 season.

The strike called by the umpires union was a historical first and came at a critical moment in major league baseball. The previous two seasons had been marred by a players' union strike that canceled the 1994 World Series. After the players' strike, attendance at ball parks and the ratings of televised games dropped significantly. But as the season ended in 1996, fan interest was beginning to rebound as several favorite big-city teams made it to the playoffs, including the Yankees, Dodgers, Indians, Padres, Cardinals, Braves, Rangers, and Orioles. Then the Alomar incident and umpires' decision to strike suddenly cast a dark, strike-related cloud over baseball. It was a very difficult decision for the umpires, who had much to lose in terms of fan support and postseason earnings. But union President Richie Phillips provided the basis for the strike decision: "Deferring the imposition of a penalty until next season is an unmistakable signal that the American League is willing to tolerate this type of behavior from its players."

American League President Budig responded to the umpires' decision to strike by noting that the umpires' contract contained a "no strike" clause that prohibited them from a work stoppage. The umpires' contract also provided a grievance mechanism to resolve disputes. Thus the umpires were contractually obligated to work during the playoffs.

Questions

1. Did the umpires act reasonably in calling a strike over the Alomar incident?
2. How should American League President Budig and Baseball Commissioner Bud Selig have responded to the union's announced strike?
3. What could the Baltimore Orioles organization have done to avert the strike?

Source: Hal Bodley, "Umps: Alomar Plays, We Sit," *USA Today*, October 1, 1996, p. C1.

CHAPTER 4

Establishing a
Bargaining Unit

In a 1982 contract vote, one Ford Motor Company employee
wore his opinion of the agreement on his back.

AFL-CIO: Signs of Revival through Organizing Campaigns

The labor movement under new AFL-CIO President John Sweeney may be turning a corner in its membership loss with a new emphasis on winning organizing campaigns that add bargaining units and employees. In a major shift in strategy under Sweeney, the organizing campaigns have largely focused on low-paid employees such as poultry workers, janitors, food service workers, and public employees. For the first time since the 1930s the AFL-CIO and national and local unions are pouring resources into organizing new workers. Historically, low-wage workers are hard to organize, but union leaders have seen the middle-class decline in numbers and a new "class struggle" rise because the number of low-paid employees is increasing.

Among lower-paid workers, a growing number are willing to challenge their bosses by organizing because other low-paid jobs are readily available. "We have a massive opportunity for organizing," claimed Wade Rathke, a union organizer for the Service Employees International Union.

The AFL-CIO under its new president, Sweeney, is spending up to $60 million per year, or one-third of its annual budget on new organizing efforts. In the 1970s and 1980s under presidents George Meany and Lane Kirkland the AFL-CIO spent almost nothing on organizing and instead focused on politics and foreign affairs—while membership constantly declined.

The new 1990s effort has been likened to the one in the 1930s, when millions of unorganized industrial workers were ignored by the craft unions and were all but written off during the Great Depression. Under John L. Lewis and the CIO, however, they rose up and organized virtually every major manufacturing industry in the United States. Low-wage service workers just might be the 1990s equivalent of the industrial workers of the 1930s, according to Robert Ziegler, a labor historian.

Adapted from Pascal Zachary, "Signs of Revival: Some Unions Step Up Organizing Campaigns and Get New Members," *Wall Street Journal*, September 1, 1995, p. A1.

The collective bargaining process is at the heart of the employer-employee relationship. That process, however, is not a simple one. The 1935 National Labor Relations Act as subsequently amended defines the process and limits the parties to it.[1] A group of employees cannot simply present their requests to the employer. Procedures must be followed to determine if those particular employees are protected by the act. A union purporting to represent the employees must prove that it does indeed represent them. And any particular group of employees who feel that they have the same interests and desires and therefore should negotiate together may not satisfy the requirements of the act as an "appropriate" unit of employees for collective bargaining purposes. This chapter explores the particulars of the act to learn when and how it can be used to determine parties subject to its provisions.

THE NATIONAL LABOR RELATIONS BOARD (NLRB)

The stated purpose of the National Labor Relations Act was to minimize industrial strife interfering with the normal flow of commerce. Using the authority of the Commerce Clause of the U.S. Constitution, Congress legislated a federally protected interest in the internal operations of certain industries.[2] That interest was in setting the legal process by which labor and management would bargain.

The act created a five-member National Labor Relations Board (NLRB) to administer its provisions. These board members are appointed for five-year terms by the president of the United States, with the advice and consent of the Senate. The members' authority under the act enables them, through a wide range of remedies, to effectuate the purposes of the act and "to protect the rights of the public in connection with labor disputes affecting commerce."[3]

Four basic principles of the act guide the NLRB's administration:

1. Encouragement of labor organizations and collective bargaining
2. Recognition of majority representation
3. Establishment of a prompt administrative machinery for enforcement instead of criminal sanctions
4. Imposition of sanctions or punishments even if other sanctions or punishments are found in other jurisdictions[4]

Jurisdiction of the National Labor Relations Board

Congress established certain jurisdictional tests to satisfy expected practical and legal criticisms of the act. The NLRB has jurisdiction over persons when there is a labor dispute affecting commerce or when there is a controversy involving an employer, employee, or a labor organization. This jurisdiction has been found broad enough to include all representation and unfair labor practice proceedings. The tests must be met before the board is empowered to act.

Persons. The definition of a *person* under the National Labor Relations Act is all-inclusive and involves "one or more individuals, labor organizations, partnerships, associations, corporations, legal representatives, trustees, trustees in bankruptcy, or receivers."[5]

Because the definition is so broad, few problems arise with finding a person in most disputes. However, entities otherwise exempt from the act because they are not considered as "employers" (namely, political subdivisions and railroads) have been able to invoke protections of the act against union-sponsored activities.[6]

Labor Dispute.   A labor dispute must exist for the board to exercise jurisdiction. The act defines *labor dispute* as "any controversy concerning terms, tenure, or conditions of employment."[7] Labor disputes have been held to include employee-concerted activities such as strikes, walkouts, and picketing; unfair labor practices such as employers' refusal to bargain; and interference in employee rights. The term has also been interpreted to include investigation of the health and safety facilities of a work environment.

Included in the definition are controversies "concerning the association or representation of persons in negotiating, fixing, maintaining, changing, or seeking to arrange terms or conditions of employment."[8] These controversies are usually addressed by the NLRB in its representation cases.

Affecting Commerce.   A broad definition of *commerce* under the statute gives the board authority in all but purely local disputes.[9] The board has jurisdiction if the labor dispute directly affects commerce. In addition, if the employer's operation affects commerce, any labor dispute involving that employer falls within the board's jurisdiction. The NLRB, using this authority, has taken jurisdiction over a manufacturer whose goods were to be transported interstate even though the manufacturer was not engaged in out-of-state commerce.

To judge the substance of a dispute, the board has established jurisdictional standards using annual specific dollar amounts for different types of businesses. For example, for nonretail enterprises, a gross outflow or inflow of at least $50,000 in revenue is required for the NLRB to take jurisdiction, while retail establishments need gross business volumes of at least $500,000 per year and substantial interstate purchases or sales. This limitation is not absolute, however, and the board may enter cases of significant impact regardless of the dollar volume involved. An example is the NLRB's decision to examine handicapped workshop operations on a case-by-case basis. If the NLRB determines the operation is essentially rehabilitative, it will not take jurisdiction, but it will if the workshop is primarily industrial with an economic purpose.[10]

The board has also judged the substance of a case and has removed itself from some controversies because of the type of employer involved, for example, employers whose employees are subject to laws of a foreign country.[11] The board at one time removed itself in a case in which a company did not have sufficient control over employment conditions because of its contractual arrangement with the U.S. Department of Labor.[12] However, recent board decisions reversed that trend, and the board has determined that even in circumstances in which some of the conditions cannot be negotiated, other areas can be.[13]

Employees.   Employees, as included in the statutory definition, are entitled to the rights guaranteed by the act. Those include the right to self-organization; to form labor organizations; to bargain collectively; to engage in concerted activities for purposes of collective bargaining; and to refrain from such activities, unless there is a contract requirement to pay labor organization dues as a condition of employment.

The definition of *employee* is liberally construed, so stated exclusions in the definition become important in determining who is *not* an employee. The types of workers not covered are agricultural workers; domestic servants; persons employed by a spouse or a parent; independent contractors; supervisors;

individuals who work for employers subject to the Railway Labor Act; and employees of the U.S. government, the Federal Reserve Bank, the states or their political subdivisions.

Employers.   Employers under the act are subject to the unfair labor practices section, which emphasizes the duty to bargain collectively with employee representatives. The definition of *employer* also takes on broad connotations by listing those persons who are *not* employers: the U.S. government or a wholly owned government corporation (with the exception of the U.S. Postal Service by virtue of another federal law), the Federal Reserve Bank, a state or political subdivision, anyone subject to the Railway Labor Act, or any labor organization.[14]

Labor Organizations.   *Labor organizations* are most commonly labor unions, but the NLRB recognizes other kinds of employee committees that represent their employees to employers.[15] Labor organizations are also subject under the act to the unfair labor practices section that places some limitations on strikes supported by the organization.

Preemption

A question of preemption arises when a field of activity, such as collective bargaining or labor relations, is subject to regulation by both the federal and state governments, and a decision must be made as to whether concurrent jurisdiction exists or if the federal government enjoys exclusive jurisdiction. The Constitution is clear that federal law is the supreme law of the land, so a factual determination must be made as to whether Congress has entered and completely covered a field or activity.

If Congress has entered and completely covered the field, then an individual who wants to bring a lawsuit concerning that issue *must* bring it in the federal court rather the state court. Or, even if the individual is allowed to litigate in state court, the law applied will be the federal law. In many instances, an individual might consider the state court procedure more "user-friendly" than that of the federal court, or the remedies provided under a state law more generous than the federal law. Preemption, however, is a legal determination that *only* the federal law applies and an individual is not allowed to make that determination—the court makes it.

The U.S. Supreme Court decided the preemption issue as it relates to the labor-management relationship in a series of cases.[16] If an activity is the subject of state action and is clearly protected under Section 7 of the National Labor Relations Act, the state is totally preempted from the field and federal law controls. Section 7 provides employees the rights to self-organization; to form, join, or assist labor organizations; to bargain collectively; to engage in other concerted activities; or to refrain from doing all of these. If the activity sought to be regulated by the state clearly is prohibited by Section 8, the unfair labor practices section, the state is also totally preempted from the field. The Court went even further when it decided that the state would be preempted if the activity was arguably protected or prohibited by the act. However, the arguably protected or prohibited test was not to be applied in what the Court described as a rigid manner.[17]

This area has recently led the Supreme Court to weaken the preemption issue in some employer-employee disputes. One major advantage for an employee covered by a collective bargaining contract is the job protection it offers. Most, if not all, contracts prohibit discharge of an employee except for just cause. Just cause is discussed in detail in later chapters. For purposes of the preemption issue, one can assume that *just cause* means for a good, job-related reason.

Traditionally, employees *not* covered by a union contract could be fired for *any* reason. Since the advent of federal and state discrimination laws, however, union and nonunion employees have been protected from being fired for discriminatory reasons, such as race, gender, handicap, or age. A union employee fired from a job for a prohibited discriminatory reason prior to 1988 was bound by the union contract provision and Section 301 of the Taft-Hartley Amendments to seek *only* redress under the federal labor laws. However, the Supreme Court in *Lingle v. Norge Division of Magic Chef, Inc.*[18] changed that policy. In this case a union employee was fired, she alleged, for making a workers' compensation claim. A state law protected employees from retaliation by an employer for making a workers' compensation claim and allowed an injured party to seek money damages. The remedy for the employee under the union contract and federal labor law was limited to reinstatement to the job lost and back pay. Reversing previous holdings, the Supreme Court allowed the worker to bypass the contractual remedies and the application of federal law for the remedies sought under the state law.

The Supreme Court's reasoning was that the state court cause of action, retaliatory discharge under a specific state law, could be adjudicated without *any* examination, interpretation, or discussion of the labor contract or established labor-management relations law. Therefore, allowing the employee a choice in forums did not undermine the public policy issues supporting the preemption doctrine.[19]

NLRB AUTHORITY IN REPRESENTATION CASES

The National Labor Relations Board (NLRB), in carrying out its lawful responsibilities, decides representation cases. Section 9(b) of the Labor-Management Relations Act authorizes the board to decide on a case-by-case basis the appropriate unit of employees for collective bargaining. The board exercises this power to guarantee employees the fullest freedom under the act—mainly, the right of self-organization.

The NLRB does not have rigid or constrictive regulations for dealing with recognition cases. It has wide discretion in its decisions, which courts will uphold absent a finding that the board acted arbitrarily.[20] Both the board and the courts recognize that more than one unit sometimes may be appropriate for collective bargaining. The board is not required to choose *the* most appropriate unit, only *an* appropriate unit.

Under Section 3(b) of the Labor-Management Relations Act, the board may delegate its authority to determine an appropriate unit to its regional directors, allowing itself discretionary review of such decisions. The board will review a decision if a substantial law or policy is raised because of the absence of, or departure from, an officially reported board precedent; a regional director's decision on a substantial factual issue is clearly erroneous on the record, and it affects the party's rights; the conduct of the hearing resulted in a legally prejudicial error; or there are compelling reasons for the board to reconsider a previously stated rule or policy.[21]

Although there are no hard and fast rules in the act to determine appropriateness, there are certain limitations on the types of units and on workers to be included and excluded from units. Certain fundamental and logical policies should be followed in determining a unit.

Bargaining Unit

The **bargaining unit** is defined as "that group of employees that is represented by the union in collective bargaining. The union has exclusive bargaining rights for all employees within the unit, and it has no rights for those employees outside, including managerial and nonmanagerial." The determination of exactly which employees are within the bargaining unit may have a great effect on the outcome of the organizing campaign. The union seeks a unit in which it feels it can win a majority of the vote in a representation election.[22]

When the employer and union cannot agree on the unit, the NLRB, under Section 9 of the NLRA decides on "the unit appropriate for the purposes of collective bargaining."[23]

Appropriate Unit

The basic underlying principle for the NLRB's determination of an appropriate unit is that only employees having a substantial mutuality of interest in wages, hours, and working conditions can be appropriately grouped in that unit. The logic is that the greater the similarity of working conditions, the greater the likelihood the unit's members can agree on priorities and thus make the collective bargaining process successful.[24]

The following criteria are most often used in deciding what constitutes a rational unit:

1. Community of interest
2. History of bargaining
3. Desire of employees
4. Prior union organization
5. Relationship of the unit to the organizational structure of the company
6. Public interest
7. Accretion
8. Stipulated units
9. Statutory considerations

Community of Interest.   The **community of interest doctrine** attempts to quantify, by means of descriptive criteria, when workers should feel that their individual interests are so similar that collective bargaining will be fruitful. The board has at various times enumerated these criteria: similarity of job functions and earnings, in benefits received or hours worked, and/or in job training or skills required; a high degree of contact and interchange among the employees; and/or geographic proximity and common supervision.[25] All of these can indicate a common interest or interests that, coupled with the other listed criteria, establish an appropriate unit.

History of Bargaining.   If a bargaining unit and a particular employer have a history of bargaining, the board will recognize the appropriateness of the unit, in the absence of compelling reasons to the contrary, to ensure the employees' right of self-organization and to provide the stable labor relations sought by the board.

History of bargaining usually becomes a question when the board receives a request for decertification to allow for smaller or different bargaining units or when a new class of employer has come under the board's jurisdiction, such as when the National Labor Relations Act was extended to the health-care industry in 1974.

Although prior bargaining relationships are favorably considered by the board, such histories are not absolute. The board has disregarded history of bargaining in several cases when that history contravened the board's policy of mixing clerical and production and maintenance personnel; when it was based on oral contracts; and when it reflected racial or sexual discrimination.[26]

Employee Wishes. The **Globe doctrine** established the National Labor Relations Board policy to give weight to employee wishes when determining an appropriate bargaining unit.[27] Although the board cannot delegate the selection of a bargaining unit to employees, it may use the election process as a way to consult employees. In one such case,

> the Board provided for special balloting to determine the representation wishes of the employees. The situation involved a bargaining unit determination by the Board where a smaller craft unit and a larger industry unit were equally plausible. By permitting the employees in the smaller unit to indicate their preference, the Board was able to decide whether to leave the craft group in the smaller bargaining unit or to combine it with the larger group.[28]

Such consultation is especially helpful if two or more bargaining units are considered appropriate by the board's otherwise objective standards.

Employee Unionization. The NLRB will consider the extent of unionization by a bargaining unit as one factor in unit determination but not as a controlling factor. The question is still one of appropriateness and not of whether the wishes of a union can be honored. If the bargaining unit is otherwise appropriate, prior unionization can again indicate employee wishes. There is no prohibition to recognition as long as the unit is not otherwise prohibited.

The Unit and Company Organizational Structure. As discussed earlier, the considerations used to determine appropriateness are not legally binding formulas but an exercise in rational examination of the facts of an individual case. The NLRB recognized this distinction from its earliest decision. In *Bendix Products Corporation*, the board stated, "The designation of a unit appropriate for the purposes of collective bargaining must be confined to evidence and circumstances peculiar to the individual case."[29] Under such a philosophy, a particular company may, because of its relationship to branch offices or its particular reporting policies, make an otherwise inappropriate unit appropriate for its employees.

The board must examine, in some cases, the internal operations of a company to ascertain those peculiarities. However, the board's decision may not be final, as can be seen in Case 4-1.

Public Interest. One consideration added by the courts for review by the board is the public interest. Without much guidance provided by the courts, the board is to ascertain when its decision will serve the public interest. In making this determination, the NLRB must not be affected by the desires of the parties involved.[30]

APPROPRIATE UNIT

Employer is an industrial food service contractor supplying food service to 19 cafeterias at 10 United Aircraft Corporation locations. The employer considers these 19 cafeterias to be a single operating unit. The unit has a district headquarters where its administration is centralized. All facets of the food service to these 19 cafeterias are identical.

The union sought to organize a collective bargaining unit composed of three of these 19 cafeterias. These three cafeterias are located five miles apart, have a combined workforce of about 50 employees, and share a manager. The National Labor Relations Board found the unit appropriate on the following basis:

1. The employees were under the common immediate supervision of a single manager.
2. The three cafeterias were grouped together as a cost center for accountability.
3. The unit manager retained control over day-to-day operations, especially in matters of hiring and firing.
4. The cafeterias were five miles apart, while the other 16 cafeterias were 14 miles away.
5. There was little employee interchange.

6. There was no bargain history and no union seeking recognition for all 19 cafeterias.

The employer appealed the board's ruling.

Decision

The court recognized that the National Labor Relations Board has primary responsibility in determining a unit appropriate and such determination should be overturned only if arbitrary, unreasonable, or not supported by substantial evidence. It reviewed the board's reasons for determining the unit appropriate and found that the board relied too heavily on the geographic proximity and the extent of union organization over the complete integration of the employer's managerial structure and labor relations policy. The cost center referred to by the board was merely an informational subdivision not indicative of financial independence; the responsibilities attributed to the local manager were overrated. In fact, the labor relations policy for all the cafeterias emanated from the district office. On the basis of these considerations, the court overruled the board's decision.

Adapted from *Szabo Food Services, Inc. v. National Labor Relations Board*, 550 F.2d 705 (1976).

Accretion. The **doctrine of accretion** allows the NLRB to add new groups of employees to existing units if their work satisfies the same criteria as the original unit; that is, community of interests, bargaining history, interchange of employees, geographic proximity, common supervision, and union wishes. However, such a determination is not automatic. If the new class of employees retains a separate identity, perhaps by virtue of its newness, it can be determined an appropriate unit.

Accretion usually occurs when an employer expands operations, builds a new facility, or merges with another employer. It is often to the advantage of the union to have an accretion.[31]

Accretion offers the board a conflicting choice. Adding new employees to an established union preserves the stability so important under the act, but squeezing in new employees, under perhaps narrow similarities, constricts the employees' freedom of choice.

Stipulated Units. The board's authority to determine an appropriate unit is not without limitations. A company and a union may stipulate to the board what they consider an appropriate unit. The courts have said that the board may not alter the unit in such cases. However, a **stipulated unit** may not violate principles in the National Labor Relations Act or established board policy, for example, by including supervisors.[32]

Statutory Considerations. The NLRB is limited by specific sections of the act in determining appropriate bargaining units. Workers not included under the act's definition of employee may not be included in a unit. Moreover, the board may not determine a unit appropriate with both professional and nonprofessional personnel unless a majority of the professional employees has approved such a designation. A craft unit can seek recognition even if it previously had been part of a larger unit unless a majority of the employees in the craft votes against separate representation. Finally, guards cannot be included in a unit with any other employees.[33]

Other types of workers are excluded from appropriate units because of various board and court interpretations. Excluded are managerial employees, defined in board rulings as "those who formulate and effectuate management policies by expressing and making operative the decisions of their employer."[34] Confidential employees are excluded if the nature of their work has a labor nexus; that is, if it involves the formation, determination, or execution of labor relations management policies and if it involves access to confidential information concerning anticipated changes resulting from collective bargaining.[35] Temporary employees and, in some instances, part-time employees may also be excluded from appropriate units.

The lines drawn by court rulings and board interpretations are never totally clear. In *National Labor Relations Board v. Yeshiva University*, it was determined that the faculty members were managerial employees because of their input into the academic product of the university.[36] As managerial instead of professional employees, they did not come under the protection of the National Labor Relations Act and could therefore not be recognized. Such a determination has a negative effect on unionization in the academic sector.[37]

Two recent Supreme Court decisions, however, expanded the definition of employees. In *Holly Farms Corp. et al. v. NLRB*,[38] the Court upheld a board decision that the employees of "live-haul crews" (chicken catchers, forklift operators, and truck drivers) employed by a vertically integrated poultry producer are covered by the NLRA. The Court found that the workers who collected and transported the chickens were part of the company's processing operations not engaged in agriculture.

In *NLRB v. Town and Country Electric*,[39] the Supreme Court rejected an employer's contention that union-paid organizers who applied for nonunion positions with the employer's electrical company were not employees under the NLRA. The employer argued that these union members could not serve two masters and that the union would direct the employees' work. The Supreme Court ruled that union employment did not inherently create a conflict. If the employee failed to do the job as directed by the employer, then the employee could be dismissed.

Types of Units

Certain types of units have evolved within the established principles of appropriateness. The act itself lists employer units, craft units, plant units, or their subdivisions.

Craft Units. A **craft unit** is composed exclusively of workers having a recognized skill, such as electricians, machinists, and plumbers. Recognition questions for craft units usually come before the board when a group of craft employees wants to break away from an existing industrial union, an action called craft severance. Congress has established the policy that the board cannot determine a craft unit inappropriate on the grounds that a different unit has been established by prior board determination, unless the majority of the employees in the craft unit vote against separate representation.

Despite this legislative policy, the NLRB has severely limited craft severance elections through a number of decisions. Under the *National Tube* doctrine,[40] the board identified certain industries whose operations were so integrated that craft workers could not be taken from the unit without affecting the stability of labor relations. And in the *Mallinckrodt Chemical Works*[41] decision, the board outlined the criteria it would use to allow craft severance; the application of these standards has greatly reduced incidents of craft severance.

The NLRB requires that the craft group be distinct from others in the unit by virtue of the skilled, nonrepetitive nature of its work. The board will examine the extent to which the group has retained its identity or, as the alternative, actually participated in the affairs of the larger unit. The impact of separating the craft unit from the whole is also a factor in the board's determination. Consideration of the particular bargaining history of the larger unit, as well as the history of collective bargaining in the industry as a whole, must be part of the board's deliberations. In some instances, the NLRB decision will be influenced by the degree to which the craft work is integrated with the unskilled work and is therefore essential to the production process. Finally, the board may examine the qualifications of the union seeking to represent the craft union for its experience as an agent for similar groups.[42]

Departmental Units. Similar to a craft unit, a departmental unit is composed of all the members of one department in a larger organization. The board uses standards similar to those used for craft severance in determining one department an appropriate unit separate from the entire plant or company. An examination of the difference in skills and in training, the degree of common supervision, the degree of interchange with employees outside the department, and different job performance ratings have been used to allow a departmental unit to exist.[43]

One Employer, Multiple Locations. Many employers have plants, facilities, or stores at more than one location. In determining if a single location can be an appropriate unit or whether all locations should constitute a single unit, the NLRB considers the prior bargaining history (once a unit has been recognized it is not easily changed), the physical proximity of facilities (less distance allows for coordinated bargaining efforts), and labor policy (a centralized administration of personnel is more likely than a decentralized adminstration to be a multilocation unit).[44]

In 1995 the NLRB proposed a new set of rules for determining if two or more locations of one employer should be a single bargaining unit or multiple units. Under the rules, a single site unit is appropriate if:[45]

- The group was previously unrepresented by a union
- 15 or more employees are employed in the requested unit
- No other worksite is within one mile of the requested unit
- The employer has a supervisor, as defined by the NLRA, at the location

Thus, for example, it would be possible for two fast-food locations of the same chain to be separate units if they were more than one mile apart even if they were managed and operated jointly.

Multiemployer Units. Although the Wagner Act favors localizing a unit within one employer, collective bargaining can be conducted between a group of related employers and representatives of their employees.[46] Factors to be considered in such a designation are whether there is an express or implied approval of all parties to enter into such bargaining relationship, or if the history of the bargaining in the industry implies an intent to consent to multiemployer units. The employer can withdraw from a multiemployer collective bargaining relationship before the date for modification or negotiation of a new contract. After bargaining has begun, an employer may withdraw only with the union's consent or upon showing unusual circumstances. The union consent ensures the stability necessary under the National Labor Relations Act, and unusual circumstances have been found by the board when there is a genuine bargaining impasse.[47]

Residual Units. Workers do not always fit into neat packages, and the board has sometimes given recognition to odd collections of employees because of their common working situations or the proximity of their working sites. The NLRB policy is that employees are entitled to separate representation if they are left unrepresented after the bulk of employees are organized. Employees who do not fit anywhere else—such as sales and service personnel, porters, janitors, and maids—are **residual units**.

Remaining Units. Employee groups that are separate from primary production and maintenance units can be classified as **remaining units**. Because of exclusions contained in the act itself, professional employees and guards often have professional and guard units. Technical units contain employees with a high degree of skill and training who exercise independent judgment but fall short of professional status. The factors to be considered in determining a technical unit are the desires of the party, the bargaining history, the existence of a unit seeking self-representation, the separate supervision of the technical employees, the location of the workplace, similarity of work hours, and employee benefit packages. It often becomes a question of who should be included on the basis of the level of skill and training, employee contact and interchange, and similarity of working conditions. Departmental units are treated the same as craft units in severance cases. Office clerical units are commonly separated from production and maintenance units in a large plant because the board recognizes the common interest of office clerical employees regardless of previous bargaining history.

Health-Care Institutions Units. The 1974 Health-Care Amendments extended coverage of the act to employees of nonprofit hospitals. In hearings concerning the amendments, Congress directed the NLRB to give "due consideration . . . to preventing proliferation of bargaining units in the health-care industry."[48] However, this direction was not specified in the language of the act itself.

Since 1974, the board has applied the usual standards for unit determination and approved eight basic units for the health-care industry:

1. Physicians
2. Registered nurses (RNs)
3. All other professional employees, including licensed practical nurses
4. Technical employees
5. Business office clerical employees
6. Skilled maintenance employees
7. Guards
8. All other nonprofessional employees

Exclusive physician units were accepted by health employers, but RN bargaining units separate from other professional employees were not. The per se acceptance of an exclusive RN unit by the board came under considerable court attack.[49] Unions attacked this attitude and blamed it for stymieing union organizing efforts. In April 1989, the NLRB confirmed its regulations involving the eight **health-care units** and opened the door to organizing the health-care industry.[50]

In *American Hospital Association v. NLRB*,[51] a health-care employer challenged the ruling of the NLRB that established the eight bargaining units on three grounds. First, the employer charged that predetermining the appropriateness of bargaining units was a violation of the NLRA's language that gave the board the duty to decide "appropriateness" on a case-by-case basis. Second, finding eight units acceptable violated the objective of Congress of limiting the proliferation of bargaining units in the health-care industry. Third, the NLRB's decision that eight units for bargaining was appropriate was arbitrary and not based on sound reasoning.

In deciding the case in favor of the NLRB, the U.S. Supreme Court responded to the three points as follows. First, the Court upheld the NLRB's authority to decide "appropriateness" by a general *rule*, pointing out that even its examination of individual cases for the "appropriateness" of a bargaining unit is based on its established *standards*. Second, the Court pointed out that the direction Congress gave the NLRB *not to allow* proliferation of bargaining units was *not* in the law. It reasoned that Congress intended the direction as a warning, and that *if* proliferation occurred, the act could be amended. Third, although the Supreme Court would not go so far as to agree with the wisdom of the board's determination that eight bargaining units are appropriate in the health-care industry, it did say the decision was based on sufficient evidence.[52]

In a 1994 decision, however, the Supreme Court reversed an NLRB holding regarding nurses' units and severely reduced opportunities for growth of unions in the health-care industry. In *NLRB v. Health Care & Retirement Corporation*,[53] the corporation had challenged the certification of a nurses' unit on the grounds that the nurses acted as "supervisors" and were, therefore, exempt from the act. The NLRB disagreed and said that in the case of nurses the assignment and direction of other employees by itself does not make the nurse a supervisor if the activity is to ensure high quality and efficient service. The Supreme Court, however, reversed, saying that the NLRA defines a supervisor as someone using independent judgment to assign and direct the work of other employees in the interest of the employer, which a nurse would do. Most nurses were, therefore, supervisors and exempt from the NLRA.

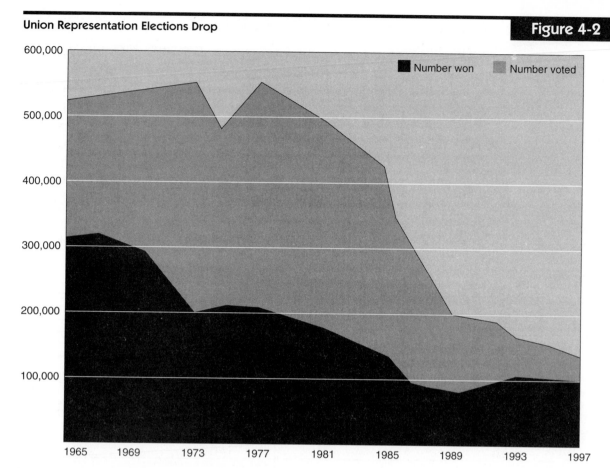

Union Representation Elections Drop

Source: Organizing for Change, Challenging to Organize. A report from the AFL-CIO Leadership Task Force on Organizing (Washington, DC, 1996), p. 5.

Management's goal is simply to keep the union out of the workplace. Its strategy is to convince the workers that unionization will do them more harm than good. Management may attempt to assure workers that their present pay and benefits are competitive and may show data to prove it. Emphasizing a philosophy of fair dealings with all employees, management may discuss the union's involvement in violent or corrupt activities if such has been the case. Management will also enumerate the costs of union membership, which include initiation fees, dues, and other assessments. The workers will be reminded that wages will be lost should a strike occur.

Election Procedures

The steps in a representation election are described in the following paragraphs.

Step 1: Representation Petition. The first step in the election process is to file a representation petition at the office of the appropriate regional director (see Figure 4-3). A union must present evidence of employee support before a

FORM EXEMPT UNDER 44 U S C 3512

FORM NLRB-502
(5-85)

DO NOT WRITE IN THIS SPACE	
Case No.	Date Filed

INSTRUCTIONS: Submit an original and 4 copies of this Petition to the NLRB Regional Office in the Region in which the employer concerned is located. If more space is required for any one item, attach additional sheets, numbering item accordingly.

The Petitioner alleges that the following circumstances exist and requests that the National Labor Relations Board proceed under its proper authority pursuant to Section 9 of the National Labor Relations Act.

1. PURPOSE OF THIS PETITION (*If box RC, RM, or RD is checked and a charge under Section 8(b)(7) of the Act has been filed involving the Employer named herein, the statement following the description of the type of petition shall not be deemed made.*) **(Check One)**

☐ **RC-CERTIFICATION OF REPRESENTATIVE** - A substantial number of employees wish to be represented for purposes of collective bargaining by Petitioner and Petitioner desires to be certified as representative of the employees.

☐ **RM-REPRESENTATION (EMPLOYER PETITION)** - One or more individuals or labor organizations have presented a claim to Petitioner to be recognized as the representative of employees of Petitioner.

☐ **RD-DECERTIFICATION** - A substantial number of employees assert that the certified or currently recognized bargaining representative is no longer their representative.

☐ **UD-WITHDRAWAL OF UNION SHOP AUTHORITY** - Thirty percent (30%) or more of employees in a bargaining unit covered by an agreement between their employer and a labor organization desire that such authority be rescinded.

☐ **UC-UNIT CLARIFICATION** - A labor organization is currently recognized by Employer, but Petitioner seeks clarification of placement of certain employees: (*Check one*) ☐ In unit not previously certified. ☐ In unit previously certified in Case No. _____

☐ **AC-AMENDMENT OF CERTIFICATION** - Petitioner seeks amendment of certification issued in Case No. _____ *Attach statement describing the specific amendment sought.*

2. Name of Employer	Employee Representative to contact	Telephone Number

3. Address(es) of Establishment(s) involved (*Street and number, city, State, ZIP code*)

4a. Type of Establishment (Factory, mine, wholesaler, etc.)	4b. Identify principal product or service

5. Unit Involved (*In UC petition, describe* **present** *bargaining unit and attach description of proposed clarification.*)	6a. Number of Employees in Unit:
Included	Present _____
	Proposed (*By UC/AC*) _____
	6b. Is this petition supported by 30% or more of the employees in the unit? * _____ Yes _____ No
Excluded	*Not applicable in RM, UC, and AC

(*If you have checked box RC in 1 above, check and complete EITHER item 7a or 7b, whichever is applicable*)

7a. ☐ Request for recognition as Bargaining Representative was made on (*Date*) _____ and Employer declined recognition on or about
(*Date*) _____ (*If no reply received, so state*).

7b. ☐ Petitioner is currently recognized as Bargaining Representative and desires certification under the Act.

8. Name of Recognized or Certified Bargaining Agent (*If none, so state*)	Affiliation
Address and Telephone Number	Date of Recognition or Certification

9. Expiration Date of Current Contract, If any (*Month, Day, Year*)	10. If you have checked box UD in 1 above, show here the date of execution of agreement granting union shop (*Month, Day, and Year*)

11a. Is there now a strike or picketing at the Employer's establishment(s) Involved? Yes _____ No _____	11b. If so, approximately how many employees are participating?

11c. The Employer has been picketed by or on behalf of (*Insert Name*) _____, a labor organization, of (*Insert Address*) _____ Since (*Month, Day, Year*) _____

12. Organizations or individuals other than Petitioner (*and other than those named in items 8 and 11c*), which have claimed recognition as representatives and other organizations and individuals known to have a representative interest in any employees in unit described in item 5 above. (*If none, so state*)

Name	Affiliation	Address	Date of Claim (*Required only if Petition is filed by Employer*)

I declare that I have read the above petition and that the statements are true to the best of my knowledge and belief.

_____
(*Name of Petitioner and Affiliation, if any*)

By _____   _____
(*Signature of Representative or person filing petition*)   (*Title, if any*)

Address _____   _____
(*Street and number, city, State, and ZIP Code*)   (*Telephone Number*)

representation election will be held. The NLRB requires designation by at least 30 percent of the bargaining unit employees, usually in the form of signed and dated authorization cards. The NLRB also accepts designations in the form of signed petitions and union application cards.[56]

National Labor Relations Board actions have several kinds of petitions. An **RC petition** can be filed by an employee, a group of employees, or a union representing employees seeking certification of an appropriate unit. An *RM petition* can be filed by an employer if one or more labor organizations claim representation status in an appropriate unit and the employer questions the representative's status. Also, when an employer has objective proof that the union no longer represents the majority of the employees, he or she may file an RM petition. An employer, employee, other individual, or a union may also use an *RD petition* to determine whether a recognized union still has the support of employees.

Other types of petitions available are the *UD petition* that 30 percent or more of the employees file to rescind a union shop agreement; a *UC petition* requesting clarification of the composition of a bargaining unit currently certified; and an *AC petition* requesting that a change of circumstances be recognized, such as a change of union name or affiliation on a previous NLRB certification.

Petitions demonstrate sufficient employee interest or the actual type of representation case so the board may decide if it has jurisdiction. The board will assume the requisite employee interest and will accept an expedited election petition if it is filed within 30 days of the beginning of a recognitional or organizational picket.

Petitions requesting certification or decertification will normally be accepted by the board only if 30 percent of the employees in a unit favor such an election. This 30 percent is usually demonstrated by presenting cards authorizing the union to act as the employees' agent for collective bargaining. It can also be shown by a certification listing at least 30 percent of the employees of the represented unit as members in good standing of a union.

Another union may enter an election with a **showing of interest** that represents 10 percent of those in the unit in question. A cross-petition from another union may also be filed claiming representation of an appropriate unit different from the original unit but including some of the same people.[57]

Step 2: Investigation. The second step occurs when the regional director conducts investigations and a hearing, if necessary, to determine whether to proceed with an election. The employer's business must sufficiently affect commerce so as to rest jurisdiction in the NLRB. An actual representation question must exist, and sufficient employee interest must be demonstrated. The requested unit is deemed appropriate and the bargaining agent qualified. Certain statutory time periods must be honored.

Step 3: Secret Ballot Election. The third step is the secret ballot election (see Figure 4-4). The NLRB has the responsibility to ensure that a representative election is fairly and honestly conducted. In a 1948 case, the board stated that its function in representation proceedings was "to provide a laboratory in which an experiment may be conducted, under conditions as nearly ideal as possible, to determine the uninhibited desires of the employees."[58] But the board recognized that the standards for election cases had to be judged against realistic standards of human

Figure 4-4   **Request to Proceed with Election**

FORM NLRB-4551
(10-62)

UNITED STATES OF AMERICA
NATIONAL LABOR RELATIONS BOARD
REQUEST TO PROCEED

In the matter of _____   _____

                                                 (Name of Case)   *(Number of Case)*

The undersigned hereby requests the Regional Director to proceed with the above-captioned representation case, notwithstanding the charges of unfair labor practices filed in Case No. _____ . It is understood that the Board will not entertain objections to any election in this matter based upon conduct occurring prior to the filing of the petition.

Date _____

                      _____

                      By _____

                                        (Title)

                                                            GPO 939-544

conduct. When improprieties occur, certain factors should be weighed, such as the size of the unit, the circumstances of any alleged misconduct, and the real or apparent influence of the interfering party. In general, the NLRB will consider objectionable conduct in determining the validity of an election only if it occurs during the critical period, that is, between the filing of an election petition and the election itself.

An employer may cause an election to be invalidated by threatening reprisals, offering promises of benefits during an election, indicating that the election itself is futile, or stating that a successful election will result in strikes and layoffs.

For example, in two 1996 cases, the NLRB ruled that employers could not pay employees who were not scheduled to work on the day of a union certification election in order to get them to come in to vote. In one case, the employer paid for two hours of work and in the other, four hours of work.[59] Although a previous NLRB ruling allowed for such compensation as a reasonable reimbursement for travel and time costs,[60] the board said it believed that these offers were more substantial than merely reimbursement and that employees might feel obligated to vote against the union because of the employer's action. Later the board clarified the issue further when it ruled that it was all right for a union to give employees $25 to reimburse them for their time and travel because that amount was reasonably related to an actual cost.[61]

Employee actions may also influence the election certification. A union's agreement to waive union fees before an election has been considered an unfair labor practice. However, the facts presented in Case 4-2 reveal that such a union waiver was held not to have interfered with a valid election. Yet in another case, a union was held to have invalidated an election by offering free medical screening characterized as the "first union benefit" two days before an election.[62]

ELECTIONS

The union petitioned the National Labor Relations Board for certification as the bargaining agent for a unit composed of the hospital's nonprofessional service, maintenance, and technical employees. The hospital objected to the unit as overly broad, but the National Labor Relations Board found the unit appropriate and ordered the election to be held.

The union won the election, and the hospital filed objections to the election, charging that the union: offered economic inducements to employees who supported it by waiving initiation fees; misrepresented to employees various conditions of employment and their rights in the event of strikes; and misrepresented the government's role in the election by leading employees to believe that the board supported the union.

The board found no grounds for the hospital's objections to the election and ordered it to bargain with the union. The hospital appealed.

Decision

The court noted that the board has wide discretion in determining whether an election was conducted fairly. The hospital must offer evidence of events from or about specific people and show that those events tended to or did influence the outcome of the election. In this case

the union won by a wide majority, so the influence would be very difficult to prove.

Offering to waive initiation fees for employees who sign authorization cards prior to an election can invalidate an election unless the offer extends to those who join after the election as well. In this case, the hospital said the offer was ambiguous; therefore, employees could have thought it was limited to before the election. The court found some ambiguity but not enough to show an undue influence on the outcome of the election.

The hospital's charge that the union misrepresented the employees' conditions during a strike was also dismissed by the court because the hospital had had an opportunity to, and did, rebut those union statements in a speech and in letters sent to employees.

In the matter of government support of the union, the hospital submitted a union pamphlet depicting Uncle Sam standing behind a union member with the caption, "Remember, Uncle Sam Stands Behind You." Although union conduct creating the impression that the government *encourages* employees to form unions may constitute grounds for setting aside an election, this leaflet did not exceed the bounds of permissible campaign propaganda. The pamphlet merely conveyed the message that the government protects the right to join a union.

The court upheld the election.

Adapted from *Vicksburg Hospital, Inc. v. National Labor Relations Board*, 653 F.2d 1070 (1981).

Elections may be voided because of misrepresentation or trickery, but they will not be set aside solely because of misleading campaign statements or misrepresentation of fact. However, if parties use forged documents so that the nature of the publication cannot be discerned, or if NLRB documents are altered to indicate its endorsement, the election can be voided.[63]

Actions of third parties also may influence and invalidate an election. Employees who are not union agents will not influence an election if the union neither authorizes nor condones the conduct. Supervisors may exhibit pro-union sentiment unless it leads employees to believe that the employer favors the particular union and they are expected to support it. Outside groups, newspapers, and public-interest organizations may be considered in board hearings on elections if their activities have exacerbated employee fears of employer retaliations or reprisals. Even the NLRB agent may cause an election to be set aside if his or her action tends to destroy confidence in the election process or can be reasonably interpreted as impinging on the board's impartial election standards.

The board's rules prohibit both unions and employers from making speeches to mass groups of employees on company time within 24 hours of an election. However, such meetings within 24 hours of an election do not violate these rules if voluntarily attended on the employee's own time.

Employers may assemble their employees and speak to them on company time if it is prior to 24 hours to the election and if the employer does not prevent, by rigid no-solicitation rules, access to the employees by the union representatives. On election day, prolonged conversations between either party and the voters are prohibited as are traditional campaign activities at the polling place. In recent studies of employee participation in representative elections, some questions have been raised as to what degree even a legal campaign discourages such participation.[64] If an employee perceives that an election will be won or lost regardless of his vote, that employee may choose not to vote at all.[65]

In cases in which an election involves three choices—for example, Union A, Union B, or no union—a **runoff election** may be required if none of the choices receives a majority of the votes cast. The two top vote getters are placed before the members of the bargaining unit again, and the one receiving a majority vote can be certified.

> Under NLRB rules and regulations, "A runoff election is conducted only where: (a) the ballot in the original election contained three or more choices [i.e., two labor organizations and a 'neither' choice]; and (b) no single choice received a majority of the valid votes cast. Thus there can be no runoff where the original ballot provided for: (1) a 'yes' and 'no' choice in a one-union election; or (2) a 'severance' election." The ballot in the runoff election provides for a selection between the two choices receiving the largest and second largest number of votes in the original election.[66]

Step 4: Certification of Election Results.   If the board is satisfied that the election represents the employees' free choice, the election is certified, the fourth step. Either no union is victorious or, if a union has gained a majority of those voting, that union is certified as the bargaining agent for the unit.

Certification benefits a union in a number of ways. It closes any challenges to the union's status as the exclusive bargaining agent for the particular unit. Its status is binding on the employer for at least one year, during which time the employer must bargain with it. After the first year the employer must continue to bargain unless there is reasonable doubt that the union will continue to enjoy a majority vote of the unit. The board will not entertain petitions regarding rival certification for that unit within the one-year certification, nor within three years, if a valid contract is in effect. The certified union may strike against the employer under certain circumstances without fear of an unfair labor practice charge.

A union may seek recognition by the board to obtain the benefit of certification even if its status as an exclusive bargaining agent has not been challenged and the employer has agreed to bargain. The NLRB considers such a request as raising a question of representation.

Voluntary Recognition

Election, although the most accepted way by which employees select their representatives, is not the exclusive method condoned by the NLRB. An employer may recognize the union as the bargaining agent without an election—this *voluntary recognition* is rare. In a Supreme Court decision upholding a board bargaining order, the Court recognized two other valid means by which a union may establish majority status and thereby place a bargaining obligation upon the employer: (1) through a show of support through a union, called strike, and (2) when a union collects authorization cards from a majority of the unit members. The cards are often submitted to a third party for a "card check" to verify the names against payroll. If an employer agrees to the card check, then, if the third party finds a majority for the union, the employer must bargain.[67] For example, in September, 1996, in a small town near Boston a small group of Latina workers showed up for work at the Richmark curtain manufacturing plant. They began distributing leaflets supporting an organizational campaign and were immediately fired. Then, in support of the fired workers, 40 others walked off the job in an unfair labor practice strike. Over the next several weeks, all of the 170 women who worked at the plant picketed and united community support for "direct action" and presented Richmark a demand for card check recognition. The picket lines kept up a daily protest, local churches collected money and food for the striking families, and Latino centers provided assistance and facilities. Finally, on October 8, 1996, 13 community leaders met with the Richmark president—and were arrested for refusing to leave. Only two days later the company agreed to recognize the union without an election, reinstate the strikers, and give them full back pay.[68]

In the **Gissel doctrine**,[69] the Court gave a stamp of approval for authorization cards as a substitute for an election *when* an employer's actions amounted to an unfair labor practice. The Court recognized that, if traditional remedies could not eradicate the lingering effects of the employer's conduct and permit the holding of a fair election, the union's authorization cards were a more reliable indicator of the employees' desires than an election, and a bargaining order should be issued. The board is strictly limited in imposing a Gissel Bargaining Order to cases in which the union actually gained majority status through the authorization cards. Regardless of how outrageous the employer's actions, unless such a majority is demonstrated, no order to bargain can be issued.[70] The board has also issued bargaining orders when the employer has gained independent knowledge of the union's majority status or has acknowledged the union's right to represent employees.

Voting Patterns

Significant time and money have been spent by unions and management researching why employees vote as they do in certification and decertification elections. In general, employees will vote in what is perceived to be their best interest. Those who abstain from voting either do not desire a change in the status quo or plan to leave the organization. Aspects of their work life that influence their vote include compensation issues, work rules, and sources of grievances. Election campaigns by employers and unions appear to have little influence on the outcome of representation elections except among those employees who are initially undecided or indifferent. In general, if employees are satisfied with their work environment, they vote against change—whether it is to keep an existing union or to bring one in to represent them. If dissatisfied, they tend to vote for a change.[71]

Recent statistics on both certification and decertification elections cause problems for union organizations. In 1966 unions won 62 percent of the certification elections held. In 1970 the percentage dropped to 56 percent, and in 1980 to 45.7 percent. In 1989 there was a slight improvement to 49.8 percent, but still, unions were not able to win elections in over 50 percent of their attempts.[72] The trend downward continued when, in 1994, unions won 49.2 percent of the representation elections, but only 48.2 percent in 1995. More troublesome for the unions was the fact that the number of representation elections fell 11 percent from 1994 to 1995.[73]

Can employees exhibit loyalty to both the union and their employer? Research indicates that such dual commitment is strongest when a positive relationship exists between the employer and the union. However, when labor-management relations are poor, employees may be forced to choose, and often employees give their loyalty to the union. When they perceive that labor is too adversarial and they tire of divided loyalties, employees may choose union decertification (voting out the union) to end their strife.[74]

Decertification Elections

Also allowed under the act and supervised by the NLRB are **decertification elections** whereby the members of the unit vote to terminate an existing union's right to represent them in collective bargaining. Decertification elections most commonly occur when the initial year of union representation ends with no collective bargaining agreement, an existing contract will expire within 60 to 90 days, or a contract has expired and no new agreement is being negotiated.

The rules for a decertification election are similar to those for certification, with some exceptions. Only employees can file a decertification petition, which must include 30 percent of the eligible members of the unit. Again, the NLRB investigates the validity of the petition. If the union feels that there is a problem with the petition or that an employer has unlawfully helped in the petition, it may file a blocking charge and delay the election until the unfair labor charge is resolved.

Although an employer can in no way aid the filing of a petition, afterward, the employer, the employees who filed the petition, and the union may all engage in an election campaign. The rules for conducting a decertification election are the same as those for a representation election.

After the votes are counted, if a majority of the employees vote against the union, it is decertified. A tie vote counts against the union because it no longer enjoys a majority status. If the union wins, it continues to represent the unit, and another election is barred for at least a year.

Why do workers vote to decertify their union? One or more of the following factors are usually present in situations in which unions are decertified:

1. The employer has recently treated employees better.
2. The employer waged an aggressive anti-union campaign.
3. The employer moves to a traditionally nonunion geographic area.
4. The union is perceived by a majority of its members as being unresponsive.
5. Female, minority, and younger workers lose confidence in the union because of its declining public image and aging leaders.[75]

The percentage of all representation elections that were decertification (versus certification) elections remained almost insignificant (less than 5 percent) until 1970. However, the percentage has steadily risen each year since 1970 until about 20 percent of all elections held are now decertification elections. Unions have lost approximately 75 percent of the more than 800 decertification elections held each year.[76]

Decertification elections held recently showed a slight improvement in union victories. In 1994, unions won 30.9 percent of the decertification elections, and in 1995 unions prevailed in 29.7 percent of the challenges. More important, the number of elections to decertify a union decreased to 488 in 1994 and 458 in 1995.[77]

The significant rise in the number of decertification elections in recent years is most likely attributable to employers' efforts to make their workers aware of their rights. Table 4-1 shows 40 years' of statistics on the success of decertification elections.

The effects of a decertification election on the labor movement can be seen in a 1991 case. After more than 60 years of representation, the Seattle employees of Nordstrom, Inc., a department store chain, voted to end their representation by the United Food and Commercial Workers Union. The vote in the five stores was more than two to one to decertify. Former union members said that they voted the union out because they had tired of the union's publicity war against Nordstrom. The union was battling Nordstrom's intent to take mandatory union membership out of the next contract. Employees felt that the union's fight was not on their behalf but was a fight to preserve union dues supporting the union organization—a goal that more than a majority of the workers failed to share with the union.[78]

Exclusive Representation

When a labor union is recognized as the exclusive bargaining agent for a unit of employees, two major issues come into play. The first is union security, that is, preserving the union's continued representation of the employees. The second is what representation by a union means to an individual employee.

Exclusive representation is both a practice and a principle of law. The practice predates the law. As discussed in earlier chapters, the very roots of the labor-management relationship depended on the workers' agreement to join together to make demands on the employer. Without such solidarity, employers would have gone to other workers willing to work for what the employer wanted to pay.

Decertification Elections, 1948–1988 — Table 4-1

Years	Elections Held	Voted "Yes" to Decertify	Percentage Decertified
1948–1957	1,257	848	67.5%
1958–1967	2,232	1,514	67.8
1968–1977	4,610	3,251	70.5
1978–1988	9,129	6,829	74.8

Source: Used by permission of David M. Savino and Nealia S. Bruning, "Decertification Strategies and Tactics: Management and Union Perspectives," *Labor Law Journal* (April 1992), pp. 201–210. Reprinted from the April 1992 issue of *Labor Law Journal*, published and copyrighted 1992 by CHH Incorporated, 4025 W. Peterson Avenue, Chicago, IL 60646. All rights reserved.

Union

Three ways a union organizer can generate sufficient interest at a workplace to organize employees:

Organizing at the workplace is not much different from organizing in the community, or on campus, or anywhere else for that matter. The key to successful organizing efforts is finding the connection between the prospective "members" and the "organization" seeking their allegiance. For employees, traditionally this connection was easy: better compensation for their labor, health benefits, and job security. As we go into the twenty-first century, this connection must be based on other things as well. The basics exist for many workers whether by existing collective bargaining or by legislation. Where the basics do exist, the emphasis must shift to (1) employment security, (2) employee-employer partnership in providing quality products and services, and (3) employee political power in the elective and legislative processes. It is necessary to find out what the workers want and to show them how the union is the vehicle for attaining what they want.

Management

What are three ways an employer can legally discourage employees from organizing?

a. Good communication, from suggestion programs (boxes for employees to write questions to be answered by top management, for example, Winn Dixie's "I want to know" program, in which the CEO personally responds to any question within 24 hours; anonymous questions can be answered in company newsletters or publications specifically geared for that purpose), to reward programs in which employees compete for the best idea for cost-cutting or similar measures, to simply training supervisors in how to best field questions and issues around which union organizing attempts focus and how to proclaim the company's union-free philosophy without interrogating the employee in the process.

b. Active participation, from joint employee-management quality teams dealing with specific workplace issues, to bonus incentives for every employee when both the company and the individual employee exceed their performance objectives, to employee representation in the development of critical personnel policies (such as the disciplinary system).

c. Instituting an internal grievance appeal process, to remove the last (assuming *a* and *b* are followed) appeal the union has.

Before this practice became law in the Wagner Act, labor organizers and union members had to "strong-arm" some employees who might otherwise break ranks.

Because part of the goal of the Wagner Act was to eliminate labor unrest, the lawmakers agreed that if a majority of the employees working in a defined unit voted to be represented by a union, then *all* the employees would be covered. This rule gives real power to the union's bargaining position and simplifies the bargaining process.

The value of exclusive representation in negotiating collective bargaining agreements cannot be overemphasized. Without it, the process simply will not work. If even a few employees ignore the union and gain individual benefits from the employer, the need for a union can be questioned. Or if individual members of a bargaining unit take unsanctioned action—such as a wildcat strike—an employer's confidence that the union's agreement not to strike if gains are made at the negotiation table may be destroyed. And if exclusive representation were not the rule, the administration of a contract among like employees in an inconsistent manner would be disruptive to the labor-management relationship.[79]

The preservation of existing strength and influence is a major issue facing unions as we near the year 2000. Security and the structure of the present organizations affect union preservation.

Union security refers to a union's ability to grow and to perform its exclusive collective bargaining role without interference from management, other unions, or other sources. A key element to a union's security is a provision in the collective bargaining agreement requiring employees to join the union and pay union dues as a condition of continued employment. Such a provision assures the union and its members that all the employees who share the benefits of collective bargaining agreements pay for the union's cost. Required union membership increases the financial base of the union and may increase its ability to represent its members at the bargaining table.

Unions are concerned about their security for many reasons. For instance, a union is certified as the **exclusive bargaining agent** for only one year following a representation election. Rival unions may not seek to organize its members during that short time. Although a union security provision cannot prevent such raiding after the year, loyalties are developed and strengthened by participation in the union for that year.

Laws

The 1935 NLRA protected union security in several ways. Company unions were prohibited because the act's proponents saw them as a major threat to employee rights.[80] Yellow-dog contracts, whereby employees agreed not to join unions in order to get hired, and blacklisting of union sympathizers were made illegal. The act allowed an employer to make an agreement with the union requiring union membership as a precondition to employment. As a result, the **closed shop** clause became common.

Union security increased union membership. Automatic **check-off provisions** in the contract authorizing the employer to withhold dues from a member's wages ensured that the union would receive payment.

Public reaction to the growth of union membership and numerous labor-management conflicts following World War I led to the 1947 passage of the Taft-Hartley Amendments to the National Labor Relations Act. Added to Section 7, which guaranteed freedom of organization, was a guarantee of the employee's right *not* to organize and engage in union activity. The closed shop was outlawed, although the amendments allowed **union shops** to be negotiated in future contracts. A union shop required union membership on or after 30 days of employment. The hiring power was, therefore, restored to the employer. However, although the act allowed union shops, it also permitted states to outlaw union shops. The so-called **right-to-work laws** permitted states to prohibit agreements requiring membership in a labor organization as a condition of employment. The Taft-Hartley Amendments also limited the dues check-off practice by requiring a written authorization from each union member.

Finally, court decisions have limited the application of a union shop provision by narrowing the meaning of union membership. The Supreme Court has long held that being a union member for the purpose of complying with a union shop provision could not require more of a person than paying dues. A union could not require attendance at meetings or participation in union activities.[81]

In a 1988 decision, **CWA v. Beck,** the Supreme Court limited a union shop requirement for the paying of dues as a union member to only that portion of the union's dues that represented the cost of bargaining and representation. Union dues that represent a union's political or fraternal activities cannot be included.[82] In 1995, the NLRB expanded the *Beck* holding to include an affirmative duty on the part of a union to inform its members of their rights under *Beck* to object to the expenditure of their dues for political or fraternal activities.[83]

Forms of Union Security

Union security clauses may take several basic forms:

1. **Closed shop**. Outlawed by the Taft-Hartley Amendments, the closed shop provision allowed the employer to hire only union members. In order to get a job, a person first had to join the union.
2. **Open shop**. No employee is required to join or to contribute money to a labor organization as a condition for employment under the open shop.
3. **Union shop**. A union shop provides that within a specific period of time, usually 30 to 90 days, an employee must join the union to continue the job with the company. Union membership under such a provision must be available on a fair and nondiscriminatory basis, and fees and dues must be reasonable and can be limited to an amount reflecting only the cost of bargaining and representation. The National Labor Relations Act allows a majority of employees to vote to rescind the union shop authorization. This form of union security clause along with the check-off provision are most commonly found in collective bargaining agreements.[84]
4. **Union hiring hall**. A union hiring hall provision is typical of the construction, trucking, and longshoring trades. This form requires an employer to hire employees referred by the union, provided the union can supply a sufficient number of applicants. As long as the union refers union and nonunion members alike and does not require membership before the seventh day of employment, such provisions are legal.
5. **Agency shop**. Agency shop provisions require employees to contribute a sum equal to membership dues to the union, but they are not required to join the union. The union is provided with the financial support of employees who benefit from their collective bargaining, but the employee's right not to join the union is retained.
6. **Maintenance of membership**. The maintenance of membership provision requires those who are union members at the time a union contract is entered into to remain union members but only for the duration of the agreement. Nonunion members are not required to join.
7. **Miscellaneous forms of union security**. A *preferential shop* requires the employer to give hiring preference to union members. The **check-off** of union dues from an employee's paycheck operates as a union security form because it protects the source of union funding and automatically keeps the employees in good standing with the union. This form of union security is often the only legal device available in right-to-work states. **Superseniority** gives union leaders top seniority for layoff purposes and indirectly increases union security by ensuring the continuity of its leadership.

Recent board and court decisions threaten some of these traditional areas of union security. Superseniority rights are now limited to those union officials who are necessary to the actual administration of a collective bargaining agreement; being an officeholder is not enough.[85] In addition, increased restriction on the expenditure of union funds raised through agency shop agreements to those items directly related to collective bargaining has created financial difficulties for unions already suffering membership losses.[86]

Right-to-Work

Section 14(b) of the National Labor Relations Act states:

> Nothing in this act shall be construed as authorizing the execution and application of agreements requiring membership in a labor organization as a condition of employment in any state or territory in which such execution or application is prohibited by state or territorial law.

This provision allows states to enact laws prohibiting the union or agency shop forms of union security, as seen in Case 4-3. Only 21 states, mostly in the West and the South, have done so.[87] Right-to-work legislation understandably evokes great emotions from both proponents and opponents.

Opponents contend that right-to-work legislation is an attempt to change the bargaining power at the negotiating table in management's favor. In addition, "right-to-work" as a slogan is misleading. Such laws guarantee no one a job and in their opinion confer rights only upon employers.[88] The phrase implies the union's concomitant right to prevent a person from working. According to union advocates, the requirement of union membership as a condition of employment is no more restrictive of an individual's freedom than the requirement of specific hours of work or of certain minimal job qualifications. Union members contend that employees should support the union primarily because of the benefits that union and nonunion employees alike receive through collective bargaining agreements.[89] Finally, opponents point out that the per capita income in states not having right-to-work laws is higher.

Proponents of the right-to-work legislation believe that it affirms the basic rights of a person to work for a living whether he or she belongs to a union or not.[90] They contend that no private organization should be able to tax a person and use that money to support causes with which all the members may not agree. Compulsory union membership can mean that a union does not need to be responsive to its members. And, according to proponents, right-to-work legislation encourages economic development since employers are not as likely to lose income from strikes over union security issues. A recent study contends that union security arrangements "have not had a significant effect on the wage settlements unions negotiate" and supports the proponents of the right-to-work legislation.[91]

A 1986 right-to-work referendum election was held in Idaho. Both sides waged extensive media campaigns and focused the debate on the issues of lower wages and growth in the Idaho economy. Whether someone should be forced to join a union became a peripheral issue in the campaign. Idaho had been targeted by the National Right to Work Committee since 1976, when it successfully pushed passage of the Louisiana right-to-work law.[92] Right-to-work states have several characteristics that differ from union shop states. These characteristics include

RIGHT-TO-WORK LAWS

A class action suit was instituted in a Florida state court by four nonunion employees who sought injunctive relief against an employer and a union who had agreed to an agency shop arrangement in a collective bargaining agreement. The agreement did not require the employees to join the contracting union, but it did require them to pay an initial service fee and monthly service fees to the union as a condition of employment. On the basis of the Florida right-to-work law, the Florida Supreme Court held that the agency shop clause involved was illegal. The union appealed on the grounds that the National Labor Relations Act specifically allows agency shop provisions in collective bargaining agreements, prohibiting only agreements requiring membership. Because this agency shop agreement did not require membership in the union, the state's law should not be allowed to forbid it.

Decision

The Supreme Court upheld the Florida court's decision in finding that the agency shop clause was prohibited by Florida's right-to-work law. The Court found that Section 14(b) of the National Labor Relations Act, which allows states to prohibit agreements requiring membership in a labor organization as a condition of employment, could not be so narrowly construed as the union had requested in this case or else the section would have no meaning. The state's right-to-work law had to be interpreted to preclude any type of union security agreement allowed under federal law if the purpose of the act and the Taft-Hartley Amendments were to be effective.

Adapted from *Retail Clerks International Association v. Schermerhorn*, 375 U.S. 96, 11 L.Ed. 179, 84 S.Ct. 219 (1963).

(1) low union membership, (2) little heavy industry, and (3) a high level of agriculture. Idaho shared these characteristics with the 20 right-to-work states.[93]

Union membership in Idaho was about 70,000 out of a population of 1 million. Idaho is surrounded by other right-to-work states: Wyoming, Utah, and Nevada. The referendum election was initiated by organized labor in an effort to overturn a 1985 law that was passed despite the governor's veto and made Idaho the twenty-first right-to-work state. Opponents of right-to-work began their campaign with the message: "The real intent of right-to-work is to damage unions and lower wages for all Idaho employees—both union and nonunion." Supporters of right-to-work pushed the message: "Should you be free to hold a job . . . whether you belong to a union or not?" Each side then began to muddle the issues by bringing in actors from Hollywood—Charlton Heston for the right-to-workers, Patty Duke for the opposition. The final vote was in favor of retaining the new right-to-work law by 30,514 votes of the 385,324 total votes cast.[94]

Court rulings and right-to-work states have had the effect of creating two new categories of employees: free riders and cheap riders. **Free riders** are employees who are in a unit represented by a union and are covered by a collective bargaining agreement but do not join the union. The collective bargaining agreement is binding on them, but they may not have any influence over its creation. **Cheap rid-**

ers are employees who, again, are covered by a collective bargaining agreement but are not union members, but they are required to pay something to the union for the bargaining and representation services they receive. The share employees pay under union and agency shops where nominal membership or financial support is required ranges from 20 percent to 85 percent of a regular member's dues.

The advent of free and cheap riders is a relatively new development, and union leaders will need to find out why a worker might choose to be a union member rather than a free rider. The results of one study could not be very encouraging for union advocates. The 1988 analysis of a U.S. Census Bureau *Current Population Survey* (CPS) indicated that employees in bargaining units might join the union as opposed to becoming free riders because they did not know they had a choice. Obviously, the union does not educate employees about this right, and employers may be accused of unfair labor practice for educating them. Employees also believe that union members get preferential treatment through the union's more diligent representation of members' interests at the bargaining table and when faced with grievance procedures. Although a union has a duty to represent fairly members and nonmembers alike, few employees believe that union officials can maintain such impartiality. Finally, some employees choose union membership over being a free rider because of the stigma associated with free rider status.[95]

Duty of Fair Representation

INDIVIDUAL RIGHTS WITHIN UNIONS

The certified union for a bargaining unit is granted an exclusive right under the National Labor Relations Act to represent *all* of the employees in that unit, members and nonmembers alike. Individuals within that bargaining unit may not contract privately with the employer but must be represented by the recognized bargaining agent. In the traditional factory setting this **exclusivity rule** posed no particular problem for the individuals as long as the bargaining unit was appropriately formed. But today, nontraditional union members such as profootball players, lawyers, and architects may find representation by the bargaining agent disadvantageous if the member is considered a superstar. Under this rule, a famous quarterback may have to accept the same salary as a member of the forward line, if that was the negotiated agreement.

The exclusivity rule giving the union the right to represent all members, however, is essential to the union's ability for proper representation at the bargaining table. Along with this right goes the **duty to represent fairly** *all* of the employees of the unit. Fair representation must be found both in the negotiation of the collective bargaining agreement and in its enforcement.

In a leading Supreme Court case, **Steele v. Louisville and N.R.R.**, a black railroad fireman asked the Court to set aside a seniority agreement negotiated by his union because it discriminated against minorities who were part of the bargaining unit.[96] Although the Railway Labor Act under which the union had exclusive rights to bargain for the employees did not explicitly do so, the Court held that the act implicitly imposed a duty on the union to exercise its powers fairly on behalf of all those it acted for. Later court decisions found that the National Labor Relations Act imposed that same duty on its unions.

However, court decisions have acknowledged that contracts may have unfavorable effects on some members of the unit. The law does provide that such unfavorable effects cannot be the result of discriminatory treatment based on irrelevant or insidious considerations such as union membership or race. Guidelines on the resolution of such thorny issues as seniority, access to training programs, or promotion, without a breach of the fair representation duty, basically come from court decisions. A union must consider all employees and make an honest effort to serve their interests in good faith and without hostility or arbitrary discrimination. The courts have held, in fact, that absent such a finding, the courts may not question the actual bargain struck by the union. It cannot be a breach of duty unless it is so far outside the range of reasonableness as to be wholly irrational.[97]

An employee must use the grievance procedure controlled by the union, but the employee does not have an absolute right to have a grievance pursued. In **Vaca v. Sipes**, the Supreme Court noted that a procedure giving the union discretion to supervise the grievance machinery and to invoke arbitration establishes an atmosphere for both parties to settle grievances short of arbitration.[98] The parties are assured that similar grievances receive similar treatment; thus, problem areas under the collective bargaining agreement can be isolated and perhaps resolved. Therefore, a breach of the duty to represent an employee fairly occurs only if the union's conduct toward the member is arbitrary, discriminatory, or in bad faith.

In a historic Supreme Court case, **Bowen v. The U.S. Postal Service**, the Court apportioned the damages due the wrongfully discharged employee between the union and the employer by using the date of a hypothetical arbitration decision.[99] All back pay prior to that hypothetical date was due from the employer; all back pay from that date to the time of settlement was due from the union.

The Court reasoned that if the employee had been properly represented, the employer's liability would have ended at the arbitration decision. All back pay benefits from that point forward were caused and should be paid by the union.

SUMMARY

The National Labor Relations Act regulated the industrial relations of employers whose activities affect interstate commerce. The act guaranteed employees the right to self-organization and required the employer to bargain collectively with employee representatives. The National Labor Relations Board was established to enforce the act.

The board, in order to protect the employee rights guaranteed by the NLRA, determines on the appropriateness of the selected bargaining units. The board also regulates and conducts union elections to ensure that employees exercise their freedom of choice.

Labor relations, as regulated by the NLRA, is considered the exclusive domain of federal law. With a few exceptions, the National Labor Relations Board has primary jurisdiction in any labor dispute affecting commerce. State laws and regulations are not controlling. Unions seek to improve their members' living standard through better wages, job security, and social legislation. To do this, unions must seek their own security as the exclusive representative of the worker.

The organizing drive conducted by a union wishing to represent a unit of employees is very important. In recent years unions have had a decreasing rate of success in certification elections and in defeating decertification elections. That trend, along with the erosion of union security protections, has had a very negative effect on unionization.

A union seeks union security clauses in collective bargaining agreements ranging from union shops to dues check-off provisions, to ensure both the exclusive nature of its representation and its financial security. State right-to-work laws undermine that security and pose a great threat to unionization.

Individual employees have certain protections as members of labor unions, including guidelines on how they are to be represented in negotiation with the employer and in grievance procedures.

DUTY OF FAIR REPRESENTATION

Facts

In 1981, the company laid off more than 100 employees because of an economic recession. The existing contract already provided that laid-off employees would accrue "continuous service" credit for two years and would retain "continuous service" credit for an additional five-year period. In addition, the union negotiated additional benefits for these laid-off employees. One of the benefits was a commitment by the company that these laid-off employees would be "offered future employment opportunities" with the company in the event positions opened up.

Eleven years later, in 1992, the company needed employees and it notified the former employees and offered them interviews. Some were rehired. However, 16 former employees, who were still union members, were not rehired. They sought the help of their union in filing a grievance against the company, claiming that the company had violated the contract by not rehiring them. The union declined, saying that because these union members were no longer employees of the company, they were not part of the bargaining unit and the union had no duty to represent them. The 16 former employees argued that under the agreement ne-gotiated by the union while they were employees, they had acquired certain protections and it was the union's duty now to enforce those protections. Because the former employees could not pursue the grievance without the union, the negotiated protections would be meaningless if the union failed to represent them. The 16 former employees sued the union.

Questions

1. If the court rules that the union has no duty to represent these former employees, they cannot pursue their grievance against the company. Discuss why this result is fair or unfair to all three parties: the company, the union, and the former employees.
2. When the union bargained for the laid-off employees, the employees were told they would have future employment opportunities with the company. Do you think it was unreasonable for these laid-off employees to expect the union's help 11 years later? Why or why not?
3. If the company and the union had known that 11 years would pass before positions opened up at this plant, do you think they would have provided this "future employment opportunities" provision?

Adapted from *Smith v. ACF Industries*, 149 LRRM 2693 (1995).

CASE STUDY 4-2

GISSEL BARGAINING ORDER

Facts

The union lost a representation election by a vote of sixteen to five, with seven challenged ballots. The union charged the company with unfair labor practices and, on the basis of the Gissel Bargaining Order, asked the NLRB to order the company to bargain with the union anyway. The NLRB found unfair labor practices and did so order. Although the company denied unfair labor practices, its appeal involved primarily the Gissel Bargaining Order.

When an election is set aside because of unfair labor practices of the employer, the NLRB can order the company to bargain with the union if the union has obtained authorization cards from a majority of the employees in an appropriate unit.

The company contended that the union did not have enough cards; the union contended that it did. There were four employees in dispute. The company contended that the unit consisted of 31 employees; the union, 29. The company also contended that one of the 16 authorization cards was invalid.

1. The union sought to exclude two members of the unit—one who was on sick leave and one who performed clerical duties. It was the union's position that, although a member on leave would normally be considered part of the unit, the company had instituted a new personnel policy automatically terminating anyone on leave for more than 21 days. The employee in question had been on sick leave for more than four months at the time of the unit count. The company pointed out that obviously the new personnel policy was not applied to this employee because he had worked for one day during his extended leave, and had been paid for it, and throughout his leave, he had enjoyed all the fringe benefits of an employee. As for the clerical worker, the union pointed out that clerical workers were excluded from the unit, and the employee was off the line doing clerical work 30 percent of the time. The company contended that her clerical time in the office was minimal and was performed between 8:00 A.M. and 8:45 A.M. and at lunchtime. Her other clerical duties were done in the line area and were associated with the production line.

2. The company challenged the authorization card of one employee. In a Gissel case—because cards substitute for a secret ballot election—the signatures on the card must be obtained only by proper means. The company contended, on the basis of the employee's testimony, that he was harassed for two or three days before signing the card, that he repeatedly stated that he did not want to sign the card, and that he was told that signing the card was just for an election. The union claimed that its admittedly repeated requests to the employee were not harassment but permissible preelection campaigning and that, although he was told in one instance that the card was only for an election, at a general meeting he was told that the cards would be presented to the company for recognition that the company could accept or reject.

Questions

1. If you were deciding this case, would you include the two employees in the unit total? Explain your answer.
2. If you were deciding this case, would you have accepted the disputed authorization card?
3. In this instance, the union had 15 unchallenged authorization cards requesting an election but lost by obtaining only five unchallenged votes. Discuss some of the factors during an election campaign that could bring about this result.

Adapted from *Medline Industries Inc. v. National Labor Relations Board*, 593 F.2d 788 (7th Cir. 1979).

KEY TERMS AND CONCEPTS

REVIEW QUESTIONS

1. What are the purpose and the jurisdiction of the NLRB?
2. Summarize the rights of employees and employers as provided by the National Labor Relations Act.
3. When are states totally preempted from regulation of the labor field, according to Supreme Court decisions?
4. What criteria does the NLRB consider when determining whether an appropriate unit of employees has substantial mutuality of interests?
5. How does the National Labor Relations Act limit the board's determination of the appropriate bargaining unit?
6. What are the steps the NLRB follows in a representation election?
7. How does certification benefit a union? Under what circumstances might the NLRB invalidate a certification election?
8. What factors might contribute to employees' voting to decertify a union?
9. Define *union security* and explain its importance to labor leaders.
10. Discuss why labor leaders have tried to repeal Section 14(b) (the right-to-work section) of the Taft-Hartley Amendments since its passage in 1947.

TAKE IT TO THE NET

We invite you to visit the Carrell/Heavrin page on the Prentice Hall Web site at:

http://www.prenhall.com/carrellr

for this chapter's World Wide Web exercise.

What Do You Really Know about Right to Work?

Purpose:
To give students an understanding of the right-to-work issue.

Task:
The term *right-to-work* is one of the most basic and yet misunderstood concepts in labor relations. Many labor experts would agree that whether a state is a right-to-work state generally sets the labor climate within the state. To determine what you know and do not know about right-to-work, complete this quiz. Your instructor will then lead a discussion about the questions.

1. The term *right-to-work* is contained in which federal law?
2. Right-to-work states do not allow union shops: true or false?
3. Right-to-work states do not allow open shops: true or false?
4. What is the provision of the National Labor Relations Act that allows states to enact laws prohibiting union or agency shop security?
5. Opponents of state right-to-work laws often contend that free riders are created in the open shops of right-to-work states. Why?
6. Proponents of state right-to-work laws often contend that they encourage economic development within a state. Why?
7. Is the argument that right-to-work legislation stops compulsory union membership usually made by opponents *or* by proponents of right-to-work legislation?
8. Is the state in which you work a right-to-work state? If not, what is the closest right-to-work state?
9. On the map below, place an *X* on each right-to-work state in the United States.
10. Which states do you think might become the next right-to-work states? Why?

Purpose:
To understand how bargaining units get started.

Task:
AmberCraft Toy Co. manufactures, sells, and distributes toys in eight western states. They have the following job classifications:

Administrators	Assembly-line workers	Inside sales
Managers	Truckers	Outside sales
Supervisors	Maintenance workers	Security guards
Clerical workers	Janitorial workers	

AmberCraft has four manufacturing plants (with about 300 employees in each) located in California (San Diego, Fresno, Oakland, and Fort Bragg). BEST union wants to organize the AmberCraft employees in the San Diego location. AmberCraft has no previous union history. Each location is largely run independently by a plant manager, but all personnel policies are set by the central office in Fresno. Hiring and other labor activities are conducted by the plant managers.

Questions
1. Does the San Diego plant meet the 1995 NLRB rules for one employer–multiple locations?
2. Do you think that the San Diego plant is an appropriate unit?
3. If BEST were organizing all four sites, which job classifications would be combined into the appropriate bargaining unit(s)?

If you are using Smith/Carrell/Golden *Collective Bargaining Simulated, 4E,* with this text, please refer to the following:

p. 14, Article II: Recognition, which specifies the bargaining unit; and Article IV: Union Shop.

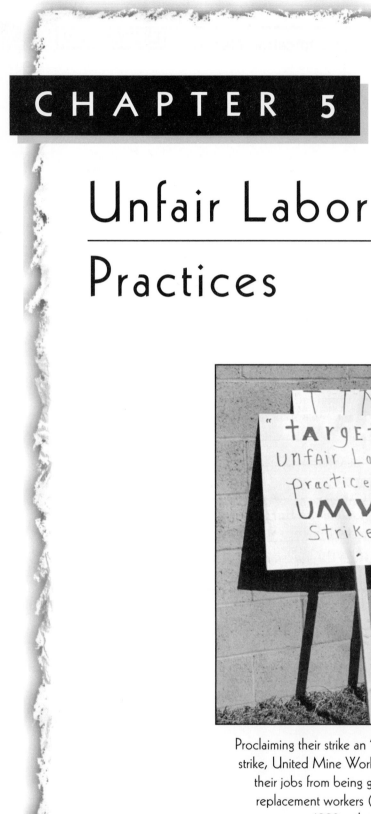

CHAPTER 5

Unfair Labor
Practices

- Unfair Labor Practices
  by Employers
- Unfair Labor Practices
  by Labor Organizations
- Duty to Bargain
  in Good Faith
- Summary

Proclaiming their strike an "unfair labor practices"
strike, United Mine Workers hoped to protect
their jobs from being given to permanent
replacement workers (scab labor) in this
1993 strike action.

Big Labor's Next Target: Las Vegas

The AFL-CIO decided in 1997 to mount its largest organizing campaign in decades. The target is not a single manufacturing or service industry, but the city of Las Vegas. If the campaign is successful, Las Vegas will become the symbol of a "revitalized labor movement" according to labor expert, Harley Shaiken. The organizational effort is focusing on three industries that are prominent in the town: hotels, hospitals, and construction.

At first glance, Las Vegas might appear to be an unlikely target because it is in a very conservative right-to-work state. But as Mark Smith, president of the Chamber of Commerce notes, it has a booming economy—and employers tend to not fight as hard in boom times; its jobs cannot be moved elsewhere; and it is a very "visible" city, which should give the AFL-CIO a great deal of free publicity if it is successful. The AFL-CIO plans on spending at least $6 million on paid organizers with the materials unions, which are involved spending millions more. The unions involved include the Hotel and Restaurant Employees Union, the Service Employees International Union, and the Building Trades Council. The AFL-CIO money "allows us to do things on a scale we couldn't do before," says Mark Kay Hewiz, a union organizer. The final result—which will not be known for years—could be a good indication of the future rate of union growth in the United States.

Adapted from G. Pascal Zachary, "AFL-CIO Mounts Organizing Drive in Las Vegas," *Wall Street Journal*, January 27, 1997, pp. A1, 4.

The collective bargaining process requires the employer and the employee to meet and negotiate terms and conditions of employment. It is an uneasy relationship that requires give and take. Often one side does not choose to participate or to participate fully. The National Labor Relations Act recognizes that reluctance and by its terms seeks to legislate the behavior of the parties. Certain actions are deemed to be unfair if they run counter to the purposes of the act, and bad faith might be evidenced in the negotiation process by other actions. This chapter explores aspects of unfair labor practices and breaches of the duty to bargain in good faith to see how such behavior frustrates successful collective bargaining.

UNFAIR LABOR PRACTICES BY EMPLOYERS

One of the primary objectives of the National Labor Relations Act was to encourage collective bargaining to minimize the industrial strife adversely affecting the free flow of commerce. To that end, the NLRB gave employees certain protected rights. Section 7 of the act, as amended by the Taft-Hartley Amendments, enumerates these rights:

1. To self-organize
2. To form, join, or assist labor organizations
3. To bargain collectively through representatives of their own choosing
4. To engage in other concerted activities for the purpose of collective bargaining or other mutual aid or protection
5. To refrain from any or all of the above[1]

The act also lists **employer** activities considered **unfair labor practices** in violation of those rights:

1. Interference with, restraint, or coercion of employees in rights guaranteed under Section 7
2. Domination or interference with the formation or administration of a labor union
3. Discrimination against union members for their union membership
4. Discrimination against an employee for pursuing the rights under the act
5. Refusal to bargain collectively with representatives of its employees[2]

The basic right of employees to join together has always been protected under the freedom of association provision of the First Amendment to the U.S. Constitution. Prior to the National Labor Relations Act, however, no federal law protected the employee in the exercise of that right. The passage of the National Labor Relations Act balances the employers' property rights and the employees' organization and recognition rights according to the dictates of law and fact.

The Authority of the NLRB

An unfair labor practice charge comes to the National Labor Relations Board through procedures similar to election petitions. The party claiming injury files an appropriate form with a regional office of the NLRB (see Figure 5-1). An initial investigation is held, and if merit is found to the charge and the regional director

FORM NLRB-501 (11-88)	UNITED STATES OF AMERICA NATIONAL LABOR RELATIONS BOARD **CHARGE AGAINST EMPLOYER**	FORM EXEMPT UNDER 44 U.S.C. 3512

	DO NOT WRITE IN THIS SPACE	
	Case	Date Filed

INSTRUCTIONS:
File an original and 4 copies of this charge with NLRB Regional Director for the region in which the alleged unfair labor practice occurred or is occurring.

1. EMPLOYER AGAINST WHOM CHARGE IS BROUGHT

a. Name of Employer	b. Number of workers employed

c. Address *(street, city, state, ZIP code)*	d. Employer Representative	e. Telephone No.

f. Type of Establishment *(factory, mine, wholesaler, etc.)*	g. Identify principal product or service

h. The above-named employer has engaged in and is engaging in unfair labor practices within the meaning of section 8(a), subsections (1) and *(list subsections)* _____ of the National Labor Relations Act, and these unfair labor practices are unfair practices affecting commerce within the meaning of the Act.

2. Basis of the Charge *(set forth a clear and concise statement of the facts constituting the alleged unfair labor practices)*

By the above and other acts, the above-named employer has interfered with, restrained, and coerced employees in the exercise of the rights guaranteed in Section 7 of the Act

3. Full name of party filing charge *(if labor organization, give full name, including local name and number)*

4a. Address *(street and number, city, state, and ZIP code)*	4b. Telephone No.

5. Full name of national or international labor organization of which it is an affiliate or constituent unit (to be filled in when charge is filed by a labor organization)

6. DECLARATION

I declare that I have read the above charge and that the statements are true to the best of my knowledge and belief.

By _____ _____
    (signature of representative or person making charge)   *(title, if any)*

Address _____
                                    (Telephone No.)   *(date)*

WILLFUL FALSE STATEMENTS ON THIS CHARGE CAN BE PUNISHED BY FINE AND IMPRISONMENT (U.S. CODE, TITLE 18, SECTION 1001)

| Table 5-1 | Disposition of NLRB Cases–1989 | | |

Disposition	Number of Cases	Percentage of Cases
Regional director to issue complaint	10,411	100%
Settled *before* complaint issued	6,473	62
Settled *after* complaint but *before* hearing	3,598	24
Withdrawn after complaint issued	273	2
Decided by ALJ (administrative law judge) board or court decision	798	7
Dismissed after hearing	269	2

Source: Matthew M. Franckiewicz, "How to Win NLRB Cases: Tips from a Former Insider," *Labor Law Journal* (January 1993), pp. 40–47. Reprinted from the January 1993 issue of the *Labor Law Journal*, published and copyrighted 1993 by CHH Incorporated, 4025 W. Peterson Avenue, Chicago, IL 60646. All rights reserved.

cannot convince the parties to settle, a hearing is held before an administrative law judge. The decision of the administrative law judge may be appealed to the NLRB, which will decide the case through a subpanel of three members randomly selected by its executive secretary.[3]

A party who disagrees with an NLRB decision can appeal to a federal court. Recent statistics, however, show that less than 3 percent of the unfair labor practice cases brought to the NLRB actually ended up in a litigation process, either in the NLRB or in federal court. The study demonstrated how cases are resolved through the NLRB process. When a complaint is filed it is assigned to an agent of the regional director in the NLRB region with jurisdiction over the parties. The agent is under tight time restraints to investigate the charges and make a recommendation to the regional director. Statistics show that the decision of a regional director to issue a complaint or not almost always determines the ultimate outcome of the charges. With that in mind, the practice of the NLRB regional directors is to let the parties know which way the decision is going to go and to give the losing party a choice of withdrawing (if the charging party is going to lose) or offering a settlement (if the charged party is going to lose).[4] The success of this precharging process can be seen in the statistics in Table 5-1 showing the disposition of NLRB cases in a typical year.

As presidential appointees, board members are part of the political process, and their decision making should not be viewed as a pure exercise in administrative law. Recent studies indicate a high probability that board decisions in unfair labor practices reflect the appointing president's political philosophy toward labor-management relations. Frequent board turnover can influence the stability of decisions, having a negative impact upon the national labor-management relations policy.[5] Critics and supporters alike noted a dramatic shift in board decisions beginning with the Reagan administration. Union attorneys cite a number of those decisions as undermining employees' basic rights under the NLRA,[6] whereas management attorneys saw the shift as the proper return to a middle ground with the board recovering from a pro-union bias.[7]

Union advocates cheered the return of a Democrat to the White House as the opportunity to change the direction of the NLRB. It has been noted that, although

WILLIAM B. GOULD IV, NLRB CHAIRMAN

The nation's basic labor law is in need of reform to encourage worker-manager cooperation and to make union organizing easier, but such reform is unlikely, says William B. Gould IV, Chairman of the National Labor Relations Board. Gould adds, however, that politics is the reason that the change will not occur.

"Politically, it would take a shift in Congress" to the Democrats for labor law reform to occur, he said. "Bare majorities will not provide a margin, because in the Senate you're faced with a filibuster." Instead, Gould hopes for a slim Democratic majority, which would mean "we are not faced with these constant attacks which threaten our existence and viability as an agency and the basis of our statute," the 1935 National Labor Relations Act.

Gould supports:

1. Rewriting labor law to allow union representation elections to proceed first, with challenges to ballots and results afterward. "That's one of the most important reforms Congress could do," Gould says, since employers delay many elections for months or years through legal challenges, hoping to wear out the unions.
2. Establishment, probably by state laws, of state-run workplace councils to deal with issues such as safety and health, discharge and discipline. Gould's model is safety and health councils, with workers and managers, in Washington State and Oregon.
3. Amending labor law to "promote voluntary creation" of groups of "minority representation" on specific workplace issues.
4. Mandatory arbitration for first contracts. Too often, after unions win representation elections, companies refuse to bargain on first contracts.
5. Larger fines. Gould says employers who violate labor law should be fined "double or triple back pay for egregious misconduct." Right now, employers are fined only back pay and damages, minus any pay the injured workers have earned while their cases were tried.

Adapted from UAW, *The Unionite*, August 28, 1996.

both management and government attorneys had been appointed to the NLRB, since the mid-1960s *no* union attorney has been appointed.[8] However, President Clinton's appointment of William Gould (see Profile 5-1) has given the NLRB a pro-labor chairman, for the first time in decades.

Section 10(j): Court Injunctions

Section 10(j) of the NLRA permits the NLRB to seek a federal court injunction in situations in which the action of the union or employer might cause substantial harm to the other side. The court in response can then order either party to resume or desist from a certain action. In general, the NLRB must demonstrate that the unfair labor practice, if left alone, will irreparably harm the other side before a final NLRB decision can be administered, or "justice delayed is justice denied." In the 1994–1996 baseball strike, for example, players would have found their abilities slipping with increasing age, so a U.S. District Court ordered the owners to abide by the old contract and to "play ball" until a new one was reached. Some baseball

Figure 5-2

Drabble

Source: DRABBLE © United Feature Syndicate, Reprinted by Permission.

fans believed that the NLRB saved the game (see Figure 5-2). Most Section 10(j) cases fall within the following 13 categories:[9]

1. Union organizing campaign interference
2. Subcontracting work to outside employers
3. Withdrawing recognition of the union
4. Undermining or denigrating the members of the union's bargaining team
5. Granting exclusive representation to a minority union
6. Successor employer refusing to recognize and bargain
7. Bad faith conduct during negotiations
8. Picketing violence
9. Strike or picketing notice or waiting period violations
10. Employer refusal to allow protected activity on private property
11. Retaliation for NLRB processes
12. Close down of operations during litigation
13. Union coercion to achieve unlawful object

Union Organizing Campaigns

Employer Interference with Employee Rights.   The violation of Section 8(a)(1) of the National Labor Relations Act, dealing with interfering, restraining, or coercing employees in the exercise of their rights guaranteed by Section 7, can be direct through numerous types of interfering activities or indirect through violations of enumerated unfair labor practices actions.

To determine an unfair labor practice by an employer, the NLRB must find that the act interfered with, restrained, or coerced an action protected under the law. It must also be determined, under a reasonable probability test, that the employer's conduct could have an interfering, restraining, or coercive effect on employees. Within some constraints, the employer's motivation also must be weighed. Protected activities will be illustrated in specific examples.

The NLRB's reasonable probability test eliminates the need to prove *actual* interference, restraint, or coercion by the employer if it can be shown that the activity *tends* to interfere with the free exercise of protected rights.[10] The courts, however, distinguish between inherently discriminatory or destructive violations of employee rights when an employer could foresee the unlawful consequences, and those not so blatantly in violation. A hostile motive may be necessary to establish proof of an unfair labor practice if the activity itself can be objectively viewed as nondestructive. The kind of practice that most often evokes the need to prove intent is one motivated by a legitimate and substantial business justification.[11] In such cases, an actual intent to frustrate the purposes of the act must be found to warrant an unfair labor practice charge.

In a 1953 case, *Peerless Plywood Co.*[12] the NLRB detailed a **24-hour rule**, which it has maintained for more than 40 years. The 24-hour rule prohibits employers and unions from making organizational campaign speeches on company time to large assemblies of employees within 24 hours of a scheduled election. It does not prohibit voluntary assemblies on or off company time or written material.[13]

Protected Activities. The right of self-organization and participation in a labor union includes the right to engage in organizational campaigns. In many cases, the exercise of that right directly opposes the employer's right to maintain a work environment. The courts have devised rules, based on the NLRB's opinion that working time is for work, to balance the two interests. However, time outside working time is personal and may be used without unreasonable restraint, even on the employer's property. This includes lunchtime, break time, rest periods, and before and after the regular workday. The Supreme Court upheld this opinion in **Republic Aviation**, stating that rules prohibiting union solicitation by employees outside working time, even on employer's property, were an unreasonable impediment to self-organization.[14]

The courts, however, have long viewed organization by employees and organization by nonemployees as distinct when deciding on the right of access to employer premises. Rules prohibiting nonemployee union organizers from solicitation on the employer's property have not been considered an unfair labor practice if there were other *reasonable* means to reach employees. With a Supreme Court decision in 1992, however, this standard has changed. The Supreme Court in the **Lechmere** case decided that an employer would not be committing an unfair labor practice when barring nonemployees access to its property if there was *any other* means to reach the employees.[15] In the *Lechmere* case, the employer banned union organizers from leafleting cars in the employer's retailer parking lot, which was clearly open to the public. But because the union organizers were able to picket on a public space outside of the parking lot, Justice Clarence Thomas wrote in his opinion that the nonemployee union organizers had reasonable access to the employees outside the employer's property. Because such access existed, there was to be no "balancing" of the employer-employee rights used in other cases.

A 1996 federal appeals court decision reaffirmed the *Lechmere* decision and, to a certain extent, expanded it. In *UFCW Local No. 880 v. NLRB*, the court ruled against a union's request to find the employer, a retail store, guilty of an unfair labor practice when the employer refused the union access to its parking lot to distribute boycott information to the store's customers. Relying on the Lechmere reasoning, the Court noted that the availability of mass media alone to reach the store's customers gives the union a reasonable alternative to what the court termed "trespass access."[16]

Activities protected under the National Labor Relations Act include the following:

1. **Solicitation and distribution.** Oral solicitation by employees is allowed on the work premises during nonworking times. But distribution of union literature is restricted to nonworking times and areas. The board based this decision on employers' representations that such literature could clutter the workplace. No rule, however, is without exceptions. If justified by the nature of the business, a no-solicitation rule restricting employees even on nonworking time can be defended. Examples include department stores, restaurants, and patient care areas of hospitals where the public nature of the working area would prohibit normal interaction between employees. Conversely, an otherwise valid rule aimed only at nonemployees or employees during work time might be found an unfair labor practice by the employer if the institution of such a rule coincides with intensive union activity, the first violator of the rule is a union employee, other solicitations during work time are allowed, or a pattern of conduct hostile to union organization has been found. Table 5-2 demonstrates the application of no-solicitation and no-distribution rules for both employees and nonemployees under current board decisions. Work *time* refers to that time when an employee is actually working and no solicitation may occur. Work *hours*, on the other hand, are those hours when the company is open, including personal times such as lunch and breaks, during which the employee may be solicited.

2. **Union buttons or insignias.** Another protected activity is the wearing of union buttons or insignias. This right is balanced against the employer's right to conduct business. If a button or insignia should in particular circumstances cause a disturbance, present a health hazard, distract workers, cause damage to a product, or offend or distract customers, it may be prohibited. The NLRB in 1985, however, refused to allow an employer to discharge a construction employee who had a union insignia sticker on his helmet because no special circumstance existed to make the removal necessary to maintain production or discipline or to ensure safety.[17]

3. **Bulletin boards and meeting halls.** Employees have no statutory right to use an employer's bulletin board. However, if the employees are allowed access to the bulletin board, the employer cannot censor the material to exclude union solicitation. Meeting halls fall under the same rule. If access has been allowed to employees on an unrestricted basis, use by employees for union organization cannot be the *only* exception. Also, if the physical location of the business makes other meeting places inaccessible, and the employer does not normally give employees access to the hall, her subsequent refusal might result in an unfair labor practice charge. In one 1986 case, the NLRB found an unfair labor practice when the company denied the union access to employee mailboxes that the union had been using to distribute literature for 40 years. Although the company claimed that the union could reach employees by other means, their denial was found discriminatory because other groups were allowed access to the mailboxes.[18]

Prohibited Conduct.   Several employer activities constitute violations of the act (*prohibited conduct*) because of their attempt to frustrate or to further union organizational efforts. Some common examples of prohibited conduct follow:

1. **Campaign propaganda and misrepresentation.** In the conduct of representation elections, the board routinely ignores rhetoric, realizing that it is part of

| **Table 5-2**

Rule	Employee Status	Time	Place	Legal Presumption
No solicitation[1]	Employee and nonemployee	Work "time"	Work or nonwork	Valid
No solicitation[1]	Employee and nonemployee	Work "hours"	Work or nonwork	Invalid
No solicitation[1]	Employee and nonemployee	Nonwork	Work or nonwork	Invalid
No distribution[2]	Employee	Work	Work	Valid
No distribution[2]	Employee	Nonwork	Work	Invalid
No distribution[2]	Employee	Work	Nonwork	Invalid
No distribution[2]	Employee	Nonwork	Nonwork	Invalid
No distribution[3]	Nonemployee	Work	Work	Valid
No distribution[3]	Nonemployee	Nonwork	Work	Valid
No distribution[3]	Nonemployee	Work	Nonwork	Valid
No distribution[3]	Nonemployee	Nonwork	Nonwork	Valid

[1]For no-solicitation rules governing employees and nonemployees, *work* versus *nonwork* time was the key factor under *Essex,* and the *place* was irrelevant. Under DRW all such rules without clarification are presumptively invalid. Now, under *Our Way* the rule returns to *Essex.*

[2]For no-distribution rules governing employees, *workplace* is still a factor.

[3]In the case of no-distribution rules governing nonemployees, neither the time nor the place is a factor and all are presumptively valid where other means are available to reach the employees.

Source: Adapted from Thomas F. Phalen Jr., "The Destabilization of Federal Labor Policy under the Reagan Board," *Labor Lawyer* 2, no. 1 (Winter 1986), p. 31.

any election campaign and usually will be disregarded by employees in making decisions. But such an attitude is flexible if the rights of the parties to an untrammeled choice are in jeopardy. In the **Midland National Life Insurance Company** case, the NLRB stated that it would intervene in cases in which forgery would render the voters unable to discern the propagandistic nature of a publication.[19] Also an employer was found to have interfered with an election when it provided a $250 prize to the employee who scored highest on a test that determined knowledge of the process used in decertifying a union.[20]

Misleading information on wage and fringe benefit data, proffered by the union to encourage unionization, is often seen by the board as exaggeration, but if viewed by the courts as more serious, it can cause the election to be invalidated.[21]

2. **Threats and loss of benefits.** Unlike mere campaign rhetoric, the actual reduction or withholding of benefits as a method of combatting an organizational drive constitutes interference. Direct threats of economic reprisals issued to thwart a representation election will result in an unfair labor practice finding (see Case 5-1). These include discharge; loss of pay or benefits; more onerous working conditions; and threats of plant closure, physical violence, or permanent replacement of strikers. It is more difficult to ascertain an unfair labor practice when threats of reprisals or promises of benefits are merely implied.

Under the *Gissel* case, an employer is not prohibited from communicating general views about unionism or predictions of the effect of unionization on the company, as long as such predictions involve consequences outside of the employer's control.[22] The Court added a subjective test of what the speaker intended

CASE 5-1

UNFAIR LABOR PRACTICE BY AN EMPLOYER

For 20 years the experienced and apprentice wire weavers of the company had been represented by a union. But after a 13-week strike, the relationship ended. For almost 13 years thereafter the employees were not represented by any union.

A new union began organizing employees and, having reached majority status, requested that it meet with the company. The company refused to recognize the union. An election was held, and the union lost by a vote of seven to six. The union petitioned the NLRB to set aside the election because the preelection conduct of the company's president was an unfair labor practice. The board agreed, set aside the election, and entered an unfair labor practice charge. The company appealed.

Decision

The court examined the preelection conduct of the president. He had on numerous occasions, orally and in writing, urged the 14 employees to reject the union. He claimed that the union's only weapon was a strike, and that the last strike had nearly ruined the company. He also warned that the company was still not financially secure and that a strike could close the plant. He denounced the particular union and its top officials as corrupt and strike-happy. He added that the wire weavers' age and lack of education would make it difficult for them to find other jobs. The company defended the preelection remarks on the grounds that the remarks were true.

The court pointed out that an employer's predictions of economic consequences must be demonstrable and not just based on the feelings of the employer. It also stated that the test of the coercive effect of such statements includes the total circumstances surrounding them.

The court affirmed the board's finding that the president's conduct interfered with the employees' exercise of a free and untrammeled choice in the election.

Adapted from *National Labor Relations Board v. Sinclair Company*, 397 F.2d 157 (1968).

and the listener understood to ensure that veiled threats would not coerce employee actions. To determine the coercive nature of a statement, a court should examine the total context in which the statement is made. Elements to be reviewed include the presence or absence of other unfair labor practice incidents, the actual content of the communication, the exact language used, the employer's history of dealing with unions, and the identity of the speaker.[23]

A 1996 NLRB decision outlined a new test to be utilized in cases involving employer threats of loss of benefits during a representation election. The new test provides that employers may not distribute propaganda regarding possible loss of benefits if workers are unionized *within 24 hours of the opening of the polls* in an election. In the *Kalin Construction Co.* case the employer distributed two separate "paychecks" to workers as they approached the polls in a representation election. One "check" showed what the average worker would earn if the union won, the second showed those benefits that would be lost if the union won. The union lost the election and filed an unfair labor charge. The NLRB agreed that workers' freedom of choice had been affected and ordered a new election.[24]

3. **Promise or grant of benefit.** The promise of economic benefits by the employer if employees reject unionization will violate the National Labor Relations Act, as will the promise or grant of economic benefits during an organizational

campaign to influence the outcome of an election or to discourage organizational activities. The fact that there is no direct link between receipt of the benefit and a vote against the union is unimportant; the courts look to the implication of such largesse. The employee may be impressed with the power of the employer's discretion to give and presumably take away benefits. However, the granting of benefits during a union campaign has not always been held a violation of the act. The board does not favor a per se approach but will examine each case within context. Clearly, offering money while urging a vote in a particular way will be considered coercive. In other cases, the board has found interference when salary increases were made in the context of repeated references to unionization, made effective just before an election, or announced before an election when there was no particular reason to do so.[25] On the other hand, a salary increase has been found not to interfere with the employee's right to organize when the timing, amount, and application of the increase were consistent with past practice.[26]

Some employers' benefits, such as free access to vending machines, have been found to be too minimal to affect the outcome of an election. Also, benefits provided to multiple locations—including some outside a campaign—can be permitted.[27]

Unions can also be charged with unfair labor practices pertaining to promises. If the promise is within the bounds of what union representation can do for employees in relationship to their employer, it is probably not legally objectionable. However, promising economic benefits from the union itself, such as life insurance coverage or a waiver of union dues, has been found to be coercive.

4. **Interrogation and polling of employees.** The NLRB originally viewed all employer interrogation of employees as to union sympathy as unlawful per se for two reasons: Such interrogation instills a fear of discrimination in the mind of the employee, thereby restraining freedom of choice, and no purpose could be served by such inquiry except to identify employees with union sympathies.

The courts, however, chose not to view employee interrogation as a per se violation and instead examined it within the context of the inquiry. As a result, the board set its standard for polling of employees in the ***Struksnes Construction Co. case***:

> Absent unusual circumstances, the polling of employees by an employer will be violative of Section 8(a)(1) of the act unless the following safeguards are observed: the purpose of the poll is to determine the truth of a union's claim of majority, this purpose is communicated to the employees, assurances against reprisals are given, the employees are polled by secret ballot, and the employer has not engaged in unfair labor practices or otherwise created a coercive atmosphere.[28]

Individual or isolated questioning of employees is not a per se violation of the act. Tests of noncoercive questioning are whether an employer has a legitimate interest in the information sought, the employee is assured that no reprisals will result from the answer, and there is no evidence of coercion in the interrogation itself. Such interrogation can arise when an employer attempts to prepare a defense for a National Labor Relations Board unfair labor practice proceeding. However, if under all the circumstances the interrogation reasonably tends to restrain or interfere with employees in the exercise of their rights, it will be held unlawful. Previously the board had held that questioning of open and well-known union adherents was inherently coercive, but under its decision in ***Rossmore House***, the totality of the circumstances must now be examined to determine if a violation has occurred.[29]

The board has developed the following detailed criteria to protect the interests of both parties:

a. The purpose of the questioning must be communicated to the employee.
b. An assurance of no reprisal must be given.
c. The employee's participation must be obtained on a voluntary basis.
d. The questioning must take place in an atmosphere free from union animus.
e. The questioning itself must not be coercive in nature.
f. The questions must be relevant to the issues involved in the complaint.
g. The employee's subjective state of mind must not be probed.
h. The questions must not otherwise interfere with the statutory rights of employees.[30]

5. **Surveillance.** Surveillance in almost any form has been held a violation of the unfair labor practices section of the National Labor Relations Act. The board has such an aversion to surveillance it will uphold findings even if the employees know nothing about it or the surveillance was only an employer's attempt to foster an impression of scrutiny. Encouraging surveillance and eavesdropping by union members has also been condemned by the NLRB.

6. **Poll activity.** The NLRB prohibits any electioneering at or near the polls in a campaign. In fact, in *Milchem, Inc.*, the NLRB applied a strict rule that conversations between company or union officials in the polling area is prohibited, regardless of what is discussed. Although the exact distance within this rule varies, the NLRB often sets a radius of 100 feet around the polls.[31]

Employer Domination of and Assistance to Labor Organizations

Under the National Labor Relations Act, employers' domination of and assistance to labor organizations are unfair labor practices. This provision obviously reflects the historical aversion to company unions of the 1930s, which were used to discourage outside union organization. The National Labor Relations Act views employer interference in the internal workings of a union as a threat to the employees' free exercise of guaranteed rights.

The unlawful domination and assistance pertains only to labor organizations. Employee recreation committees, credit unions, social clubs, and the like may be initiated and supported by the employer without violation.

Employer Domination and Interference. Once a labor organization is identified, the board will look for prohibited domination or support. *Support* is mere assistance to a favored union, whereas *domination* means actual control of the union. An employer-created organization falls within the prohibited controls section of the act. Domination of a union may also be found when a union is not created by the employer. The employer's behavior toward an existing union may result in the employees' freedom of choice being unlawfully infringed. Courts have found domination when supervisors solicited union membership, the employer's attorney acted for the union in drafting its constitution and bylaws, and the employer allowed union officials on company time and property to pursue a union organization drive. Tests for domination are subjective from the standpoint of the employees.[32]

Another violation of this section is employer interference by friendly cooperation with the creation or operation of a labor organization. A suggestion in and of itself by an employer that a union be formed is not an unfair labor practice, but interference may be found if the suggestion is timed to counter an organizational drive by an outside union. After a union has been recognized, a violation may occur if supervisors and company executives who gained membership status prior to their promotions remain in the union.

Employer Support and Assistance.   Although domination and control of a labor organization clearly violate the act, support and assistance of a labor organization by the employer present a different problem. Often the suspect activities may be a manifestation of the employer's legal cooperation with the union. If the support does not have any effect on the employees' exercise of their rights guaranteed by the act and is trivial, no violation will be found.

Assistance or support that does violate the act is employer aid to one of two competing unions. The employer can unlawfully favor one union by giving direct assistance to its campaign drive, by allowing it exclusive use of company facilities, by supplying the union with employee names to aid in a raid of the other union's membership, and by assessing and collecting union dues without signed authorization cards. Prior to 1982, continuing to recognize an incumbent union when an election challenge is pending would have been a violation of the act. The board determined in that year that the mere filing of a representation petition by an outside union does not require or permit an employer to withdraw from bargaining with the incumbent union.[33] Financial support of a union, either directly by donating money or indirectly by, for instance, allowing the union to receive the profits from company-owned vending machines, are other violations of the support and assistance provisions. In Case 5-2, employer-employee cooperation came under NLRB scrutiny for a determination as to whether the support involved employer domination.

Employee Teams.   The emergence of total quality management and teamwork principles in the workplace, as discussed in chapter 2, has created a new area for charges of unfair labor practices. The NLRB decided in two publicized cases in 1992, *Electromation*[34] and *duPont*,[35] that the employer-employee committees formed to make recommendations on improvements to the workplace violated the domination provision of the NLRA.

In *Electromation*, a nonunion company announced several changes in its personnel policies, including no wage increase for the upcoming year. In reaction to employee complaints over these changes, the employer established five action committees made up of management representatives and employees who volunteered to participate. The employer scheduled the meetings during the regular workday. It was anticipated that the recommendations of the committees would be implemented. A union-organizing campaign was begun *after* the action committees were functional. The union brought an unfair labor charge, and the NLRB ruled in the union's favor, noting that the committees were obviously *labor organizations* under the act and dominated by the employer.

In the *duPont* case, an employer-sponsored employee participation program with unionized employees was also found to have been an unfair labor practice. duPont created employee-management committees to deal with safety and

DOMINATION

The professional employees of a medium-sized architectural firm voted to be represented by a union. More than a year later, after months of unsuccessful negotiations, an employee petitioned for a decertification election.

The union lost the election. Immediately after the election, a partner in the firm called a meeting of partners and professional personnel to ask for suggestions on ensuring management-employee dialogue.

An employee suggested a committee system whereby five in-house committees, composed of five employees and one management representative, would examine a different area of employee concern, such as wages. Two employees seconded his idea, and the plan was overwhelmingly approved. An employee suggested that the partners vote on the proposal, too. They did, and it passed unanimously. The committees met on company time without loss of pay. On some committees the managers voted; on some they did not.

The union filed an unfair labor practice charge against the employer for supporting and dominating a labor organization. The National Labor Relations Board agreed and ordered the employer to withdraw recognition and support of and to disestablish the employees' committees. The employer appealed.

Decision

The Supreme Court pointed out that there is a line between employer cooperation, which the act encourages, and employer domination, which the act condemns. That line is crossed when, from the standpoint of the employee, freedom of choice has been stifled.

The Court found that the totality of circumstances in this case did not show such domination. Allowing the committees to meet on company time alone is not unlawful support. The Court noted that the idea for the committee system came from an employee and was supported and approved by other employees. Placing a management representative on the committees was also an employee's idea. The Court noted that the manager's vote, when he has a vote at all, is just one of six.

Under these facts, the Court reversed the board's finding.

Adapted from *Hertzka & Knowles v. National Labor Relations Board*, 46 L.Ed. 2d 106 (1975).

recreation issues at one of its plants. The union charged duPont with an unfair labor practice for creating and dominating a labor organization. Again, the NLRB agreed and ordered the committees disbanded.[36]

Could, in fact, participation by employees in such programs or teams affect their attitudes toward unions and the need for collective bargaining? In a survey of 200 organizational campaigns, Professor James Rundle of Cornell University found that 7 percent of the companies had employee participation programs in 1988 and 32 percent in 1994. He also found that in almost half of the elections in companies with *no* employee organization the union won the organizational campaign, whereas in companies with employee participation groups the success rate was less than one-third.[37]

Remedies. If employer control or interference in a labor organization is so extensive that it results in employer domination, the board will disestablish the union. To ensure the removal of the employer from union activities, the board requires a public announcement that the company will cease bargaining with and will withdraw its support from the union. The employer must take no part in any reorganization by employees.

If only support and not domination is found, the NLRB applies a less stringent remedy. Union recognition is withdrawn until the employer's support is eliminated and a new certification election is held.

Discrimination in Employment

Discrimination against employees, based on their union activities, is an unfair labor practice and an obvious deterrent to successful collective bargaining. A violation of the act occurs when an employer encourages or discourages membership in any labor organization by hiring or tenure practices or by using membership as a term or condition of employment.

Discrimination occurs when a union member is treated differently from a nonunion worker because he or she is involved in union activity. In general, the fact that a particular incident took place is not an issue. It is easy to ascertain that a refusal to hire, a discharge, or a change in an employment condition has occurred. The question for the board to resolve is whether the action was motivated by a desire to encourage or discourage union membership and thereby discriminate against the member.

An employer has a right to select employees and take disciplinary action to maintain good business conditions. The NLRB must weigh claims of discrimination by the employee against claims by the employer that certain actions were taken for cause.

Discrimination cases fall into two categories. In **dual-motive cases**, the employer puts forth two explanations for the action complained of. One constitutes a legitimate business reason and the other is a reason prohibited under the act. In a **pretext case**, the employer puts forth only the legitimate business reason, but the complainant asserts that the prohibited reason is the true cause for the action. Approximately 60 percent of the unfair labor practice cases presented to the board involve a charge of discrimination for union activity. Prior to 1980, the board's test in these cases was to decide if the anti-union animus of the employer played a part in the complaint. If so, the employer was found to have violated the act. Since then, however, the board has required the employee to present a prima facie case that the anti-union animus of the employer played a substantial or motivating role in the complaint before requiring the employer to justify the action taken.[38]

Discriminatory acts by the employer in compliance with a *union shop* provision in a collective bargaining agreement do not violate the act. The act specifically allows a collective bargaining agreement to require that new employees join the union within 30 days of employment.

Applicants for jobs as well as persons already employed are protected by the act. The language, "discrimination in regard to hire," could stand no other interpretation. Therefore, it is an unfair labor practice for an employer to refuse to hire an applicant because of union activities. It is also a violation to offer employment on the condition that the applicant will not join or participate in a union.

Obvious acts of discrimination against employees regarding wages, hours, and working conditions will lead to charges of unfair labor practices. As discussed earlier, withholding benefits pending union recognition elections is an unfair labor practice if the purpose is to influence the election.

Discrimination can arise when an employer treats striking employees differently from nonstriking employees. For example, discrimination may be found if an employer announces that he or she will pay vacation benefits under an expired agreement to returning strikers, nonstriking workers, and strike replacements, but not to strikers.

Concerted Activities.   Employers that discriminate against employees for engaging in concerted activities violate the interference, restraint, or coercion provisions of the unfair labor practices section of the act and also violate the discrimination for purposes of discouraging union membership provision.

Concerted activity is any action by employees to further legitimately their common interests pursued on behalf of or with other employees and not solely by and on behalf of an individual.[39] The most common form of concerted activity is the strike. Concerted activity need not involve union leadership or membership to be protected. To establish concerted activity, certain elements must exist: The issue involved must be work-related; the goal is to further a group interest; a specific remedy or result is sought; and the act itself must not be unlawful or improper.

The work-relatedness requirement is not stringently applied. The board has found many activities protected under the act:

1. Employees assisting another employer's personnel to unionize
2. Union resolution condemning employer's opposition to another union's strike
3. Union support of workers' compensation law changes
4. Union lobbying against the National Immigration Policy
5. Union lobbying against right-to-work laws[40]

Unprotected concerted activities occur when the employees are violent, act in breach of contract, or engage in activities otherwise prohibited by the act, such as jurisdictional strikes or secondary boycotts. Employees can lose the protection of Section 7's concerted activities if they take actions disproportionate to the grievance involved. Disparaging an employer's product without clarification of the context of the dispute is such an action.

A **primary strike** is a type of concerted activity protected under the act if it is called for economic reasons or to protest unfair labor practices. Any retaliation against employees participating in a primary strike is therefore an unfair labor practice. However, if the employer has replaced strikers participating in an economic strike, he or she need only reinstate those for whom there are vacant positions. In contrast, employees participating in a strike to protest an unfair labor practice are entitled to reinstatement and back pay, even if they have been replaced. Unlawful activity during a strike may be grounds for discharging an employee and would not subject an employer to an unfair labor practice charge. Also, an employer who discharges employees for breaching a collective bargaining agreement will not be guilty of an unfair labor practice. However, discharging or otherwise discriminating against an employee for filing charges or giving testimony is, under the National Labor Relations Act, specifically designated as an unfair labor practice.

Other employee concerted activities protected under the act are bringing a civil action against the employer unless done with malice or in bad faith; circulating a petition among coworkers calling for a union meeting to discuss current contract negotiations; complaining to local government authorities; and under

Union

What are the three most common unfair labor practices committed by employers and how should a union respond?

In the public sector right now, we find that a lot of our unfair labor practices involve giving away our unit work: subcontracting and privatization. We also find that there are numerous times where management treats union activists differently from other employees (anti-union animus) in efforts to silence or dampen the enthusiasm of union activists. Third, I guess we do see a lot of unilateral changes of terms and conditions of employment without management's meeting its bargaining obligations. As for the union response: it can only be to press the issue through whatever informal and formal mechanisms it has under its contract, before its labor board and even in the courts if appropriate. For a union to "sit on its rights" is to "sow the seeds" of its own undoing.

Management

What are the three most common unfair labor practices management should avoid and how can it do so?

a. Charge: 8(a)(3), discriminating against a union sympathizer/organizer/officer as regards discipline, especially termination. Avoid by either not touching those persons for violations of work rules (which makes managing the workforce very difficult) or (preferably) being doubly cautious in enforcing violations of work rules by such persons, that is, making absolutely certain that the violation and similar treatment for nonunion violators is well documented before taking action.

b. Charge: 8(a)(5), refusal to bargain/surface bargain intentionally or inadvertently, such as in unilaterally implementing a drug and alcohol policy. Avoid by scheduling sufficient numbers of negotiation sessions; being prepared and willing to make and listen to proposals; making some movement on at least some issues; not making public announcements either before bargaining commences or during the process (prior to impasse) that "X" is the company's position and that the union can go fly a kite or whatever if it thinks it will get any more, etc. With respect to the inadvertent stuff, make sure human resources and legal are working together in the implementation of any new or major changes to current policies or benefits to ensure no unintentional unilateral changes in terms or conditions of employment.

c. Charge: 8(a)(1), interference with employees in the exercise of their Section 7 rights. Avoid through soliciting information, spying, crossing over the line in an organizing campaign. Make sure thorough supervisory training is repeated regularly and supported by an adequately staffed and respected labor relations department available for immediate assistance, when necessary.

some circumstances, refusing to cross a picket line.[41] In addition, under the **Weingarten rule**, an employee's insistence on union representation at an investigatory interview, which the employee believes might result in disciplinary action, is protected concerted activity.[42]

However, the original *Weingarten* decision has been narrowed by subsequent board decisions. For example, the *Weingarten* protections apply only to union members;[43] the union employee cannot refuse to attend a meeting with management without a union representative because until the meeting begins the employee cannot know it is an investigatory interview;[44] and, a union steward can be expelled from an investigatory interview if the steward interferes with the employer's legitimate right to investigate.[45]

Concerted activities not considered protected are serious trespass, destruction of property, violence, and participating in an unlawful strike in violation of a no-strike clause in an applicable collective bargaining agreement.[46]

The Taft-Hartley Amendments to the National Labor Relations Act were a response to the perceived power of organized labor during the 1940s to dictate to the employer instead of meeting at the bargaining table as an equal. One aspect not previously covered by the National Labor Relations Act was the imposition of **unfair labor practice standards** against **labor organizations**. Figure 5-3 is a form used in filing charges against unions.

Restraint or Coercion of Employees

Unfair labor practice standards were applied to labor organizations to enforce an employee's right to refrain from union activities, which was granted by the Taft-Hartley Amendments. This right includes protection to work without restraint from strikes, to refuse to sign union dues check-offs, and not to be coerced into accepting a particular union or any union at all.

The amendments did not impair the right of a labor organization to prescribe its own rules on members in good standing. And if a union shop provision is part of a current collective bargaining agreement, an employee can be compelled to join the union after being hired and to pay dues or fees to retain employment. Nonetheless, in *Pattern Makers League v. National Labor Relations Board* the Supreme Court held that a union was guilty of an unfair labor practice when it attempted to fine its members for resigning from the union and returning to work during a strike. The Court believed that such fines were an attempt to compel membership in the union in violation of Section 8(b)(1)(A) of the act.[47]

The section of the amendments prohibiting unfair labor practices by unions can be violated only by a labor organization or its agent. Actions by individual employees not sanctioned by a union cannot subject the employee to an unfair labor practice charge.

The unfair labor practices provision prohibiting a union from restraining or coercing employees in the exercise of their guaranteed rights is not as broadly stated or as strictly enforced as the mirror provision affecting employers. Violent or otherwise threatening behavior, or clearly coercive or intimidating union activities are necessary before the NLRB will find an unfair labor practice. Union propaganda and peer pressure present in a situation in which employees belong to a union will not cause an unfair labor practice charge. Examine Case 5-3 for its facts in light of this criterion.

Specific activities are deemed to be in violation of the amendments:

1. Physical assaults or threats of violence directed at employees or their relatives
2. Threats of economic reprisals
3. Mass picketing that restrains the lawful entry or leaving of a worksite
4. Causing or attempting to cause an employer to discriminate against employees
5. Discriminating provisions in collective bargaining agreements (union shop being an exception), for example, superseniority clauses for union members that do not exist for a legitimate purpose[48]

Union Interference with Elections

The activities that concern representation elections, including the 24-hour rule, electioneering near polls, and coercion, apply equally to unions and employers. In addition, unions, under Section 8(b)(1)(A) of the NLRA are prohibited from the

FORM NLRB-508
(6-90)

UNITED STATES OF AMERICA
NATIONAL LABOR RELATIONS BOARD
**CHARGE AGAINST LABOR
ORGANIZATION OR ITS AGENTS**

FORM EXEMPT UNDER 44 U.S.C. 3512

DO NOT WRITE IN THIS SPACE	
Case	Date Filed

INSTRUCTIONS: File an original and 4 copies of this charge and an additional copy for each organization, each local, and each individual named in item 1 with the NLRB Regional Director of the region in which the alleged unfair labor practice occurred or is occurring.

1. LABOR ORGANIZATION OR ITS AGENTS AGAINST WHICH CHARGE IS BROUGHT	
a. Name	b. Union Representative to Contact

c. Telephone No.	d. Address *(street, city, state, ZIP code)*

e. The above-named organization(s) or its agents has *(have)* engaged in and is *(are)* engaging in unfair labor practices within the meaning of section 8(b), subsection(s) *(list subsections)* _____ of the National Labor Relations Act, and these unfair labor practices are unfair practices affecting commerce within the meaning of the Act.

2. Basis of the Charge *(set forth a clear and concise statement of the facts constituting the alleged unfair labor practices)*

3. Name of Employer	4. Telephone No.

5. Location of plant involved *(street, city, state and ZIP code)*	6. Employer representative to contact

7. Type of establishment *(factory, mine, wholesaler, etc.)*	8. Identify principal product or service	9. Number of workers employed

10. Full name of party filing charge

11. Address of party filing charge (street, city, state and ZIP code)	12. Telephone No.

13. DECLARATION

I declare that I have read the above charge and that the statements therein are true to the best of my knowledge and belief.

By _____   _____
(Signature of representative or person making charge)   (title or office, if any)

Address _____
(Telephone No.)   (date)

WILLFUL FALSE STATEMENTS ON THIS CHARGE CAN BE PUNISHED BY FINE AND IMPRISONMENT (U.S. CODE, TITLE 18, SECTION 1001).

UNFAIR LABOR PRACTICE BY A UNION

A union decided to try to organize employees of four direct mail companies. A plan was devised whereby a union organizer, accompanied by a group of persons acting on behalf of the union, would descend upon the four companies without permission and distribute union literature during working hours.

The nature of the union's conduct is illustrated by the following:

1. In the first incident, 25 men and women swarmed into the plant, moved to where employees were working, and began talking to employees about the union. All production stopped as a result of the commotion. When asked to leave, a union member suggested they call the police.

2. Two days later at another plant, 25 men and women entered by the front entrance and began talking to employees in the same manner as just described. At the same time, 12 men entered the plant from the rear and pushed by a manager who attempted to stop them. Again, work came to a halt.

3. One company, fearing it would be next, hired a uniformed guard. Twenty-five union members found the door unlocked, pushed past the armed guard, threatened to kill him with his own gun, and created a commotion.

The board found that the union had violated the National Labor Relations Act section prohibiting unfair labor practices by labor organizations. The union appealed.

Decision

The court upheld the board.

The act forbids a union from restraining or coercing employees in the exercise of their rights. The court noted that one right is to refrain from collective bargaining activities. The union's conduct, which included threats and physical violence, constituted illegal coercion.

Adapted from *National Labor Relations Board v. District 65, Retail, Wholesale & Department Store Union, AFL-CIO,* F.2d 745 (1967).

---

threat or use of violence against nonsupportive employees. Threats, if made by union organizers or merely supportive employees, may cause the NLRB to overturn an election.[49] For example, in *United Broadcasting Co. of New York*, a union steward told an employee he would be blacklisted and could never work again in New York—the union victory was overturned.[50]

DUTY TO BARGAIN IN GOOD FAITH

The National Labor Relations Act established a national policy to encourage collective bargaining as a way to eliminate or to mitigate industrial strife obstructing commerce. Employees seek strength in numbers by joining employee organizations to ensure equal bargaining powers. Under the National Labor Relations Act, employee organization is a *right*, protected and preserved. However, once that right is exercised, a duty is placed on both the employee organization and the employer to proceed to **bargain in good faith**.

Nature of the Duty

The Wagner (National Labor Relations) Act itself made it an unfair labor practice for an employer to refuse to bargain with representatives of his employees.[51] The NLRB, in enforcing that provision, imposed a good faith efforts test as a condition for compliance with this duty. The criteria established by the board included the following:

1. Active participation in deliberations with an intention to find a basis for agreement
2. A sincere effort to reach a common ground
3. Binding agreements on mutually acceptable terms[52]

The board found indications of less than good faith when employers met directly with employees outside the bargaining process to reach an agreement not sanctioned by their representatives, when an employer refused to put the agreement in writing even after all issues were agreed to, or when an employer refused to make counterproposals.[53]

The comprehensive inclusion of unions in the unfair labor practices section of the National Labor Relations Act by the Taft-Hartley Amendments placed an equal obligation to bargain in good faith on employees. In addition, the board-imposed test of good faith to determine whether either party had refused to bargain was included in the amendments.[54]

The amendments also clarified what was meant by bargaining: to meet at reasonable times; to confer in good faith with respect to rates of pay, wages, hours of employment, or other conditions of employment; and to execute a written contract if the parties reach an agreement. However, the obligation to bargain does not compel either party to agree to a proposal or to make a concession.

In addition, the amendments imposed on the employer the duty to bargain in good faith when the collective bargaining representative requests that the employer meet for purposes of collective bargaining. The completion of a representation election alone does not trigger the bargaining process. Until the employer has been asked, there can be no breach of the duty to bargain.

When the duty to bargain has arisen, the amendments require that negotiations be conducted in good faith with the view of reaching an agreement. Merely going through the motions without actually seeking to adjust differences does not meet this stipulation.

Totality of Conduct Doctrine

A **totality of conduct** test is applied to determine the fulfillment of the good faith bargaining obligation. If, in total conduct, a party has negotiated with an open mind in a sincere attempt to reach an agreement, isolated acts will not prove bad faith. On the other hand, actions that are not per se unfair labor practices may indicate bad faith bargaining when viewed in the totality of the bargaining process.

Boulwarism. **Boulwarism** is a "take-it-or-leave-it" bargaining technique. Its name derives from Lemuel R. Boulware, a vice president for the General Electric Company, who negotiated for that company in the late 1940s. Using this technique, a company presents a comprehensive contract proposal that, in its opinion, has included all that is necessary or warranted. This form of negotiation eliminates any need to compromise in the employer's mind. Such a proposal is presented at the outset with the understanding that nothing is being held back for later trading, and employees are notified it is a final offer. This practice places the employer in the untenable position of not being able to negotiate. The NLRB declared an attitude of boulwarism a violation of the duty to bargain. It noted that, although the formality of bargaining is followed—no illegal or nonmandatory subjects are insisted upon, and an intent to enter into an agreement is exhibited—there exists no serious intent to adjust differences and to reach a common ground.

A 1964 decision (confirmed in 1969) involving this procedure as practiced by the General Electric Company gave the NLRB a chance to examine the technique in detail. The company had examined all relevant facts and had anticipated union demands. It actively communicated its position to employees prior to the negotiation session. It presented what it considered a fair and firm offer, although representations were made that new information could alter its position. The company was found to have failed in its duty to bargain in good faith because it failed to furnish information requested by the union; it had attempted to bypass the international union and to bargain directly with local unions; it had presented a "take-it-or-leave-it" insurance proposal; and it had, in its overall attitude and approach as evidenced by the totality of its conduct, failed in the good faith test.[55]

By the examination of the totality of conduct, the court expanded the understanding of the duty to bargain collectively by emphasizing the *collective* nature of the duty as contained in the National Labor Relations Act. Involvement is a bilateral procedure, allowing both parties a voice in the agreements reached. It is in direct opposition to the intent and purpose of the act for a party to assume the role of decision maker; an exchange of options must be presented and received with an open mind.

The technique of boulwarism, although most often used by an employer, has also been used by unions. In *Utility Workers (Ohio Power Company)*, the board found a union violating the duty to bargain in good faith when the union insisted that identical offers be made to several bargaining units and conditioned acceptance in any single unit upon submission of identical offers to all units.[56]

Surface Bargaining. Another violation of the good faith duty can be evidenced by **surface bargaining**; that is, simply going through the motions without any real intention of arriving at an agreement. A totality test is used to determine surface bargaining. Surface bargaining can occur when a party has rejected a proposal and offered its own and does not attempt to reconcile the differences, or it can be used when a party's only proposal is the continuation of existing practices.[57]

Extensive negotiation in and of itself will not justify a finding of surface bargaining because the National Labor Relations Act does not compel parties to agree to proposals or to make concessions. Hard bargaining on a major issue does not exhibit bad faith because a party is not required to yield on a position fairly maintained. Even if open hostility is exhibited by the parties, surface bargaining may not be charged if the totality of the bargaining process complies with the dictates of the act.

The National Labor Relations Board uses these factors when considering an unfair labor charge for surface bargaining:

1. Prior bargaining history of the parties
2. Parties' willingness to make concessions
3. The character of exchanged proposals and demands
4. Any dilatory tactics used during negotiations
5. Conditions imposed by either party as necessary to reaching an agreement
6. Unilateral changes made during the bargaining process in conditions subject to bargaining
7. Communications by employer to individual employees
8. Any unfair labor practices committed during bargaining[58]

Although the National Labor Relations Act does not require a party to make concessions, courts have consistently viewed a *willingness to make concessions* as evidence of good faith. Parties are encouraged to engage in **auction bargaining**, in which parties state their positions, make proposals, and then trade off on those proposals to arrive at agreeable terms. Refusal to make any concessions, evidenced by inflexibility on major issues, can be held as bad faith. An intransigent attitude on some issues may be acceptable if bargaining continues on other issues.[59]

The degree to which either party stalls or uses **delaying tactics** to avoid collective bargaining is considered by the NLRB in its totality review. Obviously, a complete refusal to meet and to bargain violates the act. Scheduling meetings infrequently or canceling scheduled meetings can also evidence bad faith. Prolonged discussions on formalities designed to thwart the collective bargaining process will be considered bad faith. The number or length of negotiation sessions alone cannot determine good or bad faith, but the NLRB frequently reviews meeting history to determine an employer's charge of bad faith. Also, although there is no hard-and-fast rule as to how many or how long, a review of case decisions shows the *board's* preference for frequent meetings—79 in 11 months, 11 in 5 months, 11 in 4 months, 37 in 10 months.[60]

Employers may be guilty of bad faith if they unilaterally change conditions, such as employees' wages, rates of pay, or hours of employment, during contract negotiations. If such changes in benefits are considered better than those being offered at the table, bad faith is clearly evidenced.[61] The act seeks to avoid this attempt to bypass the union and to deal directly with employees. However, there are exceptions to this rule. If an impasse is reached that is not the result of the employer's bad faith, a unilateral increase of benefits is not evidence of bad faith.

An increasing number of employers have tried to present a "business necessity" defense for making unilateral changes when a collective bargaining agreement is not in effect. Such a defense has been successful in limited cases in which the employer demonstrated a good faith inability to maintain the status quo because of necessary business considerations.[62]

Bypassing the bargaining representation by attempting to **negotiate with employees** will often be held as a violation of the duty to bargain in good faith. The courts, in reviewing the National Labor Relations Act, found it was the employer's duty to recognize the union and conduct negotiations through the union rather than deal directly with employees. This is an obligation even if the employer traditionally had contracts with individual workers. The collective bargaining contract will supersede such contracts.[63] One exception to this rule is that if a union refuses a final offer, the employer may communicate that offer directly to employees.

The good faith test includes the duty to send negotiators to the table with sufficient **authority** to carry on meaningful negotiations. All attempts to delay commitment by the recourse of management representatives to check with some final authority are scrutinized closely for evidence of bad faith. However, the obligation of the union representative to take a contract back for a vote of union members before acceptance is not a violation of the duty to bargain in good faith.

Unfair labor practices during contract negotiations evidence bad faith. Threats to close a plant or to engage in discriminating layoffs during bargaining have been held to be in bad faith. To encourage the decertification of a union or to assist employees in the decertification process has also been found to obstruct the bargaining process.

Duty to Furnish Information

The employer has a duty to furnish information to the union enabling it to carry on the negotiation process. Often, the employees are unable to collect relevant data about an employer's business without the employer's cooperation. If the National Labor Relations Act did not support this duty to furnish information, much of the collective bargaining process would be futile. As with the duty to bargain, the duty to furnish information arises only after a request for information is made in good faith. A union may be subject to a charge of an unfair labor practice if it requests information only to harass or humiliate the employer.

1. **Relevancy.** Within liberal interpretations, the NLRB has said that information requested must be relevant to the union's right to represent its members. The union need not prove that the particular information requested is related to a currently discussed item if the subject matter is part of the overall negotiations.

2. **Financial information of company.** When an employer claims financial inability to meet a union wage demand, the financial information of the employer's company becomes relevant. The Supreme Court held that if such a claim by the employer is important enough to be made at the table, it requires some proof of its accuracy.[64] The board has extended this rule to actual claims of financial inability. Refusal to grant wage increases because the employer claims it could not stay competitive or would lose the profit margin was held by the board to invoke financial inability. Therefore, financial data become relevant. In the absence of such a claim, an employer's financial records can be denied the union's bargaining team. Nondisclosure of financial information may be seen by the employer as a reaffirmation of management prerogative and by the employees as an obstacle to effective bargaining.[65] In a very narrow interpretation of previous Supreme Court decisions, the NLRB has denied a union's right to financial information when the employer merely claimed it could not meet the

union's wage demands and stay competitive.[66] A more recent federal court opinion, however, ruled that an employer had asserted an "inability to pay" when it said that "competitive pressures" prevented it from agreeing to union contract demands.[67]

3. **Prompt delivery of information in workable form.** Bad faith may be evidenced if requested information is not delivered in a timely manner or is delivered in an unreasonable, useless form. An employer may claim that compiling requested data is unduly burdensome, but he or she must be flexible and should suggest alternatives. If the information is given in a form generally accepted in business, a union's request for a different form will not be binding on the employer. And when the employer allows the union access to all its records, it need not furnish information in a more organized form.

4. **Information that must be furnished.** Almost all areas touching upon mandatory bargaining have been open to union requests for information. However, employers frequently refuse requests by the union to furnish wage information. The board, supported by lower courts and the Supreme Court, has found little if any justification for such refusals. The statutory requirement that wages be subject to collective bargaining extends to wages paid to particular employees, to groups of employees, and to methods of computing compensation. The union's right to information may include employees even outside of the bargaining unit or in other plants operated by the employer.

Refusal to Bargain

The labor organization, like the employer, is charged with a duty under the Taft-Hartley Amendments to bargain in good faith. Failure to do so can result in an unfair labor practice charge. Basically, the good faith requirement is the same as for employers and involves having an open mind in meeting and conferring with employers to reach an ultimate agreement. Refusal to sign an agreement the union and employer have come to terms on is an unfair labor practice. Insistence on being recognized as the exclusive bargaining agent for an inappropriate unit or when majority status is not held is also an unfair labor practice. Other unfair labor practices charged against a union are explored in the contract negotiations discussed in the next chapter.

Employer unfair labor practices impede the collective bargaining process. Unfair labor practices, as contained in the National Labor Relations Act, include the interference with employees in the exercise of their rights; the domination of an employee union; the discrimination against union members; and the refusal to bargain. **SUMMARY**

The NLRA imposed a duty in good faith on the employer and the labor organization, subject to its provisions. That good faith is evidenced by the total conduct of the parties toward the collective bargaining process.

Because the NLRA guarantees employees the right to refrain from union activities, attempts by labor unions to coerce employees to join is a violation. A union must fairly represent all of its members, and a breach of that duty is an unfair labor practice. The same is true of a union's duty to bargain in good faith with the employer.

UNFAIR LABOR PRACTICE BY AN EMPLOYER

Facts

The employer manufactures automobile parts and supplies those parts to major auto manufacturers. The UAW filed a representation petition to unionize the employer's workforce. Between November 14, 1994, when the petition was filed, and January 12, 1995, when the election was held, the employer did the following:

1. The Human Resource Director distributed a letter to employees asserting that two-thirds of the 600 plants that had closed in their state over the past 20 years had been unionized.
2. The employer distributed an article concerning Ford's decision to move a parts contract from a supplier whose workforce had gone out on strike, emphasizing that the striking union was the UAW.
3. Around Christmas, the employer relocated production of a Ford part to another one of its plants at a location not subject to the pending election petition. The employer offered no explanation for the move.
4. The employer told the employees that negotiations on a renewal contract with a customer were being held in abeyance until the outcome of the union election, although the customer also had issues of quality and delivery to discuss.
5. The employer displayed large photo posters of closed manufacturing plants and distributed a letter noting that all of the plants had been unionized.
6. On January 9, 1995, the president of the company sent a letter to employees telling of his concern that its manufacturing partners would become nervous and go elsewhere if the company developed "a reputation for not being dependable because of labor problems, a UAW-led strike, or even the possibility of a strike every time the contract comes up for renewal."
7. On January 10, 1995, the division manager told employees that the employer was concerned about the impact of the union vote on its manufacturing customers. On January 9 and 10, one such customer did a very visible "walk-through" inspection of the facility accompanied by numerous managers.

When the ballots were counted, the union lost 196 to 154. The union filed an unfair labor charge against the employer, charging that its campaign tactics had violated the NLRA and invalidated the results.

Questions

1. Which, if any, of the employer's actions might the Court find violated the National Labor Relations Act and therefore might cause the election to be set aside?
2. Recognizing that this election took place in 1995, do you think the Court might find that the employees could have seen through the employer's tactics and vote the way they wanted despite of the employer's actions?
3. Would *you* have been swayed by the employer's actions to the point you could not have voted with "freedom of choice"?

Adapted from *SPX Corporation*, 151 LRRM 1300 (1995).

UNFAIR LABOR PRACTICE BY A UNION

Facts

A decertification election was held at a plant owned by a Japanese company. The appeal to the NLRB by the company and one employee was that the election, in which the decertification petition was defeated, be set aside on the basis of the union's unfair labor practice. The company and the petitioning employee charged that the union's patterns of threats and intimidation, as well as its racially oriented acts, were so extensive and persuasive that they prevented the employees' exercise of free choice.

The company presented testimony at the hearing regarding the following activities:

1. An employee's tires were slashed after he had been identified in the union's newsletter as withdrawing his union membership. In addition, one of his wheels fell off when he left work; he discovered that the lugs had been removed and were only a few feet from where the car had been parked.

2. Another employee, who had headed up the decertification petition, received numerous anonymous obscene telephone calls.

3. A union steward intimidated an employee along the roadway by slowing down so the employee would pass, then speeding up and quickly slamming on the brakes, causing the employee to do the same and swerve in order to avoid an accident. The union steward had used the same harassing highway tactics on another employee, who was driving with her daughter and five grandchildren.

4. One employee was followed home and found her fuel line cut the next day.

5. Another employee discovered a scratch down the entire side of her car, which had been parked at the plant.

6. An employee wearing a "Vote No" button was threatened with physical harm by a fellow employee.

7. Several employees received intimidating telephone calls at their homes from both union agents and anonymous callers. Some of the calls were answered by the employees' children, and threatening statements were then made to the children.

8. Two employees were overheard discussing the rumors of threats surrounding the campaign, and one of the employees said, "Sometimes it takes this kind of thing to get the point across."

9. At two union organizing meetings, at which more than 100 employees were present, a union official ended his speech with the following quote: "We beat the Japs after Pearl Harbor, and we can beat them again." Anti-Japanese graffiti appeared on bathroom walls, and a steward wore a shirt and work tags printed with the phrases, "Remember Pearl Harbor" and "Japs go home."

The union's position was that it should not be charged with an unfair labor practice because of the alleged activities of individuals who were not acting at the union's direction. Union membership and support for the union can cause emotions to run high; it happens in every election. But there was no evidence that the employees were prevented from exercising their free choice in the election itself. The anti-Japanese statements were unfortunate but mere rhetoric. Such rhetoric violates none of the established NLRB standards for conducting a fair election.

Questions

1. Would you set aside the election results and order another election? Explain your answer.
2. How could the union have stopped individuals from the intimidating actions that allegedly went on in this case?
3. Does the racial nature of the rhetoric involved in this case put a heavier burden on the union than does the usual rhetoric about an employer? Explain your answer.

Adapted from *YKK (U.S.A.), Inc.*, 115 LRRM 1186 (1984).

auction bargaining
authority
boulwarism
concerted activity
delaying tactics
dual-motive discrimination case
Electromation
employer unfair labor practices
good faith bargaining
labor organization unfair labor
    practices

negotiating with employees
pretext discrimination case
primary strike
prohibited conduct
Republic Aviation case
Section 10(j)
surface bargaining
totality of conduct doctrine
24-hour-rule
Weingarten rule

REVIEW QUESTIONS

1. What might the NLRB consider to be a breach of the good faith bargaining principle?
2. How does the NLRB review an unfair labor practice charge of surface bargaining?
3. Is an employer always required to furnish any data requested by a union during negotiations? If not, list some exceptions.
4. What are the rules employers and union organizers must follow during an organizational campaign?
5. Under what circumstances can an employer poll employees to determine their desire to join a union?
6. What is the difference between an employer's support of and domination of a union?
7. When is an employer illegally discriminating against employees because of their union activities?
8. What union activities are prohibited under the Taft-Hartley unfair labor practices provision?

TAKE IT TO THE NET

We invite you to visit the Carrell/Heavrin page on the Prentice Hall Web site at:

http://www.prenhall.com/carrellr

for this chapter's World Wide Web exercise.

EXERCISE 5-1

Protected and Prohibited Organizational Practices

Purpose:
To familiarize students with unfair labor practices.

Task:

During the organizing campaign, the two sides may try different activities to help them convince employees to vote in their favor. For each of the 10 following common activities, determine if it is *generally* prohibited or protected (allowed by the NLRB during an organizational campaign).

Place an *X* at the appropriate column:

Allowed   Prohibited   Activity

1. Union places literature on employees' desks.
2. Union posts flyers on employee bulletin boards previously accessible for any purpose.
3. Employees wear union buttons on a uniform specifically prescribed by policy.
4. Union distributes meeting announcements in employee mailboxes not previously restricted to company mail.
5. Employees discuss specific election issues during lunch breaks.
6. Supervisors discuss their personal opinion of the union during breaks.
7. Management asks for a "show of hands" from employees indicating their support or nonsupport of the union.
8. Employer grants a new "personal leave" paid holiday.
9. Employer institutes a "no-distribution" rule (of union literature) by employees during nonwork times on company premises.
10. Employer issues the annual bonus checks to employees on the basis of the profit formula used in past years.

Unfair Labor Practices EXERCISE 5-2

Purpose:

To learn about real-world unfair labor practices that have occurred or have been claimed to have occurred in your community.

Task:

Find newspaper articles that discuss possible unfair labor practices by employers or unions. For each of three separate practices define: (1) the exact activity in question that may have violated the NLRA; (2) the union's position; (3) the employer's position; (4) why *you* believe the activity was or was not an unfair labor practice.

If you are using Smith/Carrell/Golden *Collective Bargaining Simulated, 4E,* with this text, please refer to the following:

p. 8 for a discussion of past labor relations at Ohio Metals.

CHAPTER 6

Negotiating
an Agreement

- The Bargaining Process
- Bargaining Techniques
- Impasse
- Summary

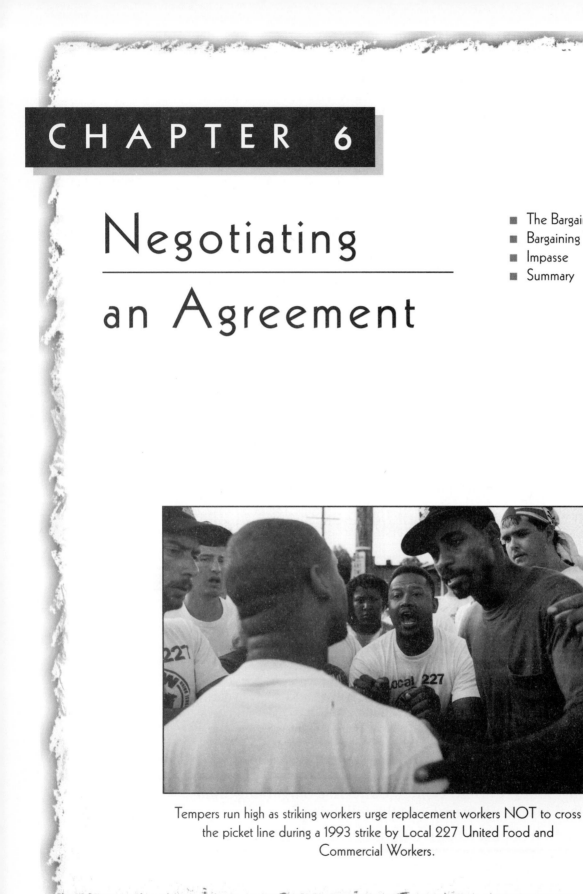

Tempers run high as striking workers urge replacement workers NOT to cross
the picket line during a 1993 strike by Local 227 United Food and
Commercial Workers.

"9 to 5"

Karen Nussbaum, a union organizer, got a telephone call from "a woman who had been fired because she got her boss a sandwich on white bread instead of rye bread and then refused to take it back." Nussbaum could not help the woman get her job back, but she did organize a picket of her boss's office by 40 coworkers. Outraged at the incident, Nussbaum quit her job at Harvard University and founded the organization "9 to 5" at age 23 to assist secretaries in similar situations. In 1976, 9 to 5 received a charter from the Service Employees International Union and began organizing secretaries. The movement was the inspiration behind *9 to 5,* the 1980 movie starring Jane Fonda, Dolly Parton, and Lily Tomlin. The movie centers on three secretaries who kidnap an abusive boss and turn the organization into a good, fair place to work. The movie brought a great deal of attention to the plight of secretaries and the organization. Today, 9 to 5 represents 9,000 workers nationwide. Karen Nussbaum, at 46, was appointed by the AFL-CIO in 1996 to head the new Working Women's Department.

Adapted from Diane E. Lewis, "Founder of 9 to 5 Gets a New Job at AFL-CIO," *Wall Street Journal*, June 10, 1996, p. B6.

Central to the collective bargaining process are the actual negotiations carried out by the parties to reach an agreement. Artful use of this process can improve the relationship between an employer and the employees and result in a profitable agreement for both parties. Unsuccessful negotiations can lead to work stoppages and a loss of profits and benefits. This chapter examines different techniques of bargaining, details of the bargaining process, and solutions to the bargaining impasse.

The bargaining process usually begins when one party wants to terminate or amend an existing contract. Most agreements provide for the automatic extension of an existing contract past the expiration date, usually for one year. Either party may initiate new negotiations by providing written, explicit notice to the other party. A clause specifying automatic renewal and the process to begin new negotiations is included in 90 percent of labor agreements.[1]

THE BARGAINING PROCESS

The collective bargaining process begins long before the parties meet across the bargaining table. As discussed in previous chapters, the organization of units and the selection of the agent is a lengthy process necessary in determining the parties to a collective bargaining relationship.

People Who Bargain

Union Representatives. Although there are as many types of negotiators as there are negotiations, some generalizations can be made. National agreements require large negotiating teams, with members from several union offices, staff, and locals (see Figure 6-1 for the 1996 membership of the UAW national negotiating team at Chrysler). The majority of negotiating takes place at the local level—either after a national agreement decides certain issues or because no national agreement exists.

A local union's negotiating team is made up of certain ex-officio members, such as the president or one or more elected officers of the local union, and a chief steward or grievance committee member. In most negotiations involving craft unions, the business agent is part of the negotiating team and often the chief negotiator. For industrial unions, an international union representative, who is a professional negotiator, is often available to guide and counsel local union officials.

Although international representatives have no official status during local negotiations, their experience often puts them in a leadership role. They give guidance on the grievance process and set the tone for negotiations and, in the case of impasse, for pressure tactics. They play the role of mediator or assume a militant stand to allow the local representatives to appear reasonable.

Whatever the makeup of the union's negotiating team, its authority is somewhat limited by the membership. The union members usually delegate only provisional and temporary authority to the negotiating team to make a settlement. Usually, any final settlement must be presented to the total membership for a vote.

Management Representatives. The authority of the management negotiating team comes from top management and is generally a more complete delegation. Policymakers are often a part of the team. In negotiations involving a single employer, representatives may be the company's labor relations director or a production person and line executive, or there may be staff advisers such as the per-

Figure 6-1

UAW's 1996 National Negotiating Team at Chrysler

Musick · *Massaron* · *Yokich* · *Laskowski* · *Paula* · *Guinan*

Rossen · *Britnell* · *Horne* · *McAllister* · *Patterson* · *Coakley*

Hoffman · *J. Davis*

Mirer · *Glenn*

This is the UAW's national negotiating team whose efforts — along with the assistance of the UAW Chrysler Department and other UAW office, technical, and professional staff — led to the achievement of a tentative new agreement between the UAW and the Chrysler Corporation. **Stephen P. Yokich** is president of the International Union, UAW; **Jack Laskowski** is vice-president and director of the UAW Chrysler Department; **Paul Massaron** is top administrative assistant to Yokich; **Leonard J. Paula**, **John Guinan**, and **Joan Patterson** are administrative assistants to Laskowski; **Frank Musick** is director of UAW special projects; **Chuck Britnell**, **Jack Horne**, and **Dave McAllister** are assistant directors of the UAW Chrysler Department; coordinators are **James Coakley**, **James Davis**, **Decoris Glenn**, **Ron Gossett**, **Jim Jensen**, **Steve Jones**, **Larry Leach**, and **Kenneth L. Young**; **Jordan Rossen** is UAW general counsel; **Gerald Lazarowitz** is director of the UAW Research Department; **William Hoffman** is director of the UAW Social Security Department; **Frank Mirer** is director of the UAW Occupational Health & Safety Department; **Michael Allen**, of Local 624, Syracuse, NY, is chairperson of the UAW Chrysler National Negotiating Committee and represents Subcouncil 3 (engine/axle); **Randall Pearson**, Local 140, Warren, MI, is committee vice chair, Subcouncil 1 (assembly, instate); **Mary Jo Rawlings Meida**, Amalgamated Local 889, Warren, MI, is committee secretary, Subcouncil 7 (office & clerical); other members are **Jerry Quinn**, Local 1268, Belvidere, IL, Subcouncil 1 (assembly, outstate); **Willie Davis**, Local 122, Twinsburg, OH, Subcouncil 2 (stamping); **Ricardo Rios**, Local 1435, Toledo, OH, Subcouncil 4 (forge/foundry); **Larry Williams**, Local 1413, Huntsville, AL, Subcouncil 5 (miscellaneous); **Timothy Bressler**, Local 260, Tappan, NY, Subcouncil 6 (parts); **Derek Thiery**, Amalgamated Local 412, Warren, MI, Subcouncil 8 (engineering); and **Curt Wilson**, Local 72, Kenosha, WI, Subcouncil 9 (skilled trades).

Lazarowitz · *Gossett*

Leach · *Allen* · *Pearson* · *Rawlings Meida* · *Quinn* · *W. Davis* · *Jensen*

Young · *Rios* · *Williams* · *Bressler* · *Thiery* · *Wilson* · *Jones*

Source: UAW–Chrysler *Newsgram*, October 1996, p. 28. Used by Permission.

sonnel director, financial officer, and a company lawyer. When a multiemployer association is involved, the companies often employ a labor relations adviser and negotiator, who is equivalent to the international representative. This professional serves a role similar to that of the union counterpart by promoting the multiemployer organization, by preparing management counterproposals, and by conducting negotiations.

Negotiating Skills. Successful negotiations depend upon the knowledge and skill of the negotiators. They must, through careful preparations, become knowledgeable about their own and the other side's positions on the bargaining issues. They prepare and propose workable, attainable, and realistic issues within the framework of the negotiations. For example, negotiators may develop strong economic positions to give the parties bargaining room during the negotiation process.

To use the acquired knowledge wisely, a negotiator develops an understanding of the opposition. Listening skills and the ability to communicate clearly are two cultivated techniques. A thick skin may be helpful because the other side may engage in personal attacks at some point in the negotiations. A negotiator realizes that such attacks are often necessary in satisfying a constituency.

The successful negotiator possesses personal integrity and courage.[2] At some point in the negotiations, agreements must be made. A negotiator's word or handshake is the basis for the agreement until it is committed to paper. The untrustworthy or faint of heart cannot bring collective bargaining negotiations to a successful conclusion.

Suggested attributes of the successful negotiator include the following:

1. Sets clear objectives
2. Does not hurry
3. Calls for a caucus when in doubt
4. Is prepared
5. Remains flexible
6. Examines continually why the other party acts as it does
7. Respects face-saving tactics employed by the opposition
8. Attempts to ascertain the real interest of the other party by the priority proposed
9. Actively listens
10. Builds a reputation for being fair but firm
11. Controls emotions
12. Remembers to evaluate each bargaining move in relation to all others
13. Measures bargaining moves against ultimate objectives
14. Pays close attention to the wording of proposals
15. Remembers that compromise is the key to successful negotiations; understands that no party can afford to win or lose all
16. Tries to understand people
17. Considers the impact of present negotiations on the future relationship of the parties[3]

Preparation and Choice of Bargaining Items

Many unions affiliate with larger international unions. If a master agreement is negotiated by the international, then the international controls all but local concerns. Preparation for negotiations on a master agreement is virtually nonstop, and the next year's preparations begin as soon as a contract is signed. Preparation for contract negotiation on a local level, although not that extensive, is still necessary.

The first stage, preparation, involves analysis and planning. In **analysis**, information is gathered and bargaining items are decided upon, narrowing the issues to a manageable size. **Planning** forces the parties to evaluate and set priorities and to make realistic decisions about their demands. The parties' attention is focused on achievable goals. The parties are then ready for the second stage, the bargaining stage, which leads to the final stage, resolution (see Figure 6-2).

Analysis. It is a function of law and common practice to decide what items to include in the collective bargaining session. The National Labor Relations Act provides that bargaining shall include rates of pay, wages, hours of employment, and conditions of employment.[4] Under enforcement of the unfair labor practice charge of refusal to bargain, the National Labor Relations Board determines which subjects fall under the law. The board and later the courts recognized three categories of bargaining subjects: those that will be discussed, those that might be discussed, and those that cannot be discussed.

In the early years of the act, the board based its decisions on what constituted bargaining subjects by evaluating the history of the agreements. However, to protect unions and the collective bargaining process in its formative stage, the board found the discussion of union recognition clauses compulsory. Hence, union shops, dues check-offs, and the treatment of employees after a strike became part of the collective bargaining discussion.

In a case-by-case method, the board began to establish the list of subjects to be covered. The Supreme Court, in 1958, decided the *Borg-Warner* **case**, which distinguished between the treatment accorded subjects determined by the board to be mandatory and the treatment accorded subjects determined to be permissive or illegal. The Court noted that, although the attitude of the parties is important in determining the good faith required by the act, the issues being discussed are also important.[5] It became a legal question as to whether a proposal was one the parties were obliged to discuss.

If the subject is **mandatory**, a party may insist on its inclusion and the other party cannot refuse to discuss it. Although compelled to bargain in good faith, neither party is legally obligated to compromise its stated position on a mandatory subject, and each party may even push the bargaining situation to an impasse. A legal impasse in negotiations can only occur when the parties cannot agree on a mandatory issue. The employer can, if there is a bona fide impasse, unilaterally implement its final offer to the union. If any permissive issues are also unresolved at the time of impasse, they can be implemented with the mandatory issue.[6]

Subjects deemed mandatory by the National Labor Relations Board include those issues actually listed in the act: rates of pay, wages, hours of employment, and other conditions of employment. Also included are issues the NLRB considers related to the subjects listed in the act. After the Borg-Warner decision, the Supreme Court refined the definition of mandatory bargaining subjects to include subjects that "vitally affect" employees.[7] In recent years, several issues critical to unions, such as liquidation of a business, partial plant closings, subcontracting work, and plant relocations, have been litigated to determine whether they are mandatory or permissive subjects of bargaining.

Figure 6-2   The Three Stages of the Bargaining Process

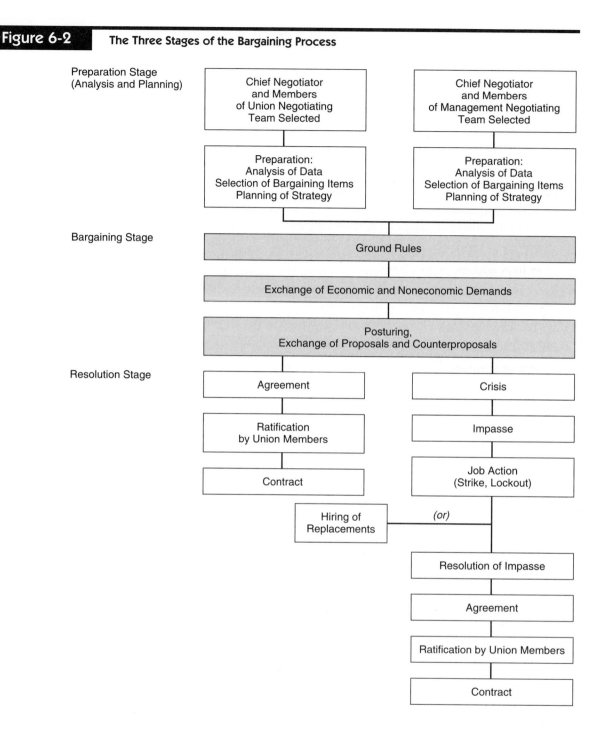

After some confusion that was generated by board decisions during the Reagan years, recent board rulings list subcontracting and plant relocations in the mandatory list if such acts mean to substitute other workers for the bargaining unit members. Partial plant closings or other "going out of business" decisions are not subjects of mandatory bargaining because there is no intention to replace the bargaining unit members.[8] Table 6-1 delineates mandatory, permissive, and illegal subjects.

Because neither party may pursue a permissive issue to impasse, seldom can concessions be gained over a permissive subject.[9] Designating plant closings and other business issues that focus on the economic profitability of a business as permissive[10] has had a profound impact on unions' ability to win concessions on such issues at the negotiating table or to alter major decisions affecting union security.

The board has defined wages as "direct and immediate economic benefits, flowing from the employment relationship."[11] Included in the discussion of wages are hourly pay rates, overtime pay, piece rates, incentive plans, shift differentials, paid holidays and vacations, and severance pay. Other forms of compensation are also included by the NLRB under the wage category and are therefore considered mandatory; they include the following:

1. **Pensions and insurance benefits**. Whereas employers considered pensions and insurance benefits as separate from wages, the NLRB considered them as payment for services rendered and found an inseparable nexus between employees' current compensation and future benefits. However, retirement and pension plans are mandatory subjects for *active* employees only, and not for retired members.

2. **Profit-sharing plans**. Profit-sharing plans are also considered as payment and enhancement of economic benefit. Such plans are usually structured to increase benefits to employees when company profits go up.

Bargaining Items | | **Table 6-1**

Mandatory	Permissive	Illegal
Rates of pay	Indemnity bonds	Closed shop
Wages	Management rights as to union	Hot cargo clause
Hours of employment	affairs	Separation of
Overtime pay	Pension benefits of retired	employees by
Shift differentials	employees	race
Holidays	Scope of the bargaining unit	Discriminatory
Vacations	Including supervisors in the	treatment
Severance pay	contract	
Pensions	Additional parties to the	
Insurance benefits	contract, such as the	
Profit-sharing plans	international union	
Christmas bonuses	Use of union label	
Company housing, meals,	Settlement of unfair labor	
and discounts	changes	
Employee security	Prices in cafeteria	
Job performance	Continuance of past contract	
Union security	Membership of bargaining team	
Management-union	Employment of strike breakers	
relationship	Employer child care	
Drug testing of employees	Plant closings	
Subcontracting or relocating		
union members' work		

3. **Christmas and other bonuses**. A one-time or performance bonus may be a mandatory subject. The board has devised a test to determine whether such a bonus is a gift or part of the employees' compensation. The decision is based on

- The consistency or regularity of the payment
- The uniformity of the amount of payment from bonus to bonus
- The relationship between the amount of the bonus and the pay scale of the employee
- The taxability of the payment as income
- The financial condition and ability of the employer to give the bonus

The board will determine it is a gift if

- The bonus has been awarded intermittently over a very few years
- The amount of the bonus is not uniform from year to year
- The amount is not tied to the employees' salary
- The awarding of a bonus depends on the present financial condition of the employer

4. **Stock purchase plans**. Employers contend that stock purchase plans are not employee benefits but are simply an incentive for the employee to invest in the company. The National Labor Relations Board rejects that argument and deems such plans are a form of bargainable compensation.

5. **Merit wage incentives**. A company may consider merit increases management's prerogative, but the NLRB has said that because merit raises involve the formation and application and standards affecting all wages, they must be considered a mandatory bargaining subject.

6. **Company housing, meals, and discounts**. The inclusion of these in the list of mandatory subjects depends upon the situation. Such items would be mandatory if the job required living or eating on company-owned premises.

Provisions detailing hours, daily and weekly work schedules, and requirements for overtime premiums are found in virtually all contracts.[12] Specific start and stop times, lunch and rest periods, and other scheduling rules are usually included. Although scheduling work is normally a management prerogative, any change from the hours specified in the contract, no matter how minimal, is considered an unfair labor practice, even if it does not affect the employee's pay.

The board has stated that the phrase "conditions of employment" refers to terms under which employment status is given or withdrawn rather than physical working conditions. Conditions must have a material and significant impact directly affecting the employment relationship. Four major areas include the following:

1. **Employment security**. This covers all aspects of hiring and firing and granting tenure. Hiring and probationary periods, seniority, job-bidding procedures, promotions, and transfers must all be bargained, except for the nondiscriminatory promotion of employees to supervisory positions. The order and manner of layoffs and recalls, issues surrounding the discharge and retirement of employees, and contracting out work normally performed by members of the bargaining unit are also mandatory. In some instances, plant closings and relocations must be

bargained. Although courts have said that a company is not required to negotiate an economically motivated decision to close or relocate a plant, the effects of such an action must be bargained.

2. **Job performance**. The day-to-day relationship between employer and employee is a mandatory subject of bargaining and includes absenteeism, work breaks, lunch periods, discipline, and dress codes. Although safety practices must be discussed, management may still have the final say. Decisions concerning workloads and the number of employees necessary for a task are considered mandatory and, under recent board and court decisions, drug testing of employees is considered a mandatory bargaining subject although the decision to test job applicants is not.[13]

3. **Union security**. The protection of the union's representation status is a mandatory subject for bargaining. Such protection requires a 30-day grace period before an employee must join the union, discontinuance of a union shop according to majority vote, and a prohibition against discharge of an employee for nonmembership in a union for any reason other than failure to pay dues.

4. **Management-union relationships**. All principles governing the discharge of collective bargaining duties and enforcement of collective bargaining agreements, including grievance and arbitration procedures, are considered mandatory.

If the subject is **permissive**, a party must withdraw it from bargaining if the other party does not voluntarily agree to its inclusion in the discussion. Both parties must agree for permissive subjects to be bargained. Examples of permissive subjects include performance or indemnity bonds, which protect the employer from liabilities in the quality of the union's work, and management's right to have an impact upon the internal affairs of the union.

Subjects deemed **illegal** by the act or the NLRB may not be proposed for discussion, and even if agreed to by both parties, would not be enforced by any court. These include violations of public policy, otherwise unlawful issues, and items inconsistent with the principles of the National Labor Relations Act. A closed shop requiring union membership before an employee is hired, racial separation of employees, and discrimination against nonunion members are illegal bargaining subjects.

If in the future a portion of the contract becomes illegal under a state or federal law, the **separability clause** in the contract becomes effective. The separability clause usually states that any portion of a contract conflicting with state or federal law is declared null and void without affecting other provisions. Separability clauses appear in 68 percent of all contracts. About half provide that the offending section is null and void; the other half call for renegotiation of the issue.[14]

Sources of Bargaining Items.   In general, it is the unions who introduce new items to be discussed at a collective bargaining session, and management reacts to such proposals. Management can, however, initiate new items for discussion.

Union negotiation teams solicit member input in formulating demands. This solicitation can be done at general union meetings, at meetings with union stewards, or through written or electronic questionnaires. The results of a

Teamster survey (Figure 6-3) of member concerns—especially section 4, Job Security, (b) create more full-time jobs—led president Ron Carey to call the historic 1997 strike against UPS. Often, bargaining items are formulated through analysis of the types of grievances filed and from recent arbitration awards. Problems detected at a lower level are passed on to be included in the collective bargaining talks. Management will often add line supervisors' suggestions on working conditions to its economic positions during negotiations.

Both union and management can also look to external sources for bargaining items. Recent contracts within the same industry can give both parties ideas on realistic, attainable proposals. Often the overall economic condition of the nation and that of the particular industry limit or expand bargaining demands.

Information necessary to support proposals and counterproposals can be obtained from such sources as the U.S. Department of Labor (Bureau of Labor Statistics) and the Federal Reserve System, which publish economic data. National organizations such as the National Labor Relations Board, the Federal Mediation and Conciliation Service, and the Federal Labor Relations Council are directly involved in collective bargaining and can contribute primary information. Publications of the Bureau of National Affairs, Commerce Clearing House, and Prentice Hall show national trends in contract settlement for comparison with local proposals. Special-interest groups representing both labor and management collect a wide variety of information to help in contract negotiations and include the National Association of Manufacturers (NAM) and the AFL-CIO.

In addition to general sources, each party is entitled to certain types of information from the opposition. Under the duty to bargain in good faith, a union may demand relevant information from the employer in preparing wage demands.

Planning. Planning may be the most critical element in successful negotiations. In general, negotiators plan effectively by:

1. **Anticipation**. Each side, through research and members' input, must correctly assess those issues critical to both sides. The general mood greatly affects the early stages of negotiations. The key issues for each side and the possibility of a strike or other actions should be anticipated and a response prepared. A response such as a detailed counterproposal or a package of several items can center the conflict on the issues rather than personal emotions.

2. **Realistic objectives**. Preparation on all items of interest can help avoid costly mistakes during heated and lengthy negotiations. Negotiators should prioritize all objectives and develop a settlement range. Logical trade-offs among items of interest can be analyzed and prepared.

3. **Strategy**. Each party must evaluate the opponent's current needs as well as its own, review the bargaining history between the two parties, and prepare an overall strategy for negotiations. Important aspects to consider include personalities of negotiators; current financial and political position of each party; and outside influences such as the economy, product sales, and public support of unions. Strategy formulation helps both sides develop realistic expectations of how negotiations will proceed and what the final agreement will be. For example, senior union employees may be most unhappy with the current pension program, but a significant increase in the pension formula would require costly increases for all future retirees. Thus, in developing its strategy, management

Dear Teamster Member at UPS:

In just a few months, the Teamsters National UPS Negotiating Committee will begin bargaining with UPS management for a new National Master Agreement.

These negotiations will be about issues that directly affect your wages and working conditions at UPS. Some key issues to be discussed include:

- Reducing the pay gap for part-timers and creating more full-time job opportunities
- Putting stricter limits on subcontracting
- New increases in pension and health fund contributions from the company
- More protection for workers' safety and health

We need your opinions on bargaining priorities to help guide your negotiating committee as it prepares for bargaining with the company.

Please take a few minutes to fill out and electronically send this membership survey.

Our success in these negotiations will depend on Teamster unity and membership involvement. We will keep you informed during the negotiations and explain what is going on and why. Thank you for your involvement. We look forward to hearing your views.

In solidarity,

Ron Carey
Chair, Teamsters UPS National
Negotiating Committee

Ken Hall
Director, Parcel & Small Package
Package Trade Division

- Answer the questions by clicking with your mouse or typing the requested information in the appropriate space.
- When you are done, click on the "send survey" box to complete the process.
- All responses are strictly confidential and will be used only to set our bargaining strategies for the 1997 UPS negotiations.

Part A: Bargaining Priorities

We need to be prepared and united for negotiations to win a new 1997 contract. Every member's opinion counts and we need to know your priorities for upcoming negotiations.

INCREASES

1. A negotiated increase may be divided between wages and benefits. Please rank the following list of wage and benefit improvements from 1 (your top priority) to 5 (your lowest priority). Mark the box in Column 1 for your top priority issue; mark the box in column 2 for your second priority issue; continue through all five issues. For example, if wage increases are the least important to you then mark the box in column 5 for wage increases.

a. Wage increases	1	2	3	4	5
b. Cost of living adjustment	1	2	3	4	5
c. Health care improvements	1	2	3	4	5
d. Improved pensions	1	2	3	4	5
e. More paid time off	1	2	3	4	5

BENEFITS

2. During the 1993 contract negotiations, UPS tried to take our pension and health care benefits and put them under company control. In the end, Teamster unity kept our benefits out of UPS's hands and helped us win the largest contributions increase in history.

(continued)

Figure 6-3 **1996 UPS Teamster Bargaining Survey (continued)**

As a result, pensions were improved in most areas and health benefits under Teamster Plans remained secure. Which pension and health care benefit improvements are the most important to you? (Please rank your priorities as in question 1).

a. Improved 25 & Out Pensions	1	2	3	4	5
b. Improved 30 & Out Pensions	1	2	3	4	5
c. Improved pensions for part-time employees	1	2	3	4	5
d. Maintain Teamsters Health Plans	1	2	3	4	5
e. Long-term disability	1	2	3	4	5

3. Improving wages and benefits is important, but so is having enough time off to spend with your family and friends. Which time-off improvements do you want the most? (Please rank your priorities as in question 1).

a. More sick leave	1	2	3	4	5
b. More vacation leave	1	2	3	4	5
c. More paid holidays	1	2	3	4	5
d. Restrictions on mandatory overtime	1	2	3	4	5
e. Paid family leave to care for a parent or child	1	2	3	4	5

Job Security

4. Teamsters at UPS are the most productive workers in the industry. That's why UPS profits topped $1 billion in 1995. But while we keep working harder, UPS keeps trying to use third-party contractors and its own nonunion subsidiaries (like Worldwide Logistics and Sonic Air) to do our work. We need more full-time jobs at UPS, not more work with fewer union employees. How important to you is each of the following job security issues in the next contract? (Rate your choice on each issue using a scale from 1 to 5, with 1 = "very important" to 5 = "not important".)

a. Put stricter limits on subcontracting	1	2	3	4	5
b. Create more full-time jobs	1	2	3	4	5
c. Protect against job loss due to new technologies	1	2	3	4	5
d. Prevent transfer of union work to nonunion employees or subsidiaries	1	2	3	4	5

Grievance Procedure

5. The grievance procedure is the way many disputes between the company and the union are resolved. How important to you is each of the following grievance procedure improvements? (Please rate each issue from 1 = "very important" to 5 = "not important".)

a. Right to strike over deadlocked grievances at the national level	1	2	3	4	5
b. Require UPS to arbitrate national cases within fixed timeliness	1	2	3	4	5
c. Require UPS to make more timely payment of settled grievances	1	2	3	4	5
d. Paid time-off for stewards to handle grievances	1	2	3	4	5

Figure 6-3

Accurate Paychecks

6. Although UPS spent over $200 million last year on new technologies, they have problems giving us accurate and on-time paychecks. How often does UPS give you an inaccurate or late paycheck?

Weekly   Once a Month   Occasionally   Never

Source: The Teamsters Union Website, 1996. Used by Permission.

could develop an economic package including alternative combinations of one-time lucrative early retirement options with pay increases loaded toward younger employees.

4. **Agenda**. Both parties should develop an agenda for discussing all items in a logical manner and incorporate it into the written ground rules. For example, after settling problems with the current contract's wording (which may have arisen through grievance), negotiators can exchange noneconomic proposals and settle as many as possible. They should follow this settlement with an exchange of economic proposals dealing with smaller-cost items first, keeping on the table the highest priority economic and noneconomic items.

Expectations must be established at the same time priorities are set. Successful collective bargaining may be impossible if the highest priority of one party is an item the other party is unlikely to negotiate.

To establish realistic objectives, the party considers patterns and trends in contract settlements of other employers in the industry and the local community. In an economy where a 4 percent cost-of-living raise is almost universal, a request for 12 percent would be unrealistic. The parties also examine their current and past bargaining relationship, along with their relative strength. For example, if contract negotiations have already been concluded with other employers in the same industry and this employer always follows their lead, it may be unrealistic to expect major deviations.

Negotiation Sessions

The rules of the collective bargaining session are set usually by the parties at the opening session. If the parties have a longstanding relationship, establishing procedures can be very routine. But when the collective bargaining process is relatively new or when the parties have had bad labor relations, setting procedures can be as difficult, and as important, as bargaining on the issues.

Ground Rules. The parties decide where, when, how often, and how long to meet. These and other procedures are often agreed to in writing as **ground rules** for negotiations. Exactly what is included in the ground rules varies greatly according to the desires of the negotiators and the bargaining history of the two parties. The following are examples of ground rules:

1. All negotiation sessions will commence on the time, date, and location heretofore agreed upon by the parties.
2. The chief negotiator for the company and the chief negotiator for the union shall be the chief spokespersons for the respective parties' interests. However, others present may speak as required or called upon by the negotiators.
3. Insofar as practical and reasonable, the data introduced by either party at negotiations shall be made available to the other party.
4. If either the company or the union intends to add a new member to its respective bargaining committee, the party adding the new member will notify the other party.
5. Proposals and counterproposals will be made on typed copies as reasonable and will be signed and dated by the appropriate party. The parties shall simultaneously exchange initial noneconomic and economic proposals at the appropriate times.
6. Individual items agreed to by both parties shall be signed and dated and removed from the table. Any attempt to reintroduce or discuss those items shall be viewed as a breach of good faith.
7. The company's chief negotiator and the union's chief negotiator shall have the authority to agree in substance on contract language and provisions. However, any agreement is preliminary and contingent upon a final contract. All preliminary agreements made regarding individual contract provisions shall be initialed and dated by both chief negotiators.

TIPS FROM THE EXPERTS

Union

What are the three most important things for a union to do to prepare for negotiating a collective bargaining agreement?

a. Its homework as far as defending its own proposals
b. Its homework as far as anticipating management's proposals
c. Its homework as far as the politics of the negotiations: its own negotiating team as well as management's

You can never be overprepared for negotiations. Whether it is an art or a science, effective negotiation takes tremendous understanding of the substantive issues, a lot of creativity, and thoroughness, as well as keen understanding of people and power. Successful negotiations require looking beyond what is in place to what is possible to create, so as to achieve a result that gives everyone what they need in a way that they can say "yes."

Management

What are the three most important things an employer must do in preparing for negotiations?

a. Select a spokesperson both for the team and for public statements; someone familiar with labor law as well as the company/industry/labor relations issues and someone who has the respect of both the union and management teams (whether in-house or an outside counsel or consultant).
b. Establish specific goals and directions, including "drop-dead" points.
c. Gather input from line management in terms of what is or is not working in current collective bargaining agreement (or practice, if this is the first collective bargaining agreement to be negotiated) and from budget folks as to cost of changes and impact of same.

8. If mediation is agreed to by both parties, the mediator picked by the parties shall be agreeable to both.

Negotiating teams are established. Neither side may dictate the membership of the other's negotiating team, but rules may be established as to how many members are allowed on each side and as to their official roles, such as spokesperson, recording secretary, and doorkeeper, who makes sure only authorized persons attend the negotiations. Negotiating teams are often kept as small as possible to allow for productive discussion. Each side must have a designated leader who makes commitments for the respective parties. Traditionally, union negotiating teams can only agree to propose the contract to the membership for acceptance.

Exchange of Initial Proposals. A bargaining agenda is set to establish exchange of initial proposals, the order of discussion of bargaining items, and, if possible, how long to continue with one item if agreement is not forthcoming. A stalemate in the early stages of bargaining can sour the process, making agreement impossible. The number and length of bargaining sessions may indicate a party's reluctance to bargain in good faith, as in Case 6-1. If feasible, the agenda lists less controversial issues first so that an atmosphere of agreement is fostered.

Economic and noneconomic proposals are usually separated. Noneconomic proposals are often negotiated first. If economic data can be agreed upon, economic issues are easier to resolve. In general, economic issues are negotiated as a

---

CASE 6-1

NEGOTIATING PROCEDURES

The company operated a wholesale and retail financing of motor vehicles in San Juan, Puerto Rico. The union organized 18 field representatives in the San Juan branch in the fall and in November was certified as the employees' bargaining representative. Collective bargaining began on December 12. The negotiations lasted for 18 months but were characterized by long delays between sessions when the company attempted to eliminate the union by withholding merit increases and soliciting letters from employees to repudiate the union. At the beginning of the negotiating sessions in December a year later, the company scheduled only three half-days for bargaining and advised the union that if it wanted to continue to negotiate, it could go to the home office in New York.

In February, the union filed an unfair labor practice charge for refusal to bargain. The company refused to meet with the union again until the charge was withdrawn. The union withdrew the charge, and the company agreed to meet in March for two more half-days. In April, two half-day sessions were held; in May, three half-days; in June, one day; and then negotiations broke down. The union again filed charges against the company for refusal to bargain in good faith.

Decision

The National Labor Relations Board found that the company had refused to bargain in good faith. The board's rationale included the following: allowing only 10 half-days for bargaining during a six-month period, attempting to continue negotiations hundreds of miles from the plant, and attempting to circumvent the collective bargaining unit and deal directly with employees.

Adapted from *General Motors Acceptance Corp.*, 79 LRRM 1663 (1972).

---

package to ensure a balanced settlement. Agreement is more easily reached on individual noneconomic issues than on a package.

Usually a decision is made on how to keep records of the negotiations. An accurate record keeps both parties honest during negotiations and when the final contract is proposed. A single outline of items discussed, proposals made on those items, and what was agreed to or where disagreement arose is prepared by one party and initialed by the other.

The negotiation site has private space to allow for a caucus by either party. It is decided in the initial session what the caucus and adjournment rights of both parties are to be. Misunderstanding in this area can lead one or the other party to stage a needless walkout when a strategic retreat could have served as a positive catalyst to settlement. Finally, parties should decide early on the role of a mediator, if they intend to resort to one in case of an impasse.

Posturing.   The atmosphere of a collective bargaining session depends on the attitudes of the parties involved. Their attitudes are influenced by their prior relationships, the economic circumstances of the employer, the basic employer's attitude toward unionization, and the leadership of the union. The relationship of the employer to the local union's international may also be a factor.

Whatever the particular atmosphere, labor negotiations follow a common pattern. The initial working sessions are no more than monologues wherein both parties present their list of demands. Often these sessions are open to the public, or at least they are well publicized to satisfy the negotiators' constituencies that proceedings are on the right course. The laundry list proposed by the parties purposely includes bargaining items that can, and will, be bargained away during the negotiations with varying degrees of reluctance. This **posturing** is very important. It allows a certain amount of face-saving to the party who comes to the bargaining table with the least amount of bargaining power.

Within the posturing of negotiations, there are several common aspects of bargaining that should be anticipated by the participants:

1. **Interdependence**. One element of negotiations is conflict, which can cause tempers to rise as parties become emotionally involved. However, both sides need to remember that their goals are interdependent. Neither side can achieve success without the other.[15]

2. **Concealment**. During negotiations parties often conceal their real goals and objectives from the other side to enhance their opportunity for the best possible settlement. This is a characteristic of the negotiation process and should be expected. Every negotiator must decide how open and honest to be in communicating needs and preferences. If a negotiator is completely open and honest, he or she often will settle for less than if he or she conceals goals and fights harder for a better settlement. However, if a negotiator is completely deceptive about goals, the talks may never move in the direction of a settlement. This dilemma of trust poses a key problem for negotiators: First discussions may reveal little of their true needs, with disclosure offered only in an effort to move discussions forward. As both sides begin to trust each other, this process becomes easier.[16]

3. **Packaging items**. It is difficult to achieve an agreement on all issues at one time. As many as 50 economic and noneconomic issues may be involved during negotiations; if all are left on the table at the same time, the process may become unwieldy. Instead, a few items may be packaged together, agreed to, and removed

from further discussion, allowing both sides to achieve their goal on one or more items and thus establish trust in the process. The number of unresolved issues decreases as more packages are agreed to, moving negotiations toward completion. Packaging may at least narrow the list of disputed items to the high-priority issues for each side. The ground rules may require each chief negotiator to "sign off" on a package—signing and dating a written counterproposal detailing the items agreed to—thereby removing them from further discussions.

4. **Throwaway items**. Negotiators, in their list of initial demands, may include items of no real value to their side, thus providing items to trade in exchange for others of high priority to their side. Throwaways can be the basis of a successful bluff if the other side believes it has won a concession on an important item. The throwaway items may have real value, but they simply are not of high priority in comparison with other issues. A throwaway item for one side may, in fact, be a high-priority item for the other side.

5. **Caucusing**. Much of the negotiating time is spent in the two parties' meeting separately. After a proposal or counterproposal is received, a team usually asks for a caucus. There they can openly discuss the merits of the proposal and their willingness to accept it, or they can formulate a counterproposal. A major part of the strategy may be *not* to reveal at the table how the party feels about a proposal received from the other side. Even an obviously desirable proposal may lead to a caucus, in which the team accepts the proposal without emotion. An expression of happiness over one item may lead the other side to believe they need not give on further items. Caucusing is also used for resolving disagreement among members of the same team and gathering additional information about unanticipated or costly proposals.

6. **Flexibility**. The successful negotiation process requires the exchange of many proposals and counterproposals. Every proposal received should be studied and responded to by acceptance or a counteroffer. Immediate rejection of a proposal implies inflexibility and a response of "we will only accept our position." This attitude angers the other side and may in fact be bad faith bargaining. Also, most proposals must be carefully evaluated before their merits can be accurately estimated.

7. **Compromise**. The key to successful negotiations is compromise by both parties. If either side believes they will achieve every goal, then most likely no settlement will be reached. Instead, both parties must realize that their goals are in direct conflict; if one side gains on an issue then the other side loses. If one side loses on too many issues, they may not sign the agreement, or if forced to sign then they certainly will be looking to "even the score" during the next round of negotiations.

At the end of most negotiations, spokespersons for each side are likely to say to the public, "We achieved the best contract we could—we wish we could have done better." Both sides will list issues they believe they won and issues on which they desired something different. Because both sides achieved some of their goals, their negotiators save face with those they represent. Neither side declares itself or the other side winners or losers but rather "tough negotiators."

Exchange of Proposals and Counterproposals. After the posturing, the real working sessions begin. Agreements are often made almost immediately on less important items. Usually these are noneconomic items that both parties wish to resolve. When the bargaining on economic issues begins, the parties tend to back away from item agreement and look to total packaging. During negotiations, changing proposals must be analyzed for their cost. Until the total economic agreement is seen, neither party can be sure of its position. Negotiators can use different approaches to reach an actual agreement. Some examples follow.

1. The parties can separate economic and noneconomic issues and agree on the noneconomic issues first. Changes improving grievance procedures, work rules, job evaluations, and similar items are often sought by both parties and can be more readily agreed to than issues involving costs and benefits.
2. The parties can separate and discuss economic and noneconomic issues. Items can then be traded, with each side winning one item and giving up another until all the issues have been resolved.
3. The parties can discuss each economic and noneconomic issue separately but may not agree to anything until all items are agreed upon. This total packaging approach, while perhaps more difficult, allows both parties the opportunity to evaluate the entire collective bargaining agreement before making a commitment.

Point of Crisis.   Finally, negotiators reach a decision. Once all of the proposals and counterproposals are on the table, the parties either agree or stop talking. If agreement cannot be reached, this may be the point of crisis. Various techniques such as mediation and arbitration are available to bring the parties back to agreement. Job actions such as strikes and lockouts, although they receive a great deal of publicity, are seldom used to resolve contract disputes.

Tentative Agreement.   As the last paragraph of Profile 6-1 states, all tentative agreements reached by representatives of management and the union are just that—tentative. At this point, the union leadership will hold informational meetings to present the details of the tentative agreement to the members and to answer questions.

Then the agreement must be ratified (receive a majority positive vote) by the members of the union. If the union negotiators have done a good job of determining the priorities of the members, keeping them informed during the negotiation process, and estimating what they will or will not accept in a new contract, then this step is routine. To show solidarity with their leadership, members usually accept the contract offered to them as the "last, best, and final" one. The ratification process involves a secret-ballot process that can take several days to allow all members at all occasions the opportunity to vote. The process can be complicated, however; for example, in 1996 the International Longshoreman's and Warehouse Union rules required a 60 percent majority of all voting members across the United States because the Los Angeles and San Francisco local union leaders vetoed the proposed contract.[17]

Contract.   Once agreement has been ratified, the contract is written. The contract language is very important and should accurately state the parties' agreement since they are expected to abide by it through its duration. Many griev-

THE NEGOTIATING PROCESS, AS DESCRIBED BY THE UAW

The Union Makes Us Strong: Collective Bargaining

The collective bargaining process gives workers power in decisions that affect their everyday lives on the job as well as the economic security of their families. Collective bargaining has been called the "art of the possible"; and the UAW, more than any other union, has pushed the boundaries of what is possible in collective bargaining.

For example, the UAW negotiated the first fully funded pension plan, the first employer-paid health insurance plan for industrial workers, the first employer-paid health insurance plan for retired workers, the first cost-of-living adjustments (COLA), and the first Supplemental Unemployment Benefit (SUB) program. In the 1980s, the UAW pioneered joint union-company education and training programs. In the 1990s, the UAW won an unprece-

dented role for workers and their union in decisions affecting product quality and, at the Big 3 U.S. auto makers (Ford, GM, Chrysler), a landmark job and income security program protecting workers against volume-related layoffs.

The UAW's collective bargaining goals are set democratically—by bargaining unit members at the local level and by elected delegates to the Collective Bargaining Convention at the international level. The written collective bargaining agreement typically covers wages, benefits, working conditions, grievance procedures, seniority, union representation, hours of work, vacation and holidays, dues check-offs, and union security.

All tentative agreements must be voted on by secret ballot by the members. Ratification requires a majority of votes. Informational meetings to review and discuss the tentative agreement are held before the ratification vote.

"How the UAW Works," http://www.uaw.org/faqs/howuawworks/collective.html (January 7, 1997).

ance and arbitration actions stem from ambiguous contract language; the parties may even disagree on whether the language reflects what they negotiated.

The four areas most contracts cover are union security and management rights, the wage and effort bargain, individual security, and contract administration.

BARGAINING TECHNIQUES

Labor and management meet across a negotiating table because of the National Labor Relations Act. The act requires that the parties bargain in good faith but provides that neither party has to agree to any particular proposal as long as it continues to bargain in good faith. Thus, the act establishes the boundaries of the negotiation process but leaves the internal workings to the parties involved.

Over the years, the bargaining process has changed from an adversarial confrontation between the forces of capitalist and worker into a stylized ritual between the representatives of management and labor. Collective bargaining may be nothing but a process by which the negotiators seek to make the main terms of the agreement, which are already decided, acceptable to the parties.

Whether or not that observation is correct, collective bargaining has certainly changed from mere confrontation to a process by which labor and management sincerely attempt to resolve conflicting interests. Respect for the process, however, does not eliminate the conflict. The resolution of this conflict has been analyzed in numerous ways.

Labor negotiation has often been inaccurately compared to playing games. Games have a definite set of values and rules, so parties know when they are winning and, more important, when they are losing. There are no rules in negotiation except for those set by the parties, and the rules are often a part of the negotiation itself. The most important difference, however, is that **negotiation** *is the art of compromise*, assuring that neither party wins or loses everything.

Studies of the collective bargaining process seem to separate styles of bargaining into three categories. Styles focus on the *parties* involved (psychological or behavioral), on the *issues* to be decided (economic or analytical), and on the relative bargaining *power* of the parties (game theory or pressure bargaining).[18] Each approach has its strengths and weaknesses.

To focus on the parties making the decisions is perhaps the most realistic approach because the bargaining process is only as successful as the people who carry it out. However, analysis of the collective bargaining process through the relationship of the parties assumes a rational negotiator who compares benefits with the costs of a particular course of action and undertakes that course only when benefits exceed cost. It also assumes that the negotiator is in total control, the parties have good information available, and all their assumptions are correct.

A study of collective bargaining assessing only the issues discussed can be comforting because of its simplicity. For example, comparing the cost of a strike for the employer and employee in order to arrive at each party's breaking point would seem an exact science. Still, this approach lacks an understanding of the emotions and knowledge of the parties involved.

A study of collective bargaining focusing exclusively on the relative bargaining power of the parties can overlook the personalities and the strengths or weaknesses of their positions on the issues. The focus is on muscle and how it is used to control the process.

The collective bargaining process is in reality a combination of the three styles. The parties interact on the issues using whatever advantage they have to achieve their goals. The key to successful bargaining lies in flexibility and in understanding and controlling the process. The following approaches are written in a "how-to" style, designed as a starting point for understanding the collective bargaining process.

Distributive Bargaining

Two parties are involved in distributive bargaining when they view the negotiations as a "win-lose" situation—the goals of one party are in direct conflict with those of the other party. Resources are viewed by the negotiators as fixed and limited, and each side wants to maximize its share of the limited resources. Every negotiator should understand distributive bargaining because (1) many collective bargaining situations are distributive and (2) many negotiators use distributive strategies almost exclusively.[19]

In collective bargaining, both sides may view the process as distributive bargaining. The limited resources include the monetary assets of the firm, which can be used for a variety of purposes—new equipment or machinery, divided payments, higher wages, and so on. Another limited resource would be unfilled positions, so deciding who is promoted or transferred can be the subject of distributive bargaining. Other noneconomic issues, such as union security, employee grievances, and plant rules, can also be included. Both labor and management view any positive change from the current contract as something to be gained at the negotiation table and as a loss to the other party.

The distributive bargaining process can best be explained by five key elements:

1. **Target point.** The optimal goal or objective a negotiator sets for the issue, the target point, is the point at which the negotiator would most prefer to conclude negotiations.
2. **Resistance point.** The resistance point is a maximum or minimum beyond which the negotiator will not accept a proposal. This is the negotiator's bottom line.
3. **Initial offer.** This is the first number or offer the negotiator presents as a written formal proposal.
4. **Settlement range.** The difference between the resistance points of labor and management is the range in which actual bargaining occurs, because anything outside the range will be quickly rejected by one party.
5. **Settlement point.** The heart of negotiations is the process of reaching agreement on one point within the settlement range, the settlement point. The objective of each party is to achieve a settlement point as close as possible to its target point.[20]

An example of the distributive bargaining process is illustrated in Figure 6-4. First, both sides develop and keep confidential their target and resistance points. Labor has surveyed its members, reviewed similar contracts recently negotiated, and estimated the company's financial situation. Within a generally favorable economic package, the labor negotiators set 4.5 percent as their target point but are willing to consider any offer above 3 percent, the resistance point, if the total package contains other economic benefits. They honestly believe that the members would vote against any contract with less than a 3 percent increase because inflation since the last negotiation has averaged 4 percent and recent contracts in the industry have included raises between 3 and 5 percent. Management negotiators set their target point at 3 percent, the lowest increase negotiated by any of their

Distributive Bargaining Negotiation: First-Year Base Wage Increase (percentage) — **Figure 6-4**

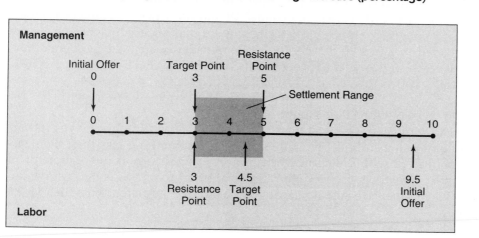

competitors. The company president has authorized them to accept an offer of up to 5 percent, the resistance point, if the total economic package is within a certain dollar amount.

Next, both sides choose their initial offers. Management decides that a proposed wage giveback (decrease in base wage) might be considered bad faith bargaining because the company is in a reasonably good financial condition, so it initially offers a 0 percent increase, the lowest possible given the circumstances. Labor knows that no similar union has received more than 6 percent and therefore feels that 9.5 percent (just under double digits) is as high an initial offer as can be made within the context of good faith bargaining. Both sides realize that their initial offers must be different from their target point to allow room for negotiation "give and take" while also staying within what the other side would consider a reasonable and good faith offer. At the same time, both sides realize that the other side's initial offer has left them room to negotiate and is not their last, best, or final offer.

Negotiations between the two sides now center on the 0 to 9.5 percent range. Each side begins trying to convince the other to move from its initial offer. Neither side knows the target or resistance point of the other side. Both sides will, however, through bargaining table discussion, begin to estimate the target and resistance points of the other side to determine if a settlement range exists and therefore a settlement point can be found. At the same time, each side strives to convince the other of the validity of its own position. By presenting factual information such as company records, copies of recent contracts, and industry data—as well as persuasive information such as employee survey data— negotiators hope to influence the perceptions of the other party. Management may try to convince labor that to remain competitive and avoid layoffs, the company cannot afford an expensive settlement and is willing to take a strike if necessary. Labor may try to convince management of the members' determination to negotiate a high increase and their willingness to put on a successful strike.

Eventually, both sides believe that they know, indirectly or directly, the other side's resistance point. For example, management might state, "We will seriously consider an offer under 5 percent if the total package is right," or labor might indicate, "Our members know that no other local has settled for less than 3 percent." Now the negotiations center on the settlement range, both sides realizing that there are many possible settlement points within the range.

Now the "hard" bargaining begins. Within the 2 percent settlement range, each side carefully proposes a settlement point that, especially when wages are considered, may include other economic items in a package. And, most important, each negotiator is careful to propose only a settlement that he or she is prepared to accept. Within this range any offer might be accepted if both sides have a settlement point. Once the settlement point has been proposed and accepted, it is too late to "hold out for a little more."

The settlement point is finally reached when one side achieves its target point or when both are willing to accept something less than their target points but within the settlement range. Factors such as the arguments of the other side, the total package, fatigue, or belief that "this is the best we can do," may influence negotiators to accept a settlement different from their target point.

Principled Negotiations

A process called **principled negotiations** was developed by the Harvard Negotiations Project and published in a book titled *Getting to Yes*. The essential element of the process is to be "hard on the merits, soft on the people."[21] The goal is to decide the issues presented at the negotiating table on their merits rather than through the traditional haggling process that focuses on what each side says it will or will not do. Substituting principled negotiations for the traditional pressure bargaining will theoretically result in a wiser agreement through a more efficient process that improves the relationship of the parties.

The key element in principled negotiations is to separate the people from the problem, an approach that ensures a focus on interests not on positions; it generates a variety of possible options before a decision on a given position is made; and it insists that the result of the bargaining is based on some objective standard.

People. Under the principled negotiation model, the first objective is to *separate the people from the problem*. This objective is accomplished by accepting the human element involved in negotiations. An understanding of the attitudes and perceptions of the parties is vital, along with the realization that not *what* is true but what the parties *believe* to be true is important. Neither party can convince the other of the legitimacy of its position without understanding the other party's perception of that position. Therefore, the first task of a negotiator is to understand the other party's perception. It is best to discuss these perceptions openly and to understand their importance to both of the parties. For example, during hard economic times, a union's noneconomic demands for job security may be more important to the union than management perceives. If management can understand that importance, it should be easier to reach a mutually satisfactory agreement.

Perceptions can be changed. Consistent with the old adage, "Actions speak louder than words," behavior inconsistent with the other party's perception can help change that perception. Unions expect management to approach the bargaining table determined to maintain the status quo. Thus, if management were to present original proposals to improve employee performance and so give an employee more job satisfaction, the union's perception of management might change.

Once a party's attitude is understood but cannot be changed, a proposal couched in terms consistent with that attitude may lead to agreement. The compromises involved in negotiation often mean a loss to one party or the other. Enabling the party not to perceive such a compromise as a loss may successfully separate the person from the problem.

Emotion strongly affects the collective bargaining process. Both parties come to the negotiating process with personal feelings: There may be strong negative feeling generated by a historically bad labor climate, or a strong positive feeling of power may prevail. Emotions must be recognized, and the parties must be allowed to express their pent-up frustrations. Releasing steam may defuse an otherwise explosive situation.

Finally, negotiating parties must learn to communicate.[22] Too often they are not really trying to converse but are simply going through the motions. To communicate effectively, a party must first actively listen and acknowledge what is being said. If necessary, a party should repeat in its own words what the other party has said to ensure understanding. When speaking, a party should remember that the goal is to persuade. Dialogue should be simple, with each side expressing its own position and then remaining silent so the parties can digest what was said.

People can also be prevented from becoming a problem by building a working relationship before negotiations begin. A not-so-subtle tactic is mixing the seating of the two teams at a negotiating session. This arrangement increases the possibility that the parties will attack the problem rather than each other.

Interests. *Attacking the problem* is the second objective of principled bargaining. The parties are to focus on interests not on positions. In general, parties come to the negotiating table with a laundry list of demands. Because a party has invested time, energy, and thought in that list, there is a strong tendency to defend it no matter how absurd it may be.

In principled negotiations, the parties are to develop an understanding of their real desires, concerns, and interests rather than simply to list demands. The achievement of those interests is left for future resolution. Both sides have multiple interests, and if those interests can be identified without the parties' hardening into a particular position, conflict is eliminated.

Options. Once interests are identified, the third objective is for both parties to *seek as many options as possible in solving their conflicting interests*. More often than not, the interests of both parties can be satisfied in numerous ways. If creative thinking is applied, interests can overlap, allowing both parties to reach a successful compromise.

In order to seek numerous options, both parties must be willing to accept that there *is* more than one right answer. In seeking new solutions, a party must separate the acts of inventing and judging options. A proposal does not make a hard-and-fast position.

Options must be broadened. The belief that one party's gain will always result in the other party's loss often prevents successful bargaining. Therefore, options must be presented so that both parties are allowed some advantage. When possible, identify interests that the parties share. For example, underlying every relationship between employer and employee is a shared interest in the health of the employer's industry; this fundamental interest must be present at the negotiating table. A creative negotiator will find ways to identify and explore shared interests, even as conflicting interests are negotiated.

Objective Criteria. The fourth objective in principled negotiating is to have the *validity of each party's proposals judged by objective criteria*. For example, the parties could agree to ask for expert advice when discussing technological changes that might affect workers' jobs. Working together to understand the expert's advice can more easily lead to agreement than working in opposition can; either party can criticize the other party's proposal or defend its own without destroying the relationship. This approach puts the parties in side-by-side negotiations against an objective third party, the criteria, instead of in a head-to-head confrontation. Agreement becomes easier when the basis of the agreement is recognized criteria.

Obviously, principled negotiation has its negative aspects. Realistically, parties in a negotiation do not often have equal bargaining power, so the temptation to engage in pressure bargaining may be strong. A party can try to keep the negotiations in a principled negotiations model by refusing to participate in pressure bargaining. Real communication is possible if the parties focus on the issues and resist reacting to attacks. Attacks on a position can be treated as an attack on the problem; the counterattack can then be limited to reasoned questions or criticisms on the issue involved.

Collective Bargaining by Objectives

Another method proposed as an alternative to pressure bargaining is **collective bargaining by objectives** (CBO). CBO is an adaptation of management by objectives (MBO) techniques to the collective bargaining process. In his book *Collective Bargaining by Objectives*, Reed C. Richardson proposes a framework for negotiators in accomplishing the common, ordinary tasks involved in collective bargaining.[23]

Table 6-2 contains the suggested outline to prepare for the collective bargaining process. Under this model, the subjects to be discussed at the bargaining table are listed in the first column. In the second column, the party rates the items, establishing priorities. The next three columns, entitled Range of Bargaining Objectives, enable the party to evaluate objectively the strength of a particular demand. The range of bargaining objectives includes what the party will accept (pessimistic); what the party believes it will get (realistic); and what the party would like to get (optimistic). The initial bargaining position is stated in the sixth column, leaving the last three columns to record the results of the collective bargaining process.[24]

Collective bargaining by objectives demands that the parties make certain assumptions and, on the basis of those assumptions, set priorities and establish an

Collective Bargaining by Objectives   **Table 6-2**

Bargaining Items[1]	Priorities[2]	Range of Bargaining Objectives			Initial Bargaining Position[3]	Evaluation Results[4]		
		Pessimistic	Realistic	Optimistic		P	R	O
Financial								
Holidays	8	8 days	7 days	6 days	6 days	X		
Wages	1	10¢ first year; 10¢ second year	5¢ first year; 10¢ second year	5¢ first year; 10¢ second year	12¢ over three years		X	
Nonfinancial								
Union security	12	Union shop	Modified union shop	Agency shop	Agency shop			X
Probationary period	20	30 days	60 days	90 days	120 days		X	

[1]Classify items in two groups: Financial and nonfinancial.
[2]Priority of each bargaining item relative to all bargaining items.
[3]Actual visible position taken at opening of negotiation (union initial proposal or company response or counteroffer).
[4]P, pessimistic; R, realistic; O, optimistic.
Source: From Reed C. Richardson, *Collective Bargaining by Objectives* (Englewood Cliffs, NJ: Prentice Hall, 1977), pp. 109–110.

acceptable range of agreement before the negotiation process begins. Although it stresses a rational and positive approach, this method recognizes the essentially adversarial nature of collective bargaining.

By establishing priorities, a party identifies those items it can bargain away and those having little or no room for compromise. Understanding priorities, therefore, allows the party to plan its strategy before the heat of negotiations so actions are based on real goals and values and not on emotions. Clearly delineating the objectives also puts the party in a position of confidence and certainty aimed at eliminating irrational actions during the negotiating process. The structural approach to priorities and the range of objectives allow for more complete delegation of authority to the bargaining team.

Certain guidelines must be followed in using CBO. The confidentiality of the information concerning priorities and the range of objectives must be preserved. As the basis for strategy and compromise, the priorities and range become useless if the other party becomes aware of them. Also, this model does not include strike or lockout considerations. According to Richardson, "The objectives approach, while not ignoring pressure tactics, is based primarily on the achievement of goals through sound preparation and a careful, systematic approach to negotiation."[25]

Pressure Bargaining

An understanding of the use of pressure during labor negotiations is necessary in any study of collective bargaining. The bargaining power model assumes that settlement in the collective bargaining process is determined by the relative bargaining power of each party. Simply stated, if it costs more to disagree than to agree, the party *will* agree. It is therefore an objective during collective bargaining to determine the costs associated with negotiations. Subsequent chapters discuss how to estimate costs for various contract proposals and provisions. However, the cost of agreeing or disagreeing *during* the collective bargaining process can be quite different.

The ultimate test of strength in the negotiating process is the union's ability to strike and the company's ability to take a strike. Before such action is undertaken, both sides, either formally or by instinct, decide on a range within which settlement can be achieved. If either party refuses to enter that range, pressure must be applied.

In the **pressure bargaining** model, as with any model for collective bargaining, the parties must make sound assumptions. Miscalculations of the target point can lead to costly and futile actions. Even under the pressure bargaining model, certain techniques such as those that follow lessen the chance of confrontation.

Pressure Tactics. The use of certain tactics during pressure bargaining is often designed to pressure the other party into accepting something they would normally refuse. Often these tactics *work*, but they can *backfire* when the members of the other side find them offensive or recognize them for what they are and use a good countertactic. The most frequently used pressure tactics are described here.

- *Good Guy/Bad Guy*. Similar to the "good cop/bad cop" routine seen on television police shows. One negotiator opens with tough, often unrealistic, positions, which are presented with threats, foul language, and obnoxious behavior. Then, while the first, "bad" negotiator leaves the room, the "good" negotiator tries to reach a quick agreement on an issue before the bad partner returns. In some negotiations the bad roles are assigned to supervisors or union members on certain issues they are likely to be particularly concerned about, and the chief negotiator plays the good role.

- *Highball/Lowball.* This tactic relies on a ridiculously high (or low) opening offer. The other side then reevaluates its position on the issue and moves closer to the resistance point, while the opening negotiator has not moved at all.
- *The Nibble.* This tactic occurs when a negotiator asks for a small concession on an item not yet discussed in order to "close the deal" on a large issue. For example, a union negotiator agrees to accept management's profit-sharing proposal, the last unresolved issue, if management will "throw in" new safety shoes. The union negotiator may claim to be embarrassed about "forgetting" the shoes until the end. Management negotiators must determine whether their profit-sharing proposal would be accepted anyway—or are the safety shoes a "deal buster"?
- *Chicken.* Named for the car-swerving contest, this tactic is a high-stakes game. Management, for example, threatens to close operations and go out of business if the union does not accept its "last, best, and final" offer. It may be a bluff, but can the union risk it? Can management risk *not* closing down if the union calls the bluff? This may be the strongest pressure tactic of all.[26]

How can a negotiator successfully deal with other negotiators who use one of these pressure tactics? Some proven methods include:

1. *Ignore them.* Simply not responding to unwarranted pressure tactics is usually the best response.
2. *Acknowledge and discuss.* "I see you are using the old good cop/bad cop routine. Well, we can play that routine if that's what you want."
3. *Respond in kind.* Counter with another hardball tactic, such as walking out while shouting obscenities.
4. *Befriend the other party.* This tactic often disarms people who might otherwise use pressure tactics. It is far more difficult to attack friends than it is to attack adversaries.[27]

IMPASSE

No matter what method of negotiations is followed, the parties at some point must agree or face an **impasse** (a stalemate). There are many reasons why negotiations could result in an impasse. The most obvious is that the interests of the two parties have not been reconciled. Another reason is that one party has no real intention of settling. Their overall strategy might include going to an impasse to show how inflexible the other party is. Also, during pressure bargaining, a strategic impasse may appear necessary to move the two parties closer together, and a genuine impasse results by simply miscalculating how close the parties really are.

Both parties have numerous options when an impasse occurs. One option is third-party intervention such as mediation or fact finding that could keep union negotiations open and workers on the job. Both sides may agree to continue the old contract on a day-to-day basis, maintaining wage and benefit levels, and preventing a strike or lockout. Or union members can continue to work without a contract, taking whatever benefits the employer hands them. The employer can continue benefits at the previous contract level, increase them, or, theoretically, it could decrease benefits. The last usually indicates negotiating in bad faith. Another option is a lockout staged by an employer: He or she withholds employment to resist worker demands or gain concessions. Still another option is a strike called by a union.

Usually, economic pressures during negotiations are initiated by the employees because the union's goal in contract negotiations is to increase benefits whereas management's goal is to maintain the status quo or gain concessions. A strike, however, may be called and endured for reasons other than a genuine inability to agree. One party may merely have miscalculated the breaking point of the opposition and increased a demand or refused a request once too often. Errors in strategy or in the interpersonal relations of the negotiator could preclude an opportunity for compromise. Management may want to liquidate surplus inventory while production is stopped by a strike. Union leaders may want to consolidate workers' support for their leadership, proving that a future strike threat has to be respected. Union leaders may feel the need for union solidarity that can be fostered only by a picket line. Often a strike is needed to vent member frustration over an inevitable but unsatisfactory contract settlement.[28]

An impasse may result after the negotiation teams have reached a tentative settlement and union membership rejects the contract. Such rejection may stem from a misjudgment of membership wishes by union officials or an inability to sell the agreement.

Calling a Strike

Whatever the reason for an impasse, a decision to strike is not made lightly. In many instances the union negotiating team has called for a strike vote early in the negotiating process to prove its bargaining power when it becomes necessary to apply pressure. Although such a vote strengthens the negotiator's position, it needs to be carefully worked so that a strike deadline is not imposed, thereby tying the negotiator's hands. Slow-moving negotiations could become deadlocked; the deadline could destroy the negotiating atmosphere.

A union must weigh the cost of a strike against the probable benefit. A strike means loss of wages when wages may be quite high after years of successful union negotiations. Strike benefits also can be a drain on union funds. Workers risk losing their jobs, and even if they return to work, a strike can damage or destroy a good relationship with the employer. In addition, a union risks the loss of public sympathy. The success or failure of previous strikes and the availability of other jobs must also be considered.

Today, union leaders are far less likely to call a strike than in past years. In fact, the Bureau of Labor Statistics reports that in 1995 the number of major U.S. strikes (1,000 or more employees) fell to 31, the fewest since 1947, when it began recording strike data. The loss of wages and potential permanent loss of their jobs are reasons why fewer union members and leaders are willing to call for a strike. But the general sentiment is one of cooperation as expressed by Marilyn Lewis, a Chrysler employee and union officer: "We'd like to see a wage increase, and we do want to fight for our issues, but we want to compromise and make everyone happy. No one wants a strike."[29]

The union must also keep in mind a 1988 U.S. Supreme Court decision disallowing food stamp benefits for striking workers. Thus, most striking workers must rely solely on personal savings and union strike funds to withstand a strike. Union members who financially cannot hold out any longer may choose to resign from the union during a strike and cross the picket line to work. In most situations, unions cannot discipline members for crossing picket lines after resigning even if the members have agreed to union rules prohibiting crossing picket lines.[30] However, peer pressure from union strikers makes the decision to resign and return to work extremely difficult for most strikers.

Management Response.   The majority of strikes occur when the existing contract expires, then employers have ample notice to prepare a strike plan. However, many wait until negotiations begin to break down, which is too late. A strike plan often focuses on how the employer will shut down operation during the strike, continue to operate with only management personnel, or hire replacement workers. Strikers may not be fired during a strike, but they can be replaced with permanent replacement workers.

Employers may not lawfully discharge a striking worker *until* they have hired a replacement worker to fill the position. In one case, supervisors telephoned bargaining unit employees to see which would be striking. The employees were told that if they did strike, replacements had been hired. A federal appeals court upheld the company's actions when the union filed an unfair labor practices charge because contract negotiations were under way.[31]

President Clinton's historic Executive Order 12954 (discussed later), signed March 8, 1995, penalizes employers for permanently replacing lawfully striking employees. The order, however, applies only to employers with federal contracts of $100,000 or more.

Both sides should keep in mind the possibility of an eventual settlement calling for the recall of striking workers even after replacements have been hired and the possibility of "bonuses" being paid to them to compensate them for lost income. Although such events are rare, the Steelworkers Union, in 1996, reached an agreement with Bridgestone-Firestone two years after the union workers went on strike. The agreement provided for the recall of almost all the workers at five U.S. plants and the payment of $15 million in bonuses to them. The Japanese-owned company had been charged by the Steelworkers with illegally replacing the 6,000 striking workers.[32]

Predicting Strikes.   Empirical research about the possible causes of strikes has produced conflicting conclusions. To date, a model of the collective bargaining process accurately predicting or explaining strikes in the United States has not been produced.[33] Perhaps the causes are too numerous and unpredictable to be easily explained. Some research has shown that the state of the economy and political forces in labor relations are significant predictors of strike activity. Thus, when negotiators believe that these factors are in their favor, they are more likely to call a strike. These predictors are limited in their usefulness because they do not account for the specific factors involved in each individual strike decision.[34] Other studies have shown that strikes are more likely to occur when either management or labor fails to estimate correctly the other party's level of interest in critical factors.[35] Management, for example, may underestimate the union members' concern over job security and the need for retraining rights or their perceived erosion of real wages due to inflation. Labor may not correctly estimate management's perceived need to adhere to a certain product-pricing policy or pressures from nonunion or foreign market competition.

The cost of a strike has also been shown to affect the likelihood and length of a strike. The employer considers costs such as loss of output, overtime costs to fill back orders, and the possible short-term and long-term effect on consumers and therefore market share. Some consumers may temporarily change to other products or supplies during a strike. Then, because of their satisfaction with the new product or service or as an expression of dissatisfaction with the striking company, they never return as customers. Profits and losses, increased legal and associated fees, and public image are also of concern to employers. The workers are primarily concerned with their loss of income during a strike. Union strike funds and government assistance seldom provide income equal to their previous take-home pay. Also to be carefully considered is the possible permanent loss of their jobs due to the eventual shutdown of the company or replacement by strike-breakers. Both sides consider their own strike costs in comparison to possible negotiation gains resulting from a strike. If the strike costs for the two parties are obviously unequal, that inequality translates into bargaining power for the side facing lower costs.[36]

A study of 1,050 negotiations in the United States revealed other possible strike determinants. Several factors were found to significantly affect the likelihood of a strike: (1) the proportion of males in the workforce, (2) product demand in the marketplace, (3) size of bargaining unit, (4) union density in the industry, and (5) the extent to which wages kept pace with inflation over the prior contract. Unions were most likely to strike when they contained more male than female members, product demand was high, the bargaining unit was large and located in a union-dominated industry, and wages had not kept pace with inflation.[37]

The circumstances that cause workers to strike and form a picket line are often tense and thus can easily provoke strikers to "let off steam," an impulse that can easily lead to serious misconduct. Workers on strike may resort to conduct that the employer believes is improper—conduct that causes damage to property, or in some cases, even bodily harm. The NLRB has held that activities of striking employees constitute serious misconduct when they "reasonably tend to coerce or intimidate employees."[38] The application of this standard has led the courts and the NLRB to consider physical acts or threats of physical harm directed at nonstriking employees (called *scabs*) to be serious and warrant possible discharge. Actions that have been ruled as serious misconduct include the throwing of rocks or eggs, vandalizing a supervisor's car, carrying a gun or a club on the picket line, and threatening physical harm.[39] In *Clear Pine Mouldings, Inc.*,[40] the NLRB ruled that verbal threats alone could warrant the discharge of a striker who, while carrying a gun, threatened to kill a nonstriking employee. In most cases, the isolated instance of obscenities or name calling alone will not be considered as serious strike misconduct. If an employer fires striking employees because of serious misconduct, the employer is not required to show that all of the employees engaged in the activity if they were "actively cooperating" in the misconduct. And violent activity can result in the removal of the participants from the protection of the NLRA. An examination of misconduct cases led one labor attorney to conclude that arbitrators are generally tolerant of strikers' misconduct, particularly if the employer provoked the incident.[41]

Although the number of strikes in the United States is far fewer today than it was before the 1981 PATCO strike (discussed later), each year hundreds of thousands of people are affected by economic strikes. For example, in a typical year—1993–1994 as illustrated in Table 6-3—more than 320,000 employees and 600 employers were directly affected by strikes in just the 10 largest U.S. unions.[42]

Types of Strikes

Economic weapons such as a strike are necessary to the collective bargaining process. Many such actions are protected under the National Labor Relations Act. The **primary strike** is a strike between an employer and employee. For employees to be protected under the act, a labor dispute must exist between the striking employees and their employer.

The act recognizes two types of strikes and handles them differently. An **economic strike** is called to effect the economic settlement of a contract under negotiation. An **unfair labor practice strike** is called to protest an employer's violation of the National Labor Relations Act. For example, if a union member was fired for union activities, workers could stage a strike until the discriminatory practice was remedied.

Under either strike action the worker retains status as an employee and thereby remains under the protection of the National Labor Relations Act. The worker's right to reinstatement after a strike will depend on the type of strike. After an economic strike, the employee is not entitled to reinstatement if the employer filled the job with a permanent employee during the strike. However, as demonstrated in Case 6-2, if the job has not been filled or becomes vacant when a replacement leaves, it can be reclaimed by the worker. Employees are entitled to reinstatement after an unfair labor practice strike even if the employer has filled their positions. Strike misconduct by the employee in either case can disqualify the worker from reinstatement.

Strikes in Top 10 Unions (September 1, 1993, to August 31, 1994) — Table 6-3

Union	Number of Strikes	Number of Workers Affected
Teamsters	131	87,563
Steelworkers	62	20,442
Machinists	42	26,177
United Auto Workers	37	60,692
United Food and Commercial Workers	24	28,365
National Education Association	20	4,284
Electronic Workers	17	2,262
Operating Engineers	16	1,273
Service Employees International Union	15	1,448
Retail/Wholesale	15	832
Total strikes—all unions		601
Total workers—all unions		321,395

Source: Brenda Paik Sunoo, "Managing Strikes, Minimizing Loss," *Personnel Journal*, January 1995, p. 52.

ECONOMIC STRIKES

The company is a manufacturer of mobile homes with approximately 110 employees. As a result of the breakdown in collective bargaining negotiations between the company and the union, about half of the employees went on strike. The company cut back its production and curtailed its orders for raw materials. The strike ended, and a contract was signed. The union requested reinstatement of its strikers. The company explained that it could not reinstate the strikers because of the curtailment of production caused by the strike but that it intended to increase production to the full pre-strike volume as soon as possible. Six strikers who applied for reinstatement were not hired. However, within six months of the strike six new employees who had not previously worked for the company were hired to fill jobs the striker applicants were qualified to fill. At a later date, the six strikers were reinstated. The employees filed charges against the company, claiming it was an unfair labor practice to hire the new employees instead of the six strikers.

The NLRB trial examiner agreed with the employees and recommended that the company make the six employees whole for loss of earnings. The NLRB upheld the trial examiner's findings. The company appealed to the Court of Appeals. The court reversed the board's finding on the basis of the fact that the company did not have jobs for the six strikers on the date they applied for reinstatement; thus, not hiring them on that date was not a violation. The employees appealed the court's decision.

Decision

The Supreme Court found that the company did commit an unfair labor practice by not hiring the six striking employees when jobs became available. The Court found no merit to the fact that there were no jobs on the first date the employees applied. The Court stated that the basic right to jobs cannot depend on job availability at the moment when applications are filed because the status of the striker as an employee continues until he or she has obtained regular and substantially equivalent employment. The Court recognized that frequently a strike affects the level of production and the number of jobs and that it is normal for striking employees to apply for reinstatement immediately after the strike and before full production is resumed. Then, when a job becomes available for which the striker is qualified, he or she is entitled to an offer of reinstatement. This right can be defeated only if the employer can show legitimate and substantial business justification for not reemploying. The company obviously had the applications of the striking employees on file and could show no legitimate business reasons for not hiring them when the jobs became available.

Adapted from *National Labor Relations Board v. Fleetwood Trailer Company, Inc.,* 389 U.S. 375 (1967).

A strike beginning as an economic strike may become an unfair labor practice strike if the union can prove that an employer is refusing to bargain in good faith. It is obviously to the union's advantage to do so, as it is to management's advantage to keep the strike an economic strike by continuing to negotiate in good faith. Management then has the option to hire replacement workers during the strike and keep the plant open, thereby lessening any adverse impact caused by the strike. At the end of the strike, the replacement workers can be retained, and the employer may have upgraded the workforce with minimal disruption.[43]

A strike technique that has recently gained favor with unions whose members work at numerous locations for the same employer is the **rolling strike**. A rolling strike targets one location at a time for a union walkout. The location, however, can change daily, making hiring replacements or covering locations with management nearly impossible.[44]

It is interesting to note that courts will not allow an employer to assume that permanent replacement workers hired during a strike are anti-union. In *NLRB v. Curtin-Matheson*, the Supreme Court upheld the board's rule that permanent replacement workers must be treated as any other group of employees when determining whether they wish to be represented by a union. That they took jobs while union employees were on strike does not create a presumption that they are anti-union.[45]

Permanent Striker Replacement.   This distinction between how striking employees are treated as a result of an economic or an unfair labor practice strike was established by a Supreme Court decision in 1938.[46] Before the 1980s, however, companies seldom replaced striking workers with permanent replacements for a number of reasons. Frequently, an economic strike was determined, after the fact, to be an unfair labor practice strike and the replacement workers were displaced. Often the company used the issue of allowing the strikers to return to their jobs as a way to settle an economic strike.

Economic factors of the 1980s led companies to use permanent replacement workers more than ever before.[47] Mergers, downsizing, and companies going out of business provided many employers with available trained workers during a strike. High unemployment and a weakening of union membership caused workers to cross picket lines willingly and to take jobs at wage rates *lower* than union-bargained rates.

Organized labor's response to this increased use of **permanent replacement workers** was to lobby Congress to amend the National Labor Relations Act to make such action on the part of an employer an unfair labor practice. The Workplace Fairness Act, as it has been called by its proponents, was a major showdown between management and labor when it came before Congress. Advocates for the act used the following arguments for their position:

1. Employees should not lose their jobs for exercising a very basic right protected under the NLRA—the right to strike.
2. Employers can often keep their business open during a strike without using permanent replacement workers.
3. Hiring scab labor and leaving them in the workplace after the strike leads to hostility and ill will, which the NLRA was supposed to eliminate.
4. Employers use the hiring of permanent replacement workers not for balancing the scales during a strike but as an opportunity for union busting.[48]

Opponents of the amendment to the NLRA warned that changing the rules regarding replacement workers could result in many companies' closing their doors. The only effective weapon a company has when faced with an economic strike is to keep operating without the unionized workers. Some companies can continue to function with supervisors and their other nonunion employees, but many must hire workers to stay in operation. Being able to attract quality employees requires these companies to offer permanent jobs.[49]

When Congress took up the proposed change in 1994, the U.S. House of Representatives passed the amendment, but it died in the Senate. Some people believe that the outcome of the striker replacement issue will determine the future direction of the collective bargaining process in the United States.[50]

In a 1995 attempt to support labor's position on striker replacements, President Clinton issued Executive Order 12954. This order authorized the federal government to disqualify employers who hired replacement workers from receiving certain federal contracts. The U.S. Chamber of Commerce challenged the Executive Order and the U.S. Supreme Court ruled that it was preempted by federal labor laws and, therefore, was illegal.[51]

Illegal Strikes. Strikes undertaken by unlawful means or purposes are not legal, and employees can be fired. Unlawful means of conducting a strike include the following:

1. **Sit-down strike**, a takeover of the employer's property. This action is seen as a violation of the owner's property rights.
2. **Wildcat strike**, an economic strike conducted by a minority of the workers without the approval of the union and in violation of a no-strike clause in an existing contract. Although courts try to discourage such actions to ensure the continued credibility of the union, these strikes may be sanctioned if actually called to protect one of the union's aims.[52]
3. **Partial strike**, various types of job actions such as a work slowdown, refusal to work overtime, or an organized effort to have all workers call in sick. This action is seen as a violation of the owner's property rights. In the absence of an absolute strike, the employer cannot replace the workers to keep the operation going, although the employer continues to be responsible for the workers' wages.

The National Labor Relations Act requires that a union desiring to terminate or modify an existing contract may not strike for 60 days after giving written notice to the employer or before the termination date of the contract, whichever occurs later. Also, the appropriate federal and state mediation agencies must be notified within 30 days. Any strike held during the 60-day period is unlawful.

The National Labor Relations Act outlaws some consequences for which workers might strike. The following are unlawful ends that make a strike illegal:

1. **Jurisdictional strike**, called because two unions are in dispute as to whose workers deserve the work. For example, an electrical union could strike a construction site in protest of laborers' being used to unload electrical supplies.
2. **Featherbedding strike**, when a union tries to pressure the employer to make work for union members through the limitation of production, the amount of work to be performed, or other make-work arrangements.
3. **Recognitional strike**, when a strike is called to gain recognition for another union if a certified union already represents employees.[53]

Picketing

The use of picket lines during a strike varies according to the type of union involved. A craft union strike generally uses only two or three pickets. The purpose of the picket is simply to inform other craft union members that a strike is in progress. Because craft union workers are skilled laborers, they cannot easily be replaced by workers who will not honor a picket line. Craft unions may employ larger picketing groups when protesting the use of a nonunion contractor.

An industrial union strike, however, often requires an active and large picket line to discourage unskilled laborers from keeping the production lines in operation. Mass picketing generally takes place at least at the start of a strike to persuade union members to join the strike and to keep strikebreakers away.

An employer may respond to mass picketing by obtaining a court injunction against the union to refrain from certain activities. An injunction, usually in the form of a temporary restraining order, is possible if the strike activities have included incidents of violence, personal injury, or damage to property. In such cases, the court can order specific restraints on the union's use of pickets—limiting, for instance, their number and location.[54]

Today, picket lines have lost the power they once provided unions. In years past, a picket line in front of a plant, store, or construction site could cause a major financial loss to the employer. Union and nonunion workers would "honor" the picket line. Crossing the line was the equivalent of pushing an old lady off a curb. Labor sympathizers would refuse to enter picketed workplaces as employees or customers. When unions represented 36 percent of the labor force, almost every adult had at least one union member in the family—and thus was sympathetic to labor's cause. Today, that just is not the situation. Even Rachelle Pachtman, the daughter of a union man, raised on union wages and benefits, crosses picket lines. "If there's a meeting in a hotel where workers are striking . . . I'm going to the meeting. . . . But I feel terrible."[55]

Prominent Strikes

The number of economic strikes has declined sharply in recent years. The news media, however, still keep them in the headlines when they occur.

The 1981 PATCO Strike. The first declared strike against the federal government was called by the Professional Air Traffic Controllers Organization in 1981. The 13,000 strikers thought they were irreplaceable; President Ronald Reagan, however, quickly hired permanent replacements after his return-to-work deadline was ignored. His success and public support made other employers take notice—and started the current trend of replacing strikers.

The 1983 and 1989 Telephone Workers' Strikes. Nearly 700,000 unionized telephone workers broke a 12-year labor peace on August 7, 1983. This strike was partially the result of an order by federal judge Harold Greene to divest AT&T into 22 local operating companies. The federal order, combined with the company's need to increase its use of high technology to remain competitive, gave union members ample reasons to fear future loss of jobs. Thus, their demands centered on employment security, although higher wages and benefits were also issues. Union negotiators asked that management and the unions jointly finance broad training and retraining programs to give members the necessary skills for the high-technology jobs of the future. Management felt that such a request went far beyond normal provisions for job security to a requirement of career security.[56]

The effects of modern technology at AT&T were strongly felt as a result of the strike. After the first two weeks, the company reported almost no interruption in service except for new installations. Ninety-seven percent of the calls were handled by automated computer systems, which had also enabled management to reduce the ratio of supervisors to workers from five-to-one to two-to-one in less than 20 years. By scheduling supervision on 12-hour shifts and by postponing some work, AT&T was able to keep the strike from affecting most of its customers.

Management's ability to endure the strike by means of automated equipment and longer shifts of supervision was something new. Harley Shaiken dubbed it **telescabbing**, using modern technology as a substitute for labor during a strike instead of hiring scab labor.[57] Shaiken further stated that many industries, including oil, steel, and utilities, will be able to maintain high production levels during strikes because of automation, thus taking away the unions' ability to disrupt production by striking.[58] Unions had lost one of their most important collective bargaining tools as a result of high technology. Although repair work, new installations, and some long-distance calls were affected by the strike, union leaders underestimated the ability of the company to continue its normal operations.

This six-year labor peace ended in August 1989, when nearly 157,000 telecommunications workers went on strike after contracts expired between the Communication Workers of America (CWA) and the International Brotherhood of Electrical Workers and three of the seven Bell companies (created in the 1984 breakup of AT&T). The strike against Pacific Bell in California, Bell Atlantic, and NYNEX in New England centered on the issues of wages, job security, and the financing of health benefits. The striking workers faced the same critical problem they first witnessed in 1983—telescabbing.

The 1986–1987 Steel Industry Negotiations. For the first time in 30 years, the major U.S. steelmakers decided in the spring of 1986 not to bargain jointly. The prior use of **coordinated bargaining** enabled all the major steel producers to negotiate common wage rates and benefits with the United Steelworkers of America. All parties (including 450,000 workers) had also enjoyed relative harmony with an industrywide no-strike agreement. However, foreign competition and weakening demand due to newer and cheaper steel substitutes had caused the industry to lose more than $1 billion in the previous two years. Thus, each steelmaker decided to negotiate separately a contract that could mean survival or bankruptcy.[59] USX and the union had the longest strike in steel history.

The 1989 Eastern Airlines Strike. In March 1989, the International Association of Machinists (IAM) went on strike against Eastern Airlines and was joined by the pilots and flight attendants as Eastern filed for bankruptcy. The strike was triggered by Eastern's demands for large wage concessions from the machinists. In reality, however, the discontent that fueled the strike may have begun when Texas Air Corporation, an obscure airline owned by Frank Lorenzo, staged a takeover of Eastern Airlines in November 1988. In 1983, Lorenzo, a self-proclaimed "union-buster," took Continental Airlines into bankruptcy proceedings, imposed significant wage cuts, and broke the pilots' and machinists' strikes. Continental survived as a profitable, low-cost (and low-paying) airline. The machinists and pilots at Eastern saw what was coming and decided to strike even if it broke Eastern.

Late in 1989, the Eastern Airline pilots voted to return to work, leaving only the IAM out on strike. The Eastern strike is a good example of how even highly trained and technical employee unions have a difficult time sustaining a strike.

1993 United Mine Workers. In early May 1993, the United Mine Workers began a selective strike against coal producers after contract negotiations failed to result in a new master agreement with the Bituminous Coal Operators Association (BCOA). The primary goal of the union during the talks was to stem the coal operators' practice of opening new, nonunion mines.

1994 Baseball Players Strike. The most disastrous strike in sports history canceled the 1994 World Series and cost the sport many fans (see page 103).

1996 General Motors Strike. A local labor dispute in one plant eventually crippled the world's largest automobile company. UAW local in Dayton, Ohio, went on strike over outsourcing—the employer practice of giving business to nonunion suppliers that usually will eventually mean fewer union jobs. The strike gained national prominence and historical significance because the Dayton General Motors plant supplied 90 percent of the brakes for GM cars and trucks. Thus, within weeks more than 72,000 workers at 21 of GM's 29 North American auto assembly plants were idled at a cost of $45 million per day (see Figure 6-5). This method of using a **selective strike** had been used by the UAW with Ford and Chrysler, but not nearly as effectively. The new UAW strategy was to avoid large national strikes by thousands of members, which drain support and the strike fund. A selective strike can have the same effect yet pose less risk and cost to a union.[60]

1997 UPS Strike. The Teamsters Union strike idled over 180,000 workers and crippled delivery of packages worldwide. A central issue was part-time versus full-time jobs. The union won 10,000 new full-time jobs and focused national attention on this issue.

The Spreading Impact of the March, 1996 GM Strike **Figure 6-5**

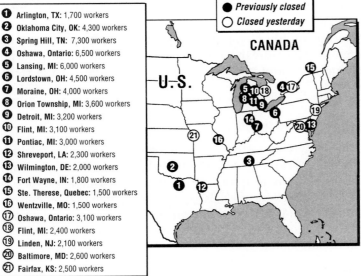

Assembly plants where production has been halted

❶ Arlington, TX: 1,700 workers
❷ Oklahoma City, OK: 4,300 workers
❸ Spring Hill, TN: 7,300 workers
❹ Oshawa, Ontario: 6,500 workers
❺ Lansing, MI: 6,000 workers
❻ Lordstown, OH: 4,500 workers
❼ Moraine, OH: 4,000 workers
❽ Orion Township, MI: 3,600 workers
❾ Detroit, MI: 3,200 workers
❿ Flint, MI: 3,100 workers
⓫ Pontiac, MI: 3,000 workers
⓬ Shreveport, LA: 2,300 workers
⓭ Wilmington, DE: 2,000 workers
⓮ Fort Wayne, IN: 1,800 workers
⓯ Ste. Therese, Quebec: 1,500 workers
⓰ Wentzville, MO: 1,500 workers
⓱ Oshawa, Ontario: 3,100 workers
⓲ Flint, MI: 2,400 workers
⓳ Linden, NJ: 2,100 workers
⓴ Baltimore, MD: 2,600 workers
㉑ Fairfax, KS: 2,500 workers

● Previously closed
○ Closed yesterday

Source: Rebecca Blumenstein, Nichole Christian, Oscar Suris, "GM Local Labor Dispute Spins Out of Control," *Wall Street Journal*, March 13, 1996, p. B1. Used by Permission.

Lockout

Although less frequent than strikes, an employer **lockout** may also result in a labor dispute. The employer may withhold employment to resist union demands or actually to force concessions from the union. The lockout can be accomplished by layoffs, shutting down, or bringing in nonunion workers. The employer again must measure the same factors involved in withstanding a strike when deciding to lock out the employees: loss of profits, cost of continued operations, possible loss of customers, and the effect on future labor negotiations. Employer lockouts can be in violation of the National Labor Relations Act as an unfair labor practice if they are invoked to prevent unionization or to preclude collective bargaining before it begins.

Courts have supported both defensive and offensive employer lockouts under the Taft-Hartley Amendments. In *defensive* actions, employers are justified in a lockout if a threatened strike caused unusual economic loss or operational difficulties. In multiemployer bargaining, a strike against one employer can justify a lockout by the others to preserve the integrity of the multiemployer bargaining unit. *Offensive* economic lockouts have been justified after an impasse has developed during collective bargaining negotiation or if the lockout was used to pressure employees to end the labor dispute on grounds favorable to the employer. The courts reasoned that an economic strike by employees seeks the same end, and therefore the lockout is protected.[61]

The use of replacement workers during a lockout is governed by the same rule as using replacements during a strike. Permanent replacements may be hired during a lockout to affect the economic outcome of a contract under negotiations but not if the lockout is a result of an unfair labor practice by the employer.[62]

In a recent case, the NLRB was asked to rule on whether a lockout was an unfair labor practice by the employer. The parties were in negotiations but unable to reach agreement on a contract renewal. The employer undertook a lawful lockout and replaced union workers with nonunion workers under a "temporary" agreement. However, as negotiations with the union resumed, the employer decided to permanently replace the union workers. The board found the employer guilty of an unfair labor practice. It ruled that the lockout and permanent replacement of the employees would have been legal had the employer originally taken this action. However, the conversion from temporary to permanent after resuming negotiations was an attempt to pressure the union into accepting the employer's position at the bargaining table and was "inherently destructive" of the rights protected under the act.[63]

No-Strike, No-Lockout Provisions

Most agreements contain provisions restricting the union's ability to call a strike and management's ability to stage a lockout. Usually either both or neither type of provision is negotiated since they are reciprocal in nature. No-strike and no-lockout clauses often contain similar, if not identical, language, falling into two general categories: (1) unconditional bans (63 percent of agreements) on interference with production during the life of the contract and (2) conditional bans that permit strike or lockout under certain circumstances, usually one or more of the following:[64]

Exhaustion of grievance procedure
Violation of arbitration award
Refusal to arbitrate dispute

OPEN LETTER TO UNION MEMBERS

Non-union companies are the winners in the strike by the local union. Customers don't stop using products just because a union is on strike. They are turning to non-union companies to fill their needs. Every day the strike continues, union companies are losing business to non-union companies.

Learn a lesson from history!!! After the last strike, over one hundred union companies never reopened.

This strike is unfair to union members. As customers turn elsewhere union jobs are put at risk. We want a contract that preserves union jobs by making our company competitive with non-union companies.

The only way to achieve job security is to be competitive. The only way to get a competitive agreement is for union leaders to return to the bargaining table.

The question is not "Who is winning this strike, union or management?" Non-union companies are!! How much more will they win at the expense of our company and the workers?

JOHN DOE
President
Union Company

Paid Advertisement

Noncompliance with portion of agreement
Deadlocked contract reopener

The discipline or discharge of employees participating in illegal strikes under a no-strike provision may be permitted in the agreement. Most of these clauses provide for appeal by the employee.[65]

No-strike clauses are usually highly sought by industry, but severe circumstances may alter their value. As discussed above, since 1956 the U.S. steel industry enjoyed an industrywide no-strike agreement. In 1986 the six major U.S. steelmakers decided to bargain separately with the United Steelworkers of America. The firms' fierce competition for survival forced them to give up the safety of joint negotiations and the continuance of the no-strike pact, and led to the longest steel industry strike in history.[66]

Resolution of Impasse

When possible, an impasse should be avoided. Parties to negotiations can decide early on to seek a mediator to encourage joint problem solving. Bargaining techniques such as principled negotiations and collective bargaining by objectives can be used to avoid pressure tactics. Entering into negotiations long before the contract expiration date can relieve some of the deadline pressure. The use of joint labor-management study committees before and during the contract negotiations also can alleviate much of the conflict present in traditional bargaining sessions.

Still, an impasse often cannot be avoided, and resolution becomes one of the stages of negotiations. Sometimes a pressure tactic works and one of the parties reactivates negotiations more favorable to the opposing party. Often informal communication through a neutral third party enables the parties to resume talks to a successful conclusion. Traditionally, however, an impasse is resolved by resorting to **mediation** and **arbitration** services.

1. **Mediation**. These services are available through the Federal Mediation and Conciliation Service (FMCS) and similar state agencies. A mediator assists in rescheduling negotiation sessions, reopening discussions, and making suggestions on possible areas of agreement. If an impasse has been caused by a mere misunderstanding of the parties' positions, an unbiased third party can often show them how close they actually are to agreement. If the impasse is caused by the substantive distance between the parties, a mediator must try to bring the respective proposals closer together.[67]

The mediator can only bring the parties together and keep them talking. He or she has no independent authority and will be successful only if trusted by both sides. Studies have confirmed that the qualities likely to aid a mediator in reaching a settlement are knowledge, expertise, impartiality, and sincerity.[68]

2. **Interest arbitration**. Although infrequently used in the private sector, this method involves the selection of an arbitrator or panel to listen to both sides of a dispute and to make a final and binding decision on the details of the final agreement. This process substitutes a person or panel for the negotiating parties in formulating a written contract.

3. **Final-offer arbitration**. This method requires both parties to submit their final offer to an arbitrator or a panel that has the authority to select one of the proposals. Final-offer arbitration gives the parties the motivation to make their final offers reasonable. Both parties realize that an unreasonable offer will have a lower chance of selection. Therefore, they strive to make their offer appear as fair and reasonable as possible.

In 1987, Detroit Tiger Jack Morris won a $1.85 million contract dispute through final-offer arbitration. The baseball players' union and major league owners had agreed to begin using the impasse resolution technique in 1974 to settle salary disputes. When the Tigers and their star pitcher could not reach a salary agreement, they each presented their final offer to an arbitrator who could choose only one of the two offers and could not choose a compromise. The Tigers' last offer was $1.35 million—$500,000 larger than the previous largest final-offer arbitration award. Morris proposed $1.85 million based on his 123–81 record (most wins in the majors in the 1980s) and his performance in the 1984 World Series.

4. **Mediation-arbitration**. A combination of items 1 and 2, in this method parties agree to bring in a mediator with authority to arbitrate *any* unresolved issues. Since the parties must agree to abide by the mediator-arbitrator's decision, they will likely agree on the substantive issues as well.

5. **Fact finding**. This method lies between mediation and arbitration. A hearing, similar to the one used in the arbitration process, is used to assemble and make

the facts public through the media. But the fact-finding panel, like a mediator, can only recommend how an impasse may be resolved. Fact finding can be used to delay a strike, bring an unreasonable demand to the public's attention, create an atmosphere for new ideas, and, if reasonable recommendations are made, pressure a party into acceptance. This technique is used mostly in the public sector, where such pressure is useful in forcing the parties to reach an agreement, especially if the facts show that one side is unreasonable.

Individuals representing labor and management are involved in the collective bargaining process. Negotiators prepare for the negotiations, set priorities, and proceed in an honest and thorough manner. The National Labor Relations Act delineates areas of mandatory, permissive, and illegal negotiations. A good negotiator must also understand and value the human element, which is an integral part of the negotiating process. For some parties, the give and take is as important as the end result. Knowing that, although every demand was not met, the position and point of view at least being heard by the other party can be part of a successful negotiation.[69]

SUMMARY

Bargaining styles used in the collective bargaining process can focus on the relationship of the parties, on the issues to be decided, and on the relative bargaining power of the two sides. Principled negotiations emphasize getting the people involved in the negotiations to communicate on the issues. Collective bargaining by objectives borrows management by objectives techniques and proposes a framework for the negotiators by setting priorities and reasonable goals before the collective bargaining process is begun. Parties often use pressure bargaining techniques to further their bargaining objectives.

When the collective bargaining process breaks down, an impasse is reached. The parties can react to that impasse in various ways, with strikes being the most widely publicized reaction. Most often, however, mediation, arbitration, and fact finding are used to resolve impasses.

CASE STUDY 6-1

SURFACE BARGAINING

Facts

The company was charged with an unfair labor practice for failure to bargain in good faith. The union alleged that the company was engaged in surface bargaining with no intention of entering into a collective bargaining agreement. The company had begun meeting with the union after it had been certified by the NLRB. Eighteen bargaining sessions were held over an 11-month period. The negotiations did not result in a contract. The parties did reach agreement on a recognition clause; the numbers, rights, and duties of union stewards; the use of a bulletin board by the union; pay for jury duty and other leaves of absence; a procedure for processing grievances and arbitrations; and plant visitation by union representatives.

The administrative law judge hearing the case found that the company met at regular intervals and bore no anti-union animus. The company's conduct away from the bargaining table did not indicate that the company had no intention to conclude an agreement with the union. As there was no evidence of a failure to meet to discuss terms and conditions, the arbitrator had to examine the proposals by the company and by the union to see if their substance

(continued)

indicated good faith bargaining. The company's proposals are briefly outlined as follows:

1. *Wages.* The company insisted that it remain in total control over wages. Wage increases were to be determined on the basis of semiannual merit reviews, in which the union would have no participation. The union had proposed a specific wage schedule, but the company would not adopt it.

2. *Management rights.* The company retained absolute right to subcontract work; to assign it to supervisors; to abolish jobs; and to transfer, discontinue, or assign any or all of its operations to others. It required the union to relinquish the employees' statutory right to notice in bargaining over such actions and their effects. Actions taken under the management clause were subject to the grievance procedure only if that right was limited by express contract provision, and there was no such limitation.

3. *Zipper clause.* The company proposed a zipper clause, which waived the union's right to bargain during the life of the agreement over anything that could have been considered mandatory or permissive under existing law.

4. *No-strike clause.* The company proposed a no-strike clause, including prohibition against a strike for unfair labor or unfair employment practices.

5. *Discipline and discharge.* The company rejected the union's proposal of a standard right to discipline an employee for "just or sufficient cause only." The company intended to reserve exclusive authority over discharges and discipline in the management rights clause.

6. *Layoff and recall.* The company proposed that the layoff and recall of employees would be at the company's sole discretion.

7. *Dues check-off.* The company rejected a union proposal that a dues check-off clause be included in the contract.

8. *Nondiscrimination clause.* The company rejected a union proposal that stated that the company was not allowed to discriminate against union members. The company's position was that since discrimination was illegal, a clause forbidding it did not need to be included in the contract.

Questions

1. Was the company bargaining in good faith? Explain your answer.
2. Which company proposal was the most important in determining the "in good faith" issue?
3. Suggest how either principled negotiations or collective bargaining by objective techniques could be utilized in this case.

Adapted from *A-1 Kingsize Sandwiches,* 112 LRRM 1360 (1982).

CASE STUDY 6-2

NEGOTIATING

Facts

The company is an interstate trucking company with 98 percent of the stock owned by its president or his relatives. The president makes almost all of the company's decisions. The union received a bargaining order from the NLRB in October 1972, and bargaining began in November 1972. Between November 1972 and December 30, 1974, when negotiations ceased, the parties met 25 times. The principal union negotiator was its president, who attended all the negotiating sessions but the last. The principal management negotiator was a vice president of operations, who attended all the meetings accompanied by two lawyers.

(continued)

The company president attended the initial meeting and the last three.

At the first meeting when the union negotiator advised the company that any negotiated agreement was subject to the approval of the employees, the company president stated that the company's executive committee would have to ratify any agreement also. There was, however, no executive committee and the president alone intended to exercise the right of ratification.

The union's initial proposal was its master agreement covering over-the-road drivers. The company responded that the master agreement was written for dry-freight haulers and this company hauled wet freight. The union agreed to keep that fact in the negotiations. The negotiations bogged down for nine months on whether owner-operators were part of the unit. A decision by the NLRB that they were not was finally reached. Though slowed by this dispute, negotiations continued, and some issues were agreed upon.

After the fifteenth and the twentieth sessions, in January and March of 1974, status sheets prepared by the company negotiator were given to the union negotiator. One such sheet appears in Table 6-4.

Although the president was not directly involved in the negotiations, in late April he reviewed the negotiations file kept in his office and began to rewrite portions of the draft agreement. He arrived at a negotiation session and proposed his draft, which caused the union negotiator to object and accuse him of bad faith bargaining. The president asserted he was acting pursuant to his right of ratification. Two more sessions were held with more changes from the president. The negotiations stopped at the December 30, 1974, meeting when the president received a petition from 80 to 90 percent of the unit employees stating that they no longer wanted representation by the union.

The union charged the company with a violation of the duty to bargain in good faith.

The company's position was as follows:

1. The president lawfully reserved the right of ratification at the first meeting.
2. A great deal of spade work was necessary because of the unique nature of the company's business.
3. That spade work was not done until the summer of 1974.
4. The president's entering into negotiations at that time was reasonable.
5. The president was merely exercising his right of ratification.

The union's position was as follows:

1. The negotiations prior to the president's involvement had resulted in tentative agreements on numerous noneconomic issues. These agreements had been reached through a give-and-take process involving mutual compromises. The president's alternative proposals, late in the negotiations, were either a return to the company's original position or to an even more management-oriented position. His proposals bore no resemblance to any of the spade work that had been done over two years of negotiating.

2. Although the individual proposals had been only tentatively agreed to, *major* changes to previously agreed-to provisions evidence bad faith. In this instance the president's proposals were harsher than the company's original proposals.

3. The uniqueness of the company's product would not necessitate two years of spade work on an issue such as a grievance procedure and then a totally different proposal by the president.

4. Negotiators must have some authority to speak for the company. In this case, the company's chief negotiator had not even seen the president's proposals prior to the negotiating session in which they were presented.

5. If the company's negotiating position was to be totally in the president's hands, he should have communicated his positions to his negotiators *before* the two years of meetings.

(continued)

| Table 6-4 | Negotiations Status Sheet | | |

Name of Section	Status	Date
Preamble and existing operating practices	OK	3-8-73, 2-21-74
Contracting practices	OK	12-11-73
Bargaining unit	OK	1-11-74
Scope of agreement	Hold but OK	Discussed 1-11-74
Separability and savings	OK	12-11-73
Workweek and workday	Hold	Set 5-10-73
Meals	OK	1-10-74
Unassigned employees	Withdrawn	1-11-74
Pay period	OK	1-10-74
Wages	Hold	Discussed 12-11-73
Holidays	Hold	Discussed 12-11-73
Vacation	Hold	Discussed 12-11-73
Seniority	OK	1-10-74
Federal and state regulations	OK	12-11-73
Nondiscrimination	OK	4-25-73
Stewards	OK	12-11-73
Management rights	OK	12-11-73
Work rules	OK	2-21-74
Grievance/arbitration	OK	12-11-73
Work stoppage/lockout	OK	2-14-74
Sick leave	Hold	Set 3-9-73, 4-4-73
Jury duty	OK	3-9-73
Discipline	OK	2-14-74
Interchangeability	Hold	Discussed 2-14-74
Employee examinations	OK	2-17-74
Maintenance of standards	OK	1-11-74
Existing operating practices	? See Preamble	2-14-74
Hiring of personnel	OK	1-10-74

Note: As of 2-21-74 the following articles or topics are either being held for economic reasons or have not been specifically discussed during negotiations.

1. Wages	6. Pension
2. Holidays	7. Workday/workweek
3. Vacation	8. Overtime
4. Sick leave	9. Length of contract
5. Health and welfare	10. Check-off

6. Using a negotiating session after two years of bargaining to present the company's position and then claiming it as his right of ratification was clearly bad faith bargaining.

Questions

1. Would you rule for the union or the company? Why?
2. Could the union have used either principled negotiations or collective bargaining by objectives techniques to resolve this disagreement? Explain your answer.
3. Could establishing more specific ground rules have helped negotiations in this case? Explain your answer.
4. If the company president intended to stall the negotiations, what, if anything, could the union negotiator have done to prevent it?

analysis
arbitration
Borg-Warner doctrine
collective bargaining by objectives
coordinated bargaining
economic strike
fact finding
ground rules
illegal bargaining subjects
impasse
jurisdictional strike
lockout
mandatory bargaining subjects
mediation

negotiation
permanent replacement workers
permissive bargaining subjects
planning
posturing
pressure bargaining
primary strike
principled negotiations
rolling strike
selective strike
separability clause
telescabbing
unfair labor practice strike
wildcat strike

1. What are the different styles used by negotiators?
2. Why are perceptions so important during the negotiation process? Why is listening critical to negotiators?
3. Can management by objectives be effectively used in labor negotiations? How?
4. Who are the principal parties involved in the collective bargaining process? What are their roles?
5. List some guidelines negotiators can use in aiding the negotiation process.
6. Why do negotiators use posturing during labor negotiation sessions?
7. Distinguish between mandatory, permissive, and illegal bargaining subjects.
8. What types of strikes could result in employees' being legally fired?
9. Describe commonly used methods for resolving a negotiation impasse.
10. Explain the significance of the proposed change to the NLRA that would prohibit an employer from replacing striking workers with permanent replacements.

TAKE IT TO THE NET

We invite you to visit the Carrell/Heavrin page on the Prentice Hall Web site at:

http://www.prenhall.com/carrellr

for this chapter's World Wide Web exercise.

Surface Bargaining at St. Matthew's Hospital   EXERCISE 6-1

Purpose:
To help students understand the bargaining process.

Task:

The union became the certified bargaining representative for the employees at St. Matthew's Hospital. The company was contacted by the union on December 2, 1990. The union stated that it would like to begin contract negotiations as soon as possible. The representatives for the company responded to the union's request, stating that they would not be ready to negotiate for the next two months but could possibly begin in March 1991. The union responded that the waiting period was too long and the negotiations should start sooner or the union would file an unfair labor practice charging the company representatives with refusal to bargain. The company then reluctantly agreed to begin negotiations on December 15, 1990.

The two sides met and set forth their initial demands. The company initially refused to bargain on the union's proposal. The company's initial proposal was extremely low, cutting back in benefits that the employees had received previously. For counterproposals, the company hardly moved from its initial proposals. During negotiations the union would state a demand and provide supporting statistics, primarily data from other hospitals. Management would ignore the union's proposal and bring up an entirely unrelated issue.

On the union's wage proposal, the company responded with an outright no. The chief negotiator said there was no way the company could come close to accepting the proposal. The only wage proposal offered by management was the current wage rates, and it was stated that there was no room for negotiation on this item. The union requested financial information from management, and management negotiators said they would be happy to furnish all relevant financial data to the union. Three weeks later the company gave the following information from the previous year: Revenue = $3,596,700; Operating Expenses = $2,700,000; Fixed Expenses = $560,000. The union requested a further breakdown, which the company never furnished. The union requested a final meeting in which both sides would sincerely attempt to settle, or the union would call a strike. They met and again could not agree on anything. The union called a strike. Has the employer committed any unfair labor practices? Explain. What could the employer and the union have done differently to avoid the strike?

| EXERCISE 6-2 | **Bargaining Techniques** |

Purpose:
To help students identify how some of the bargaining techniques discussed in the chapter can also be found in everyday negotiation situations as characterized by the following Dilbert cartoon.

Task:
Identify how each of the following negotiation techniques is illustrated in the Dilbert cartoon.

Example:

Technique	*Explanation*
Win-win negotiating	The buyer has obviously been taken, but he thinks he "won" a good deal and even a free hood ornament.

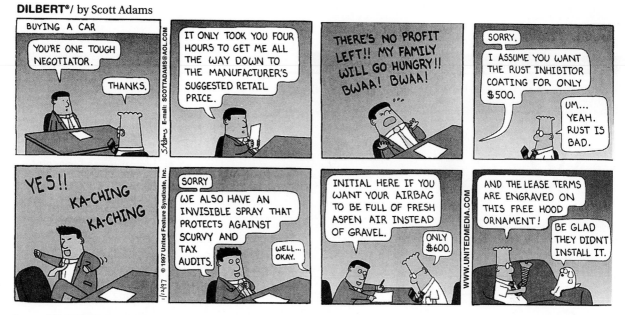

Source: DILBERT © United Feature Syndicate. Reprinted by Permission.

Technique	Explanation
1. Posturing	_____
	_____
	_____
2. Throwaway items	_____
	_____
	_____
3. Concealment of objectives	_____
	_____
	_____
4. Face saving	_____
	_____
	_____
5. Strategy	_____
	_____
	_____
	_____

If you are using Smith/Carrell/Golden *Collective Bargaining Simulated, 4E*, with this text, please refer to the following:

p. 9 for the survey of employee economic and non-economic preferences, and pp. 29–34 for a description of bargaining team member roles.

CHAPTER 7

Wage
and
Salary Issues

- Union Wage Concerns
- Management Wage Concerns
- Negotiated Wage Adjustments
- Wage Negotiation Issues
- Wage Surveys
- Costing Wage Proposals
- Union Wages and Inflation
- Summary

Wages are often considered the most important and difficult collective bargaining issue, and relief is evident on the faces of these negotiators when workers and management shake hands on a new contract.

Historic UAW–GM, Ford, Chrysler 1997–1999 Agreements

A historic round of negotiations between the Big 3 automobile makers—General Motors, Ford, and Chrysler—and the United Automobile Aerospace and Agricultural Implement Workers of America (UAW) set a new precedent in the automobile industry. Negotiations in 1996 occurred with no "strike target" being declared by the UAW. In past years the UAW's designation of a strike target had always led to bitter strikes. But the cooperative negotiations of 1996 led to agreements that met all of the UAW's top concerns:

- *Job security.* A guarantee that union employment will not fall below 95 percent of the level at the time of the signing.

- *Outsourcing.* The auto makers agreed to replace any jobs lost to outside suppliers, with a few exceptions for GM.
- *Bonuses and wage hikes.* A lump-sum $2,000 bonus to eligible workers, with 3 percent wage increases in the last two years.
- *Retirees.* Rare cost-of-living protection was provided to inactive members.
- *Employee tuition plans.* First-time assistance up to $3,800 per year for high school, college, and other targeted courses of study.
- *Veterans holiday.* The new holiday increases the 1997–1999 paid holiday total to 16 per year.

Adapted from *UAW-Chrysler Newsgram*, October 1996.

Wages and other economic benefits for employees are undoubtedly the meat and potatoes of collective bargaining in labor relations. To the employee, they represent not only their current income and standard of living but also potential for economic growth and the ability to live comfortably during retirement. Wages are often considered the most important and difficult collective bargaining issue. When negotiated settlements are reported to the public, the first item specified is the percentage wage increase received by employees. In fact, in many cases that may be the only item employees consider critical or an absolute must as they vote to ratify a tentative agreement.

> There is a feeling these days among employees that [the company] is a good place to work and the benefits are good [but] it's just not enough. You can't feed a family on good working conditions. . . . Right or wrong, shortsighted or not—because of inflation money seems to be the prime motivator and driving force.[1]

According to industrial research, pay level is positively related to employee satisfaction.[2] Employees consider their pay to be a primary indicator of the organization's goodwill. Many in our society consider the salary or income one receives as a measure of one's worth. Employees can get an exact measure of their salary, which can easily be compared with the salaries of fellow employees and those in other organizations and occupations. Therefore, most of us consciously or subconsciously compare our income levels not only with inflation and our cost of living but also with incomes of other individuals.

Wages and benefits are also a prime collective bargaining issue to the employer. They represent the largest single cost factor on their income statement. Although many management negotiators would like to pay high wages to employees, the reality of competition and the knowledge that competitors may be able to secure less expensive labor make it difficult to survive. Unlike many costs, such as capital and land, wages constantly rise, and they are not as easy to predict. Wages are the single most important source of tax revenue to federal, state, and local governments and in general are a strong indicator of the economic vitality of a community.

The total economic package of wages and benefits may be negotiated as a complete item rather than treated individually, enabling both sides to estimate accurately the total cost of the contract to the organization in terms of increases over current salary and benefits. In this chapter we will discuss wage issues; employee benefits are covered in Chapter 8. Wages and benefits are separated to draw a distinction between the two; however, negotiators consider them part of a total economic package.

Labor and management negotiators normally define pay by either time worked or units of output. **Pay for time worked**, or an **hourly wage** or **annual salary**, has become the predominant means of employee compensation in the United States. Most labor contracts contain specific job titles and associated wage scales agreed upon by labor and management. An example is Figure 7-1, an agreement between the Anaconda Aluminum Company division of the Atlanta Richmond Company and the United Steelworkers of America AFL-CIO. *Pay for units produced*, usually referred to as **piecework**, is still utilized in many industries as not only a means of wage determination but also a motivational technique. Many piecework systems today provide a guaranteed salary with an additional rate established for units of output above a certain production level.

Group		Department
I	Die Repair	Maintenance
II	Maintenance	Maintenance
III	Cage Attendant	Material Handling
	Checker	Shipping
	Head Loader	Shipping
	Guillotine Operator	Window and Prime
	Brake Operator	Millroom and Prime
	Crane Operator	Material Handling
	Automatic Bander	Door and Prime
	Automatic Saw-Punch Machine	Millroom and Prime
IV	K. D. Material Handler	Material Handling
	Utility	Door and Window
	Thermal Break Operator	Prime
	Large Glass Cutter	Specialty
	Large Punch Press Operator	Door and Millroom
	Loading and Receiving	Shipping
	Plant Truck Driver	Shipping
V	Salvage	Material Handling
	Material Handler	Material Handling
	Janitor	Maintenance
	Loader-Unloader	Paint Line and Prime
	Schlegeler	Door, Millroom, Prime and Specialty
VI	(None)	
VII	Glass Cutter	Window, Specialty, Prime and Insulated Glass
	Glass Puller	Door
	Sample Builder	Sample
	Glass Washer and Assembler	Insulated Glass
	Spacer Assembly	Insulated Glass
	Sealant Applicator	Insulated Glass
	Parts Puller (Sash, Screen, Frame)	Window
	Saw Operator	Door, Millroom, Prime, Specialty and Insulated Glass
	Belt Line	Door
	Door Prehanger	Door
VII	Screen Pre-Assembler	Door, Window, Specialty and Prime
	Screener	Door, Window, Specialty and Prime
	Sash Builder	Door, Window, Specialty and Prime
	Frame Builder	Window, Specialty and Prime
VIII	Small Punch Press Operator	Door, Millroom, Specialty and Prime
	Processor	Door, Millroom, Specialty and Prime
	Jamb Wrapper	Door
	Window Wrapper	Shipping
	Miscellaneous Jobs	
IX	Packaging	Material Handling
XXIII	Paint Equipment Operator	Paint Line
XXIV	Assistant Paint Equipment Operator	Paint Line

(continued)

| Figure 7-1 | Job Classifications and Wage Rates (continued) |

Group	Hire Rate Effective June 1, 1982	Rate after 35 Working Days Effective June 1, 1982
I	$7.80	$8.05
II	$7.62	$7.80
III	$7.28	$7.62
IV	$7.28	$7.54
V	$7.28	$7.48
VI	$6.95	$7.28
VII	$6.95	$7.18
VIII	$6.95	$7.13
IX	$6.95	$7.07
XXIII	$7.62	$7.86
XXIV	$7.62	$7.78

Source: Agreement between Anaconda Aluminum Company and United Steelworkers of America (Sugarcreek, Ohio, 1982), pp. 45–48. Used with permission.

As the nature of jobs changes, more agreements provide annual salaries expressed in pay grades. In Figure 7-2, for example, all of the clerical, engineering, and technical jobs at Chrysler Corporation will be negotiated to the pay grade that best reflects their value and maintains internal equity. All new employees will start at the minimum salary for the grade for their job and each year will receive an automatic step increase until they reach the top progression rate. To reach the maximum for the grade, they must be given merit pay increases.[3]

UNION WAGE CONCERNS

"A fair day's pay for a fair day's work" is a commonly used phrase summing up the expectations of many employees. Employees expect and even demand to be treated fairly and honestly by the organization. Although most are reasonable in their pay expectations, a few feel that they are being underpaid. If employees perceive that they are unfairly treated by the organization, particularly in pay matters, they typically will react by leaving the workplace either temporarily through absenteeism and tardiness or permanently through seeking employment at another organization; by reducing the quantity or quality of their production; or by filing a grievance or enacting a work stoppage through the union. Eventually their pay dissatisfaction will be brought to the bargaining table, leading ultimately to either higher wages or an economic strike. Or they may change their perceptions by simply accepting the inequity, although this response may become a permanent morale factor.[4]

Obtaining pay equity in the workplace is difficult. The slogan "equal pay for equal work" is a guide union and management leaders follow and employees expect to be maintained. Obviously not all jobs involve work of equal value to an organization. The first-year bookkeeper does not expect the same pay as a tax accountant; the same is true for a punch press operator and a maintenance attendant. Employees understand that the value of the work leads to different pay grades and classifications for different jobs. As shown in Figure 7-2, labor

Figure 7-2   Pay Grades for Salaried Union Jobs at Chrysler Corp.

Chrysler Corporation
Clerical—Engineering—Technical
18-Grade Structure

	Effective Date of Agreement				Effective September 15, 1997				Effective September 14, 1998		
Grade	Minimum	Top Progression Rate	Maximum	Grade	Minimum	Top Progression Rate	Maximum	Grade	Minimum	Top Progression Rate	Maximum
1	$470.33	*	$774.99	1	$492.33	*	$805.99	1	$515.13	*	$830.17
2	$472.53	*	$787.96	2	$494.53	*	$819.48	2	$517.33	*	$844.06
3	$475.76	*	$799.52	3	$497.76	*	$831.50	3	$520.56	*	$856.45
4	$530.05	*	$824.91	4	$552.05	*	$857.91	4	$574.85	*	$883.65
5	$546.49	$799.57	$860.87	5	$568.49	$831.55	$898.70	5	$591.29	$856.50	$925.66
6	$555.28	$808.42	$888.50	6	$577.49	$840.76	$927.16	6	$600.29	$865.98	$954.97
7	$560.96	$821.61	$908.04	7	$583.40	$854.47	$947.28	7	$606.20	$880.10	$975.70
8	$568.24	$825.46	$930.86	8	$590.97	$858.48	$970.79	8	$613.77	$884.23	$999.91
9	$587.95	$850.80	$950.17	9	$611.47	$884.83	$990.68	9	$634.27	$911.37	$1,020.40
10	$595.72	$854.98	$981.02	10	$619.55	$889.18	$1,022.45	10	$642.35	$915.86	$1,053.12
11	$614.77	$870.13	$1,000.64	11	$639.36	$904.94	$1,042.66	11	$662.16	$932.09	$1,073.94
12	$622.59	$882.28	$1,023.82	12	$647.49	$917.57	$1,066.53	12	$670.29	$945.10	$1,098.53
13	$639.91	$908.61	$1,045.99	13	$665.51	$944.95	$1,089.37	13	$688.31	$973.30	$1,122.05
14	$656.17	$926.70	$1,080.62	14	$682.42	$963.77	$1,125.04	14	$705.22	$992.68	$1,158.79
15	$662.49	$937.28	$1,100.22	15	$688.99	$974.77	$1,145.23	15	$711.79	$1,004.01	$1,179.59
16	$689.78	$962.20	$1,131.84	16	$717.37	$1,000.69	$1,177.80	16	$740.17	$1,030.71	$1,213.13
17	$706.51	$975.32	$1,162.16	17	$734.77	$1,014.33	$1,209.02	17	$757.57	$1,044.76	$1,245.29
18	$748.51	$1,032.97	$1,193.01	18	$778.45	$1,074.29	$1,240.80	18	$801.80	$1,106.52	$1,278.02

*Automatic progression to the maximum rate in Grades 1, 2, 3, and 4.
Source: UAW-Chrysler Newsgram, October 1996, p. 3. Used by permission.

agreements commonly provide for different job classifications's being assigned different pay grades according to level of skill and work demanded. As long as pay grades are fairly structured and evenly applied, employees have no trouble accepting differential pay based upon job classification and internal wage levels.

Some wage systems provide for higher wages to employees with more longevity. Thus, seniority helps employees not only in bidding for open jobs but also in receiving higher pay. Even though less senior employees perform the same work, everyone realizes that longevity pay serves as an incentive to stay with the organization.

Industrial Differentials

Industrial wage differentials also provide a logical basis for differences in pay among employers in the same labor market. Employees recognize that the relationship between labor and total production costs affects their wage levels. Organizations in highly labor-intensive industries are usually less able to provide wage increases than organizations that are in more capital-intensive industries. For example, if a specialized chemical processing plant that has few competitors increased its wage rates by 10 percent, it would need to raise prices by only 0.6 percent to absorb the wage increase because only 6.0 percent of its total production costs would be attributable to labor. However, if a southern textile firm raised its wages by 10 percent, it would need to raise prices by 7 percent because its labor costs would equal 70 percent of total production costs. A 7 percent price increase could be disastrous to the highly competitive textile organization. Employees accept and understand that not all employers, because of their profitability or current competitive position within the marketplace, can be the highest-paying organization in the industry. If profits decrease so much that the organization suffers losses, wage demands usually will reflect the reality of the economic times.

Unions affect wages to some extent in many industries. The variation of union power and ability to raise wage levels across industries appears to be related to several factors. Union wage gains are generally greatest where (1) employers' ability to pay is high because of discretionary pricing power and profitability, (2) unions practice centralized bargaining, and (3) unions avoid fragmentation.[5]

There is a correlation between more unionization and increased wage rate when local industries, such as supermarkets, are studied. Increased unionization in basically national industries, such as the aerospace industry, will not be the cause of increased union wages in that industry.[6]

MANAGEMENT WAGE CONCERNS

Wage and benefit changes have an impact on the cost of the production of goods and services. Management must consider how a change in wages will affect its pricing policy and ability to compete in the marketplace. It is often mistakenly inferred that management wants to minimize its labor costs for no particular reason or because employees are not appreciated. The reality is that management needs to maintain competitive labor costs to produce and price products successfully within their industry. Thus, maintaining a competitive position is a primary aim of management in negotiations.

Accurate assessment of competitors' wages and total payroll costs is critical for management in anticipating the future of pricing changes within the industry. Labor-intensive industries find comparable wages to be even more necessary for long-run success. Thus, when national unions seek to negotiate equal pay increases among employers in the same industry, it is beneficial to management from the standpoint of maintaining a current, competitive position. Union leaders, of course, find it beneficial to offer all members the same wage increases. More competitive and less organized industries, however, cannot provide this type of consistency.

This practice, known as **pattern bargaining**, can be highly successful for both management and labor. Steel and auto industries, as well as meat packing and textile industries, have utilized pattern bargaining in the past. Typically, the union leaders choose what they perceive as the weakest company—the one most susceptible to granting wage increases—and begin negotiations. Once negotiations are completed, the union insists that other firms in the industry agree to equal wage and benefit increases.

Pattern bargaining, however, does not prevent firms from negotiating differences according to local labor conditions and the profitability of a particular employer. Instead, when negotiated wage and benefit increases are equal for several employers, they maintain their same relative competitive position with regard to labor costs. However, during the recent economic recession, pattern bargaining has declined in such hard-hit industries as steel, rubber, and automobile. The individual profitability of affected firms becomes more important in many negotiations.

The conclusion of the Caterpillar strike in May 1992 was seen by some labor experts as the end of pattern bargaining. The union ended the strike after agreeing to drop its demand that the company accept the same contract the union had reached with Deere & Co. Caterpillar's threat to hire permanent replacement workers proved to be an effective bargaining tool, forcing the union back to work.[7]

Management is also concerned about the **value added**, labor's theory that wages should equal the contribution of labor to the final product. Out-of-hand labor costs may hamper management's ability to replace and maintain equipment and machinery. It may be tempting in the short run to absorb labor increases by reducing these kinds of expenditures. However, lack of competitive technological improvements and modern machinery can erode productivity. Thus, management wants the value added kept in proportion with the wages paid. The value added by labor to the total product and the value added by capital and equipment cannot be totally separated because of their interrelationship. One is not useful without the other, and each affects the other's increase or decrease in productivity. Determining labor's share of the value added to the product is a difficult and often debated point in labor negotiations. Sometimes subcontracting bids for specific work can be used to estimate the true value labor has added.

Wage Laws

A number of federal laws outside the NLRA affect wage rates. The major compensation legislation regulating employers is the Fair Labor Standards Act (FLSA) of 1938, as amended. It governs the items discussed below.

Table 7-1			U.S. Minimum Wage Changes under FLSA				
1938	*1945*	*1950*	*1956*	*1962*	*1967*	*1974*	*1978*
$0.25	$0.40	$0.75	$1.00	$1.15	$1.40	$2.00	$2.65
1979	*1980*	*1985*	*1990*	*1991*	*1996*	*1997*	
$2.90	$3.10	$3.35	$3.80	$4.25	$4.75	$5.15	

Minimum Wages. Under the FLSA, employers must pay an employee at least a minimum wage per hour, as shown in Table 7-1. The minimum wage per hour in 1938 was $0.25 and has been increased several times to $5.15 in 1997. Exempted from the act are small businesses whose gross sales do not exceed $500,000. Also exempted are organizations that operate within one state. However, several states have minimum wage laws that parallel the federal minimum wage provisions. The 1990 amendments to FLSA also provided for a training wage for employees under 20 years of age set at 85 percent of the minimum wage. Three studies conducted after the increase in the minimum wage rate and the creation of a training wage for teenagers showed that increases in the minimum wage caused no increase in unemployment.[8] The training wage section of the FLSA amendment expired in April 1993.

Is there really a minimum wage today? Profile 7-1 reveals that some employers would pay a lower hourly rate—and some do so illegally.

PROFILE 7-1

SWEATSHOPS IN THE 1990s

Immigrants work seven days a week sewing clothes for pennies per garment. Workers are treated as machines not as humans; they are given 15-minute meal breaks, which must be taken at the sewing machine. They are subjected to tirades from a boss who will fine someone for asking questions. Minimum wage, overtime, and workers' compensation are unknown concepts, as are doctored payroll records (to reduce hours paid). Is this a scene from the 1930s? No, some say it's the 1990s garment industry in California—today's sweatshops.

A study of 69 randomly selected garment factories in California found that 50 percent did not pay minimum wage, 68 percent did not pay overtime, and 90 percent had health and safety violations. They exist from San Francisco to San Diego. Some employees were paid only $2.97 an hour for 40 of the 60 hours they worked per week.

A typical raid, according to California Labor Commissioner Vickie Bradshaw found about 50 workers hunched over sewing machines making cotton T-shirts. At the sight of the labor inspector, the shop's owner yelled in Spanish that immigration officials had come to take workers away, so the workers ran. The employer had no records. The federal Labor Department attempts to intercept garments produced by scofflaw contractors before they are delivered to the large garment makers who hire dozens of the small contractors. If garments produced by scofflaw contractors get past the Labor Department, the large companies that buy them can be levied fines to cover back wages to contractors' workers. One of the larger fines—$500,000—was paid by GUESS?, the jeans company.

Adapted from Associated Press, "Sweatshops Thrive in California," *Omaha World-Herald*, July 31, 1994, p. B1.

Overtime Compensation. The FLSA stipulates that certain employees must receive overtime pay of one and one-half times the normal rate when they work over 40 hours per week. Certain kinds of employees are exempt from the overtime provision of the act. In and of itself, a job title is not a sufficient basis for **exemption**. Rather, the actual work performed and the primary duties of the employee are what count. A person with an executive title who does not primarily manage a department or a function may not meet all conditions for exemption.

All workers are **nonexempt** unless proven exempt by the employer. Typically, exemption is determined by referring to a series of salary tests and other requirements that must be met. These are specified for four basic groups of employees: executive, administrative, professional, and outside salespeople. The test for executive, administrative, and professional employees includes a minimum salary and, most important, a primary-duty condition requiring that more than 50 percent of the employee's time is to "customarily and regularly exercise discretion and independent judgment." In addition, less than 20 percent of said employee's time can be spent on routine, manual, or clerical work.

Some organizations have tried to lower their overtime costs by classifying more employees as exempt. The restaurant, tourist, and medical industries are exempt from the overtime provision, as are agricultural workers. In overtime calculations, a workweek is 168 consecutive hours or seven consecutive days, not necessarily a calendar week. Special provisions allow hospitals to use a 14-day period instead of a seven-day period.

An employer's refusal to pay overtime may lead to a successful union organization effort. In 1995, for example, workers at the Fisherman's Outlet Restaurant in Los Angeles asked to be paid overtime. The owner refused and said workers confused work times with break times in calculating overtime. After organizing a union and using a time clock, workers averaged an extra $35 to $60 per week for an average of 10 hours of overtime. Although most employers correctly pay overtime, it is estimated that $19 billion per year in overtime pay in the United States is not paid.[9]

Many of the technical violations of the act result from newer compensation plans that include pay incentives such as attendance bonuses, productivity bonuses, and commissions. Employers are often unaware that such bonuses and commissions must be included in the regular rate of pay when computing the overtime rate of pay. As a general rule, the act requires that all compensation be included in the employee's regular rate of pay, with seven specific exceptions:[10]

1. Gifts
2. Christmas bonuses
3. Special occasion bonuses
4. Profit-sharing payments
5. Thrift plan payments
6. Savings plan payments
7. Irrevocable contributions made to a bona fide trust

About 98 percent of all agreements contain some premium pay for overtime above the FLSA requirement. *Daily overtime* premiums are provided in 93 percent of agreements. *Sixth-day premiums*—the sixth consecutive day of work is eligible for a premium payment—and *seventh-day premiums* are found in about 26 percent of contracts. The **pyramiding** (being paid for more than one premium pay on the same hours) of overtime pay is prohibited in 69 percent of contracts because of management's concerns that the same hours might either become eligible for both daily and weekly overtime or become eligible for more than one type of premium. An example of the latter might be holiday pay plus double time on a seventh day worked. Most agreements also specify how overtime should be distributed among workers: "Equal distribution as far as practical" or on a strict seniority basis are common provisions.[11]

The American 40-hour workweek with time and one-half for hours over 40 may end. This workweek standard since the FLSA was passed in 1938 has been questioned by President Clinton and the 105th Republican Congress. They proposed in 1997 to pass a new workweek law that would allow flexible work schedules by employees and that would not be limited by the 40-hour standard. Employees, for example, might work four 12-hour days with a three-day weekend and be paid the standard hourly rate for all 48 hours, sacrificing eight hours of overtime pay. Union leaders strongly oppose the change; they fear that employees would be coerced into working longer hours and giving up overtime pay. Under one proposal, employees could choose time and one-half compensatory time (hours taken off at a later date) or overtime pay. How do most workers feel about the issue? A Roper poll found that women would prefer the flexible hours (44 percent versus 32 percent) but men would not (38 percent versus 42 percent), and about one-third reported that they already have flextime.[12]

The Davis-Bacon Act. The Davis-Bacon Act of 1931 regulates employers who hold federal government contracts of $2,000 or more for federal construction projects. It provides that employees working on these projects must be paid the prevailing wage rate. In most urban areas, the union wage is the prevailing wage for that particular geographic area. If the local union wage for plumbers is $10 per hour, then any plumbers hired to work on federal construction projects in the area must be paid $10 per hour. The reasoning behind the Davis-Bacon Act is that often governments will award contracts to the firm submitting the lowest bid for certain construction specifications. By requiring all employers in construction projects to pay the prevailing wage, the Davis-Bacon Act puts bidders on an equal basis and ensures that craft workers will not be underpaid.[13]

Walsh-Healey Act. The Walsh-Healey Act of 1936 covers employees with federal contracts of over $10,000. It requires employers to pay overtime for any hours worked over eight per day at a rate of one and one-half times the normal hourly rate. If an employee works days of more than eight hours within a 40-hour week, he or she will receive greater compensation for the same total hours worked.

NEGOTIATED WAGE ADJUSTMENTS

Standard Rate, Pay Range Systems

How wage rates are to be defined in the agreement is a critical issue. Most agreements contain a **standard rate**, or *flat rate*, of pay for each job classification effective during the life of the agreement, as in Figure 7-1. Some agreements provide a *pay range* for each job: The person may be paid one of several steps within the range. Usually management will seek flexibility in wage administration by using a range of pay for each grade or category. A common practice in the nonunion sector, this allows management to reward individual differences in employees according to seniority, merit, or quality and quantity of production.

Management usually wishes to hire new, inexperienced employees at the minimum pay rate and allow them to advance during their tenure with the company through merit and seniority increases. Management may argue that it makes little sense to pay exactly the same wage rate for a job regardless of the performance level of the employee. The highest-performing employee and the lowest-performing employee in a standard rate system receive the same wage rate, a system that tends to undermine individual motivation.[14] Union leaders argue that merit increases, which are the primary reason to have pay ranges instead of standard rates, are useful management tools in theory but actually run into severe problems. Union leaders feel that, because these systems are normally based on a supervisor's performance appraisal, they are subject to supervisor bias. The subjectivity and imperfections of performance appraisal systems, which cannot be denied by management, lead most union leaders to argue against a merit pay increase system. Management may then counter with the argument that an imperfect performance appraisal system is better than no system of rewarding individual performance. An example of an arbitrated grievance over an employee's step increase within a pay range is provided in Case 7-1.

Piece-Rate Systems

An alternative pay system is a **piece-rate system**. Straight piecework is the most common and easily understood individual incentive plan. If an employee is paid $0.025 per unit produced and completes 100 units in an hour, then the hour's gross earnings will be $2.50. Variations of straight piecework include falling piece rate and rising piece rate. Table 7-2 is a comparison of the various piece-rate plans.

CASE 7-1

SALARY ADJUSTMENT

In the contract governing the 1980–1981 school year, the parties had agreed that teachers who attended 93 or more calendar days in any school year would be advanced on the salary schedule for the following year. The number of days required for advancement was changed in the contract governing the 1981–1982 school year to 130 days. The school board did not advance teachers in the 1981–1982 school year who had more than 93 days but less than 130 days' attendance in the 1980–1981 school year. The union grieved the school board's action.

The arbitrator was presented with the following positions. The union claimed that provisions of the 1980–1981 collective bargaining contract controlled and had to be honored because the employee who attended the required 93 days had already earned the step increase

for the 1981–1982 school year. The school board claimed that as the 1981–1982 contract was in effect before the school year began, its provisions controlled any salary advancements for that school year, and therefore the 130-day rule had to be honored.

Decision

The arbitrator decided in favor of the union. His opinion was based on the fact that the 1981–1982 collective bargaining agreement did not specifically provide for retroactivity in the computation of the earned step increase. And, although such retroactivity would have been valid if agreed to by the parties, it must be clearly stated in the contract and cannot be presumed if the contract is silent on the issue.

Adapted from *Bremen Community High School District*, 79 LA 778 (1982).

Table 7-2

A Comparison of Piece-Rate Plans
($100 per worker overhead cost per hour)

Standard Piece-Rate Plan

Number of Pieces	Piece Rate	Worker's Earnings	Per Piece Overhead Cost	Total Cost
100	$ 0.025	$2.50	$1.000	$1.025
120	0.025	3.00	0.833	0.858
140	0.025	3.50	0.714	0.739
160	0.025	4.00	0.625	0.650
180	0.025	4.50	0.556	0.581
200	0.025	5.00	0.500	0.525

Falling Piece-Rate Plan

Number of Pieces	Piece Rate	Worker's Earnings	Per Piece Overhead Cost	Total Cost
100	$ 0.025	$2.50	$1.000	$1.025
120	0.024	2.88	0.833	0.857
140	0.023	3.22	0.714	0.737
160	0.022	3.52	0.625	0.647
180	0.021	3.78	0.556	0.577
200	0.020	4.00	0.500	0.520

Rising Piece-Rate Plan

Number of Pieces	Piece Rate	Worker's Earnings	Per Piece Overhead Cost	Total Cost
100	$ 0.025	$2.50	$1.000	$1.025
120	0.030	3.60	0.833	0.863
140	0.035	4.90	0.714	0.749
160	0.040	6.40	0.625	0.665
180	0.045	8.10	0.556	0.601
200	0.050	10.00	0.500	0.550

Source: Leonard R. Burgess, *Wage and Salary Administration* (Columbus, OH: Merrill, 1984), pp. 241–242.

Plans that use a **falling piece rate** involve a standard time and rate of production. If the employee produces more than the standard, the gain is shared between the employer and the employee. The employee's hourly earnings increase with output above a standard of 100, but the rate per piece falls at various predetermined levels. Thus, an employee who has produced 140 units (40 percent above standard) receives only $3.22 (29 percent more) and not $3.50, which would be the case if the $0.025 rate were maintained. The employer receives the remainder of the gain, effectively lowering the overhead cost per piece.

Plans that use a **rising piece rate** also involve a standard time and rate of production. But as Table 7-2 illustrates, the worker who increases output by 40 percent has a greater than proportional increase in hourly earnings. After earning $2.50 for the first 100 pieces, the worker earns $2.40 ($4.90 − $2.50) for the next 40 pieces, or 96 percent of the base hourly pay. The increase occurs because the worker earned $0.025 per piece for the first 100 pieces and $0.035 per piece for the next 40. Management benefits nevertheless: The total cost per piece still declines as more pieces are produced because the fixed overhead cost is spread out over more pieces.[15] Why would management agree to a rising piece-rate system? If the higher hourly earnings are sufficiently motivational, the total cost per piece could be cheaper than under a falling piece-rate plan. For example, if under the falling piece-rate plan of Table 7-2 the employee is only slightly motivated and averages 120 units per hour, then management has an average total piece cost of $0.857. But if the rising piece-rate plan is slightly more motivational and the employee averages 140 units per hour, management averages $0.749 total per unit cost while the employee averages $4.90 per hour instead of $2.88 (falling rate of 120 pieces).

Piece-rate systems have the advantages of being easily understood, simple to calculate, and motivational. But many jobs do not easily lend themselves to such a pay system because the output of the employee cannot be directly and objectively measured. Also, most employees' output is affected by the output of others, so their productivity is not directly proportional to their input. Finally, union and management negotiators may have a difficult time agreeing on what is a fair production standard. Changes in standards by management can easily lead to union grievances.

Standard hour plans are similar in concept to piece-rate plans except a "standard time" is set to complete a particular job instead of paying the employee a price per piece. For example, an auto mechanic might be given a standard time of two hours to tune up an eight-cylinder car. If the worker's hourly rate is $8.00 per hour and three eight-cylinder tune-ups are finished in six hours, then the employee earns $48.00. If a so-called Halsey 50/50 incentive plan is used, the worker and employer share equally in time saved by the employee. Thus, after completing the three tune-ups in five hours, the employee would be paid $52.00 ($48.00 + $4.00 [1/2 hour saved at $8.00/hour]), and the employer has an additional hour's work time.

Deferred Wage Increases

Many multiyear collective bargaining agreements provide increases in wage rates that are deferred to later years rather than taking effect immediately. Together with the preferred use of cost-of-living adjustments (COLAs; see next section), such **deferred wage rate increases** often make multiyear contracts desirable for both sides. Management can predict labor costs further into the future with a greater degree of accuracy, and union members feel that their buying power is protected for a longer period of time and do not have to worry annually about possible strikes.

Deferred wage provisions specify increases in the base pay to take effect on future dates during a multiyear contract. Negotiating multiyear increases often hinges on whether they are *evenly distributed* over the life of the contract, as in the following example of a three-year contract (5 percent increases) starting July 1, 1997, or whether they are front-end loaded.

Pay Classification	Wage Rate on July 1, 1997	Wage Rate on July 1, 1998	Wage Rate on July 1, 1999
I	$12.00	$12.60	$13.23
II	$10.00	$10.50	$11.03
III	$9.00	$9.45	$9.92

Front-end loading refers to a deferred wage increase with a larger proportion of the total percentage increase in the first year of the agreement. Thus, a three-year total wage increase package might be evenly distributed, with an equal percentage provided at the beginning of each year: 5 percent–5 percent–5 percent; or it could be front-end loaded: 10–3–2. Many contracts provide front-end loading, including providing the total increase in the first year: 15–0–0.

Management generally prefers to spread the increases out over the life of the agreement for cash flow purposes and because the total cost of the agreement is substantially less since higher wages paid only in later years are avoided in early years. For example, the two alternatives for the three-year, 15 percent increase when applied to a $20,000 current wage produce the following wages paid:

Year	Equal Increases 5%–5%–5%	Front-End Loaded 10%–3%–2%	Difference Each Year
0	$20,000	$20,000	—
1	$21,000	$22,000	+$1,000
2	$22,050	$22,660	+$ 610
3	$23,153	$23,113	−$ 40
			+$1,570

Union negotiators often prefer front-end load wage rate increases so that their members receive the additional wages ($1,570) and realize a large increase in pay the very first year. However, negotiators acknowledge from past experience that front-end loading may produce long-term problems. Members who were quite happy with a 10 percent increase during the first year of an agreement can easily become dissatisfied with the two subsequent years of small increases, especially during periods of high inflation. Thus, "What have you done for me lately?" becomes a real problem for union and management leaders alike. Also, the annual wage rates at the end of the agreement can easily be lower under a front-end loaded provision than under an evenly distributed provision, as in the previously cited examples. The union may demand a **wage reopener** provision providing for the reopening of contract talks to discuss only wage rates. Such discussion during the later years of the agreement may become necessary because of unpredictable inflation or company financial success. Management is not obligated to agree to higher wage rates under such a reopener but realizes that this agreement may be necessary to obtain a long-term contract. Also management negotiators realize that they will likely be faced with the demands, particularly when they are valid, during the next negotiating session anyway.

Before the 1980s, virtually all collective bargaining agreements with multiyear settlements included front-end loaded wage increases. However, foreign and domestic nonunion competition in the 1980s forced management negotiators to seek a variety of cost-curbing measures including **back-loaded contracts**. A back-loaded contract provides a lower wage adjustment in the first year, with higher increases in later years of a multiyear contract. For example, a 10 percent three-year wage adjustment could be 2–4–4. In many back-loaded contracts, workers receive no wage increase in the first year. For example, the 1997–1999 UAW-Chrysler agreement provides for a 0–3–3 distribution with a $2,000 bonus.[16]

Cost-of-Living Adjustments

Union negotiators have for years emphasized the need for **cost-of-living adjustments (COLAs)** during the life of an agreement. They contend that the *real wage*—the purchasing power negotiated in an agreement as a wage rate—is eroded by inflation during the life of the agreement. Therefore, it is necessary to provide the COLA in an escalator clause so that wage rates will keep pace with inflation. General Motors first proposed a COLA clause during negotiations with the UAW in 1948.

Unions and employers were leery of COLAs until the 1950s. Both feared that COLAs would include pay cuts, which might have occurred because declines in the consumer price index (CPI) were at the time quite possible. Union leaders also disliked COLAs because they represented a "substitute for bargaining," meaning they would receive less credit for increases with a COLA. Unions preferred wage reopeners that put them back at the bargaining table. However, by the mid-1950s, both sides worried less about deflation and more about their ability to estimate correctly rising inflation. In addition, in 1950 General Motors and the United Auto Workers signed a historic wage formula that combined deferred wage adjustments with a COLA—a practice previously avoided by GM but soon followed by many negotiators.[17] The percentage of agreements that contained COLAs steadily increased and peaked in 1979 at 48 percent, but low CPI increases in the 1990s have seen the percentage slip to only 34 percent of agreements.[18]

Both labor and management negotiators are careful to specify exact COLA provisions during the agreement. Several critical issues must be carefully spelled out.

1. **Inflation index**. Most provisions use the consumer price index determined by the Bureau of Labor Statistics (BLS) as a standard for measuring change in inflation. In 1978 the Bureau of Labor Statistics broke the CPI into two entities: the urban family index, or CPI-U, for urban families and the urban wage earner index, or CPI-W, for urban wage earners and clerical workers. Starting in January 1999, the BLS will change the CPI-W base from 1967 = 100 to 1993–1995 = 100.

Increases in the CPI are linked to increases in wages by an adjustment formula. The two most commonly used formulas are a *cents-per-hour* increase for each point increase in the CPI or a *percentage increase* in wage rates equal to some percentage increase in the CPI. The most commonly used formula provides for a 1 cent increase in wages for each 0.26 of a point increase in the CPI. An example of this provision is found in Figure 7-3, from the agreement between the UAW and Ford Motor Company.

2. **When the increases are to be provided**. The majority of agreements provide for inflation adjustment four times a year subsequent to the reported increase in the CPI. This quarterly increase provision is also included in the UAW-Ford agreement. Other labor agreements provide for adjustments to be made twice a year (semiannually) or once a year (annually).

Figure 7-3   COLA Provision

Section 4. Cost-of-Living Allowance

(a) **Payment of Allowance; Effect on Other Payments**

Effective **September 30, 1996**, and thereafter during the period of this Agreement, each employee **hired on or before September 30, 1996**, shall receive a cost-of-living allowance as set forth in this Section.

Employees hired or rehired after September 30, 1996, shall receive the Cost-of-Living Allowance amount effective during the three-month period in which they are hired until their first base rate adjustment. Concurrent with each subsequent base rate adjustment employees shall have their Cost-of-Living Allowance amount changed to the then current Cost-of-Living Allowance payable as specified in subsection (d)(2).

The cost-of-living allowance shall not be added to the base rate for any classification, but only to each employee's straight-time hourly earnings (including the earned rate only of employees on an incentive basis of pay).

The cost-of-living allowance shall be taken into account in computing overtime and shift premiums, and in determining call-in pay and pay for vacations, unworked holidays, jury duty, bereavement and short-term military duty.

(b) **Basis for Allowance**

(1) The amount of the cost-of-living allowance shall be determined and redetermined as provided below on the basis of the Consumer Price Index for Urban Wage Earners and Clerical Workers (revised, CPI-W, United States City Average) published by the Bureau of Labor Statistics (1967 = 100).

(2) Continuance of the cost-of-living allowance shall be contingent upon the availability of the Index in its present form and calculated on the same basis as the Index for July, 1996, unless otherwise agreed upon by the parties. If the Bureau of Labor Statistics changes the form or the basis of calculating the Index, the parties agree to ask the Bureau to make available, for the life of this Agreement, a monthly Index in its present form and calculated on the same basis as the Index for July, 1996.

(3) **The Cost-of-Living Allowance provided herein will be determined in accordance with changes in the Consumer Price Index for Urban Wage Earners and Clerical Workers, CPI-W, (United States City Average) published by the Bureau of Labor Statistics, and calculated in accordance with the Letter of Understanding signed by the parties. For the nine adjustments beginning in December 1996 and continuing through December 1998, the BLS's CPI-W (1967 = 100) reference base will be used in such calculations. Thereafter, beginning with the March 1999 adjustment, the BLS's CPI-W (1993–95 = 100) reference base will be used to determine the Cost-of-Living Allowance.**

(c) **Redeterminations**

Adjustments during the period of this Agreement shall be made at the following times:

Effective Date of Adjustment	Based Upon Three-Month Average of the Consumer Price Index for:
December 2, 1996	August, September, and October, 1996
First pay period beginning on or after March 3, 1997 and at three-calendar-month intervals thereafter to June 7, 1999.	November, December, 1996 and January, 1997 and at three-calendar-month intervals thereafter to February, March, and April 1999.

Figure 7-3

(d) **Amount of Allowance**

(1) The amount of cost-of-living allowance beginning **September 30, 1996**, and ending December **1**, 1996 shall be five cents (5¢) per hour.

(2) Effective December **2**, 1996 and for any period thereafter as provided in Subsection (c), the cost-of-living allowance shall be in accordance with the following table:

Three-Month Average Consumer Price Index	Cost-of-Living Allowance
457.9 or less	None
458.0–458.1	1¢ per hour
458.2–458.4	2¢ per hour
458.5–458.6	3¢ per hour
458.7–458.9	4¢ per hour
459.0–459.2	5¢ per hour
459.3–459.4	6¢ per hour
459.5–459.7	7¢ per hour
459.8–459.9	8¢ per hour
460.0–460.2	9¢ per hour

and so forth with one cent (1¢) adjustment for each 0.26 **point** change in the Average Index **(1967 = 100)** as calculated in accordance with the Letter of Understanding signed by the parties **continuing through the adjustment effective in December 1998. Thereafter, beginning with the adjustment effective in March 1999, and beginning with the first next 1¢ that may become payable, the above table will be changed to reflect a conversion in CPI-W reference bases, from 1967 = 100 to 1993–95 = 100, and modified to provide that 1¢ adjustments in the Cost-of-Living Allowance shall become payable for each 0.06 change in the Average Index, as calculated in accordance with the Letter of Understanding signed by the parties.**

Source: Agreement between UAW and Ford Motor Co., vol. 1, 1997–1999, pp. 99–102.

3. **Change in base pay**. If COLAs are treated as additions to the base pay, then other wage adjustments such as shift differential and overtime will increase after a COLA because they are usually a fixed percentage of a base pay. Thus, the company will find its personnel cost increased by an amount greater than the percentage COLA. The alternative is to treat the COLAs given during the life of the agreement as a benefit and not as an addition to the base pay, see Figure 7-3 for an example.

4. **COLA maximums**. Some labor agreements provide for a maximum COLA increase made by the company during the life of the agreement. This maximum is usually referred to as a *cap* put on the cost-of-living provision. The cap assures management that wage increases due to CPI increases will not go beyond a certain total.

Critics of COLA provisions state that such provisions fuel inflation. However, only a little more than 10 percent of the civilian nonagricultural workforce in the United States is covered by COLA provisions and is therefore able to keep pace with inflation. Although more than 80 percent of the workforce are thus excluded from COLA provisions, critics still contend that employers who pay COLAs increase their prices to reflect the increase in labor costs. A circular situation develops that ultimately results in increased prices or higher inflation. Inflation causes the CPI to go up, the higher CPI causes COLA provisions in labor agreements to be enacted; COLA provisions cause an increase in wage rates.

Labor leaders are quick to point out, however, that since only a small portion of the total labor force is covered by COLA provisions, the effect on inflation must not be very great. They also believe that their members should be protected against inflation. Labor leaders point out that government's tying of Social Security increases and federal employee retirement increases to the CPI has much more of an impact on inflation than do labor agreement COLA adjustments.

A significant problem with COLA adjustments that concerns both union leaders and management is that, once given, the increases are taken for granted by employees. Members may believe that the wage increases they receive on the basis of COLA provisions are not negotiated increases and therefore they want further wage increases. Union and management negotiators may believe that they are not given credit for these negotiated increases. Because members come to expect automatic adjustments for inflation, they tend to ask labor negotiators and management, "What have you done for me lately?" Finally, management complains that COLA provisions prevent them from forecasting future labor costs. Management contends that it cannot adequately predict the total product cost, and COLA costs hamper the ability to bid successfully on projects or priced items.

History indicates that the percentage of union workers covered by COLAs is most likely to increase in the three-year period following a period of higher inflation as union negotiators strive to regain lost buying power. Since the COLA has been generally intended for this purpose, this is a logical result. However, it appears that recently COLAs have not been a prime negotiating target for labor or management. When either is in a generally strong negotiating position, neither party has significantly altered the percentage of union workers covered by COLAs in the direction expected. This would seem to be the natural result of a few years with low inflation.[19]

Relatively small increases in the CPI over the 1980s caused a shift away from COLA provisions in negotiated agreements. When the inclusion of COLA clauses in agreements covering a thousand or more workers from 1973 to 1993 were compared, the results showed that workers covered by COLA agreements dropped from 60 percent to 28 percent. In 1991 alone, bargainers discontinued COLA clauses in 24 agreements and did not add them to any new agreements.[20]

Profit Sharing

Compensation systems whereby management agrees to make a lump-sum payment to employees in addition to their regular wages are termed **profit-sharing** or bonus plans. The payments may be based on the profits of the company using an agreed-upon formula (profit sharing) or an amount specified in the contract based on production or sales levels (see Figure 7-4 for the UAW-Ford formula based on sales). Both are preferred by management over base-wage changes because negotiated increases do not automatically carry over to future years and do not increase the cost of associated benefits such as overtime rates and pension payments, which are typically based on base-wage earnings.

FORD MOTOR COMPANY PROFIT SHARING PLAN FOR HOURLY EMPLOYEES IN THE UNITED STATES

The purpose of this Plan is to make provision for profit sharing distributions by the Company to eligible hourly employees, thus affording them a means of participating in the growth and success of the Company resulting from improved productivity and operating competitiveness as well as providing new sources of income for such employees.

(a) "Eligible Hourly Employee" or "Participant" shall mean, with respect to any Plan Year, any person who met all of the following requirements at any time during such Plan Year:

    (i) such person was employed **full-time** at an hourly rate in U.S. Operations on the active employment rolls maintained by the Company in the United States (except that any such person who was so employed on a temporary part-time basis shall be excluded from the definition of "Eligible Hourly Employee" and "Participant"); **and**

    (ii) such person, if represented by a Union, was covered by an agreement making this Plan applicable to such person or, if such person was not represented by a Union, such person was employed in a unit to which the Company had made this Plan applicable;

including any person who met such requirements at any time during such Plan Year and (1) was on layoff or approved leave, incuding expired medical leave, at the end of such Plan Year, or (2) retired during such Plan Year, (3) died during such Plan Year, or (4) was terminated by the Company during such Plan Year as a result of the sale by the Company of the operation, or a controlling interest in the operation, in which such person was employed; provided, however, that any person who terminated during such Plan Year (without being reinstated at the end of such Plan Year), for any reason other than death, retirement, sale of an operation, or a controlling interest in an operation, or any voluntary termination of employment program developed under the Job Security Program—GEN (Appendix M of the Agreement) shall be excluded from the definition of "Eligible Hourly Employee" and "Participant".

II. Determination of Total Profit Share

For any Plan Year in which there are Profits, the Total Profit Share for such Plan Year shall be determined as hereinafter provided. Such Total Profit Share shall be the sum of the following:

(a) 6.0% of the portion of the Profits for such Plan Year which does not exceed 1.8% of such Sales;

(b) 8% of the portion of the Profits for such Plan Year which exceeds 1.8% of Sales for such Plan Year but does not exceed 2.3% of such Sales;

(c) 10% of the portion of the Profits for such Plan Year which exceeds 2.3% of Sales for such Plan Year but does not exceed 4.6% of such Sales;

(d) 14% of the portion of the Profits for such Plan Year which exceeds 4.6% of Sales for such Plan Year but does not exceed 6.9% of such Sales; and

(e) 17% of the portion of the Profits for such Plan Year which exceeds 6.9% of Sales for such Plan Year;

provided; however, that the Total Profit Share for any Plan Year in which there are Profits shall in no event be less than the amount determined by multiplying (×) $50 by (y) the sum of (i) the number of Eligible Hourly Employees for such Plan Year, (ii) the number of persons who would have been Eligible Hourly Employees for such Plan Year except for the fact

(continued)

that they were employed in a unit which was represented by a Union that had not agreed with Ford or a Subsidiary that this Plan shall apply to such unit, and (iii) the number of Salaried Employees for such Plan Year.

III. Determination of Allocated Profit Share

1. A portion of the Total Profit Share, if any, for each Plan Year shall be allocated to this Plan as hereinafter provided. The portion to be so allocated shall be determined by multiplying such Total Profit Share by a fraction, the numerator of which is the sum of (x) the number of Eligible Hourly Employees for such Plan Year, and (y) the number of persons who would have been Eligible Hourly Empoyees for such Plan Year except for the fact that they were employed in a unit to which the Company had not made this Plan applicable or employed in a unit which was represented by a Union that had not agreed with Ford or a Subsidiary that this Plan shall apply to such unit, and the denominator of which is the sum of (a) the numerator, and (b) the number of Salaried Employees for such Plan Year. The amount determined pursuant to this Paragraph for any Plan Year is hereinafter called the "Allocated Profit Share" for such Plan year.

2. If any person shall come within the definition both of "Eligible Hourly Employee" and "Salaried Employee" for any Plan Year, such person shall be treated, for all purposes of this Plan, as both an Eligible Hourly Employee and a Salaried Employee.

Source: Agreement between UAW and the Ford Motor Company, 1997–1999, pp. 111–121.

Profit-sharing plans appear in about 10 percent of agreements.[21] Management favors profit sharing to COLAs as a wage supplement for several reasons: (1) Payments are made only if the company makes a profit and thus is usually financially strong; (2) unlike COLAs, payments are not tied to inflation, which is not related to the company's financial status and may require increases during difficult times; (3) workers' pay is linked to their productivity and not just to the number of hours they work, giving them a direct incentive to see the company become more profitable; and (4) workers may feel more a part of the company and develop increases interest in reducing waste and increasing efficiency in all areas as well as their own jobs.

In 1990, for example, the Ford Motor Company distributed $153 million in annual profit-sharing checks to U.S. employees. The average worker received $1,025, a decrease from the 1989 average of $2,800, when Ford reported higher profits, and in 1994, $1,350. Peter Pestillo, Ford's personnel chief and chief labor negotiator noted, "We think it's money well spent. They get more, and they get more done. We think we get a payback in the cooperation and enthusiasm of the people." The 1984 Ford–United Auto Workers master agreement was the first to contain a profit-sharing provision pushed by management as a means of avoiding the UAW-proposed 3 percent annual raises.[22] The concept of profit sharing within the auto industry is not new, however. Douglas Frasier, former president of the UAW, noted that the union first asked for a profit-sharing plan more than 40 years prior to the 1984 agreement and during several other negotiations, but none of the U.S. auto giants were interested until they were losing money in the 1980s.[23]

Scanlon Group Incentive Plans

A group incentive plan designed to achieve greater production through increased efficiency with accrued savings divided among the workers and the company was developed by Joseph Scanlon. Scanlon at the time was the research director of the United Steelworkers and later joined the faculty at the Massachusetts Institute of Technology.[24] The **Scanlon plan** became the popular standard in U.S. group incentive plans. It has since become a basis for labor-management cooperation above and beyond its use as a group incentive plan. The plan contains two primary features: (1) Departmental committees of union and management representatives meet together at least monthly to consider any cost-savings suggestions, and (2) any documented cost savings resulting from implemented committee suggestions are divided 75 percent to employees and 25 percent to the company.[25]

Most other group incentive plans involve programs that set expected levels of productivity, product costs, or sales levels for individual groups and then provide employee bonuses if the targeted goals are exceeded. One widely recognized example is the Nucor Corporation. In one year the company reported a staggering growth of 600 percent in sales and 1,500 percent in profits over 10 years due to a production incentive program. The company actually developed four separate incentive programs: one each for production employees, department heads, professional employees, and senior officers. Their theory was that "money is the best motivation."[26]

Two-Tier Wage Systems

A wage system that pays newly hired workers less than current employees performing the same or similar jobs is termed "two-tier." Since the **two-tier wage system** was established in 1977 at General Motors Packard Electric Division in Warren, Ohio, many more union-management negotiations have resulted in similar systems.[27] The basic concept is to provide continued higher wage levels for current employees if the union will accept reduced levels for future employees. Union leaders believe that they must accept the two-tier system or face greater layoffs in the future. Management usually claims that the system is needed to compete with nonunion and foreign competition. Two-tier systems appear in about 30 percent of contracts today, mostly in the retail, foods, transportation, equipment, and electrical machinery industries.[28]

Although a two-tier system is contrary to the historical union doctrine of "equal pay for equal work," or **pay equity**, when a system is first negotiated, the union representatives can claim that they have avoided disaster and saved the jobs or wage levels of current members (who must vote on the contract). It is relatively easy to sell such a concept because no workers at that point are accepting the "lower tier." However, five or ten years later, when many workers are paid lower wages for the same work as their affiliated union members, it can become a source of conflict and resentment. In some cases the lower-paid workers express their feelings with lower product quality and productivity records than their higher-paid counterparts.[29] In these bargaining units, the conflict could present even greater problems to both union and management leaders as the number of lower-tier workers approaches 51 percent of the bargaining unit and they demand equity.

Examples of two-tier agreements that were negotiated in the past include the following.[30]

- At Packard Electric, new hires were brought in at 55 percent of the wages of current employees.
- At General Motors' Delco Products plant in Rochester, New York, new assemblers earned almost $3.00 per hour less than current employees.
- Newly hired journeymen at the Ingalls Shipbuilding Company in Pascagoula, Mississippi, earn $1.00 less than the senior employees. The wages of new hires were to catch up after 2,000 hours.
- Giant Food negotiated a new entry-level wage of $2.00 less an hour than the old contract.
- The Allied Industrial Workers of America union accepted from Briggs & Stratton a wage rate almost $3.00 less for new workers on a lower tier.

Do employees hired into a lower-tier pay position perceive their treatment as equitable? A study of about 2,000 employees found that low-tier employees perceived the employer as being significantly lower in pay equity and perceived the union as being of little use in obtaining fair pay for its members. In addition, compared with the high-tier employees, the low-tier employees felt a lower level of commitment to their employer—which might affect their productivity and tenure with the organization. These perception problems can be controlled, the research results suggest, if low-tier employees are assigned to new work locations where there are few high-tier employees and if they are hired to part-time instead of full-time work. Employees hired under these conditions do not report equity perception problems.[31] Another method of minimizing the morale problems of low-tier employees is to provide eventual merging of the two tiers.

Studies also indicate that the high-tier employee is dissatisfied with the two-tier system. In a survey of over a thousand employees in a 14-store food outlet company, researchers found that employees at the high end of a two-tier pay scale feared replacement by the lower-tiered employees. In addition, they believed the two-tier system had a detrimental effect on any wage increases they might feel entitled to receive.[32]

Many two-tier wage systems allow newly hired employees to reach the higher tier within 90 to 180 days. Some two-tier systems are permanent because the contract does not provide for any means by which employees hired at the lower tier wage can progress to the higher tier. The presence of permanent systems in a contract puts a great deal of pressure on union negotiators to achieve a merger of the two tiers, which is found in 60 percent of all two-tier contract clauses.[33] For example, the two-tier provision in the UAW–Ford Motor Co. 1993–1996 contract states that new employees are hired at 75 percent of the current workers' rates with a merger after three years. The UAW was able to retain full employer-paid health-care benefits in exchange for the two-tier provision.[34]

Management and union leaders share the belief that two-tier pay systems will continue to exist for many years despite union objections. Unions continue to place a high negotiating priority on preserving jobs. Two-tier pay systems, lump-sum bonuses in lieu of merit wage increases, and health insurance cost-reduction plans are three major cost-saving approaches negotiated by management in exchange for a job security provision. Unions continue to resist two-tier systems because of morale problems that develop as more lower-tier workers are hired.

Pros and Cons of the Two-Tier Wage System		Table 7-3
Pros	**Cons**	
Significantly reduced labor costs	Resentment, low quality, and low productivity from low-tier employees	
Maintenance of higher employment levels	Higher absenteeism and turnover of low-tier employees	
Relief from wage compression between senior and junior employees on the same job	Intensification of the preceding problems as low-tier employees increase in number	

However, when employees are faced with wage cuts or layoffs as the only other means of significantly reducing employer payroll costs, two-tier systems appear more desirable to current union members. Although two-tier systems may come under increasing pressure from employees and labor leaders, management in those industries where such systems have been adopted are not likely to grant the pay increases necessary to raise the lower tier to equality with the higher tier. Cost pressures from deregulation, nonunion competition, and foreign competition are likely to increase, not decrease, in the future. Thus, labor and management often must consider the low-tier pay level a reality and adjust to it or consider across-the-board pay or benefit cuts for high-tier employees that would produce equal cost savings. Such across-the-board concessions, combined with profit-sharing bonuses and job security, may easily appeal to low-tier employees, but can they be sold at the bargaining table to senior, high-tier employees? Table 7-3 outlines the pros and cons of the two-tier wage system.

Lump-Sum Payments

As illustrated in Table 7-4, **lump-sum payments** and two-tier systems are relatively new methods of providing general wage increases and are increasing in their use, whereas COLAs and wage reopeners have declined in use. Lump-sum payments are often preferred by management to COLAs or profit-sharing plans because their total cost during the contract is easier to predict and they do not increase hourly wage rates. Unions may prefer they be paid early in the weeks of a new contract to provide quick benefit to members.

Wage Trends in Contracts (frequency expressed as percentage of contracts)											Table 7-4	
	1954	1957	1961	1966	1971	1975	1979	1983	1986	1989	1992	1995
Deferred increases	20	33	58	72	87	88	95	94	80	77	89	88
Cost-of-living adjustments	25	18	24	15	22	36	48	48	42	35	34	34
Wage reopeners	60	36	28	13	12	8	8	7	10	9	5	8
Lump sums	—	—	—	—	—	—	—	—	—	22	23	22
Two-tier pay	—	—	—	—	—	—	—	—	17	28	27	29

Source: Bureau of National Affairs, *Basic Patterns in Union Contracts*, 14th ed. (Washington, DC: BNA Books, 1995), p. 111. Used by permission.

WAGE NEGOTIATION ISSUES

During the negotiation process one or both sides may utilize different wage-level theories to stress their economic proposals. One or both sides will bring to light one or more wage theories and issues having an impact on the negotiation of rates. Which issues might be stressed during negotiations and whether they are even presented depend on the history of the company's labor relations and the personalities of the negotiators. In general, either side would utilize an issue it felt was valid or simply useful in providing a significant point for its list of arguments.

Productivity Theory

One of the oldest and broadest negotiation issues concerning wages involves the **productivity theory** that employees should share in increased profits caused by greater productivity. At the heart of the issue is the commonly accepted proposition that the organization's production is a combination of three factors: machinery and equipment, employee labor, and managerial ability. Union and management leaders agree that all three share in the creation of profits since they contribute to the organization's productivity. Whenever figures show that productivity or profits have risen, then the question becomes what percentage is attributable to employees' labor as opposed to machinery and equipment or managerial ability. Labor leaders commonly request that their members get their fair share of the increased profits. Management may request that the value-added concept be applied.

Determining labor's fair share then becomes the problem. Management may contend that all it asks is for employees to perform assigned work at stated times and at accepted levels of performance. The union usually counters that employees seek to improve quality and quantity of output, reduce cost, and minimize the waste of resources. If specific production standards are established through negotiation, it is much easier to negotiate accepted wage increases. Yet separating out and measuring profit resulting from individual and group productivity as compared with management and capital equipment are almost impossible.

Ability to Pay

The issue of **ability to pay** is commonly expressed during wage negotiations. In principle, this issue is similar to the productivity theory. Union leaders emphasize that labor is one of the primary inputs into a company's productivity and therefore profitability. Labor negotiators conclude that if the company is experiencing high profits, it can better pay its employees who have contributed to the good financial conditions. For example, 1996 was the most profitable year in the history of the airline industry. Thus when it came time to renegotiate labor contracts "a spirit of militancy" swept through the ranks of airline workers. "American Airlines is making record profits, and it's time our wages reflect that," said Rob Held, a pilot. American Airlines pilots, in fact, overwhelmingly rejected a contract offer their own union leaders had called generous. United Airlines mechanics rejected an offer of a 10 percent wage increase. However, these same unions only a few years earlier had accepted layoffs, wage cuts, and longer hours during hard financial times in the airline industry.[35]

The ability to pay concept, however, has severe limitations according to management negotiators. First and foremost, unions will not press this issue during hard times when profits have decreased or when the company is suffering temporary losses. Unions seldom want to apply the ability to pay doctrine consistently in both good and hard times; instead, they expect wage levels to be maintained during hard times and increased during good times. Second, management will argue that higher profits must be applied back into the company in capital investments. Third, although profit levels fluctuate greatly, negotiated wage rates do not vary accordingly. If higher wage rates were negotiated on the basis of a six-month crest of high profits, the company might find it extremely difficult to maintain the higher wages during a period of sluggish profitability. Unfortunately, wage rates are negotiated for the future, and profit information is available only for the past. Thus, estimating the company's future ability to pay during the life of the new contract is quite difficult.

Companies are usually reluctant to share extensive financial information with the union during collective bargaining sessions. Unless a company claims that it is *unable* to pay the demanded wage rates, the union is not entitled to the financial information. If a company merely chooses to say at the negotiating table that it *does not want* to pay the demanded wage rates, the union cannot get the financial information from the company.[36]

One very important number in contract negotiations is the *estimated total profits available* during the term of the new contract. Table 7-5 provides a sample calculation of total profits available for a metals firm. During their preparations, both management and labor will project sales, production costs, overhead, changes in productivity, and so on, that will occur during the life of the new contract. They can then project the total profits available to pay increased wages and benefits that might be negotiated. Determining labor's fair share of the total profits available is a difficult task; a starting point is usually the current labor cost as a percentage of total revenue (30.4 percent in Table 7-5). The union will try to negotiate a higher percentage using the productivity theory based on management's ability to pay (35 percent in Table 7-5). Management may cite higher production costs, cost of new equipment, or additional management costs as reasons to keep the percentage the same or even to lower it under the new contract. Both sides therefore enter negotiations with this dollar figure playing an important role in their negotiation strategy. Management uses it as an absolute maximum cost of the new contract, which they cannot exceed without endangering the future profitability of the organization. The union uses the figure as a goal that they hope to achieve in order to realize for their workers a fair share of future profits. During negotiations, both sides carefully keep a running total cost of all economic items negotiated and compare that figure with an estimated amount available developed before negotiations. If management produced these estimates, it would set $1.4 million as a maximum cost for the entire economic package, essentially wages and benefits, for the first year of a new contract. Thus, management might accept a total economic proposal that was far less than $1.4 million. If the union produced these estimates, it would set $1.4 million as a realistic target for negotiations, hoping to achieve at least that amount in new economic items.

Many calculations in Table 7-5 could easily vary and of course affect the $1.4 million estimate. Total sales revenue is a critical and often difficult estimate, particularly if the company sells directly to consumers. Labor costs are already projected to increase by nearly $1.5 million ($15,890,000 − $14,390,000), which includes the projected 6 percent increase in total wages paid due to more hours worked to achieve higher levels of production (*not* higher wage rates, which have not yet been negotiated). Similar increases in overhead and administrative costs can only be estimated for the projected level of production. Included in Table 7-5 are the estimated

Table 7-5	Estimated Profits Available under a New Contract*

Potential Profits Available from Current Operations

	Current	Projected
1. Sales revenue	$46,324,064	$52,056,000
2. Production costs	−23,100,000	−26,565,000
3. Labor costs (wages and benefits)	−14,390,064	−15,890,000
4. Labor costs as a percent of sales	30.4%	30.52%
5. Administrative and selling costs	−2,800,000	−3,080,000
6. Overhead	−1,550,000	−1,705,000
7. Net profits before taxes	5,484,000	4,816,000
8. Income tax	−2,020,000	−1,774,000
9. After-tax profit	3,464,000	3,042,000
10. Dividends paid	−400,000	−400,000
11. Profits with current operations	3,064,000	2,642,000

Potential Increased Cost Savings Due to New Equipment

	Current	Projected
12. Increased output: 10% (reduced product costs: $23,100,000 × 0.10)	2,310,000	2,656,500
13. Costs of new equipment = $6,400,000 × 0.10 (current interest rate)	640,000	640,000
14. Related new equipment costs	640,000	660,000
15. Total cost of new equipment	1,280,000	1,300,000
16. Savings due to new equipment (savings available to *all* organizational needs)	1,030,000	1,356,500

Potential Profits Available from Future Operations and Savings Due to New Equipment

	Projected
17. Potential profits available for all corporate needs (11 + 16)	$3,998,500
18. Percent of profits available for labor	35%
19. Profits available for increased labor costs under new contract	1,399,475

*This example might be used by either management or labor to calculate the dollar amount each believes will be available for labor under the new contract. Of course, each side might make different assumptions about the firm's future sales, profits, and productivity.

costs of the purchase of new production equipment and the projected savings, which both sides will include in their projections for the new contract. Management may be able to produce more accurate estimates since it can more easily obtain information such as sales forecasts and production costs. Reaching a settlement may be very difficult if the two sides produce substantially different estimates.

Job Evaluation

Job evaluation is the process of systematically analyzing jobs to determine their relative worth within the organization. The process is generally part of *job analysis*, the personnel function of systematically reviewing the tasks, duties, and responsibilities of jobs, usually to write job descriptions and minimum qualifications

RECLASSIFICATION OF JOBS

The company manufactures refrigerators and dehumidifiers. The grievance concerns assembly-line workers who installed foil wrap around the wired socket on certain food liner tops. The company instituted an operational modification that substituted fiberglass insulation for foil in the assembly operation. The grievants were classified as Class III Assemblers. Their grievance was a request to be reclassified to the higher classification of Hand Pack Insulation workers. The Hand Pack Insulation classification was specifically created in the early 1960s to cover personnel who must work with fiberglass insulation.

It was the union's position that the grievants regularly worked with fiberglass insulation and therefore should be classified to the higher classification. The workers do not have to spend more than 50 percent of their time handling fiberglass insulation before they can be classified as Hand Pack Insulators because there are Hand Pack Insulators who cut up fiberglass insulation on only two days per week. By creating the new classification, the parties had recognized that employees generally do not like to work with fiberglass insulation because it causes the workers to itch.

Using the management rights clause as its basis, the company contended that it had the right to change the materials being used in particular operations and to assign different tasks to appropriate classifications. The company pointed out that many assembly-line workers had occasionally come into contact with fiberglass materials during the 20 years preceding this grievance and no prior claims or grievances had been made regarding reclassification. It contended that the jobs performed by the two grievants were not meaningfully changed by the substitution of fiberglass for foil. In fact, the job description for the Class III Assemblers mentions that the personnel must deal with insulation, indicating that they may be expected to handle some fiberglass.

Decision

The arbitrator found that, although it is apparent that the Hand Pack Insulation classification was created to cover personnel who spend a significant amount of their time handling fiberglass insulation, the history of the plant indicates that there were numerous assembly-line workers in other classifications who continued to handle some fiberglass insulation without job reclassification. The arbitrator cited the basic rule that when jobs are classified by titles and the parties have not negotiated a detailed description of job content, management will be permitted wide authority to assign work that is reasonably related or incidental to the regular duties of the job. The arbitrator also put heavy emphasis on the fact that other personnel had not previously sought reclassification of their jobs to Hand Pack Insulator, even though they did handle some fiberglass insulation.

Adapted from *Magic Chef, Inc.*, 84 LA 15 (1984).

---

as well as to provide information for job evaluation. In general, the result of a job evaluation effort is a pay system with a rate for each job commensurate with its status within the hierarchy of jobs in the organization.[37]

Job evaluation procedures do not include analyzing employee performance; that is referred to as *performance evaluation* or *performance appraisal*. Nor is job evaluation an attempt to review the employees within a position. Rather, the position is reviewed for several carefully selected criteria to determine the relative worth of the job to the organization in comparison with other jobs in the labor market.

Union leaders as well as members of management can use job evaluation techniques as guides to negotiate wage agreements and explain paid differentials to employees. An example of how an agreement can provide for the use of job evaluation procedures during the life of a labor contract is shown in the following labor agreement between the Lockheed-Georgia Company and the International Machinists and Aerospace Workers:

> The job descriptions for each of the factory and for each of the office and technical classifications which are in effect on the date of execution of this agreement, or which are placed into effect pursuant to Paragraph 2 [next paragraph] herewith, shall be a part of this agreement.
>
> In the event that a new job or position is established or there is a substantial change in the duties or requirements of an established job, the company shall develop an appropriate job description and establish within the existing rates structure provided in Section 2 of this article, the basic rates to apply to such job. The company shall furnish the union with the new job description and shall submit for its approval the rate established for such job. In the event that an agreement is not reached within seven calendar days from the date of such submission or within such additional days as may be mutually agreed upon, the company may place the new job description and rate in effect subject to continuing negotiation of rate. Within five working days from the date the job was placed into effect, the union may proceed in accordance with Step 3 of the grievance procedure established in Article 3, Section 1 of this agreement.[38]

Job classification is common in labor agreements, and when an agreement contains a rigid classification, the employer may not unilaterally change it. When no explicit provision exists, it is generally recognized that management has the right to make classification changes or to add new jobs. However, even if the agreement contains a job classification, arbiters have recognized management's need—and right—to make changes as long as established pay rates are used, the union is allowed to file complaints through the grievance procedure, and management follows any procedures agreed to in the contract.[39] Case 7-2 illustrates a typical dispute over job classification.

WAGE SURVEYS

Both labor and management conduct their own **wage surveys** to provide information on external labor market conditions. The job evaluation process is utilized to maintain internal equity for wage rates, but it is also important to maintain external equity. That is, both sides want to offer wages competitive with the labor market and industry so that the firm can attract and retain qualified, productive employees. Union leaders want to provide evidence during negotiations to management and their own members that the wage rates they are negotiating are fair and justified by market conditions.

Negotiators seek wage survey information from three general sources. The first source is published labor market information from federal agencies, primarily the U.S. Department of Labor, which provides wage and salary information to all organizations by metropolitan statistical area. In general, the government's employment information is considered complete and accurate. Negotiators in specialized industries may wish to use the second source, industry wage surveys, published by various interested parties within the industry. Or negotiators may choose a third source: their own survey, which is a costly and time-consuming process. One side of the table is less likely to accept the figures produced by the other side unless they have a very strong working relationship or have participated in the survey process.

Conducting their own wage survey can be expensive and difficult for either negotiating team. Job titles alone are no longer acceptable in comparing positions among other organizations. Instead, the surveyor must compare job descriptions and receive detailed information on the duties and responsibilities of various jobs reported in the survey. The wages paid for each job included in the survey must be specifically defined. Information such as initial hiring salary ranges, the value of related benefits, and cost-of-living increases, as well as other wage increases, must be specified so that wage rates among different organizations can be compared fairly. Information concerning seniority provisions, paid vacations, sick leave, and other paid time-off work is critical for a valid analysis. Any other paid benefits such as uniform allowance or tuition reimbursement must also be included.[40]

Using wage surveys in negotiations primarily involves two types of problems. First, because survey information is available from many sources, including industry data, the Bureau of Labor Statistics, employer associations, and union groups, it is often difficult to agree which source contains jobs and data applicable to a particular firm. This problem may be compounded if negotiators use survey information from different cities and therefore must agree on an acceptable cost-of-living difference between the areas as well. One solution is to combine relevant data of two published surveys to determine averages.[41] But even if negotiators agree on wage survey information, a second problem involves the question of how the negotiating company should compare itself with other firms. Survey information usually provides an average as well as a range of wages paid for different jobs. Negotiating parties must then agree on whether they want to pay higher, average, or lower wages than the competition.

Thus, wage survey information will not resolve the issue of appropriate wage rates but will at least provide ballpark information to negotiators. Management may argue that what it lacks in wages it makes up in liberal benefits, working

TIPS FROM THE EXPERTS

Union

What are three wage issues union negotiation team members should look for at the negotiating table?

a. Fairness at both ends of wage/salary scale
b. Rewards for performance as well as for service
c. Equal pay for equal work

Management

What are some practical forms of wage concessions to use at negotiations that will not break an employer?

a. Swap indirect benefits and apply to direct labor (e.g., switch a holiday for a specific wage increase).
b. Lengthen the term of the collective bargaining agreement (perhaps in combination with item c).
c. Stagger wage increases with minimum or no increase at the front end but load up near the end of contract (perhaps in combination with item b).
d. Give concessions in an area that will be utilized infrequently but is a big morale booster, such as extended family leave (unpaid, event).

conditions, or advancement opportunities. Labor leaders may counter that these advantages are available in higher-paying organizations and do not make up for the lack in take-home pay.

COSTING WAGE PROPOSALS

Many of the changes in contract language may result in indirect or direct long-range cost to the company. However, most changes in wages, benefits, and cost-of-living adjustments are direct and usually substantial cost increases. Other types of changes such as layoff provisions, seniority determination, and subcontracting may result in indirect cost increases to the company. The process of determining the financial impact of a contract provision change is referred to as **costing**.

The costing of labor contracts is obviously a critical aspect in collective bargaining negotiations. Both sides need to estimate accurately the cost of the contract provision so it can be intelligently discussed and bargained for by either side. If it is an item that ultimately is given up by one side so another provision can be gained, then its relative weight is best estimated by knowing its costs.

Although costing is a critical aspect of collective bargaining, it has been neglected in labor relations literature. Two important factors may contribute to this neglect. The proprietors of some successful costing models are unwilling to share their knowledge with the opposition or potential competitors. In addition, although some models have been developed at substantial costs and are quite valuable, collective bargaining maintains a general atmosphere of secrecy as a part of negotiating strategy.[42]

All economic provisions can be reduced to dollar estimates, whereas noneconomic items cannot be as easily valued by either side. The costing process enables both sides to compare the value of different contract provisions and, it is hoped, helps them arrive at a contract agreement. In most cases, accurate costing processes will be accepted by both sides with little disagreement over the methods employed.

The largest single cost incurred by most corporations is labor cost. Even in capital-intensive organizations such as commercial airlines, labor costs account for about 42 percent of total cost; but in labor-intensive organizations, such as the U.S. Postal Service, labor may account for more than 80 percent of total cost. For most organizations, labor's impact on profits is critical, and relatively small changes in labor costs greatly affect profitability. Therefore, accurate costing of wage proposals in contract negotiations is critical to future cost control for many organizations.[43] Figure 7-5 shows how a typical company might cost the wage provisions of a contract.

Accountant Michael Granof outlines the four most commonly used methods of costing union wage provisions:

1. **Annual cost.** This is the total sum expended by the company over a year on a given benefit; usually the sum excludes administrative costs. Most companies make computations similar to those illustrated in Figure 7-5 to arrive at the annual cost of a wage agreement or benefit.

2. **Cost per employee per year.** This is determined by dividing the total costs of the benefit by either the average number of employees for the year or the number of employees covered by a particular program.

Data

90 employees at $8.00/hr
60 employees at $6.50/hr
20 employees at $5.75/hr

Proposed wage increase = 6% across the board = 1,900 average number of production hours per year

Annual Cost
Current: 90 × $8.00 = $720
         60 × 6.50 =   390
         20 × 5.75 =   115
                       $1,225/hr

Current annual cost is $1,225 × 1,900 hr = $2,327,500

Proposed: 90 × $8.48 = $763.20
          60 × 6.89 =   413.40
          20 × 6.09 =   121.80
                        $1,298.40/hr

Proposed annual cost is $1,298.40 × 1,900 = $2,466,960
Total cost of proposed increase is $2,466,960 − $2,327,500 = $139,460

Cents per hour
$8.48 − 8.00 = $0.48/hr for 90 employees
$6.89 − 6.50 = $0.39/hr for 60 employees
$6.09 − 5.75 = $0.34/hr for 20 employees

Roll-up (Average ÷ Employee)
Cost of benefits per person = $2.00/hr
$1,225 current cost ÷ 170 employees = $7.20 cost of wages/hr
$2.00 benefit cost ÷ $7.20 wages = 27.77% roll-up

Total Cost of Proposed Wage Rates + Roll-up
$139,460.00 + 38,728.04 (27.77% × 139,460.00) = $178,188.04 wages + roll-up

3. **Percent of payroll**. This is the total cost of the benefit divided by the total payroll. Companies may include all payments to all employees in the total payroll, but some exclude overtime, shift differential, or premium pay.

4. **Cents per hour**. This is derived by dividing the total cost of the benefit or wage provision by the total productive hours worked by all employees during the year.[44]

The two most commonly discussed economic figures are the annual cost figure and the cents per hour figure. When the contract is being negotiated, the total value of all additional wages and other economic items is included so that the annual cost of the entire package can be accurately estimated. All sides want to know the exact figure of the negotiated wages and benefits. The management negotiator may even offer a lump-sum amount, giving the union negotiators the choice of how to divide it among the various proposed economic enhancements. The cents per hour figure is perhaps the single most important item to employees in the new contract. Because employees can quickly estimate their additional take-home pay by using the cents per hour figure, it becomes vital when they vote on contract ratification. Granof found that most management negotiators agree that the primary goal in bargaining is to minimize the cents per hour direct wage increase.[45]

Employers are usually aware that any negotiated economic increases will have to be duplicated for nonunion and management personnel. This **spillover** effect is often quite costly. However, most costing models do not include the spillover costs; unions do not want to consider them part of the contract cost.[46]

Base

The first step in determining compensation costs is to develop the **base** compensation figure. During negotiation, this figure is essential in determining the percentage value of a requested increase in wages. For example, a $500 annual wage increase means a 2.5 percent wage increase on a $20,000 base and a 5 percent increase for an employee with a $10,000 base. The base may be thought of as the employee's annual salary; however, it seldom represents the total payroll costs incurred by the company for that employee. For example, the average salary cost, or *base salary*, for a nurse in a city hospital was $14,073. Under the terms of the contract, a nurse may have also received an average of the following: longevity pay of $505.00, overtime of $486.75, shift differential of $1,033.68, vacation cost of $636.76, holiday pay of $560.72, hospitalization insurance of $515.72, a clothing allowance of $150.00, and pension benefit of $965.89. The total additional paid benefits were $4,854.52 for each nurse, equal to about 34 percent of base pay. These additional costs, when added to the base of $14,073.00, produced what many think of as the nurse's true gross salary of $18,927.52.[47]

Figure 7-6 illustrates the Chrysler Corporation-UAW agreement base rates for three jobs. At the end of the old agreement the base rates were $17.44, $17.92, and $21.11 for the janitor, assembler, and tool and die job classifications. At the start of this 1996 negotiation it was agreed to "fold-in" or add to the old base rates, the COLAs that had been given, thereby creating new base rates that would stay in effect during the new three-year agreement (1997–1999). If the CPI increased 2.9 percent each year, the new COLA adjustment and negotiated deferred wage increases of 3 percent in the second and third years would cause the hourly wage rates to increase as reflected in Figure 7-6.

The new base rates for each year are determined by adding the wage increase and COLA to the previous year's base rate. For example, the base rates for the janitor job classification start at $18.47 to start the new contract and for the next three years are: $18.88, $19.95, and $21.06.

The one absolutely essential figure that every negotiator should have in mind at all times is *how much a wage increase of 1 percent will cost the employer in thousands of dollars per year.* Although the overall dollar cost of a contract settlement is important for budget purposes, most negotiators do not consider such costs to be especially pertinent. They find the total cents per hour cost of the negotiated wage increase more relevant, and they bargain in those terms. Settlements are also evaluated by their superiors in terms of cents per hour, but they need to be able to convert cents per hour to total dollars for accurate costing.[48]

	Janitor	Assembler	Tool & Die
Base rate: contract end	**$17.44**	**$17.92**	**$21.11**
COLA fold-in	<u>$1.03</u>	<u>$1.03</u>	<u>$1.03</u>
New agreement base	**$18.47**	**$18.95**	**$22.14**
Beginning COLA float	$0.05	$0.05	$0.05
1st-year COLA	<u>$0.36</u>	<u>$0.36</u>	<u>$0.36</u>
End 1st-year wage	**$18.88**	**$19.36**	**$22.55**
2nd-year wage increase	$0.55	$0.57	$0.96*
2nd-year COLA	<u>$0.52</u>	<u>$0.52</u>	<u>$0.52</u>
End 2nd-year wage	**$19.95**	**$20.45**	**$24.03**
3rd-year wage increase	$0.57	$0.59	$0.69
3rd-year COLA	<u>$0.54</u>	<u>$0.54</u>	<u>$0.54</u>
End 3rd-year wage	**$21.06**	**$21.58**	**$25.26**

Chrysler-UAW Examples: Base Rate, COLA Adjustments, Wage Adjustments — Figure 7-6

Source: UAW-Chrysler Newsgram, October 1996, p. 3.

Roll-Up

As hourly wages increase, many benefits also directly increase because they are directly tied to the wage rate or base pay of employees. This direct increase in benefits caused by a negotiated wage increase is referred to as the **roll-up**. Examples of some of these benefits are:

1. *Social security and unemployment insurance contributions.* The employer's contribution is computed as a percentage of each employee's wage up to a maximum annual figure. Any negotiated wage increase up to this maximum will cause a direct increase in the employer's contribution.

2. *Life insurance.* Often the amount of life insurance coverage paid by the employer is based on the employee's annual earnings. Therefore, as annual earnings are increased, the cost of the insurance automatically increases.

3. *Overtime pay and shift premium.* Overtime compensation and shift premium are often computed as a percentage of base wage. Thus, these also increase with the base wage.

4. *Pension benefits.* The pension benefit formula normally includes employees' average annual wages. An increase in wages increases the employer's funding liability for the pension.[49]

Negotiators often determine an agreed-upon percentage attributable to roll-up. The roll-up percentage is computed by dividing the cost of the directly increased benefit by the cost of the wage rate increase. For example, if a $0.50 per hour increase in the base wage directly causes a $0.10 per hour increase in benefits, then the roll-up percentage is $0.10 divided by $0.50, or 20 percent. Therefore, if negotiators agreed to increase employees' base wage by $0.50 per hour, from $5.00 per hour to $5.50 per hour, the 10 percent negotiated wage increase would cause a direct cost increase of 12 percent, or $0.60, when the roll-up costs were added.

Total Negotiated Costs

At all times during negotiations, both labor and management maintain their estimated cost of wage and benefit items upon which they have reached agreement. Therefore, as additional economic items are proposed, both sides know exactly the total cost of the new contract; they can then decide if the cost of the new items would increase the total cost of the agreement beyond an affordable level. In Table 7-6, the total cost of all new wage and benefit enhancements for the metals firm example in Table 7-5 is $1,318,049 at some time in the negotiations. Management had previously determined that the profits available for increased labor costs under a new contract was $1,399,475 (also shown in Table 7-5). Therefore, management would likely agree to the total package of items presented in Table 7-6 or might even be willing to agree to additional economic enhancements *if* their total cost is less than $81,426. The union might, for example, propose increasing the clothing allowance by another $150 per year to reach a final agreement. Although the total cost of this proposal would be only $100,500, or about one-half of 1 percent of the total wages and benefits that management estimates would be paid under the new contract, it would increase the total costs of all negotiated items to $1,418,549. Thus, the new total would exceed the maximum management believes it can afford under a new contract. In such a situation, management might either (1) reject this proposal and therefore signal to the union that the total cost is close to the maximum; (2) respond with a counteroffer of an additional $50 clothing allowance, which would be less than the $81,426 that management believes it has left to bargain; or (3) accept the final proposal by the union if it would secure a contract and hope that the $19,074 by which management exceeded its estimate will not critically affect future operations. If management believed that the union would press other economic issues after the clothing allowance increase was accepted, management would most likely reject the proposal. Otherwise, the union could keep proposing small additional increases and possibly exceed the maximum cost estimate by a large amount.

Table 7-6	Estimated Costs of Negotiated Wage and Benefit Increases	
Item	First Year, New Contract	Estimated Additional Cost
Wages (wage rate + roll-up)	3%	$361,000
Paid holidays	1 new day	40,505
Funeral leave	New provision: 3 days/death	121,515
Health insurance	Increase in employer share: ($120/year)	128,100
Clothing allowance	Additional year: ($50/employee)	33,500
Profit sharing	New provision: 10% of net	399,850
Pension benefits	Additional $50/month	100,000
Paid vacation	Two additional days/year for employees with less than two years service	24,712
Shift differential	Increased from 10% to 12%	108,867
Total cost of negotiated wage and benefit increases		$1,318,049

Computerized Costing

Merlin P. Breaux of the Gulf Oil Corporation in Houston sums up the role of the computer in collective bargaining today:

> Access to computer data banks has significantly shortened our research time prior to negotiations. And the application of software spread sheets has made contract cost analysis a much easier and more accurate process. In the future of collective bargaining, more development of computer skills is a necessity.

During contract negotiations, the terms of the contract are constantly changing. Negotiators often quickly revise their demands for wages, benefits, and other cost-related items. The time span of a contract is also negotiable. The negotiator needs to estimate the impact of these changes on the total cost of the contract. A labor or management negotiator may ask: What if a time period or other critical contract item is changed? What would the impact be on the bottom line? Thus, a computer is essential in making these quick, accurate, and detailed calculations.[50]

Knowing how *sensitive* a contract is to its individual terms allows the negotiator to manipulate those variables having the least cost to avoid bringing high-cost items to the bargaining table.[51] Company negotiators can use historical records to calculate quickly the cost of the benefits, as, for example, when the union bargains for an additional holiday. The value of this holiday may be the cost of one day's production because the factory will be closed or the salary and overtime necessary to pay workers required to work that day. The advent of computer spread sheets gave negotiators a significant tool to quickly and accurately estimate the costs of proposals.

Unionized wages are often characterized as the spark behind wage-price spirals in the United States. The general public is made aware of large union wage increase settlements, often after any economic strike. Salary increases received by management and nonunion employees, however, do not receive such publicity. Also, the use of COLA provisions in negotiated settlements has received criticism as being a prime cause of inflation.

Many labor critics have claimed that union wage increases have an effect far beyond the organized portion of the labor force. The contention is that nonunion employers, to remain unorganized, follow the lead set by union contracts. However, survey data suggest that such a practice depends on the size of the employer. Large nonunion employers do tend to match the union scale of all levels of unionism in their industry. Medium-sized nonunion employers tend to match the union scale only if unionism is a strong presence in their industry. Small nonunion employers tend to maintain wage levels below the union scale regardless of the presence of unionism in the industry.[52] Thus, it is difficult to show that union wage increases are followed by a large proportion of employers who may be raising employees' wages for any of several other good reasons.

Daniel Mitchell, director of the UCLA Institute of Labor Relations, suggests that during negotiations employers *offer* lower wages than they really intend to pay, or than they would pay if the company were nonunion, and then they *agree* on higher union-demanded wages. Thus, it appears to the public that the final outcome was a victory for the union, which bargained for more than the employer was willing to give. But the outcome might be similar to what the employer's

UNION WAGES AND INFLATION

wage determination would have been without a union. Unions may substantially affect only difficult-to-measure, noneconomic items such as work rules, working conditions, and grievance procedures.

SUMMARY

Wages and benefits represent the heart of the collective bargaining process. Guarantee of a certain standard of living and a reasonable return for their productive efforts is the major concern for most union members. At the same time, management realizes what large percentages of its total costs are wages and benefits. Through job evaluation, wage surveys, and other methods, both sides negotiate either a standard rate or a pay range for each job covered in the agreement. Also, future cost-of-living adjustments are negotiated.

Both labor and management begin negotiations by estimating sales, production costs, overhead costs, and other significant economic variables, which can then produce the predicted total revenue available for negotiated wage and benefit enhancements. This figure can be used as a target figure during negotiations and can therefore be constantly compared against estimated total cost of negotiated increases. Management can thus ensure that the organization will be able to afford negotiated future labor costs, and the union can obtain a fair share of future profits for its members.

The accurate costing of all negotiated wage changes is critical to successful bargaining and to management's cost containment efforts as well as to predictions of future labor cost. Roll-up costs must be included in any estimate when wage increases have been agreed upon. The computer has given both management and labor a negotiating tool to add speed and accuracy to the costing of proposals.

CASE STUDY 7-1

WORK SCHEDULES

Facts

The company is a manufacturer and packager of certain veterinary products. The company's operation utilizes an automatic liquid packaging (ALP) machine that requires a continuous nine-hour operation. The machine is prepared prior to the 8:00 A.M. shift and then runs for nine hours with approximately two and one-half hours of cleanup time after the run is complete. The employees had worked a regular 8:00 A.M. to 4:30 P.M. shift, with the employees on the 8:00 A.M. shift completing the cleanup of the machine *on overtime*. The company changed the work schedule of three employees on that regular 8:00 A.M. shift to a 10:30 A.M. to 7:00 P.M. shift, two days a week. The employees were allowed to work either the 8:00 A.M. to 4:30 P.M. shift or the 10:30 A.M. to 7:00 P.M. shift on the three days the machine was not running. The collective bargaining agreement provided in Article V, HOURS OF WORK: "The regular workweek shall consist of five consecutive or regularly scheduled days of eight hours each."

The union grieved the change in schedule, stating that it violated the contract, which required a regular workweek of eight hours a day. The union claimed that the regular workweek was 8:00 A.M. to 4:30 P.M. and that any other change was not allowed under the contract. The company's position was that the three employees had a regularly scheduled workweek, which consisted of five scheduled days of eight hours each. The start and finish time was set on each of those five days. The union asked the arbitrator to find that, al-

(continued)

though the company had the prerogative to schedule work under the agreement, the irregular work schedule was in violation of Article V. The union relied heavily on the definition of a regular workweek in making this argument. The definition of *regular* from *Black's Law Dictionary* is "steady or uniform in course, practice, or occurrence; not subject to unexplained or irrational variation. Usual, customary, or general." The definition of *regularly* is "affixed and certain intervals. Regular in point of time. In accordance with some consistent or periodic rule or practice."

Questions

1. Did the company violate Article V by having employees begin and end their workdays at different times?
2. Would the union be able to make the same argument in this case if the schedule for the affected employees had been changed to 10:30 A.M. to 7:00 P.M. for every day of the week?
3. The loss of overtime pay was obviously a concern in this case. How could the company have handled the issue differently and avoided the grievance?

Adapted from *Fort Dodge Laboratories, Inc.*, 87 LA 1290 (1986).

INCENTIVE PAY

Facts

The company had an incentive pay rate in place that could increase the employees' pay by 30 percent over their base pay. Citing changed circumstances, the employer eliminated the incentive pay for one department. The union appealed. The collective bargaining agreement in place at the time of the grievance reserved all management rights to the company unless restricted by the language of the agreement.

Article V of the agreement established wages to be paid and specifically continued during the term of the agreement "all incentive rates" in existence at the time of the agreement; excepting only the company's right to "establish new incentive rates or to adjust existing incentive rates" under certain conditions listed in the agreement. Those conditions included changes, modifications, or improvements made in equipment involved in an incentive pay area; new or changed standards of manu-

facturing; and changes in job duties of those affected by incentive pay.

Procedures on how the company was to proceed to establish new or changed incentive rates were also included in Article V of the agreement, unless changes to the incentive rates were a result of the changed circumstances previously cited. If this was the case, employees affected by the changes were given the right to grieve the application of the changed incentive rate. When the incentive pay was totally eliminated for one department, the union grieved on behalf of those affected employees.

It was the company's position that significant changes of equipment and operations in the affected department authorized the unilateral elimination of the incentive pay under the agreement. A new mechanical device had eliminated the need for fracture tests of a furnace. The employees in the department had been reduced from 6 Head Operators, 22 Attendant Carburizing, and 4 Recorder Optical

(continued)

Pyrometers to 3 Head Operators and 4 Attendants. The classification of Recorder Optical Pyrometer was completely eliminated because the duties were no longer needed. The company's interpretation of the contract language was that these changed circumstances allowed the company to eliminate unilaterally the incentive pay for the remaining employees.

The union's position was that the collective bargaining agreement contemplated the incentive pay's being kept in place as part of the employee's wages, and the company could not unilaterally eliminate the incentive pay. New or changed rates could be negotiated as circumstances dictated, but eliminating the pay completely was not allowed.

The following are the relevant contract provisions:

ARTICLE V—WAGES
A. Wage Rates

. . . such hourly wage rates, together with all incentive rates now in existence, which altogether constitute the wage structure applicable to existing occupations in effect on August 28, 1983, shall remain in effect during the term of this agreement, except as any of such rates may be changed, adjusted, or supplemented in the manner prescribed in this Article. . . .

B. New and Changed Rates

. . . It is recognized that the company, at its discretion, may also find it necessary or desirable from time to time to establish new incentive rates or to adjust existing incentive rates because of any of the following circumstances:

1. Changes, modifications, or improvements made in equipment, material, or product. If there is any such change, modification, or improvement in existing equipment or material or on an existing product, the company may change the elements of the rate or rates affected by such change, modification, or improvement but will not change the elements not affected by such change, modification, or improvement.

2. New or changed standards of manufacture in (a) processes; (b) methods; and (c) quality.
3. Changes in the duties of an occupation covered by incentive rates that affect the existing incentive standards.

Whenever it is claimed by any employee that any of the changes or events have occurred that are outlined in Paragraphs 1, 2, and 3 of the preceding Section B of this Article V, any employee who is affected thereby, either (1) by the production of product or (2) by being employed on an occupation affected by such claimed changes or events outlined in said paragraphs, may request the establishment of a new rate by discussing such request with his supervisor. In the event that no agreement is reached in respect to the employee's request, grievance may be filed by such employee within 10 calendar days after such changes or events have occurred.

If, as the result of a grievance being processed under this Section B, it is determined that the company did not have the right to establish a new or adjusted rate, the rate structure in effect prior to the new or adjusted rate shall be reinstated as of the effective date of the new or adjusted rate. The company will calculate retroactive payment to the extent possible under the applicable rate structure.

Questions

1. Did the changes made in the department satisfy the circumstances cited in the agreement that would allow the company to eliminate the incentive pay?
2. Did the affected employees have a legitimate grievance under the collective bargaining agreement language?
3. If you were the arbitrator, would you allow the company to eliminate the incentive pay? Explain your answer.

Adapted from *Timken Co.*, 85 LA 377 (1985).

ability to pay
annual salary
back-loaded contract
base
Cost-of-living adjustment (COLA)
costing wage proposals
deferred wage rate increase
exempt
falling piece rate
front-end loading
hourly wage
job evaluation
lump-sum payment
nonexempt
pattern bargaining
pay equity

pay for time worked
piece-rate system
piecework
productivity theory
profit sharing
pyramiding
rising piece rate
roll-up
Scanlon plan
standard rate
standard hour plan
two-tier wage system
value-added concept
wage reopener
wage survey

1. What are the general wage concerns that management and employee representatives bring to the negotiating table?
2. Why have profit-sharing plans replaced COLAs in some recently negotiated agreements?
3. Why does management often prefer profit-sharing increases or bonuses to deferred wage increases?
4. How can wage surveys be effectively used in collective bargaining?
5. Why are labor and management negotiators likely to respond to consideration of the company's ability to pay higher wages?
6. What are some problems with negotiated cost-of-living adjustments?
7. Why must labor and management be able to determine accurately the cost of wage proposals?
8. How should negotiators treat the roll-up costs when negotiating wage changes?
9. Why might union negotiators favor front-end loaded deferred wage increases? Are there potential drawbacks?
10. Why do you think profit-sharing and lump-sum provisions have increased in usage in recent years, while COLAs and wage reopeners have decreased in use?

TAKE IT TO THE NET

We invite you to visit the Carrell/Heavrin page on the Prentice Hall Web site at:

http://www.prenhall.com/carrellr

for this chapter's World Wide Web exercise.

Current Wage Issues

Purpose:
To familiarize students with wage and salary issues that are currently being discussed by unions and employers.

Task:
Through news articles, journals, the Internet, and other sources, identify 10 current wage issues, and summarize the general position of labor and management on each issue.

Example:

Issue	*Management*	*Union*
Increased hourly rates	Management will propose only a percentage it believes future revenues can safely provide without exceeding rates paid by the competition.	The union will vote the increased inflation rate and wage rate increases negotiated by others to support a high-percentage increase.

1.
2.
3.
4.
5.
6.
7.
8.
9.
10.

Source: Adapted from M. Carrell, F. Kuzmits, and N. Elbert, *Personnel*, 3rd ed. (Columbus, OH: Merrill Publishing, 1989), pp. 601–602.

EXERCISE 7-2 **Wage Provisions**

Purpose:
To help students understand the necessity of using precise language when drafting a contract.

Task:
Divide the class into management and labor, and assign each wage topic below for students to write a mutually agreeable contract term.

1. COLA provision for a three-year contract
2. Profit sharing in a small engineering firm
3. Two-tier wage system for a teacher's contract
4. A 0–3–3 deferred wage increase.
5. A lump-sum payment of $2,000.00 to all eligible unit employees.

If you are using Smith/Carrell/Golden *Collective Bargaining Simulated, 4E*, with this text, please refer to the following:

p. 21, Article XX: Wages, and pp. 25–28 for the costing of key economic features.

CHAPTER 8

Employee
Benefits Issues

- Concession Bargaining
- Required Benefits
- Negotiated Benefits
- Income Maintenance
  Plans
- Medical Care
- Pay for Time Not Worked
- Premium Pay
- Employee Services
- Summary

Cafeterias with restaurant-style menus and inviting atmospheres are frequently
provided by employers as an employee benefit.

United Steelworkers/ Inland Steel Precedent Contract

Faced with tough foreign and nonunion domestic competition, the Inland Steel Industries Corp. and the United Steelworkers negotiated a historic contract that became a model for 1990s labor agreements. The contract reflected a new attitude by both labor and management. The reason for the new attitudes at the negotiating table? "We have dragons to slay together and this sets the context for very close company-union cooperation," said Inland President Maurice S. Nelson. The union chief negotiator, Jack Parton, added: "I think this is the way of the future for the industry and for all industries. For the union the precedent-setting contract provides:

- *No-layoff clause.* The union's top priority is job security for its members.
- *Union participation.* This is at all levels of management including a seat on the board of directors.

Adapted from Dana Milbank, "Inland Steel Sets Accord with Steelmakers," *Wall Street Journal*, May 28, 1993, p. A2.

- *Wage and benefits increases.* Wages will keep up with inflation during the contract.

For management the contract provides:

- *Six-year contract* that will provide stability in the labor force and is a record length for steel industry contracts.
- *Elimination of most work rule restrictions,* enabling management to redesign jobs for greater efficiency.
- *Managed health-care plan,* which should enable management to hold the line on cost increases.
- *25 percent workforce reduction,* only through attrition, enabling Inland to become more competitive.

Today, negotiated employee benefits, once referred to as fringe benefits, represent a critical part of the total economic package. Employers may easily find that between 25 and 45 percent of the total economic package now consists of benefits rather than direct compensation. Yet benefits are not usually designed to meet the same employee objectives as the wage portion of the negotiated agreement. From the employee standpoint, the wage portion of the economic package provides income needed for the necessities of life such as food, shelter, and clothing, as well as some luxuries. Management views wages as a means of attracting, retaining, and motivating employees and therefore maximizing their productivity.

Benefits, however, often have different objectives for management as well as the union. For example, many benefits are designed to guarantee employees a stream of income regardless of unforeseen circumstances such as layoff, automation of work, death, or illness. A major effect of a strong benefit package is the reduction of turnover. A substantial cost borne by workers in changing jobs is the loss of associated benefits. A worker leaving behind a pension may forfeit several thousands of dollars of retirement income, along with sizable losses in vacation, insurance, and other benefits.[1]

Retirement income is usually the most expensive negotiated economic benefit. Additional pay for time not worked, such as vacation, holiday, and sick leave, is commonly negotiated as is premium pay for unusual circumstances such as overtime and call-in pay.

As a percentage of the total compensation provided by management, benefit costs have grown dramatically in recent years. From 1975 to 1985, for example, the cost of benefits provided by employers increased 105 percent, from an average of $77 per week to $157 per week.[2] Also, the most expensive areas of employee benefits continue to be pensions, Social Security, insurance, and paid time off work. Unions have generally led the way in benefit changes in this country regarding the types of benefits provided by employers and their relative value. Negotiated benefits in collective bargaining agreements generally set the standard for the nonunion sector.

Does collective bargaining affect the benefits received by union members? A comparison of more than 10,000 union and nonunion establishments found that unionism had a sizable impact on total benefit expenditures as well as on the straight-time wage rate. The average dollars spent per hour on voluntary benefits is 140 percent higher ($0.70/hour versus $0.29/hour) in private union firms (versus nonunion).

CONCESSION BARGAINING

The 1980s ushered in a new era in negotiated wages and benefits. High levels of unemployment prompted unions in severely affected industries to seek ways to protect jobs. Through collective bargaining, unions seek to stop further layoffs. Employers are willing to agree to increased employment security only at the high price of wage or benefit freezes. In several cases, reductions in benefits, particularly paid time off work, are required to guarantee employment levels.[3] Thus, givebacks, or **concession bargaining** techniques, were born out of necessity.

Concession bargaining first gained national headlines in November 1979 when Chrysler negotiated more than $200 million in givebacks. On the brink of bankruptcy, Chrysler used the United Auto Worker concessions to negotiate more than $1 billion in long-term, federal government loans. Although some concessions were in the area of deferred wage increases, the majority of the savings came in the reduced employee benefits of paid holidays, paid sickness and accident absences, and pension funds.[4] In return, Chrysler gave the UAW a seat on its board of directors and a no-layoff guarantee.

The giveback negotiations of the UAW and Chrysler were historic in the labor relations field. The negotiations set a pattern for several other unions and showed that unions preferred reductions in previously negotiated benefits such as paid time off work to reductions in wage levels. The negotiations also proved that a giant corporation and a major union could work together to keep the company operating.

In 1982, Ford Motor Company and the UAW negotiated a break-through in greater job security for union members. At that time, 55,000 Ford workers were on indefinite layoff while the remaining 105,000 feared for their future employment. The UAW agreed to defer cost-of-living increases for 18 months and to eliminate nine previously negotiated personal paid holidays each year. In exchange, Ford Motor Company agreed to a two-year moratorium on plant closings, which would have resulted in subcontracting the manufacturing of parts to non-UAW suppliers.

Of particular significance in the Ford agreement was the new **guaranteed income stream** program in which laid-off employees with 15 years or more of service would be guaranteed 50 percent of their hourly rate of pay until age 62 or retirement. In addition, Ford agreed to undertake an experimental *lifetime job security* program at two plants so that jobs would not be eliminated because of technological change or the economy.

In the meat-packing industry, giveback bargaining began in 1981 when the United Food and Commercial Workers Union and Armour and Company agreed on a wage and benefit package. Armour had lost almost $6 million in 1980 and had closed 24 plants in the past 10 years. The workers gave up specified wage increases and agreed to suspend semiannual cost-of-living pay adjustments. The Food and Commercial Workers Union negotiated similar terms under what was referred to as the "Armour pattern" with several other employers, including Wilson Foods Corporation, George A. Hormel and Company, and Rath Packing Company. Similarly, in 1981, the Teamsters, with nearly half of its members indefinitely laid off, negotiated a 37-month national master freight agreement calling for a freeze on general wages. The agreement provided for a reopening of negotiations in 1984 only if the parties agreed that the financial status of the industry had substantially changed. The tire, steel, and airline industries, as well as others, also began similar concession bargaining agreements.[5]

An analysis of successfully concluded concession negotiations showed that in more than half, the union agreed to wage and benefit reductions. In the remaining contracts, unions consented to a wage and benefit freeze. The most common concession, found in 40 percent of the contracts, was an agreement to give up paid holidays. The second most common concession involved a work rule or production change. In exchange, employers generally agreed to future wage and benefit improvements and greater job security.[6]

In the 1990s, an increase in concession bargaining took place in a number of industries. The United Steelworkers reached a precedent-setting agreement with Inland Steel Industries, Inc., in 1993. In this agreement, which was heralded as the wave of the future, the union exchanged the elimination of decades-old work restrictions for a seat on the board of directors and a no-layoff clause. Wages and pension benefits also increased during the term of the six-year agreement. Inland

Steel, under the agreement, was allowed to reduce personnel levels, loosen job descriptions, reduce the workforce by 25 percent through attrition, and manage the plan so that it could compete with nonunion mills.[7]

Concession bargaining in the 1990s could also be found in the airline industry. In an effort to keep Northwest Airlines from bankruptcy, the International Association of Machinists and the Teamsters agreed to $428 million in labor cost savings through concessions at the bargaining table. The unions agreed to wage cuts from 6 to 12 percent in exchange for a 30 percent equity stake in the company and three of 15 board seats.[8]

In 1992, the International Union of Electrical Workers (IUE), which represents autoworkers at *one* General Motors plant in Moraine, Ohio, found itself at odds with the United Auto Workers (UAW). Threatened with a shutdown at its plant, the IUE agreed to major concessions in its contract with GM. Overwhelmingly approved by the 3,100-member workforce, the agreement reduced job classifications, added a third shift, and let new hires be paid at 55 percent of the wage rate of current employees.[9]

In the sagging aerospace and defense industry, concession bargaining continued into 1993. The International Association of Machinists (IAM) agreed to let Pratt & Whitney devise productivity improvement plans and to tie pay to meeting such plans as well as to forego raises and cost-of-living adjustments during the term of the contract. In exchange, the company eliminated 6,700 jobs rather than the 9,000 originally targeted and kept four plants in the state of Connecticut open.[10]

Successful concession bargaining hinges on management's ability to convince labor of impending financial crisis that could cause a significant loss of jobs or total shutdown of the operation.[11] However, economic adversity alone may not be enough to bring about concessions. Union negotiators expect management concessions and programs to enhance labor-management relationships. Thus, employers as well as unions have made concessions during giveback negotiations, many aimed at increasing quality of work life and worker participation in decision making. Economic concessions have often centered on management's sharing of future "good times" through profit sharing or gain sharing in exchange for immediate union givebacks.[12]

In many cases concessions are not called "concessions" so that neither side appears to have lost or won in negotiations. Most negotiations involving givebacks require both labor and management to make some concessions in a true give-and-take process.[13] Often, for example, if management demands givebacks in wages and benefits, union negotiators will demand similar reductions in management salaries and benefits. If management requests greater flexibility in work rules and scheduling, labor negotiators might demand greater union participation in management decisions.

In a similar vein, employers may try to protect the investment they have made in their employees by including **payback agreements** in the negotiations. Payback agreements require an employee who voluntarily quits before a specified period of time (usually one year) to pay the employer the cost of certain benefits. The most common benefits specified include relocation costs for newly hired employees, training program costs, and tuition assistance costs. Companies such as American Airlines (pilot training costs of about $10,000), Electronic Data Systems Corporation (relocation costs), and Lockheed Corporation (tuition assistance) have successfully sued employees who refused to honor their agreements.[14]

Some unions have criticized the agreements: The AFL-CIO has noted their similarity to indentured servitude (a person required to work for another as a servant). However, not all unions dislike the concept. The Sheet Metal Workers Union has required those who complete the union training program to repay the program costs if they work for a nonunion shop within 10 years.

Union concessions generally involve wage, benefit, or work rule changes, with reduced benefits generally more acceptable to employees than wage concessions, although future wage increases may be renegotiated. Often work rule changes are easier to sell to employees and have a more lasting effect. Employers, however, must expect to pay the price of these concessions through one or more of five areas of negotiation:

1. **Increased job security.** The union will most likely try to extract a promise not to close plants or not to subcontract with nonunion producers. The Ford Motor Company example of a guaranteed income stream will be pursued by many unions. Such restrictions can be very expensive and limiting to employers.
2. **Increased financial disclosure.** The employer will have to make a claim of inability to pay or financial hardship. Although the company's financial information normally need not be disclosed in collective bargaining, when the employer puts profitability or financial condition in contention, the financial data must be provided to substantiate the position.
3. **Profit-sharing plans.** Union members generally feel that sharing in austerity now should mean sharing profits in the future. For example, Chrysler Corporation's employees demanded a share of the record profits after the UAW made major concessions to guarantee the federal loan to Chrysler. In 1994, workers were expected to receive an average of $4,300. More than 160,000 union and nonunion employees of the Ford Motor Company received an average of $1,350 in 1994 as their part of the Ford-UAW profit-sharing plan.
4. **Equality of sacrifice.** Employers must demand the same sacrifices from management and nonunion employees as union employees. For instance, General Motors tried to increase its executive bonus program just after the UAW made major concessions in 1982. The UAW and its members demanded, and got, the increases rescinded.
5. **Participation in decision making.** Unions may seek greater participation in various management decisions, including plant closings and the use of new technological methods. If properly utilized, this concession can help develop greater understanding and improve employee relations.[15]

The essence of successful and continued concession bargaining is the development of mutual trust and respect by both parties. The union must be willing to give up some gains made through the years, especially in terms of nonproductive paid time off and other expensive benefits. The employer, in somewhat of a role reversal, must convince the union of the need to negotiate concessions to guarantee survival of the business. The obvious and ultimate proof is that the company is losing money, which usually must be verified by an objective third party such as an outside auditor.

REQUIRED BENEFITS

Some employee benefits are required by law and are therefore not negotiated. However, both labor and management representatives need to be cognizant of these benefits and their impact on other benefits that can be negotiated. Some negotiated benefit plans are designed to supplement those required by law to guarantee the employee a greater level of benefit. In recent years, some union leaders opposed government-imposed benefit programs such as the Occupational Safety and Health Act of 1970, the Pension Reform Act of 1974, and the Health Maintenance Organization Act of 1973 because the benefits provided were previously only for union employees. Union negotiators also felt that the government diluted their ability to bargain for even better benefits. Uniformly provided benefits restrict negotiators' ability to bargain for specific programs preferred by their membership.

Unemployment insurance, Social Security, and workers' compensation are three costly and important government-required benefits. **Unemployment insurance** programs have been operating since 1938. States provide unemployed workers with benefits by imposing payroll taxes on employers. The amount paid normally varies according to the state's unemployment rate. The unemployed person must have worked for a certain period of time and must register with the state bureau of employment to receive benefits.

About 97 percent of all workers are included in the federal-state unemployment insurance system. Employers pay a payroll tax on each employee's wages. There are no federal standards for benefits, qualifying requirements, benefit amounts, or duration of benefits; the states each develop their own formulas for workers' benefits. Under all state laws, a worker's benefit rights depend on work experience during a "base period" of time. Most states require a claimant to serve a waiting period before receiving benefits.[16] Workers are usually required to be available for work, able to work, and seeking work actively to receive benefits. Claimants are disqualified for voluntarily leaving without good cause, discharge for misconduct, or refusal to accept suitable work.

In 1935, Congress established the **Social Security** system to provide supplemental income to retired workers. Initially intended to supplement private, often union-negotiated pension plans, Social Security would help retirees live in dignity and comfort. The cost of the system is carried by employers and employees who pay an equal amount of taxes into the system, which then uses the funds to pay benefits to currently retired individuals. Technically, Social Security taxes are Federal Insurance Contributions Act (FICA) taxes. Management often points out that the employees pay only half the cost of the system yet receive all the benefits.

Recently, another phase of the Social Security system was added to provide disability, survivor, and Medicare benefits. To become eligible for retirement benefits, individuals born after 1928 must contribute for 40 quarters (10 full years). Required contributions to receive medical benefits vary according to age.

Since the Social Security Revision Act of 1972, the benefits paid to retirement income recipients increase each year by a percentage equal to the increase in the consumer price index. This automatic and liberal increase has been one of the main causes of the shaky financial condition of the Social Security system.[17] It has also provided management's primary weapon in not increasing employees' private pensions. Employers complain that Social Security taxes have increased each year along with raised salaries, because the tax is a percentage of the employees' salary. In addition, Congress raised the employers' and employees' Social Security tax rate from 4.8 percent in 1970 to 7.65 percent in 1990.[18]

Laws requiring **workers' compensation** were enacted by states to protect employees and their families against permanent loss of income and high medical bills due to accidental injury or illness on the job. The primary purpose of most state laws is to keep the question of the cause of the accident out of court. The laws assure employees payment for medical expenses or lost income. Workers' compensation primarily consists of employer contributions into a statewide fund. A state industrial board then reviews cases and determines employee eligibility for compensation for injury on the job.

Union leaders have played an important role in ensuring that workers' compensation laws are updated and employee interests are protected. Their efforts protect not only the interests of the union workers but also those of the nonunion sector.

Most benefits included in labor agreements are not required by law, although most are mandatory issues for negotiations. However, any such paid benefits must be gained at the negotiating table. In general, these benefits can be grouped into four categories as illustrated in Figure 8-1: (1) income maintenance, (2) employee health care, (3) pay for time not worked, and (4) premium pay. A fifth group includes employee services.

NEGOTIATED BENEFITS

Benefit Issues

Figure 8-1

Type of Issue	Issue	Relevant Items
Required	Social Security Unemployment insurance Worker's compensation	
Negotiated	Income maintenance plans	Pensions Wage employment guarantees Supplemental unemployment (SUB) plans Guaranteed income stream (GIS) Severance pay Death and disability
	Employee health care	Health insurance Dental, optical, prescription drugs Alcohol and drug treatment Wellness programs Employee assistance programs
	Pay for time not worked	Paid holidays Paid vacations Sick leave Paid leaves
	Premium pay	Reporting pay Shift differential Call-in pay/on-call pay Bilingual skills Travel pay
	Employee services	Flexible benefit plans Child care Credit union

INCOME MAINTENANCE PLANS

Income maintenance provisions have become commonplace in collective bargaining agreements. These plans are negotiable and include supplemental unemployment benefits, severance pay (also called *dismissal* or *termination pay*), and wage employment guarantees. In addition, these plans protect employees from financial disruptions. Private pension plans provide for income during retirement, along with Social Security.

Pension Plans

Private pension plans have become one of the most sought-after and most expensive employee benefits. In the early stages of the U.S. labor movement, the benefit provided motivation for senior employees to remain with the organization and thus increase their retirement income. Later both labor and management negotiators accepted management's obligation to provide income to employees beyond their productive years. Acceptance of this obligation occurred largely as a result of a 1949 decision by the Supreme Court, *Inland Steel Company v. NLRB*, in which the Court declared that pension plans are mandatory collective bargaining subjects. Today, pension plans are provided in almost all labor contracts.[19] The number of private pension plans throughout the United States has increased dramatically since the *Inland Steel* decision. Fewer than 1,000 private pension plans were in operation in 1940; by the mid-1980s, more than 700,000 were in operation.

However, many American workers never collect from their pension plans. For example, Christine Clark was a tobacco worker for more than 30 years for several companies with private pension plans. Yet she could not receive a single penny in retirement benefits. The reason: Clark never became **vested**—had enough years to become eligible for company pension benefits—with any employer. Although she worked for Liggett & Meyers Tobacco Company in Richmond, Virginia, for 23 years, only seven years counted toward the pension plan: not enough to qualify her for the minimum of 10 years. After several odd jobs, Clark worked for eight and one-half years for American Tobacco Company in Richmond, Virginia: again not long enough to become vested with the pension plan. At the age of 53 and having worked for 34 years, Clark had no retirement income other than her Social Security.[20]

Many U.S. workers will not receive private pensions because they change jobs and leave employers frequently during their productive years. They miss being covered by any one company's pension plan. For other employees, the company either shuts down, lays them off, or dismisses them before they become vested. The lack of pension planning is particularly a problem in the service sector of our economy, which has grown rapidly in recent years.

Unions have been successful in providing private pension plans for their members; private pension plans are not as commonly found in the nonunion sector. One major study concluded that unionization has significantly affected the retirement systems of private employers, increasing the likelihood that an employer will offer a pension.[21] However, unions apparently are not able to raise actual employer expenditures for pensions once they are established.[22]

Union-negotiated pension plans compared with nonunion plans provide beneficiaries the ability to retire at an earlier age, greater benefits when they retire, and larger increases in their benefits after they retire. Combined with the greater inclusion of union workers in pension plans compared with nonunion, union membership is the dominant factor in determining the private pension dollars received by a retired worker in the United States.[23]

Most workers plan to retire at the age when they first become eligible for full private pension benefits.[24] In the past that age, most commonly 65, was also the mandatory retirement age and the age at which full Social Security benefits would first be available. In the future the typical retirement age may be difficult to estimate. Many workers are living longer and choosing to work longer. The amendment to the Age Discrimination in Employment Act of 1986 made it illegal for employers to require retirement at any age,[25] and the 1983 Social Security Amendment changed the age of full benefits eligibility from 65 to 67. Thus, the worker is faced with a more complex decision when choosing a retirement date.

Private pension systems will play an even more important role in the retirement decision. Undoubtedly, management will consider changing the full benefit eligibility age to match Social Security benefits and reduce its cost of retirement benefits. In the absence of unexpected events such as sudden wealth or failing health, most workers faced with the choice of working as long as they desire will consider the age at which they first become eligible for full pension benefits to be a critical decision point. Pension plans often use increased benefits to encourage workers not to retire early at reduced benefits, for example, at age 62, but to continue working and each year receive a higher proportion of their total benefits. Labor and management leaders alike are now faced with the reality of no mandatory retirement age and a change in Social Security. Thus, they can more easily consider changes in pension benefits, significantly affecting the age at which their workers choose to retire and therefore the cost of the pension system. Just as employee health-care plans have seen a great deal of change in recent years, private negotiated pension plans are likely to experience significant change in the future.

The popularity of company-financed pension plans rapidly declined in the early 1990s. Whenever possible, employers are transferring the financial risks and costs, as well as choices, to employees. Many companies now offer 401(k) savings plans, named after the Tax Code section, which provides that money put into a 401(k) plan is not taxed as income. In 1993 it was estimated that 36 million Americans were covered by 401(k) plans whereas only 26 million Americans were covered by traditional pension plans. Although the advantage to employers is easy to see, employees choose a 401(k) plan over a traditional pension plan because they have not benefited from the traditional plan.[26]

Employee Retirement Income Security Act (ERISA)

In 1974 Congress passed the **Employee Retirement Income Security Act (ERISA),** also known as the Pension Reform Act. The law was passed in response to alleged abuses and incompetence in some private pension plans. ERISA provided a sweeping reform of pension and benefit rules. The lengthy and complicated law primarily affects the following aspects of pension planning:

1. Employers are required to count toward vesting all service from age 18 and to count toward earned benefits all earnings from age 21. (Prior to the Retirement Equity Act of 1984, accrual toward vesting began at age 22, toward earnings at age 25.)
2. Employers must choose from among three minimum vesting standards (Sec. 203).

3. Each year employers must file reports of their pension plans with the U.S. Secretary of Labor for approval. New plans must be submitted for approval within 120 days of enactment.
4. The Pension Benefit Guarantee Corporation (PBGC) was established within the Department of Labor to encourage voluntary employee pension continuance when changing employment. This is accomplished by providing **portability**—the right of an employee to transfer tax-free pension benefits from one employer to another.
5. Pension plan members are permitted to leave the workforce for up to five consecutive years without losing service credit and allowed up to one year maternity or paternity leave without losing service credit.[27]

ERISA substantially reduced the number and scope of pension issues left at the bargaining table. The law has been criticized by employers and labor leaders because it is quite complex and may have encouraged some employers to provide no retirement plan at all.[28] However, ERISA gave employees protection when an employer, Continental Can, engaged in a complex nationwide scheme to avoid pension payments by laying off its employees just before they became eligible for benefits. A settlement of $415 million enabled more than 3,000 victims of the scheme to recover benefits.[29]

Issues in Pension Negotiations

Vesting. The conveying of employees' nonforfeitable rights to share in a pension fund is termed vesting. As illustrated in the example of Christine Clark, many individuals never receive private pension funds because they leave employers before working enough years to become vested.

Section 203 of ERISA provides that employers choose from among three alternatives of retirement age and service. One alternative is to provide 100 percent vested rights after five years of service. The other two provide less than 100 percent vested rights with fewer years of service. Union negotiators are very interested in the plan chosen by management. However, no single plan is always preferred by employees.

Qualified Plan. A *qualified plan* generally refers to a plan that meets standards set by the Internal Revenue Service (IRS). By qualifying under the IRS provisions, an employer can deduct pension contributions made to the qualified plan as business expenses for tax purposes. This, of course, is a major reason employers seek to qualify their pension plans whenever possible. Employees, however, also benefit because they do not pay taxes on any dollars either they or the employer invest in the plan under current income. Instead, income taxes are paid when the retirement benefits are received. A *nonqualified plan* would not provide the tax advantages of the qualified plan but would be required to meet the strict guidelines set by the IRS.

Funding Methods. There are four general methods of funding pension plans. Each method may provide some particular advantage to management:

1. **Trusted or funded plans.** Employers create a separate account or fund and invest dollars annually to provide the future retirement benefits for employees.

The fund is usually administered by a bank or separate board that makes decisions as to the investment of the funds and the payment of retirement benefits to individuals. Usually the fund is kept financially sound by an actuarial study of the estimated financial liability of the plan as well as its expected wealth of current assets. If the actuarial study determines that the fund does not have enough money to guarantee benefit payments to both present and past contributing employees, the employer adds the additional money necessary to keep the fund financially sound. This review of actuarial soundness is normally done annually. In some years if the number of retirement employees decreases and the number of new employees changes, it may not be necessary for the employer to add any additional money to the fund, whereas in other years employers may have to add substantial amounts (see Figure 8-2, the Ford-UAW fund example).

2. **Current expenditure plans.** Treating the retirement benefits paid to previous employees as a current expense and therefore paying it out of operating income is known as a *nonfunded*, or *pay-as-you-go*, funding method. This method is not actuarially sound and guarantees no fund available to current employees to provide later retirement benefits. Yet, for many employers, the possibility of providing the trusted or funded plan is very small because such plans usually require a large amount of capital to begin operation and create a large fund. The **current expenditure** system can simply provide that the employer will meet an additional expense each year: that is, the retirement benefits due its previous employees, as it meets other expenses. The largest nonfunded plan in the world is the Social Security retirement system.

3. **Insured plans.** Insurance companies often provide pension plans to employers. Normally the insurance company treats the provisions of the pension plan for the employer as it would any other type of collective insurance: The employer pays a premium and the insurance company administers the plan, pays out all benefits due, and assumes future payment liability. Although the employer may pay more to the insurance company than might be necessary under a trusted plan, the expertise and the experience of the insurance company may be well worth the additional fee to the small or medium-sized employer.

4. **Profit-sharing plans.** Some companies provide a pension plan that is funded; however, the funds are provided only through a percentage of company profits. This represents a unique compromise between the current expenditure and the funded methods. Management feels that employees will be more interested in the profitability of the company if their pensions share in the risk of profitability of doing business. Companies with stable profitability and growth have little trouble funding a pension plan through the profit-sharing approach. Sears Roebuck and Company and other firms in this country have successful profit-sharing plans. However, if profits substantially decrease or become nonexistent over several years, the plan may eventually become financially unsound.

Union leaders prefer the trusted and insured methods of funding pension plans that provide greater security for the future retirement benefits of their members. Even if the company had to shut down, most properly funded plans would continue to provide retirement benefits to employee participants.

Contributory Plans. All pension plans are either contributory or noncontributory. In a **contributory plan**, the employer pays a portion of the funding and the employee pays the other portion. The percentage paid by employer and employee

Figure 8-2 · UAW-Ford Motor Co. Pension Fund Provision

Section 5. Company Contributions

(a) (i) For the period commencing January 1, 1980 and thereafter during the term of this Agreement, the Company shall make contributions to the Pension Fund which, together with its contributions heretofore made, shall be sufficient to fund (A) and (B) below, based upon estimates made by a qualified actuary[1] for each Plan year starting January 1, 1980 and ending with the termination of this Agreement: (A) the normal cost[2] of the Plan (excluding the cost of benefits under Article VI of the Plan[3]) and (B) the respective unfunded lump sum past service costs of the Plan (excluding the cost of benefits under Article VI of the Plan) for such period on the basis of a method of funding, approved by a qualified actuary, according to the following schedule:

  (1) December 31, 2009 with respect to the portion of such unfunded lump sum past service cost[4] attributable to the benefit structure in effect prior to January 1, 1980,

  (2) thirty years after the end of the Plan year in which a revision of the benefit structure established by amendments to the Plan effective on or after January 1, 1980 becomes effective with respect to the portion of such lump sum past service cost attributable to such revision.

 (ii) For the period commencing September 1, 1965 through the date of termination of this Agreement, the Company shall make contributions to the Pension Fund to fund the cost of benefits under Article VI of the Plan on any basis from time to time approved by a qualified actuary; provided that the total of such contributions available in any calendar year shall be at least equal to total payments of benefits under Article VI of the Plan in such year.

(iii) The "past service effective date" for the original lump sum past service cost of the Plan shall be March 1, 1950. The effective date of each revision in the benefit structure of the Plan (except benefits under Article VI of the Plan) which shall affect the cost substantially shall be the "past service effective date" for the additional lump sum past service cost attributable to such benefit revision, except that commencing on or after November 19, 1973, the "past service effective date" of each such revision in the benefit structure (including benefits under Article VI of the Plan) shall be the date on which benefits under such revised benefit structure first become payable.

(iv) Nothing herein shall be deemed to prevent the Company from making contributions towards the lump sum past service cost greater than those required under this Section (or required under the basis of funding being used to fund the cost of benefits under Article VI of the Plan), nor shall a greater contribution in any year be construed to reduce the maximum funding period established as provided above.

All of the foregoing is subject to the understanding that (i) the Company shall be required to make in any year no contribution in an amount which is greater than the amount which is deductible for tax purposes in that year, and (ii) except as required by ERISA on and after January 1, 1980, the Company shall not be obligated to make additional payments to the Fund to make up deficiencies in any year arising from depreciation in the value of the securities in the Fund resulting from abnormal conditions.

The Company may elect to defer payment of its contributions for any year after 1981 to a date not later than the date on which such contributions are permitted by law to be paid for purposes of crediting such contributions to such year under the minimum funding standards of ERISA.

(b) The Company will cause the Union to be furnished annually with a statement, certified by a qualified actuary, that the amount of the assets in the Pension Fund is not less than the amount then required by Subsection (a) of this Section to be in such Fund. That amount shall be computed by a qualified actuary on the basis of the normal cost and the respective lump sum past service costs of the Plan, disregarding benefits under Article VI of the Plan, and then in use for funding purposes, and, with respect to the cost of benefits under Article VI of the Plan on the basis being used for funding such benefits.

Source: *Agreement* between Ford Motor Co. and UAW, 1997–1999.

becomes of keen interest during collective bargaining. Also of interest is the type of benefit plan provided. In a *noncontributory plan*, the employer pays all the administrative and funding costs. Therefore, the question of how much is to be paid by the employer does not arise during collective bargaining; rather, the benefit package provided by the plan becomes the central issue.

About 82 percent of the plans are contributory in manufacturing firms. Management feels that having employees share some of the cost of the pension plan reminds them of the expense of the plan and motivates them to stay with the firm once they have become vested. Union negotiators would prefer that all plans be noncontributory; however, they realize that many employers, particularly small firms, cannot bear the entire cost of a financially sound retirement system.

Age or Service Requirement.   Most pension plans require a minimum age or years of service before an employee becomes eligible to receive retirement benefits. The plan may simply require a minimum age such as 55 or 60 at which the retired employee begins receiving benefits or a minimum of 25 or 30 years of service. Other plans require a minimum of both, such as 25 and 60, meaning 25 years of service and 60 years of age. Under such a plan, the employee who began work with the company at age 20 must work for 40 years before becoming eligible to receive retirement benefits, even though he or she could become eligible at age 45 under the service requirement. Some systems provide for an option of retirement minimums. For example, an employee may receive 50 percent of the benefits if he or she retires at age 55, 70 percent at age 60, 80 percent at age 62, or 100 percent at age 65. Management realizes that the percentages and ages can be changed to motivate employees to retire at an earlier age or to stay with the company longer. A similar type of provision can be created for years of service. The minimum age or service requirement is an item of great interest during contract negotiations. If union membership is heavy with senior employees close to retirement, changing the minimum requirement becomes an even greater goal of the union negotiators.

Benefit Formula.   Perhaps the most important pension item in collective bargaining is the *benefit formula*, in which benefits due each retiree are calculated. A common benefit would appear as follows:

Benefit dollars = Years of service × Base pay × _____ %

The three variables of importance in the formula are years of service, employee's base pay, and a percent to be applied. The percentage is usually a fixed figure that is seldom negotiated to change; 2 to 3 percent is often used, but the percentage can be as high as 5 percent or as low as 1 percent. The number of years of service is determined by the individual employee. The determination of the base pay, therefore, becomes critical to many contract negotiations. For many years, base pay was defined to be the average of the employee's annual gross wage received. However, in recent years with high inflation causing rapid salary increases as well as moves through promotion and transfer, base pay often receives other definitions.

Contracts today commonly define **base pay** as the average yearly salary for the last three or five years worked or the average yearly salary for the highest three of the last five years. The most liberal definition of *base pay* would be the employee's highest gross salary received in any one year. The more years included in averaging base pay, if one assumes a steadily increasing salary, the lower the average and therefore the lower the benefit. Union negotiators also want to include vacation time and time taken for personal leave as well as time worked in a definition of *base pay*. Management will naturally resist any redefinition of base pay that would increase its calculated total and the pension benefit in the formula.

Union leaders are keenly aware that private pension plans fail to keep up with inflation. Therefore, their demand priorities for pension benefits usually center on providing fully funded plans with a base defined to be the average of the highest three years of employee service with future benefits tied to increase in the consumer price index. As our workforce grows older and union members increasingly get closer to retirement years, their interest in providing cost-of-living adjustments to pension plans will probably increase. However, many plans today still provide for a flat-rate pension benefit as determined by the formula, which never increases during the retirement years. At the same time, however, management negotiators claim that employers cannot afford increases in pension benefits because they are required to pay substantial increases in the Social Security taxes. Social Security benefits are also tied to the consumer price index and provide for automatic increases as the index rises, so management reasons that private pension plans need not provide similar increases.

Determining the cost of a change in pension plan negotiated through collective bargaining is difficult. Normally such changes cannot be made without an actuarial study to estimate their impact on the total pension plan and possible increase in the company's insurance premium or additional cash contribution. The actual cost of a plan benefit cannot be determined until the employee is deceased. Therefore, costs are always estimated and may change. Negotiators may avoid some of the problems in estimating proposed changes in pension plans by assigning cost determination to outside consulting actuaries or trusted employees.[30]

Wage Employment Guarantees

In recent years, union negotiators have fought vigorously for an income maintenance benefit previously provided only to white-collar workers—that of guaranteed income throughout the year regardless of available hours of work or actual work performed. Union negotiators feel that their members should also have the security and convenience of regular pay periods. The problems and frustrations of fluctuating income make the guaranteed wage a high priority for many union leaders.

Wage employment guarantees (WEGs) ensure employees a minimum amount of work or compensation during a certain period of time, usually for the life of the contract. Normally all full-time employees who have at least one year's service are eligible. The United Auto Workers contracted a guaranteed wage in its agreement with Ford Motor Company in 1967, a major step for union negotiators in the industry. Today WEGs appear in 16 percent of all agreements.[31] A wage employment guaranteed provision might read: All regular, full-time employees shall be guaranteed a minimum of 40 hours of work per week or compensation in lieu of work being provided.

When negotiating to provide a guaranteed annual wage, management often will insist on an **escape clause** to suspend the guarantee for production delays beyond the control of management, such as natural or accidental disasters, voluntary absences, employee discharge, or strikes.

Supplemental Unemployment Benefits

In the 1950s, steel and automobile industry union leaders began to negotiate for supplemental unemployment benefits (SUB) plans. These plans provide additional income to supplement state unemployment benefits to employees who are laid off. Union negotiators normally contend that state unemployment benefits do not enable employees to maintain adequately their style of living. SUB plans are designed to be directly supplemental; employees receive a certain percentage of their gross pay for a maximum number of weeks when unemployed. For example, if each employee subjected to a layoff during the period of the contract receives 75 percent of normal base pay, with the company providing the additional funds necessary to the employee's state unemployment benefits, an employee making about $266 a week would receive a total of $200. This 75 percent figure would include $150 per week of state unemployment benefits, with the remaining $50 being provided by the company.

Some negotiated SUB plans will provide only 50 to 75 percent of gross pay; few go beyond 75 percent. Most will provide the additional unemployment benefits for at least a period equal to the state's unemployment, often exceeding up to one year in length. Employees must have at least one year's service before they are eligible for SUB benefits; they do not receive such benefits if they are on strike or under disciplinary action. Most SUB plan provisions include the escape clauses discussed under wage employment guarantees.

Management usually strongly opposes implementing a SUB plan. Management negotiators emphasize that the company already pays into the state unemployment fund as required by law and that union leaders should lobby their state legislature to increase those funds. Management will also argue that additional unemployment benefits decrease its ability to make technological changes and to provide new equipment and processes because of the additional benefits paid to displaced employees.

Although some SUB plans were negotiated as early as 1923 by Procter & Gamble and 1932 by Nunn Shoe Company, the great increase in the number of plans providing coverage for employees came after the 1955 negotiated SUB plan between the Ford Motor Company and the United Auto Workers. Today most plans are within the primary metals, transportation, electrical, rubber, and auto industries.[32]

Guaranteed Income Stream

The relatively high unemployment rate and severe layoffs in the 1970s and 1980s caused job security to become a top priority for union negotiators and members.[33] Several innovative provisions in contracts have the intent of improving employment security. One of the most interesting and publicized is the **guaranteed income stream** (GIS) plan in the auto industry.

The GIS plan is an alternative to the traditional supplemental unemployment benefits (SUB) plan, although the goal of income maintenance for employees is the same. The typical GIS plan differs from SUB plans in three important areas. First, GIS plans furnish benefits to eligible workers until they retire and thus have been called a "guaranteed lifetime wage," whereas SUB plans end after a short period of time, usually two years. Second, qualification for a GIS plan is based on earnings not on employment, which encourages laid-off workers to seek other employment. Third, the benefits provided by a GIS plan are only partially offset by outside earnings until a "break-even" point is reached. Under most SUB plans, benefits are completely offset by outside earnings—a deterrent to laid-off workers seeking outside jobs. Thus, GIS plans create incentives for laid-off workers, unlike SUB plans, which tie them to their former employer. Both sides may benefit from GIS plans. If laid-off workers find new jobs, the amount of GIS benefits paid by the former employer may be reduced as they are partially offset by the outside income. However, the employer is encouraged to avoid layoffs by the long-term eligibility aspect of a GIS plan. When layoffs are necessary, the employer has an additional financial incentive to help workers find new employment. The GIS plan may eventually replace SUB plans because both management and labor can realize important advantages.[34]

Severance Pay

Severance pay, sometimes called *dismissal pay*, is income provided to employees who have been permanently terminated from the job through no fault of their own. Although similar to SUB in its appearance and formula for provision in determining benefits, severance pay is given under quite different circumstances. SUB pay enables the employee who is temporarily laid off to feel minimum impact from the layoff and anticipate a return to work and full pay. Employees who receive severance pay, however, realize that they have no hope for future work with the company. It is not normally provided to employees who are terminated for just cause or who quit.

The purpose of severance pay is to cushion the loss of income due to plant closing, merger, automation, or subcontracting of work. Union negotiators contend that management should shoulder some of the financial burden while the employee is seeking other permanent work.

The provision of severance pay and advance notice of layoffs varies by industry. It is most common in industries that have incurred past layoffs during hard economic times, such as manufacturing (74 percent of all contracts) and utilities; contracts for professional and technical employees seldom (16 percent) provide severance pay and advance notice.[35]

The amount of severance pay is usually specified by a formula guaranteeing a percentage of base pay determined by number of years of service with the company. The percentage normally increases as the employee's number of years increases to a maximum percentage. To be eligible, employees are normally required to have a minimum number of years of service, usually one, except in a case of disability. Management negotiators have been somewhat more sympathetic to severance pay provisions because management controls its cost completely. However, as the economy, technology, and mergers force changes in many of our industries, management negotiators may be likely to resist further increases in severance pay provisions.

If severance pay is included in an agreement, it is considered an employee right. In the case of a merger, plant closing, relocation, or the sale of the company, the liability for severance pay may become a most important issue. Court decisions have upheld the legal right of employees to receive severance pay from the parties involved. In such cases severance pay owed workers is generally regarded as a legal liability of the company.[36] Unions have a legal right to file suit on behalf of employees denied negotiated severance pay under the Labor Management Relations Act, Section 301.[37]

Death and Disability Plans

Union leaders have also strongly negotiated for death and disability benefits to supplement Social Security. The negotiated benefit may provide for coverage up to a maximum, or it may provide benefits independent of others received by the employee. The need for negotiators to be very specific about what is provided by these benefits is illustrated in Case 8-1, in which misunderstandings about a program led to arbitration. However, negotiators are aware of the benefits made available upon death or disability to employees by the Social Security system, and employers remind union officials that they contribute to the Social Security system and therefore provide funding for its death and disability benefits as well as those received through the collective bargaining process. An example of the negotiated benefit is included in an agreement between Anaconda Aluminum Company and Aluminum Workers Local 130 and the Aluminum Workers International Union, AFL-CIO.

ARTICLE 19
Group Insurance

a. The company will provide without cost to the employee the following group insurance and benefits.
b. Terms and conditions of the coverage called for in paragraph(s) of this article will be contained in the contract between the company and the insurance company with details in a separate booklet which will be furnished to each employee.
c. Life Insurance—On the fifteenth of the month, following the completion of his probational period, the employee will be covered by $12,000 life insurance. Included in the policy are provisions for coverage after retirement, layoff, and in the event of disability. Retiree benefits do not apply for deferred vested pension.[38]

The company commonly bears the entire premium cost of death and disability insurance. However, often it may be negotiated that employees will be offered

DISABILITY PENSION

The agency's pension plan and agreement for the employees provided that an applicant for disability pension would be subject to a medical examination and evaluation by the agency doctors to determine if the applicant was qualified for a disability pension. The decision, however, would be made by the Disability Pension Board, which is made up of three representatives from the company and three representatives from the union.

The employee in this case became disabled and was unable to drive a bus, which was her job. The employee had been diagnosed by her own doctor as suffering from temporomandibular joint syndrome (TMJ). The employee applied for disability pension, and the board voted on her application. The six-member panel was deadlocked: The three company trustees voted no, and the three union trustees voted yes. The position of the union was that the employee suffered from permanent disability and, under the collective bargaining agreement, should be allowed a pension.

The applicable provision of the collective bargaining agreement stated that employees with 10 years or more of service who become permanently physically or mentally incapable of performing their job could retire and begin receiving benefits. Any such pensioner who regains his health or mental capacity shall have his pension discontinued and he shall be restored to his former position with full seniority rights.

The union pointed out that, although the collective bargaining agreement pension rules required an employee to be examined by an agency physician when applying for permanent disability, the decision of whether the employee qualified was left to the trustees. The trustees had admitted that they did not take into consideration the opinions of the employee's private physicians that the employee suffered from TMJ and could be considered permanently disabled. The position of the company, however, was that the examination by the agency physician failed to decide conclusively the issue of the permanency of the disability. On the basis of one examination, the agency physician determined that the employee was unable to drive a bus *at that time* but could not find any physical impairment that would justify classifying the employee's condition as permanent disability.

Decision

The arbitrator found that to rely only on the agency physician, who had admittedly performed a relatively short and cursory exam, was not sufficient. The arbitrator found that the grievant did meet the disability requirement under the pension plan and should be awarded pension benefits.

Adapted from *Bi-state Development Agency*, 90 LA 91 (1987).

additional group insurance through the group plan at reduced rates. Union members, of course, often benefit from such a plan by an amount greater than the premium paid by the company in their behalf. Usually the company can obtain group insurance at a rate cheaper than each individual could purchase on his or her own.

Employee life insurance plans are included in more than 99 percent of negotiated plans. Most provide a specific benefit, often $10,000.[39] Another common type of benefit provides an amount directly related to the employees' annual earnings. Plans that relate the amount to earnings most often provide a maximum benefit equal to total yearly earnings; some provide twice the earnings.[40] The cost of life insurance coverage is paid entirely by the employer in most agreements.

One of the most common, and most expensive, negotiated benefits is medical care. The continued rise of health-care costs and complexity of the issue have caused health care to become a top concern for union and management negotiators alike. In the 1990s, a major change in agreements' provisions has been the rise in comprehensive medical care plans to 70 percent of all contracts in 1996, up from 21 percent only 10 years earlier. Basic hospitalization and surgical benefits have correspondingly fallen; they now are found in only 30 percent of agreements (see Figure 8-3).[41] Most comprehensive plans specify an initial deductible of $100 to $200. Many contain a family deductible. Most provide, after the deductible, for 80-20 coinsurance with a maximum expenditure per individual. A maximum lifetime coverage of $500,000 to $1,000,000 is also a common provision.[42]

Hospitalization plans are either commercial insurance or hospital service plans. *Commercial insurance* involves a contract between an employer and an insurance company providing fixed cash benefits for hospital room, board, and other hospital charges. The employer agrees to pay the premiums to cover the insurance provided by the contract, and the insurance company assumes the liability of qualifying employees. The commercial insurance plan pays directly to the insured company, which reimburses the hospital for costs; this plan can be tailored to the needs of the company as specified by contract.

Under the *hospital service plan*, a nonprofit organization such as Blue Cross–Blue Shield provides coverage for hospital services including room, board, and other costs. The insurance company is directly billed for the covered costs. Blue Cross covers hospital costs; Blue Shield covers physicians' fees. An example of the hospitalization, medical, and surgical insurance as well as the major medical insurance negotiated between the Anaconda Aluminum Company and the Aluminum Workers International Union AFL-CIO follows.

ARTICLE 19
Hospitalization, Medical, and Surgical Insurance

d. Hospitalization, Medical, and Surgical Insurance—The plan covers the employee and his dependents, as defined in the booklet, for actual charges for room and board up to the hospital's most common semi-private room rate for up to 730 days; surgical benefits at reasonable and customary charges; outpatient hospital benefits for accidents, illness or surgery; and maternity benefits. Retirees and their spouses will have the same basic coverage (group hospital and surgical coverage) as an active employee. Coverage will cease for the

---

Medical Care Provisions (percentage of agreements) | | | | **Figure 8-3**

	Hospitalization	Major Medical	Comprehensive Medical	Sickness and Accident
All industries	30	24	70	88
Manufacturing	30	23	70	93
Nonmanufacturing	32	28	69	74

Source: Bureau of National Affairs, *Basic Patterns in Union Contracts*, 14th ed. (Washington, DC: BNA Books, 1995), p. 13. Used by permission.

spouse when the retiree dies. Retiree benefits do not apply for deferred vested pension.

e. The plan of paragraph (d) above also provides for benefits for six months following a layoff for employees with two years seniority; for one year for employees who become disabled because of sickness or injury; and for retiring employee and spouse.

f. Sickness and accident benefits in accordance with the following schedule for a maximum of 26 weeks for any one illness or injury, subject to a 7-day waiting period in case of non-hospitalized sickness.[43]

Note that the hospitalization provision specifies that actual charges for room and board will be reimbursed, indicating an insurance plan rather than the service benefit. Also the number of days for which an employee can be reimbursed for a semiprivate room rate is specified. The major medical plan covers 80 percent of employee expenses to be paid by the employer, and a cash deductible of $50 paid by the employee with an annual maximum of $100.

The Consolidated Omnibus Budget Reconciliation Act

A federal law entitled the **Consolidated Omnibus Budget Reconciliation Act (COBRA)** was passed April 7, 1986. This law provides for the continuation of medical and dental insurance for employees, spouses, and dependents in the event of termination of employment, death of the employee, divorce, legal separation, or reduction of hours, which results in the loss of health plan eligibility. This coverage must be elected by the employee or dependents, and they must pay 100 percent of the full cost of the plan selected. The intent of this law is to alleviate gaps in health-care coverage by allowing the employee or beneficiary to elect to continue medical or dental insurance for up to 18 or 36 months, depending on the circumstances of their employment separation. The passage of the act was a major victory for unions, which had been seldom able to obtain similar provisions from employers at the bargaining table.

Under COBRA, one of the six events that requires an employer to continue group health coverage is termination of employment or a reduction in hours. Under federal regulations, a strike is within this category of events; thus, management is required to provide continued health-care coverage to striking employees and their families at the employees' expense. COBRA also requires management to notify in writing each employee and spouse of their right to continued coverage. The employee then has 60 days to choose continued coverage. If the employee chooses to continue coverage, under COBRA, the employer must provide the same group health-care coverage that was provided before the strike.[44]

Dental, Optical, Prescription Drugs

The provision of dental insurance has become common in agreements (85 percent); optical care (43 percent) and prescription drugs (43 percent) are less common. Most dental provisions contain a $50 deductible and a maximum coverage for periodic checkups and cleanings, X-rays, fillings, extractions, reconstruction, and orthodontic care. Most plans (96 percent) provide family coverage. Optical care typically includes annual eye exams, lenses, and frames. Most plans (92 percent) include similar family coverage. Prescription drug provisions usually require a minimum deductible with equal dependent coverage.[45]

Alcohol and Drug Treatment

A rapidly growing medical care provision is for alcohol and drug abuse treatment. In 1995 69 percent of agreements provided for such care, up from only 32 percent in 1986. Most plans provide for inpatient treatment in a hospital or rehabilitation facility for up to 30 days.[46] Only a few years ago drug and alcohol problems were considered personal problems. However now both employers and unions realize that substance abuse can cost millions of dollars by increasing absenteeism and accidents and by causing strained relations. Rehabilitation rather than immediate dismissal is encouraged.[47]

Health Maintenance Organizations

In 1973 Congress passed the Health Maintenance Organization Act, which provided for the creation of **health maintenance organizations (HMOs)**. An HMO is simply a local medical facility that provides routine checkups, shots, and treatments for injuries or illnesses to employees and their families. In addition, it includes many other services, such as maternity care, family planning services, vision testing, mental health services, and services for alcohol and drug abuse, not normally found in major medical-hospitalization plans.[48] Many HMOs contract with local hospitals when extensive specialized surgery and other unusual medical treatment are needed.

The act established standards for private individuals to receive federal financing to create HMOs to provide an alternative health-care system for employees. Once they become established, the HMOs should become self-sufficient through premiums received from employees and their employers. The act also requires companies that employ 25 or more employees and that currently offer a medical benefit plan to offer the HMO option to employees if a federally approved HMO exists in the local area.

Among the advantages provided by HMOs is comprehensive health care. The plan allows for preventive medicine and includes routine visits to a physician and less expensive periodic health assessments and immunizations. HMOs also provide health care to a family at lower annual total cost than a typical insurance plan. The HMO plan includes many of the additional health-care costs families normally incur that are not covered in their group health insurance. Physicians try to prevent unnecessary hospitalization costs by doing many procedures in the office and on an outpatient basis. In addition, HMOs can often be easily administered. Because there is no expensive and time-consuming third-party claim review process, the employer finds it easier to provide HMO insurance to employees. A monthly premium check is paid to the HMO for services to the covered individuals with no other financial transactions or vouchers.

However, some union leaders view HMOs as restricting their ability to negotiate benefits because employees contend that private insurance benefits are needed when extensive specialized surgery and other unusual medical problems arise. Employees may not accept HMOs because their choice of physicians and location of facilities are limited to the HMOs in the area. Many employees simply feel more comfortable with physicians they know and trust and believe that it is unfair for management to put a price tag on the cost of quality health care.

Health-Care Cost Containment

General Motors spends more money for employee medical benefits than for steel from its main supplier. Indeed, employers pay almost half the nation's health-care bills through insurance programs.[49] Provisions designed to lower the cost of health care are included in more than 83 percent of 1995 labor agreements—an indication that management and labor are serious about health-care cost containment. Most of the measures are designed to reduce hospitalization costs by requiring surgery on an outpatient basis when possible and requiring second opinions before scheduling surgery.[50]

A Bureau of Labor Research analysis of current health insurance trends indicates a continued expansion of cost-control measures. First, employers are raising their employees' share of the total health-care bill by eliminating "first-dollar" coverage and requiring increased cost sharing by employees through higher deductibles and coinsurance provisions. Second, the higher cost of hospital rooms has encouraged more employers to include extended care facilities and home health care as alternatives to hospital care. Third, an increasing number of employers are changing sources of coverage from traditional commercial insurance companies to self-insurance or health maintenance organizations. Finally, entirely new cost-cutting measures include requiring a second opinion before elective surgery, routine physical examinations, and greater testing before hospital admittance. Whereas most benefits have not changed in recent years, two notable exceptions are dental coverage and increased major medical maximums that increase employee protection against catastrophic "out-of-pocket" expenses.[51]

The shift from traditional hospital service plans to more competitive comprehensive coverage plans has also enabled management to design plans carefully to cut costs and negotiate with several health-care providers for the lowest cost. One such strategy is the preferred provider organization (PPO). A PPO is usually a specific contract among the employer, insurance carriers, hospitals and health-care providers, dentists, and physicians. The contract allows certain services to be provided at a discount in exchange for a guaranteed number of patients. The employees can be assured of receiving needed health care, and management is given the flexibility to negotiate a low-cost program.

One area of major concern to both labor and management is which, if any, of the various health-care cost-containment programs available should be used. Both sides recognize the need to control cost increases. However, some techniques such as self-insurance and expanding coverage to extended care facilities and home health care may be far more palatable to unions than those that directly increase workers' share of medical bills such as higher deductibles or coinsurance provisions.

Wellness Programs

Company-provided **wellness programs** have dramatically risen in number. Most are expanded physical fitness or alcohol and drug rehabilitation programs, but many complete wellness programs include stress management, high blood pressure detection, cancer detection and treatment, and individualized exercise programs. Examples of successful wellness programs include the following:

- Mesa Petroleum Company: Medical costs for participants in the fitness program averaged $173 per person compared with $434 for nonparticipants.[52]

- General Motors: An employee assistance program cut medical benefit payments by 60 percent after only one year.[53]
- Campbell Soup Company: A colon-rectal cancer detection program resulted in a savings of $245,000 in medical payments.[54]
- Burlington Industries: Its "health-back" program decreased absenteeism from 400 days to 19 days annually.[55]

Company-sponsored physical fitness programs (PFPs) have become a popular part of wellness programs. Few existed before 1975, but they are common today among large employers. A PFP may only be a basketball hoop in the employee parking lot—or Kimberly Clark Company's $2.5 million physical fitness center.[56]

Both union and management negotiators view the issue of a company-provided PFP or wellness program as a desirable addition to the workplace. Thus, the issue at the negotiating table may be reduced to who designs, runs, and pays for the program. What do workers think? A Ford Motor Company employee and UAW member noticed the positive effect on morale: "They've taken out 500 lockers and put in exercise equipment, and two hourly employees get paid to run the room. Those things help make the camaraderie stronger."[57]

Employee Assistance Programs

Beginning in the early 1970s, the number of **employee assistance programs (EAPs)** significantly increased. Today nearly half of all employees have programs in almost every type of service, industrial, and nonprofit organization.[58] The number increased apparently because many labor relations managers believe that they can save money by helping employees resolve personal problems that affect job performance. EAPs also provide the union evidence of management's concern for employees' well-being, which should be a strong boost to employee relations. But the primary reason for more company-sponsored EAPs is that they may enhance a company's profitability by reducing absenteeism, turnover, tardiness, accidents, and medical claims.[59]

Many EAPs grew from alcohol-treatment programs. The typical program addresses psychological and physical problems, including stress, chemical dependency (alcohol and drug), depression, marital and family problems, financial problems, health, anxiety, and even job boredom. The procedure in virtually all EAPs is (1) problem identification, (2) intervention, and (3) treatment and recovery.

An example of a successful referral program is the EAP at Bechtel Power Corporation in San Francisco. When a supervisor believes an employee's performance has been adversely affected by personal problems, the supervisor phones the EAP office. (An alternative first step would be an employee self-referral.) Once the supervisor and EAP specialist discuss the particulars of the situation—performance record, absenteeism, and so on—the supervisor is normally advised to suggest that the employee use the EAP. It is carefully explained to the employee that participation is voluntary and does not affect the discipline process, which may be implemented if required by poor work. Strict confidentiality is guaranteed.[60]

Unions have often taken an active role in designing EAPs. Usually both labor and management agree that the troubled employee is a valuable asset and, if rehabilitated, can remain a valuable employee after treatment. However, the EAP is generally not viewed by the union or management as an alternative to the disciplinary process, and at some point an employee may be forced to choose between treatment or termination.

Future Medical Care Negotiations

Unions generally have responded positively to cooperative management programs designed to trim health-care costs. Since 1958, the Teamsters Union has worked with the city of New York by operating the Teamster Center Services, an advice and referral unit that provides information on alcoholism, drug abuse, second surgical opinions, insurance, vocational reeducation, and legal and financial matters. In 1986, General Motors and the United Auto Workers announced that they had reduced health-care costs by $200 million in a single year. Their cost reduction program promoted the use of health maintenance organizations, outpatient surgery, and the elimination of unnecessary surgery.[61]

Even though unions are reluctant to abandon their traditional medical insurance coverage, there are a number of strategies management negotiators can use that may result in cost-cutting agreements. Among those successfully used are the following:

- Proposing to offer coverage equal to the current plan, except under company administration. This strategy may result in lower administrative costs and greater company control.
- Eliminating dependent coverage. This tactic may be successful if the workforce tends to be married and the spouses have comparable benefits that can cover the family at lower cost.
- Freezing company costs, either fully or partially. Such an agreement would require members of the bargaining unit to share in the increases in coverage during the life of the contract or to establish deductibles for emergency room visits to discourage the use of the emergency room "as an outpatient clinic or as a substitute for the family doctor."[62]

In the fall of 1993, President Bill Clinton announced his proposed overhaul of the health-care industry in the United States. The plan as presented to Congress included universal health-care coverage for all Americans, financed largely by employers and a tax on tobacco products. Reactions from around the country were mixed. The prediction was that Congress would enact some changes to the way health care is regulated but not necessarily the president's plan. Employers and unions watched the progress of the proposal through Congress closely. The Republican Congress, led by Bob Dole (R-Kansas) eventually killed Clinton's plan and made it a 1996 campaign issue.

PAY FOR TIME NOT WORKED

What has become one of the most sought-after employee benefits by union members is **payment for time not worked** on the job. Employees today have come to expect to be paid for holidays and vacations, as well as many other absences. These *time-off-with-pay* components of labor agreements are many and varied and include the following:

Holidays
Vacations
Jury duty

Civic duty
Military duty
Funeral leave
Marriage leave
Maternity/paternity/family leave
Sick leave
Wellness leave (no sick leave used)
Blood donation
Grievance and contract negotiations
Lunch, rest, and break periods
Personal leave
Sabbatical leave[63]

Paid Holidays

More than 99 percent of labor agreements provide for *paid holidays*. Union nego-tiators' demand for increased paid holidays has been great and continues to in-crease the average number of paid holidays provided by the agreements. In 1950, the average number of paid holidays in labor agreements was three; 40 years later the average was closer to 11.[64] Most contracts provide for between eight and 13 paid holidays, as illustrated in Table 8-1.

Normally, employees required to work on holidays receive double or even triple pay in the contract provision. In the chemical, hotel, and restaurant indus-tries that operate every day, employees may be given double pay for working hol-idays and another day off during the following week. If a holiday falls during an employee's paid vacation, the employee usually receives an extra day of sched-uled vacation. Employees on layoff during a paid holiday usually do not receive pay for that holiday.

The **personal day**, or "**floating holiday**," started in the rubber industry. Float-ing holiday provisions allow the selection of the day on which the holiday is

Trend in Number of Holidays (frequency expressed as percentage of contracts) — **Table 8-1**

	1957	1966	1975	1986	1995
None specified	1	1	1	2	1
Fewer than 7	36	16	6	3	4
7–7½	48	39	10	6	4
8–8½	12	31	12	8	7
9–9½	4	7	29	9	12
10–10½	4	7[1]	20	23	18
11–11½	—	—	12	18	24
12–12½	—	—	10[2]	14	16
13 or more	—	—	—	19	16

[1]10 or more.
[2]12 or more.
Source: Bureau of National Affairs, *Basic Patterns in Union Contracts*, 14th ed. (Washington, DC: Bureau of National Affairs, 1995), p. 58. Reprinted with permission.

observed to be left to the discretion of the employee or to be agreed upon mutually between management and the employee. Management has resisted the concept of a floating holiday on the theory that there is little difference between a floating holiday and an additional vacation day.

Many labor agreements have observed the **Monday holiday** practice provided by the federal government. The observance of Monday holidays is, in theory, designed to give employees more three-day weekends during the year for additional rest and relaxation. In practice, however, the Monday holiday has increased absenteeism, the chief administrative problem caused by paid holidays. Employees can easily see that being absent on Friday or Tuesday would provide them a four-day weekend or almost a complete week's vacation.

An agreement provision for a paid holiday should specify the following:

1. **Eligibility.** As illustrated in the duPont agreement, Figure 8-4, Section 2(b), employee eligibility, which requires employees to work the last working day before the holiday and the first scheduled working day after the holiday, helps to minimize the problem of employees' stretching holiday periods.
2. **Holiday rate.** If employees are scheduled to work on what was agreed to be a paid holiday, they will receive premium pay, as in Section 1 of Figure 8-4.
3. **Which days are paid holidays.** The days determined to be paid holidays should be specified in the agreement as in Section 1 of Figure 8-4.
4. **Holidays falling on nonwork days.** As specified in Figure 8-4, provisions for the holiday should be made in case the holiday falls on a nonwork day such as a Sunday.

Paid Vacations

The practice of providing employees with *paid vacations* in labor agreements has become not only commonly accepted but also expected by union employees. About 92 percent of labor contracts provide for paid vacations of two to six weeks duration.[65] Employers believe that, unlike paid holidays, paid vacations are effective in increasing employee productivity. Employees, by taking a physical and mental break from the workplace, are able to return to work refreshed and rejuvenated.

Four types of vacation plans are commonly negotiated: the graduated plan, the uniform plan, the ratio-to-work plan, and the funded plan. By far the most popular type of plan is the *graduated plan*, which provides an increase in the number of weeks of vacation according to length of service. The *uniform vacation plan* provides all workers with the same length of vacation. This is most commonly found in manufacturing firms that shut down for specified periods to retool or change product lines, giving employees vacations during the shutdown. The *ratio-to-work plan*, commonly found in the printing and transportation industries, relates the length of vacation to the number of hours or days the employee works during a given time period, usually the year preceding the allocation of vacation. The *funded plan* requires employers to contribute to a vacation fund from which employees may draw vacation pay during periods when no work is available. This is most often found in the construction and apparel industries.

ARTICLE VII

Holiday Pay

Section 1. An employee who works on any one of the holidays listed below shall be paid, subject to the further provisions of Section 3 of this Article, overtime pay at one and one-half (1½ times his regular rate for hours worked in addition to a holiday allowance equivalent to his regularly scheduled working hours not to exceed two and one-half (2½ times his regular rate for such holiday hours worked, whichever yields the greater pay.

New Year's Day	Labor Day
*Washington's Birthday	Thanksgiving Day
Good Friday	Day after Thanksgiving Day
Memorial Day	Christmas Eve
**July Third	Christmas Day
July Fourth	

*A choice of either Washington's Birthday or Martin Luther King's Birthday will be offered provided the COMPANY and UNION have not agreed, prior to December 31 of the preceding year, that another day shall be designated as a holiday in lieu of either Washington's Birthday or Martin Luther King's Birthday.

**July Third shall be one of the recognized holidays except when July Fourth falls on Thursday in which case July Fifth shall be the holiday.

When any of the foregoing holidays, except Christmas Eve or July Third fall on Sunday, the following Monday will be observed as the holiday. When Christmas Eve or July Third falls on Sunday, the following Tuesday will be observed as the holiday. When any of the foregoing holidays fall on Saturday, the preceding Friday shall be observed as the holiday for all employees who normally are scheduled to work Monday through Friday. Saturday shall be designated as the holiday for all other employees. When Christmas Day or July Fourth falls on Saturday, and is observed on Friday by employees normally scheduled to work Monday through Friday, the December Twenty-Fourth holiday or the July Third holiday shall be observed on the preceding Thursday.

Holiday hours shall correspond to the hours of the regular work day.

Employees will be informed at least one (1) week in advance if they are expected to work on a holiday.

Section 2. Pay for hours equivalent to regularly scheduled hours not to exceed eight (8), at the employee's regular rate, shall be paid to an employee for each of the holidays designated above on which he does not work, provided such employee:

(a) Does not work the holiday for the reason that:
    (1) He is required by Management to take the day off from work solely because it is a holiday, or
    (2) The holiday is observed on one of his scheduled days of rest (an employee on vacation, leave of absence, or absent from work for one (1) week or more due to a shutdown of equipment or facilities or conditions beyond Management's control shall not be considered as having "scheduled days of rest" during such periods of absence), and
(b) Works on his last scheduled working day prior to the holiday and on his next scheduled working day following the holiday, except when the employee has been excused from work by Management.

If an employee who is scheduled to work on the holiday fails to work, he will receive no pay for the holiday if his absence is not excused.

(continued)

Section 3. If an employee works only part of his scheduled working hours on the holiday, and he is required by Management to take off the remaining part of his scheduled hours or is excused by Management because of personal illness, serious illness in his immediate family, or other unusual conditions, he shall be paid overtime pay at one and one-half (1½) times his regular rate for the hours worked plus a holiday allowance equivalent to his regularly scheduled working hours not to exceed eight (8) at his regular rate. If the employee works only part of his scheduled working hours and is not required or excused by Management for the above reasons to take off the remaining part of his scheduled hours, the employee shall be paid overtime pay at two and one-half (2½ times his regular rate for hours worked but no holiday allowance.

Section 4. Holiday hours paid for but not worked shall not be used in computing hours worked in excess of forty (40) in the work week.

Source: *Agreement* between E. I. duPont de Nemours and Neoprene Craftsmen Union, 1994, pp. 20–22.

An example of a graduated vacation plan is provided in the agreement between Anaconda Aluminum Company and the Aluminum Workers International Union, AFL-CIO.

ARTICLE 8

Vacations

a. An employee with one year or more of service with the company and who has worked at least one thousand hours since the employee's anniversary date in the preceding calendar year projecting work hours (if necessary) to the employee's next anniversary date shall receive a paid vacation on the following basis:

Employee's Service	Vacation Pay	Weeks Vacation Leave
One year, but less than two	$52.00	One
Two years, but less than three	$74.00	One
Three years, but less than five	$100.00	Two
Five years, but less than ten	$168.00	Two
Ten years, but less than fifteen	$180.00	Three
Fifteen years, but less than twenty	$200.00	Three
Twenty years, but less than twenty-five	$210.00	Four
Twenty-five years or more	$240.00	Five

b. The amount of vacation pay for each employee shall be computed at his regular bid rate as of January 1 of each year, multiplied at the appropriate number of hours set forth in the table in the paragraph above.

c. An employee entitled to a vacation shall receive his vacation pay on the payday preceding his vacation leave, but no later than the second pay period in December.

d. Vacation shall be taken during the period from January 1 to December 31 each year. Preference of vacation period shall be according to seniority but subject to planned operation schedule. The company shall discuss a vacation schedule with the union regarding preference by seniority. Nothing in this article shall restrict the company from scheduling all or part of a planned shutdown for vacation purposes, should business conditions permit.[66]

This example includes several provisions that should be specified in the labor agreement, including the eligibility for vacation leave and pay, how long the employee has to be with the company to qualify, and any other requirements for vacation leave. Duration of vacation leave must be determined, along with any additional vacation pay such as premium pay or bonuses. Also, the scheduling of vacations, a critical aspect of the contract, must be specified. Normally, scheduling is done on the basis of seniority; however, management often tries to retain some right in the determination of employee scheduling so that adequate skills and abilities can be maintained in the workplace. In the agreement between Anaconda Aluminum and the union, the company retains the right to schedule vacations during a planned shutdown that might become necessary for business reasons, an important provision for management to retain.

Determining the annual cost of any negotiated increase in the number of vacation days or holidays is relatively straightforward. One common method is to multiply the number of additional vacation or holiday hours by the base wage rate of employees covered. Another method would be to determine the appropriate percentage of the amount charged to the holiday or vacation pay account from the previous fiscal year. For example, if the company estimates that employees averaged 11 days of paid vacation in the previous year at a total cost of $1,200,000, then the average cost per day was $109,090. Thus, if one additional vacation day is negotiated, the total cost for the next year will be $1,309,090.[67] One problem in determining the cost of additional vacation or holiday benefits is that the cost of continuing production as usual is not provided in the two alternatives. Industries such as the chemical and utility companies that provide around-the-clock service require many employees to work on holidays for premium rates. Thus, it may be necessary to add additional factors to the estimate of negotiated increases in vacation and holiday pay.[68]

Sick Leave

Sick leave is normally accrued by employees at a specific rate such as one day per month from the first day of permanent employment. The subject of many arbitration cases, sick leave is intended to provide for continuation of employment when employees are physically unable to report for work. To minimize grievances and other problems associated with sick leave provisions, the labor agreement should specify the procedure for taking sick leave—the time sick leave must be reported by during the beginning of the work shift and what verification by a physician or other individuals is required; a definition of *sick*; and the accumulation rights. Some contracts provide that unused sick leave can be accumulated without any maximum to cover employees who require extended sick leave for serious illnesses. A doctor's certification is usually needed only when an employee uses extended sick leave. Many contracts specify a maximum number of days of sick leave that can be accumulated by an employee.

Paid Leaves of Absence

Most agreements provide for *paid leaves of absence* for a variety of other purposes including military service, education, and union business, as well as personal reasons. Personal leave may result from a variety of causes such as jury duty, appearing as a witness in a court case, or attending a family funeral. In negotiations

SERIOUS DISTRESS PAY

The grievant and his wife were both employed. They were the parents of a three-year-old child. On a Saturday evening, the child became ill with a high fever. On Monday morning, the fever had not subsided, and the mother stayed home from work and took the child to the doctor, who diagnosed the illness as an upper respiratory infection. He suggested that the child be kept at home and be given bed rest, cool sponge baths, and acetaminophen to reduce the fever. The mother decided to stay home from work again Tuesday and Wednesday because the fever had not subsided. At the conclusion of the workday on Wednesday, the child's parents conferred, and the child's father informed his supervisor that he would stay home from work on Thursday and probably Friday to care for his son. The grievant requested that his leave be classified under the "serious distress" provision of the contract. *Serious distress* was defined in the contract as "a serious condition which requires the personal attention or presence of the employee at a time over which the employee has no control and which cannot appropriately be served by others, or attended to by the employee at any other time when the employee is off duty."

The supervisor informed the grievant that he did not consider it a serious distress situation, but the grievant remained at home on Thursday and Friday anyway. The child's fever did not break until Saturday evening, and by Monday he was well. In defending the grievant's request for serious distress pay, the union argued that the situation met the requirements of the contract. The child's illness required the personal attention and presence of his father at a time over which he had no control and which could not appropriately be served by others. The union felt that had the grievant been the mother and not the father, the company would have routinely paid the claim. The company argued that an emergency situation has to be demonstrated to invoke the serious distress pay provision of the contract. Because the child had been ill since Saturday, and the father was not needed until Thursday and Friday, he had adequate time to arrange for someone else to care for the child. Therefore, although the father's presence was preferable, it was not required as the term *requirement* relates to the serious distress pay provision. It was also the company's position that it is up to the claimant to establish entitlement to a special benefit such as that provided by the "serious distress" provision of the contract.

Decision

The arbitrator noted that, although the child's usual babysitters were not available the week of his illness, it was not impossible for the parents to decide to use a professional nurse, and such services were available. The arbitrator found in this case that the grievant had not established his entitlement in that the child's illness was not a sudden emergency situation but one for which the parents could have made alternative arrangements, had they so desired. Although it was in their power to determine the type of care the child should receive, it was the company's decision on whether the situation warranted serious distress pay.

Adapted from *Indiana Bell Company, Inc.*, 84 LA 255 (1985).

for a funeral leave benefit, it is important to specify for which family members the leave should apply. Personal leave may also include the awarding of personal days that employees may take without specifying why they missed work or giving advance notice. Military leave is often negotiated for employees in the United States Armed Forces Reserve Units.

There is little consistency among or even within industries as far as what types of leaves are negotiated and the number of paid days of work provided for. The most commonly negotiated paid leave is for the conducting of union business, with 78 percent of agreements providing this paid benefit. Usually the conducting of union business provision would include contract negotiation as well as handling grievances for arbitration proceedings. Paid leave for military services is included in 74 percent of labor agreements, leave for personal reasons in 76 percent; maternity/paternity leave in 36 percent; and civic duty leave in 81 percent of labor agreements.[69] The provision for paid leave of absence varies greatly by industry but is generally most prevalent in the manufacturing industries.

In general, the labor agreement for paid leave of absence provisions must include employee eligibility requirements; payment received—base wage plus other wages as well as whether additional outside income such as pay for jury duty or reserve pay is to be deducted from the employee's wage; and scheduling considerations. Case 8-2 is an example of how such paid leaves of absence can result in a grievance.

PREMIUM PAY

Virtually all labor agreements provide a specific work schedule and require **premium pay** for any hours worked beyond the normal schedule. More than 67 percent of labor agreements provide for premium pay for Saturdays and Sundays not part of the normally scheduled workweek, and 99 percent provide for specified overtime premium pay rates on either a weekly or daily basis.[70] Overtime premiums are often provided on a daily basis for time over eight hours, as shown in Table 8-2. Such additional pay was termed *penalty pay* in the past because it was intended to discourage employers from requiring employees to work additional hours or weekends. Today employers are anxious to maintain their rights in scheduling additional hours so that overtime costs in premium payments can be minimized.

Negotiated increases in overtime in premium pay benefits cannot easily be costed because the actual cost increase per year will be determined by management's scheduling of overtime hours. Therefore, the best estimation of negotiated cost increases is made by multiplying the percentage increase in the benefit by last year's total dollars allocated to that particular benefit. For example, if management spent an additional $550,000 in overtime pay and the overtime rate is increased by 5 percent during the next year, the additional cost of the increase to management will be $27,500 annually.

The **pyramiding of overtime** pay is prohibited in most contracts. Pyramiding is the payment of overtime on overtime, which can occur if the same hours of work qualify for both daily and weekly overtime payment. In contracts that prohibit pyramiding, provisions specifying how such hours will be paid are usually included.

How overtime work is distributed among employees is also discussed in most labor contracts. The most common provision is a general statement to the effect that overtime will be distributed equally as far as practical. Other provisions assign overtime on the basis of seniority or by rotation. Many agreements limit overtime distribution to employees within a department, shift, job classification, or those specifically qualified.[71]

Premium pay for other undesirable work situations may also be negotiated. **Shift differentials** are negotiated additional hourly rates of pay provided to

Overtime Provisions

	Daily	Weekly	6th Day	7th Day	Saturday	Sunday
All industries	93%	72%	26%	29%	51%	64%
Manufacturing	96	74	27	33	63	74
Nonmanufacturing	88	68	25	24	32	48

Second-Shift Differentials

	Cents per Hour						Percentage of Hourly Pay					
	1–10¢	11–20¢	21–30¢	31–40¢	41–50¢	Over 50¢	1–3%	4–6%	7–9%	10–12%	13–15%	Over 15%
All industries	7%	29%	28%	15%	11%	10%	10%	40%	10%	24%	5%	12%
Manufacturing	5	34	26	18	10	6	10	45	3	31	—	10
Nonmanufacturing	10	11	33	7	13	24	8	31	23	8	15	15

Third-Shift Differentials

	Cents per Hour						Percentage of Hourly Pay					
	20¢ and under	21–30¢	31–40¢	41–50¢	51–60¢	Over 60¢	1–3%	4–6%	7–9%	10–12%	13–15%	Over 15%
All industries	16%	24%	22%	15%	11%	13%	3%	12%	18%	39%	15%	12%
Manufacturing	18	26	23	13	9	10	—	14	23	41	9	14
Nonmanufacturing	11	16	16	20	16	20	9	9	9	36	27	9

Reporting Pay

	Guaranteed Hours							
	1	2	3	4	5	6	7	8
All industries	2%	13%	4%	65%	1%	1%	—	13%
Manufacturing	—	5	4	79	1	1	—	9
Nonmanufacturing	5	31	4	31	1	1	—	22

Call-Back, Call-In Pay

	Guaranteed Hours							
	1	2	3	4	5	6	7	8
All industries	—	17%	13%	64%	—	1%	—	3%
Manufacturing	1	14	11	71	1	1	—	3
Nonmanufacturing	—	24	19	50	—	1	—	3

Source: Adapted from Bureau of National Affairs, *Basic Patterns in Union Contracts*; 14th ed. (Washington, DC: Bureau of National Affairs, 1995), pp. 53, 115, 116, 117.

employees who work the least desirable hours. Usually specified in cents per hour in the labor agreement, the cost of the increase in a shift differential would be calculated similarly to that of an overtime premium pay increase. More than 90 percent of all late-shift factory workers receive a shift differential premium over their day-shift counterparts. Usually the differential is provided in the contract clause on a cents per hour addition to day-shift rates, averaging about 25 cents per hour or 8 percent of the day-shift rate. Third-shift rates often are several cents per hour higher than second shift. Employers are willing to pay the higher personnel costs not only because production volumes can be increased but also because they receive maximum use of plant and equipment and may receive lower utility rates for night usage. Continuous process industries such as basic steel and chemical require 24-hour operation to avoid high start-up and shutdown costs. Thus, shift differentials are most common in capital-intensive industries. On the other hand, workers often resist late-shift employment because of biological, psychological, and social problems related to night work.[72]

Still other premium payments often negotiated include reporting pay, call-in pay, and on-call pay. Particularly common in the manufacturing and construction industries, **reporting pay** is the minimum payment guaranteed employees who report for work even if work is not available. If employees have not been given adequate notice of, usually, 24 hours not to report to work, they are eligible to receive either the minimum amount of work or payment usually equal to four hours of scheduled work.

A supplemental payment given to employees called back to work before they were scheduled is usually termed **call-in pay**. Most labor agreements provide a lump-sum amount or an amount equal to a minimum number of hours of pay for employees called in during other than scheduled work hours. Thus, employees receive a bonus for being called in before their next normal reporting time.

On-call, or *standby*, **pay** is given to workers available to be called in if needed. This type of pay is commonly negotiated in companies such as the chemical industry or airlines that must provide continuous production or service. Usually a lump-sum amount is paid to employees on a daily basis when they must be available to work, whether they are called in or not.

Bilingual Language Skills

The 1996 agreement between the National Treasury Employees Union and the U.S. Treasury Department provided premium pay of 5 percent to about 7,000 customs agents who are bilingual. The new premium pay provision was one of the first in U.S. collective bargaining agreements. Other employers agreeing to pay a bilingual premium pay include Delta Air Lines to flight attendants and MCI, which pays a 10 percent bonus to workers who are required to speak a second language more than one-half the time. In general, more unions are pressing for new bilingual premium pay if the skill is needed a substantial percentage of the time in job-related communication.[73]

Travel Pay

In industries that require workers to regularly travel to different job sites, a premium is paid for excessive travel. The construction industry may provide, for example, a specified home office and a "free zone" of several miles from that office in which workers will travel to sites for free. Beyond that zone they receive a premium (see Figure 8-5).

Figure 8-5 | Travel Pay

ARTICLE 10—TRAVEL PAY

Branch Office
Ashland, Kentucky

Travel pay on all jobs covered by this Agreement are as outlined below, and all miles shall be measured from the office of Millwright Local 1031 by use of the most direct route, using only improved or hard surface, non-toll roads.

> 5 miles free zone.
> All jobs outside the free zone shall be
> $.25 per hour additional for each hour paid.

Source: *Agreement* between District Council of Carpenters and Tri-State Contractors Association, 1995–1998.

EMPLOYEE SERVICES

A wide variety of employee services have been negotiated in labor agreements. In general, they are not as commonly found as the previously discussed employee benefits; however, most labor agreements provide for at least a few employee services. Some of the more traditional employee services include sponsoring social and recreational activities such as picnics and athletic events. The cost of these services has been reexamined in recent years because only a relatively small percentage of employees utilize them.

Subsidized food services are a popular employee benefit. Both labor and management feel that providing dining facilities, low-cost meals, or vending machine products minimizes time away from the job spent on breaks or at mealtime, in addition to improving employees' diet. Company-sponsored credit unions are another employee service often sought by union negotiators. Although a credit union is normally operated completely independently from the employer, the employer's cooperation in establishing it and providing payroll deductions is critical and must be negotiated.

In recent years, some of the newer employee services negotiated include counseling for employees with medical, financial, or drug and alcohol problems; services minimizing work-related costs such as transportation to and from the job; and clothing and tool allowances.

Flexible Benefit Plans

An alternative to negotiating a fixed combination of employer-provided benefits is a flexible benefit package. In a typical **flexible benefit plan**, employees are allowed to choose the benefits they believe will best meet their needs. Their choices are limited to the total cost the employer has agreed to pay in the collective bargaining agreement. Thus, for example, employees may be given a monthly benefit-dollar figure and told that they can allocate the dollars to the benefits they select from a list. In many programs, employees may exceed their benefit limit, but they must pay the difference between what the employer provides and the cost of what they wish, or if employees choose to allocate fewer dollars than their maximum, they may be allowed to keep all or part of the savings as additional monthly income.

Union	Management
What are the three best benefits employees can try to get from their employers?	*What three benefits should an employer avoid?*
a. Employment security (as opposed to job security)	a. COLA (cost-of-living adjustment) or any benefit plan with fixed benefits unrelated to costs or a future plan with fixed entitlement
b. Family coverages (health insurance, appropriate leave opportunities, child and elder care)	b. Discretionary overtime
c. Opportunity for employee growth through retraining, promotion, education, literacy, and recognition for performance	c. Premium pay for time not worked or any other pay for nonproductive time, such as on-call pay

Flexible benefit plans have had an on-again, off-again, on-again life. In the 1960s, **cafeteria plans**, which also allowed employees to choose some benefits from a "menu" of benefits, started to spread among employers. However, the cafeteria approach ran into problems. Employees found it confusing and difficult to make decisions, and employers (without today's computer programs) found the administration of the programs expensive and difficult.

In recent years, employers are increasingly implementing flexible benefit plans. A survey of the top 150 *Fortune* 500 companies found that 45 percent either had flexible benefit plans or were considering implementing them.[74] The primary reason employers are switching from fixed to flexible plans, in addition to better meeting their employees' needs, is to contain their medical costs. In fact, flexible benefit plans may be the most effective means employers have of containing medical costs. A survey of 330 employers with flexible plans found that almost half (49 percent) had achieved their medical-cost target, an additional 43 percent reported it was too soon to tell whether their targets would be met, and only 8 percent reported that they could not meet their target. The survey also reported that better than 87 percent of employers met employees' needs.[75]

An important feature of a flexible plan is the opportunity for each employee to spend employer dollars as personally desired. By contrast, many so-called flexible plans are fixed. They either offer the employee the opportunity to choose among limited alternatives or offer a "take-it-or-leave-it" approach. For example the employer offers to pay a portion of an employee's medical insurance if the employee pays the balance. But if the employee does not choose medical insurance (possibly because of a spouse's coverage), then the employer's contribution is lost. A true flexible plan credits the employee with the employer's share, which could be applied to another benefit.

Types of Flexible Plans. There are at least three major types of employee flexible benefit plans. First, the *core cafeteria plan* provides employees with "core" (minimum) coverage in several areas and allows employees to choose either additional benefits or cash, up to a maximum total cost to the employer. In the core cafeteria

Figure 8-6   Employee Flexible Benefit Plans

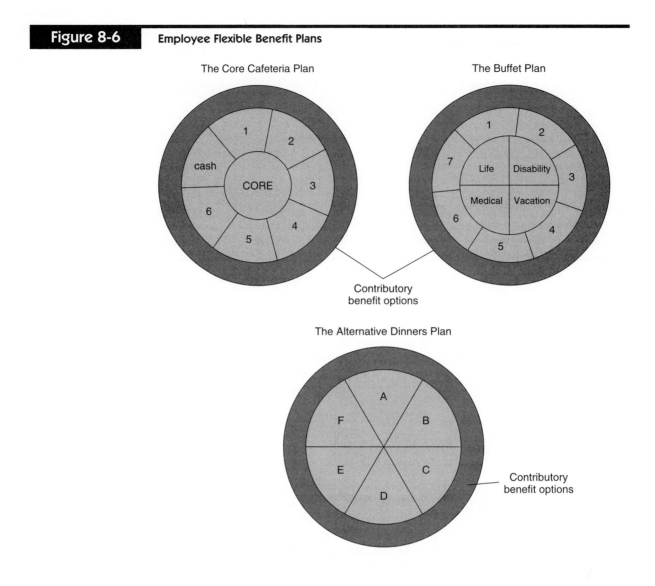

The Core Cafeteria Plan

The Buffet Plan

Contributory
benefit options

The Alternative Dinners Plan

Contributory
benefit options

plan of Figure 8-6, employees have a choice of items 1 through 6 and cash. This plan strikes a balance between giving employees complete freedom to choose among benefits and the employer's need to protect employees against poor decisions. Second, the *buffet plan* starts employees with their exact current benefit coverage and allows them to decrease coverage in some areas (life insurance, medical insurance, and so forth) in order to earn credits for other benefits (dental care, day care, and the like). Third, the *alternative dinners plan* provides a number of packages ("dinners") from which to choose. For example, one package might be aimed at the employer with a nonworking spouse and children, another at the single employee, and a third at an employee with a working spouse and no children. The total cost of each "dinner" would be approximately the same as the cost of any other. The employer pays for whatever basic plan is chosen, and the employee can augment the basic benefits package at his or her own expense (contributory benefits options).

Advantages of Flexible Plans.   Originally created to better meet the needs of employees, flexible plans have become increasingly effective in matching employees' needs to their benefit plan. Among the advantages of flexible plans are the following:

1. **Control benefit costs.** Of employers with flexible plans, 78 percent reported that a major objective in their initiating a plan was to contain rising health-care costs. With health-care costs continuing to rise, this effective containment method is likely to spread among employers.

2. **Improve benefits offered.** Employers can better meet the needs of their employees by expanding the variety of benefits offered to employees. Child care is a good example: Employers can pay a portion or all of the cost of providing child care at an off-site facility through a voucher system. In choosing the coverage, employees must either reduce the coverage of another benefit or have the increased cost deducted from their pay. (Employers generally, however, provide a portion of child care.)

3. **Attract and retain employees.** The changing workforce is causing employers in some industries to consider flexible benefits as a tool in the recruitment and retention of employees. Just as flexible work schedules can be utilized to attract and keep employees, flexible benefit plans can be included in recruitment and advertising.

4. **Avoid duplicate coverage.** Another aspect of the changing labor force is the increased number of working married couples with duplicate benefit coverage from separate employers. Flexible benefit plans may allow a married couple to save thousands of dollars in wasted duplicate coverage.[76]

Child Care

Although many employers have addressed the child-care needs of their employees, child care, according to the National Labor Relations Board (NLRB), is not a mandatory subject for collective bargaining. As the workforce continues to include more single parents and dual-career couples, the direct link between employment and child care might cause the NLRB to reconsider its position. A survey conducted by the U.S. Department of Labor listed the following *employer benefits* from a child-care policy:

1. Greater ability of the employer to keep and attract good employees
2. Less employee absenteeism
3. A lower job turnover rate
4. Improved employee morale

Employer-sponsored child-care programs are varied.

Child-Care Centers.   Some employers provide in-house child-care services by establishing a child-care center in the workplace. The company must have available space and a sufficient number of interested employees for this service to work. Often, smaller employers join together and create a nonprofit center off the premises for all employees.

Financial Assistance.   A number of employers choose to participate in their employees' child-care needs by providing financial assistance. Employees can afford quality child care with the assistance offered by the employer. Many communities lack the resources necessary to provide quality child care, however, and employers often find it necessary to actually provide the centers.[77]

Credit Unions

One of the oldest and most common employee services is the credit union. Most agreements provide that the employer will initiate a payroll deduction process, but the union assumes responsibility for enrolling members, investing funds, and administering the program. In general, employers wish to stay apart from the process and have "the credit union assume complete responsibility."[78]

SUMMARY

Employee benefit costs have constantly risen in recent decades. The four most expensive types of benefits in agreements are: (1) income maintenance, (2) medical care, (3) pay for time not worked, and (4) premium pay. Still, a variety of employee benefits have increased in recent years as employees and union leaders initiate new benefits in labor negotiations. By necessity, some benefits are unique to particular industries. For example, the agreement between the UAW and Ford Motor Company includes a safety belt user program, which pays $10,000 to the beneficiary of a participant who dies in an automobile accident while "properly using a qualified passenger restraint."[79]

Although no one can predict the future of benefit negotiations between management and labor, the spiraling increases in employee benefits have slowed down as concession bargaining has become commonplace. Employers continue to seek methods of containing health-care costs and to make concessions on work rules, outsourcing, and management rights in exchange for higher wages and benefits and greater job security.

CASE STUDY 8-1

PAID LEAVES OF ABSENCE

Facts

The collective bargaining agreement between the company and the union contained the following provisions:

Overtime/Compensatory Time: . . . Employees may elect to use compensatory time off in lieu of a cash payment. Compensatory time is paid at time and one-half (1½). The scheduling of compensatory time, if such be elected by the employee, must be approved by the employee's supervisor. . . .

Eligibility for Sick Leave: . . . Each permanent employee who has earned sick leave credits shall be eligible for sick leave for any period or absence from employment which is due to illness . . . of members of the immediate family (defined as . . . children of the employee or his/her spouse. . . .)

The company allowed employees who worked overtime to either be paid time and one-half for each hour worked or earn time off at the rate of one and one-half hour for each hour worked. The employees accrued eight sick days and 10 vacation days a year.

Prior to February 13, 1995, employees were allowed to use compensatory time when they were absent because of illness, and prior ap-

(continued)

proval for the use was not always required. However, on February 13, 1995, the company issued a directive stating that "supervisors will no longer approve utilizing compensatory time for sick leave absences. An exception may be made by a supervisor if the employee does not have any sick leave hours available but does have a compensatory balance."

The employee's son became ill on February 28, and she left a note for her supervisor that she might not be in on March 1. She did in fact take the day off. On March 2 she called in and said she would not be at work and she said she would be using a vacation day. When she filled out her time sheet, she listed March 1 as a compensatory day. On the basis of the company's directive, her supervisor required the employee to use a sick day for March 1 but allowed the use of a vacation day for March 2. The union pursued this grievance on her behalf.

The union's position was that a past practice of allowing the employees to use compensatory time for leaves due to illness without the prior approval of the supervisor had been established and that the company could not change that practice unilaterally. The employees had acquired a "benefit" through that past practice and the collective bargaining agreement did not give the company the right to take away that benefit.

The company position was that the past practice argument was not controlling in this case. Rather, the precise language of the collective bargaining agreement required the use of sick leave for illness and required a supervisor's approval for use of compensatory time. Because the collective bargaining agreement is definitive, past practice does not create additional rights. In addition, the management rights clause of the agreement allows the company to make changes in the way it manages the workplace. Controlling leave time would be included under that clause.

Questions

1. The union claimed that the employees lost a benefit when the company changed the use of compensatory time for illness. In light of the fact that the use was permitted if the employee had no sick leave available, how were the employees damaged?

2. The company paid employees the same wage whether the time was credited against accrued sick leave, compensatory time, or vacation. Why would the employer care which leave was used?

3. As the arbitrator, give your reasons for ruling in the union's favor. Now give your reasons for ruling in the company's favor.

Adapted from *Sheboygan County*, 105 LA 605 (1995).

VACATION PAY

Facts

The company and the union had a collective bargaining agreement in effect from November 2, 1973, to October 31, 1976. No agreement for a new contract was reached by the October 31, 1976, expiration date, and the employees

went on strike. The strike lasted until July 11, 1979—two years and eight months.

In June of 1977, the union asked for accrued vacation pay for the 10-month period before the strike (January 1976 through October 1976) for all eligible employees. The company refused, stating that under its interpretation of

(continued)

the contract no vacation pay was yet due. The contract provisions in question are as follows:

SECTION VII. VACATIONS

A. *Eligibility*—To be eligible for a vacation in any calendar year during the term of this Agreement, the employee must have one year or more of continuous service.
B. *Length of Vacation and Extra Vacation Pay*
1. An eligible employee who has attained the years of continuous service indicated in the following table in any calendar year, on the anniversary of his employment with the Company, during the term of this Agreement shall receive a vacation corresponding to such years of continuous service as shown in the following table. . . .
D. *Vacation Pay*—An employee granted a vacation will receive, for each vacation week, two percent (2%) of his earnings from January 1 to December 31 of the year previous.
E. *Vacation Allowance in Lieu of Vacation*— While it is recognized that the purpose of the vacation provided by this Section is to grant the employees vacation with pay as annual periods of rest and recreation, the Company may require an employee to work during his vacation, in which event he shall be paid his vacation pay in addition to his regular pay.

The union charged that the company committed an unfair labor practice by withholding the vacation pay, and the NLRB agreed. The company appealed.

In defending its position, the NLRB relied on court-tested standards for determining an unfair labor practice when an employer discourages union membership by means of discrimination.

If the conduct complained of could naturally and foreseeably have an adverse effect on employee rights, then the conduct is "inherently destructive." In such cases, there is no need to find actual anti-union motivation, and showing a legitimate business purpose will not relieve the employer of the unfair labor charge. In this instance, the NLRB contended that the company's refusal to pay previously earned vacation benefits to striking workers was "inherently destructive" of important employee rights.

The NLRB further contended that the company's interpretation of the contract was incorrect, and therefore there was no legitimate or substantial business reason for its conduct. Because the conduct was "inherently destructive," however, neither the lack of anti-union sentiment nor a legitimate business purpose was relevant.

The company's position included the following points:

1. Its interpretation of the contract was legitimate and in good faith.
2. The board overstepped its role by disagreeing and substituting its own interpretation of the contract.
3. In the past, vacation rights were not determined by expired contracts but by the contract in effect at the time of payment.
4. Vacation pay was withheld from strikers and nonstrikers alike; no one received the pay.
5. Payment of benefits was contingent upon reaching an agreement on the contract not on the employees' return to work.

Questions

1. Did the company's action of withholding vacation pay illegally affect the employees' right to bargain collectively? Explain your answer.
2. Would you have reached a different decision if nonstriking employees had received vacation benefits? Explain your answer.
3. If you were the union, how might you propose changing the eligibility clause to avoid future problems?
4. Should striking employees be paid for accrued vacation time?

Adapted from *Vesuvius Crucible Co. v. National Labor Relations Board*, 668 F.2d 162 (3d Cir. 1981).

cafeteria plans
call-in pay
concession bargaining
Consolidated Omnibus Budget Recon-
    ciliation Act (COBRA)
contributory plan
current expenditure pension plan
employee assistance program (EAP)
Employee Retirement Income Security
    Act (ERISA)
escape clause
flexible benefit plan
guaranteed income stream
health maintenance organizations
    (HMOs)
Monday holiday provision

on-call pay
pay for time not worked
payback agreements
personal day (floating holiday)
portability
premium pay
pyramiding of overtime
reporting pay
severance pay
shift differential
sick leave
unemployment insurance
vested
wage employment guarantee
wellness program
workers' compensation

1. How can negotiators reduce health-care costs and maintain good health-care benefits?
2. In recent years, management negotiators have increased their resistance to increases in private pension plan funding. Why?
3. Why might workers be ineligible for retirement funds from a private pension plan, even though they have worked all their lives?
4. What is meant by *eligibility* in a holiday clause?
5. Why do workers try to negotiate wage employment guarantees? Supplemental unemployment benefits (SUBs)?
6. How does a GIS differ from SUB pay?
7. What type of health-care plans are normally negotiated? How can a health maintenance organization (HMO) be considered as an alternative to such plans? What are the purposes of HMOs?
8. Why do employees today place a high priority on paid time off? How has the Monday holiday caused administrative problems? How can holiday provision problems be minimized?
9. What paid leaves of absence are usually provided by labor agreements?
10. Why does management dislike pyramiding of overtime?

TAKE IT TO THE NET

We invite you to visit the Carrell/Heavrin page on the Prentice Hall Web site at:

http://www.prenhall.com/carrellr

for this chapter's World Wide Web exercise.

Flexible Benefit Decisions

Purpose:
To help students gain an understanding of the philosophy behind flexible benefit plans and the individual decision making involved.

Task:
Management is increasingly striving to negotiate flexible benefit plans as a means of controlling the total cost of employer-paid employee benefits.

If *today* you were given $1,000 per month in benefit dollars to allocate among the following, what package of benefits would you choose? Complete the following chart by placing a dollar amount for each benefit you choose in the left column.

Benefit Plan *Benefit*
Pension plan (matched by employer 50/50 up to $500/mo)
Paid holidays ($50/day)
Guaranteed maternity or paternity leave ($50/day for 2 weeks per year)
Medical insurance ($250/employee, $450 family)
Elder care ($50/week; provides daily care for 1 adult)
Health maintenance organization health-care option ($200/employee, $350 family)
Legal insurance ($50/month)
Vision care ($50/month per employee or $75/month per family)
Child care ($75/week per child)
Cafeteria lunches ($50/month)
Tuition reimbursement ($50/month maximum)
Funeral leave (3 days/death, 6 days/year; maximum, $50)
Company-sponsored social events (annual picnic, parties, etc., $10/month)
Life insurance ($50 for $100,000)
Disability insurance ($50/month)
Dental insurance ($50/employee; $75/family)
Reserved parking ($50/month)

If the total is less than $1,000 the employee and employer split the difference, 50/50. If the total is over $1,000 the employee pays the excess.

Paid Holiday Clause

Purpose:
To practice negotiating positions.

Task:
Write a paid holiday provision for a collective bargaining agreement. Assume that the workers are employed by a local manufacturing company, are paid average wages, and receive average benefits.

Steps:

Study the contracts of local companies to determine what is commonly provided. Organize students in groups to write the provision. Assign some groups the position of management and other groups the position of labor. Negotiate the provision. The clause should contain the following:

1. Holidays recognized
2. Pay rate received for the holidays
3. Pay received for work performed on the holidays
4. Eligibility requirements for the paid holidays
5. What happens if the holiday falls on a nonworking day or during a vacation period

If you are using Smith/Carrell/Golden *Collective Bargaining Simulated, 4E,* with this text, please refer to the following:

pp. 15–22, Article VIII: Vacations, Article VI: Reporting and Call-In Pay; Article XIII Group Insurance; Article XIV: Holiday Pay; and Article XXIII: Pensions.

Job Security
and Seniority

Scenes like this closed factory highlight the fact that job security
must be given top priority by negotiators.

Both Sides of "Replacement Workers" Issue

Labor News

Historically, unions have counted on their ability to put on a successful strike as a means of gaining new wages and benefits at the negotiation table. Employers feared that a lengthy strike could cost them substantial market share or even put them out of business if customers supported the union or simply changed to competitors' products.

The 1981 Air Traffic Controllers Strike, however, in which President Reagan permanently replaced striking workers with nonunion employees, began a new era in labor relations. Many employers began hiring replacement workers as soon as a strike was called—often forcing the union to agree to their demands. In 1992, the United Auto Workers (UAW) became the victim of such a strategy when it staged a strike against Caterpillar, the last unionized U.S. manufacturer of heavy equipment. When the UAW called the strike, Caterpillar advertised for replacement workers, and thousands of would-be strikebreakers responded. UAW quickly canceled the strike without gaining a concession at the negotiating table and after losing thousands of union jobs.

In contrast to the experience of UAW, a 1993 strike by American Airline flight attendants negated the use of permanent strike replacements by utilizing a limited duration strike. Having been engaged in very difficult negotiations, the Association of Professional Flight Attendants and the management of American Airlines reached an impasse in early November 1993 over pay, medical benefits, staffing, and work rules. Management refused to continue the meetings until the union agreed to certain concessions. The union decided to go on strike. A strategic decision was made to start the strike a week before Thanksgiving, thereby disrupting the holiday travel plans of millions of customers. In addition, the union announced that the strike would be a limited duration strike to last only 10 days. The timing of the strike was guaranteed to cripple one of the nation's largest airlines during one of its busiest times of the year, and the short duration of the strike ensured that no replacement workers for the strike period could be hired.

On Sunday, November 21, four days into the strike, President Bill Clinton intervened and convinced the president of American Airlines that it was in his company's and the country's best interest to cut the strike short. President Clinton persuaded both sides to agree to binding arbitration on the issues still in dispute. Labor leaders praised the union's strike strategy as a way to reshape the traditional strike tactic to make it, once again, an effective weapon to use in a labor dispute.

In 1997 a declared strike by American Airlines pilots was only hours away when President Clinton invoked a seldom-used section of the 1926 Railway Labor Act to halt the strike in the interest of avoiding an interruption of commerce.

Adapted from Dana Milbank, "Unions' Woes Suggest How the Labor Force in U.S. Is Shifting," *Wall Street Journal*, May 5, 1992, pp. A1, 4; and "Clinton's Intervention Halts American Strike: Flight Attendants' Union and Airline Agree to Arbitration in 4-Day-Old Work Stoppage," *Louisville Courier-Journal*, November 23, 1993, p. D1.

Over the years, workers' interests and demands regarding job security have never waned. Together with wages and benefits, job security is seen by negotiators as a top priority in good and bad economic times. Job security is viewed by many as simply meaning the guarantee of work. However, in reality it means much more, including the rights to remain employed during times of layoffs, to promotion, and to a fair hearing in cases involving discipline; and the need to have work performed by employees within the company rather than subcontracting or increasing the use of automatic equipment. The ultimate job security employment situation occurs in some foreign countries where, after a probationary period, employees are guaranteed a job with good wages and benefits for their entire careers as long as they continue to produce satisfactorily. At the other end of the continuum is the hypothetical lack of job security situation, in which management might fire, promote, or lay off employees without rationale or consideration for experience and productivity. Negotiating for better wages or working conditions would be meaningless if management could, without reason or with biased intentions, terminate employees or remove jobs from the workplace.

The concept of job security has also been termed **industrial jurisprudence** by Sumner Slichter. Slichter's concept contains the primary ingredients of job security in today's collective bargaining: seniority as a determining factor in layoffs, promotions, and transfers; control of entrance to the organization or trade; seniority as a determining factor in job assignments; negotiated management change and work methods and introduction of new machinery; and negotiated wage rates.[1] Industrial jurisprudence generally embodies the principle that the operation of the organization will not be determined by a single individual or group of top management officials. Instead, the employees are given some rights to guarantee input into important decisions regarding their employment.

Guarantees of work and promotion opportunities are less important in some industries such as local government and public utilities that have very little variation in the numbers they employ. However, in most manufacturing industries that are heavily unionized, employment variations are great because of changes in consumer demands; thus job security is a primary concern.

The precedent-setting 1997–1999 UAW-Chrysler agreement, for example, provided a new job employment guarantee program that created a "snapshot" of the workforce at the start of the contract. Then three 100 percent "baseline" employment levels were established at the unit, group, and companywide levels. The agreement then provides that attrition (death, retirement, quitting) cannot allow the employment level to fall below 95 percent of each unit's baseline. When it does positions are filled by (1) active employees, (2) recall of laid-off employees, and (3) new hires.[2]

The ultimate labor-management conflict over job security is a basic and important one. Management believes that it needs to have a free hand in the operation of the workplace to maximize profits and exercise its abilities. In contrast, labor believes that employee experience and skills are critical to productivity. Employees require some protection against unreasonable managers as well as guarantees that important decisions such as promotions and layoffs will be made on a rational basis, and favoritism or union busting will be avoided.

Beginning in the 1930s, seniority-based procedures, such as the **last hired, first fired** rule, became common layoff and recall decision criteria. Various theories support this rule, including the *human capital theory*, in which employees increase their productivity with experience and rational employers want to retain the more productive employees; the *implicit contract theory*, in which the career strategy of employers encourages employees to commit themselves to steady, productive work, thus laying off senior employees would cause worker distrust in any career planning; and the *internal labor market theory*, in which collective bargaining produces rules and procedures to ease the tension between the parties. Seniority-based layoff procedures are a prime example of such rules in limiting management's actions and increasing employee loyalty.[3]

Permanent layoffs are of particular concern to employees because layoffs result in significant reductions in earnings over the course of employees' work lives. Thus, employees have even stronger expectations that, during economic downswings, employers will reward loyalty.[4] The last hired, first fired rule has caused lower permanent separation rates among union workers in comparison with nonunion workers, along with more frequent temporary layoffs in the union sector due to senior union members' preference for short layoffs, allowing them to maintain their seniority.[5]

SENIORITY

A *seniority system* is a set of rules governing the allocation of economic benefits and opportunities on the basis of service with one employer.[6] It is by far the most commonly negotiated means of measuring service and comparing employees for promotion and employment decisions.

Seniority is perhaps the most important measure of job security to employees, and the issue of seniority is popular among unions and viewed as critical to job security. Seniority is highly visible because it is so easy to define and measure. Normally, it is calculated in terms of days, beginning with the employee's date of hire, and, with a few exceptions continues over the years during the employee's tenure. Union negotiators will vehemently claim that management, in the absence of a job seniority system, will make promotion, layoff, and other decisions solely on the basis of possible short-run cost savings or individual biases rather

---

PROFILE 9-1

LIFETIME EMPLOYMENT GUARANTEE

General Motors in its 1996 contract negotiations with the UAW made a historic offer—lifetime employment guaranteed to current workers—in exchange for the ability to reduce its total workforce as those members retire. Certainly the demographics of GM's aging workforce make the offer reasonable. The ultimate job security proposal, however, would have been unthinkable only a few years ago even though it would have provided most UAW workers their top job demand. Perhaps ironically the concept of lifetime employment was until recently found only in Japan, whose automakers have taken much of the U.S. market away from the Big 3. The Japanese recession of the 1990s caused many major employers there to end the practice of guaranteed lifetime employment, just at the time that GM proposed beginning the policy in the United States.

Adapted from Rebecca Blumenstein, Nichole Christian, Angelo Henderson, "GM Offers Lifetime Employment in UAW Talks," *Wall Street Journal*, September 12, 1996, p. A3.

than on the objective criteria that seniority easily provides. These criteria include the employee's loyalty to the company and his or her skills and productivity, which increase with time spent on the job.

Management may argue that time worked on the job is only one measure and that the employee's performance record, as well as other criteria, especially performance appraisals completed by supervisors, should be considered. However, performance appraisal systems, even at their best, are heavily dependent on supervisors' objectivity and ability to evaluate honestly and thoroughly individual performance—something that is often very difficult to do. Therefore, performance appraisals are subjective and do not guarantee employees the objectivity and consistency they expect when promotion or layoff decisions are made.

In nonunionized organizations, it certainly is not unheard of for employers to terminate or lay off senior employees who have worked into higher pay grades or junior employees who have unjustifiably suffered a supervisor's contempt. A seniority system provides a means of job security and requires that if a supervisor feels that an employee is unproductive or unable to produce successfully, the supervisor must defend and subject his decision to an agreed-upon process. Also, the seniority system utilizes a basic and fair premise that employees who have stayed with the organization longer and provided more service than other employees should be given first preference when all other aspects of the employment decision are equal.

To define fully the concepts of seniority, it may be helpful to distinguish between unionized and nonunionized employer-employee relationships. Seniority is not required by federal or local laws, nor is it an inherent right of employees. However, seniority is a mandatory subject in the collective bargaining process. Strict formal seniority systems are commonplace in virtually all unionized organizations, but they are rare among nonunion employers. The latter employer typically maintains total decision-making control in all aspects of employment that are partially or totally governed by seniority systems in the unionized organization. A Bureau of National Affairs survey of more than 400 labor contracts found that 91 percent of the agreements provided for the seniority system, including 99 percent in the manufacturing industries and 79 percent in the nonmanufacturing industries. In most of the contracts surveyed, seniority played a critical role in the determination of promotion, transfer, and layoff decisions.[7]

CALCULATION OF SENIORITY

In general, seniority is considered to be the process of giving preference in employment decisions on the basis of the length of continuous service with the company. When seniority is involved in promotion considerations, it may be defined as preference in employment on the basis of the length of continuous service and the ability and fitness of the employee to perform the job. New employees generally begin acquiring seniority on the date they are first hired. In the case of two or more employees hired on the same date, seniority may be determined by the exact time of hire or the alphabetical listing of their last names. Often, however, seniority is not awarded to employees until after the probationary period, even though they begin accruing seniority from their date of first hire.[8] The contract clause that specifically defines seniority can be quite fairly detailed as in the example of the agreement between E. I. duPont Co. and the Neoprene Craftsmen Union in Figure 9-1. Some clauses may be fairly brief, as the following seniority

ARTICLE IV

Seniority

Section 1. Seniority accrued prior to the effective date of this Agreement shall be that shown on the seniority rosters as of the effective date hereof. Seniority accrued following the effective date of this Agreement shall be an employee's total length of employment acquired since the first day of his last period of unbroken employment or since the effective date of this Agreement, whichever is later, within the bargaining unit, unless otherwise specified in this Article. Such seniority acquired since the effective date of this Agreement shall be calculated and adjusted in the following manner:

(a)   The seniority of an employee shall be broken and automatically terminated in case of:
    (1)   Discharge for just cause;
    (2)   Voluntary quit;
    (3)   Absence in excess of sixteen (16) days unless covered by leave of absence;
    (4)   Failure to return to work following expiration of leave of absence;
    (5)   Termination because of lack of work.

(b)   No seniority credit will be given for the time between termination because of lack of work and re-employment. The Plant seniority an employee had at the time of termination because of lack of work shall be used in offering re-employment for a period of three (3) years after date of such termination. A former employee who has been terminated because of lack of work for less than three (3) years will be offered re-employment in accordance with his Plant seniority before new employees are hired, provided such former employee is basically qualified to do the work to be performed. A former employee who has been terminated because of lack of work and who is re-employed shall be credited with the seniority he had prior to his termination; provided that an employee who has not completed his probation period shall begin a new one hundred and twenty (120) day probation period. A former employee who has been terminated because of lack of work will not be eligible for credit of prior seniority nor for other offers of re-employment under the provisions of this Section 1 (b) if he fails to notify the COMPANY of his intent to return to work within one (1) week after notice to return to work has been sent by registered letter to his last known address, or if he fails to report for work within two (2) weeks after notice has been sent by registered letter to his last known address.

(c)   Service outside this bargaining unit in other parts of this Plant will be credited only (a) if such credit was given under prior Agreements between the parties and is included in seniority shown on the seniority roster as of the effective date hereof, or (b) if such credit is provided for by other provisions of this Article.

(d)   Plant seniority shall be the employee's total creditable seniority within the bargaining unit. If two (2) or more employees have the same Plant seniority date, their names shall be listed in alphabetical order. The name change of an employee shall not affect such listing.

Section 2. An employee shall exercise Plant Seniority only in the Master Division and unit in which he is employed. For the purpose of this Article the four (4) Master Divisions and the units which comprise these Divisions are as follows:

   Engineering Master Division
     Each Individual Engineering Unit

(continued)

Figure 9-1   **Agreement on the Terms of Seniority (continued)**

Operations Master Division
　Monomer Operations
　Poly Operations
　"Freon" Operations
　Laboratory
　Power and Refrigeration Operations
Auxiliary Master Division
　Poly Clean-up Operators (Including Water Blasters and Leader-Water Blasters)
Stores Attendants
Monomer Helpers
Diesel Railroad Crew
Labor Unit (Including Power Helpers and Maintenance Helpers)
Service Unit (Including Laboratory Stores Attendant)
Fireman Master Division

Section 3.
(a)　An employee may transfer from one Master Division to another only under the provisions of Section 5 (c) pertaining to re-employment and return, or Section 5 (d) pertaining to job bidding, Section 3 (b), or Section 7 pertaining to reduction of force, of this Article except that the transfer of an employee with a disability may be negotiated between parties. On a case-by-case basis the parties may agree on the transfer of an employee from one seniority unit to another.
(b)　An employee's "home" unit shall be that unit in which he was first employed. However, if thereafter he has been transferred to another unit because of disability or in accordance with Sections 5 (c), (d) or 5 (e) of this Article, then his "home" unit shall be the unit as indicated in these Sections 5 (c), (d), or (e).

Section 4. Seniority rosters shall be maintained by the COMPANY, kept in the Employment Office and shall be available to the UNION. Such rosters shall show each employee's relative position within their Master Division and unit.

Section 5. When job vacancies in a unit occur, they will be filled in the following order:
(a)　By Promotions. Promotions shall be made within a given unit on the basis of Plant seniority provided the employees have approximately the same qualifications and are qualified to perform the job.
(b)　By the voluntary return of eligible employees within the Master Division to their "home" units. Eligible employees are those who have been involuntarily displaced from their unit. Employees will be offered the vacancy and if they refuse this opportunity, their present unit will become their "home" unit. Employees who volunteer shall be returned to their "home" unit in Plant seniority order, the employee with the most seniority returning first.
(c)　By return of employees outside of Master Division to their "home" Master Division.
(d)　By job bidding. Job bidding, subject to agreement by the parties on a case-by-case basis, may be limited to the employees of a Master Division, but if not so limited, shall be on a bargaining unit basis. A general announcement regarding vacancies will be posted at least two calendar weeks in advance of selection of successful bidders. Ability, skill, knowledge and training being approximately equal, the candidate having the most Plant Seniority within the bargaining unit shall be selected to fill such vacancy, provided he meets established requirements of the job vacancy. Successful candidates will be transferred to the bid job as soon as it is practical to do so. Each will be notified of his transfer date as much in advance as practical. This provision will not require the COMPANY to drop below a minimum level of experience and skill necessary to properly perform the work in any unit. An employee may job bid to any job with a higher straight-time rate. However, a new employee, or a successful job bidder,

may not job bid to a job which does not have a higher straight-time rate for a period of three (3) years from the date they are declared a successful bidder. All of the above notwithstanding, subject to agreement of the parties on a case-by-case basis, an employee who has been transferred in accordance with his bid may be returned to his former Master Division.

(e)   Re-employment shall be in accord with Section 1(b) of this article and in Plant Seniority order with the qualified former employee having the most such seniority returning first. They shall have indefinite return rights to their "home" Master Division and shall be offered one opportunity to return to that Division that (A) vacancy occurs; provided, they are still basically qualified for the vacant job. Eligible employees will be offered the vacant job and if refused, their present unit will become their home unit.

(f)   By hiring of new employees (at management's discretion).

Section 6. When new jobs are established on the Plant, they will be filled in the following order:

(a)   By job bidding as provided in Section 5 (d) of this Article.

(b)   By re-employment and hiring as provided in sections 5(e) and (f) of this article.

Section 7. Plant Seniority shall be used to select employees for transfer in a reduction of force in a Master Division, provided employees to be retained in the Division must have collectively sufficient qualifications to perform all the jobs in the Master Division.

Source: *Agreement* between E. I. duPont de Nemours and Company and the Neoprene Craftsmen Union, 1994.

provision from the agreement between Anaconda Aluminum Company and the Aluminum Workers Trades, AFL-CIO:

> *Section 1.* Plant seniority is defined as an employee's length of continuous service at Anaconda Aluminum Company, division of the Anaconda Company, Columbia Falls reduction plant in Columbia Falls, Montana.
>
> *Section 2.* Departmental seniority is defined as employee's length of continuous service in a department of the plant.
>
> *Section 3.* Granted leaves of absence, vacations and jury duty will not be considered as a break in service. Re-employment rights of employees who enter the armed forces shall be determined by the applicable federal and state laws.[9]

Seniority List

Most agreements have the company prepare and post a **seniority list** (or roster, as in Section 4 of Figure 9-1) so that there will be no question about employee, department, or plantwide seniority. There must be total agreement as to the exact calculation and order of employees on seniority lists (see Case 9-1). The method of displaying seniority lists is usually a matter for local negotiation between labor and management. Many contracts provide that seniority lists be updated monthly and that they contain the employee's name, occupational group or department, any specific skilled trades date of entry, and related seniority. Any disputes over seniority lists are taken through the grievance procedure for resolution.

Depending on the particular labor agreement, seniority rights are vested within a variety of employee units. The most common unit is **plantwide seniority**, in which an individual employee receives credit that becomes applicable whenever that employee competes with any other employee from another unit for

SENIORITY LIST

The union protested the inclusion of administrators on a school district seniority list. The list included the accumulated seniority of former administrators who had returned to teaching and present administrators who were formerly teachers. The union conceded that teachers promoted to administration retained the seniority accumulated while in the bargaining units, but it objected to their accumulating seniority as administrators for the purposes of bumping into the bargaining unit. The school district admitted that administrators are not in the bargaining unit but defended their demands on the basis of the contract and past practices.

Decision

The arbitrator considered the contract language involved and found that when a teacher is promoted to an administrator's position he or she leaves the bargaining unit for purposes of seniority and does not accumulate seniority for the time spent working as an administrator. In addition, a person who begins employment as an administrator does not accumulate seniority if and when he or she becomes a teacher. This decision was based on interpretation of the seniority section specifying that systemwide seniority would be computed from the date of employment. The school district contended that the provision is so broad it allows continuation of seniority accumulation when a teacher is promoted to an administrator's position, but the arbitrator found that the reference to "teachers with the highest seniority shall be the last to be laid off" reiterated the union's position that the seniority provisions applied only to members of the bargaining unit. In addition, the arbitrator relied on interpretation of other contracts in the same field that defined *systemwide seniority* as the continuous service with the district. In interpreting the contract language, the arbitrator found that it did not speak to how seniority would be continued, just from what date it would begin.

Adapted from *Clarkston Community Schools,* 79 LA 48 (1982).

the same position. Plantwide seniority first appeared in the duPont contract in Figure 9-1 in 1943. That year, according to union negotiator Archie V. Carrell, it was the top priority of the members, who wanted job security over members of a new unit. Thus the provision in 1943 stated that "with respect to reduction of force," seniority shall be determined by "length of continuous service at the plant," therefore providing security to current union members over those of the new unit.[10]

Other common seniority units include departmental, trade, classification, and companywide. In a **departmental seniority** system, employees accrue seniority according to the amount of time they worked within a particular department, and that seniority credit is valid only within that department.[11] For example, an employee with 11 years seniority in department x could not successfully compete with an employee with seven years in department y for an open position in department y.

Classification seniority, similar to departmental seniority, provides for employee seniority only within the same job classification. *Companywide seniority* systems combine all employees from various locations and types of facilities. When two employees compete for an open position in a companywide system, individual experience, length of service, and related departments or job classifications are not considered, but only the seniority with the company. This provision makes companywide seniority the most impractical and infrequently used.

Companies often use a seniority system combining plantwide seniority with departmental seniority. Plantwide seniority may be utilized for determining layoffs, vacations, and other specific benefits. Departmental seniority is often used to determine eligibility for a promotion or a transfer so employees with specific skills and related job experience can be considered for new positions. However, in the case of layoffs, it is often believed that employees' total work experience, and therefore their plantwide seniority, is the most important job security factor.

In situations involving layoffs, seniority systems often use **bumping** (63 percent of all contracts). Bumping occurs when employees with greater seniority whose jobs have been phased out have the right to displace employees with less seniority. Most bumping clauses require that employees be qualified to perform the job they bump into.[12]

Superseniority

Union officers and committee personnel may be given preferred seniority rights for layoff and recall situations. This is often referred to as superseniority and is granted in the collective bargaining agreement so that union stewards and other labor officials will continue to work during periods of layoff, thus enabling the union to continue to operate effectively. When agreeing to superseniority for the union, management may ensure that certain labor relations personnel be similarly protected against layoffs. Some superseniority clauses require that protected union officials have the ability to perform available work or that superseniority is provided only within departments or job classifications. Others limit superseniority to those union officials who perform stewardlike duties such as grievance processing and contract administration.[13]

The value of superseniority depends on the frequency and degree of layoffs typically experienced by the company. In some cases, it is virtually meaningless because union stewards and officials have high levels of seniority from their many years of experience with the union and company.

The labor agreement should explicitly specify under what conditions an employee might lose seniority. Virtually all contracts provide that employees lose seniority if they voluntarily quit or are discharged. Employees who do not report back to work after a vacation or other leave of absence for an excessive period of time may also be deprived of their seniority. Usually employees on layoff will retain and accumulate seniority for a period of time specified within the agreement.

PROMOTIONS

Management often disagrees with the use of seniority to determine promotion decisions. The Bureau of National Affairs estimates that seniority is a determining factor in promotional policies as provided by collective bargaining agreements in 67 percent of labor contracts. However, only 5 percent call for promotion decisions based on seniority as the sole determiner. Another 49 percent provide that the most senior individual will receive promotion among those equally qualified, and 40 percent provide seniority as one factor along with "skill and ability."[14]

Some contract clauses that allow promotion according to seniority simply state that promotions to fill vacancies or new job positions on a permanent basis will be based on length of service within the company and employee skill and ability. Determining which employees have the required skill and ability is difficult and subjective. Management generally contends that promotion should be

PROMOTIONS

The company operates a plant in Mississippi. A position came open as a result of the resignation of the incumbent. The open position was posted, and four employees bid on the job and were interviewed concerning their interest. Employee Studdard, whose plant seniority date was November 17, 1980, was selected. Another employee, Welch, whose seniority date was September 9, 1980, filed a grievance. The union's contentions in Welch's grievance were that management had violated the contract concerning job promotions that stated that the job was to be assigned within seven calendar days to the bidder who had the apparent ability to perform the work and the greatest plant seniority. The union contended that the company had passed over a senior employee without showing that the employee was incapable of performing the job in favor of an employee who was admittedly more qualified. But since the collective bargaining agreement only requires that the bidder with the greatest plant seniority have the apparent ability to perform the work, the company violated the agreement.

The position of the company was that it was not a stringent seniority clause and allowed the company some discretion in selecting the bidder who had the most experience, qualifications, and leadership abilities to perform the job.

Decision

The arbitrator in this case decided for the union. He found that, although the seniority clause concerning promotions in this contract was a modified seniority clause, it did give the senior employee preference. Although some modified clauses compared the relative ability of a senior and junior employee and promoted the senior only if those abilities were equal, this particular collective bargaining agreement clause required that the senior employee be given preference if he possessed only sufficient ability to perform the job. Therefore, the company was to determine the seniority date of the employees bidding on the job and whether the most senior employee had the apparent ability to perform the work. The interpretation of *apparent* was understood merely to exclude obviously unqualified bidders and not to allow for comparison among those bidding. If the most senior employee apparently had the ability to perform the job, he would have to be appointed.

Adapted from *American Sawmill Machine Company*, 79 LA 106 (1982).

based on an employee's individual performance and required skills rather than on length of service.

When labor agreements provide that promotional decisions will be made according to seniority and job skills, it is difficult to determine the weight of each factor and the measurement of individual skills. Although seniority is a factor in promotion decisions in most labor contracts, it is usually not considered to be as important as ability to perform the job. Quite frequently ability becomes more dominant. When management decides to promote a less senior employee on the basis of higher demonstrated ability, employee grievances may result, as in Case 9-2. Management must prove that the more senior employee does not have the ability to perform the job.

Managers may argue that making important promotional decisions solely on length of service takes away employee incentive. Employees will tend to perform at the status quo knowing that they cannot be promoted before all the senior employees, and when their turn comes, no one can take the promotion away from them. Labor leaders point out that seniority can be objectively and easily measured. Therefore, promotion decisions based on seniority are far less subject to supervisor bias or inability to assess correctly individual performance and skills.

Arbitrators have generally held that management has the right to judge, weigh, and determine qualifications as long as the methods are fair and nondiscriminatory. However, if a clause provides that seniority alone is the deciding factor, then management cannot promote a "better qualified" person if the senior employee is "capable of doing the work." When ability and seniority are equal factors, arbitors generally allow management the right to make the selection, subject to a union challenge that the decision was unreasonable (given the facts), capricious, arbitrary, or discriminatory. In most disputed cases, the employer's decision is supported, and when the position is a supervisory one, management has unquestioned authority. Contract clauses dealing with promotion apply only to positions within the bargaining unit.[15] Why? It is generally held that management has complete authority to "select its own."

What weights are given to seniority and ability in actual promotion decisions? Is there a difference between union and nonunion employers? An analysis of more than 600 U.S. firms indicated that 60 percent give the person with greater seniority a preference in promotion decisions. In practice, both union and nonunion employers reported giving length of service more weight in promotion decisions than required by written policy or union contract. Although union employers reported using seniority to a greater extent, the difference in comparison with nonunion employers was not significant.[16]

Nonunion organizations often have promotion policies based primarily on promoting from within to boost employee morale and assure individuals that they can work hard and get ahead. Like union organizations, they hesitate to promote a less senior employee unless there is concrete evidence to show that a more senior employee is less capable. The effect of such a promotion on general employee morale, as well as on the individual involved, also needs to be determined.

Job Bidding

It is quite common for the job bidding process to be detailed in the labor agreement to minimize misunderstandings and grievances and to increase employee morale. An example of a detailed **job bidding** process follows:

1. When a new classification is created or an opening occurs in the existing classification, the opening will be posted on the official bid bulletin boards for a period of four working days, Saturdays, Sundays, and holidays excluded.
2. Bids for such openings will be received from any permanent employee. Temporary employees will not be allowed to bid.
3. Bids will be awarded on an up-bid, down-bid, or lateral-bid. An **up-bid** is a bid from a lower to a higher pay grade or from a pool classification to a specific line classification. A **lateral-bid** is from one classification to another classification in the same pay grade, or from one pool position to another regardless of pay grade. A **down-bid** is from a higher pay grade to a lower pay grade or from a specific line classification to a pool classification.
4. Bids will be based on plant seniority and competency with the following regulations applying:
   a. Bids to be classifications and specific lines of progression: an employee awarded a job bid in one specific line cannot bid again for one year from the date qualified in the specific line job except on an up-bid basis within his specific line progression.

b. Bids to classifications in the pool: an employee who down-bids from a specific line of progression to a pool position cannot bid again for a period of six months from the date classified except to a specific line. Or an employee classified in a pool position who down-bids or laterally bids to another pool position cannot bid again for a period of six months from the date classified except through a specific line.

c. Down-bids from classification and pay grades 12 and above will be limited to a maximum of one down-bid per classification in any one 60-day period.[17]

LAYOFF AND RECALL ACTIONS

Employers also question the use of seniority as the sole decision criterion in layoff and **recall** situations. Employers argue that ability should be a greater factor in determining layoff and recall of employees. However, since layoff and recall situations are usually seen as temporary, management's argument against the use of seniority is considerably weakened. Also, in layoff and recall situations, there is less of a question of the employee's ability since he or she had been performing the job satisfactorily before a layoff occurred. Thus, management has little room to argue that seniority is not more important in layoff and recall than in promotion decisions.

In most labor contracts, probationary employees will be laid off first, with further necessary layoffs being made in accordance with plantwide seniority. Laid-off employees may be given the opportunity to exercise their plantwide seniority and bump employees at the bottom of the seniority list rather than be laid off. When skilled trades or other specialized job classifications are involved, layoffs will commonly occur by seniority within the trades or classifications. Most agreements also provide that the company give reasonable notice and reasons for upcoming layoffs to the unions. If the workforce is increased after a layoff, contracts usually provide that laid-off employees will be recalled according to plantwide seniority for appropriate jobs.

Contract layoff procedures may fall into three general categories: layoff based entirely on seniority, layoff based on seniority among those employees who management feels are capable of performing the work, and layoff based on seniority only if ability and other factors are equal among affected employees. When the last two methods of layoff and recall procedures are utilized, grievances are likely to be filed because of the subjectivity of determining employee ability to perform work, especially when bumping is used and employees are performing new jobs.[18] If a contract provides that seniority and equal ability shall govern in layoff and recall decisions, arbitrators are likely to interpret *equal* as meaning not exactly equal but relatively equal. When contracts provide that ability should be part of the determination in layoff and recall decisions, arbitrators' awards have suggested certain guidelines be considered.[19] Some of the guidelines include the following:

1. When seniority is considered a governing criterion if ability to perform the work is relatively equal, then only the employee's seniority should be considered.[20]
2. A junior employee could be given preference over a senior employee if the senior requires a much greater amount of supervision in performing the job.[21]
3. Senior employees can be required to demonstrate ability to perform the work by passing a test that would qualify them for jobs held by junior employees.[22]

In cases involving temporary or emergency layoffs, management is often given more flexibility in selecting employees than in indefinite layoffs. If the contract does not specify differences in procedure involving temporary layoffs and indefinite layoffs, arbitrators have generally held that ordinary layoff procedures must be followed even where the lack of work lasted only a few hours or one to two days. However, the more common ruling of arbitrators in such situations has been that cumbersome seniority rules need not be followed to the letter in a brief layoff. Arbitrators have even held that in layoffs caused by emergency breakdowns or natural or unforeseen disasters, seniority rules can be disregarded if necessary. However, if the application of seniority rules in the contract does not cause a hardship during the emergency, the employer is advised to follow the contract layoff procedures.[23] The following is a concise layoff and recall contract clause setting forth the procedure and notification requirements and possible emergency exceptions:

ARTICLE 10
Reduction of Forces

a. The company agrees that in the event of a reduction in force, plant seniority shall govern and employees covered by the terms of this agreement shall be laid off in the inverse order of seniority, provided that the employee retained has the ability to fill the job. He shall have a reasonable length of time to demonstrate his ability to hold the job.
b. If an emergency such as fire, flood, storm, or major breakdown occurs during a workweek, every effort will be made to avoid loss of work and/or to reassign employees on a basis of seniority. However, it is recognized that a layoff out of seniority not exceeding one day may be necessary to avoid a payment of penalty pay.
c. Whenever a reduction in force is necessary, the company will post the names of the employees to be laid off at least three days, excluding Saturday, Sunday, and holidays, prior to such reduction unless cancellation of orders, changes in customer's requirements, breakdowns, or accidents or other emergencies make such notices impossible, in which case a union will be immediately notified.

   When the company again adds to the number of employees, those laid off shall be reemployed in the order of their seniority. A notice of recall or restoration shall be sent by registered mail to the last known address of the employee, and a copy of the notice, before it is mailed, shall be given to the properly designated officer of the union. It shall be the duty of the employee to keep the company informed as to his correct address.[24]

Typically, the only exceptions to the use of seniority as the total or partial determinant in layoff and recall decisions occur when probationary employees are laid off first without any discussion of ability to perform or in cases involving superseniority when union officials are laid off last.

A recent development in the issue of seniority rights involves layoffs by companies or governmental agencies subject to court-ordered affirmative action plans. The U.S. Supreme Court, in *Firefighters Local Union No. 1784 v. Stotts*, upheld a seniority system even though the resulting layoffs adversely affected blacks hired under a consent decree to remedy past discrimination. The Court would not allow the consent decree, which had not dealt with the layoff issue, to be given preference over a collectively bargained seniority system. Advocates of affirmative action plans fear that this decision, reaffirming the "last hired, first fired" philosophy, will undermine equal opportunity employment strides made in the last few years. Labor leaders, however, defend the protection afforded by seniority systems as necessary to preserve a basic negotiated job right. They argue that changed hiring practices giving women and blacks more job opportunities will eventually lead to *their* seniority in the various systems. Increased employment and secure job rights will accomplish the desired affirmative action goals without adversely affecting the senior worker.

In some situations, the hiring of temporary workers may be a key to an employer's remaining competitive. Management may negotiate the right to hire a higher percentage of temporary workers. The union may want the ability to add the temporary workers to its membership and collect dues from them. Most contracts will restrict management's use of temporary workers but allow a higher percentage if the union approves. The union is more likely to approve if the temporaries might be transitioned to additional permanent workers within the bargaining unit.[25]

Worker Adjustment and Retraining Notification Act

In 1989, the **Worker Adjustment and Retraining Notification Act**[26] **(WARN)**, more commonly known as the *Plant Closing Act*, became effective. The general purpose of the law is to "warn" workers and local communities of plant closing or mass layoff decisions by requiring employers to provide advance notice in either situation. The AFL-CIO and other labor forces lobbied for a similar bill, which was vetoed in 1988. However, the pressures of the 1988 presidential election contributed to President Reagan's decision to allow WARN to become law without his signature. The U.S. Chamber of Commerce strongly opposed the plant closings bill. However, corporate officials at Ford Motor Company, Eastman Kodak, Whirlpool Corporation, and other companies noted that WARN mandates less notice than most firms have voluntarily given workers.[27]

The act requires employers to provide 60 days' advance written notice of either a plant closing or a mass layoff once the decision is made by management. A *plant closing* is defined as the permanent shutdown of a single site or one or more operating units that causes an employment loss of 30 days or more for 50 or more employees, excluding part-time workers. Written notification is required by law even when other employees remain working if 50 or more are included in the shutdown. Advance notice of a temporary shutdown decision is required if the action affects, for more than six months, at least 50 employees and 33 percent of all employees—or whenever 500 or more employees are affected. Advance written notice of 60 days is also required when mass layoff decisions will affect at least 50 full-time workers and 33 percent of all employees or whenever 500 or more are affected.

Employers covered by the act include most private sector and nonprofit organizations that employ 100 or more full-time workers. Federal, state, and local government operations are not included in the law. Major exemptions from the law include sudden and unforeseen economic circumstances, natural disasters, and faltering companies actively raising capital to keep a facility open.

These exemptions could bring the effectiveness of WARN into question. For example, one company claimed that it could not give the 60-day warning because of unforeseen circumstances when, in fact, the company had one major client, and that client had begun pulling back its business in late March and continued to do so in increments until late June, when the plant closed. The court accepted the company's representation that up to the day of the plant closing it could not have predicted the event.[28] Unions achieved an important section within the law, which provides that the act does not supersede state laws or collective bargaining agreements that require additional notice or assistance to workers. Thus union negotiators might argue that WARN is a starting point in negotiating benefits to laid-off or terminated employees.

The greatest advantage of advance notification is that workers and their community are given time to prepare for the action. For example, workers near retirement may inquire as to the status of their pension and decide to retire without unnecessary psychological strain. Other workers may choose to enter retraining programs offered by the employer or community agencies, and some will secure new jobs and thus avoid weeks or months of unemployment. In some cases, the additional notice can provide the time necessary for community, union, and company leaders to find a means of keeping the plant open.

A most persuasive argument is simply the humanitarian issue. Studies show that the incidence of alcoholism, suicide, child abuse, ulcers, and heart attacks increases to an alarming extent when workers are subject to plant closure.[29] In 1982, General Motors Corporation shut down its Fremont, California, automobile assembly plant, giving only three weeks' notice. A year later, Ford Motor Company shut down the nearby San Jose, California, plant, giving six months' notice and an extensive program of counseling, job training, and job search assistance. The total suicides at General Motors was eight—at Ford, none.[30]

The U.S. Chamber of Commerce and other employer lobbyists were very critical of the Plant Closing Act. They claim that advance notice of a closing may hurt a company's credit rating or reduce new customer orders. They also point to lower employee morale, absenteeism, and other problems as workers look for new jobs. A 1993 study of the effectiveness of the law by the General Accounting Office of the federal government pronounced it a flop. About half of the plants that closed in the preceding year were exempt from the law because of their size, and many of the rest did not provide enough notice or any notice at all. Noncompliance was blamed on a lack of knowledge about the law among employers and on the fact that no federal agency was charged with enforcement.[31]

In a landmark 1996 decision the U.S. Supreme Court recognized a new role for unions under WARN. In *United Food and Commercial Workers Union Local 751 v. Brown Group, Inc.*, the Court ruled that if an employer fails to give sufficient notice of a plant closing, the union may sue on behalf of the affected workers. The decision increased the authority of unions and will likely lead to similar suits because employees are usually hesitant to sue former employers for fear of retaliation. In the *Brown* case the company had sent a letter to the united Food and Commercial Workers Union indicating a plan to shut down operations in two months. However, the union filed a suit under WARN because Brown Shoe Co. had already laid off some workers. The union won 60 days' back pay for each of its workers.[32]

In another case, the Court found that, because the federal act had no time limitations on the bringing of a suit under it for failure to comply with its provisions, the laws in each state would be applied to determine the timeliness of the lawsuit. This interpretation will mean that in one state an employee might have one year to bring a suit against his employer for failure to notify him of a plant closing and in another state an employee could have five years.[33]

SHARED WORK/ SHORT-TIME COMPENSA- TION

Workers who have their work time (and therefore pay) reduced have become more numerous as management strives to cut personnel costs and remain competitive. This **shared work** concept has affected workers who had their hours cut one day per week (short-time) but at least retained their jobs and 80 percent of their income. Union leaders pressured to accept this proposal can rationalize that it is preferable for 100 percent of the employees to work 80 percent of their regular hours than to have 80 percent work 100 percent of their regular hours and have 20 percent laid off. Before the 1980s, short-time workers were ineligible for any unemployment insurance benefits because they continued to work a reduced number of hours each week. Thus, a "pro-layoff" bias existed because many would prefer total layoff, which would enable them to receive unemployment benefits.

Overall, the AFL-CIO has supported the short-time compensation concept as a means of reducing the number of workers who must experience the extreme hardships of total unemployment. However, the AFL-CIO does not endorse long-term use of shared work or view it as an alternative to the creation of permanent full-time jobs. In general, management has been slow to endorse the concept.[34]

DETERMINING ABILITY

In general, the burden of proof is placed on the employer to show that a bypassed senior employee is not competent for the job during promotions or layoff or recall actions. However, employers are not required to show that junior employees are more competent. When seniority and ability are given practically equal weight in contract clauses, arbitrators expect the employer to prove whether the ability factor was given greater weight than the seniority factor. In general, even though arbitrators may speak in terms of burden of proof when management's decision regarding ability is challenged, both parties are expected to produce any evidence supporting their respective continuances.[35]

Although it is generally agreed that management has the right to determine how ability is to be measured in cases involving promotion or layoff and recall decisions, there is no federal law or agreed-upon formula to specify exactly how such decisions should be made. Management generally uses a variety of factors to determine the ability to perform a job.[36] The specific factors may be limited by the contract clause prevailing in a given situation. However, the absence of any such clause gives management the freedom to determine its own factors and measurements. The factors or criteria most commonly used to determine an employee's ability to perform the job and make decisions of promotion or recall are summarized here.

1. **Tests**. Appropriate written, oral, and aptitude tests have been used to determine the ability of competing employees. Most arbitrators look very favorably upon the use of appropriate tests as fair and objective means of determining employee fitness to perform the job. Arbitrators have generally held that tests, in order to be used validly to determine ability, must be job-related, fair and reasonable, administered fairly without discrimination, and evaluated properly and objectively. Management should be prepared to show that the tests are directly related to the skill and ability required in the performance of the job. Also, employers should be able to prove that the tests were administered fairly and without discrimination.

2. **Experience**. This is the extent to which an employee has performed the particular job or relevant type of work and is completely separate from seniority. In most situations, experience is an important, related factor considered by management to determine an employee's fitness and ability to perform the job. If other factors are approximately equal, and the senior employee had had satisfactory experience performing the job in some capacity, experience may be considered the most important criterion. However, experience on the particular job in question is far more valuable than experience on related jobs.

3. **Trial period**. Some contract clauses provide that a trial period be given to the senior employee so his or her ability to perform the job is directly tested. The absence of such a specific provision gives management more flexibility in deciding whether to give the senior employee a trial period. Some arbitrators consider a fair trial period the best test of an employee's ability. However, management is not required to give the employee training on the job but instead allows a temporary period to determine if the employee has the ability. Thus, arbitrators have generally concluded that if there is a reasonable doubt as to the ability of the senior employee, a trial period should be granted, unless it would cause serious inconvenience to the company. Some labor contracts provide for a specific amount of time for the trial period; others only require a reasonable qualifying period and leave such determination to management.

4. **Opinion of supervisor**. The opinion of the supervisor to determine ability is seriously considered only if supported by factual evidence such as production records, merit ratings, or other specific job-related information. Periodic performance evaluations by supervisors are often an essential part of this documentation. Such merit ratings or rating scales generally include factors such as quality of work, knowledge of the job, cooperation with others, ability to accept orders, and attitude. If supervisory ratings include personal biases, the ratings are given less weight in employment decisions.

5. **Educational background**. Employee training on or off the job can be considered an important criterion. Such training must be job related to the specific job in question. The employee's formal education can also be considered if it is pertinent to the job.

6. **Production records**. Management may rely heavily upon an employee's production record as evidence of fitness and ability to perform the job. Certainly, an employee's past output reflects not only skills and abilities but motivation and effort. If there is a considerable difference among competing employees, arbitrators have held that management can consider production records as the sole factor if the selection is based upon ability.

7. **Attendance records**. If a senior employee has a particularly poor attendance record, he or she may be bypassed. The promotion of a junior employee over a senior employee on the basis of great differences in their attendance records has been generally upheld by arbitrators. The same is true if the senior employee has a poor disciplinary record.

8. **Physical fitness**. Contracts may specify physical fitness as a job requirement. Arbitrators will generally favor recent medical evidence and discard dated medical records. Unless prohibited by contract, management can require competing employees to take physical examinations, if all employees are required to take such examinations, and the results are job-related. A particular physical defect or limitation limiting the employee's ability to perform the job can be considered a pertinent reason to bypass a senior employee. Arbitrators have even upheld management's decision to bypass a senior employee on the grounds of obesity, if it has to some extent affected the employee's past work performance. An employee's temperament or nervousness, as exhibited in past job performance, may also disqualify a senior employee.[37]

COMPANY MERGERS

When separate companies or different entities merge, how the seniority lists of the two are combined is a critical question. The merger must specify which principle of combining seniority lists will be utilized. The most commonly used methods include the **Surviving Group Principle**, in which seniority lists are merged by adding the names of the employees of the acquired company to the bottom of the acquiring company. Thus, all the employees of the acquiring company receive greater seniority consideration than any employee of the acquired company. Another method, the **Length of Service Principle**, is used when an employee's length of service is considered, regardless of which company he or she worked for prior to the merger; therefore, the two seniority lists are combined with no employee losing any previously earned seniority. With the **Follow the Work Principle**, employees are allowed to continue previously earned seniority on separate seniority lists when their work with the merged company can be separately identified. The **Absolute Rank Principle** gives employees rank positions on the merging seniority lists equal to their rank position on the prior seniority lists. Therefore, two employees will be ranked first, followed by two being ranked second, followed by two being ranked third, and so on. The **Ratio-Rank Principle** combines seniority lists by establishing a ratio based on the total number of employees in the two groups to be merged. If Group A has 150 employees and Group B has 50 employees, the ratio is three to one and, of the first four places on the new seniority lists, the three ranked highest in Group A will be given positions one, two, and three, and the highest ranked position in Group B will be given rank four.[38]

A combination of methods is often used to combine seniority lists of merged units or companies, with weight being given to the different principles. For example, in merging two airline pilot seniority lists, one-third weight was given to the Ratio-Rank Principle and two-thirds to the Length of Service Principle.[39]

Subcontracting, Outsourcing, and Relocating

Although few problems arise when there are specific contract restrictions on management's rights to subcontract, management's insistence on freedom in this area often leads to grievances. A grievance over management's right to subcontract (or outsource) work during the agreement often results in arbitration. In the past, many arbitrators held that management has the right to subcontract work through independent contractors; however, in recent years, this practice has been somewhat restricted by arbitrators.

What is subcontracting? It has been termed the "Twilight Zone" of management rights in collective bargaining and is considered a headache by both labor and management. Basically, **subcontracting** may be defined as arranging to make goods or perform services with another firm that could be accomplished by the bargaining unit employees within the company's current facilities.[40]

Contract provisions against subcontracting may carry over to new employers, as when the Communication Workers of America won a $6 million settlement from AT&T over subcontracting. The 130 workers who won reinstatement of their jobs claimed that AT&T had violated the subcontracting clause contained in their agreement with Pennsylvania Bell. The breakup of the Bell system shifted the workers to AT&T, where they were laid off and their work, primarily wiring and installation of telephones, was contracted out. The union won reinstatement of their jobs and back pay for the 130 workers, and in addition, won back pay for another 900 workers and resolved more than 100 pending arbitration cases.[41]

Many union leaders and arbitrators believe that the recognition clause recognizing the union as the exclusive bargaining agent implies an agreement that the employer may not remove work from employees in the unit by subcontracting it to others during the life of an agreement. However, others argue that the National Labor Relations Act requires recognition of the union as a representative of people and not work; the purpose of the recognition clause is to enunciate the legal status of the bargaining unit required by the act. The clause merely describes the unit of the employees for whom the union speaks and thus delineates the agreement in terms of those employees covered. Therefore, it does not deal with and has no bearing on any specific employment terms or conditions. The decision was made, however, in a 1964 Supreme Court ruling, *Fibreboard Paper Products Corp v. NLRB*, that subcontracting was a mandatory subject for collective bargaining.[42]

An example of a contract clause limiting the ability of management to subcontract is provided in Figure 9-2. This example, however, will allow management to subcontract work. Management could subcontract work currently being performed by employees of the bargaining unit through another employer that has an agreement with the union. Thus no union jobs are lost to lower-paid, nonunion workers.

The historic agreement between the UAW and Ford Motor Company in 1996 included a unique outsourcing provision. As Figure 9-3 describes, the provision requires confidential notification by Ford when outsourcing is considered, the work involved, the reason for outsourcing, the impact on the workforce, and, most important, the promise by management to "work with and assist the union at both local and international levels to preserve jobs, replace jobs which may be lost by outsourcing action, and to create jobs for laid-off employees."[43] If this new

---

Subcontracting Provision   **Figure 9-2**

ARTICLE 6—SUBCONTRACTING

SECTION A: The Employer agrees that where portions of the Employer's contracts for construction, repair, or alteration are sublet or assigned to subcontractors, the subcontractor shall be required by the Employer to conform to all of the terms and conditions of this Agreement. The Union will not recognize a contractor's manpower request without first having a signed Agreement.

The Employer will not subcontract any work within the jurisdiction of the Union which is to be performed at the job site except to a subcontractor who holds an Agreement with the Union, or who agrees in writing, prior to or at the time of the execution of his subcontract, to be bound by the terms of this Agreement.

SECTION B: A contractor, company, or Employer acting in the capacity of a Construction Manager agrees that it, or any of its subcontractors, will not contract or subcontract carpenter work to be done at the site of construction, alteration, repair of a building, or structure except to a person, firm, or corporation party to a current Labor Agreement with the Union.

Source: *Agreement* between the Kentucky State District Council of Carpenters, Local Union 472 and Tri-State Contractors Association, 1995–1998.

Figure 9-3   Outsourcing Provision

FORD–UAW MEMORANDUM OF UNDERSTANDING SOURCING

The Company will work with and assist the Union at both the Local and International levels to preserve jobs, replace jobs which may be lost by outsourcing action, and to create jobs for Protected employees in GEN and laid off employees. It is an objective of the Company to grow the business and to continue to rely upon its employees and facilities as the source of its products. During the term of the 1996 Agreement, the Company will advise, in writing, the Union members of the sourcing group of the monthly **FAO Sourcing Council** meeting results, including the number of potential jobs affected. Additionally, data regarding work brought in-house and work outsourced will be given to the International Union in a quarterly meeting. (The Company will provide this data on a computer disk in addition to providing hard copy.) In this manner, the parties can judge the success of mutual efforts toward improved job security. The Company further agrees to address its sourcing during the 1996 Agreement, in accordance with the guidelines herein.

The rationale for sourcing actions will consider the criteria of quality, technology, cost, timing, statutory requirements, occupational and related environmental health and safety issues, the impact on long-term job stability, the degree to which the Company's resources can be allocated to further capital expenditures, the overall financial stability of affected facilities, and the impact on related facilities. Other factors considered by the Company before a final sourcing decision is made will include the effect on employment, and job and income security costs, on both a short and long term basis. The National parties will jointly further develop the above criteria to be used to address sourcing issues. In developing financial criteria appropriate Corporate return on investment and burden will be considered. Pertinent criteria will be applied consistently in comparisons of internal and external supply capability.

. . .

In addition the following specific commitments have been made to address sourcing-related job security concerns of UAW members:

1. **Insourcing**

    The National Committee and, where appropriate the Local Committee, will discuss the practicality of insourcing, in whole or in part, work previously outsourced or new work which the Union identifies as that which might be performed competitively within the location based on the criteria outlined above.

    If it is established that certain work can be performed competitively, judged by the above criteria, Management will adopt the Committee's proposal and, barring unique or unforeseen circumstances, bring the work in-house. The Union shall thereafter obtain any necessary approval or ratification within 30 days of the decision to bring the work in-house.

    . . .

2. **Outsourcing**

    Outsourcing as used herein means the Company's sourcing of work from Ford-UAW locations, including work connected with current, new or redesigned vehicles, fabricated parts, powertrain, and component products. When a market test is initiated, the International Union and the Local Union at the affected location(s) will be notified in writing by the Company. At such time as the sponsoring activity has received the results of a market test (or a similar point in the sourcing process when a market test is not applicable) and an outsourcing decision is contemplated, the International Union and the Local Union will be given written notice. **The notice shall be provided to the Union as far in advance as possible or promptly following FAO Sourcing Council approval, and**

consistent with the timing requirements of the Ford Product Development System.
The notice will **provide, on a confidential basis,** the reason for the outsourcing, a description of the work involved, the impact on the workforce, the identification of the sourcing authority, **the quality status of the recommended supplier, and a copy of all data contained in the financial analysis submitted to the FAO Sourcing Council.**

a. When such an outsourcing decision is contemplated at any level of the Company, the written notice will be given to the **Vice President and** Director of the National Ford Department. A copy of such notice will be given to the Chairperson of the Unit Committee at the same time.

b. When such a contemplated outsourcing decision is initiated by the Company at a level external to the affected location(s), the Company will provide sufficient advance written notice to allow the designated Management representative at the affected location(s) to comply with the notification procedure.

c. Additionally, International Union and Local Union input will be sought by the Company as early as possible in the outsourcing decision-making process. The intent of the evaluation period and Union input being sought as early as possible is to allow for more thorough discussion and to permit the parties to assess better the impact of outsourcing on the long-term job stability of employees and the financial viability of given Company locations.

d. The Company will not enter into a contractual relationship with a non-Ford-UAW supplier until such time as the designated Management representative of the affected location provides written verification that the above notification procedure and discussion by the local Committee has taken place.

　　Proposals to keep the work in-house will be made by the Union within 90 days of the receipt of the written notice. If it is established that the work can be performed competitively, judged by the criteria listed earlier in this Appendix, Management will, barring unique and unforeseen circumstances, keep the work in-house. The Union shall thereafter obtain any necessary approvals or ratification within 30 days of the decision to keep the work in-house.

e. The Company agrees to a full disclosure to the International Union of the procedures utilized in the sourcing decision-making process.

Source: *Agreement* between the UAW and the Ford Motor Company, 1996, pp. 236–240.

approach to outsourcing, peacefully negotiated between the union and management withstands the tests of time, economic downturns, and grievance arbitration, it could provide the model for what some have described as the most divisive labor issue of the 1990s.

Another, related, historic first occurred in 1996 when General Motors Corporation offered a lifetime employment guarantee (see Profile 9-1 on page 317), to the UAW—perhaps the ultimate job security provision.

Management's right to subcontract is usually judged by arbitrators against the recognition of the bargaining unit, seniority, wages, and other clauses within the agreement. Standards of reasonableness and good faith are applied in determining whether clauses in the contract have been violated by subcontracting. In general, management's right to subcontract is recognized, provided it is exercised in good faith. Arbitrators often recognize that signing a contract does not establish an agreement that all of the jobs will continue to be performed by members of the bargaining unit unless this condition is specified within the contract. However, the company cannot undermine the unit by subcontracting for the sole purpose of getting rid of work done by union employees in favor of nonunion employees who are paid lower wages. The standards that arbitrators generally apply to subcontracting cases are summarized here:

1. **Past practices**. Whether the company has subcontracted work in the past (64 LA 101, 63 LA 1143, 61 LA 526)
2. **Justification**. Whether subcontracting is done for reasons such as economy, maintenance of secondary sources for production, plant security, etc. (62 LA 421, 61 LA 530)
3. **Effect on union**. Whether subcontracting is being used as a method of discriminating against the union and substantially prejudicing the status and integrity of the bargaining unit (64 LA 602)
4. **Effect on unit employees**. Whether members of the union are discriminated against, displaced, laid off, or deprived of jobs previously available to them, or to lose regular or overtime earnings, by reason of the subcontract (63 LA 798, 62 LA 1000, 62 LA 895, 61 LA 333)
5. **Type of work involved**. Whether it is work that is normally done by unit employees, or work that is frequently the subject of subcontracting in the particular industry, or work that is of a marginal or incidental nature (62 LA 474)
6. **Availability of properly qualified employees**. Whether the skills possessed by available members of the bargaining unit are sufficient to perform the work (65 LA 598, 65 LA 431, 63 LA 883)
7. **Availability of equipment and facilities**. Whether necessary equipment and facilities are presently available or can be economically purchased (64 LA 1244, 63 LA 82, 62 LA 505)
8. **Regularity of subcontracting**. Whether the particular work is frequently or only intermittently subcontracted
9. **Duration of subcontracted work**. Whether the work is subcontracted for a temporary or limited period, or for a permanent of indefinite period
10. **Unusual circumstances involved**. Whether an emergency, special job, strike, or other unusual situation exists, necessitating the action
11. **History of negotiations**. Whether management's right to subcontract has been the subject of contract negotiations.[44]

Case 9-3 is a typical grievance about subcontracting.

An issue intertwined with subcontracting is management's decision to relocate work previously done at one location by union workers to another location that is generally nonunion. A Supreme Court decision in 1981, *First National Maintenance Corporation v. NLRB*, said that a management decision to *eliminate* work previously done by union workers was not a mandatory bargaining issue *if* the decision to eliminate the work was for economic reasons.[45]

The NLRB decided in *Milwaukee Spring II*[46] and in *Otis Elevator II*[47] that the decision to *relocate* work for economic reasons was akin to eliminating work for economic reasons and, therefore, was not a mandatory bargaining subject. Nonetheless, although a decision to relocate either all or part of the business is not a mandatory subject of bargaining, a company must bargain over the effects of such a decision.[48]

SUBCONTRACTING

Until January 1982, the company was in the business of installing and servicing equipment on trucks and selling parts. Since the 1950s the employees were classified as mechanic welders, painters, and utility men and were covered by collective bargaining agreements. It is undisputed that the company was losing money since 1979 and that by 1981 three of the four remaining unit employees were on layoff status.

In 1981, the company was approached by two individuals with an offer to take over the company's mounting and service work under a subcontract. An agreement was worked out, and the company hired the two parties as independent contractors for providing mounting and service work. The company was to lease its facilities and equipment to them. The subcontractor was to pay a percentage of the company's rent and utility bills and to provide various kinds of liability and other insurance. The company reserved the right to hire other subcontractors but reserved no right to exercise control over the employees of the subcontractor. The company notified its employees and the union of the subcontract agreement, citing the dire economic conditions that required the subcontract. The union grieved the layoff of employees as a violation of the contract, protesting that outside employees were performing work normally done by members of the bargaining unit. While the grievance was in progress, the union conducted an audit of the company's books and confirmed that the company was in a poor financial condition. The union offered to consider wage concessions to get the laid-off employees back to work, but the company declined because it deemed the concessions insufficient to address the cash flow problems. The company, citing the NLRB's reversal of the *Milwaukee Spring* decision, stated that before it can be found that a company has violated the act by subcontracting during the term of the contract, a specific term contained in the contract must be identified that prohibits such sub-

contracting. In addition, under the *Otis Elevator Company* case, a management decision to subcontract was not subject to mandatory bargaining because the essence of the decision turned upon a change in the nature or direction of the business and not upon labor costs.

The company stated that its decision to contract out service work turned not on labor cost but on a significant change in the nature and direction of the business; therefore, the company had no duty to bargain. The company's decision to subcontract was to reduce its overhead cost across the board so that it could remain in business. To that end, the subcontractor agreed to pay a specified percentage of the rent paid by the company for use of the premises, plus a monthly fee for the rental of the equipment. In addition, the subcontractor agreed to pay a specified percentage of utility bills, to produce liability insurance, and to maintain workers' compensation and other insurance. The company had made a decision to abandon its service and mounting operations. Therefore, on the basis of *Otis Elevator*, the company had no duty to bargain regarding its subcontracting decision.

Decision

Although the NLRB agreed that the company did not have to bargain its decision to subcontract, it found that the company unlawfully failed to bargain with the union about the effects of the subcontracting decision on union employees. The NLRB found that the company's notice to the union that the subcontract had been entered into, and its failure to meet with the union and laid-off employees for two months after the subcontract, was not sufficient notice and a meaningful opportunity to bargain with the union about the effect of subcontracting on unit employees. The employees were awarded back pay as is the customary remedy in such cases.

Adapted from *Gar Wood Detroit Truck Equipment*, 118 LRRM 1417 (1985).

Union

What are some practical protections against employers' relocating, outsourcing, or subcontracting?

Good contract language is the best protection against these employer actions. Good language would ensure no loss of jobs as the result of any of these actions during the life of the contract. It would also include processes for meaningful union input into the debate prior to these decisions' being made and into plans to ensure no adverse effect on present employees from such decisions if they are made. These processes would address plans for retraining and redeployment of existing staff if necessary, outplacement services, severance packages, re-employment rights, insurance and pension protections, and reasonable notice of any adverse action.

Management

What are the best ways an employer can outsource, relocate, or subcontract without violating the law or a collective bargaining agreement?

a. Retain specific management rights in each area in the collective bargaining agreement, with no restrictions or limitations.
b. Develop a credible business plan for when outsourcing, relocating, or subcontracting is necessary, in conjunction with budgeting, marketing, production, sales organizations, etc., with buy-in from all who assist in its development, which is defensible to the employees, the media, the public, and whatever board, arbitrator, or judge will ultimately hear the issue.
c. Give timely and appropriate notice to union leadership and then to employees as well.

In 1991 a newly constituted NLRB reconsidered its previous decisions and determined that a decision to *relocate* work was more akin to subcontracting than to eliminating work. Therefore, in *Dubuque Packing Co. v. NLRB*, the board determined relocating work to be a mandatory bargaining subject.[49]

However, unless an agreement contains specific language barring subcontracting, a union will have difficulty stopping it. They are generally not successful in winning arbitration cases based on a mere implication that it harms the bargaining unit.[50]

EMPLOYEE ALCOHOL AND DRUG TESTING

The use of **alcohol and drug testing** of job applicants and employees has become a complicated and critically important job security issue. Management often claims that the employee use of illegal drugs is a problem that is growing out of control.

Some estimates of substance abuse costs in the workplace are as high as $100 billion annually. One company, Motorola Inc., became a prime example of this claim in 1989. In that year the company discovered that it had an illegal drug-use problem among its 55,000 domestic workers. It estimated that lost time, impaired productivity, and health-care and workers' compensation costs attributed to drug use cost 40 percent of the company's net profit. In a year in which net profit was $500 million, the $190 million price tag for drug use was too much to ignore.[51]

Because of the huge cost, unions worry that management's approach to the problem will be an overreaction. They also fear that use of unreliable tests could result in the unjust discipline and termination of some of their members. They also claim that the tests can be biased against black and Hispanic workers and are an invasion of personal privacy.

According to a 1992 survey of 630 companies by the American Management Association (AMA), 90 percent of the largest businesses in the United States—those with more than 5,000 employees—have some form of drug testing or screening. The statistics on smaller companies, those with fewer than 500 employees, are almost as high, with 66 percent having some drug-testing program. The survey found that preemployment drug-testing programs continue to be utilized the most, with 73.5 percent of large businesses screening job applicants. Random drug-testing programs were also on the rise, with 33 percent of large businesses testing their employees. In January 1987, when the AMA began surveying the use of drug testing, about 22 percent of the firms asked had testing. In 1992, 85 percent had testing programs, and the percentage may continue to rise.[52]

In two landmark decisions, the NLRB ruled that the alcohol and drug testing of current employees is a mandatory subject of bargaining; thus, any such program must be negotiated with the union.[53] The NLRB reasoned that the test results could affect a worker's job security and therefore constituted a condition of employment; thus, the testing requires bargaining. However, in another case involving the mandatory testing of all job applicants, the NLRB ruled that management could unilaterally implement such a program without bargaining.[54] The board decided that the testing of job applicants who are not covered by a collective bargaining agreement is a management right.

Therefore, management may generally require any applicant to submit to a drug screening test, unless limited by a state law. Employers, in a statement of policy, may express their desire to hire only qualified applicants, and since the use of drugs may adversely affect job performance, they can choose to hire only applicants who pass a screening test. This concept was generally upheld by a U.S. Supreme Court decision in *New York City Transit Authority v. Beazer*.[55] The Court ruled that the safety and efficiency of the public transportation system constituted a valid business necessity and a justifiable reason to require drug testing of bus driver applicants.

Management's desire to screen all job candidates may increase because of several factors: (1) the increased use of drugs within all segments of society, (2) the reluctance of previous employers to report suspected or known drug usage of former employees for fear of litigation, and (3) the employer's liability for the negligent hiring of employees.

Preemployment testing policies often include clauses such as the following, developed by IBM and other employers:[56]

Notification. Notify applicants of the screening on the physical exam questionnaire. Notification minimizes claims of privacy invasion.

No rescheduling of test. Do not allow an applicant to reschedule a test after he or she appears at the doctor's office and realizes that it is part of the physical exam. The person may be a substance abuser who will refrain from illegal substance use before the next exam.

Test validity. In the event of a positive test result, repeat the test on the same sample in order to ensure validity. Ensure that test samples are kept by the doctor's office for 180 days in case of litigation.

Confidentiality. Maintain confidentiality by recording positive test results only on the doctor's records. On personnel records, use a code if someone fails the test. Only the applicant should be made aware of the test results, and the person can simply be informed that the results were unsatisfactory. This policy holds true for employees also.

The testing of current employees presents more difficult negotiation issues as well as the need to keep current with court and arbitration decisions. Management will generally test current employees under one of three policies:

Random testing. All employees are tested at random periodic intervals, or randomly selected employees are tested on predetermined dates.
Probable cause. An employee is only tested when his or her behavior causes a reasonable suspicion on the part of supervisors.
After accidents. All employees are tested after any industrial accident or major incident involving employees.

A 1996 case illustrates the last point. A worker involved in an on-the-job accident that damaged company property was fired after testing positive for cocaine. It was his second accident in eight months. The contract specified that termination be for "just cause" and that a prior warning was not needed if, while on duty, an employee was tested positive for illegal drugs. The union requested the worker be reinstated and asked for documentation of the chain of custody of the urine sample. The company declined to provide the documentation until the hearing. The U.S. 8th Circuit Court ordered back pay from the date of the discharge to the date of the hearing to the worker because of the company's breach of contract—to cooperate in the investigation. The court did, however, uphold the termination because there was sufficient evidence to support just cause.[57]

Employee Attitudes toward Drug Testing

Unions' institutional response to drug-testing programs originally focused on the struggle over bargaining duties; that is, could an employer institute a drug-testing program unilaterally? After the NLRB ruled that such policies have to be negotiated, unions were faced with the responsibility of representing their members' views on drug testing at the bargaining table. In the atmosphere created by government's "War on Drugs," less than a strong antidrug attitude was considered unpatriotic. Knowing that, unions no longer focused on *whether* drug testing would be done but on *how* it would be done.

Of the three policies, the use of random testing has raised the strongest criticisms by unions, largely on the basis of an employee's right to privacy. However, because of the random testing policies in the public sector and in industries regulated by the federal government, such as in the defense and transportation industries, the legal barriers to random testing have largely been removed.

Still, private sector unions in most negotiations will strongly resist random testing programs and insist on a probable cause or an accident-related program. Drug testing only when there is "probable cause" is a policy that will often be more readily acceptable by employees. Probable-cause testing has also received support from the courts and from arbitrators when the test has been given because of a reasonable suspicion of drug use. A supervisor's reasonable suspicion based on absenteeism, erratic behavior, or poor work performance can generally be accepted as reason to test.

A major accident involving employees can be considered an immediate probable-cause situation and can thus invoke required testing of all employees involved. The federal government regulation requiring railroads to test all crew members after major train accidents was upheld by the U.S. Supreme Court in the *Skinner* case.[58] The Court held that private railroads subject to federal regulations had to comply with the requirement that all members of a train crew must be tested after a major train accident. Both blood and urine tests are required.

Presented here are several negotiation issues regarding the probable-cause testing process and the use of test results:

1. **Valid testing procedure**. The burden of proof is clearly on management in questions regarding the use of confidential, fair, and valid testing procedures. Proper testing procedures include the use of an approved, certified laboratory with state-of-the-art tests. To guard against "false-positive" results leading to unfair discipline or other actions, a second, confirming test should be required. The testing procedure should also specify a "chain of custody" of the specimen. In *Amalgamated Transit Union*, for example, an employee fired for a positive drug test was able to show that the company failed to protect the chain of custody of the drug sample, rendering it useless to the disciplinary proceedings.[59]

2. **On-the-job impairment**. In cases involving discipline as a result of a positive drug test, an employee or union may contend that the tests prove the presence of a drug in the employee's body but not on-the-job use or on-the-job impairment. Indeed in *Shelby County Health Care Center*, the relevant provision of the contract limited drug- or alcohol-related major offenses to drug or alcohol use *on the employer's premises* or being "under the influence." A fired employee was reinstated because, although his drug test was positive, there was no on-the-job impairment.[60]

There is concern that positive drug tests involving illegal drugs might be used to discipline an employee for the illegal activity involved in obtaining and possessing the drug, regardless of the on-the-job effect. The employer's position is that an employee who engages in such illegal activity is not a fit employee. To date, however, arbitrators and courts often require a nexus between the employee's drug use and the behavior in the workplace before just cause for discipline is found. Such a relationship should not be difficult to find in most cases.

For example, in *Boise Cascade Corp.*, a drug-screening test was done on an employee after his involvement in an auto accident. Although the test found the presence of marijuana, the level was so low there was *no* finding of intoxication. The arbitrator, however, upheld the company's 60-day suspension and requirement that the employee join the employee assistance program. The arbitrator pointed to the employer's drug program, which the union had never challenged, that allowed that for disciplinary action "if drugs are detected." No on-the-job impairment was necessary.[61]

3. **Refusal to be tested**. Management can usually sustain the termination of an employee for failure to take a drug test in cases of probable cause. In *Warehouse Distribution Centers*, the employer was told that his employee had been seen in a car in the company parking lot "blowing a joint." On the basis of that report, the employee was directed to have a drug test taken, but the employee refused. The collective bargaining agreement provided for disciplining an employee who refused to take a drug test if there is suspicion of drug use. The arbitrator found sufficient grounds for the employer's suspicion and upheld the firing.[62] However, if there is

no probable cause for the test, an employee is within his or her rights to refuse to take the test as a protest against an unwarranted invasion of privacy. In *Gem City Chemicals*, management unilaterally added a drug screen to a negotiated annual "physical examination for environmental effects." There was no demonstrated drug problem at the plant. The grievant refused to submit to the test as part of his annual physical and was discharged for his refusal. The arbitrator reinstated the employee because requiring the test under that circumstance was not reasonable.[63]

And just as with other fireable offenses, the employee must be *warned* that failure to submit to testing will result in discharge. After a truck accident, a supervisor who smelled beer on the driver's breath asked him to take a blood alcohol test. The driver at first agreed and accompanied the supervisor to the hospital. However, before the test he changed his mind and declined to take the test. The arbitrator found no evidence that the supervisor made it clear to the employee that failure to take the test would result in disciplinary action, and the employee was reinstated.[64]

4. **Supervisor training**. A program that includes the training of all supervisors to recognize the typical signs of employee drug use is important if probable cause is the basis of testing. Any challenge to the reasonableness of a supervisor's request for a test is likely to be discounted if the supervisor has participated in an appropriate training program.[65] Although many supervisors may be able to detect alcoholic intoxication, detection of drug abuse is more difficult to recognize without training.

Whether unions are indeed representing their members' views in negotiating drug-testing programs was the subject of an interesting survey. In 1989, 930 union members were surveyed on their attitudes toward various drug-testing programs. Approximately 29 percent of those surveyed had drug-testing programs in their workplace; 71 percent did not. The survey hoped to discover if union members' attitudes regarding drug-testing programs were greatly influenced by their own personal workplace experience or if the attitudes among union members were fairly uniform.[66]

The survey results indicated that drug testing, on the whole, is acceptable to union members provided it is limited. The union members already covered by drug-testing programs, however, were somewhat less comfortable with all types of drug testing and with a policy discharging employees who failed the test than were those persons not currently covered. The survey results are summarized in Table 9-1.

Table 9-1	**Comparison of Attitudes of Union Members Who Are Covered and Not Covered by Drug-Testing Programs (as percentage of respondents by group)**		
		Covered	Not Covered
	1. Agreed to probable-cause testing	61.7	71.8
	2. Agreed to random testing	14.8	17.9
	3. Agreed to preemployment testing	69.5	71.4
	4. Agreed to discharge of employee who tested positive	28.5	38.4

Source: Adapted from Michael H. LeRoy, "The Presence of Drug Testing in the Workplace and Union Member Attitudes," *Labor Studies Journal* 16, no. 4 (Fall 1991), pp. 41–42.

If there is a change in either a collective bargaining representative or an employer, parties to an unexpired collective bargaining agreement may not be certain of their status. This situation may exist when the union becomes decertified, or because of a schism, merger, or change in union affiliation, or if the union simply becomes defunct and is replaced. Questions may arise by management when the sale of all or part of a business occurs because of a merger or corporation consolidation or if the corporation is reorganized. The courts refer to these situations as **successorship**.

The law on successorship provides that, if there is a genuine change in the collective bargaining representative, the existing collective bargaining contract, even if unexpired, is not binding on the successor representative. If a genuine change of employer exists but the employing industry remains substantially the same, the successor employer is required to recognize the existing collective bargaining unit and its representative but is not bound by the agreement.

The U.S. Supreme Court for the first time offered a test for determining the circumstances under which the successorship doctrine applies in *Fall River Dyeing v. National Labor Relations Board*.[67] A new company, Fall River Dyeing, acquired the plant, equipment, and remaining inventory of a textile dyeing and finishing plant (Sterlingware Corporation). The union that had represented the production employees of Sterlingware sought and was refused recognition by Fall River Dyeing. The union filed an unfair labor practice charge, and the NLRB upheld its claim. The Supreme Court upheld the NLRB decision and imposed a bargaining duty on Fall River Dyeing under the successorship doctrine. The Court in its decision suggested three factors that must be present for the successorship doctrine to apply to the purchaser of a business employing union members:[68]

1. **Substantial continuity**. The successor substantially continues the business operations of the predecessor. Factors considered include the purchase of real property, equipment, and inventory; employing workers on essentially the same jobs; employing the same supervisors; and continuing the predecessor's product line. In general, not all factors must be present for substantial continuity.
2. **Appropriate bargaining unit**. The bargaining unit(s) of employees must remain appropriate after the change of employers. Job duties and operational structure are critical in this determination. Significant change in the nature of jobs performed or in the means of operation may mean that the unit is no longer appropriate.
3. **Predecessor's workers**. The new employer hires a majority of its employees from the predecessor.

The new employer has several important rights even as a successor employer, including (1) the right to hire its own workers (although it may not discriminate against workers of the predecessor because of union status), (2) the right to disregard the predecessor's collective bargaining agreement, and (3) the right to set the initial terms of employment, such as wages, benefits, and working conditions, without consulting the union.[69]

A successor employer, however, may also be obligated to remedy an unfair labor practice committed by its predecessor. If it is a true successor, and if it had notice of the unfair labor charge, the NLRB may require the new owner to remedy the unfair labor practice by, for example, reinstating an employee and providing back pay.[70]

A successor employer may be obligated to arbitrate the grievances filed under the predecessor's collective bargaining agreement. So, although a successor employer is not bound by the prior employer's collective bargaining agreement, it is bound to arbitrate violations. If the collective bargaining agreement contained a *successor clause* that stated that the predecessor employer agreed to "require" a purchaser of the company to honor the collective bargaining agreement *and did not do so*, a union may be able to force the successor employer to honor that agreement through arbitration.[71]

The NLRB further delineated the successorship doctrine in the *Canteen Company* case in 1996. In this case, the NLRB found that the employer was obligated to bargain with the union about terms of employment. The employer had acquired a unionized plant from another company. The employer then interviewed and offered jobs to some employees and discussed possible new provisions with the union. The NLRB found that by making job offers to some employees and discussing the compensation package with the union, the employer had "demonstrated a clear intention" to hire a majority of its new workforce from among the workforce of the former employer; thus it had violated the NLRA by not bargaining with the union.[72]

SUMMARY

Job security and seniority are vital to collective bargaining agreements. Both labor and management strongly believe that they must maintain certain rights where job security affects the employee's ability to keep his or her job and successfully compete for higher positions. Seniority, or length of service with the organization, and the employee's ability to perform the job successfully are the two primary factors considered in layoff and promotion situations for both union and nonunion companies. An effective job security system also requires that the labor agreement contain a fair and just discipline and grievance system so that management's decisions regarding promotion or layoff and recall can be properly disputed by labor.

Seniority systems have generally been utilized because they are easy to develop and provide an objective, unambiguous means of considering employees when job openings occur. The theory behind using seniority is that if the employees are approximately equal in ability, then the employee who has the greatest length of service should be given the opportunity first. This practice is commonplace in nonunion as well as union organizations. Unfortunately, there are not always objective measures of ability to perform. The difficulty lies in determining the relative ability of competing employees.

Seniority systems and employee feelings of job security are meaningless unless contract provisions limit management's ability to subcontract work. Without such provisions, management can subcontract work temporarily and force severe hardships on employees, causing them to leave and lose their seniority. Certainly, although union leaders agree that subcontracting is necessary in some situations, it can and has been used to undermine labor unions.

The use of an alcohol- and drug-testing program on current employees covered by a collective bargaining agreement must be negotiated at the bargaining table. Unions generally will agree only to probable-cause testing and will strongly object to random testing of all workers. Both sides express great interest in several aspects of any testing program, including the testing procedure, on-the-job impairment, and basis for probable-cause testing.

If a change in employers occurs, the successor is not bound by existing collective bargaining agreements. Also, if a genuine change in business has occurred, the new employer is not required to recognize the union.

ANTINEPOTISM RULE

Facts

The employer is a Union Local of Electrical Workers with a job referral office in St. Louis. The union is the bargaining agent for the employer-union's office employees. The grievance concerns the employer-union's policy that it will not employ spouses and close relatives of its members as full-time office personnel. The St. Louis office employs a business manager, a business representative, and two office workers. When the business manager and business representative are out of town, the clerical workers, in addition to their usual tasks, are responsible for the operation of the union's hiring hall. The procedure for calling up workers under the hiring hall is that an unemployed worker signs up on the list and his or her name goes at the bottom of the list within the same classification. When employers call for referrals, the office personnel start at the top of the list to call the union workers. However, the usual order of calling up workers may be altered when the requesting employer asks for workers with a special skill or when the worker is on the list but is currently employed on a short-term job and is given the opportunity to take a longer- or better-term job.

The employer-union had a longstanding rule that it would not hire spouses or close relatives of its members to be full-time office personnel to avoid the potential for abuse and because of and the need to avoid any appearance of favoritism in the selection of workers through the hiring hall. The grievant was an office worker who was forced to resign when she married a union member.

It is the employer-union's position that the collective bargaining agreement does not prohibit an antinepotism policy; that the policy was of long standing and had been consistently applied in the past and that the grievant had prior notice; that both parties had notice of this policy prior to negotiation; and that such a policy was necessary to the business of the union in maintaining a bona fide hiring hall free from any allegations of discrimination or favoritism.

The union's position was that the grievant could have lived with her spouse without the benefit of marriage and not have violated the policy, showing that the policy was arbitrary and capricious, and that there was no basis for the employer-union to say that such policy was necessary for the efficient, orderly, and safe operation of the workplace.

Questions

1. If you were the arbitrator, would you decide for the union or the employer-union? Why?
2. Explain why control of a union hiring hall is so important to both parties in this case.

Adapted from *Electrical Workers*, IBEW, 90 LA 383 (1987).

DRUG TESTING

Facts

The company and the union had negotiated a typical substance abuse prevention and treatment program in their collective bargaining agreement. It prohibited the use of legally obtained drugs and alcohol if such use adversely affected the employee's job performance. It also prohibited the sale, purchase, transfer, use, or possession of illegal drugs "on the work premises or while on employer business." It allowed for testing in the following circumstances: for reasonable cause, after on-the-job accidents or incidents, for safety-sensitive jobs, and for reinstatement after treatment for drug or alcohol abuse. The collective bargaining agreement also stated, in a separate article, the general principle that "there is no intent to intrude upon the private lives of employees."

The employee tested positive for an illegal substance after an on-the-job accident and was enrolled in an inpatient treatment program. At the completion of the program he was reinstated subject to the normal provisions that he would continue with aftercare treatment and submit to random testing for three years. The employee was a member of a work crew that reported to work on a regular schedule and was not subject to being called in. In fact, if he chose not to report to work with his crew, there was no penalty. The employee had been called for a random drug test and had been tested eight times, all of which were negative. The ninth time he was called, he was contacted at home on a day he was not scheduled to work and was told to report for a drug test. In this instance, he tested positive and the company dismissed him. The union appealed.

The union position was that: the collective bargaining agreement prohibited intrusion into the private lives of employees; the drug policy prohibited only on-the-job impairment or abuse; random testing can be used only in relationship to the workplace (i.e., when the employee is, should or may be reporting to work, at work, or about to leave work). The employee was not scheduled to work, was not on the employer's premises or business, and was not subject to being called in to work. His reinstatement agreement to submit to random drug tests meant only those types of random tests consistent with the substance abuse policy (i.e., for on-the-job impairment).

The company's position was that: because some employees can be called into work at any time, the conduct of random testing needs to be on a 24 hours a day, 7 days a week basis; the union had not previously objected and a past practice can be argued; the employee had violated the collective bargaining agreement by drug use on the job and had agreed to submit to random testing for three years in order to be reinstated, so an argument can be made that his testing then *is* job-related; the fact that this employee could elect not to report to work on any given day reinforces the need to be able to test him on his off-duty time.

Questions

1. As the arbitrator, give your reasons for ruling in the union's favor. Then give your reasons for ruling in the employer's favor.
2. Argue for and against a decision by the employer in this case to insist on expanding the drug program to include the prohibition of sale, possession, or use of illegal substances on the employees' own time.

Adapted from *New Orleans Steamship Association*, 105 LA 79 (1995).

REVIEW QUESTIONS

1. Why is seniority considered a critical issue? What are the advantages and disadvantages of using a seniority system?
2. How is seniority generally calculated?
3. Describe the different methods by which labor agreements might consider seniority in a promotion decision.
4. Why is seniority often used in layoff and recall actions? Specifically how do contract clauses provide for the consideration of seniority in such decisions?
5. Under what circumstances might the employer bypass a senior employee and promote a junior employee when the labor agreement contains a seniority clause?
6. Why is a seniority system important to a labor group's union security?
7. Why has management's right to subcontract work been the subject of many grievances?
8. What are the key issues in an employee alcohol- and drug-testing program?
9. How does the successorship doctrine affect union security?
10. When is a successor employer required to recognize a union from the previous employer's business?

TAKE IT TO THE NET

We invite you to visit the Carrell/Heavrin page on the Prentice Hall Web site at:

http://www.prenhall.com/carrellr

for this chapter's World Wide Web exercise.

Job Security Provisions   **EXERCISE 9-1**

Purpose:
To appreciate the issue of union security.

Task:
Job security has become a critical negotiation issue for most unions. Unions have witnessed the loss of hundreds of thousands of jobs in the past 10 to 20 years because of nonunion and foreign competition, technological change, and

decertification elections. Today unions are increasingly creative in their efforts to secure their level of employment and a full work-week for each worker.

Your task is to review the specifics of labor negotiations reported in the local newspaper. Identify three different methods of job security described in the news articles. Discuss why they are job security methods and which, if any, are different from the ones discussed in this chapter.

EXERCISE 9-2 | Merging Seniority Lists

Purpose:
To utilize a group decision-making process with an issue involving seniority.

Task:
Covington Custom Window Mfg. Co. recently bought a smaller window firm, Ft. Wright Windows. Both had a job classification, aluminum workers, and were represented by locals of the Aluminum, Brick and Glass Workers International Union. Neither of the agreements, however, contained a provision on how seniority lists should be combined should a merger occur.

Your tasks, in groups of three to five, are to: First, discuss the five merger principles presented in the chapter: Surviving Group, Length of Service, Follow the Work, Absolute Rank, and Ratio-Rank. Second, combine the two lists using each of the five principles. Third, select the method you would recommend in this situation and develop a written explanation of your decision. Fourth, review the merged lists and provide a written analysis of what effects the merger principle you recommended may have on the morale of the people involved.

CURRENT SENIORITY LISTS

Covington Mfg. Co. (Est. 1988)

1. Paul Joseph (9 years)
2. Don Willen (9 years)
3. Anne Kling (9 years)
4. Carol King (9 years)
5. Mark Nutter (7 years)
6. Christy Nutter (7 years)
7. Mary Gronefeld (7 years)
8. Bill Gronefeld (7 years)
9. Peggy Gronefeld (7 years)
10. Jeremy Kling (6 years)
11. Sam Brown (6 years)
12. Steve Arvizu (5 years)
13. Gilbert Rojas (5 years)
14. Harvey Sloane (5 years)
15. Bill Stansbury (5 years)
16. Franklin Dixon (5 years)
17. Mary Anne Ryan (4 years)
18. Carolyn Hensley (4 years)
19. Peggy Breeze (4 years)
20. Wasu Chin (4 years)

Ft. Wright Mfg. Co. (Est. 1954)

1. Archie Carrell (37 years)
2. Myrtle Jaggers (35 years)
3. Shari Brown (28 years)
4. Brooks Wilson (24 years)
5. Gary Green (20 years)
6. William Ryan Jr. (17 years)
7. Robert Hatfield (15 years)
8. Donna Shipley (11 years)
9. Johnny Ryan (7 years)
10. Bob Hillard (6 years)
11. Jay Vahaly (6 years)
12. John Nelson (4 years)
13. Kathy Chicago (2 years)
14. Bob Shinn (2 years)
15. Sue Vahaly (1 year)
16. Bob Myers (1 year)

Covington Mfg. Co. (Est. 1988)

21. Francis Lamb (4 years)
22. Ping-Ping Woo (3 years)
23. Ev Mann (3 years)
24. Boyd Wang (3 years)
25. Colleen Carrell (3 years)
26. David Banks (2 years)
27. Steve Magre (2 years)
28. Amber Maureen (1 year)
29. Alexis Savannah (1 year)
30. Anna Belle Michaels (1 year)
31. Ralph Swanson (1 year)
32. Sue Clater (1 year)

If you are using Smith/Carrell/Golden *Collective Bargaining Simulated, 4E,* with this text, please refer to the following:

p. 15, Article VII: Seniority, for a definition employee seniority rights and the layoff and recall process.

CHAPTER 10

Implementing the Collective Bargaining Agreement

- Reducing an Agreement to Writing
- Contract Enforcement
- Rights and Prohibited Conduct
- Summary

Striking union workers urged passing motorists to boycott Fischer products during a 1993 labor dispute.

Clergy Leaders Renew Union Ties

Fifty-seven ministers, priests, and rabbis held a press conference in Newark, New Jersey, to pressure a New Jersey dairy to settle a strike and to criticize its two-tier wage offer as too low to support a family. Rabbi Arthur Hertzberg explained that the clergy members who support such actions believe that "people are becoming poorer and less secure . . . and people in the clergy like me who grew up during the New Deal are going back on the warpath to defend the weak. Under these circumstances, where else would you expect the clergy to be but on the side of labor?"

In Morganton, North Carolina, 25 members of the clergy prayed in front of Case Farms poultry plant. They pressed management to sign a union contract offer and to provide better working conditions. In New York a labor-religion coalition organized a 1,000-person fast in 40 cities to protest Governor Pataki's health and welfare cuts.

Not since the Great Depression in the 1930s or the farm workers' movement of the 1970s have so many religious leaders joined labor leaders in a common cause. They are pressuring employers into accepting contract offers and are denouncing sweatshops, organizing workers, and supporting higher wages and better working conditions.

Adapted from Steven Greenhouse, "Unions, Clergy Renew Ties on Behalf of Working Class," *Louisville Courier-Journal*, August 18, 1996, p. A2.

Whereas the interest of management and labor is usually focused on the months of negotiations necessary to arrive at a collective bargaining agreement, the negotiated agreement is implemented over a much longer period. It is that period of implementation that tests the success of the collective bargaining process. That success is measured not only by the fact that a contract is signed but also by the quality of its terms and the willingness of the parties to administer the contract fairly. This chapter examines implementation and includes an overview of grievance and arbitration issues; economic activity during a contract term; and the rights of labor, management, and individuals under a collective bargaining agreement.

REDUCING AN AGREEMENT TO WRITING

Duty

At some point in the labor-management relationship governed by the National Labor Relations Act, agreement is reached on wages, hours, and other terms and conditions of employment. Today the agreement is written, but when the National Labor Relations Act was passed, the act did not expressly require that a collective bargaining agreement be reduced to writing and signed by the parties. Nor did it address whether bargaining was to be a process of continuing negotiations or even what the legal status of a signed agreement might be. These questions were left to the National Labor Relations Board, the courts, and Congress to answer in piecemeal fashion.

As early as 1941, the Supreme Court imposed a **"duty to sign"**: or a *duty upon the parties in a collective bargaining relationship to reduce to writing and sign any agreement reached through the bargaining process.* A refusal to sign was declared a refusal to bargain collectively and an unfair labor practice because, the Court found, a signed agreement had long been informally recognized as a final step in the bargaining process. The Court thought it obvious that the employer's refusal to sign an agreement "discredits the [labor] organization, impairs the bargaining process, and tends to frustrate the aim of the statute to secure industrial peace through collective bargaining."[1] In the Taft-Hartley Amendments, Congress recognized the need for a written agreement and defined the bargaining duty as including "the execution of a written contract incorporating any agreement reached if requested by either party."[2]

Part of the negotiator's role in the collective bargaining process is drafting the final agreement. The negotiator should try to be clear and concise, while accurately reflecting the agreement and understanding of the parties. One author suggests that, before it is signed, the final agreement should be circulated for comment among nonnegotiating union and management personnel whom it will affect.

> Once contract provisions are committed to paper, a good test of their meaning is to have a wide variety of different individuals, wholly unfamiliar with what has transpired during negotiations, read and interpret each provision of the contract. Particularly appropriate candidates for this **provisional intent test** are those who enforce, administer, police, or are governed by the terms of the agreement—stewards, foremen, department superintendents, shop chairmen, plant managers, grievance committeemen, rank-and-file members, etc. If provisional meaning is misconstrued, revision is in order.[3]

Nature of the Labor Agreement

The agreement between a union and an employer is not an employment contract. The employment contract is between the employer and the employee. It may be expressed verbally or in writing, or it may simply be a function of the employer's job offer and the employee's acceptance. The union is not a party to this employment contract, but the agreement between the union and the employer does shape the terms of that independent employment contract by establishing company policy in the areas covered by the agreement. The labor agreement also serves to define the union's relationship with management and provides the means to enforce its provisions.

Each labor agreement is unique in terms and language, but all have basic similarities. Most labor contracts contain four main sections: union security, wage and effort bargain, management rights, and administration.

Union Security.   The contract needs to identify the parties to the agreement, the parties' authority, and the conditions and duration of their authority. The bargaining unit is described generally in terms of employees in job categories included or excluded from coverage under the agreement. By law the union is the exclusive bargaining agent for the unit described. The contract might go further than that and provide for certain union security provisions. These can include the following:[4]

1. *Union shop.* Requires that a new employee join a union after a certain period.
2. *Maintenance of membership.* Requires that union members remain members during the contract term.
3. *Agency shop.* Requires nonmembers to pay union dues and fees as if they were members, but does not require actual membership.
4. *Hiring halls.* Requires an employer to seek employees through a union hiring hall. Nonunion members can and legally must have access to the referrals and can be charged a fee by the union.
5. *Modified union shop.* Requires membership of new hires, but permits current members to remain nonunion.

A contract must run for a specific term. Most contracts contain renewal provisions, with prior notice of termination or of a time for reopening negotiations. Contracts can have **openers**—clauses that allow for negotiations to proceed during the term of the contract on one or more items, generally wages.

A majority of contracts (about 64 percent) contain three-year terms, as shown in Table 10-1. A movement from one-year to three-year terms was aided by the NLRB in a general ruling that extended the contract bar rule (see next section) to a three-year period.[5] In recent years, the number of contracts with periods extended to four or five years has steadily increased (to 30 percent, up from only 5 percent in 1986). The desire by both labor and management to provide greater long-term stability in labor relations has greatly motivated negotiators toward longer multiyear agreements.[6]

In a study conducted on 373 contracts signed in the 10-year period from 1977 to 1987, researchers concluded that there was a positive relationship between increases in wage rates and the terms of a contract. Employers were, by and large, willing to increase wage rates in exchange for a longer contract term. In addition, contracts with COLA (cost-of-living adjustment) provisions had longer terms than those without. Finally, the study concluded that the average length for all contract

Table 10-1 — Length of Contract Term (frequency expressed as percentage of industry contracts)

	Duration in Years			
	1	2	3	4 or more
All industries	1	5	64	30
Manufacturing	1	2	67	30
Apparel	—	10	81	11
Chemicals	6	6	70	18
Electrical machinery	—	28	47	25
Fabricated metals	—	—	81	19
Food	—	—	100	—
Furniture	—	—	100	—
Leather	—	—	43	57
Lumber	—	—	77	23
Machinery	4	—	77	19
Paper	—	—	100	—
Petroleum	—	—	56	43
Primary metals	—	4	56	40
Printing	13	13	75	—
Rubber	—	—	100	—
Stone, clay, and glass	—	—	70	31
Textiles	—	—	70	30
Transportation equipment	—	3	74	24
Nonmanufacturing	1	9	60	30
Communications	—	10	60	30
Construction	7	14	59	20
Insurance and finance	—	14	86	—
Maritime	—	—	38	63
Mining	—	—	58	42
Retail	—	7	59	33
Services	4	11	63	22
Transportation	—	12	60	28
Utilities	—	—	60	40

Source: Bureau of National Affairs, *Basic Patterns in Union Contracts*, 14th ed. (Washington, DC: BNA Books, 1995), p. 2. Copyright © 1995 by The Bureau of National Affairs, Inc., Washington, DC 20037. Used by permission.

terms had increased during the study period, perhaps reflecting a desire on the part of both management and union to establish some stability in labor-management relations.[7]

Wage and Effort Bargain. With or without a labor agreement, the employer-employee contract contains a wage and effort bargain. If a union exists, collective bargaining can determine the contents of that employment agreement. Areas primarily covered in this section are as follows:

1. *Pay scales*. Hourly, weekly, or monthly wage or salary paid for the job, usually determined by job classification and compensation schedules or earnings based on work output such as piecework systems

2. *The effort bargain.* Acceptable standards for the task performance measured in work crew sizes and tasks, quotas, or work rules
3. *Premium pay.* Includes overtime, call-in pay, shift differentials, and weekend work
4. *Contingent benefits.* Includes insurance, pensions, paid time off, and severance pay

Management Rights.   The area of labor relations known as **management rights** has evoked more emotion and controversy than any other single issue. At the core of the debate is the concept of management's right to run the operation versus the union's quest for job security and other protections for its members.[8] Management rights provisions are found in almost all contracts in a section labeled *management rights*; union rights, however, are usually scattered throughout a contract according to subject matter.[9]

Of course, the question of who controls the workplace is of great interest to both management and labor. Management rights generally include decisions governing the working environment, including supervising the workforce, controlling production, setting work rules and procedures, assigning duties, and the use of plant and equipment. Management generally believes that if it is to operate efficiently, it must have control over all decision-making factors of the business. Management also contends that any union involvement in the area is an intrusion on its inherent right to manage. Union advocates respond that where the right to manage involves wages, hours, or working conditions, labor has a legal interest under federal law.[10] Arthur Goldberg, former secretary of the U.S. Department of Labor and U.S. Supreme Court Justice, summarizes the management rights issue:

> Somebody must be boss, somebody has to run the plant. People can't be wandering around at loose ends, each deciding what to do next. Management decides what the employee is to do. However, right to direct or to initiate action does not imply a second-class role for the union. The union has the right to pursue its role of representing the interest of the employee with the same stature accorded it as is accorded management. To assure order, there is a clear procedural line drawn: the company directs and the union grieves when it objects.[11]

A management rights clause often appears at the beginning of a contract following the union recognition and security clauses. An example of a common management rights clause follows:

ARTICLE III
Management

The management of the plant and the direction of its working force are vested exclusively in the Company. These functions are broad in nature and include such things as the right to schedule work and shift starting and stopping time, to hire and to discharge for just cause, to transfer or lay off because of work load distribution or lack of work. In the fulfillment of these functions the Company agrees not to violate the following Articles or the intent and purpose of this Contract, or to discriminate against any member of the Union.[12]

Reserved Rights.   In addition to explicit management rights specified in the contract (as illustrated in the example), there are also residual, implied, or **reserved rights** not found in the language of the agreement. The reserved rights theory generally contends that management retains all rights except those it has expressly agreed to share with or relinquish to the union.[13] Management, under the reserved rights concept, does not review the agreement to determine which rights it has gained but instead reviews the agreement to ascertain which rights it has conceded to labor. All rights remaining reside with management.[14]

One area of management rights that has received a great deal of attention since the 1980s involves a management decision to *relocate* its operation, in whole or in part. Previous Supreme Court decisions had decided that if a company planned to "subcontract" work currently being done by union workers, that decision was a mandatory bargaining subject.[15] However, if the company was deciding to close down part or all of its operation, such a decision was *not* a mandatory bargaining subject.[16]

The NLRB, therefore, first likened management's decision to relocate part or all of its facility to the decision to close a plant, and it ruled in *Otis Elevator Co.* that relocating was *not* a mandatory bargaining subject.[17] After the federal court rejected that comparison, the NLRB, in *Dubuque Packing Co.*,[18] compared *relocating* to *subcontracting* and reversed itself, deciding it *was* a mandatory bargaining subject.[19]

Restricted Rights. Restrictions of management rights are common in contracts (87 percent) as union negotiators strive to delineate the union's rights in specific areas of decision making. Contracts may contain these **restricted rights** in a general statement restricting management from "taking actions in violation of the terms of the agreement." Specific restrictions of management rights, or conversely the providing of union rights, are most often found in the following contract clauses:[20]

- *Subcontracting* of work to outside firms (contained in 55 percent of all contracts)
- *Supervisory performance* of bargaining unit work, except for training, in an emergency, conducting experiments, developing new products (58 percent)
- *Technological changes* in work methods or equipment (such as robots) without union approval or the retraining of displaced workers (26 percent)
- *Plant shutdown or relocation* without advance notice and transfer rights to a new location (23 percent)
- *Union rights* of access to bulletin boards, pertinent information, and company premises (94 percent)

Administration. Most contracts provide for the machinery necessary to enforce the terms of the agreement. On-the-job representation is given by union shop stewards and officials. External enforcement is provided through arbitration provisions.

Contract Bar

Through its decisions over the years, the National Labor Relations Board established a **contract bar** doctrine stating that a current and valid contract can prevent another union from petitioning for an election and being certified as the exclusive representative. The board developed this doctrine as a balance between two competing interests under the National Labor Relations Act: the right of employees to choose their bargaining representatives and the need to achieve stability in labor relations through negotiation of collective bargaining agreements.

It is the NLRB's theory that if a union has negotiated and signed an agreement on behalf of its members, another union should not be allowed to seek recognition during the life of that agreement. Certain elements must be present to ensure that the contract acts as a bar to a representational election:

1. The contract must be in writing and signed by the parties. An oral agreement cannot be a bar.
2. The contract must be for a fixed term. An indefinite term expiring upon some happening in the future cannot bar an election, nor will the board honor a contract with an unreasonably long term. Currently, the NLRB views a three-year contract as reasonable. Any contract of longer term will not bar an election to change representation at the end of the three-year period.
3. The contract must provide substantive terms and conditions to ensure a stable employer-employee arrangement. If a contract covered wages alone, it probably would not operate as a bar.
4. The contract must be duly ratified if ratification by the membership is required.
5. The contract must contain only legal provisions. Clauses that discriminate on the basis of race, religion, and so on, or that clearly violate union security provisions of the act cannot bar a new election.
6. The contract must not be prematurely extended. The NLRB allows employees the right to change representation during the **open period**—the first 30-day period in the 90 days before termination of the original contract.

A 1996 case provides an example of item 6. The U.S. Supreme Court unanimously ruled that an employer had violated Section 8(a)(1) of the NLRA, which protects the union's rights, when the employer disavowed a contract. The union in the case had accepted the company's last contract proposal, but the employer disavowed the contract the next day because 16 (of 23) employees had complained about the union and 13 had resigned from the union. The Court ruled that to preserve industrial peace and stability the NLRB presumes that a union has majority support during the term of any contract, once negotiated, up to three years. Only at the end of the contract, during the open period, can employees seek to change representation.[21]

Under the contract bar doctrine, if a rival union wants to win the bargaining rights of a unit, it must petition for an election and win it during the open period—that is, between the 90th and 60th day prior to the contract's expiration. Once the end of an open period arrives without the filing of a petition, the incumbent union becomes insulated from another union's petition, and if a new agreement is reached before the old one expires, the new one presents a new contract bar.[22]

Once contract negotiations begin, the employees cannot petition for a change in representation. This **insulated period** begins 60 days before the contract is due to expire. Therefore, negotiations must not take place during the open period so that employees will have an opportunity to change representation.

CONTRACT ENFORCEMENT

Collective bargaining agreements are enforced through judicial proceedings by either the NLRB or the courts, through adherence to grievance procedures by the parties to the contract and arbitration, or through resorting to economic self-help pressure activities.

Judicial Proceedings

National Labor Relations Board. The National Labor Relations Board has the authority to investigate and prevent unfair labor practices as listed in Section 8 of the National Labor Relations Act. Violation of a provision of a collective bargaining agreement is not in and of itself an unfair labor practice. Therefore, enforcement and interpretation of a contract provision might come within the jurisdiction of the National Labor Relations Board only if the matter also involves a violation of the unfair labor practice provision. The board may be involved in contract enforcement if the contract has incorporated a statutory obligation it already has jurisdiction to enforce or if a contract has incorporated an unlawful provision it is called upon to invalidate.

For example, if an employer is accused of refusing to bargain during the term of the contract by making a unilateral change in the wage structure or other term of employment, by subcontracting work, or by refusing to supply information the union seeks, and if the employer claims that the contract justifies his or her action, the NLRB can *interpret the lawful contract clause*. The board is called upon to investigate and determine the validity of the employer's claim.

The board's interpretive power might also be apparent in a case involving a union security clause or the provisions of a grievance procedure in which a contract is used by an employer or a union to defend the discharge or disciplining of an employee, and that employee claims a violation of the National Labor Relations Act.

In representation cases, a party may claim that proper interpretation of a contract places him or her under its protection and provisions. Thus, the NLRB's definition of the parties to a collective bargaining agreement can have great impact.

The NLRB may *invalidate a contract or clause* if it finds that the union acted under an erroneous though good faith claim that it had majority representation; in a successorship situation in which one union has dissolved or merged with another; or when a business has changed hands. Contract clauses impinging upon areas prohibited by the act will come before the board for validity tests. Items tested include union security clauses, discriminatory provisions, hot cargo clauses (in which union members refuse to handle goods from a nonunion employer), and breach of a union's duty of fair representation. Also, a petition and election for representation not barred by an existing contract may invalidate an existing contract.

The NLRB may also show support of contracts and contract clauses by interpreting the contract as a waiver of statutory rights. Often, claims that a statutory right of a party has been violated, based on specific language in the collective bargaining agreement, result in an NLRB finding that the party waived those rights when entering into the agreement. Numerous cases have come before the board in which a union is found to have waived the right to bargain over such issues as employee qualifications, employer subcontracting, or administration of a merit rating system. These have been so decided because of specific language in the contract reserving those items to the employer.

The NLRB may even go past the specific language of the contract and explore the bargaining history of the parties to determine if there has been a waiver of a statutory right. The present law on waiver is summarized as follows:

1. There is a continuing statutory duty to bargain, even during the term of a contract.
2. The continuing duty to bargain embraces not only grievances but also all mandatory subjects that are not contained in a contract for a fixed period.
3. A party may waive his right to bargain, either by relinquishing a right to bring up a particular subject or by agreeing that the other party may exercise unilateral control over the subject.
4. Such a waiver must be clear and unmistakable and must indicate an acquiescence, agreement, or conscious yielding to a demand.[23]

However, a statutory right to receive information is not waived by waiving a right to bargain over the issue. In one case, the board found that, although the union gave the employer the prerogative to discharge for lack of work, it did not in the contract forestall a grievance or a claim for information to justify the discharge when the employer took such action.

The enforcement of existing collective bargaining agreements also comes under the NLRB's jurisdiction when it has been claimed that unilateral action by the employer has modified the contract. Or an employer might claim that the union has violated the act by strike action called to force bargaining on a modification of an existing contract. It is an unfair labor practice to terminate or modify an existing contract during its life except under the conditions outlined in the statute.[24]

Court Enforcement. Prior to the Taft-Hartley Amendments, employers and unions could sue in state court for breach of contract if one party believed the other party violated a collective bargaining agreement. Most state courts viewed the collective bargaining agreement as a legally enforceable obligation. Unions could obtain injunctions to restrain employers from violation of wage provisions or to require employers to abide by a union shop agreement. The employer could obtain an injunction against strikes in breach of a valid no-strike clause. Still, contract enforcement for the employer was difficult because many labor unions were not incorporated. In some states such unincorporated organizations could not be sued; thus, the employer had to sue each union member individually. Even if the unincorporated union could be sued for specific injunctive relief, monetary damages might not be available.

The Taft-Hartley Amendments were an attempt to lessen the unions' power by allowing access to federal courts on suits for collective bargaining contract violations. The amendments specifically recognized labor unions as entities that could be sued and held liable for monetary damages. The legislative intent of the Taft-Hartley Amendments was interpreted by the Senate as follows:

> If unions can break agreements with relative impunity, then such agreements do not tend to stabilize industrial relations. The execution of an agreement does not by itself promote industrial peace. The chief advantage which an employer can reasonably expect from a collective labor agreement is assurance of uninterrupted operation during the term of the agreement. Without some effective method of assuring freedom from economic warfare for the term of the agreement, there is little reason why an employer would desire to sign such a contract.
>
> It is apparent that until all jurisdictions, and particularly the federal government, authorize actions against labor unions as legal entities, there will not be the mutual responsibility necessary to finalize collective-bargaining agreements. The Congress has protected the right of workers to organize. It has passed laws to encourage and promote collective bargaining.
>
> Statutory recognition of the collective agreement as a valid, binding, and enforceable contract is a logical and necessary step. It will promote a higher degree of responsibility upon the parties to such agreements, and will thereby promote industrial peace.
>
> It has been argued that the result of making collective agreements enforceable against unions would be that they would no longer consent to the inclusion of a no-strike clause in a contract. . . .
>
> In any event, it is certainly a point to be bargained over and any union with the status of representative under the NLRA [National Labor Relations Act] which has

bargained in good faith with an employer should have no reluctance in including a no-strike clause if it intends to live up to the terms of the contract. The improvement that would result in the stability of industrial relations is, of course, obvious.[25]

Grievance Procedure and Arbitration

Later chapters of this book deal with the practical aspects of contract enforcement through grievance and arbitration procedures. The development of grievance and arbitration as a means of contract enforcement and the relationship and effectiveness of this type of enforcement as compared with court and NLRB enforcement are discussed here.

Development of Arbitration Rights.   The American common law tradition is that an employee is an employee at will, with the terms and conditions of employment established by the employer with virtually no restriction. Although this tradition allowed either party to terminate the relationship and therefore was seen as fair and equitable, the employee had little real protection from poverty. It was in the public interest, therefore, that the government enter into the employer-employee relationship. It could enter either by enacting laws to regulate terms and conditions of employment, including questions of wages, bonuses, fringe benefits, discharge and employment standards or by using legislation to regulate the relationship between employer and employee. The National Labor Relations Act reflects the latter choice. Its provisions speak to the requirement for collective bargaining but not to the substantive provisions of the employment contract, and those provisions have resulted in the development of *arbitration*, a system of private enforcement of publicly protected rights. The National Labor Relations Act itself did not embody arbitration provisions.

The real development of labor arbitration as we know it today, and indeed the virtual transformation of the usual meaning of the word, came as a result of World War II, the War Labor Board and the impermissibility of the strike weapon as a method of resolving questions of interpretation and compliance with collective agreements and of providing the interstitial lawmaking which the interpretive process implies.

As a result of this development, we have in this country a system of nongovernmental law which provides not only the rules concerning the rights of em-

---

TIPS FROM THE EXPERTS

Arbitrator

What are the three most common "drafting errors" in collective bargaining contracts that cause problems for an employer or the union?

a. *Failure to define a contractual term or phrase.* Arbitrators give words their ordinary and usual meaning unless there is an indication that the parties intended a special meaning.

b. *Failure to specify the scope of the arbitrator's authority.* For example, is the award binding, or merely advisory? Does the arbitrator have the usual authority to review the penalty imposed once he or she determines that the grievant did commit the offense with which he or she was charged?

c. *Failure to encourage resolution of grievances at the earliest possible step.* Such a failure would encourage open and full discovery and exchange of information in the lower grievance steps and could enhance the prospects of settlement or avoid the element of surprise at the arbitration hearing.

---

ployees against employers but also the system of adjudication of controversies concerning the applications of those rules.[26]

The public had become responsible for the enforcement of the right to a specific process, but it had not gained the right to substantive protections.

The collective bargaining agreements entered into by parties subject to the act after the War Labor Board Policy of World War II gave each side protective rights enforceable through the use of arbitration. In most contracts, a grievance procedure provides a union the right to seek compliance with a contract provision through a system of formal or informal meetings between union and management. Such procedures may cause the employer to comply simply because the grievance is brought to the employer's attention. However, if the grievance involves disagreement over facts, the meaning of the collective bargaining agreement, application or implementation of the agreement, or the reasonableness of an action, it might not be resolved without the intervention of a third party. Thus, *arbitration* can also be the resolution by an outside party of a grievance dispute. If the parties to a collective bargaining agreement agree to a grievance arbitration procedure in the contract, substantive rights granted under that contract are enforced by the arbitration award.

Court and Board Enforcement. As discussed earlier, state and federal courts have enforcement powers in collective bargaining agreements. In the **Lincoln Mills** case, the Supreme Court, by accepting such enforcement powers, required specific performance of an employer's promise to arbitrate in a collective bargaining agreement.[27] The Court felt that the agreement to arbitrate grievance disputes was the employer's trade-off for the union's agreement not to strike.

The role of arbitration and court enforcement of contract agreements was more specifically outlined in three Supreme Court cases known as the **Steelworkers Trilogy**.[28] These cases held that the function of the court is limited to a review of whether the issue to be arbitrated is governed by the contract. Any doubt as to the coverage should be resolved in favor of arbitration. Unless the arbitrator's award is ambiguous, it should be enforced by the courts even if the court would not have decided the substantive issue in the same way.

> The 1960 *Steelworkers Trilogy* expanded vastly upon the foundation laid in *Lincoln Mills*. Arbitration was acknowledged as the preferred, superior forum for contract interpretation and enforcement. The powers of an arbitrator were held to be bounded by the restrictions of the "four corners of the contract" but arbitral actions were largely immunized from judicial review. As repeatedly stated thereafter, arbitration became the cornerstone of the rapidly arising edifice housing the federal law of the labor agreement.[29]

The Court gave almost complete deference to arbitration as a means of contract enforcement by limiting its own review of an arbitration to whether the issue under arbitration is in the agreement.

In a study of federal and district court decisions for the 30 years following the *Steelworkers Trilogy*, it was found that the courts deferred to the arbitration process 70 percent to 74 percent of the time. Tables 10-2 and 10-3 present the results of this study by court and years.

The National Labor Relations Board also deferred its jurisdiction in certain unfair labor practice cases to an arbitration procedure established under the contract. In the **Collyer** decision, the NLRB agreed to defer jurisdiction if there was a

Table 10-2 District and Circuit Court Decisions Ordering Arbitration (1960–1990)

	Decisions Ordering Arbitration	Decisions Dismissing Petitions to Order Arbitration	Total Number of Decisions	Percentage of Decisions Ordering Arbitration
District courts: 1960–1981	68	24	92	73.9
District courts: 1982–1990	40	12	52	76.9
Total District courts: 1960–1990	108	36	144	75.0
Circuit courts: 1960–1981	23	7	30	76.7
Circuit courts: 1982–1990	16	11	27	59.3
Total Circuit courts: 1960–1990	39	18	57	68.4

Source: Michael H. LeRoy and Peter Feuille, "The *Steelworkers Trilogy* and Grievance Arbitration Appeals: How the Federal Courts Respond," *Industrial Relations Law Journal* 13, no. 1 (1992), p. 100.

Table 10-3 District Court and Circuit Court Decisions Enforcing Awards (1960–1991)

	Decisions Enforcing Award	Decisions Vacating (or Denying Enforcement to) Award	Total Number of Decisions	Percentage of Decisions Enforcing Award
District courts: 1960–1981	372	134	506	73.5
District courts: 1982–1991	352	150	502	70.4
Total District courts: 1960–1991	724	284	1,008	71.8
Circuit courts: 1960–1981	140	47	187	74.9
Circuit courts: 1982–1991	161	79	240	67.1
Total Circuit courts: 1960–1991	301	126	427	70.5

Note: Decisions that did not result in the award's being enforced or denied were omitted; 1991 cases include only decisions ruling on public policy challenges to awards.
Source: Michael H. LeRoy and Peter Feuille, "The *Steelworkers Trilogy* and Grievance Arbitration Appeals: How the Federal Courts Respond," *Industrial Relations Law Journal* 13, no. 1 (1992), p. 102.

stable collective bargaining relationship between the parties, the party defending the charge was willing to arbitrate the issue, and the dispute centered on the contract and its meaning.[30]

The board also decided to defer to an arbitration award if the arbitration procedure met the following criteria:

1. **Fair and regular proceedings**. That the proceedings are the equivalent of due process, affording parties an opportunity to be heard, cross-examine witnesses, be represented by counsel, and have an unbiased decision maker.
2. **Agreement to be bound**. Both parties must agree to abide by the arbitrator's decision. A hearing over the parties' objections would not be honored.
3. **Award not repugnant to purposes and policies of the act**. Even if due process is followed, the arbitrator's award can be invalidated if it violates the purposes of the National Labor Relations Act. For example, an arbitrator upheld a dismissal of an employee for being disloyal, but his so-called disloyalty was in seeking help from the National Labor Relations Board. The board did not uphold that award.
4. **Unfair labor practice to be considered by arbitrator**. The actual issue surrounding the unfair labor practice must be reviewed and decided by the arbitrator or the NLRB will not defer to the award. Deciding other issues between the parties is immaterial.[31]

The courts narrowly construe the ability of a court to provide a public policy exception to the enforcement of an arbitration award. The Supreme Court ruled in the *Misco* case that to vacate an arbitrator's award, it must be clearly indicated that the award violates public policy on the basis of laws and legal precedents and not on general consideration of supposed public interest.[32] The study referenced in Tables 10-2 and 10-3 confirms that since the *Misco* decision fewer federal or district courts overturned an arbitration decision on public policy grounds.[33]

Since the 1971 *Collyer* decision, the NLRB has continued to reaffirm its policy to defer to arbitration in unfair labor cases.[34] A comparison of NLRB awards and arbitration decisions and grievance settlements in one study found that when the unfair labor practice involves a complaint from an individual because of discipline of a union member, the arbitration or grievance procedure often results in the same or nearly the same result as an NLRB award. However, cases involving a charge that the employer has refused to bargain in good faith have less frequently been decided by an arbitrator or settled by the parties in the same manner as similar cases that were decided by the NLRB.[35] Case 10-1 is an example of a decision by the National Labor Relations Board to send the parties to arbitration.

Economic Activity

The resort to economic pressure as a means to enforce a contract obviously is not the preferred method, as evidenced by the support given arbitration in court decisions. A union slowdown or strike countered by an employer lockout or mass dismissal seems at odds with the National Labor Relations Act's aim of promoting industrial peace. But the resort to economic activity, or at least the ability to resort to economic activity, is a key element in the success of the collective bargaining process.

Earlier chapters detailed the use of economic weapons, strikes, and other concerted activity during recognition campaigns and during negotiations. Although

CASE 10-1

DEFERRING TO ARBITRATION

The union and the company were unable to reach agreement on a contract, and a strike ensued. A strike settlement agreement provided that all unresolved contractual issues after 30 more days of negotiations would be submitted to final and binding arbitration. This was done, and an arbitration award resolving major contractual provisions was made. The company refused to sign the contract and instead announced that it would close down its plant. In preparation for such closing, it began to lay off employees. The union grieved and alleged that the company was discriminating in its layoffs against union members who had participated in the strike. The arbitrator began hearing the cases but examined the layoffs only from the standpoint of discharge for "just cause" and did not address the discrimination issue. The company requested that the union be directed to submit whatever proof it had of discrimination; the union did not comply. After the individual employees who were laid off were given

arbitration awards, the union charged the company with an unfair labor practice on the basis of discrimination, and it sought relief from the National Labor Relations Board.

Decision

The National Labor Relations Board reiterated its decisions in the *Spielberg* and the *Collyer* cases: To discourage dual litigation and forum shopping, the board would encourage parties to settle their contractual disputes through arbitration. In this case, the issue of discrimination could clearly have been presented to and decided by the arbitrator. The union chose not to do so, believing it could decide the issues of unjust dismissal with the arbitrator and then go to the National Labor Relations Board for a decision on the discrimination charge. Therefore, the board refused to review the discrimination charge because the union had failed to present it at the arbitration level.

Adapted from *Electronic Reproduction Service Corp.*, 213 NLRB 110, 87 LRRM 1211 (1974).

use of economic power to enforce an existing contract has become increasingly rare because of mandatory grievance and arbitration procedures and no-strike clauses in labor agreements, such action has not disappeared.

The Supreme Court, in the **Boys Market, Inc. case**, upheld an injunction against a union that struck over an arbitrable grievance despite a no-strike clause and a mandatory grievance procedure.[36] But the Court noted that not all such strikes would be enjoined. It adopted strict standards from an earlier case:

> When a strike is sought to be enjoined because it is over a grievance which both parties are contractually bound to arbitrate, the district court may issue no injunctive order until it holds that the contract does have that effect; and the employer should be ordered to arbitrate, as a condition of his obtaining an injunction against the strike. Beyond this, the district court must, of course, consider whether issuance of an injunction would be warranted under ordinary principles of equity—whether breaches are occurring and will continue, or have been threatened and will be committed; whether they have caused or will cause irreparable injury to the employer; and whether the employer will suffer more from the denial of an injunction than will the union from its issuance.[37]

Thus, a union does have an effective weapon despite a no-strike clause if the grievance does not factually come under the contract arbitration procedure, if the employer is not willing to arbitrate, and if the employer cannot show where he or she has suffered irreparable injury from the breach of the no-strike obligation.

The Supreme Court later upheld the right of a union to engage in a sympathy strike pending an arbitrator's decision on whether such a strike was forbidden under the particular no-strike clause of the labor agreement.[38] The strike had been called in support of another union properly engaged in an economic strike. Although the arbitration procedure could be invoked to decide the scope of the no-strike clause, the Court would not allow the union's strike to be enjoined pending that decision. The NLRB, in its decision in *Indianapolis Power and Light Company*,[39] attempted to create a presumption that broad no-strike clauses were intended to cover sympathy strikes, but the U.S. Court of Appeals overruled that presumption in 1986 in *International Brotherhood of Electrical Workers, Local 387 v. National Labor Relations Board*.[40] The court said a no-strike clause must be interpreted according to the terms of the particular collective bargaining agreement, the bargaining history, and the past practices of the parties to determine its application to sympathy strikes.

RIGHTS AND PROHIBITED CONDUCT

Certain rights and duties arise during the term of a contract. These include the rights of the individual under the collective bargaining process, the duty to bargain during a contract term, and the duty to refrain from prohibited economic activities.

Individual Rights

Right to Refrain from Union Activities. Because of the National Labor Relations Act, labor relations has developed into a stylized system of employer-union relations. In an election decided by majority rule, a union is given the authority to represent all the employees of an appropriate unit in negotiation and administration of a contract. Individual employees who may have voted against the union still find their employment contract affected by the negotiations, and, although the union has a duty to represent fairly all employees during the negotiation process, absent a showing of actual hostile discrimination, the court will accept a wide range of reasonableness when a question of a breach of that duty arises.

Originally the National Labor Relations Act allowed an employer to make an agreement with a union to require union membership as a prior condition of employment—that is, the closed shop. All forms of union security were permitted, as long as the agreement was made with a bona fide union representing the bargaining unit. Closed-shop clauses became common in collective bargaining agreements. Although these clauses protected and promoted the growth of unions, abuses of the system against individuals who were denied job opportunities led to the Taft-Hartley Amendments. These amendments made the closed shop an unfair labor practice and added the right *not* to organize and engage in union activity. Although union shop clauses still could be negotiated and enforced against existing employees, the employee need only pay dues to abide by that contract clause; no other activity was required. The amendments also allowed state right-to-work laws to outlaw even the union shop requirement.

The union hiring hall is another practice that appears to give equal consideration to union and nonunion personnel. Although a hiring hall operating as a closed shop was technically outlawed by the amendments, a union can still negotiate a contract clause that requires the employer to hire through the union's exclusive referral system. It is then up to the nonunion individual to claim and prove discriminatory referrals. Case 10-2 illustrates the fine line between union discrimination and discrimination in general in union hiring halls.

Union security clauses are not the only prohibited behavior violating the individual employee's right to refrain from union activity. The courts consider union intimidation, reprisals, or threats against employees as restraint and coercion.

Duty of Fair Representation. Under its duty of fair representation, a union must consider all the employees in the bargaining unit when negotiating an agreement and must make an honest effort to serve their interests. This must be a good faith effort, without hostility or arbitrary discrimination. But the end result of such negotiations may still unevenly affect one, several, or a class of employees without the union's being considered in breach of its duty.

CASE 10-2

UNION HIRING HALL

The union and the companies signed a three-year collective bargaining agreement that included a provision relating to the hiring of casual or temporary employees as follows:

> Casual employees shall, wherever the union maintains a dispatching service, be employed only on a seniority basis in the industry whenever such seniority employees are available. . . . Seniority rating of such employees shall begin with a minimum of three months service in the industry, irrespective of whether such employee is or is not a member of the union.

The union did indeed maintain such a hiring hall and would refer casual laborers to the employers upon request. One union member who had customarily used the hiring hall was employed without going through the hiring hall. When the union complained to the employer, the union member was fired. The union member filed charges against both the union and the employer to the NLRB, and the NLRB found that the hiring hall provision in the contract was unlawful per se and that the discharge of the union member at the union's request was a violation of both the employer's and the union's duty not to discriminate against union members. The board further ordered that the company and the union cease using the hiring hall provision. The union appealed the board's ruling to the federal courts.

Decision

The district court reversed the NLRB decision and found in favor of the union. The court pointed out that Congress had not outlawed the hiring hall, although it had outlawed the closed shop and the use of hiring halls as a de facto closed shop. As the language of the hiring hall provision itself provided that nonunion members would not be discriminated against, the board could not find that the hiring hall arrangement was discriminatory per se. Although the court did find discrimination in the actual facts of the case, it was personal and not the encouraging or discouraging union membership discrimination that is outlawed by the Taft-Hartley Amendments.

Adapted from *Local 357, Teamsters v. National Labor Relations Board*, 47 LRRM 2906 (1961).

A far more litigious area concerning fair representation is in *contract enforcement*. Grievance arbitration has become the most common method of enforcing each party's promise to abide by the contract. That promise to arbitrate is enforceable by either the employer or the union. Fitting the individual into that arbitration system involves balancing conflicting interests.

The National Labor Relations Act adopted the doctrine of majority rule when it granted a union exclusive representation rights if selected by most unit members. The courts confirmed this doctrine by giving the collective agreement precedence over the individual employment contract. To balance the power of the union, the court recognized the union's duty to represent all of its employees.

But there remained a question of whether an individual employee could arbitrate against both or either party. In *Vaca v. Sipes, Hines v. Anchor Motor Co., Inc.*, and *Bowen v. U.S. Postal Service*, the Supreme Court indicated that the individual has no absolute right to have a grievance arbitrated and that the union is liable to the employee only if, in processing and settling that grievance, it violates its fair representation duty.[41]

In contract administration issues, the duty of fair representation is breached when a union's conduct is arbitrary, discriminatory, or in bad faith. A union may not arbitrarily ignore a meritorious grievance or process it in a perfunctory manner. Yet proof of the merit of a grievance is not enough under this test: Arbitrary or bad faith actions must also be proved.

The subjective nature of the fair representation test has left unions with "Hobson's choice." If a union cannot be reasonably certain that its honest and rational decision not to pursue a grievance to arbitration will withstand a *Vaca* challenge, the arbitration process will be so burdened that its effectiveness and financial viability will be undermined. At the same time, the *Vaca* rule ensures an individual that, although there is no absolute right to arbitrate a grievance, the union cannot behave in a capricious fashion, as demonstrated in Case 10-3.[42]

Due Process.   The individual employee has a right to due process of law under a collective bargaining agreement. This process includes a right to *substantive due process*, which is fair treatment by the employer in any action taken against an employee, and a right to *procedural due process*, which comprises a fair hearing on that action.

In general, in substantive due process, the policy or standard invoked must be known by the employee and must be reasonable. In addition, a violation of policies must be proved, and the burden of proof is on the employer. The application of rules and policies must be consistent; certain employees cannot be singled out for discipline. Also, actions must be impersonal and based on fact.

In procedural due process, any contractual procedures for employment actions must be followed. Equally important, the arbitration procedure must be fair. The individual must receive fair representation by the union; a hearing must be held so that the individual can be heard in an unbiased setting; and the employer's reasons for bringing the action must be made known.

Duty to Bargain During the Contract Term

The standards for good faith collective bargaining contained in the National Labor Relations Act include the duty to bargain during the contract term under certain circumstances. The duty, however, is not absolute. The language of the act

DUTY OF FAIR REPRESENTATION

The plaintiff had been discharged by the company for intoxication and abusive language. He filed a timely grievance protesting his discharge. The grievance proceeded to the third step, which required the union to file a statement of unadjusted grievance to invoke arbitration. The local union never filed such a statement, although it sought and received two extensions to do so. After the union had missed the two extensions, the company disclaimed any further obligation under the agreement to arbitrate. The plaintiff instituted intra-union procedures charging unfair representation by the union and, having lost, filed in federal court. The plaintiff alleged that a union official's hostility toward him had caused that official not to file the statement of unadjusted grievance. The lower court concluded that there was no unfair representation because the union official had merely negotiated to file the required statement and that, even if the official was hostile toward the plaintiff, the plaintiff had to show that the hostility caused the official's neglect. Therefore, the lower court concluded that the union had not unfairly represented the plaintiff because it had merely neglected to file the grievance and had not acted in bad faith.

Decision

The Supreme Court reversed the lower court's decision and found that the union had violated its duty of fair representation by violating at least one of the three tests in the *Vaca* decision—arbitrary, discriminatory, or in bad faith. It pointed out that a union must adhere to three separate standards: First, it must treat all factions and segments of its membership without hostility or discrimination; second, in asserting the rights of its individual members, the union must exercise its discretion in complete good faith and honesty; and, third, it must avoid arbitrary conduct. Any one of those standards may be violated and cause the union to be charged with unfair representation. In this case, the appropriate official's neglect in filing the third stage of the grievance procedure without deciding the plaintiff's claim was without merit, was clearly arbitrary, and was a perfunctory handling of agreements. As such, it was unfair representation.

Adapted from *Ruzicka v. General Motors Corp.*, 523 F.2d (6th Cir. 1975).

provides that a party cannot be required to discuss or agree to terminate or modify the contract during its term. In addition, the contract under which parties operate may limit the duty in the following ways:

1. **Zipper clause.** An abbreviated form of the waiver provision in a collective bargaining agreement, sometimes referred to as a "wrap-up" clause, considered to denote waiver of the right of either party to require the other to bargain on any matter not covered in an agreement during the life of the contract, thus limiting the terms and conditions of employment to those set forth in the contract. A clause of this type would read:[43]

   This contract is complete in itself and sets forth all the terms and conditions of the agreement between the parties hereto.

2. **Opener clause.** A clause that allows negotiations to take place during the contract term on certain mandatory items. Most clauses provide for the reopening of negotiations on only one specific issue while the remainder of the contract

is closed to discussions. The most common issue specified in reopeners is wages; specific benefits are also common issues.[44]

3. **Separability clause**. Most contracts contain a clause that protects the rest of the contract should one section come into conflict with state or federal law. Such a clause usually provides that the offending section becomes null and void, or, as in the following Article XIV from the agreement between duPont Co. and the Neoprene Craftsmen Union, the section must be renegotiated as needed:

ARTICLE XIV
Suspension of Provisions of Agreement

Section 1. If during the life of this Agreement there shall be in existence any applicable rule, regulation or order issued by governmental authority, which shall be inconsistent with any provision of this Agreement, such provision shall be modified to the extent necessary to comply with such law, rule, regulation, or order.[45]

Union Demand to Negotiate.   A question of bargaining during the contract term may arise when the union seeks to add new items not covered under the contract. This situation highlights the two competing views of collective bargaining. One view is that the collective bargaining agreement does not end the collective bargaining process. It is a continuous process, albeit with rules as to how the process should proceed. Many people believe that the grievance-arbitration procedures are a part of that process because those decisions shape the administration of the contract and therefore its terms. The opposite view is that the collective bargaining process must be completed with the signing of the contract to give meaning to the contract terms. Because bargaining should encompass all subjects, the final agreement should settle all subjects either explicitly or implicitly between the parties. Under this view, the grievance-arbitration procedure only interprets the contract and adds nothing to its terms. The National Labor Relations Board's attitude to a union demand for bargaining on a new item during a contract term seems to be that, without a zipper clause, if the item is not contained in the contract and was not discussed during negotiations, the employer has a duty to bargain on that item.[46]

Employer's Unilateral Action.   Most often the question of the duty to bargain during a contract term arises as a result of unilateral action by the employer. Depending on the circumstances, such action may be deemed an unfair labor practice as a breach of that duty to bargain. The questions of whether a substantive or procedural provision of a contract was violated arise when an employer takes unilateral action during a contract term and makes a change in some condition of employment.

If the employer's action changes a stated term of the contract, the answer is simple. The employer has committed an unfair labor practice. However, if under a broad management rights clause the employer takes an action affecting employees in a manner not contemplated by the contract, disagreement as to breach obviously occurs. As a rule, the NLRB considers charges of unfair labor practice by a union in this instance a matter for arbitration and, under the *Collyer* decision, will defer its jurisdiction to the arbitrator.

Even under a management rights clause in which the final decision is the employer's, a contract may contain a requirement that the union must be consulted prior to any action. An employer who violates this procedural requirement is in breach of the contract and of his or her duty to bargain during its duration.

Prohibited Economic Activity

The National Labor Relations Act, as amended by Taft-Hartley and Landrum-Griffin, outlawed four specific economic pressure techniques that unions might try to employ during the term of a contract: secondary boycotts, hot cargo agreements, jurisdictional strikes, and featherbedding.

Secondary Boycotts.   Section 8(b)(4) of the National Labor Relations Act prohibits a union from engaging in, or from inducing others to engage in, a strike or boycott aimed against the goods or services of one employer to force the employer to cease doing business with another employer. This prohibition was a response to the labor movement's use of the **secondary boycott** to affect employer A by exerting economic pressure on those who do business with employer A. Primary economic activity such as a boycott by employees against an employer is not prohibited by this section, nor is a secondary boycott with an objective that is not statutorily forbidden.

The Supreme Court attempted to give guidance on the distinction between a primary and a secondary boycott. A **primary boycott** occurs when persons who normally deal directly with the work involved are encouraged to withhold their services. This type of boycott is not prohibited and includes, for example, appeals to replacement workers or delivery people not to cross a picket line, or appeals to employees of subcontractors not to continue work essential to the operation. Even if the picketing takes place at the work site of the secondary employer, it may be protected if the work involved is the object of the dispute.

However, inducement of persons indirectly related to the work in question is a *secondary boycott* and is prohibited. For example, there is a prohibition against attempting to stop a subcontractor from crossing a picket line and entering a plant site if the contractor's work has no relationship to the day-to-day operation. The fine line between a legal boycott and an illegal secondary boycott is not always easy to find. In 1974, the AFL-CIO supported a boycott of goods from the Farah Mfg. Co., Inc., of El Paso, Texas. Mass picketing demonstrations were organized from New York to Tokyo, in which pickets could legally carry signs saying, "Don't Buy Farah Parts at XYZ's" but not those saying "Don't Shop at XYZ's—they carry Farah Parts."[47] In 1988, the U.S. Supreme Court gave a significant victory to labor unions by ruling that union members may hand out leaflets in a secondary boycott action. The case, *De Bartola Corp. v. Florida Gulf Coast Trades Council*,[48] involved a union's distributing handbills in a shopping mall. The handbills asked customers not to shop at any of the stores in the mall because a construction company hired to build a new mall store was paying substandard wages. The mall was owned by the De Bartola Corporation, which then filed a complaint with the NLRB charging the union with engaging in a secondary boycott against the mall stores. The NLRB and a U.S. circuit court ruled in favor of De Bartola and ordered the union to cease and desist the action. The U.S. Supreme Court reversed the decision on the grounds that peaceful handbilling urging a customer boycott was not prohibited by Section 8 of the NLRA when unaccompanied by picketing. The key difference between this case and previous cases was the act of handbilling without picketing. The Court declared that picketing was qualitatively different and produced different consequences. Although the Court noted that both picketing and handbilling can have detrimental effects on a neutral third party, prohibiting peaceful and truthful handbilling raised questions of First Amendment rights.[49]

As a result of the Supreme Court ruling, the NLRB overruled a long-standing rule that handbilling dealing with matters unrelated to the labor dispute was an unfair labor practice. In one case, *Delta Airlines, Inc.*, the union and the independent contractor that provided janitorial services to Delta were in a dispute. The union distributed handbills at the airport reporting on Delta's bad safety record.[50] In another case, a union that was protesting a contractor's use of nonunion companies to build housing gave out handbills that pointed out the proximity of the development to an EPA Superfund landfill site.[51] The importance of the board decisions that give unions the ability to affect a labor dispute by marshaling public opinion against their opponent cannot be overstated.[52]

In any event, the secondary employer involved must be neutral for the primary-secondary distinction to be valid. Secondary and primary employers will be considered allied if the secondary employer performs work she would not be doing except for the strike or if there is common ownership, control, and integration of operation causing the businesses to be treated as a single enterprise.

A union is liable for any actual damages resulting from an unlawful secondary boycott sustained by the secondary or primary employer.

Shop-ins.   A new form of secondary boycotting was demonstrated in 1995 by a union in Massachusetts. The Teamsters Union was in a labor dispute with the August A. Busch & Co. of Massachusetts, Inc., a beer distributor. The union conducted three **"shop-ins"** involving three different retail establishments that carried Busch products. The shop-ins involved anywhere from 50 to 125 union members' converging on the stores at the same time; buying small items, such as gum or snacks; and paying with large-denomination bills. The results were crowded parking lots, delays in service, and the loss of regular customers. The union did not engage in any information sharing; that is, it did not leaflet or express an opinion regarding the Busch Co. Nor was it actually picketing. An unfair labor practice charge was made against the union, and the NLRB found this activity to be prohibited as a secondary boycott. Clearly the shop-in was conducted to pressure the retailers to not use Busch products. There was no communication to the public about Busch that would have been protected under the First Amendment.[53]

Hot Cargo Agreement.   **Hot cargo agreement** refers to a negotiated contract provision stating that union members of one employer need not handle nonunion or struck goods of other employers. Court decisions after passage of the Taft-Hartley Amendments basically allowed such agreements, stating that the prohibition against secondary boycotts did not prohibit an employer and union from voluntarily including a hot cargo clause in their agreement, but such a provision was not an absolute defense against an unfair labor practice charge. If inducements of employees prohibited by Section 8(b)(4) of the National Labor Relations Act in the absence of a hot cargo provision occurred, the inducements would still violate the act.

The need to analyze such provisions on a case-by-case basis decreased somewhat after the passage of the Landrum-Griffin Amendments, which outlawed most hot cargo agreements, except in the garment and construction industries. But there still remain numerous similarly negotiated clauses that may or may not violate the act. A picket line clause protecting employees from discharge for refusing to cross a lawful primary picket line at another employer's premises is not a violation of the hot cargo agreement prohibition. However, a struck-work clause stating that an employer will not do business with a nonunion or struck employer is in violation unless the secondary employer is an ally. Clauses completely prohibiting an employer from subcontracting are valid. But a clause forbidding subcontracting with nonunion employers may be a violation if it is aimed at a union's difference with another employer and not designed to protect union standards. A work-preservation clause is lawful if the object of the clause is to protect and preserve work customarily performed by employees in the unit. This is true even if it involves refusing to handle certain cargo, as long as it is the cargo that is refused and not the employer making the cargo. The aim of the clause must be to protect the actual employees of the bargaining unit and not union members as a group.

However, board decisions regarding **dual employer** operations must be carefully considered. This "double-breasted" issue arises when a unionized employer establishes a separate, similar company to operate on a nonunion basis. Such employers are often in the construction industry. Because the construction industry was allowed an exception to the act's prohibition against secondary boycotts, the union sought to end dual operations. A contract clause was negotiated that made mere ownership of two ostensibly separate companies sufficient to cover even the nonunion employees of one company under the provisions of the unionized company's contract. The general counsel of the NLRB, however, charged the union with an unfair labor practice for this clause, stating that it violated Section 8(e) of the act and was not covered by the construction industry exception.[54]

Jurisdictional Disputes. Prior to the 1947 Taft-Hartley Amendments, jurisdictional disputes between labor unions competing for the same work assignments caused numerous work stoppages. The amendments and later court decisions made such activities unfair labor practices and gave the NLRB jurisdiction to decide not only the unfair labor practice charge of participating in a jurisdictional dispute but also the underlying question of which union should get the work assignment. Factors the board uses to make its determinations include

> the skills and work involved: certifications by the board; company and industry practice; agreements between unions and between employers and unions; awards of arbitrators, joint boards, and the AFL-CIO in the same or related cases; the assignment made by the employer; and the efficient operation of the employer's business.[55]

Featherbedding. Another prohibited activity is **featherbedding**, which, according to Section 8(b)(6) of the NLRA is "to cause an employer to pay . . . for services not performed or not to be performed."[56] The featherbedding section is rarely used unless a union tries to cause an employer to pay for services neither performed nor intended to be performed. In such cases the NLRB may order the union to reimburse the employer and cease the unlawful activity.[57] The Supreme Court may uphold a negotiated agreement to provide pay for make-work if the work was actually done regardless of its value to the employer.

SUMMARY

The parties to the collective bargaining process have a duty to bargain in good faith, and, when agreement is reached, to commit that agreement to written form. That written agreement becomes the basis for the labor-management relationship during the contract term.

The contract is enforced at various times and for various purposes by the courts and the National Labor Relations Board through arbitration and grievance procedures and through employee job actions.

The National Labor Relations Board through its power to prevent unfair labor practices can interpret, invalidate, and enforce collective bargaining agreements in appropriate cases. The courts also have jurisdiction to enforce the labor agreement as binding on both the employer and the labor organization. As a rule, both the board and the courts defer to a grievance-arbitration process for contract administration whenever possible. The arbitration process allows the parties to resolve their differences during the life of the contract as a continuation of collective bargaining. Resorting to economic activity to enforce contracts cannot always be avoided, and the strike is one aspect of contract enforcement.

Contract administration includes recognition of rights under collective bargaining agreements. Individual workers have the right to refrain from union activity, to be fairly represented by the union, and to receive due process in their dealings with the union and the employer.

The union and the employer operate under a good faith duty to bargain during the contract term in appropriate circumstances. Neither party has the right to resort to secondary economic activities that violate the collective bargaining agreement or the law.

CASE STUDY 10-1

CONTRACT INTERPRETATION

Facts

The collective bargaining agreement contained a provision allowing for double-time pay to be paid as follows:

> For hours worked on the sixth or seventh consecutive day in a workweek, provided that the employee has worked his full assigned hours in the previous five or six workdays respectively in the workweek.

The grievant, a production worker, was 10 minutes late reporting for work on a Thursday morning. He was late because he was a passenger in a car that had a flat tire. As a result of his tardiness, he was only paid time and one-half instead of double-time for working the following Saturday. The union grieved the issue on the basis that the parties had a different understanding during the negotiating process from the company's current interpretation of the double-time section of the contract. The

union stated that at the fourteenth negotiating session, the company's negotiator had agreed not to count reasonable tardiness against the double-time provision but had refused to change the language used in the contract. The company negotiator, on the other hand, stated that the very purpose of the double-time section was to allow for double-time pay only if there was no absenteeism in the preceding week. The only comment he remembered making regarding "reasonable application" was in response to a maintenance worker on the negotiating committee who thought it was not fair that he worked his regular hours Monday through Friday but would be denied double-time on Sunday if he were a few minutes late on Saturday. The company negotiator remembers responding that, in that situation, he would agree to apply a reasonable standard to maintenance workers for Sunday double-time following a tardiness on Saturday because the 25 maintenance workers were regularly

(continued)

---

scheduled for both Saturday and Sunday, whereas the 650 to 675 production workers were rarely, if ever, scheduled to work on Sundays.

The arbitrator was faced with clear contract language but convincing evidence that the parties at the negotiating table had a different understanding of what the contract language meant. The arbitrator had to decide whether the employee should receive double-time pay for the Saturday work or be punished for the Thursday tardiness. The arbitrator could not rely on the "meeting of the minds" concept because obviously the parties disagreed as to what was contained in the collective bargaining agreement. There had been previous grievances on the same issue, but those arbitration awards were inconsistent. Explaining that it is the arbitrator's role to use judgment in a particular grievance to not only reflect what the contract says but also to give effect to the bargain, the arbitrator attempted to discover the purpose for the provision.

Adapted from *Mor Flo Industry, Inc.*, 83 LA 480 (1984).

The company stated that the double-time provision was added to the contract as a means of combatting absenteeism during the week. It was, therefore, both a carrot and a stick provision. The use by the company of the tardiness rule was in and of itself not unreasonable. The question that the arbitrator needed to resolve was whether the grievant in this case would have the incentive to avoid tardiness in order to get double-time pay under the facts as presented.

Questions

1. As the arbitrator, which fact would you consider most important in deciding this case? Why?
2. Would denying the employee his double-time pay in this instance give "effect" to the bargain of the parties? Explain your answer.
3. If the contract language is clear, why should the arbitrator even hear a case such as this?

CASE STUDY 10-2

DUTY TO BARGAIN

Facts

The company, prior to 1976, manufactured all of its products at a unionized plant in Cleveland. In 1976 it built a nonunion plant in Alabama, originally intending to duplicate the Cleveland operation. Unfavorable economic conditions, however, caused the company to transfer certain operations from Cleveland to Alabama, resulting in the layoff of seven union employees. The union filed unfair labor practice charges, which were settled when the company promised not to transfer work from the Cleveland plant without bargaining with the union. The settlement was reached during the same time the company and union were negotiating a new collective bargaining agreement.

During negotiations, the company, despite the aforementioned settlement, repeatedly submitted to the union a written statement asserting its right to decide what product "is made where by whom" and asked the union to submit any proposal it had to limit the company's right to transfer work. The union made no such proposal. It did, however, submit a severance pay proposal, which became part of the contract. That provision provided for severance pay for layoffs as a result of plant closure or operational transfers.

(continued)

A month after the agreement was signed, and again within a year, the company informed the union of certain operational transfers to the Alabama plant. The actions did not cause layoffs and the union did not object to either move. However, the next operational move did result in four layoffs, and the union objected and asserted that the company should have bargained before moving. The company disagreed. After 23 more employees were laid off, the union filed unfair labor charges against the company.

The company's position was that the union waived its right to bargain over the work transfers (1) in the language of the collective bargaining agreement, (2) during negotiations of the agreement, and (3) by acquiescing in the previous work transfers.

Language of Agreement

Company Position: The severance pay provision in the contract showed that the union accepted compensation in lieu of bargaining over work relocation. It pointed to the wording of the section, "In the event the company *determines* to . . . transfer . . . severance allowances will be payable . . ." to show that discretion to relocate was given solely to the company in return for the pay.

Union Position: The severance pay provision was in the supplemental unemployment benefits section not the management rights section, in which a union waiver would normally be located. In addition, the law requires a waiver to be "clear and unmistakable." The company's interpretation of the severance pay section gave too much weight to one word, *determines*. That word was taken out of context as to a clear union waiver of rights.

During Negotiations

Company Position: During negotiations, the company asserted that it had no restraints on its right to relocate work and asked that, if the union wished to restrict the company's right, it should propose constraints. Instead, the union proposed the severance pay provision, definitely a quid pro quo, which constituted a waiver.

Union Position: Because work transfers are a mandatory subject of bargaining, the union did not have to bargain on the subject to avoid waiving it. It was the company's duty to show an unequivocal waiver. In addition, the severance pay proposal during negotiations occurred *before* the union and the company settled the original unfair labor practice charge in which the company agreed to bargain before relocating work. Obviously the union was still interested in bargaining on the issue and did not waive it by the severance pay proposal.

Failure to Object

Company Position: The union's failure to object to the two initial work transfers constituted a waiver by acquiescence.

Union Position: The union did not object because no member of the unit was affected by the first two transfers. The union did object when the work relocation resulted in layoffs.

Questions

1. Did the union waive its right to negotiate transfers? Explain your answer.
2. Do you think the company would have allowed the collective bargaining agreement to remain silent on transfers if it had thought it would have to negotiate each transfer?
3. Should a collective bargaining agreement end the bargaining process, or should the administration of the agreement be part of the process? Explain your answer.

Adapted from *Tocco Division of Park-Ohio Industries, Inc. v. National Labor Relations Board*, 702 F.2d 624 (6th Cir. 1983).

Boys Market case	open period
Collyer case	primary boycott
contract bar	provisional intent test
dual employer	reserved rights
duty to sign a contract	restricted rights
featherbedding	secondary boycott
hot cargo agreement	separability clause
insulated period	shop-in
Lincoln Mills case	*Steelworker's Trilogy*
management rights	zipper clause
opener clause	

**REVIEW
QUESTIONS**

1. How can labor negotiators ensure that the agreement reached will be easily understood by others?
2. What are some common management rights that might be found in labor agreements?
3. Describe elements of an agreement ensuring that other unions are barred from representing a union's bargaining unit.
4. By what methods can collective bargaining agreements be enforced?
5. Assume that a union wants to end contract negotiations but (1) is concerned that in 18 months the employer may be financially stronger, and (2) wants a four-year contract. What should the union do to protect the interests of its members?
6. How did the *Steelworkers Trilogy* help clarify the role of arbitration and court enforcement of contracts?
7. What individual rights do employees have within the collective bargaining process?
8. What kind of economic pressures are illegal?
9. When is distributing handbills that request a boycott considered legal?
10. If a national union seeks to represent members of an independent local union, when can it petition the NLRB?

TAKE IT TO THE NET

We invite you to visit the Carrell/Heavrin page on the Prentice Hall Web site at:

http://www.prenhall.com/carrellr

for this chapter's World Wide Web exercise.

EXERCISE 10-1 **Agreement Provisions**

Purpose:
To familiarize students with contract provisions that deal with the administration of the contract.

Tasks:

Locate current labor agreements that contain examples of each of the following:

1. Management rights clause
2. Reopener provision
3. Zipper (wrap-up) clause
4. Separability clause
5. Duration provision

Provisional Intent **EXERCISE 10-2**

Purpose:

To become familiar with the concept of provisional intent.

Reducing an agreement to writing, the subject of this chapter, is not an easy task. Although most agreements contain fewer than 100 "short" pages, each article, page, and paragraph in each agreement is read by tens, hundreds, or thousands of people. Often these many readers are reading from different points of view. Reducing what was *intended* to be concise, clear language and writing it in a binding contract is not as easy as it may appear. This exercise is designed to help students better understand this aspect of labor relations and collective bargaining and to improve their own writing skills.

Task:

To best understand the purpose of the exercise re-read the last paragraph of the Duty section at the beginning of this chapter. Next, the class should be divided into three- to four-member teams. Each team should decide the intent of a new contract clause. The instructor may assign a topic or allow teams to select their own. Once the intent has been decided each team must reduce it to writing in clear and concise language.

The last step is for teams to exchange written provisions. Now members should play the role of union members *or* supervisors who must enforce the provision and list any potentially troublesome omissions, vague language, or other enforcement issues. The lists should be returned to their authoring teams for revision. The instructor, in conclusion, will present and discuss the first and second drafts of all provisions to the class.

If you are using Smith/Carrell/Golden *Collective Bargaining Simulated, 4E,* with this text, please refer to the following:

p. 14, Article III: Mangement, for a discussion of the company's management rights.

Grievance and Disciplinary Procedures

Because disagreements may arise during the life of a contract, grievance procedures must be in place to resolve any perceived contract violations or any complaints by an employee against an employer, or vice versa.

Dispute Resolution in the Federal Sector

Labor News

The federal workforce has been extensively organized by unions. For example, 60 percent of the general schedule (GS) and wage grade (WG) employees in the federal sector belong exclusively to recognized bargaining units. (The GS includes white-collar employees; blue-collar employees are covered in the WG.) In comparison, less than 20 percent of the private sector workforce in the United States is represented by unions. This high level of bargaining representation in the federal sector suggests that unions are in a strong position to influence personnel matters. However, a comprehensive study of federal sector labor relations indicates that a "barrier exists between labor and management in which existing bargaining processes are bogged down by litigation over minute details, plagued by slow and lengthy dispute resolution, and weakened by poor management."[1]

In 1978, Congress enacted the Civil Service Reform Act. Title VII of this act, referred to as the Federal Service Labor Management Relations Statute (FSLMRS), provided the first statutory framework regulating labor-management relations among GS and WG employees. The statute reaffirmed the right of federal employees to "form, join, or assist, any labor organization" and "to engage in collective bargaining with respect to conditions of employment" through their duly chosen representatives. In this perspective, FSLMRS is akin to the National Labor Relations Act, which provides similar rights to private sector employees under its jurisdiction. In other respects, however, FSLMRS restricts certain aspects of the bargaining process and the resolution of disputes. The FSLMRS mandates an expansive management rights clause, forbids GS and WG employees from striking, excludes matters that are determined legislatively, eliminates the right to bargain over compensation (wages, salaries, benefits), and forbids unions representing federal employees from negotiating any form of union security arrangement. The swift dismissal of thousands of striking air traffic controllers in 1981 and the decertification of the Professional Air Traffic Controllers Union indicates the severe repercussions of strike activity by federal employees and their unions. Also, the FSLMRS provides limited access to binding arbitration. The FSLMRS states that the parties (labor and management) may agree to adopt a procedure for binding arbitration but only if the procedure is approved by the Federal Service Impasses Panel. In contrast, many state public sector bargaining laws make binding arbitration of impasses compulsory.

In 1993, President Clinton directed Vice President Gore to conduct a National Performance Review (NPR) of the federal government. The NPR focused primarily on *how* government should work not on *what* it should do. An important aspect of the NPR focused on ways to reform the FSLMRS and included the following recommendations:

Good government standard. A standard should be applied that the parties (labor and management) and third-party neutrals can use in resolving disputes.

Scope of bargaining. Nonnegotiable rules should be reviewed in "partnership" councils involving senior managers and top-level union officials.

Dispute resolution. Because the existing dispute resolution process is slow and fragmented, the parties should be allowed to resolve collective bargaining disputes in a process they design themselves.

It is now up to the president and Congress to act. Given the poor state of federal labor relations, it seems necessary to revise the FSLMRS.

Adapted from Marick Masters and Robert Atkin, "Reforming Federal Sector Labor Relations: Recommendations of President Clinton's National Partnership Council," *Labor Law Journal* (June 1994) pp. 352–359.

As indicated in the preceding Labor News section, considerable differences exist between public sector and private sector collective bargaining. A major difference between the two is that a market economy does not operate in the public sector and cannot act to constrain labor and management negotiations.[2] For example, many of the services provided in the public sector such as education, police, and fire protection are provided to citizens at little or no additional cost beyond taxes. Monopolistic conditions often exist in the public sector, and public sector organizations often control the products or services rendered.[3] As an example, public education has little real competition, and fire and police departments are organizations that provide unique types of services.

In the public sector, labor relations at the state, county, and municipal levels are governed by policies, statutes, executive orders, and ordinances. At the federal level, most labor relations activities are governed by the Civil Service Reform Act (CSRA), which was passed in 1978, and the Postal Reorganization Act of 1970.

Although differences exist between public and private sector labor relations, there are also similarities. A major similarity is that the collective bargaining agreements of both sectors are often influenced by the personalities of the negotiators and their abilities to improve their bargaining power relative to the other party.[4] Also, grievances in the two sectors are generally processed in the same manner.

In the day-to-day administration of a collective bargaining agreement, the majority of time is spent on grievance handling.[5] A detailed study of the time devoted to the formal meetings required to process a typical grievance found that, on the average, more than nine direct working hours were required. This time did not include the hours of investigations and preparation spent by each side.[6] The extreme importance of a good grievance procedure has been described as the "lifeblood of a collective bargaining relationship."[7]

Regardless of the completeness and clarity of the labor agreement, disagreements will arise during the life of the contract. Thus a *grievance procedure*, a previously agreed-upon procedure to resolve such disputes, must be provided in the agreement. The grievance handling process must settle disputes arising during the term of the agreement; if it does not, strikes, lockouts, or other work disruptions may result.

A **grievance** is often defined as any perceived violation of a contract provision. This definition could be broadened to include any complaint by an employee against an employer, or vice versa. One arbitrator has said that "if a man thinks he has a grievance, he has a grievance."[8] However, a more precise definition might include any formal complaint lodged by persons who believe they have been wronged.[9] A grievance is not a *gripe*, which is generally defined as a complaint by an employee concerning an action by management that does not violate the contract, past practice, or law. For example, an employee may only have a gripe if his supervisor speaks to him in a harsh tone, but when the supervisor assigns him work outside of his job classification, he may have a grievance.

Fortunately, most collective bargaining agreements contain provisions similar to Figure 11-1 and delineate a grievance procedure that consists of a specified series of four or five procedural steps that aggrieved employees, unions, and management representatives must follow when a complaint arises. Typically, the grievant is provided with a systematic set of appeals through successively higher levels of union and management representatives. The fact that most contracts provide for specific grievance procedures clearly indicates that, although both sides try to develop a clear and precise document during the contract negotiation

ARTICLE IX
Adjustment of Grievances

A grievance shall consist of a dispute between an employee, the Union, and the Company as to the meaning or application of any provisions of this Agreement.

When it becomes necessary for a Union officer, steward or employee to process a grievance during working hours, he shall notify the foreman involved in advance and ring out his card and receive no pay for the time spent processing the grievances. It is the Union's desire that a minimum of time be spent processing the grievances during regular shift hours of the employees and the Union officers concerned.

The President of the Union, or his duly appointed representatives chosen from the Grievance Committee, shall have access to departments other than his own for the purpose of transacting the legitimate business of the grievance procedure, after reasonable notice has been given to the head of the department to be visited and permission from his own department has been obtained.

An employee ordered to report to the office for disciplinary purposes shall have the right to be represented by a Union official (steward, committeeman, or officer). The representative will be treated as though processing a grievance. The employee shall be advised of the purpose of the meeting in advance and advised of the provisions of this paragraph.

The Union Committee or Union officers shall conduct no Union activities, other than processing of grievances, on Company premises without the consent of the Company.

Step 1. Within three (3) working days after the first occurrence of the situation, condition, or actions of the Company giving rise to the grievance, the employee affected shall personally discuss his grievance with his foreman. He shall ring out his card (unless it can be discussed on an off-shift hour) and his steward shall be present.

Within twenty-four (24) hours after the grievance is discussed, the foreman shall give his verbal decision to the aggrieved employee and/or his steward.

Step 2. In the event that a satisfactory settlement has not been reached at the verbal level, the aggrieved employee, or his steward, may within 48 hours present the grievance in writing, and within 48 hours shall receive a written answer from his foreman.

Step 3. Within three (3) working days after the written decision has been given, the Local Union may present the grievance in writing to a representative designated by the Company.

All third step grievances (except discharge cases which may, if requested by the Union, be discussed at special meetings to meet deadlines) shall be considered at the next scheduled grievance meeting attended by an International Representative, unless he waives the right to be present; but upon demand by the Company, such representative shall attend at least one meeting a month to consider pending grievances.

Within four (4) working days after the grievance meeting, the Company shall give to the Local Union its written decision. The time limits in this step may be extended by mutual agreement.

The aggrieved, or in case of a group grievance, a representative of the aggrieved group, may be present at the meetings at all steps of this grievance procedure if he so requests to be present.

The Union shall certify in writing to the Company, over the signature of the Local Union Recording Secretary, a list of the officers, committeemen and stewards who are to be recognized by the Company.

The Union Grievance Committee shall consist of not less than three (3) members.

The Union Grievance Committee shall have the right to file a grievance in behalf of an employee and/or employees if there is a contract violation, and if filed within three (3) working days of the occurrence.

Source: *Agreement* between the Anaconda Company Aluminum Division and United Steelworkers of America, AFL-CIO, 1976–1979, pp. 19–23. Used with permission.

process, some areas will be subject to misunderstanding during the life of the contract. Indeed, as shown in Case 11-1, the grievance procedure itself is sometimes the subject of a grievance.

The signing of a contract spells out a new relationship between labor and management, and the agreement specifies a new set of rules legally binding labor

CASE 11-1

WHEN THE UNION FAILED TO FOLLOW THE GRIEVANCE PROCEDURE

The grievance procedure in this case contains four steps with a time period of seven calendar days at each step. For example, step 1 of the grievance procedure states that the union has seven calendar days to present a grievable incident to management. If the grievance is not resolved in step 1, then the union has seven calendar days to prepare a grievance form and move it to step 2 and so on. At step 4, if the grievance is not resolved, the union is required to prepare a written notice of intent to arbitrate and has 14 calendar days to do so. The contract specifies that the notice of intent to arbitrate shall be sent by certified mail with return receipt requested, and the postmark shall govern compliance with the time limit. The union is also required to obtain a listing of possible arbitrators from the Federal Mediation and Conciliation Service (FMCS), meet with the company, and select an arbitrator.

On November 4, 1993, a meeting occurred between the union business agent and the employer's human resources manager (HRM) concerning the discharge of two employees. The meeting was within the seven-day time period required in the contract. During the arbitration hearing, the union business agent testified that on November 9, 1993, he had hand-delivered an intent to arbitrate document to the company's HRM. Also, during the arbitration, the HRM testified that he did not remember receiving such a document from the union. On November 15, 1993, the union forwarded a request for an arbitration panel to the FMCS. On December 28, 1993, the union business agent approached the company HRM

with a list of arbitrators. At that time (December 28, 1993) the HRM informed the union for the first time that a grievance had not been properly filed. The union argued that step 1 of the grievance procedure became step 4 because of the nature of the grievance (the two employees had been discharged) and that an intent to arbitrate had been timely filed. The parties continued to differ sharply with respect to both whether the grievance was filed and its timeliness.

In November 1994, at an arbitration hearing to resolve this issue, the arbitrator was asked to make a finding as to the timeliness issue. If the grievance was determined to be timely, then the grievance would be heard on its merits. Otherwise, the matter would be dismissed. During the arbitration hearing, the company argued that a written grievance was not filed in a timely manner and that the parties' labor agreement specifically states:

> If the grieving party fails to process the grievance in accordance with the requirements of this article, the grievance is waived.

The collective bargaining agreement further states that the "arbitrator may not add to, detract from, nor alter in any way, the provisions of the agreement."

Decision

The arbitrator ruled that the union had failed to follow the requirements of the grievance procedure, and the grievance was denied.

Adapted from *Los Alamos Protection Technology*, 104 LA 23 (1995).

and management during the life of the contract. The administration of the contract is substantially provided by a formal grievance process agreed upon in the contract. Although the number and contents of the procedural steps in a formal grievance process vary from contract to contract, most grievance processes involved four or five steps.

Whatever the subject matter of a particular grievance may be, exactly *why* the grievance was filed may provide far greater understanding of the union's or employee's motives. One or more of the following situations might be a source of employee grievance.

Clarifying Contract Provisions under Changing Conditions

After contracts are agreed upon and signed by both parties, unforeseen circumstances change some operating conditions. Even with the best of intentions, both management and labor may find that they honestly disagree on the contract provision relevant to the new operations. For example, workers at the Diamond Shamrock Corporation normally worked the evening shift from 3:00 to 11:00 P.M. and received a shift differential under the existing contract. Management changed the hours of the shift to 11:00 A.M. to 7:00 P.M., resulting in a grievance requesting shift differential pay for the four new hours of work overlapping with the old hours for which they received shift differential pay. Management declined, claiming that shift differential was required by contract only when the entire shift was from 3:00 to 7:00 P.M. The arbitrator agreed with management that the contract did not provide shift differential on a per hour basis but on a per shift basis.[10]

Support for Future Negotiations

Unions often encourage their members to file grievances in certain areas to provide a file of supporting evidence during future negotiations. The negotiators may then point to the grievances as evidence of their members' concern over a particular management practice or lack of an employee benefit or service. The union does not intend to prevail in many of these cases but wants to alert management to the issue. Thus, the administration of one contract becomes a basis of negotiation for a future contract.

Rectifying a Contract Violation

Contract negotiators have one primary goal—to sign a contract. Although many contracts are quite lengthy and involved, they cannot cover every possible situation that might arise. For that reason, most contracts specify how each debatable issue should be resolved. Both sides expect that disagreements will occur during the life of the contract, which is why grievance arbitration is included.

One of the most common sources of grievances is the union's honest belief that management has violated a provision of the existing contract. For example, an arbitrator ruled that the contract clause stating that the parties may negotiate necessary schedule changes from the standard work week did not require the union's consent before changes could be made if negotiations were provided. The union believed that the contract phrase did in fact require management to gain its consent before changes were made.[11]

Show of Power

Sometimes employees and union officials file grievances to demonstrate their authority and influence. Union officials may feel a need to remind employees that they are on their side and work hard to represent their interests. After all, union leaders are elected by their members, and members expect something in return. Although the union leadership may realize that a particular employee grievance is without substantial merit, they will pursue the issue if it is of great concern to the membership. Individual employees may also, for a variety of reasons, file grievances. Some may simply be letting off steam; others may use the grievance process as a means of settling a score with management. No contract language can eliminate grievances when these kinds of motives are involved. Some management and labor relations personnel claim that such meritless grievances waste time and resources. However, critics should consider that the grievance process is partially designed to provide a safety valve to employees who might otherwise express their normal anxiety and frustration in more harmful ways, such as absenteeism, alcoholism, or even sabotage.

Increased Pay

One of labor's primary motives in bargaining is to provide assurances of pay that might otherwise be at the discretion of management. Labor negotiations have initiated many types of pay incentives and premiums not found in the nonunion sector. Many grievances result from employees' belief that they are entitled to additional pay that management believes is not required.

The union, in one instance, claimed that the contract providing that employees who worked on Sunday would receive double the straight-time hourly rate required double-time pay for all Sunday hours. Management contended that because it had begun opening on Sunday as a regular business day after a state blue law was repealed, the double-time pay was not required because Sunday became a normal workday. The arbitrator agreed with management.[12]

STEPS IN A GRIEVANCE PROCEDURE

Step 1: Employee, Steward, Supervisor

The initial step in a **grievance procedure** usually instructs the employee to discuss the grievance with the shop steward or go directly to the supervisor. The employee has the legal right to do the latter; the supervisor must resolve the grievance consistent with the contract. The supervisor must also notify the union of the grievance. The shop steward is, however, usually the first person contacted. Therefore, the steward must be experienced in handling grievance matters and familiar with the terms of the contract and its provisions. The steward must also be able to recognize grievances containing some merit as well as those that are trivial and should be dropped. A steward will encourage and help the employee to pursue a legitimate grievance, and in some cases must convince the employee that a grievance contains no merit.

The extent to which grievances are resolved at the lowest possible level is an important indicator of effective grievance handling. One means of attaining resolution at the lowest possible level is the use of feedback from previous grievance cases. The outcome of previous similar cases provides cues to both parties that tend to focus their discussion and provide a faster resolution of the grievance. In general, the purpose of feedback is not to "set precedent" but to provide both parties with an array of possible likely solutions.[13] In practice, if both sides introduce the results of previous similar grievances at the first level of grievance discussions, a compromise may well be reached more quickly than if they wait until the issue goes to arbitration.

Step 2: Written Grievance

If steward and employee agree that the grievance has some merit and should be pursued, then the grievance is reduced to writing. At this point, the grievance is said to have moved from the informal to the formal stage. A grievance form is completed by the steward and employee within 48 hours of the occurrence or within the time limit specified in the contract. The process of writing out the complaint forces the grievant to set forth the facts, contract provisions, and contingencies early on in the process.

Most company and union representatives believe it is important to formalize the grievance in written format at this stage.[14] Once the grievance has been reduced to writing, the steward and the employee meet with the supervisor to discuss the grievance in an honest effort to settle the matter quickly. Both sides can assess the strengths and weaknesses of the claim. Most grievances containing little merit will be dropped at this stage.

The steward normally investigates the grievance to provide documented facts on the case. The pertinent facts are written on a grievance form such as the one in Figure 11-2. A good rule for remembering the crucial facts in a grievance is the "5 Ws" rule:

- What happened?
- When did the event take place?
- Who was involved? (witnesses?)
- Where did it happen?
- Why is the complaint a grievance?

The written grievance is delivered to the supervisor, and a meeting of the three parties is held (the shop steward is occasionally accompanied by a personnel or industrial relations representative). In discussing the grievance, all of the parties make an attempt to settle the matter at that point. Research indicates that most grievances are settled in this step of the grievance process. If the grievance cannot be resolved at this stage, the employee may choose to appeal.

Step 3: Shop Steward, Department Head

When the shop steward and supervisor cannot resolve the grievance, then it may be appealed to the next higher level of management and union representative, usually within seven calendar days. At this point, the union representative continues to be the shop steward or business agent. However, the management representative usually represents a higher level and may be a plant superintendent or department head. At this stage, the two sides review the written grievance and try to reach a resolution.

Figure 11-2   A Standard Grievance Record Form, Step 1

GRIEVANCE NUMBER <u>97-003</u>   DATE FILED <u>4/23/97</u>   UNION <u>Local</u> <u>1233</u>

NAME OF GRIEVANT(S) <u>Davis, Henry</u>   CLOCK # <u>0379</u>

DATE CAUSE OF GRIEVANCE OCCURRED <u>4/20/97</u>

CONTRACTUAL PROVISIONS CITED <u>Articles</u> <u>III,</u> <u>VII,</u> <u>and</u> <u>others</u>

STATEMENT OF THE GRIEVANCE:

On April 20, Foreman George Moore asked Henry Davis to go temporarily to the Rolling Mill for the rest of the turn. Davis said he preferred not to, and that he was more senior to others who were available. The foreman never ordered Davis to take the temporary assignment. He only requested that Davis do so.

Davis was improperly charged with insubordination and suspended for three days. The foreman did not have just cause for the discipline.

RELIEF SOUGHT:

Reinstatement with full back pay and seniority.

GRIEVANT'S SIGNATURE _____*Henry Davis*_____ DATE *4/22/97*

STEWARD'S SIGNATURE _____*Jim Bob Smith*_____ DATE *4/23/97*

STEP 1

DISPOSITION:

Foreman Moore gave Davis clear instructions to report temporarily to the Rolling Mill for the remainder of the shift. Davis refused to do so and was warned that it could result in discipline. When he again refused the foreman's directive, he was disciplined.

The discipline was for just cause. The grievance is rejected.

SIGNATURE OF
EMPLOYER REPRESENTATIVE _____*Paul Roberts*_____ DATE *4/26/97*

_____ Grievance Withdrawn or __√__ Referred to Step 2

SIGNATURE OF
UNION REPRESENTATIVE _____*Jim Bob Smith*_____ DATE *4/28/97*

Step 4: Union Grievance Committee, Director of Personnel and Industrial Relations

At this point, the employee's grievance is reviewed by a plantwide union grievance committee that may further appeal the answer to Step 5, usually within 30 calendar days. The plant manager or department head may be assisted by the director of personnel and industrial relations in reviewing the grievance from a management perspective. As with the second step, they review the written grievance and discuss the case with the employee's representatives. The two sides continue to try to resolve the grievance honestly rather than go to the final stage of the process, final and binding arbitration. This final step is more expensive, represents a failure to reach an agreement in the matter, and brings greater tension to the grievance. Both sides realize that they may completely lose the case before an independent arbitrator.

Step 5: Arbitration

Approximately 98 percent of all collective bargaining agreements provide for a binding arbitration as the final step in the handling of grievances.[15] The contract provisions usually include that either management or labor request arbitration as a final step in resolving the grievance. This request must be made within 60 calendar days of the receipt of the answer of Step 4. The outside independent arbitrator will study the evidence and listen to the arguments of both sides before rendering a decision. The arbitrator's decision, as agreed upon in the collective bargaining contract, is final and binding on both parties and can be appealed to the courts only on the grounds of collusion, if the arbitrator's award exceeded his or her authority, or if the arbitrator's decision was not based on the essence of the labor agreement.[16]

Formal grievance procedures have been found to be the most common tool to resolve conflicts arising between labor and management during the life of the agreement. In general, the functions provided by a grievance procedure are as follows:

FUNCTIONS OF GRIEVANCE PROCEDURES

1. *Conflict management resolution.* Before grievance procedures and arbitration became popular, strikes and slowdowns were often used by employees and unions to resolve complaints over the interpretation of labor agreements. Without grievance procedures, questions would probably be resolved by a test of economic strength, harmful both to management and to the union.

2. *Agreement clarification.* All agreements contain a certain amount of unintentional ambiguity that results in questions requiring contract interpretation. The dynamics of employer-employee relationships cannot be fully anticipated by the parties at the bargaining table; thus, negotiating language often must be applied to unforeseen situations.

3. *Communication.* Grievance procedures provide a vehicle for individual employees to express their problems and perceptions. They offer employees a formal process to air perceived inequities in the workplace.

4. *Due process.* The most widely heralded function of grievance procedures is that of a third-party intervention. Most grievance procedures provide a fair and equitable due process containing binding arbitration as a final step. Without this process, management would likely have an upper hand in most grievance situations. However, employee and union strikes would be heightened, with economic measures used to balance management's authority.

5. *Strength enhancement.* The grievance mechanism helps unions to develop employee loyalty and trust. Grievance processing emphasizes union presence and strength during the term of the collective bargaining agreement and reminds employees of the union efforts to protect their interests. The formal grievance also strengthens management's and labor's communication skills, since first-level stewards and supervisors are almost always involved in the initial step of the grievance procedure. The two sides come to better understand each other's perspectives and develop a closer working relationship.[17]

Grievance Categories

Grievance categories are based on the issues that arise most frequently:

Suspension	An employee is ordered not to work for a period of time usually ranging from one day to two weeks. Almost all of these suspensions are the result of absenteeism, avoidable accidents, insubordination, or job performance.
Seniority	An employee files a grievance because of seniority bypass. Almost all such grievances are filed because an employee has been overlooked for overtime, transfer, promotion, training, or scheduling.
Transfer	An employee files a grievance because he or she has been refused a transfer for which he or she has applied. This may be because of low supervisory ratings, excessive absenteeism, medical transfers receiving priority, and so forth.
Termination	The employee is fired. Almost all actions in this category are because of excessive absenteeism, a history of avoidable accidents, insubordination, or job performance.
Disciplinary memoranda	This is essentially a warning to an employee that presumably will be followed by more serious consequences should the employee continue or repeat the incident. Ordinarily, these are a reaction to absenteeism, accidents, insubordination, tardiness, and job performance.
Vacation	This occurs because employees do not receive the vacation dates they prefer. This may be because junior employees have been given the dates of preference, or because the organization has limited the number of employees who may be on vacation at any given time.
Grievance process	The union ordinarily charges that the company has not met in good faith on a grievance. Also, a case is occasionally found when the company is alleged not to have met the conditions of a grievance settlement.

Management performing production work	The union alleges that management employees are doing work that is (or should be) restricted to union personnel.
Safety	The union alleges that a procedure or a condition involving employees is unsafe. The union is usually asking that this procedure or condition be modified.
Discrimination	This may be a forum for Title VII disagreements. However, this is not ordinarily the case. Grievances in this category are catchalls. Discrimination here means that an employee charges that he or she is not being treated the same as other employees. These grievances rarely have race, sex, or national origin overtones.
Performance evaluations	An employee charges that his or her annual performance evaluation is not a fair representation of his or her job performance over that period.
Union representation	The union files a grievance in this case because an employee, facing a disciplinary hearing, has requested union representation and has had this request denied.
Sick benefits denial	An employee who has not reported to work for some period claims to have been ill and requests sick pay compensation. For whatever reasons, the company has refused to pay this sick leave.
Pay (differentials, travel, etc.)	These grievances usually occur over the nonpayment of special pay provisions (not ordinarily hourly wages). Meal allowances, night shift differentials, and travel reimbursements are most common.
Excused or complimentary time	An employee requests time off without pay. The company has denied the request.
Work out of classification	An employee is asked to do a job that is allegedly not in his or her job description. It is argued that this particular job should be done by someone in a different job classification.
Training	An employee has requested training for some aspect of his or her job. The company has denied the request.[18]

Case 11-2 describes a grievance regarding a performance evaluation.

PERFORMANCE EVALUATION
OF A CRANE OPERATOR

The employer operates a metal processing plant that uses cranes of various sizes and capabilities to transport materials. As a result of a bid to fill a vacancy, the grievant, a 20-year employee, was selected to operate a 60-ton crane. After a two-week training program, and a 15-year tenure as a crane operator, the grievant was removed from his crane operator position.

During the arbitration hearing, the company argued that the grievant had failed to attain the necessary level of depth perception and motor skills required to perform the duties of a crane operator in a safe and efficient manner. The grievant had received prior warnings that he could be disqualified from his job if his work performance did not improve, and he deliberately failed to take advantage of several training opportunities to improve his performance. Also, at the arbitration hearing, a union employee who had been a crane operator for 20 years testified that two weeks of training was sufficient and that he had trained some 20 to 25 other crane operators. Additional testimony introduced at the arbitration hearing indicated that the grievant had dropped material, hit pilings, and "brushed" employees working on the floor with heavy dangerous objects. As a result, many of the floor employees refused to work with the grievant.

At the arbitration hearing, the grievant testified that during his first week of training, he was trained by two different crane operators and by two others during the second week of training. The grievant further testified that during the second week of his training, the two training operators refused to ride in the cab with him. The grievant also testified that his supervisors had urged him to "speed up" the operation of the crane to meet production quotas but that he had refused to do so. The grievant testified that he was never told of his unsatisfactory performance and that he was disliked by certain supervisors, several crane operators, and many floor employees. The union argued that the grievant, a black, had not been properly trained and was disadvantaged by the lack of training in an all-white department.

The parties' labor agreement gives the employer the right to demote and transfer and the right to disqualify. It stipulates, however, that disqualification will not occur in an unreasonably short period of time.

Decision

The arbitrator ruled that he could find no basis that the grievant's disqualification was based on his race. The arbitrator stated that the overwhelming evidence is that the grievant's disqualification as a crane operator did not violate the parties' labor agreement.

Adapted from *Alloys International*, 94 ARB 449 (1994).

DISCIPLINARY PROCEDURES
A primary objective of a grievance process is to provide employees with a fair review and, if necessary, an appeal of disciplinary actions taken by management. Regardless of size or industry, every company at some time must administer corrective discipline. Certain employees may need such attention only once or twice in their careers and quickly respond to fair procedures; others may never correct their behavior and will exhaust any progressive disciplinary process. However, it is important that *other* employees believe that the disciplined employee was given a fair chance and equitable punishment. In order to maintain good labor relations, both labor and management should strive for fair and effective disciplinary policies.

Employers need a comprehensive and effective discipline system to maintain control over the workforce. Otherwise, satisfactory employee attendance, conduct, and productivity could not be achieved. A well-structured and uniformly enforced discipline program also may reduce employee discontent, along with any manager's tendency to treat employees in an arbitrary or biased manner. Employees are more satisfied when they know what consequences to expect from rule violations and when they see discipline procedures consistently administered.[19]

Labor and management officials want to minimize the use of disciplinary actions, but both realize that such actions will be needed in some situations. Therefore, virtually all collective bargaining agreements outline a **disciplinary procedure**.

Other than the economic benefits of a labor agreement, the disciplinary process may be the most vital aspect of a labor-management relationship. Management views the right and ability to discipline its employees effectively as the heart of maintaining a productive workforce. If work rules can be accidentally or willfully violated by one employee, the total result could be very costly. For example, if one employee continues to neglect wearing protective goggles because they are uncomfortable or inconvenient, others may follow because they think the rule has been relaxed. The eventual penalty is OSHA citations and fines or possibly an individual's loss of eyesight in an accident because of one minor infraction.

Any degree of discipline—even if it is only an oral warning—is both stressful and embarrassing to the employee because of the economic and psychological penalties of possible layoff or termination. If such discipline was not warranted by the facts of the situation, if the employee was ignorant of any wrongdoing, or if the penalty was unusually harsh, other employees will react very negatively. Protection from biased or thoughtless supervisors in disciplinary matters has been a prime motive behind many union organizing campaigns.

A variety of disciplinary policies may be provided in the labor contract. A study by the Bureau of National Affairs suggests that these policies should be encouraged and utilized by management and labor officials.

1. *Explain company rules*. Orientation courses, employee handbooks, bulletin board notices, and other devices must be used to bring work rules to the attention of employees.
2. *Get the facts*. Interview witnesses and investigate testimony to ensure that both sides of a story are presented. Circumstantial evidence, personality factors, and unproven assumptions cannot be easily defended before arbitrators.
3. *Give adequate warning*. Most grievance warning steps are given to the employee in writing; however, all warnings, even oral warnings, should be noted in the employee's personnel record. Copies of warning notices should go to the union.
4. *Ascertain motive*. People usually have a reason for what they do. Seldom will employees intentionally and maliciously violate rules. The penalty should be adjusted to the degree the employee's action was intentional.
5. *Consider the employee's past record*. Before taking disciplinary action, consider the employee's past record. Take into account both a good work record and seniority, especially in cases of minor offenses.
6. *Discipline without discharge*. Wherever possible, avoid the use of discharge. Only when there is no hope of future improvement or the offense is severe should discharge be used.[20]

Figure 11-3   Discipline Rules to Protect Us All

Whenever people gather together, some rules and regulations are needed to help everyone work together harmoniously. This is especially true in a company such as ours which needs to have efficient operations. It is our aim to be patient and firm in running the company. Our sincere desire is to help each employee in every possible way to perform his or her job well. However, responsibilities are shared by everyone. You have the responsibility to us and to your fellow workers to conduct yourself according to certain rules of behavior and conduct. The purpose of these rules is not to restrict the rights of anyone but, rather, to define them. By keeping you informed of your rights, you will be more satisfied and the company can maintain an orderly and efficient operation. We ask for the wholehearted cooperation of all members of our team of employees in the observance of these rules which are necessary to protect the best interests of all.

The following rules are listed with their attending penalties for your information.

GROUP I

1. Failure to attend scheduled meetings.
2. Stopping work before time specified for such purposes.
3. Loitering and loafing during working hours.
4. Leaving your department or assigned working areas during working hours without permission of a supervisor, except for the use of the restrooms. (No smoking in restrooms.)
5. Failure to keep your own time card accurately or completing another employee's time card.
6. Repeated failure to be at the work station to work at starting time.
7. Creating or contributing to unsanitary conditions.
8. Posting or removal of notices, signs or writing in any form on any bulletin board on company property without permission of management.
9. Neglect or mishandling of equipment or any other supplies.
10. Unsatisfactory work and/or attitude.
11. Waste or personal use of company supplies.
12. Untidy attire, extreme makeup, and hairstyles; torn uniforms and other failure to maintain a clean, neat appearance.
13. Failure to follow any other company rule, regulation, or job requirement not specifically mentioned herein.

PENALTIES FOR GROUP I VIOLATIONS

First offense—Oral warning.
Second offense—Written warning.
Third offense—One (1) day's suspension without pay.
Fourth offense—Termination of employment.

GROUP II

1. Leaving the premises during working hours without permission of a supervisor.
2. Fighting of any type on company premises at any time.
3. Attempting bodily injury to another.
4. Two (2) days' unexcused absence during any thirty (30) calendar days.
5. Violation of the no solicitation/no distribution rule.
6. Failure to report off from work in accordance with current regulations.

PENALTIES FOR GROUP II VIOLATIONS

First offense—Written warning.
Second offense—Two (2) days' suspension without pay.
Third offense—Termination of employment.

GROUP III

1. Deliberately making or using falsified records, material requisition, passes, time cards, etc.
2. Use of intoxicating liquids or narcotics of any kind on company premises.
3. Insubordination.
4. Sabotage.
5. Theft of any property.
6. Concerted or deliberate restriction of output (slowdown, delaying other employees' work, etc.).
7. Reporting for work under the influence of any alcoholic beverage or illegal narcotic.
8. Improperly discussing or disclosing confidential information.
9. Using the eating, drinking, and smoking facilities to excess.
10. Excessive absenteeism.
11. Discourtesy to the public.
12. Refusal to accept any reasonable work assignment.
13. Gambling.
14. Immoral conduct.
15. Incompetence.
16. Gross negligence of duty.
17. Willful or consistently careless destruction of company property.
18. Violation of safety rules.
19. Sleeping on duty.
20. Profanity.
21. Possession of firearms or other illegal weapon on company premises.

PENALTIES FOR GROUP III VIOLATIONS

First offense—Termination of employment.

Source: Stephen Cabot, *Labor-Management Relations Manual* (Boston: Warren, Gorham, Lamont, 1979), chap. 16, pp. 7–9, by permission of Warren, Gorham, Lamont, Inc.

A critical aspect of the disciplinary procedure is the face-to-face counseling provided by the supervisor. Such encounters can become explosive and often lead to subjective and emotional behavior. Employees may feel that they need a union to provide them protection against what they perceive as unfair supervisory actions. Any corrective supervisory counseling should provide the employee feedback, stating the problem, the preferred action, and future expectations, as well as the disciplinary action to be taken. Figure 11-3 illustrates a disciplinary system designed to provide maximum employee control, minimum discontent, and reduced exposure to legal problems.

The Labor-Management Relations Act, in addition to civil and antidiscrimination laws, provides restrictions on employee discipline. The act prohibits disciplinary action against employees for union-related activity. Most related charges of such employer actions arise out of union organizing campaigns. The second most common source of unfair discipline charges arises from conflict between the union steward and management. The steward must file the grievances of union members and advocate their point of view. In this situation, the NLRB may view disciplinary actions against the steward as an unfair labor practice. Thus,

Cause	Manufacturing	Nonmanufacturing
Violation of leave provision	61	36
Unauthorized strike participation	47	31
Unauthorized absence	62	29
Dishonesty or theft	24	34
Violation of company rules	22	14
Insubordination	18	20
Intoxication	19	33
Incompetence	21	15
Failure to obey safety rules	14	15
Misconduct	20	11
Tardiness	13	5

Source: From Bureau of National Affairs, *Basic Patterns in Union Contracts*, 14th ed. (Washington, DC: BNA Books, 1995), pp. 7–11.

employers should have a uniformly applied and well-documented disciplinary program they can defend against possible claims of unfair labor practice discrimination.[21]

Grounds for Discharge

Employees may be terminated or discharged for "cause" or "just cause" for specific offenses. Most contracts specify the offenses that are sufficient grounds for immediate discharge, but they also provide for an appeal procedure in that event. The contract may require that the union be notified in advance of a discharge or that a predischarge hearing be held with the employee and union present. The most common grounds for discharge specified in contracts include those listed in Table 11-1. An example of a just-cause grievance is seen in Case 11-3.

NONUNION GRIEVANCE PROCEDURES

The use of formal grievance procedures in which employees may advance their complaints and problems is often recognized by organizational managers as critical in remaining nonunion. Formal grievance procedures are far less common and more varied in nonunion organizations.[22] In a survey of 1,958 *Harvard Business Review* readers, only 14 percent of nonunion workers reported that their companies had a management grievance committee.[23]

Formal grievance procedures in nonunion organizations are normally patterned after procedures in unionized organizations. An example of the grievance procedure for a nonunion organization is presented in the following:

In order to protect the individual rights of the employee, the hospitals have established and maintain a grievance procedure, whereby an employee may present what he/she considers to be a personal injustice regarding his/her employment relationship. Such a grievance must be filed by the employee within five days from the time the situation occurred that may have caused the grievance. Also the following steps should be taken in pursuing the grievance:

1. The aggrieved employee should first let his/her supervisor know of the complaint. If the employee does not receive a satisfactory reply within two working days, he/she should proceed to Step 2.

JUST CAUSE

The company posted a notice on October 24 scheduling the grievant, along with other employees, to report a half-hour early on October 28 to attend a United Way meeting. The half-hour would be scheduled overtime and paid as such. The grievant saw the notice, made no attempt to discuss the matter with his supervisor, and failed to report at the time stated in the notice. The grievant reported at his regular work time. The company put a discipline memo in his personnel file for failure to report to work for scheduled overtime. The memo noted that the grievant had not reported to work as scheduled and warned that further disciplinary action would result if he continued to violate the contract. The employee grieved the disciplinary action on the basis that he should not be required to attend a United Way meeting, as he did not agree with the principles espoused by United Way.

It was the company's position that the company was within its rights to require the employee to report a half-hour early for work and to attend the United Way meeting on company time. Furthermore, the failure of the employee to report to work on time was in violation of a contract provision. The company adhered to the established principle that the employee should "obey now, grieve later." The company argued that the employee should have attended the meeting and then grieved the factual issue of whether the company had the right to compel attendance at the United Way meeting. It was the union's position that, although the union was supportive of the United Way activity and participated with the company in the annual United Way drive, the company did not have the right to compel the attendance of the employee at the meeting.

Decision

The arbitrator found that the issue in the case was whether the company had the right to compel the grievant's attendance at a United Way meeting. Although it is a well-established rule that the employer has the right to direct the workforce—and this company had the right under its contract with the union to schedule overtime with appropriate notice—the exercise of its management rights must reasonably relate to the operation of the employer's enterprise. It was the arbitrator's belief that the United Way drive was not reasonably related to the company's operation. So, although the company may *request* attendance by the employees at a meeting and be willing to pay overtime, it did not have the authority to *require* attendance at the meeting. The arbitrator did not accept the company's position that the grievant should have reported to work and grieved the issue later because that basic premise, "work now, grieve later," is relevant only when it allows the company's operation to continue during a dispute with a grievant. As the United Way meeting was in no way related to the employer's ability to keep his operation going, there was no requirement that the employee delay his disagreement with the requirement.

Adapted from *Green Bay Packing*, 87 LA 1057 (1986).

2. At this step, the department head is notified of the complaint in writing by the employee. If the employee wishes assistance in writing the grievance, he/she may request assistance from the personnel department. If a satisfactory reply to the grievance is not received in three working days, then the employee should proceed to Step 3.

3. At this stage, the director of personnel services or his/her designate is informed of the grievance by the employee. After a review of the facts, the personnel director or his/her designate and the employee may reach a satisfactory

solution to the grievance. However, if this does not occur, then the fourth step should be taken.

4. A peer review committee composed of three impartial employees will be established to review the grievance and establish the facts of the complaint. The members of this committee are subject to the approval of the aggrieved employee. The director of personnel services or his/her designate will serve as a resource person for the committee. However, the peer review committee, alone, makes the recommendation of how the complaint is to be resolved. Within five working days of the hearing, the employee will receive the committee's written recommendation.

5. Finally, if the employee and/or the department head is not satisfied with the committee's recommendations, then the last step in the appeal process is administration where the final determination is made.

In no way, either directly or indirectly, is the employee to consider his/her job in jeopardy as a result of participating in this procedure.[24]

The example illustrates the major difference between union and nonunion procedures: the absence of binding arbitration as a final step. Also, nonunion firms are more likely to use suggestion boxes or open-door grievance procedures. The theory behind nonunion firms' having a grievance procedure in which employees, without reprisal, can seek relief against unfair practices or procedures has considerable merit. However, making it a reality presents many problems.

Most nonunion employees are relatively unsophisticated about grievance procedures and what the procedures can accomplish. Nonunion employees may believe that their company carries a smaller percentage of grievances through to the final step than do unionized organizations. In fact, nonunionized and unionized organizations usually have a similar percentage of grievances that reach the final level because the union steward effectively communicates to the employee that a grievance is without substantial merit and is not worth pursuing. The employee in the unionized firm realizes that the steward usually has the employee's best interest in mind and accepts this advice more readily than the nonunion employee, who generally does not have as much trust in management.

Formal nonunion grievance procedures raise the employees' expectations of relief and intensify their feelings about problems because they know that some of the problems will be addressed. If the grievance procedure takes a long time to resolve, employees may begin to feel that management is delaying the process. In some cases, the entire plant may become empathetically involved, and small problems may be magnified into large ones.

Nonunion employees may be more hesitant to use the formal grievance procedure since they do not have the support and understanding of union representatives. Unless both top management and the first-level supervisors enthusiastically support the grievance procedure, the employees quickly discount it as truly objective for airing complaints. In the unionized organization, the employees feel safer knowing that the union structure is supporting them. Therefore, grievances must be quickly aired and objectively heard in nonunion organizations. Management must understand that there is no union hierarchy to protect the employees' interests and views.[25]

Arbitrator

What are the best three ways to ensure a fair grievance procedure process if you are the employer or the union?

a. *Conduct a full and adequate investigation into the facts and circumstances.* The employee should be given an opportunity to explain why he or she should not be disciplined, or the employer should explain why the discipline imposed did not violate the agreement or past practice.

b. *Make full disclosures at the earliest possible grievance step.* Disclose the issues, the facts, the documents to be presented, and the names of the witnesses and what they will offer as testimony.

c. *Do not rely on the other side to make the case for you.* Develop a theory of the case, with witnesses and documents ready to support it.

TYPES OF ARBITRATION

Two major types of arbitration exist with respect to labor relations, *interest* and *rights*. **Interest arbitration** occurs when a labor contract or agreement does not exist or when a change is sought. **Rights, or contract interpretation, arbitration** involves interpretation of existing contract terms. Interest arbitration has been criticized because arbitrators may tend to "split the difference," thereby causing the parties to take more extreme positions.[26] One arbitrator contends that interest arbitration processes are too adversarial and that they are hampered by impediments to settlement.[27] Rights arbitration is found in almost every labor agreement and is used far more today than interest arbitration. Because interest arbitration tends to have a broader scope than rights arbitration, many unresolved issues are present in interest arbitration. Few parties are willing to place such responsibility in the hands of a third-party neutral.

DEMAND FOR RIGHTS ARBITRATION

There are no prescribed rules for grievance arbitration as there are in the judicial process. Arbitration procedures should be based on the wishes and needs of the parties involved to the extent possible within the judgment of the arbitrator. The arbitration process is more private and is therefore unique to the parties, as compared with the public judicial process. Also, the grievance arbitration procedure involves more sophisticated and knowledgeable parties than those in most judicial proceedings, and the arbitrator, in most cases, is more knowledgeable than the judge. Figure 11-4 is a typical example of a demand for a contract interpretation.

Although labor arbitration tends to be based on the principles of contract law, external law has specified its scope, power, and influence. The practice of arbitration has been shaped substantially by a number of decisions that have come from the federal courts. The legal foundation of the arbitration process is presented in Chapter 12.

Although many labor disputes are clearly suitable for arbitration, judgment must be exercised in deciding whether to arbitrate a particular dispute. Factors to be considered are the merits of the case, the importance of the issue, the effect of winning or losing the dispute, the possibilities of settlement, and psychological and face-saving aspects. The most popular use of labor arbitration is interpreting

Figure 11-4   Demand for Arbitration

Date: _8/8/97_

To: _ABC Company_
     (Name)
     (of part upon whom the Demand is made)
     (Address)   _10 East Street_
     (City and state)   _Pittsburgh, PA_

The undersigned, a Party to an Arbitration Agreement contained in a written contract, dated _5/6/96_, which agreement provides as follows

(Quote arbitration clause)

Any dispute, claim or grievance arising out of or relating to the interpretation or application of this agreement shall be submitted to arbitration under the Voluntary Labor Arbitration Rules of the American Arbitration Association. The parties further agree that there shall be no suspension of work when such dispute arises and while it is in process of adjustment, or arbitration.

NATURE OF DISPUTE:

The union claims that _____ _John Smith_ _____ was unjustly discharged.

REMEDY SOUGHT:

Reinstatement with full back pay and all seniority rights to the date of discharge.

You are hereby notified that copies of our Arbitration Agreement and of this Demand are being filed with the American Arbitration Association at its _Pittsburgh_ Regional Office, with the request that it commence the administration of arbitration.

Signed   _George Green_
(Title)   _XYZ Union, Local 777 International Representative_
(Address)   _122 West Street_
(City and state)   _Pittsburgh, PA_
(Telephone)   _412-555-1890_

Source: Theodore Kheel, *Labor Law* (New York: Matthew Bender, 1983), p. 21, by permission of Matthew Bender.

applications of the collective bargaining agreements. However, labor arbitration is not always the solution. Management will hesitate to arbitrate issues regarding normal prerogatives such as determining methods of production, operating policies, and finances. Labor likewise considers the settlement of an internal union conflict as a topic in which management should not participate.[28]

Public policy exceptions to labor arbitration concerns appeal rights in cases that involve both a contractual grievance and a public policy. These issues are important to the parties because of their impact on the finality of all awards. There are three kinds of public policy cases: equal employment opportunity (Title VII) and sexual harassment, public safety and criminal laws, and the duty of fair representation.

Title VII Cases

The principle stated by the courts in early Title VII Cases *(Gardner-Denver* and *Grace)*[29] is clear: Individuals may exercise a legal right based on external law that is independent of their rights under a collective bargaining agreement. An individual who takes a grievance to arbitration that involves an EEO (equal employment opportunity) matter could be entitled to a trial if he or she loses in arbitration. Case 11-4 provides a description of the *Gardner-Denver Case.*

The public policy exception has been extended into the area of sexual harassment. In a number of cases, the courts have quoted public policy extensively

---

CASE 11-4

GARDNER-DENVER

The grievant, an African American, after being discharged, filed a grievance under a collective bargaining agreement that contained a nondiscrimination clause. Prior to arbitration, the grievant also filed a racial discrimination complaint that was referred to the Equal Employment Opportunity Commission (EEOC). The arbitrator ruled that the grievant was discharged for just cause, and the EEOC determined that there were no reasonable grounds to believe that a violation of Title VII of the Civil Rights Act had occurred. The grievant then brought action in the U.S. District Court alleging that his discharge resulted from a racially discriminatory employment practice.

Decision

The district court held that the grievant was bound by prior arbitral decisions and had no right to sue under Title VII. The court of appeals affirmed, but the Supreme Court reversed, holding that an employee's statutory right to a trial de novo under Title VII is not foreclosed by prior submission of his claim to final arbitration.

From the standpoint of arbitration, footnote 21 in the Supreme Court's decision is its most controversial element because it specifically raises the specter of judicial review. The Court said:

> We adopt no standards as to the weight to be accorded an arbitration decision, since this must be determined in the court's discretion with regard to the facts and circumstances of each case. When an arbitral determination gives full consideration to the employee's Title VII rights, a court may properly accord it great weight. This is especially true where the issue is one of fact, specifically addressed by the parties and decided by the arbitrator on the basis of an adequate record. But courts should be ever mindful that Congress thought it necessary to provide a judicial forum for the resolution of discriminatory employment claims. It is the duty of the courts to assure the full availability of this forum.

Adapted from *Harrell Alexander, Sr. v. Gardner-Denver Co.*, 415 U.S. 36, 944 S.Ct. 101 (1974).

MISCO, INC.

One of misco's work rules listed as cause for discharge the possession or use of a controlled substance on company property. An employee covered by the collective labor agreement was apprehended by police in the backseat of someone else's car on the company parking lot. There was marijuana smoke in the air of the car and a lighted marijuana cigarette in the front seat ashtray. A police search of the employee's own car on the lot revealed marijuana gleanings.

Management discharged the employee for violation of the disciplinary rule. The employee grieved, and an arbitrator later upheld the grievance and ordered reinstatement. The arbitrator concluded that the cigarette incident was insufficient proof that the grievant was using or possessed marijuana on company property. At the time of discharge, the company was not aware of the fact that marijuana was found in the employee's own car, and the arbitrator refused to accept that claim into evidence.

Decision

The district court vacated the arbitration award, and the court of appeals confirmed, ruling that reinstatement would violate the public policy against the operation of dangerous machinery by persons under the influence of drugs (the grievant operated a slitter-rewinder, which cuts rolling coils of paper). The Supreme Court reversed, holding that the court of appeals exceeded the limited authority possessed by a court reviewing an arbitrator's award under a collective bargaining agreement. The high court stated that absent fraud by the parties or the arbitrator's dishonesty, reviewing courts in such cases are not authorized to reconsider the merits of an arbitrator's award. The high court also stated that the collective bargaining agreement left evidentiary matters to the arbitrator: The arbitrator's finding of fact is conclusive.

United Paperworkers International Union, AFL-CIO v. Misco, Inc., 484 U.S. 29, 108 S.Ct. 364 (1987).

as they reexamined arbitration awards. For example, the courts set aside the arbitrator's decision in *Newsday* and *Stroehman Bakeries* but affirmed an arbitration award in *Chrysler*.[30]

Public Safety and Criminal Laws

The courts appear to be less consistent in enforcing public safety and criminal law matters. The *Misco* **case** (see Case 11-5) involved marijuana use, possession, and attendant safety concerns. However, the Supreme Court upheld the arbitration award reinstating the grievant.

Duty of Fair Representation

The courts have held that it is a union's obligation to represent all members of the bargaining unit fairly. If a breach in this duty taints an arbitration award, then the arbitration decision can be set aside, and the person harmed can be compensated by both the union and the employer.

GRIEVANCE MEDIATION

Although the use of mediation to resolve employee grievances is not new in labor relations, it is less visible than arbitration. **Grievance mediation** can be defined as "the intervention of an outside mediator into a potential or actual impasse over the interpretation or application of contract terms.[31] The process should be viewed as a means of reducing the need for arbitration since it is usually utilized as the last step *before* arbitration.

The former director of the Federal Mediation and Conciliation Service, William Simkin, has suggested that mediation is a most useful means of avoiding the need for binding arbitration as a means of resolving grievances.[32] Reducing the use of expensive, time-consuming arbitration is one of the primary advantages of mediation. Small unions and employers might be particularly interested in using mediation as an alternative.[33] Also, mediation is *not* a decision process in which one side must lose. If a compromise is reached, it is far less likely that either side will bear the image of a loser than is often the case in arbitration. Mediation is not a final step, yet it allows the voluntary use of a neutral third party to help resolve the conflict without going to arbitration.

The bituminous coal industry illustrates one of the most successful uses of grievance mediation. The unionized sector of the industry has historically been plagued by wildcat strikes, expensive arbitration, and a great deal of labor unrest.[34] In the fall of 1980, several coal districts began experimenting with the use of mediation as the final step in a grievance resolution process before binding arbitration. After two six-month trial periods in four districts of the United Mine Workers of America, 89 percent of the 153 grievances taken to mediation were resolved before arbitration. Total savings were almost $100,000, and the average grievance was resolved three months earlier than it would have been under arbitration.[35]

The use of grievance mediation in the coal industry has been considered a success for several reasons. Most grievances were resolved regardless of the mechanism by which the grievance was brought to mediation (by request of one party or by mutual consent) and regardless of the nature of the issue. Mediation saved, on the average, $700 and three months per case in comparison with arbitration. Also, labor and management leaders greatly preferred the informality of mediation and their ability to control the outcome through negotiation. The key to the use of mediation was the willingness of both parties to *negotiate* a solution with the mediator and other party.[36]

The NLRB and other agencies will usually accept the intervention of grievance mediation if the guidelines, such as those recommended by mediator and arbitrator Mollie Bowers, are followed:

1. Include the grievant in any and all meetings.
2. Hold meetings in reasonable times and locations.
3. Guard against any charge that the neutral party conspired to obtain a result that conflicts with case law, the contract, or statutory law.
4. Ensure that the mediators have a good working knowledge of laws, the contract language, and prevailing practices.
5. Ensure that all parties agree on the settlement.[37]

In 1986, Bell South and District 3, Communication Workers of America, agreed to utilize grievance mediation on a one-year trial basis. Of the 64 grievances referred to mediation during that time, 69 percent were resolved. A follow-up survey of Bell South managers showed that they had a very favorable impression of the grievance mediation process even though some grievances ended in a settlement managers disliked.[38]

SUMMARY

Grievance procedures and the arbitration of disputes provide important tools to collective bargaining. Without such procedures, labor and management, as well as the community, would suffer greatly from economic recriminations, such as strikes and walkouts. Instead, issues such as a supervisor's disciplining an employee, as well as instances of "letting off steam," can be logically decided. The Supreme Court and the NLRB have given sufficient authority to agreed-upon grievance procedures and arbitration as a final step, making the practices commonplace and effective. However, specific steps to be utilized in employee grievances should be detailed in the labor agreement. Grievance mediation reduces the need for arbitration as a final step and should be considered when possible.

CASE STUDY 11-1

INSUBORDINATION OF A POLICE OFFICER
WHILE IN PURSUIT OF A STOLEN VEHICLE

Facts

The city's police department has a procedure that establishes guidelines for police officers who are in pursuit of the occupants of another vehicle. A section of the pursuit policy states that a shift commander is to be assigned as Managing Supervisor of each pursuit and has the authority to terminate a pursuit when public safety is at risk.

Patrol officers became involved in a pursuit when a man pointed a rifle at his wife, threatened her, discharged the rifle, and then, in a vehicle he had stolen, fled from investigating police officers. Sergeant D, who had been assigned as Managing Supervisor, monitored the pursuit and finally ordered it terminated. Police Officer A, however, continued to follow the suspect despite having been told by both Sergeant D and Sergeant C to stop the pursuit. Officer A apprehended the suspect when the suspect's automobile "broke down." The city charged Officer A with a violation of the pursuit procedure and suspended him for one day without pay.

At an arbitration hearing, Officer A testified that he was concerned that the suspect's automobile would break down and that, because the suspect had committed a felony (stealing a vehicle) and was armed, he might engage in a carjacking. Officer A further testified of his oath to protect the public and his belief that the public was in danger from the suspect. Officer A also testified that his emergency lights and siren were not in operation while he followed the suspect, and he never attempted to close the gap on the suspect's automobile; thus he was not in pursuit.

The city argued that Officer A had failed to obey the orders of two sergeants to terminate a pursuit and should be disciplined for his failure to obey their orders.

Questions

1. Was Officer A in pursuit of the suspect's vehicle?
2. As an arbitrator would you uphold or deny the grievance?
3. Would you change the punishment of Officer A from a one-day suspension to that of a written warning?
4. What is the value to the police command in disciplining Officer A?

Adapted from *City of San Antonio*, 95 ARB 5066 (1995).

GROOMING STANDARDS
AT SOUTHWEST AIRLINES

Facts

Ramp agents of Southwest Airlines load and unload baggage from aircraft and also collect baggage from customers as they board the aircraft. The union states that Grievant B, a ramp agent with 13 years' experience, is being discriminated against because management at its Love Field Operation in Dallas, Texas, requires him to wear his long hair tucked beneath a cap but female ramp agents and male maintenance employees are not required to wear caps.

At an arbitration hearing, the company testified that its grooming rules have been enforced on a uniform basis. All male ramp agents have been treated the same, and all female ramp agents have been treated the same. The company argues that discrimination is permissible as long as it is not unlawful and as long as differences in grooming standards that do not unreasonably inhibit work opportunities are permissible under Title VII of the 1964 Civil Rights Act. The company also states that the issue of an alleged discrimination with respect to male maintenance employees is beyond the scope of this grievance because a separate labor agreement exists between maintenance employees and the company.

Questions

1. How realistic is the company's argument regarding grooming standards?
2. Can an employer unilaterally impose a grooming rule over the objections of its employees or their bargaining agent?
3. How valid is the company's argument that the labor agreement with maintenance employees is "beyond the scope of this grievance?"

Southwest Airlines 97 ARB 3036 (1996).

		KEY TERMS AND CONCEPTS
disciplinary procedures	grievance procedure	
formal grievance procedure	interest arbitration	
Alexander v. Gardner-Denver	*United Paperworkers v. Misco*	
grievance	public policy exceptions	
grievance categories	rights arbitration	
grievance mediation		

REVIEW QUESTIONS

1. Discuss the relationship that exists between labor and management in the public sector.
2. Explain the grievance procedure.
3. Describe how the concepts of authority and influence affect the grievance process.
4. Explain the steps of a grievance. Why do these steps exist?
5. Discuss how disciplinary procedures affect the labor-management relationship.
6. How do nonunion grievance procedures compare with those commonly found in unionized situations?
7. Discuss the major types of arbitration.
8. Explain the public policy exceptions to a labor agreement.
9. What are advantages and disadvantages of grievance mediation?

EXERCISE 11-1 ## Source of Grievances

Purpose:
To understand the different sources of grievances in the workplace.

Task:
Divide the class into teams. Each group should survey one of the following types of local businesses to see what types of grievances commonly arise at their workplace. Share the results:

Type of business
Governmental unit
Manufacturer
Retailer
Professional firm
Your university
Survey

Cause of Grievance	*Number of Grievances per Year*
Violation of leave provision	
Unauthorized strike participation	
Unauthorized absence	
Dishonesty or theft	
Violation of camping rules	
Insubordination	
Intoxication	
Incompetence	
Failure to obey safety rules	
Tardiness	
Misconduct (general)	
• Drug or alcohol abuse	
• Sexual or racial harassment	
Other	

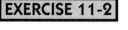

Reducing a Policy to Writing

Purpose:

To familiarize students with the critical elements of a well-written grievance policy and of the writing process, such as clarity, presentation of evidence, appeals mechanism, and the fairness of the final decision process.

Task:

Divide the class into teams of three to five students. Each team must acquire the written student grade appeal policy of a different college or university. Each team should develop a written analysis of the strengths and weaknesses of their policy in comparison with the policy used at the school where the class is being taught and then present their findings to the class. The class as a whole should then develop a "model" policy based on the preferred elements of the policies presented.

If you are using Smith/Carrell/Golden *Collective Bargaining Simulated, 4E,* with this text, please refer to the following:

p. 17, Article IX: Adjustment of Grievances, for the description of the three-step grievance process and the termination and suspension process.

The Arbitration
Process

Donald Fehr, executive director of the Major League Baseball Players Association (far left) testified on Capitol Hill in February 1995, before the Senate Antitrust subcommittee. The subcommittee was holding hearings on baseball's antitrust exemption.

Process and Content Issues in Labor Arbitration

Labor News

What are the critical variables employed in reaching an arbitration decision and award? Have these variables changed over time? Two longitudinal studies have examined these questions by examining the *process* and *content* of labor arbitration. In these studies, the process of labor arbitration is considered as a rational, comprehensive decision-making activity that describes *how* the arbitration decision and award are formulated. The content of labor arbitration in these studies deals with *what* types of decisions are made.

These two studies (the process and content of labor arbitration) replicated an earlier study and then compared the time periods to identify process and content changes in labor arbitration. The earlier study, conducted in 1975, involved a mail questionnaire of members of the National Academy of Arbitrators (NAA) regarding their perspectives on the characteristics of arbitrators, arbitration procedures, and arbitration decision criteria. The later process and content studies were conducted in 1987 and also involved a mail questionnaire of members of the NAA.

The results of the longitudinal process comparison of labor arbitration indicated that the process of labor arbitration as well as certain decision-making criteria have not significantly changed. For example, an overwhelming majority of responding arbitrators in both the 1975 and the 1987 study reported that the labor contract language and the parties' past practices were the two top factors in order of importance in arbitral decision making. The results of the longitudinal comparison of labor arbitration indicated that significant changes have occurred in the process of arbitration for the two time periods.

The results of the comparison indicated that significant changes have also occurred in the content of labor arbitration. For example, comparison of the 1975 and 1987 studies revealed that 1987 respondents tended to use fewer pages in writing their opinions, conducted fewer multiple grievances, were less sympathetic with requests for "work products,"* called fewer witnesses, and were less involved in examining witnesses than their 1975 counterparts. Although the value of posthearing briefs had not changed among arbitrators for the two time periods, 1987 arbitrators tended to leave the decision of filing briefs to the parties rather than instructing them to do so. The characteristics of arbitrators significantly changed for the two time periods. For example, arbitrators in 1987 were older in terms of age than their 1975 counterparts, had more experience, and had different backgrounds. The two time periods were not significantly different with respect to decisions awarded to either the company or the union.

*An area of controversy and sensitivity to the parties concerns whether an arbitrator should require that one party, upon demand by the opponent, disclose or produce material collected and prepared for an arbitration hearing but not submitted as evidence—commonly referred to as "work product."

The 1975 study was published in A. Dale Allen Jr., "Procedures in Labor Arbitration: Views from Arbitrators Themselves," *Labor Studies Journal* 1 (1976), pp. 190–202. The content of labor arbitration was adapted from Daniel F. Jennings and A. Dale Allen Jr., "A Longitudinal Analysis of Content Issues in Labor Arbitration: Views from Arbitrators Themselves," *Labor Studies Journal* 16 (1991), pp. 35–49. The process of labor arbitration was adapted from Daniel F. Jennings and A. Dale Allen Jr., "How Arbitrators View the Process of Labor Arbitration: A Longitudinal Analysis," *Labor Studies Journal* 18, no. 1 (Winter 1993), pp. 41–50.

The first mention of labor arbitration in American labor history, according to Professor Edwin Witte, dates to a clause in the constitution of the Journeymen Cabinet-Makers of Philadelphia in 1829.[1] The earliest recorded arbitration hearing occurred in 1865 when iron workers in Pittsburgh arbitrated their wages.[2] The first known case in which an outside arbitrator was employed occurred in 1871 in eastern Ohio. The Committee of the Anthracite Board of Trade (an association of coal operators) and the Committee of Workingmen's Benevolent Association (the coal miner's union) retained the services of Judge William Ewell of Bloomsburg, Pennsylvania, to settle their dispute on "discharging men for their connection with the Workingmen's Benevolent Association." Professor Robban W. Fleming reports that the results were successful in that the parties accepted and implemented Judge Ewell's recommendation. However, in 1874 when the two parties attempted to submit a second dispute to another judge for a decision, one company of the association refused to agree to the process and a strike developed.[3] Apparently, the other firms in the association were willing to conform to the desires of the dissenting company rather than to submit their dispute to an "outside" arbitrator. Professor Jean McKelvey writes that "arbitration" in the period from 1865 to 1931 was a "negotiation" process rather than a third-party decision-making process.[4]

HISTORY AND LEGAL STATE OF ARBITRATION

Four Supreme Court cases (*Lincoln Mills* and the *Steelworkers Trilogy*)[5] have provided the legal foundation for arbitration as it exists today in the United States. The *Lincoln Mills* decision authorized federal courts to fashion a body of law for the enforcement of collective bargaining agreements, and it promoted the view that the agreement to arbitrate is a quid pro quo for an agreement to refrain from striking during the term of a labor contract. This decision was based on the premise that arbitration provided the best route to industrial peace and provided the support necessary for the development of labor arbitration in the United States.

The *Lincoln Mills* concept that the federal courts would mandate the performance of arbitration provisions contained in collective bargaining agreements was given substance in the *Steelworkers Trilogy*, decided by the Supreme Court three years later in 1960. These four cases established the following five principles to govern the arbitration of grievances under collective bargaining.[6]

1. Arbitration is a matter of contract. The parties are not required to arbitrate a dispute that they have not agreed to submit to arbitration. The courts determine whether there is a duty to arbitrate a dispute.
2. In determining whether there is a duty to arbitrate a dispute, the courts should not examine the merits of the underlying grievance, even if it appears to be frivolous.
3. In labor contracts with an arbitration clause there is a presumption of arbitrability unless there is positive assurance that the arbitration clause is not susceptible to an interpretation that covers the dispute. Doubts should be resolved in favor of coverage.
4. As long as an arbitration award is based on the bargaining agreement, a court should enforce the award without examining its correctness.

5. In interpreting the labor agreement, the arbitrator is not limited to the words of the contract. The arbitrator is empowered to consider factors such as past practice, parol evidence,* and the "common law of the shop."

Three important issues have evolved from the *Lincoln Mills* and the *Steelworkers Trilogy* cases: the principle of general arbitrability, situations in which the contract has expired or the ownership of the company has changed, and whether the duty to arbitrate survives a change in company ownership.[7]

1. *General arbitrability.* The courts have consistently enforced the principle that if the contract provides for the arbitration of grievances, then a grievance is presumed to be arbitrable as long as the agreement does not exclude the topic under consideration.
2. *Expired contracts or changes in ownership.* The Supreme Court has ruled that the duty to arbitrate can extend beyond the life of the contract. A postexpiration grievance is arbitrable only when it involves facts and events that occurred before expiration, when the action infringes a right vested under the agreement, or when the normal principles of contract interpretation show that the disputed contractual right survives the remainder of the agreement.
3. *Successorship.* The Supreme Court has also ruled that the successor employer is not required to adopt the substantive terms of the predecessor agreement but that the successor inherits the contractual duty to arbitrate as long as there is "substantial continuity" between the old and the new companies.

In summary, the rulings by the Supreme Court on the duty to arbitrate makes it clear that if the parties' labor agreement requires the arbitration of grievances, then it will be difficult to avoid arbitration.

The U.S. Supreme Court acknowledged the superiority of arbitration in resolving labor-management disputes under collective bargaining agreements by stating:

> The labor arbitrator performs functions which are not normal to the courts; the considerations which help him fashion judgments may indeed be foreign to the confines of courts. The parties expect that his judgments of a particular grievance will not only reflect what the contract says but, insofar as the collective bargaining agreement permits, such factors as the effect upon productivity of a particular result, its consequence to the morale of the shop, his judgment whether detentions will be heightened or diminished. For the parties' objective in using the arbitration process is primarily to further their common goal of uninterrupted production under the agreement, to make the agreement meet their specialized needs. The ablest judge cannot be expected to bring the same experience and confidence to bear upon the determination of a grievance because he cannot be similarly informed.[8]

The courts stressed that arbitrators' decisions, as long as they are based on interpretation of the contract, should be final and binding and not questioned by the

---

Parol evidence, in its classic form holds that evidence, oral or otherwise, cannot be admitted for the purpose of varying or contradicting written language recorded in the labor agreement. The rationale for this rule is that the parties have spent many hours in negotiating standardized employment conditions; thus, disregarding negotiated terms would damage stable labor-management relationships and communicate to the parties that there is little or no point in reducing contract terms to writing. For an expanded discussion see Marvin Hill Jr. and Anthony V. Sinicropi, *Evidence in Labor Arbitration* (Washington, DC: Bureau of National Affairs, 1987), pp. 50–52.

OUTSOURCING OF WORK AT
GENERAL ELECTRIC RAILCAR FACILITIES

General Electric (GE) Railcar Services repairs railcars in its Texarkana, Arkansas, facility. The labor agreement between GE and the Transportation International Union, AFL-CIO includes the following management rights clause.

ARTICLE 21.1—MANAGEMENT

The management of the business and the direction of the working forces, including but not limited to the right to plan, direct and control plant operations; to schedule the working hours, lunch and rest periods; to determine employee qualifications; to hire, transfer, and promote employees, to suspend or discharge employees for cause or to relieve employees from work because of lack of work or for other legitimate reasons; to establish reasonable production standards; to require employees to work when directed; to make and enforce shop rules and regulations; to introduce new and improved production methods, materials, or facilities; to close the plant completely (but prior thereto the Company shall notify the Union and discuss the effects of such closing with the Union); and to exercise all other management rights are vested exclusively in the Company; provided, however, that such rights shall not be applied in a manner violative of any provisions of this Agreement.

The Company reserves the right to determine how, where, and by whom its work shall be performed, provided that in the case of contracting out work then being performed by the employees the Company shall discuss its intentions relating thereto with the Union Committee, prior to reaching a final decision, but in all events, it is understood that the Company reserves the right to make such final decision and proceed accordingly as in its sole judgement,

may seem advisable or to be in the best interests of the Company. The Company's obligation to discuss contracting out of work shall not apply to transfer of work between plants of the Company.

In June 1996, GE subcontracted the work of mowing grass at its manufacturing facility to "outside contractors." In August 1996, GE hired three outside contractors to work as safety observers. A safety observer works outside a confined area and observes the employees who work within the confined area. Working in a confined space such as inside a "tank" or "hopper" railcar becomes hazardous when the oxygen content of the space goes below a certain level. Also, dust, odor, and flammable or explosive gases can create a hazardous condition. In the past, the work of mowing the grass and the work of safety observers were performed by individuals who had the bargaining unit classification of General Helper.

GE's position in the arbitration hearing was that its intentions were to make the jobs of its employees more secure. Using employees with "craft" skills to perform certain work elements and lesser skilled employees to perform other tasks, the company contended, would benefit both employees and GE.

The union's position was that, in the past, GE had contracted out work only when union employees lacked the required skills. The parties' labor agreement contained an article "that all newly hired employees will be considered probationary employees and have no seniority for 45 days and that GE has the right to terminate the employment of temporary employees within the 45-day period with no grievances being filed with reference to such termination." Another article in the bargaining agreement stated "that all permanent vacancies are to be promptly posted." The union argued that GE

(continued)

had violated those two articles because the outside contractors would have no seniority after 45 days. The union also argued that the outside contractors working as safety observers had not received the proper safety training. The union further argued that GE had not acted in good faith and had violated the parties' labor agreement and that if GE were allowed to continue this course of action, then no bargaining unit job would be safe.

Decision

A prevailing principle in every collective bargaining agreement is the duty of reasonableness and good faith of the parties. Thus, a company cannot bargain with a union over jobs regularly assigned to its employees and contract out those same jobs solely for the purpose of saving money, thereby subverting the labor agreement or seriously damaging the bargaining unit. Furthermore, Arbitrator Nolan in *Uniroyal, Inc.* (76 LA 1049 [1981]) stated that

> the very presence of a negotiated labor agreement indicates that there are inherent limits on an employer's right to contract out work. An employer could not sign a labor agreement one day and then contract

out all the work the next day because it was cheaper.

The union's claim of past practice falls short in proving their case. Although bargaining unit employees have in the past performed the tasks of cutting or mowing the grass and acting as safety observer, the language of Article 21.1 clearly states that the final decision to contract out such work is reserved to the company.

In summary, the union's grievance must fail because the union has not carried its burden of proof to show a contractural violation. The union asks this arbitrator to imply too much. Given the clear language of the parties' collective bargaining agreement, the company has acted reasonably and in good faith. This arbitrator, however, notes the Union's concern regarding the extent to which the company will contract out work. The union should realize that the language in a collective bargaining agreement is developed by the parties at the bargaining table. Also as Arbitrator Hart in *Continental Fibre Drum Inc.* (86 LA 780 [1986]) stated: In labor relations the opposite of love is not hate but fear—as is apparent when a union fears for its job security without fully appreciating that the best job security is with a successful, money-making company.

Adapted from *General Electric Railcar Services*, Opinion rendered by Arbitrator Daniel F. Jennings on January 7, 1997.

courts. For example, in 1986 the seventh circuit upheld an arbitrator's decision and overturned a district court's reversal of that decision. In this case, an employee of E. I. duPont de Nemours & Company, during a nervous breakdown, attacked fellow employees and damaged company property. The arbitrator had concluded that the incident was a result of a mental breakdown (not drug use as the company contended) and would most likely not recur. The arbitrator's decision, vacated by the district court, was upheld by the seventh circuit court. The court stated, "So long as the arbitrator interpreted the contract in making his award, his award must be affirmed even if he clearly misinterpreted the contract."[9]

Another advantage of arbitration over litigation is the final and binding provision contained in most agreements to arbitrate grievances. This provides a final step for settling labor disputes in comparison with the court process requiring a series of lengthy appeals and many steps before a final decision. In addition, the technical rules of evidence found in the courtroom need not be applied to the proceedings. Arbitration hearings are less formal than litigation, and the advocates need not have legal training.

Courts of general jurisdiction are not usually well versed in problems unique to labor-management grievances. Arbitrators are presumed to be familiar with the needs and techniques of the industry, and therefore both parties are confident that they will be able to adapt to the awards of the arbitrator.[10] Case 12-1 describes a situation involving the outsourcing of certain work previously performed by union employees.

In our society, the use of voluntary arbitration to settle labor-management disputes provides an important role in minimizing disruptions of the production of goods and services. It serves as a safety valve for our capitalistic system. Society as a whole benefits greatly when disputes are arbitrated quickly without the use of strikes or walkouts.

SELECTING THE ARBITRATOR

Both labor and management pay the arbitration fees and have a hand in the choice of arbitrator; he or she is not an outside party imposed on them to resolve disputes. The arbitrator's jurisdiction evolves from the contract negotiated by the two parties. Therefore, the arbitrator's performance must generally be satisfactory; the parties can dispense with an incompetent arbitrator. The arbitrator is well aware that he or she provides a service for a fee and is expected to meet certain professional standards.

Because of the very real need to keep both parties satisfied with arbitration decisions, arbitrator decisions and awards are far from uniform on almost any issue.[11] However, no two grievance situations are the same.

The arbitrator may be a permanent umpire chosen beforehand by labor and management to decide disputes arising during the life of the collective bargaining agreement. However, most arbitrations take place on an ad hoc basis, with arbitrators selected to hear disputes case by case.

Collective bargaining agreements with arbitration normally provide for the selection process of arbitrators. If a permanent arbitrator is not designated in the contract, then an impartial agency is often agreed on as a source of arbitrators. The American Arbitration Association and the Federal Mediation and Conciliation Service are the two agencies that are the most frequent sources of arbitrators.

The American Arbitration Association has developed this process for selecting an arbitrator:

1. On receiving the demand for arbitration or submission agreement, the tribunal administrator (a staff member of the association) acknowledges receipt thereof and sends each party a copy of a specially prepared list of proposed arbitrators. In drawing up this list, he is guided by the statement of the nature of the dispute. Basic information about each arbitrator is appended to the list.

2. Parties are allowed seven days to study the list, cross off any names objected to, and number the remaining names in the order of preference. If parties want more information about a proposed arbitrator, such information is gladly given upon request.

3. Where parties are unable to find a mutual choice on the list, the association will submit additional lists, at the request of both parties.

4. If, despite all efforts to arrive at a mutual choice, parties cannot agree upon an arbitrator, the association will make an administrative appointment. But in no case will an arbitrator whose name was crossed out by either party be so appointed.[12]

The arbitrator would be required to follow the contract language regardless of any personal opinion as to the reasonableness of the agreement language if the intent of the provision is clear. However, the language is often ambiguous, and the arbitrator must interpret the provision in question.

For the interpretation of contract language, two role models for arbitrators have been developed. One role model sees the arbitrator as a judge or umpire. Under this model the arbitrator, as a judge, reviews the arguments and proofs presented by the parties and makes a decision according to the rules imposed by the contract.[13] The second role model is much broader. The arbitrator's role is that of a mediator or impartial chairperson and is there primarily to help resolve the dispute rather than to decide which party was right or wrong under the contract. The fact that the future relationship of the two parties would be stronger if they resolved their own disputes is emphasized. The arbitrator issues a binding decision only as a last resort.[14] Today the latter role is more often viewed as proper for a grievance mediator, as discussed in chapter 11. Arbitrators are more likely to serve as judges.

Qualifications of Arbitrators

Arbitrators are not required to have any specific educational or technical training unless specified by the collective bargaining agreement. If rigid qualifications are required, it may become very difficult to find an available arbitrator.

Various characteristics including experience, education, occupation, and visibility have been identified as affecting arbitrator selection. Both labor and management prefer arbitrators with specific attributes. Research has shown that age and experience are the most significant *demographic* factors affecting arbitrator decisions. Surprisingly, though, labor lawyers have not been able to distinguish between the decisions of experienced and inexperienced arbitrators.[15]

In addition to these demographic variables, other variables affecting arbitrator selection include *visibility*, such as public speaking and professional association membership, and *past arbitration decisions*. All three appear to determine which arbitrator might be selected for a case. Empirical data indicate that visibility in the community may be the single most important variable.[16]

Arbitrators are secured from a wide variety of backgrounds and include attorneys, judges, and university professors. Elkouri and Elkouri outline some general **qualifications of an arbitrator**:

1. *Impartiality.* Although no one can be absolutely free from bias or prejudice, the arbitrator is expected to divest himself or herself from personal inclinations during an arbitration, even though he or she decides cases according to his or her own judgment. The elements of honesty and impartiality are the most critical, and the arbitrator must always be able to be up front with both parties. Otherwise, he or she might not be selected again.

2. *Integrity.* Arbitrators are expected to be of the highest integrity. Both parties can review backgrounds and affiliations of prospective arbitrators; personal, financial, or business interests in the affairs of either party are primary considerations. The Code of Ethics for Arbitrators requires the arbitrator to disclose any association or relation that might reasonably bring any doubt to his or her

objectivity. Records of past decisions and whether the arbitrator has expressed strong opinions in favor of either labor or management are also reviewed. Arbitrators are expected to exercise fairness and good judgment in issuing awards and not just to please both sides by splitting awards.

3. *Ability and expertise.* A labor-management arbitrator should have a broad background, experience, and education. Maturity of judgment and a quick, analytical mind are also necessary. The arbitrator is not expected to be a subject-matter specialist; such an expert may be difficult or impossible to find. Both parties may prefer someone with general business or financial expertise.

4. *Legal training.* Labor-management arbitrators often are lawyers. Legal training may help an arbitrator to be objective and to analyze and evaluate facts without personal bias or extraneous evidence. However, not all lawyers make good arbitrators, nor are all good arbitrators lawyers.[17] Profile 12-1 describes a labor arbitrator with some unique achievements.

Tripartite Arbitration Board

The labor agreement may provide for multiple arbitrators. A **tripartite arbitration board** usually has one or more members selected by management, an equal number of members selected by labor, and a neutral member who serves as chairper-

---

PROFILE 12-1

A. DALE ALLEN JR., LABOR ARBITRATOR AND PROFESSOR OF LABOR RELATIONS, BAYLOR UNIVERSITY

To my knowledge, I hold the distinction of being the youngest arbitrator to have ever heard a labor arbitration case, and I am among the most-published authors of labor arbitration cases in the nation. The manner by which I was selected for my first arbitration cases was most unusual. In 1967, at the age of 31, I was teaching an MBA night class in labor relations at the University of Louisville. Among my students were the vice president of labor relations for a national manufacturing company located in Louisville and the business agent of the large union that represented those employees. Upon completion of the course (and having received good grades), these two men asked me to serve as arbitrator for three of their disputes. Since that beginning, I have rendered around 1,100 arbitration decisions, of which 350–400 have been published in the national arbitration reporting services. In addition, over the years, I have

served as permanent arbitrator at various times for about 40 companies and their respective unions. My university education consists of a Doctorate in Labor Relations from the University of Colorado, and an MBA and BS degree from Indiana University. Prior to becoming a university professor, I worked in industry for two companies as a line manager and labor relations specialist. Among my published research are approximately 45 articles that have appeared in the following academic journals: *Employee Relations Law Journal, Labor Law Journal, Labor Studies Journal, Personnel Journal,* and the *Journal of Industrial Engineering,* as well as in numerous management and labor relations proceedings. Despite my heavy involvement in teaching and labor arbitration, I am active in many civic, church, and community projects. I am married and have five children and eight grandchildren at the writing of this profile.

Contributed by A. Dale Allen Jr.

---

son. The labor and management members act as partisans or advocates for their respective sides and, in essence, the neutral chairperson becomes a single arbitrator.

Tripartite boards sometimes do not reach decisions unanimously. Collective bargaining agreements often provide that a majority award of the board is final and binding. Some agreements may even give the neutral member the sole right and responsibility for making the final decision. The advantage of using a tripartite board rather than a single arbitrator is to provide the neutral member with valuable advice and assistance from the partisan members. Each party may be able to give to the neutral arbitrator a more realistic and informed picture of the issues involved than may be given by formal presentation of the issues. The disadvantage of such a board, of course, is the additional time and expense incurred.[18] The following is an example of a panel selection procedure:

ARTICLE 27
Section 2

If the issue cannot be resolved by the Joint Conference Committee, a panel of seven (7) impartial arbitrators will be promptly secured from the Federal Mediation and Conciliation Service. The employer and the union shall each have the right to reject one panel of impartial arbitrators, but they must select an arbitrator from the third panel of arbitrators if they cannot agree to select from the first or second panels. The arbitrator will be selected by each party striking an equal number of arbitrators from the panel. The remaining individual shall be the arbitrator and his decision shall be final and binding on the employer, the union, and the employees. Expenses incurred in any arbitration under the provision of this article will be borne equally by the employer and the union.[19]

DETERMINING ARBITRABILITY

If both parties in a dispute submit the dispute to arbitration, there is no question of **arbitrability** since a submission by both parties identifies their agreement to go to arbitration. However, if only one party invokes the arbitration clause in a collective bargaining agreement by notice of intent to arbitrate a dispute, the other party may resist the intent to arbitrate on the grounds that the dispute is not arbitrable. Such a challenge to arbitrability is presented either to the arbitrator or to the courts. Although most questions of arbitrability are left in the hands of the arbitrator, they may be taken to the courts. The courts may be involved with arbitrability in one of three ways:

1. The party challenging arbitrability may seek a temporary injunction or stay of arbitration, pending determination of arbitrability.
2. The party demanding arbitration may seek a court order compelling the other party to arbitrate when the applicable law upholds agreements to arbitrate future disputes; the latter party then raises the issue of arbitrability.
3. The issue of arbitrability may be considered when an award is taken to court for review or enforcement, unless the parties have clearly vested the arbitrator with exclusive and final right of determining arbitrability, or unless the right to challenge arbitrability is held by the court to have been otherwise waived under the circumstances of the case.[20]

The Supreme Court in the *Warrior & Gulf* case declared that congressional policy in favor of settlement of disputes through arbitration restricts the judicial process and strictly confines it to questions of whether the reluctant party agreed

ARBITRABILITY

The City of Texas City, Texas, and the International Association of Firefighters reached agreement on a drug-testing policy for firefighters. According to the policy, the city may perform drug or alcohol testing:

1. On any employee who manifests "reasonable belief" behavior
2. On any employee who has been involved in a work-related accident that involves an injury to himself or to another while operating a vehicle or motor-driven or heavy equipment
3. On a random basis of any employee who performs duties in a safety-sensitive position
4. On any employee who is subject to drug or alcohol testing pursuant to federal or state rules, regulations, or laws

During a dispatch to an alarm in a local apartment complex, Engine Driver B scraped an unoccupied parked automobile. B immediately stopped and inspected the damage, which was slight. Captain W called the police department and reported the incident. Both B and W located the individual who owned the automobile and reported to her what had happened. The owner of the automobile did not file a claim, and there was no liability to the city.

After returning to the station, Captain W reviewed the testing requirements of the Drug and Alcohol Policy. Captain W, who had worked most of the shift with driver B, concluded that there was no cause or reason to require B to submit to a drug test. There was no reasonable belief of any impairment of B, and no injury had occurred in the accident.

Later, Captain W was contacted by telephone by Fire Chief G, who ordered that B go immediately to a drug-testing facility and submit to a drug test. Chief G had no firsthand knowledge or information of the incident or of B's work performance. B and W protested, but B submitted to a urine test, which was negative.

At the arbitration hearing, the union argued that the standards to be used to require a firefighter to submit to a drug test are clear and unambiguous and that Chief G had exceeded his jurisdiction by ignoring these standards and requiring B to submit to a drug test against the opinion of the firefighter's immediate supervisor.

The city's position was that the arbitrator did not have jurisdiction over this dispute because of a management rights clause that gives the city the right to make rules and regulations governing conduct and safety. The city argued that the language of the drug-testing policy was clear; the city has the right to require a firefighter to undergo a drug test after any incident.

Decision

Arbitrator A. Dale Allen Jr. ruled that Chief G had no basis for ordering B to submit to a drug test and that G did not properly interpret and apply the drug-testing policy. The city and Chief G were ordered to adhere to the terms of the drug-testing policy in the future.

Adapted from *Texas City, Texas*, 104 LA 534 (1995).

to arbitrate the grievance in the collective bargaining contract. A labor-management agreement to arbitrate therefore should not be denied unless a court is absolutely positive that the arbitration clause in the collective bargaining contract is not susceptible to interpretation covering the dispute. Any doubt in questions of arbitrability should be *resolved in favor of the grievance being arbitrated*.[21] Case Study 12-2 on page 434 illustrates a necessary exception to this rule.

In general, the arbitrator may rule on the question of arbitrability. That ruling is not subject to reversal by the courts as long as the arbitrator is applying the contract and acting within the scope of his or her authority. The exception to this rule occurs when the contract does not clearly demonstrate that the parties agreed to arbitrate the issue. The Supreme Court in *AT&T Technologies v. Communication Workers of America*[22] ruled that arbitrability is undeniably an issue for the courts and not the arbitrator in such cases. The Court cited a case in which the issue was whether an arbitration provision in a contract was binding after a corporate merger occurred. Thus, the question of arbitrability was one of the scope of the arbitration clause (Did it apply after the merger?) and as such was a question for the courts to decide.[23]

It is usually felt that a preliminary decision relating to arbitrability by the arbitrator is an inherent part of his or her duty. Procedurally, however, the arbitrator determines whether to rule on arbitrability before the presentation of the merits of the case or to reserve a ruling until after the full case has been presented. Therefore, the arbitrator's authority is derived from the collective bargaining agreement. Even if the courts are utilized to decide whether the contract obligates both parties to arbitrate a grievance, once that determination is made, the arbitrator decides if a particular grievance should be resolved within the framework of the contract. In other words, the court generally decides whether the union and employer have agreed to arbitration. But the arbitrator determines whether a particular grievance under a contract is arbitrable. The arbitrator also decides all procedural issues pertaining to the grievance.[24] Case 12-2 has a slightly different arbitrability issue to resolve.

HEARING PROCEDURES

The arbitrator fixes the date of the hearing after consulting with both sides and makes the necessary arrangements. The hearing procedure for the arbitration of a grievance normally follows a certain series of steps:

1. An opening statement by the initiating party (except that the company goes first in discharge or discipline cases)
2. An opening statement by the other side
3. The presentation of evidence, witnesses, and arguments by the initiating party
4. A cross-examination by the other side
5. The presentation of evidence, witnesses, and arguments by the defense
6. A cross-examination by the initiating party
7. A summation by the initiating party (optional)
8. A summation by the other side (optional)
9. Filing of briefs (optional)
10. The arbitrator's award[25]

Opening Statement

The opening statement lays the groundwork for the testimony of witnesses and helps the arbitrator understand the relevance of oral and written evidence. The statement should clearly identify the issue, indicate what is to be proved, and specify the relief sought. Sometimes parties will present the opening statement in writing to the arbitrator, with a copy given to the other side. Usually, the opening statement is also made orally so that appropriate points can be highlighted and given emphasis if doing so would be to the advantage of the presenting side.[26]

Rules of Evidence

Strict legal **rules of evidence** are not usually observed unless expressly required by the parties. The arbitrator determines how the hearing is run and how evidence is presented:

> In arbitration, the parties have submitted the matter to persons whose judgment they trust, and it is for the arbitrators to determine the weight or credibility of evidence presented to them without restrictions as to rules of admissibility which would apply in a court of law.[27]

In general, any pertinent information or testimony is acceptable as evidence if it helps the arbitrator understand and decide the issue. Arbitrators are usually extremely receptive to evidence, giving both parties a free hand in presenting any type they choose to strengthen and clarify their case.[28] The arbitrator decides how much weight to give evidence in making a decision.

Assessing Credibility of Witnesses

Included in the weighing of evidence is the arbitrator's need to assess witness credibility. An arbitrator is both judge and jury in deciding an arbitration. Conducting a fair hearing and at the same time trying to arrive at the truth from the facts presented demands keen analysis. Psychological studies regarding eyewitness testimony offer arbitrators helpful guidelines for such analysis.

An arbitrator must be aware of the following:

1. The most confident witness is not necessarily the most accurate.
2. Demeanor alone cannot reveal that a witness is lying.
3. Biases because of race, sex, or ethnic stereotyping must be eliminated.
4. The occupation or social class of a witness will not guarantee veracity.

In addition, studies indicate the following regarding the ability of a witness to recall information:

1. The more often and the longer an observer sees an event, the more accurate the recall. This factor must be weighed against the possibility that the observer's familiarity with a situation causes him or her to see what he or she expects to see from past experience.
2. Witnesses are not very accurate in estimating the duration of an event or the height, distance, or speed relevant to an event. The more emotionally charged the event, the less accurate the recall.
3. A witness's personal biases may cloud both the memory and the perception of an event.
4. Memory dims as time passes, and "after-acquired" information becomes incorporated into this memory.[29]

Presenting Documents

Most arbitration cases provide for the presentation of essential documents. Most important, of course, are those sections of the collective bargaining agreement that have some bearing on the grievance. Other documentation would include records of settled grievances, jointly signed memoranda, official minutes of contract negotiation meetings, personnel records, office reports, and organizational information. Documentary evidence is usually presented to the arbitrator, with a copy made available to the other party, but it is also explained orally to emphasize its importance.[30]

Examination of Witnesses

Each party depends on the direct examination of its own witnesses during an arbitration hearing. The witness is identified and qualified as an authority on the facts to which he or she will testify and is generally permitted to tell his or her story without interruptions and without the extensive use of leading questions as in legal cases. The witness in an arbitration proceeding is rarely cut off, and some arbitrators even ask the witness if he or she wants to add anything to the testimony as relevant to the case. Arbitrators generally uphold the right of cross-examination of witnesses, but not as strongly as courts.

The arbitrator also does not usually limit the rights of parties to call witnesses from the other side for cross-examination. However, opinion is split concerning the right of the company to call the grievant as a witness. One side believes that the application of the privilege against self-incrimination should apply in arbitration proceedings, even though there is no applicable constitutional privilege. The opposing view is that the privilege against self-incrimination in the field of criminal law is not present in grievance cases.[31]

Summation

Before the hearing is closed by the arbitrator, both sides are given equal time for closing statements. This is the last chance for each side to convince the arbitrator and to refute all the other side's arguments. Each side can summarize the situation and emphasize relevant facts and issues.[32]

Arbitrator's Award and Opinion

The **award** is the arbitrator's decision in the grievance case. Awards are usually short, are presented in written format, and are signed by the arbitrator. Even if an oral award is rendered, the arbitrator usually produces a written award later. Awards of arbitration boards must be signed by all members if a unanimous decision is required; otherwise, an award must be signed by a majority.

The arbitrator will also often present a written **opinion** stating the reasons for the decision. This opinion is separate from the award and clearly indicates where the opinion ends and the award begins. It is generally felt that a well-reasoned opinion can contribute greatly to the acceptance of the award. The Supreme Court has emphasized the need for arbitrator opinions and encouraged their use. Such opinions should be solidly based on the contract's terms; answer all of the questions raised in the arbitration without raising new questions; and address all of the arguments raised in the hearing, especially those of the losing party.[33]

CASE PREPARATION

When a grievance has reached the point of arbitration, both parties have probably gone through several steps of discussion in negotiations to resolve the issue. The issues disputed by the parties usually have been fairly well defined by the time the case reaches arbitration. To prepare the case for arbitration, the American Arbitration Association recommends the following steps in hearing preparation:

1. Study the original statement of the grievance and review its history through every step of the grievance machinery.

2. Carefully examine the initiating grievance paper (submission or demand) to help determine the arbitrator's role. It might be found, for instance, that, although the original grievance contains many elements, the arbitrator, under the contract, is restricted to resolving only certain aspects.

3. Review the collective bargaining agreement from beginning to end. Often clauses that at first glance seem to be unrelated to the grievance will be found to have some bearing.

4. Assemble all necessary documents and papers at the hearing. When feasible, make postdated copies for the arbitrator and the other party. If some of the documents are in the possession of the other party, ask in advance that they be brought to the arbitration. Under some arbitration laws, the arbitrator has authority to subpoena documents and witnesses if they cannot be made available in any other way.

5. If you think the arbitrator should visit the plant or job site for on-the-spot investigation, make plans in advance. The arbitrator should be accompanied by representatives of both parties.

6. Interview all witnesses. They should certainly understand the whole case and particularly the importance of their own testimony.

7. Make a written summary of each proposed witness's testimony. This summary will be useful as a checklist at the hearing to make sure nothing is overlooked.

8. Study the other side of the case. Be prepared to answer the opposing evidence and arguments.

9. Discuss your outline of the case with others in your organization. Another's viewpoint will often disclose weak spots or previously overlooked details.

10. Read as many articles and published awards as you can on the general subject matter and dispute. Although awards by other arbitrators or other parties have no binding present value, they may help clarify the thinking of parties and arbitrators alike.[34]

> On the basis of its extensive experience in administering arbitration proceedings, the American Arbitration Association has concluded that a party may harm its case by the following practices:
>
> 1. Using arbitration and arbitration costs as a harassing technique.
> 2. Overemphasis of the grievance by the union or exaggeration of an employee's fault by management.
> 3. Reliance on a minimum of facts and a maximum of arguments.
> 4. Concealing essential facts; distorting the truth.
> 5. Holding back books, records, and other supporting documents.
> 6. Tying up proceedings with legal technicalities.

7. Introducing witnesses who have not been properly instructed on demeanor and on the place of their testimony in the entire case.
8. Withholding full cooperation from the arbitrator.
9. Disregarding the ordinary rules of courtesy and decorum.
10. Becoming involved in arguments with the other side. The time to try to convince the other party is before arbitration, during grievance processing. At the arbitration hearing, all efforts should be concentrated on convincing the arbitrator.[35]

Decision Criteria

In surveys conducted by the National Academy of Arbitrators in 1975 and again in 1987, some interesting facts on how arbitrators decide cases were analyzed. As listed in Table 12-1, the major criteria used by arbitrators did not change over the 12-year period. The following three factors were used most by arbitrators in both groups:

1. *Labor contract language*. If the labor agreement provides clear and specific directives, obviously this is the first factor used by the arbitrators.
2. *Past practice*. In the absence of clear contract language, arbitrators rely on the parties' past practice to decide.
3. *Fairness*. Arbitrators felt some latitude to decide an issue in a fair and reasonable way regardless of contract language and past practices.

The next five factors were not used by arbitrators in 1975 and 1987 in the same order, but they were used often:

1. *Industry practice*. Even if the parties have no past practice in a particular area, the industry may have some consistent approach to an issue that an arbitrator can use.
2. *Other arbitration awards*. Arbitrators are not bound by precedent but do often review other arbitrator awards for guidance.

Influential Factors Used in Decision Making | **Table 12-1**

Item	1975 Rank*	1987 Rank*
Labor contract language	1	1
Parties' past practice	2	2
Judgment of fairness	3	3
Industry practice	4	8
Outside precedent	5	6
Future labor relations	6	4
State and federal laws	7	5
Social mores and customs	8	7

Source: Daniel F. Jennings and A. Dale Allen Jr., "How Arbitrators View the Process of Labor Arbitration: A Longitudinal Analysis" *Labor Studies Journal* 18, no. 1 (Winter 1993), pp. 41–50.
*Ranking of items most influential in making a decision (from most to least critical).
Kendall's tau statistics = 0.536, $p = 0.076$.
There is no significant difference between the two rankings.

3. *Future labor relations*. Occasionally an arbitrator decides an issue on what he or she believes will further the labor-management relationship.
4. *State or federal law*. If relevant, adherence to or violation of state or federal law will determine the outcome of an arbitration.
5. *Social mores and customs*. Seldom is an arbitration award decided on the basis of customs outside the workplace.[36]

As a counterweight to the findings on how arbitrators decide cases, a New York State Bar Association survey of labor and management attorneys found considerable criticism of some arbitrators' styles. Three-fourths of the 345 respondents felt that arbitrators should not consider outside factors in deciding a case. Such factors as the political fallout of a decision, a possible strike, or alleged abuse of power were not appropriate considerations. The respondents also felt that an arbitrator should not help one side even if that side has poor representation at the arbitration hearing.[37]

CONTRACTUAL ISSUES

Although both labor and management strive to produce a contract that results in as few disagreements as possible, contractual disputes will arise. Some of these, of course, end up in arbitration after other avenues for resolution have been explored. Historically, certain contractual issues seem to develop an agreed-upon solution mechanism that eventually enables both parties to resolve their dispute before arbitration is needed. However, many issues simply cannot be easily resolved with *any* contractual language and therefore must go to arbitration for final resolution. Some of the most commonly arbitrated issues are discussed in the following paragraphs.

Just Cause

Most collective bargaining agreements provide that management has the right to discipline or discharge employees for **just cause**. Although most labor and management negotiators can agree upon the general concept, specifying exactly what constitutes just cause appears impossible. Some contracts will specify the exact grounds that constitute just cause and usually include other less specific provisions that are open to dispute. The inability to specify exactly which employee offenses constitute just cause is a major reason why employee discipline and discharge procedures continue to be one of the most frequently arbitrated contractual issues.[38] The overwhelming majority of discipline cases also involve disagreement over the concept of just cause. Case 12-3 presents an unusual set of circumstances leading to an employee discharge later found to be unjust.

An example of the just cause provisions appears in the 1979 *Agreement* between the National Conference of Brewery and Soft Drink Workers and Teamsters Local No. 745 and the Jos. Schlitz Brewing Company, Longview, Texas:

ARTICLE V
Section 1

The right of the company to discharge, suspend, or otherwise discipline in a fair and impartial manner for just and sufficient cause is hereby acknowledged. Whenever employees are discharged, suspended, or otherwise disciplined, the

---

JUST CAUSE AT BALL-ICON

A 20-year maintenance electrician employed by Ball-Icon Glass Packaging Corporation was discharged after he physically attacked his supervisor, who allegedly had pushed the employee and slapped his face while giving him a new work assignment. Several coworkers prevented the employee from attempting to throw the supervisor over a catwalk railing (the employee and supervisor were on a catwalk approximately 30 feet from floor level).

During arbitration, the supervisor alleged that the electrician previously had threatened to beat him up and also had threatened to kill him. The current plant manager testified that there were morale problems between the supervisor and his employees. The former plant manager testified that the electrician had complained about his supervisor several times and on one occasion had said, "If things don't change, somebody is going to get hurt."

The company contented that the discharge should be upheld because the electrician assaulted his supervisor, who could have been seriously injured or killed. "No employee has the right to physically assault his supervisor with the intent to do serious bodily harm or cause death to him," the company argued.

The union's position was that the electrician was provoked. The supervisor had systematically harassed the electrician over the past four years, the union contended, and the company's inability to control the situation after it was brought to management's attention several times "puts the responsibility squarely on the company's shoulders."

Decision

Arbitrator Marlin Volz ruled that, although fighting with a supervisor is a serious disciplinary offense, the manner in which the supervisor assigned the work to the electrician had triggered the offense. Arbitrator Volz noted several factors in the employee's favor: an exceptionally good work record for 20 years, no prior disciplinary offenses, three consecutive years of perfect attendance, and no record of difficulties getting along with other supervisors.

Volz ruled that Ball-Icon did not have sufficient just cause to discharge the electrician and restored the electrician to his job with back pay.

Adapted from *Ball-Icon Glass Packaging Corporation*, 98 LA 1 (1992).

union and the employees shall promptly be notified in writing of such discharge, suspension, or other disciplinary action and the reason therefore. No discipline, written notice of which has not been given to the union and the employee, nor any discipline which has been given more than twelve months prior to the current act, shall be considered by the company in any subsequent discharge, suspension, or other disciplinary action.

Section 2

If the union is dissatisfied with the discharge, suspension, or other disciplinary action, the questions as to whether the employee was properly discharged, suspended, or otherwise disciplined shall, upon request of the union, be reviewed in accordance with the grievance procedure set forth. (pp. 13–15)

The criteria used by arbitrators for just cause will obviously vary from case to case and from arbitrator to arbitrator. However, the Bureau of National Affairs has provided tests for determining whether a company has just cause for disciplining an employee.

1. *Adequate warning.* Is the employee given adequate, oral or printed, warning as to the consequences of his conduct? Employees should be warned by the employer as to punishments either in the contract, handbook, or other means in disciplinary cases. Certain conducts such as insubordination, drunkenness, or stealing are considered so serious the employee is expected to know they will be punishable.

2. *Prior investigation.* Did management investigate the case before administering the discipline? Thorough investigation should have normally been made before the decision to discipline. When immediate action is required, the employee should be suspended pending investigation with the understanding that he or she will be returned to the job and paid for time lost if found not guilty.

3. *Evidence.* Did the investigation produce substantial evidence or proof of guilt? It is not required that evidence be conclusive or beyond reasonable doubt, except when the misconduct is of such a criminal nature that it seriously impairs the accused's chances for future employment.

4. *Equal treatment.* Were all employees judged by the same standards, with rules applied equally? The same penalty, however, may not be always given since it may be a second offense, or other factors may logically suggest a different punishment.

5. *Reasonable penalty.* Was the penalty reasonably related to the seriousness of the offense and the past record of the employee? The level of the offense should be related to the level of the penalty, and the employee's past record should be taken under consideration.

6. *Rule of reason.* Is the disciplinary action fairly administered? Even in the absence of specific provisions, a collective bargaining agreement protects employees against unjust discipline. Employees may reasonably challenge any company procedure that threatens to deprive employees of their negotiated rights.

7. *Internal consistency.* Was management enforcement of the rule or procedure consistent? The company should not selectively enforce codes of conduct against certain employees. Enforcement should be consistent, whether the company disciplines on a case-by-case basis or uses a handbook. The *past practice* of management in similar cases will be carefully reviewed by an arbitrator.[39]

The more common remedies used by arbitrators in overturning management actions in discipline and discharge cases include reinstatement with back pay, without back pay, or with partial back pay, with other rights and privileges remaining unimpaired; commuting the discharge to suspension for a specified period of time or further reducing the penalty to only a reprimand or a warning; and reversing management's assessment of suspension because the arbitrator believes the penalty is too severe. Back pay will usually be ordered consistent with the elimination of suspension.[40] Most arbitrators apply accepted common law with contracts not specifying just cause, which usually means that management action is subjected to tests of prior standards and procedural requirements. If the action meets both criteria, it will generally be found to be a valid prerogative of management.[41]

Drug Testing

A current issue regarding disciplining of employees for just cause is the use of drug-screening tests as the basis for such discipline. It is certainly an established principle that employees are subject to discipline if they are unable to perform their job while under the influence of alcohol or drugs.[42] Employees will be disciplined because of their impairment under the provisions of the management rights section of an agreement. Proving the fact of drug-related impairment through **drug testing** provides the *just cause* test necessary for the employer's action.

In 1986, intolerance of illegal drug use as it related to the workplace entered a new phase. By Executive Order 12564, President Reagan provided that use of illegal drugs off or on duty makes federal employees unfit for federal employment. The E.O. stated that random drug testing would be initiated in those agencies of the federal government in which the employees' duties involved public safety or law enforcement. Drug testing became a management-union issue separate from the right of the employer to discipline one employee for clearly demonstrated on-the-job impairment.

The Supreme Court upheld the drug-testing programs begun by the Reagan administration. By implication, their decision upholds local and state government programs involving similar personnel.[43] The NLRB has ruled that for the private employer, implementing a drug-testing program for current employees involves a mandatory duty to bargain, at least to impasse. If it is clear that the union has waived that right by contract, a drug-testing program may be implemented by the employer unilaterally. Bargaining is not required, however, prior to implementing a testing program for job applicants.[44] Arbitrators have required employers to meet a higher standard of proof in grievances over discharges for possession and use of drugs because of the stigma attached to an employee so discharged.[45]

Following are issues that are commonly considered by an arbitrator in a drug abuse case:

1. Does the drug-testing procedure violate the contract?

   In instances in which a drug-testing program is instituted unilaterally by the employer during the term of a contract, such programs have been upheld under the general management rights and health and safety provisions of the contract. The drug-testing program, however, must satisfy a just cause test.[46] Sufficient language must be found in the existing contract concerning health and safety, disciplining for drug or alcohol abuse, and management rights to justify the employer's implementing a drug-testing program unilaterally.[47]

2. Was the testing of the employee reasonable?

   Random drug screening is generally not allowed for employees not involved in public safety. There must be a reasonable basis for the suspicion or probable cause for the belief that the employee is abusing drugs or alcohol in order for the employer to require a test.[48]

3. Was the test itself fair?

   Management is held to a very high standard to ensure that the test, which might be the basis of discipline, is properly administered. Established procedures regarding "chain of custody" of the specimen, control methods for accuracy, a confirming test, and a certainty on the kinds of drugs being tested are required.[49]

4. Was there on-the-job impairment?

In cases involving discipline as a result of a positive drug test, the union may contend that the tests prove the presence of a drug in the employee's body but not on-the-job use or on-the-job impairment.[50] There is concern that positive drug tests involving illegal drugs might be used to discipline an employee for the illegal activity involved in obtaining and possessing the drug regardless of the on-the-job effect. Management's position is that an employee who engages in such illegal activity is not a fit employee. To date, however, arbitrators usually require a nexus between the employee's drug use and the behavior in the workplace before just cause for discipline is found.[51]

5. Can an employee be disciplined for refusing to be tested?

A company can sustain its firing of an employee for failure to take a drug test only if there are reasonable grounds for the belief that the employee had consumed an illegal drug.[52] If there is no probable cause for the test, an employee is within his or her rights to refuse to take the test as a protest against unwarranted invasion of privacy.[53] In addition, just as with other fireable offenses, the employee must be warned that failure to submit to a test itself will result in discharge.[54]

Seniority Recognition

The most severe limitation of managerial discretion is the negotiated requirement of seniority recognition. It significantly reduces the employer's control over the workforce and the filling of positions. **Seniority** is commonly understood to mean the length of service with the employer either on a companywide basis or within the particular unit of the organization. People retain their jobs according to their length of service with the employer or within the particular unit and will be promoted to better jobs on the same basis.

The purpose of seniority is to provide maximum security to workers with the longest continuous service.[55] Arbitrators often hear cases involving loss of seniority or management's failure to promote the most senior person. Collective bargaining agreements often provide sections describing the loss of seniority similar to this agreement between General Motors Corporation and the United Auto Workers.

> **SECTION 64**
>
> Seniority shall be broken for the following reasons: (a) if the employee quits, (b) if the employee is discharged, (c) if the employee is absent for three working days without properly notifying the management, unless a satisfactory reason is given, (d) if the employee fails to return to work within three working days after being notified to report for work, and does not give a satisfactory reason, [and] (e) if the employee is laid off for a continuous period equal to the seniority he had acquired at a time of such layoff.[56]

The agreement commonly requires management to prepare seniority lists to be made available to all employees. The seniority list usually contains each employee's name, occupational group, plant seniority date, and new seniority date if applicable. If the contract does not require the posting of a seniority list, the employer may be held to be under an implied obligation to make proper and reasonable disclosure of seniority. An arbitrator has ruled the following:

> An employee—and the union as his representative—clearly has a right to be informed of a seniority date and length of continuous service credited to him on the company's records. By the same token, since most seniority issues involve a comparison of the relative rights of two or more employees, the employee—and the union as his representative—has a right to know the seniority dates and length of continuous service credited to the other employees in the seniority unit applicable to him at any given time. The only accurate source of such information is obviously the company. It has the records. It is initiating the various transfers, promotions, demotions, thumps, layoffs, recalls, etc. . . . which are daily causing changes in those records.[57]

Absenteeism

Unexpected employee absences cause major problems for management. Supervisors who receive an employee's call notifying them of his or her absence that day must quickly transfer personnel and possibly call in additional employees. The absent employee causes several problems:

1. *Lost productivity.* Replacement employees usually cannot be as efficient on a job as those who perform it daily. If they are shifted from another area, two or more jobs may be affected by one absence.

2. *Additional costs.* Often the use of a replacement employee causes the employer to pay overtime. Thus, even if the absent employee is not paid for hours missed (which is usually not the case), personnel costs increase significantly.

3. *Benefits.* Most contracts provide that the absent employee continues to receive almost all benefits. If a replacement employee also receives some additional benefits, the hourly cost can increase significantly.

4. *Administrative time.* Several people may be needed to provide replacement help. The immediate supervisor may need not only to contact additional help but also to provide them with more instruction during the day. Personnel department people, department heads, and others may also be required to use part of their day in arranging for replacement help.

Management considers **absenteeism** a controllable problem and usually seeks to minimize the number of absences through the use of control or disciplinary techniques. Although hesitant to implement new or additional control techniques that may be abused by management, unions recognize the seriousness of the problems caused by unexpected absences and have agreed to a variety of control measures in contracts, including those listed in Table 12-2.

One example of union-management ability to control absenteeism is the case of the H. J. Scheirich Company, a cabinet manufacturer with more than 400 employees. Several years ago, the firm's management concluded that absenteeism was causing major production problems and had inflated labor costs. Together Scheirich and the union negotiated an innovative **"no-fault" absenteeism** policy. The new policy centered on the policy statement, "Action may be taken when cumulative time lost from work for any reason substantially reduces the employee's services to the company."[58]

Table 12-2   Control of Absenteeism

Method of Control	Percentage of Use
Employee call-in to give notice of absence	99
Termination based on excessive absenteeism	97
Progressive discipline for excessive absenteeism	97
Identification and discipline of employees abusing attendance policies	92
Inclusion of absenteeism rate on employee job performance appraisal	47
Consistency in applying attendance policy	83
Clearly written attendance policy	77
Requirement of doctor's written excuse for illness and accidents	89
Component on attendance in a formal employee orientation program for new hire	73
Daily attendance records maintained by supervisors	66
Screening of recruit's past attendance records before making a selection decision	66
Analysis of daily attendance information at least monthly	68

Source: Steve Markham and Dow Scott, "Controlling Absenteeism: Union and Nonunion Differences," *Personnel Administrator* 30, no. 2 (February 1985), pp. 87–102. Reprinted with the permission of *HR Magazine* (formerly *Personnel Administrator*) published by the Society for Human Resources Management, Alexandria, VA.

In practice, excessive absenteeism was considered to be about 3 percent above the plant average; however, no exact figure was used. Instead, abuses were examined on a case-by-case basis. In the first six years of the new program, 11 employees were terminated for "unavailability for work." Eight of the 11 grieved their terminations through the union; five went to arbitration. The arbitrators upheld the termination in four of the five cases, and in the fifth case the award was given to the employee only because management failed to notify her with sufficient warnings. In general, the arbitrators issued opinions stating that management has a right to terminate employees for excessive absences even when due to illness or other factors. They found the case-by-case method of comparing the employee's percentage of absenteeism against the company average to be reasonable.[59]

Managers may believe that unions present barriers to effective absenteeism programs and policies. In fact, campaigns to remain union-free often include information implying that significant differences in absence rates and programs exist between union and nonunion employers. However, a survey report of 959 employers suggested that the presence of a union is not associated with employee absence levels any higher or lower than those of nonunion employers. Also, the most common absenteeism control mechanism, employee call-in to give notice of absence, was reported by 99 percent of both types of employers. The only method reported to decrease absenteeism significantly, a monthly analysis of attendance data, was used more often by union organizations than nonunion. Nonunion employers in general had fewer control techniques than union employers.[60] Case 12-4 describes a situation in which an employee was discharged because his absences placed him in the "worst 2 percent" of all employees and an arbitrator's decision to reinstate the employee with back pay.

ABSENTEEISM AT WEBER AIRCRAFT

Weber Aircraft's labor agreement contains a no-fault attendance policy that specifies that after 80 hours of absences, an employee is subject to discharge. Vacation time, approved medical leaves, special situation absences, or holidays are not counted against the employee. On February 26, 1992, grievant A received a written notice that his 1990 and 1991 absences placed him "in the worst 2 percent of all employees in the entire plant with respect to attendance and that a failure to maintain an acceptable attendance may result in discharge without any additional warnings." The labor agreement also specifies that an employee is to be notified when 64 of the allowed 80 hours of absences are used.

Beginning in 1990, grievant A experienced heart problems and high blood pressure, which occasioned considerable absence from work during 1990 and 1991 while on approved medical leave. After these absences, grievant A received the February 26, 1992, warning letter. On March 31, 1992, grievant A was granted a medical leave of absence relating to a cyst problem. Grievant A had a cyst removed from his leg and originally believed that this procedure would not result in any loss of work. However, the stitches broke open, and A had to seek and obtain medical leave again. Grievant A's hour bank was not charged for the approved medical leave relating to the cyst problem. Beginning in June 1992, grievant A experienced considerable discomfort and symptoms (blood in his urine) related to a prostate condition. He continued to work with this discomfort until he left work at approximately 10:30 A.M. on June 15, 1992, to visit a doctor. A's shift began at 7:00 A.M., and he had obtained approval from his supervisor to leave work. His doctor advised him to take off work until June 22, 1992. On the morning of June 16, 1992, A's wife (also a company employee) took a slip signed by A's doctor to the plant nurse, who advised that A should apply for a medical leave. The nurse advised A's wife that he probably would not be granted a second medical leave but that the company would charge vacation time for the medical leave and that A would not be charged for an absence. On June 17, 1992, A received a telephone call from his supervisor advising that his medical leave had not been approved, that his allowable absence hours were exhausted, and that he was discharged. The company argued that it could not operate efficiently without the assurance that employees, within reason, will report to work. Numerous arbitral decisions were cited by the company in which an employer has the general right to discharge an employee for chronic excessive absenteeism.

Decision

Arbitrator Daniel Jennings ruled that the employer was not justified in discharging A because his work record reflected "genuine hard luck and real illnesses" rather than frequently recurring illnesses that would indicate a sickly state that might be permanent. Arbitrator Jennings noted (1) that A's problems (high blood pressure, cyst, and prostate problems) were not permanent and that no evidence was introduced to suggest that the grievant suffered from an illness that would prevent him from returning to work on a regular basis; (2) that, although the company had warned A on February 26, 1992, it had failed to discipline him for subsequent illnesses or to warn him that his employment was in jeopardy; in fact, the company had granted a medical leave for the period March 25, 1992, through April 6, 1992; (3) that the company had failed to notify A that he had expended 48 hours of his allowable 80 absence hours, and (4) that the company had failed to honor its agent, the plant nurse, who had given assurances that A's absences since June 15, 1992, would not be counted against him.

The award of arbitrator Jennings was to uphold A's grievance; A was reinstated and received back pay.

Adapted from *Weber Aircraft*, 100 LA 417 (1993).

Incompetence

Arbitrators in general recognize management's right to set reasonable production standards and to enforce such standards through discipline. However, incompetence generally should not be treated the same as a disciplinary problem because proper remedies usually include additional training, transfer, or demotion instead of warnings, suspension, or discharge. In incompetence cases arising over the reasonableness of management's action, arbitrators will consider the adequacy of the employee's training, supervision, and ability to perform the job. The arbitrator must decide if the contract has been followed. Although both labor and management have the responsibility for producing evidence supporting their case, the burden of proof is usually on management to verify the employee's incompetence.[61]

The discharge or severe discipline of an employee for incompetence will not likely be upheld by an arbitrator under the following conditions:

1. The charge of incompetence is not properly investigated or substantiated.
2. The employee is not given adequate warning and opportunity to improve his or her performance.
3. Other employees with equally poor performance records are not treated in the same manner.
4. The employee shows substantial improvement after being warned.
5. Poor work is due to inability, and there is other work available that the employee can perform.[62]

Holiday Pay Eligibility

In recent years, most contracts have come to provide for **paid holiday eligibility**. Certain contract eligibility requirements must be fulfilled to receive pay for the holiday. Since the creation of Monday holidays by the federal government has increased labor's demand for three-day weekends, employers have become even more concerned with attendance problems due to employees' trying to stretch three-day weekends into four days, substantially disrupting production. An example of a common eligibility requirement is provided in the labor agreement between the National Conference of Brewery and Soft Drink Workers and the Schlitz Brewing Company.

> **ARTICLE XII**
> *Holidays*
>
> . . . to be eligible for holiday pay, an employee must work his full shift on the day before the holiday and his full shift on the day after the holiday. Approved absence on either of these days shall not disqualify the employee for holiday pay. Holiday pay shall be at the straight time rate, excluding shift differentials.[63]

Because paid holidays represent one of the most costly benefits given to the employees, management often will pursue disagreements to arbitration. The most common dispute concerning paid holidays involves the eligibility of employees. Other disputes concern avoidance of *holiday stretching*: that is, requiring work on the day before or after the holiday. Holiday pay is generally given to workers who fail to meet work requirements through no fault of their own. For example, an employee of the John Deere Tractor Co. was awarded holiday pay by an arbitrator even though he had left work a half-hour early the day before the holiday so he could catch a train. The arbitrator felt that the employee was simply making the holiday available.[64] Also, if a contract provides holiday pay without restriction, laid-off workers continue to be employees of the company and are entitled to the holiday pay. Still another disputed topic involves holidays that fall on nonwork days. These must be paid for if the contract designates certain days as paid holidays and does not limit pay to holidays that fall on scheduled work days.[65]

Arbitrators generally agree that the common attendance requirement for employees to work the days before and after the holiday is not limited to the days immediately preceding and following the holiday. For example, a contract stated that holiday pay would be provided if the employee worked the workday previous to and following the holiday. The holiday fell on a Thursday, and the plant was closed for the rest of the week. The employee was denied pay for the holiday because he was absent the following Monday, the next scheduled workday. The arbitration board upheld the company's position that the days preceding and following the holiday do not have to fall on the same workweek.[66] In general, the prior and following workdays are considered to be the last and first scheduled workdays surrounding the holiday.

TIPS FROM THE EXPERTS

Arbitrator

What are the three most common violations by employers of the "just cause" provision of a collective bargaining agreement?

a. *Assuming that the company's rule-making authority abolishes the contractual obligation to observe just cause in imposing discipline.* It does not necessarily follow that because a unilaterally promulgated rule is reasonable on its face and is uniformly applied that all the just cause requirements have been met and the penalty is automatically justified.

b. *Failing to observe an employee's Weingarten rights.* Whenever an employee is summoned to an interview with management that he or she reasonably believes is likely to result in discipline, he or she is entitled to union representation if a request is made.

c. *Failing to afford the employee procedural due process.* This action would include such elements as giving adequate notice of a rule, conducting an adequate and thorough investigation before imposing discipline, and imposing discipline for the purpose of correcting conduct and not punishing.

What are the three most common errors unions make in challenging a "just cause" discharge?

a. *Failing to screen the facts and circumstances or to assess properly the company's case.* Before deciding to proceed with the grievance, the union needs to be thorough in its investigation and assess the possibility of losing or setting a harmful precedent.

b. *Failing to offer successful postdischarge evidence of rehabilitation.* In cases involving discharge for drug and alcohol usage a union can demonstrate to the arbitrator the rehabilitation of the employee discharged.

c. *Relying on uncorroborated hearsay evidence or bad precedents.* A union should carefully screen its evidence for corroboration and its precedents when citing prior arbitration awards to make sure they support the union's position.

Management Rights

A common issue in arbitration cases is management rights in the areas not expressly discussed in the contract. Often it is believed that in the absence of restrictive or specific provisions, managerial rights are retained by management. However, arbitrators do not always take the view that management retains *all* unstated rights.

The following contract provides a general statement of management rights covering items such as the size of the workforce and operational methods.

> **ARTICLE V**
> *Management Rights*
>
> (a) It is the intent of parties to this agreement that the employee will furnish a full fair day's work for a full fair day's pay. (b) Management shall be the sole determiner of the size and composition of the workforce. Management shall have the prerogative of controlling its operations, inducing new or improved methods or facilities, subject to the limitations set forth in this agreement. (c) Management shall retain all rights and privileges which are not specifically abridged by the terms of this agreement.[67]

Arbitrators usually impose a standard of reasonableness and good faith on managerial actions that adversely affect employees, whether or not the contract provides management's discretion in the area. Arbitrators generally agree that the union cannot block technological improvement, even if the workforce is reduced, unless there is a specific contract restriction. Likewise, arbitrators generally give management broad authority in assigning work to employees and in controlling plant operations and procedures, unless specifically restricted by the contract.[68]

The following summarizes points to consider in management rights cases:

1. If a company brought up a subject in negotiations but failed to get its demands written into the contract, it may have lost its right to take unilateral action in that area.
2. Management generally is conceded to have the right to make technological improvements, even if some workers are adversely affected, unless its contract says otherwise.
3. Similarly, a company normally has the right to eliminate a job it no longer considers necessary. The union will be watchful, though, to make sure the duties of the job aren't in fact transferred to other workers.
4. Even in the absence of a contract clause forbidding supervisors to do bargaining unit work, arbitrators sometimes have held that they could not do such work if people in the bargaining unit would be adversely affected.[69]

SUMMARY

The arbitration process has been developed and refined over many years. The selection of an arbitrator or board of arbitrators is generally specified in the labor agreement. The hearing procedure, however, which is not bound by legal precedent, is quite flexible and is subject to the arbitrator's discretion. The courts have generally left the questions of arbitrability and case decisions to arbitrators.

A great variety of important and complex issues end up in arbitration. The issue of just cause for employee discipline or discharge is difficult to define within the contract and in most cases involves emotional situations. Drug testing for substance abuse presents unique problems for an arbitrator to resolve. Seniority and absenteeism are deceptively simple yet important contractual issues. Disagreements over incompetence, holiday pay, and management rights are also common arbitration subjects.

DRUG AND ALCOHOL TESTING

Facts

The company is an insulation subcontractor that performs maintenance work for duPont. For several decades, the company had a collective bargaining agreement with a union that included employees who were sent to a duPont plant for maintenance work. The contract in effect between the company and the union had no reference to a drug-testing or substance abuse program. Prior to 1986, the company had never required its employees to submit to drug testing. In 1986, however, the company received a letter from duPont stating that duPont was developing a substance abuse policy and requiring its subcontractors to develop a similar policy to include testing procedures.

The company instituted a drug program similar to duPont's and sent it to the union for its information. The company notified the union that it was willing to meet with it to discuss the plan. At the meeting, the union met not only with its company but also with representatives from duPont concerning the drug program. The written policy stated that "the use, possession of, being under influence of, or the presence in the person's system of prohibitive drugs and unauthorized alcoholic beverages is prohibited on any company work location." Under the policy, all new employees of the company were required to sign consent forms for testing as a condition of employment. The company implemented the drug-testing policy but only as it related to the duPont plant. The union instructed its members to sign the forms consenting to drug testing with the statement that they were signing under duress.

The grievant in this case was referred to the duPont plant by the company for its maintenance work in April 1987. The employee, along with four other fellow employees, submitted to a urine test. The grievant's test was sent to the screening facility, and the initial test resulted in a positive finding of marijuana. The chain of custody for the test was not established, and the level of marijuana found in the test was extremely low. Nonetheless, the grievant was dismissed. The position of the company was that duPont made it mandatory for subcontractors to adopt minimum requirements for drug testing and that such minimum requirements for new employees were not unreasonable. The company further contended that, although it did not agree to negotiate with the union, the company gave the union ample time to study the program's policy.

The union felt that the company's policy was really duPont's policy and was adopted despite the union's disapproval solely because duPont had insisted on it. The union contended that the company made no effort to ensure the union that the policy or the enforcement of the policy was reasonable, fair,

(continued)

or accurate. The cut-off level for a positive test result was unreasonable because it did not indicate either on-the-job impairment or consistent use of marijuana. The company did not examine the grievant's prior work record or the fact that there was not prior history or evidence of drug impairment on the job. In fact, the company could not even prove that the specimen tested was the grievant's. The union further contended that even if the results of the test proved that the employee was using marijuana, on the basis of her past work history she should be given an opportunity to correct her conduct and be treated in a fair and consistent way. Discharge was clearly not appropriate.

Questions

1. Did the company have a legitimate business reason for instituting a drug-testing program during the term of a contract?
2. Did the company conduct the drug-testing program properly?
3. As the arbitrator, would you reverse or uphold the dismissal of the grievant? Explain your answer.

Adapted from *Young Insulation Group*, 90 LA 341 (1987).

CASE STUDY 12-2

ARBITRABILITY

Facts

In September 1981, the union grieved the company's announced intention to lay off 79 employees from its Chicago location. The union contended that there was no lack of work at that site and that under the contract the company can lay off from the site only when there is a lack of work. Despite the grievance, the company laid off the employees and transferred approximately 80 employees from other locations to the Chicago location.

The union demanded that the dispute be arbitrated, and the company refused. The company claimed that the "management functions" clause of the contract gives it the prerogative to determine "lack of work" and so long as it lays off in the order prescribed by the contract, there is nothing to arbitrate. The union contended that certain provisions of the contract modified the "management functions" clause and requested the court to order arbitration.

The lower court found that there were arguable issues to arbitrate and ordered the parties to arbitrate the arbitrability issue; in other words, an arbitrator would decide if she had jurisdiction under the contract of the issue in dispute.

Before this could happen, the company appealed the lower court's ruling. The company argued that the lower court erred in not simply deciding whether the dispute was subject to arbitration. It contended that under the *Steelworkers Trilogy* cases the *courts*, not the arbitra-

(continued)

tor, must decide if the issue is subject to arbitration. The company proposed the following points:

1. Arbitration is a matter of contract, and parties cannot be forced to submit issues to arbitration that they have not agreed to submit.
2. Unless the contract clearly provides otherwise, arbitrability is a judicial determination.
3. In deciding arbitrability, the court is not to decide on the merits of the claim.
4. Where the contract has an arbitration clause, the presumption is for arbitrability.

The lower court pointed out, however, that the exception to the rule is found when deciding the arbitrability of the case would also involve the court in interpreting the substantive provisions of the labor agreement.

The union's position was that the layoffs were subject to arbitration, and they pointed to sections of the labor agreement to prove this. The "management functions" clause, the "adjustment to the working force" clause, and the "arbitration" clause must be read together and interpreted. The court could not decide arbitrability in this case without interpreting these sections and therefore deciding the substantive issue. It is for an arbitrator to decide the substantive issues.

Questions

1. Should the court decide whether there is an issue to arbitrate, or should an arbitrator? Why?
2. Give the reasons you think arbitration is a superior resolution process to court action in contract disputes.
3. Give the reasons you think a court action is a superior resolution process to arbitration in contract disputes.

Adapted from *Communication Workers of America v. Western Electric*, 751 F.2d 203 (7th Cir. 1984).

KEY TERMS AND CONCEPTS

absenteeism
arbitrability
arbitrator's award
arbitrator's opinion
drug testing
holiday pay eligibility

just cause
qualifications of an arbitrator
rules of evidence
seniority
tripartite arbitration board

REVIEW QUESTIONS

1. Describe how the legal foundation for arbitration as it exists today in the United States was developed.
2. Discuss the five principles that govern the arbitration of grievances under collective bargaining.
3. Explain how the change in ownership of a company affects the duty to arbitrate.
4. What is the process normally utilized in the selection of an arbitrator? How does the selected arbitrator interpret ambiguous contract provisions?
5. How is binding arbitration superior to the courts in settling labor disputes? How does it differ from mediation and conciliation?

6. What information can be presented as evidence during arbitration proceedings? What are the usual hearing procedures?
7. Can a party harm its own case during arbitration proceedings? If it can, explain how.
8. How does an arbitrator determine that a company had just cause for taking a disciplinary action? What remedy might an arbitrator choose if a company did not have just cause?
9. How do labor contracts prevent holiday stretching?
10. Discuss the issues an arbitrator might use in deciding a discharge case involving drug abuse.

TAKE IT TO THE NET

We invite you to visit the Carrell/Heavrin page on the Prentice Hall Web site at:

http://www.prenhall.com/carrellr

for this chapter's World Wide Web exercise.

EXERCISE 12-1 | **Alternative Dispute Resolution**

Purpose:
To expose students to alternative dispute resolution procedures.
Task:
Research current periodicals for examples of ADR (alternative dispute resolution) procedures. Compare and contrast an alternative procedure to an arbitration procedure.

EXERCISE 12-2 | **Use of the Arbitration Process**

Purpose:
To enable students to learn how the arbitration process is being utilized in areas outside of the labor relations field.
Task:
Using the library, Internet, and other reference sources, identify three fields outside labor relations in which the arbitration process is utilized. Write a two- to three-paragraph summary explanation of each use of the arbitration process. Finally, list the elements of the processes in the fields cited that are similar to the arbitration process discussed in this chapter.

436   Part Four The Labor Relations Process in Action

If you are using Smith/Carrell/Golden *Collective Bargaining Simulated, 4E,* with this text, please refer to the following:

p. 18 for a discussion of the arbitration process agreed to in the contract.

CHAPTER 13

Labor Relations
in the Public
Sector

Mike Kurtsinger, president of the Local Firefighters Union (left), leads
the negotiations at a bargaining session with City of Louisville (Kentucky) officials.

What Is AFSCME?

The American Federation of State, County and Municipal Employees **(AFSCME)** is the second largest public union in the United States and the second largest national union in the AFL-CIO, with over 1.3 million members. AFSCME represents public employees and health-care workers throughout the United States, Panama, and Puerto Rico. They include employees of state, county, and municipal governments, school districts, public and private hospitals, universities, and nonprofit agencies who work in a cross section of jobs ranging from blue collar to clerical, professional, and paraprofessional. White-collar employees account for one-third of the membership; health and hospital workers constitute the largest sector, with more than 325,000 members. About 325,000 AFSCME members are clerical and secretarial employees, making AFSCME the largest union of office workers. One hundred thousand members are corrections officers, making AFSCME the largest union in that profession.

AFSCME is organized into more than 3,400 local unions, most of which are affiliated with one of 63 councils. Local unions and councils have their own constitutions, elect their own officers, and administer a wide variety of local affairs. The international union coordinates issues of concern to all AFSCME members and provides research, legislative, legal, organizational, educational, public relations, and other services.

AFSCME began as a number of separate locals organized by a group of Wisconsin state employees in the early 1930s. By 1935, 30 locals had become a separate department within the American Federation of Government Employees. In 1936, AFSCME was chartered by the American Federation of Labor. By 1955, at the time of the AFL-CIO merger, AFSCME had 100,000 members. The following year, the union merged with the 30,000-member CIO Government and Civic Employees Organizing Committee. In 1957, AFSCME moved its headquarters from Madison, Wisconsin, to Washington, D.C. With the affiliation of the 220,000-member Civil Service Employees Association (CSEA) of New York State in 1978, AFSCME membership surged to the 1 million mark. Recent organizing successes have brought the union's membership past the 1.3 million mark.

Adapted from "About AFSCME." www.afscme.org/afscme/about/index.htm, February 28, 1997.

The National Labor Relations Act, passed in 1935, established a national labor policy to be enforced by federal action. This policy recognized the need for collective bargaining as a way to eliminate and mitigate industrial strife. The act established equality of bargaining power between employers and employees and gave employees substantive rights to organize into labor unions, presenting themselves to the employer for recognition. Employers were required to meet with their employees at the bargaining table to discuss the terms and conditions of the job. The right to strike was given government protection and served as an economic equalizer for the employee.

Public employees, however, were not guaranteed rights under the National Labor Relations Act. This chapter examines the development of labor relations in the public sector, how the parties and the interests differ from those in the private sector, and how disputes are resolved.

Today, public sector unions are the fastest-growing unions in the United States. National public unions such as the American Federation of Teachers (AFT), American Postal Workers Union, American Federation of Government Employees, and American Federation of State, County and Municipal Employees (AFSCME) are some of the largest and most influential members of the AFL-CIO.

The unionization of public employees has borne witness to a basic change in the character of the American labor movement. For instance, in 1953, public employees constituted only 6 percent of union membership. By 1997, approximately 44 percent of union members were public employees, and public sector unions will soon enroll a majority of union members in the United States. Actually, public sector unions will be predominant in the AFL-CIO if the National Education Association (NEA), the nation's largest public sector union, becomes affiliated with the AFL-CIO. As will be explained shortly, however, it is a fundamental mistake to think of public sector bargaining and public sector unions as merely an extension of private sector concepts to the public sector. Politically, teacher unions are major players at all levels of government. One of every 10 delegates to the 1996 Democratic National Convention was a member of the NEA or the AFT, and no serious observer doubts their important role in state and local politics. Inasmuch as elected officials shape policy on noneducational as well as educational issues, the political influence of teacher unions extends far beyond the field of education. Although teacher unions are usually the most influential interest group on educational issues, their impact on noneducational issues may be even more important from a public policy perspective.[1]

EVOLUTION OF PUBLIC SECTOR LABOR RELATIONS

Congress excluded federal, state, and local government employees from the provisions of the National Labor Relations Act until the Postal Reorganization Act of 1970 allowed postal workers to come under the National Labor Relations Act's provisions.[2] In the traditional sense, Congress did not view government as an employer but as a representative of the people, supplying certain necessary services. Therefore, people employed by the government were not employees but public servants, and they were protected from the arbitrary actions of private employers by already existing systems. Such systems addressed basic employee concerns—wages, benefits, job security—even as the sovereignty of the government was maintained.

Such was not always the case. In the early 1800s, citizens were scandalized by the use of party patronage in federal, state, and local governments. This **spoils system** caused a turnover of government workers on the basis of their political affiliation not their ability or dedication. Government workers were expected to support political candidates with time and money or fear losing their jobs. The government lost continuity and efficiency because of the repeated replacement of trained employees.

In 1871, the first Civil Service Commission was established to propose reforms in the national government. Congress, however, failed to make an appropriation for the commission and it disbanded. In 1883, an outgoing Republican Congress passed the **Pendleton Act**, which provided for a bipartisan three-member Civil Service Commission to draw up and administer competitive examinations to determine the fitness of appointees to federal office. The act protected federal employees from being fired for failure to make political contributions and actually forbade political campaign contributions by certain employees. The Pendleton Act affected only about 10 percent of the federal employees at the time, but it enabled the president to broaden the merit system and was the foundation of the present federal civil service system.

Many states followed the federal government's lead and instituted civil service merit systems for their employees. Thus, the **civil service system** provided job security for government workers. Rules governing hiring, firing, and discipline protected the worker from arbitrary actions. Due process hearings gave workers a forum to protest an employer's actions.

The Pendleton Act also gave Congress the right to regulate wages, hours, and working conditions of public employees. These employees began to lobby Congress for wage increases and improved benefits. In the early 1900s, Presidents Theodore Roosevelt and William Howard Taft issued restrictive executive orders aimed at preventing such lobbying. But in 1912, Congress enacted the Lloyd-LaFollette Act allowing unaffiliated organizations to present their grievances to Congress without fear of retaliation.[3]

In the public sector, organizations of government employees, such as the National Federation of Employees formed in 1917 and the American Federation of Government Employees formed in 1932, concentrated on lobbying to obtain legislation favorable to their members. For most government workers, such lobbying proved to be successful. Although income was modest, fringe benefits such as vacations, paid holidays, paid sick leave, and pensions offered the public employee rewards not found in the private sector. Before the National Labor Relations Act was passed, public employees, represented by employee associations and organizations, could boast of an indirect participation in decisions affecting their employment. Unlike their counterparts in the private sector, their employer also could be reached in the legislatures and at the ballot box. However, the growth of public employment at every level soon began to erode that accessibility.

The Rise of Public Sector Unions

During the 1930s and 1940s, private sector unionization flourished under the protection of the National Labor Relations Act. These unions sought job security, higher wages, improved benefits, grievance procedures, arbitration rights, and, more important, recognition as participants in the decision-making process. Because many public employees already had these conditions, unionization held no attraction for them. The successes of private unions, however, began to surpass the public employees' ability to lobby, and changes in their job classifications and numbers gave an impetus to public sector unionization.

In the private sector, wages and benefits improved year after year, and job security was increased through the establishment of grievance and arbitration procedures in collective bargaining agreements. The organized worker also became cognizant of the respect a union could demand from an employer. Because strikes were protected under the act, the employer did not hold all of the bargaining strength.

Public employees discovered that lobbying efforts alone could not provide them with the controls and benefits of collective bargaining. Their swelling ranks made the lobbying process increasingly cumbersome and contributed to the rise of public sector unionism.[4] From 1956 to 1976, state and local government employment increased 140 percent, and federal employment increased by 23 percent.

The organizational size and complexity of government contributed to mismanagement and job dissatisfaction. It became increasingly difficult for employees to influence legislative action because the numerous layers of bureaucracy freed politicians from responsibility. In addition, the civil service systems developed to protect public employees were perceived as employer-recruited, employer-directed personnel mechanisms. As one expert observed, "It is the labor-management inadequacy of the civil service system that has been a prime cause of the remarkable thrust of union organization among public employees in recent years."[5] The 1939 Hatch Act also limited the political activities of most public workers (see Profile 13-1).

The Sovereignty Doctrine

As discussed in earlier chapters, the key to employers' resistance to collective bargaining in the private sector was the desire to protect their private property rights. The National Labor Relations Act tried to balance the employer's private property rights against the employee's right to organize and to bargain collectively. Although the purpose of the act was to place employees in an equal bargaining position, employers still held all rights not taken from them at the bargaining table.

In the public sector, governments were able to resist collective bargaining because of the **sovereignty doctrine**. *Sovereignty* is defined as "the supreme, absolute, and uncontrollable power by which an independent state is governed."[6] In a democracy, the source of that supreme power is the people who have vested their government with rights and responsibilities as caretakers of that power. The sovereignty doctrine requires that the government exercise its power unfettered by any force other than the people—all of the people. Collective bargaining was seen as a threat to that sovereignty doctrine if government were to share decision-making authority with employees. Obviously, decisions made at the collective bargaining table would affect the way government provides services and the amount those services would cost the taxpayer.

But the sovereignty doctrine had numerous weak points. Government contracts extensively with members of the private sector, and negotiation of those contracts takes place bilaterally. This practice disputes the claim that government must make its decisions unilaterally. Government's voluntary recognition of the employee's right to bargain collectively with it has also weakened the sovereignty doctrine. And the sovereignty doctrine can no longer be used to support the theory that government—the ruler—can do no wrong when numerous court deci-

HATCH ACT
(1993 AMENDMENT)

In 1993, President Bill Clinton signed a bill amending the Hatch Act and removing restrictions on federal workers' partisan political activity that had been in place for over 50 years. The **Hatch Act** was passed in 1939 after politicians used their control over Works Progress Administration (WPA) programs to influence elections. Workers were solicited for contributions and were pressured to change their party registration and to work for the election of candidates selected by the WPA politicians. In an effort to clean up the WPA, the Hatch Act was proposed. The act placed prohibitions on the federal employees, limiting their rights to take an active part in partisan elections, rather than placing any strictures on those who solicited the employees. The act passed and was signed into law by President Franklin Roosevelt. Almost immediately it was amended to include state and local government employees working under federal contracts and was put under the U.S. Civil Service Commission for enforcement.

Labor unions seeking to organize federal employees in the 1950s found the Hatch Act to be a deterrent. The threat, or perceived threat, of being accused of violating the Hatch Act because of union organizing activities became a major issue. One union, United Federal Workers of America (UFWA), decided to challenge the law. Arguing the case two times to a divided Supreme Court, the union contended that the Hatch Act went too far. The act's infringement on the First Amendment rights of federal employees was not necessary in order to guard against corruption. The Court disagreed and upheld the act as a reasonable restriction on activity necessary to ensure orderly management of the federal government free of political partisanship.

After years of seeking amendment, federal employees can now engage in a wider range of political activities off-duty, including managing political campaigns. In addition, federal sector union members may solicit other union members for contributions to union-based PAC funds. However, federal employees are still barred from running for office and from soliciting for other types of political contributions.

Adapted from Gilbert Gall, "The CIO and the Hatch Act," *Labor's Heritage* 7, no. 1 (Summer 1995), pp. 4–21; "Federal Service Labor and Employment Law," *Labor Lawyer* 10, no. 3 (Summer 1994), p. 373.

sions have ruled against the sovereign. The Supreme Court has allowed citizens to claim civil rights, torts, and contract violations against state and local governments, subjecting such institutions to monetary damages and remedial actions. In some states, federal judges have taken over the responsibility for administering the prison system until court-mandated improvements are made.

Laws

Executive Orders. In January 1962, the President's Task Force on Employee-Management Relations reported that one-third of the federal employees belonged to labor organizations. It recommended that the government officially acknowledge this fact and respond affirmatively to employees' desire for collective bargaining. President John F. Kennedy signed **Executive Order 10988**, which recognized the rights of federal employees to join or to refrain from joining labor organizations, granted recognition to those labor organizations, and detailed bargaining subjects. Although this executive order can be cited as having established the framework for labor-management relations in the federal government, comparison to its private sector counterpart, the National Labor Relations Act, showed glaring deficiencies.

What is important about Kennedy's original order of 1962 is the lightning effect it had on organizing drives among federal, state, and municipal employees. The order served as a signal to organize public workers as much as the Wagner Act of 1935 had stimulated the growth of industrial union membership in the CIO and AFL. The effect of E.O. 10988 was to send public sector union membership rolls soaring. Before 1962, only 26 union or association units in the executive branch of the federal government had union shops, and they represented only 19,000 workers. Six years after the Kennedy order, there were 2,305 bargaining units, with a total membership of 1.4 million employees. A number of unions represented federal workers, the largest being the American Federation of Government Employees (AFGE). From 1962 to 1972, the AFGE grew from 84,000 members to 621,000. The Postal Workers and the Letter Carriers also experienced growth in that period. For state and local public employees, the 1962 Kennedy order also spawned growth in unionization, although the order did not apply to them directly. The fact that union membership grew, however, did not mean that all state or local governments recognized or bargained with unions.[7]

As in the National Labor Relations Act, the right to organize was granted to federal civilian employees under E.O. 10988. However, the head of an agency could determine that a bureau or office was primarily performing intelligence, investigative, or security functions, and the employees of that bureau or office could be excluded from the executive order for national security reasons.

Under the National Labor Relations Act, a labor organization receiving a majority vote of the members of the bargaining unit gains exclusive recognition. Under E.O. 10988, exclusive recognition could be gained in the same manner, but two other types of recognition were also proffered. The first type granted formal recognition if there was no exclusive representative for the bargaining unit and the organization had at least 10 percent of the employees in the unit. Such an organization would represent only its members. A second type consisted of informal recognition of an employee organization that did not meet the majority vote or 10 percent of membership qualifications. This system generated much confusion because an agency might have to deal with two unions representing the same class of employees. For example, 10 percent of the service personnel could gain formal recognition while a different 8 percent could claim informal recognition. The agency would be negotiating with two unions consisting of 18 percent of one class of employee.

In the private sector, bargaining subjects protected by the act included wages, hours, and conditions of employment. Under E.O. 10988, bargaining subjects were limited. The employees could not mandate negotiations on economic issues. A management rights clause reserved the government's power to direct and discipline employees. And the grievance procedure could not result in binding arbitration.

Another deficiency in E.O. 10988 was the lack of a central authority to determine bargaining unit recognition and to resolve disputes. Many decisions were left to agency heads who were the immediate employers of the labor organization's members.

The most significant difference between the National Labor Relations Act and E.O. 10988 was the right to engage in work stoppages. Strikes were specifically denied the public labor organizations.

The Civil Service Reform Act of 1978. Currently, federal employee labor relations are governed by the provisions of Title VII of the **Civil Service Reform Act of 1978** and Reorganization Plan No. 2 of 1978.

Title VII, Federal Service Labor-Management Relations, is modeled after the National Labor Relations Act. Central authority was placed in a three-member panel, the Federal Labor Relations Authority. This panel oversees labor-management relations within the federal government; its three members are appointed by the president of the United States. The president also appoints a general counsel empowered to investigate alleged unfair labor practices and to file and prosecute complaints.

The Federal Labor Relations Authority oversees creation of bargaining units, conducts elections, decides representation cases, determines unfair labor practices, and seeks enforcement of its decisions in the federal courts. The Federal Service Impasse Panel was continued by the act and provides assistance in resolving negotiation impasses.

The unfair labor practice provision of Title VII generally mirrors the unfair labor practice provision in legislation for private employers and employees. The government is prohibited from the following practices:

1. Restraint and coercion of employees in the exercise of their organizational rights.
2. Encouragement or discouragement of union membership
3. Sponsorship of labor organizations
4. Refusal to bargain in good faith with a recognized organization
5. Refusal to cooperate in impasse procedures
6. Discipline of a union member who files a complaint
7. Enforcement of a new regulation that conflicts with an existent collective bargaining agreement[8]

A labor organization is prohibited from these actions:

1. Interference with an employee's right to organize or to refrain from organizing
2. Discrimination against or causing the employer to discriminate against employees because of union activity
3. Refusal to cooperate in impasse procedures
4. Refusal to bargain in good faith
5. Calling for or engaging in a work stoppage or slowdown[9]

Unlike private sector labor laws, Title VII mandates inclusion of a grievance procedure with binding arbitration as a final step in all federal collective bargaining agreements:

(B) Any negotiated grievance procedure referred to in subsection (A) of this section shall
1. Be fair and simple
2. Provide for expeditious processing
3. Include procedures that
   (a) Assure an exclusive representative the right, in its own behalf or on behalf of any employee in the unit represented by the exclusive representative, to present and process grievances
   (b) Assure such an employee the right to present a grievance on the employee's own behalf, and assure the exclusive representative the right to be present during the grievance proceeding
   (c) Provide that any grievance not satisfactorily settled under the negotiated grievance procedure shall be subject to binding arbitration which may be invoked by either the exclusive representative or the agency[10]

Title VII codifies presidential policies toward federal labor-management relations and improves the opportunities for the growth of collective bargaining in the public sector.

National Partnership Council, 1993.   In 1993, President Bill Clinton enacted Executive Order 12871 as part of the reengineering of government programs. It was hailed as a significant and fundamental change in federal sector labor-management relations. The goal was to change the relationship and alter the process by which the managers and unions reached decisions. A team of federal managers and union representatives worked on the plan. It created a National Partnership Council (NPC) to advise the president on labor-management issues. The NPC is made up of union leaders, representatives from the Federal Labor Relations Board, the Federal Mediation and Conciliation Service and executive branch directors. The order directs each agency to establish labor-management partnerships at appropriate levels to change the way government operates.[11]

State and Local Government Laws.   Title VII does not cover state and local employees, who must look to state and local laws for their collective bargaining rights. More than two-thirds of the states have enacted legislation granting public sector collective bargaining rights to some groups, such as teachers, police, and firefighters. Local, county, and municipal governments may also adopt collective bargaining laws or, by practice, recognize and bargain with employee organizations.

Although state and local laws differ as to particulars, some patterns do emerge. Legislation is more favorable to collective bargaining in the northern, northeastern, midwestern, and far western parts of the United States. The Sunbelt states located along the lower Atlantic coast, the southeast, southwest, and southwestern Rocky Mountain states generally do not have comprehensive public sector labor laws.

State legislation usually includes bargaining over wages, hours, terms of employment, and working conditions. Unfair labor practices and limits on or prohibitions of the right to strike also are legislated. The bargaining obligation is enforced by an administrative agency, and procedures are established should there be an impasse.[12]

A developing campaign to include state and municipal employees under federal legislation was substantially undermined by the Supreme Court decision in *National League of Cities v. Usery*.[13] That case reconfirmed the specific state's sovereignty over its own employees and denied that the commerce power of the federal government could be invoked to regulate that relationship. A recent study of the growth of teacher bargaining concluded that, although teacher bargaining in large cities typically starts before collective bargaining laws are passed, the passage of the laws spurs subsequent union growth.[14]

BARGAINING PARTIES IN THE PUBLIC SECTOR

Public Employment

Unlike employees in the private sector, public employees provide education, police, fire, and sanitation services and maintenance of public improvements. In recent years, legislation has increased government jobs for social workers, clerical and office employees, and computer technicians. Citizens depend on the services of these employees. The nature of the services provided—Social Security checks, food stamps, recordkeeping—are such that private industry is unable or unwilling to offer them; thus, a government monopoly is created.

The lack of competition by the private sector can cause collective bargaining problems. Without consumer control, quality can suffer, subjecting the public employee to adverse public sentiment. The lack of another provider makes the continuation of the public service critical; it prevents the employees from using economic pressure to reach a collective bargaining agreement. The absence of marketplace control on costs might also encourage intemperate collective bargaining settlements by public employers. The public employer, often an elected official, might give more than the tax dollars warrant to a certain project and then let a succeeding administration solve the deficit.

Public sector collective bargaining also differs because of its extensive unionization of professional employees. Measures of productivity are more difficult to devise for professional employees than for production and maintenance employees. In addition, the use of a service in the public sector cannot be related to the need for such service when participating in collective bargaining. Since providing public transportation is necessary, a bus driver should not be expected to have his pay affected by the number of people who choose to use that service.

The Public Employer

The public employer represents and provides services to the public. That employer is either an elected official serving for a limited term or someone placed in a position by that official. Although the legislative and executive branches of governments are almost always separate, the government as an employer is a combination of the two. Their roles may be clearly distinguished or may merge as the employee seeks the decision maker for collective bargaining rights. The source of funds available to the public employer may be limited by totally external factors—Proposition 13–type taxing limitations or grants of funds from a higher government level with constraints on their use, for example, the Job Training Partnership Act of 1982.[15]

By using the sovereignty doctrine, the public employer may seek to control the collective bargaining process by limiting the issues to be bargained. Also, the public employer can be influenced by a lack of competition in the necessary services.[16]

Bargaining Unit Determination

Under Title VII of the Civil Service Reform Act, the Federal Labor Relations Authority must determine an appropriate bargaining unit. Borrowing from court decisions under the National Labor Relations Act, the federal law applies a community of interest test to identify an appropriate unit on an agency, plant, installation, functional, or other basis. The criteria used to determine a clear and identifiable community of interest include common skills, similar working conditions, common supervision, common worksite, and identical duties. An appropriate unit must promote effective dealings with the agency; the extent of unionization by a bargaining unit is not a factor in its recognition. At the federal level, confidential employees, managers, supervisors, and personnel employees are excluded from the bargaining unit. Professional employees are excluded from nonprofessional units unless the professional employees vote in favor of their own inclusion.

A community of interest test is also used in state and local government to determine an appropriate unit. Guidelines for such determination may or may not be outlined in the legislation. The following criteria have been developed by the Advisory Committee on Intergovernmental Relations (ACIR) to define community of interest:

1. Similar wages, hours, working rules, and conditions of employment
2. Maintaining a negotiating pattern based on common history
3. Maintaining the craft or professional line status
4. Representation rights, which involve the inclusion or exclusion of supervisors or nonprofessionals (this refers to organizations such as police or fire departments)[17]

On the state and local level, the inclusion of supervisory personnel within the bargaining unit has presented a difficult question. Those in favor of such inclusion point to the need to consolidate employees and to limit the number of unions involved. It has been suggested that supervisors moderate demands and create less militant organizations. In some instances, supervisory titles in the public sector do not reflect actual supervisory authority because of the way decisions are made in the public sector, as illustrated in Case 13-1. In addition, all supervisory and nonsupervisory career employees share common interests, especially in money issues. Those who oppose the inclusion of supervisory personnel point out that supervisors face a potential conflict of interest when they themselves are affected by a contract they must enforce. Also, in pursuing grievance procedures, the distinction between management and employee needs to be clear, and supervisors may need to continue an operation during a work stoppage by the bargaining unit.

The size of a public employee unit can give a strategic advantage to either side. The public employer may encourage a larger unit, hoping the diverse interests and backgrounds of a larger unit will prevent the union from gaining majority status. Larger units prevent or reduce the possibility that multiunion negotiation will be used against the employer. The time and cost of bargaining are greatly reduced with larger units. Still, employers realize that the political power of public employee unions may be increased if the unit is very large. Because unions seek to represent the unit most likely to give it majority status, size is not the only determining factor in their organization efforts.

In addition, because of the mix of service and clerical employees being organized on a local or state level, the employees often have to choose between two labor organizations—a trade union and an employee association. Their choice will have significant impact on the labor-management relationship.[18]

Although modeled after private sector campaigns, union elections conducted in the public sector have some differences. Public sector employers may not be able to prohibit nonemployee union agents access to the workplace because the workplace is a public area.[19] Rules governing public employer preelection activities during an organizational campaign generally mirror private sector restrictions, although some states and local governments have encouraged less restrictive standards particularly when applied to employers expressing an opinion on the effect of unionizing. In effect, this approach balances the employer's right of free speech with its duty not to be coercive.[20]

BARGAINING UNIT DETERMINATION

The union in this case was recognized as the exclusive bargaining representative of a group of public employees who worked in mass transit. The city appealed this finding because the bargaining unit contained certain employees who the city claimed were supervisory and should not be included. The State Department of Labor had reviewed this contention by the city and had found that those employees were properly a part of the unit. A lower court reversed that finding and the union appealed.

Decision

The Court overruled the lower court and reinstated the Department of Labor's finding. It pointed out that the lower court had based its reversal of the Department of Labor's decision on the fact that the department had not followed its own procedures in determining which employees were supervisory. The Court stated that the lower court was wrong in requiring that those procedures be followed because, unlike the National Labor Relations Act, which excludes supervisory employees from bargaining units, the state law excludes only employees designated as deputy, administrative assistant, or secretary who have a confidential relationship to the executive head of the actual bargaining unit. Therefore, even though the Department of Labor may have applied some type of past procedure in determining the supervisory nature of the public employee, the state law merely excludes the employees in those three classifications who maintain a confidential relationship with the director.

Adapted from *Seattle v. Amalgamated Transit Union Local 587*, 1977–78, P.B.C. para. 36,046.

The Scope of Negotiations

Management Rights.   More management rights are reserved for the employer in the public sector than in the private sector. Under the sovereignty theory, government avoids many issues at the bargaining table. For example, in Title VII, an agency is given the right to make a unilateral decision to determine the mission, budget, organization, number of employees, and internal security practices. Questions of hiring, employee assignment, promotions, firings, suspensions, and other disciplinary actions are all at the agency's discretion. A union may be able to negotiate procedures for actions taken by the employer and appropriate arrangements for adversely affected employees, but, as stated earlier, the basic content of a grievance procedure is also legislated. Most state and local governments use similar language to ensure that policy and quality of service remain the prerogative of management.

Union Security.   *Union security* refers to the ability of the union to grow and to perform its collective bargaining role without interference from management or other unions. As the exclusive representative of certain employees, a union enjoys a high degree of security. But unions seek more. In the private sector, union security provisions include automatic dues deductions, a union or agency shop, and maintenance of membership provisions. These ensure a dependable source of revenue.

**BARGAINING
INTERESTS
IN THE PUBLIC
SECTOR**

Automatic dues deduction is used as a **public sector union security** provision. Each employee is asked to sign an authorization card; union dues are withheld from the employee's checks and are transmitted to the union.

An agency shop provision requires financial support of the union, whether the employee joins or not. This is a popular provision in public employee contracts because it assists the union financially, but it does not require compulsory unionization. As demonstrated in Table 13-1, agency shop provisions are the most commonly accepted union security clause in public sector contracts.

A union shop requires that the employee join the union after being hired, and a maintenance of membership clause keeps the employee in the union during the life of the contract. Both of these provisions can run afoul of employee rights under civil service or merit systems in which an employee can be discharged only for a job-related reason. The agency shop provision came under some question in a Supreme Court decision, *Abood v. Detroit Board of Education*, limiting the amount of dues to be paid by nonunion members to the amount actually spent on collective bargaining, contract administration, and grievance adjustment.[21]

In recent years, state and local governments have been subjected to numerous civil rights actions in which allegations have been made that the power of the government was used to deprive a citizen of a constitutional right.[22] Such actions have led many public officials to believe that union security and maintenance of membership clauses could subject the governmental entity to a civil rights charge of depriving the employees of their property rights in employment.

Claims that such union security clauses can violate merit principles and possibly the employee's civil rights reinforce the public employer's aversion to such clauses.[23] The employer also recognizes that the bargaining power of the employee increases with the security of the union.

Privatization. Perhaps the greatest threat to public unions and their members today is outsourcing, or **privatization**. In the past outsourcing full-time public sector jobs was unheard of; it was something "big business does, not us." In the

Table 13-1

Percentage Distribution of Union Security and Impasse Resolution Provisions by Duty to Bargain: State and Local Government Sample (excluding police and fire)

Variable	Duty to Bargain	No Duty to Bargain
Agency shop		
Right to work	3.6	19.3
No agency provision	9.2	18.8
Agency shop authorized	43.0	2.1
Agency shop mandatory	4.1	0.0
Compulsory check-off		
No compulsory check-off	25.9	4.3
Compulsory check-off	36.1	33.7
Impasse resolution		
No binding method	40.8	0.0
Compulsory arbitration	2.2	0.0
Right to strike	19.0	0.0

Source: Greg Hundley, "Collective Bargaining Coverage of Union Members and Nonmembers in the Public Sector," *Industrial Relations* 32, no. 1 (Winter 1993), p. 76.

1980s and 1990s, however, as public agencies became strapped for funds, governments looked to lower their personnel costs. In Indianapolis, for example, outsourcing reduced the city's number of public employees by 40 percent in only three years. Sunnyvale, California, used a temporary Manpower company for 25 percent of its workforce. Some states, such as Pennsylvania, have developed their own pool of temporary workers, and large state community college systems use as many as 66 percent contract workers instead of full-time faculty. The International Personnel Management Association, the nation's largest group of public sector human resource managers, estimated in 1996 that 24 percent of local and state governments used temporary or privatized workers, up from only 9 percent in 1993. The employees most commonly affected are shown in Table 13-2.[24]

Outsourcing has become so widely used so quickly in the 1990s that many public employee unions and some public officials have become alarmed. The most effective response by unions is to negotiate a provision in their agreements that prevents any civil service status employee from losing his or her job to such action. Although legal, these provisions are difficult to negotiate if management intends to outsource. Managers recognize that privatized workers can be treated quite differently from permanent employees; some make as little as one-third the wages of full-time public sector employees, and they get no health benefits, paid vacations, holiday pay, or sick leave. Some observers see outsourcing as another factor eroding the middle class:[25]

> "Everyone sees outsourcing as a way of gaining for the government the advantages and flexibility of the private sector, but this creates problems for society," says Frank McArdle, managing director of the General Contractors Association of New York. "When you drive down wages through outsourcing, you undermine your tax base and you add to the burden on government services." Adds Sal Albanese, a New York City Council member: "In the past, the government provided a tremendous opportunity for people to elevate themselves into the middle class. We're in danger of losing that."

Wages and Fringes.   In most cases the negotiation of wages and fringe benefits is a union's principal function. Public employee unions, however, often find this subject out of their reach. Under Title VII, the federal statute governing employee rights, the right to bargain collectively is limited to issues concerning conditions of employment and excludes wages and fringe benefits. For most state and

Privatized Jobs (percentage of public services handled by contract workers)		Table 13-2

	1987	1995
Waste collection	30	50
Building maintenance	32	42
Bill collection	10	20
Data processing	16	31
Health/medical	15	27
Street cleaning	9	18
Street repair	19	37

Source: Mercer Group Inc. As printed in the *Wall Street Journal*, August 6, 1996, p. A1.

municipal employees, union contract negotiations take place during or after the respective legislative body has determined a budget. Unions may be limited to a negotiation on how the available dollars are to be divided among classes of employees or distributed as base wages, fringe benefits, bonuses, and incentive pay. Despite these limitations, collective bargaining does have an impact on public sector wage levels.

An analysis of wage rates demonstrated that collective bargaining was a strong determinant of earnings in the public sector. In a comparison of public and private, and federal, state, and local government wages, the study determined that the union wage premium was over 20 percent in every category, with the private sector being the most significant. Table 13-3 summarizes these findings. Local and state government workers fared better than federal government workers in overall union wage premiums.[26]

Hours. The nature of the job performed often determines the amount of flexibility available in the negotiation of hours. Police, fire, and other emergency services must operate around the clock. Transportation and public utilities cannot be subject to variation. Determination of total hours of employment, therefore, is jealously guarded by the public employer as a basic policy decision.

Working Conditions. Unlike in the private sector, negotiation of working conditions in the public sector does not center on promotions, discipline, and production standards. Working conditions directly affect the provision of service to the public. Therefore, the number of police in a patrol car or firefighters on a fire alarm run are issues that may be decided at a negotiating table. Classroom size, the number of bus routes, or the frequency of trash pickup are determined by the public employer, often through negotiations. The public employee is often better able to determine the quality of service than the manager.

Grievance Procedure. Under the federal statute, a grievance procedure must be included in federal contracts. That procedure includes binding arbitration if necessary. State and local government contracts, although containing grievance procedures, frequently stop at advisory arbitration. A review of impasse resolution

Table 13-3	Union Earnings Premiums for Public and Private Sector Employees		
	Group	Earnings Differential	Number of Observations
	Federal workers	23.36%	271
	State government workers	29.69%	278
	Local government workers	29.70%	344
	Private sector workers	34.99%	3,255
	All workers	31.00%	4,151

Source: Javed Ashraf, "Union Wage Effects in the Public Sector: An Examination of the Impact across Alternative Governmental Structures," *Journal of Collective Negotiations in the Public Sector* 21, no. 4 (1992), p. 296. Reprinted with permission, Baywood Publishing Company, Incorporated, Amityville, NY 11701.

procedures in state and local government contracts (excluding police and fire) found few that called for binding arbitration. Table 13-1 includes those results.[27]

Public employers may believe that the sovereignty doctrine prohibits the delegation of decision-making authority to a nonelected body. That legal theory weakens, however, when the binding arbitration concerns only adjudication of contract provisions already negotiated and agreed to by the public employers.

> Although not entirely dead, the sovereignty and extraloyalty theory are moribund; and it is clear that the federal policy in favor of grievance arbitration in the public sector, as well as recent state legislation, has had a considerable influence on state court decisions involving public sector arbitration. The trend is strongly in the direction of upholding the legality of voluntary agreements to submit grievance to final and binding arbitration and of enforcing such agreements.[28]

Public Employee Drug Testing

As discussed in chapters 9 and 12, random drug testing of employees began in the public sector under President Reagan's administration. The armed services began random urine testing in 1981 and *Executive Order 12564* followed in 1986, extending random testing to various federal employees. Urine testing by the public employer raises the Fourth Amendment constitutional issue of an unreasonable search. The Fourth Amendment provides that

> The right of the people to be secure in their persons, houses, papers and effects, against unreasonable searches and seizures, shall not be violated, and no warrants shall issue, but upon probable cause, supported by oath or affirmation, and particularly described being the place to be searched, and the person or things to be seized.

Custom department and railroad employees challenged the random drug testing program as an unreasonable search. The Supreme Court ruled that the tests were searches covered under the Fourth Amendment, but for certain employees whose duties involved public safety or law enforcement, such searches were not unreasonable.[29]

In a related case, railroad employees challenged Conrail's unilateral institution of a drug testing program for its employees as a violation of its collective bargaining agreement under the Railway Labor Act. The Court found that, because Conrail's policy of conducting periodic physical exams already existed in the collective bargaining agreement, the inclusion of drug testing in all physical examinations was a minor dispute under the act and, therefore, subject to arbitration, not judicial review.[30]

Two recent court rulings in cases involving drug policies and public agencies have increased exceptions to the Fourth Amendment prohibitions. A federal court ruled that, because the NLRB had determined that drug testing was a mandatory subject for collective bargaining, a public employee union may consent to drug testing on behalf of the employees it represents. Such consent will restrict an employee's right to claim a violation of the Fourth Amendment.[31] The Supreme Court lowered the constitutional test used to determine if drug testing in the absence of probable cause is legal. The Vernonia School District instituted a drug policy that authorized random urinalysis drug testing of its athletes. When one student refused, he was not allowed to participate in the school's football program. The Court said that, although state-compelled drug testing programs are subject to the Fourth Amendment's protections against warrantless searches, sometimes "special needs" exist to support suspicionless drug testing. In this instance, the Court found that student athletes have lower expectations of privacy than other students or adults; the procedure used for the testing was not invasive; and the school's interest in not having student athletes use drugs, while maybe not a compelling interest, was "important enough."[32]

Negotiating the Public Employee Contract

As collective bargaining has gained acceptance in the public sector, the contract has become increasingly important to the public "helping" professions, such as the police.

> In many of today's law enforcement agencies, collective bargaining and labor relations have been and can continue to be a catalyst for changing old methods and old attitudes. Police agencies are reflections of society and the career professional police officer demands to be heard and considered. Police departments and public sector administrators have an obligation through collective bargaining, to change with the changing times, or risk the possibility of stagnation, unrest, and dissatisfaction, both in the ranks and in the eyes of the public.
>
> Police officers are no longer the ultraconservative public employees who will grudgingly accept whatever they are given without regard for personal needs and wants. Police officers have been conditioned through the sixties and seventies of seeing others accomplish missions by united action. With public demands of law enforcement at its highest level, collective bargaining has and must be the avenue to demonstrate the ability to discuss with administrators and bargain in good faith, to improve upon economic conditions, hours, and improvement of the hazardous working conditions.
>
> When there is a reluctance of police officers to use collective bargaining, normally, it is the uncertainty of what it is, and what it can do, due to the many historical myths surrounding the process. The public sector process goes beyond actual bargaining. It should be an ongoing, daily process designed to administer contractual provisions, resolve personnel grievances, and most importantly—promote an atmosphere of harmonious relationships, which ultimately will provide an efficient and productive police agency.[33]

The Bargaining Process. Fundamental ideas regarding bargaining theories and the bargaining process in the private sector hold true for the public sector with a few variations. As outlined in Chapter 6, union negotiators derive their authority to negotiate from their membership. That authority is generally limited in that the contract must be taken back to the membership for a vote. On the other hand, management negotiators have the authority to commit to a negotiated agreement at the bargaining table. This situation is often referred to as **bilateral bargaining**. In the public sector, where *management's* authority to negotiate flows from the people, the decision cannot be made by one official and is referred to as **multilateral bargaining**.

Multilateral Bargaining. The governmental entities involved in collective bargaining fall into two categories: a council form and an executive-legislative form. For example, an elected or appointed *council* of a school district acts as a board of directors for a corporation that appoints its own chief executive officer. The public negotiator for management may find his or her role similar to that of the negotiator for labor; that is, he or she is charged with returning a negotiated agreement for approval to the final authority. Such approval is usually given because of the close relationship between the negotiator and the council.

In an **executive-legislative** form, the executive authority resides with a president, governor, or mayor who is the *manager* of the governmental entity. The legislative authority resides with a congress, a legislature, or a council that is the *lawmaker* of the governmental entity. Together, the two parties make up *management*; both are employers to the public employees. This joint management authority is seldom a problem because the executive manages personnel policies on a day-to-day basis under directives put in place by the legislators. During labor negotiations, however, when the decisions affecting employees are subject to collective bargaining, conflicts can arise. The negotiator is employed by the executive branch and may be understood to be negotiating on behalf of the executive branch. Settlement may be reached by the negotiator and endorsed by the executive (mayor, governor, etc.), but it must be approved by the legislative body. The legislative body may not approve the negotiated agreement, thereby undermining the collective bargaining process.

Obviously, the disadvantage of multilateral negotiations to the employer is the union's ability to appeal to the legislative body for a more favorable settlement before, during, or after the negotiations, thus undermining the work of the executive. On the other hand, the executive and legislative branches may not agree on a settlement, leaving the union up in the air while each side blames the other for indecision.[34]

The legislative body may seek to play the role of a mediator between the executive branch and the union when an impasse develops.[35] The legislative body is a part of management and, as such, has no legitimate role as mediator. Because the legislature has the authority to determine the budget, involvement at an impasse stage of negotiations represents a new level of negotiation rather than mediation. That level may involve a restatement of the executive's position or a new offer by the legislative branch. Such a practice undermines the public employer's negotiating posture. Intervention after the fact by a third party may destroy the fairness of a negotiated agreement and the commitment to compromise so important to collective bargaining.

Open Negotiations. Public employee collective bargaining makes news. Press coverage of public employee collective bargaining can harm the bargaining process in several ways. If an impasse is reached, the parties may try to explain their side to the media, hoping to influence public opinion and in turn the negotiating process. Rushing for media coverage may cause a party to present proposals publicly before it has presented them to the other party at the negotiating table. By emphasizing the differences between the parties instead of the points of agreement, reporters can actually prolong the posturing stage. In the normal course of events, agreement of public employees and employers at the collective bargaining table is not newsworthy; therefore, media coverage often will be confined to reporting on the items separating the parties and not the items of agreement. Publicity might also encourage the negative tactic of turning to the legislative body for impasse resolution. Coverage reinforces the bad feelings too often present in negotiations in a way the private sector rarely experiences.

Sunshine laws may require that collective bargaining sessions be open to the public, often thwarting the parties' ability to compromise[36] (see Case 13-2). Some initial posturing is necessary on both sides so that the negotiator's constituency is assured that he or she is acting on their behalf. Negotiators may find it difficult

NEGOTIATING IN OPEN SESSION

The members of the City of Springfield Public Utilities Board were negotiating with several labor unions. During the course of those negotiations, the board held numerous meetings with its principal negotiator to discuss issues remaining in dispute. These meetings were not announced to the general public, and it was voted they go into closed session. A newspaper reporter filed suit charging that the board could not meet in closed session to discuss the contract negotiations because of the state's Open Meetings Act.

Decision

The court found that, although the state's Open Meetings Act was applicable to the utility board and it held no specific exemption for collective bargaining sessions, such sessions were not subject to the act. The court based this decision on an interpretation of the rights granted public employees to bargain collectively under another state law. It was the court's opinion that the public employees' right to meaningful collective bargaining would be destroyed if full publicity were accorded at each step of the negotiations. However, the final agreement negotiated by the parties would be subject to an open session.

Adapted from *City of Springfield, Missouri v. John C. Crow, Judge,* 1979–80, P.B.C. para. 36,815.

to stop posturing if they are under constant scrutiny. At any particular juncture during the negotiation process, it may seem as if one side or the other is winning or losing. A fear of "loss of face" by either side may endanger the fair compromise so necessary to successful negotiations.

However, press coverage of public sector collective bargaining is necessary because the ultimate decision does rest with the public. Without contribution by the public at some point during the process, the parties will not be able to gauge its reaction. By making the progress of negotiations public, elected officials and union members are able to get a response and so can modify their positions. For example, if a union representing teachers learned through news coverage of their negotiations that the public would support tax increases to improve the teacher-student ratio but not to raise salaries, its posture during the negotiations might change.

The Right to Strike. In the private sector, an impasse in collective bargaining negotiations can result in a strike. The National Labor Relations Act reserves that right to the employee as an economic weapon. In the public sector, the right to strike is usually denied to the public employee either by the collective bargaining statute or by court actions.

The right-to-strike issue is to the public sector what the right-to-work issue is to the private sector. Those who believe the public employee should have the right to strike cite the following reasons:

1. Despite legislation to the contrary, public employees do go on strike.[37] Attention is then focused upon the strike issue and not upon the reason for the disagreement, thereby thwarting resolution of the impasse.

2. Strikes, or at least credible strike threats, facilitate agreement at the bargaining table. Good-faith bargaining alone cannot equalize the parties' bargaining power.[38]

3. Strikes test the union's strength as a bargaining representative; this strength can be used as a bargaining strategy.

4. Nonessential public employees should have the same rights as their counterparts in the private sector to strike.[39]

Those who believe that public employees should not have the right to strike cite the following reasons:

1. The primary reason for prohibiting public employee strikes is that the services provided by employees are essential to the general welfare. A distinction between police and fire services and motor pool operations may or may not be made. Case 13-3 points out the public's interest in curtailing the right to strike.

2. Under the sovereignty theory, giving unions the right to strike places too much power in the hands of the employees rather than in the elected representatives of the people.

3. Since there are no market controls on government services, the strike threat could cause public employers to make unwise agreements at the expense of the taxpayer.[40]

Despite the traditional bias against public employees' right to strike, some states allow public workers to strike either directly or by not prohibiting it.[41] The percentage of state or local contracts that allow public employees to strike from a sample of public employers is close to 20 percent, as shown in Table 13-1.

The Professional Air Traffic Controllers (PATCO). In 1968 a group of New York controllers formed the Professional Air Traffic Controllers Organization (PATCO). Increased frustration with the Federal Aviation Association's (FAA) poor management of the air traffic control system led to a slowdown beginning in New York and spreading to other cities. In 1969, PATCO counsel F. Lee Bailey discussed the controllers' frustrations with overcrowding in the skies on the *Tonight Show* and said, "I'd start walking, if I were you."[42] The next day several hundred controllers conducted a work stoppage, and the FAA suspended 80 of them. In 1970 almost 3,000 controllers informally went on strike; 52 were fired, and 1,000 were suspended.[43]

Several other instances gave PATCO the reputation of being an independent and feisty union. Certainly some of their members' feelings of independence were rooted in the belief that they were highly skilled professionals who could not easily be replaced. Then in 1981, PATCO leaders called the first declared national strike against the federal government.

However, at least 22 strikes *unauthorized* by law against the federal government occurred before the 1981 PATCO strike, including these:

1962	Tennessee Valley Authority craft workers' strike. Eighty were fired, none rehired.
1969	Sick-in by 500 PATCO members over F. Lee Bailey's remarks. No disciplinary action taken.
1969	Postal workers in Massachusetts strike over wages. No disciplinary action taken.
1970	More than 2,300 PATCO members engaged in a two-week sick-in during contract negotiations. Sixty were fired, 59 rehired.

THE RIGHT TO STRIKE

On the eve of Labor Day weekend, the union called a strike of its members, preventing public employees who normally ran ferry services to a tourist island from providing such services over the holiday weekend. The strike was called to protest the change in the wording of a contract under negotiation after the union believed agreement had been reached on the language. The strike was held to be in breach of an existing collective bargaining agreement and was voluntarily ended after the weekend. Members of the public who resided or owned businesses on the islands and were left without a ferry system filed suit against the union, claiming inconvenience and economic harm as a result of the strike. The plaintiffs claimed damages from the union in excess of $1 million.

The plaintiffs based their case on the union's action as being a tortious interference with their business relationships. The plaintiffs also held that they were third-party beneficiaries of the public employee contract and that the union had breached its duty to them.

The union protested that the plaintiffs were seeking to create a new law to hold public employee unions strictly accountable to the public if anyone was injured by their strikes.

Decision

The court held that the plaintiffs, as members of the public, were not third-party beneficiaries of the collective bargaining agreement between the union and the public employer. To create third-party beneficiary rights, the contract between the first and second party must convey such rights to the third party. In this instance, the purpose of the collective bargaining agreement between the union and the employer was to improve the relationship between the employer and its employees. As to the plaintiffs' contention that the strike was a tortious interference in business relationships, the court found no such intent. The court held that, although the strike does affect members of the public, the purpose is to use economic force to gain bargaining leverage during contract negotiations. The court also declined to create a tort doctrine to permit public collection of damages from strikes. It felt that decisions affecting resolution of public employee labor relations issues should be left to the legislature. Although a tort doctrine would not hold up in court in this instance, citizens could still require that employees either resume their work or be held in contempt of court.

Adapted from *Burke and Thomas, Inc. v. International Organization of Masters, Mates, and Pilots*, 1979–80, P.B.C. para. 36,785.

1970	More than 152,000 postal workers strike for nine days for higher wages. The issue was negotiated. No disciplinary action taken.
1970	One-day strike by 1,400 Printing Office workers over wages. Issue was negotiated. No disciplinary action taken.
1971	Library of Congress employees' strike. Thirteen were fired, none rehired.
1973	Tennessee Valley Authority craft workers' strike. One hundred ninety-two were fired; all were rehired.
1974	New Jersey postal workers (475) walkout. Federal judge orders arbitration of issue. No disciplinary action taken.
1978	California and New Jersey postal workers (4,750) engage in wildcat strike. Two hundred twenty-six were fired, 104 rehired.[44]

Therefore, when more than 13,000 air traffic controllers followed PATCO's call for the first nationwide declared strike, a critical moment in U.S. history had arrived. Never before had so many federal workers directly violated the no-strike clause of their contracts and endangered the lives of Americans.

President Reagan quickly warned that such direct disobedience of the law would not be tolerated. He stated, "There is no strike, what they did was to terminate their own employment by quitting."[45] Reagan gave workers a deadline that most ignored; then he fired all but the few who returned to work. Not one controller was given amnesty or rehired until President Clinton took office in 1993.

The success of the Reagan administration in replacing such highly skilled workers, together with widespread public support, left little doubt in the minds of government workers as to what might happen if they went on strike. PATCO miscalculated its ability to gain concessions by striking. It sacrificed a substantial pay increase, a generous benefits package, and its very existence in its attempt to legitimize strikes in the public sector.[46]

Some union leaders point to the PATCO strike as the signal for employers to replace striking workers with permanent employees.[47] An anticipated teachers' strike in California in 1990, for example, led the Santa Maria Joint Union School District to advertise for replacement teachers even before the strike began.

IMPASSE SETTLEMENT PROCEDURES

Legislation that allows public sector collective bargaining but prohibits strikes often details the procedures available to resolve an impasse.

Mediation is provided in almost all states with collective bargaining in the public sector. As with the private sector, the mediator has no independent authority but uses acquired skills to bring the parties back together. It has been suggested that the mediator represent the public's interest at the bargaining table. Such a role does not seem to facilitate resolution of a dispute.

Fact finding and *advisory arbitration* can be far more successful in the public sector than the private because of political pressures. Under fact finding and advisory arbitration, an unbiased third party examines the collective bargaining impasse and issues findings and recommendations. The findings may move the process by simply eliminating the distrust one party feels for the other party's facts or figures. Reasonable recommendations may also pressure a party to accept an offer that otherwise would not have been considered.

Interest arbitration allows a panel to make a final and binding decision on a negotiation dispute and has been used in the public sector to resolve impasses. However, the legality of allowing a third party to set the terms of the contract has been questioned.[48]

The use of such a compulsory mechanism seems incompatible with collective bargaining. A fundamental tenet of American industrial relations is that the bargaining outcome be determined by the parties to the greatest extent possible. Interest arbitration violates that tenet by substituting a third party's decision for that of the negotiating parties. Interest arbitration can become a substitute for the arduous demands of bargaining and can discourage the concessions so necessary to negotiations. The award merely becomes a compromise between the parties' final positions.[49]

Proponents of interest arbitration, however, believe that the threat of arbitration, like the threat of a strike, provides an incentive to negotiate when the parties understand and appreciate the final offer procedure.[50]

The 1984 interest arbitration involving the U.S. Postal Service (USPS) and its two largest unions, the American Postal Workers Union and the National Association of Letter Carriers, was historic. The five-member arbitration panel's award covered more than 500,000 employees, a record number for a single arbitration in the United States.

The postal negotiations were the first postal labor talks since the landmark air traffic controllers' (PATCO) strike in 1981. The tone of the talks was set when the USPS Board of Governors proposed a two-tier wage structure with a new scale 33 percent below the current scale. The unions believed the wage concession was unwarranted by the financial condition of USPS. Negotiations quickly went to impasse and led to binding arbitration as provided for in the 1970 Postal Reorganization Act.[51]

The central issue was the interpretation of a section of the 1970 act that gives USPS the ability to maintain compensation and benefits "on a standard of comparability" to the private sector. The arbitration award provided for a three-year agreement with 2.7 percent annual increases for incumbent employees. New employees in a two-tier system would start at wage levels below those of current employees.

THE PUBLIC EMPLOYEE CONTRACT

Reducing the Contract to Writing

Title VII of the Civil Service Reform Act requires that any agreement must be incorporated into a written document if either party requests it.[52] The subjects covered in a public sector collective bargaining agreement may differ from those in the private sector. An analysis of the differences can be made using four contract groups: union security and management rights, wage and effort bargaining, job security, and contract administration. Union security will generally be included in the collective bargaining agreement as an automatic check-off provision or agency shop. The federal statute mirrors the National Labor Relations Board in regard to a valid contract as a bar to an election for recognition by a different union. State and local statutes are usually not that comprehensive. The management rights issue is indirectly addressed by detailing procedures to be followed by the employer.[53]

Although wages and benefits are not subject to negotiation, such items as merit raise systems and premium pay may be covered. Local government and state contracts may include wage provisions and often include procedures for testing standards of performance.

Job security, seniority, and due process often are covered under merit and civil service systems already in place. If the contract touches upon those areas at all, the rights and procedures would be in addition to the civil service system.

In the area of contract administration, federal law requires that a grievance procedure with binding arbitration be part of each contract. Such procedures usually stop at advisory arbitration at the state and local level.

Contract Enforcement

The Federal Labor Relations Authority performs the same role in federal labor contract enforcement as the private sector National Labor Relations Board. If a contract interpretation or violation issue is also an unfair labor practice, the authority has jurisdiction. However, unlike the NLRB, the authority has jurisdiction in all the arbitration awards appealed to it, regardless of the issue involved. The authority performs a quasijudicial role when it determines if the arbitrator's award is contrary to any law, rule, or regulation or if it is deficient "on other grounds similar to those applied by federal courts in private sector labor-management relations."[54]

Grievance Arbitration

Grievance arbitration in the private sector has proved to be a more effective means of contract enforcement than strikes, in addition to continuing the collective bargaining process through the life of the contract. At the federal, state, and local levels, the grievance arbitration procedure has borrowed heavily from the private sector.[55]

The expense of grievance arbitration is of concern to employers in the public sector just as it is to those in the private sector. A study was done on the attitudes of union stewards toward filing grievances in the public sector to see if costs could be reduced. It was demonstrated that grievance rates tended to be reduced when management negotiators were perceived as accommodating rather than combative during negotiations. Grievance rates tended to increase or decrease depending on whether union stewards perceived their union members to be combative or cooperative toward their government managers. The study also found that if an informal method of communication existed fewer grievances were filed. Surprisingly, the clarity of a collective bargaining agreement had little effect on the number of grievances filed. If the relationship between the parties tended to be combative or cooperative, disagreements over contract language followed that same pattern.[56]

In the area of discipline and dismissal, however, public sector labor law has developed along completely different lines because of the constitutional protection afforded government employees. When government acts at any level to discipline or dismiss an employee, a form of state action has occurred. The power of the state over an individual is curtailed by the Bill of Rights, and if any constitutionally protected right is infringed upon by the discipline or dismissal of an employee, that employee has a valid claim against the governmental entity regardless of contractual rights. Examples of constitutionally protected rights include the following:

1. Privilege against self-incrimination
2. Freedom of association
3. Right to participate in partisan politics
4. Freedom of expression

These constitutionally protected rights, as well as specific statutes allowing government employees to appeal to various courts, have assured public employees of multiple forms of relief not available to private sector employees. Although this protection tends to weaken the grievance-arbitration system, it guarantees the rights of the individual over those of the unions.[57]

SUMMARY

Widespread unionization in the public sector developed later than in the private sector. Presently, unionization is still somewhat limited because of the sovereignty doctrine curtailing the scope of collective bargaining in the public sector.

Under Executive Order 10988, as updated under the Civil Service Reform Act of 1978, federal employees are granted limited collective bargaining rights.

The nature of public employment affects the bargaining units, along with the scope and conduct of negotiations. The restriction on the ability to strike in the public sector further limits the effectiveness of the collective bargaining process, even though that restriction is not always followed.

Drug screening of public employees continues to be a major area of concern for the employees, the governments, and the public that relies on the services provided by the public employers.

Alternative remedies available to the public employee prevent the grievance-arbitration procedure from becoming the predominant means of contract enforcement as in the private sector.

CASE STUDY 13-1

RELIGIOUS DISCRIMINATION

Facts

The Federal Bureau of Investigation (FBI) discharged the employee for insubordination and violation of his oath of office. The employee refused to conduct an FBI investigation into vandalism that occurred at military recruiting facilities in the Chicago area. The FBI directive to the employee included "Silo Plowshares" and "Veterans' Fast for Life" as possible suspects for the property damage incidents.

The employee objected to the classification of this investigation as a domestic security-terrorism case and stated that on the basis of his religious beliefs, he would not participate in the investigation. He was advised by his supervisor that his refusal to investigate would leave the FBI with no alternative but to dismiss him. The employee testified that he was a Catholic who in the early 1980s experienced a spiritual awakening that prompted him to oppose the U.S. military posture and nuclear weapons policy. He had been told by his supervisor, he testified, that if problems developed regarding this spiritual awakening, he should put it in a memo and give those problems to his supervisor.

The employee argued that his refusal to undertake the investigation was based on religious beliefs and that the FBI made no effort to accommodate his religious beliefs by *not* assigning him to that type of case.

In order for the employee to establish a prima facie case of religious discrimination he must show the following:

1. He holds a sincere religious belief that conflicts with employment requirements.
2. He has informed the employer of the conflict.
3. He was discharged or disciplined for failure to comply with the employment requirement.

Once the prima facie case is established, the employer must prove that it cannot reasonably accommodate the employee without incurring undue hardship.

The FBI contended that the employee was insubordinate in refusing to obey an order that a superior officer had given him. Relying on past decisions, the FBI pointed out that an employee of the FBI must obey an order unless it would place him in a clearly dangerous situation. At a later time, the employee can take whatever steps he thinks appropriate to challenge the validity of the order. In addition, the FBI stated that the employee violated his oath of office because his duties included the investigation of violations of U.S. laws. The employee violated his oath when he refused to carry out the investigation. As to the contention of the employee that the FBI discriminated against him because of his religion, the FBI introduced evidence showing that any accommodation for the employee's religious belief would create an undue hardship on its business. It would not be possible to plan investigations concerning violation of U.S. laws, which is the heart of the FBI's mission, around the religious beliefs of this or any other agent.

Questions

1. Would you find that the employee was insubordinate and violated his oath of office? Explain.

2. Did the FBI discriminate against the employee for his religious beliefs?

3. Is it reasonable for the FBI to accommodate religious beliefs in assigning cases?

Adapted from *John C. Ryan v. Dept. of Justice*, (Docket No. Cb 07528810010, February 2, 1988, T. Christopher Heavrin, A.J.).

BARGAINING UNIT

Facts

A bargaining unit consisting of principals, assistant principals, coordinators, and department heads had been represented by the Wellesley Teachers Association for a number of years and had been recognized by the school board. After the effective date of a state statute granting collective bargaining rights to certain public employees, the school board stopped bargaining with the union on the grounds that the employees in the unit were managerial employees and were excluded from coverage of the state act.

The state statute in question defines *managerial employees* as those who (a) participate to a substantial degree in formulating or determining policy; (b) assist to a substantial degree in the preparation for or the conduct of collective bargaining for the public employer; and (c) have substantial authority to act independently in an appeal under a collective bargaining agreement.

The parties to this suit analyzed the facts as to the powers, duties, and responsibilities of the unit members quite differently from the statutory requirements.

A. Policy Formation

FACT: Members of the unit attended and participated in periodic discussions with higher administrators. The meetings were characterized as "input" meetings, and some members were consulted before policy was implemented. Two committees made up of unit members met regularly with the superintendent to discuss policy. Suggestions formulated at these meetings could be forwarded to the school board for action.

UNION POSITION: Unit members participated only in an advisory and consulting role, *not* with authority to make a final decision. Therefore, their participation was not to a "substantial degree."

SCHOOL BOARD POSITION: Statute includes "participation . . . in formulating" policy as well as determining policy. These meetings were for that purpose and put the employees in the "managerial" group.

B. Collective Bargaining

FACT: One principal, a member of the unit, attended one negotiating session between the board and the secretaries' union. Members of the unit were asked for their opinions on administering the teachers' and secretaries' contracts. The superintendent wanted members of the unit to participate with the board in negotiating teachers' and secretaries' contracts.

UNION POSITION: Members did not participate in collective bargaining for the public agency.

(continued)

SCHOOL BOARD POSITION: The positions of the members of the unit as principals and department heads made them uniquely qualified to assist the board in contract negotiations with other groups, and their status as "nonmanagerial" obviously presented a conflict of interest to those duties.

C. Administering Collective Bargaining Agreement

FACT: Members of the unit are part of the grievance procedure in the collective bargaining agreements of teachers and secretaries. In the two grievances filed under those agreements, the principal was not actually allowed to settle the grievances but served as a conduit to pass them on to the superintendent.

UNION POSITION: The members of the unit do not possess "substantial responsibility," because the actual authority exercised is perfunctory, clerical, routine, or automatic.

SCHOOL BOARD POSITION: Regardless of the actual authority previously exercised, the collective bargaining agreements state the potential authority of the principals to settle grievances. That potential is enough to satisfy the statute.

Questions

1. If you were the judge would you decide the employees are "managerial employees" and therefore not eligible for collective bargaining? Explain your answer.
2. Would the fact that these are public employees influence your decision?
3. Do you think the employees in this case would have sought bargaining rights if their participation in management had been as substantial as the school board argued it was?

Adapted from *School Committee of Wellesley v. Labor Relations Commission*, 1977–78 P.B.C. para. 36, 404.

KEY TERMS AND CONCEPTS

AFSCME
bilateral bargaining
Civil Service Reform Act of 1978
civil service system
Executive Order 10988
fact finding
Hatch Act
interest arbitration

mediation
multilateral bargaining
PATCO strike
Pendleton Act
privatization
sovereignty doctrine
spoils system
sunshine laws

REVIEW QUESTIONS

1. How are public employees provided the right of collective bargaining? Do state and local government employees have the same rights as federal employees?
2. Why did the government resist collective bargaining?
3. How do public employees' rights and interests differ from those of private sector employees? How do management rights differ between the public and private sectors?
4. What factors are considered in the public sector that are not considered in the private sector when drug testing is instituted?
5. Can the news media affect the bargaining process in the public sector? Should their news coverage be curtailed?
6. Give some valid reasons for and against giving public employees the right to strike.
7. Why has privatization increased in the public sector? Should most public jobs be privatized?

We invite you to visit the Carrell/Heavrin page on the Prentice Hall Web site at:

http://www.prenhall.com/carrellr

for this chapter's World Wide Web exercise.

State and Local Collective Bargaining Rights | EXERCISE 13-1

Purpose:
Most states have enacted legislation that guarantees (or prohibits) the collective bargaining rights of state employees. In addition, most states have enacted legislation that allows (or prohibits) county and municipal governments from passing ordinances providing collective bargaining rights to their employees. Millions of teachers, police officers, firefighters, sanitation workers, clerical workers, parks workers, and other employees are affected. The purpose of this exercise is for you to become familiar with the collective bargaining laws in your state, county, and city that cover public employees.

Task:
Contact the appropriate office of a governmental body and request a copy of all statutes or ordinances pertaining to the collective bargaining rights of its public employees. Then write a summary of the rights provided to public employees by that level of government. Include a discussion of how broad or limited their rights are in comparison with private employees. For example, are public employees allowed to negotiate a union shop provision? To go on strike? To negotiate all wage and benefit issues?

Right to Strike | EXERCISE 13-2

Purpose:
To enable students to distinguish between rights afforded public and private employees.

Task:
Invite all or some of the following individuals to your class to discuss the general rule that public employees should *not* be allowed to strike:

Teacher
Principal
Firefighter
Police officer
Local elected official
Sanitation worker
Local government manager
Letter carrier
Local representative of U.S. Postal Service

Unions
and Workforce
Diversity

Workforce 2000: Work and Workers for the 21st Century, a 1987 study funded by the U.S. Department of Labor, predicted that women would make up 61 percent of new workers by the year 2000 and that people of color would provide 29 percent of the new century's beginning workforce.

AFL-CIO's New President: John Sweeney, a Man with a New Vision

John Sweeney became only the sixth person to head the world's most powerful labor organization—the AFL-CIO. Sweeney, the former president of the Service Employees International Union, defeated Thomas Donahue, the interim president, after a bitter fight. Sweeney clearly represents a "new vision" for the AFL-CIO. That vision is one of growth in membership based on aggressive organizing campaigns and political hardball. His record indicates he can be successful. As president of the Service Employees he led a growth in membership to 1.1 million from 626,000 in 15 years while most of the AFL-CIO's 78 unions were losing members. Most of the gains came through recruiting members in low-paid industries, such as janitors and nursing home employees, and through mergers.

A key to Sweeney's election was his decision to add 10 women and minorities to the almost all male and white AFL-CIO Executive Council. Among those newly named to the council were Joe Greene, the African-American head of the American Federation of School Administrators; Sumi Haru, the Asian-American president of the Screen Actors Guild; and Arturo Rodriguez, the Hispanic president of the United Farm Workers of America. Other union presidents gaining executive council posts were Randy Babbitt of the Air Line Pilots Association, Patricia Friend of the Association of Flight Attendants, and Robert Wages of the Oil, Chemical and Atomic Workers union.

Adapted from Robert L. Rose and Asra Q. Nomani, "Sweeney Wins Bitter Fight for President of AFL-CIO," *Wall Street Journal*, October 26, 1995, p. A2.

The history of the labor movement in America is one of competing agendas. Focus on societal changes doomed the National Labor Union, the Knights of Labor, and the Industrial Workers of the World, while focus on trade and industrial unionization and workplace representation preserved the AFL and CIO. Although studies show that the altruistic nature of labor unions is a factor in workers' approval, the bread-and-butter issues of collective bargaining rights are of more importance.

The labor movement, then, has been caught between the proverbial "rock and a hard place" in its relations with the groups that make up the new diverse workforce. In the past, the labor movement had a number of opportunities to react to these groups: for African-Americans, during abolition and the 1960 civil rights movement; for women, during the suffrage movement and the various stages of the women's movement; and for immigrants at the turn of the twentieth century and after World War I.

UNIONS AND DIVERSITY

African-Americans and Unions

The abolitionist movement could not claim major support from American white workers. Trade unionists protested the move the federal government was making toward war over the issue of slavery in 1861 with the slogan "Concession, Not Secessions."[1] After the Civil War the labor movement struggled with the influx of cheap labor into the labor pool, eroding power to keep wages high. Freed slaves and immigrants were a part of that cheap labor pool. The National Labor Union originally encouraged freed slaves to unionize, but they were not invited to actually join the NLU.[2] The relationship between the freed slaves and the white workers in the industrial centers deteriorated. African-Americans began forming their own trade union locals, including the National Colored Labor Union (NCLU). Headed by Isaac Myers, the NCLU organized in the South in 1870 and applied for affiliation with the NLU, stating that, "The day has passed for the establishment of organizations based upon color."[3] Unfortunately, the white labor movement did not agree.

Rebuffed by the white labor unions, the NCLU joined forces with the Republican Party in the South in hopes of gaining ground in its racial emancipation movement. Labor eventually joined forces with the Democratic Party, the party seen as the "working man's party," as a reaction to big business. The split between African-American workers and white workers widened when African-Americans were used as strikebreakers. Because racial discrimination in the South limited African-Americans' job opportunities, they fell victim to the opportunities big business offered when they were recruited to go north and west to provide scab labor to break union-supported strikes.[4]

The antagonism between African-American workers and white workers continued as the labor movement matured. The effects of racial discrimination and the use of blacks as strikebreakers drove an almost insurmountable wedge between the two. In addition, at the same time the white upper classes in the South created the "Jim Crow" laws. These segregation laws kept African-Americans at the lowest rung of the economic ladder by convincing poor whites that their place one step up the ladder was dependent on keeping blacks down. Institutional racism kept white and black workers apart.

As trade unions began to gain strength in the 1920s and 1930s and came south to organize workers, the unions did not include African-American workers. AFL unions in Memphis, Tennessee, for example, excluded black carpenters, and white railroad brotherhoods organized teams of assassins to shoot black workers. The CIO's performance was not much better, although African-Americans were allowed to participate in the unions of the lowest level of unskilled laborers such as hod carriers and construction laborers.

Despite the lack of acceptance, African-American industrial workers, such as those in Memphis, Tennessee, in the 1930s, supported the union movement. They saw the union movement as a chance to change the power relationship between them and their employers. One example of how they were treated can be seen in an "A, B, C" wage system instituted in one Firestone factory in 1937: "Adult white males (A) received 32 cents an hour while boys (B) between 18 and 21 and the 'colored' (C) made 28 cents an hour."[5] But because the "Jim Crow" system continued to give white workers an advantage, unions excluded African-Americans. This exclusion gave AFL-organized unions dominance over CIO-organized unions in union elections through the 1930s. However, white industrial workers began to abandon the AFL for the CIO when it began to dominate the labor movement under John L. Lewis. Because black workers made up a significant part of the unskilled labor force, some African-American participation resulted. However, even black labor leaders suffered from discrimination when a hotel, in 1948, which was to house a labor negotiation session, refused admission to a black member of the union's negotiating team.[6]

The pre–civil rights days for African-American workers were a series of advances and defeats. When the growth of the CIO began to slow down and the AFL-CIO united to preserve the labor movement, the AFL's exclusionary policies seemed to dominate so that identification of unions with the civil rights movement declined.

The labor movement was again confronted with the needs of African-American workers during the 1960 civil rights movement. The civil rights movement was to give African-Americans shut out from the job market by segregation and discrimination an opportunity to work. Their need to integrate workplaces was coupled with their need to integrate unions.

Although labor leaders were seen as supportive of the civil rights movement, such support did not go deep into union membership. Trade unions that sponsored apprenticeship programs excluding African-Americans were not alone in their discrimination. Industrial unions did not help the African-American worker. Reacting to the nonresponsiveness, civil rights leaders and organizations simply regrouped and organized African-American workers into unions as part of their civil rights activities. The **Maryland Freedom Union** (MFU) and the Mississippi Freedom Labor Union organized and engineered strikes and demonstrations to improve the lot of African-American workers who had been shunted to low-paying jobs. A boycott of a small retail chain in a white neighborhood of Baltimore, Maryland, in 1966 led to the MFU's first success. When AFL-CIO officials learned that the MFU had been recognized as the exclusive bargaining agent for the employees of the retail chain, they objected. Walter Reuther, then head of the AFL-CIO's Industrial Union Department, pressured the leadership of the Congress of Racial Equality (CORE), a major civil rights organization, to sever its support of the MFU.[7] The MFU, like the activist civil rights organizations, peaked in the late 1960s and disappeared in the 1970s.

Although the AFL had supported African-American membership in affiliate unions, it was not until 1964 that the last affiliate of the AFL-CIO removed the "whites only" clause from its bylaws and constitution. Case 14-1 gives a brief look at how the vestiges of discrimination still exist today. African-Americans today are more unionized (15 percent of organized labor) than the workforce as a

CASE 14-1

AFRICAN-AMERICANS

The duPont plant opened in 1941 under the World War II regulations of the U.S. government. In 1949 those regulations were suspended. The 1950 collective bargaining agreement with the Affiliated Chemical Workers (ACW) union segregated African-American and white workers in the plant into two seniority units, and transfers between the units were prohibited. By 1956 the workers were represented by the Neoprene Craftsmen Union (NCU), and the Collective Bargaining Agreement permitted job bidding between the two seniority units. In 1958 the Collective Bargaining Agreement created four classifications of employees for seniority purposes: operations and engineering (high-paying jobs), classified and maintenance (low-paying jobs).

Although the Collective Bargaining Agreement allowed for crossovers, as of 1974, when a race discrimination suit was filed, only 3 percent of the jobs in operations and none of the jobs in engineering were filled by African-Americans.

The company and the union denied any discrimination and pointed out that the Col-

lective Bargaining Agreement *did not* discriminate in the way the seniority system operated. The reason given why so few African-Americans were promoted was that the African-American employees did not want to transfer to the other classifications.

Decision

The Court dismissed the company and union defenses as ridiculous. One would have to believe in the stereotype of a "happy" African-American worker satisfied in a low-paying job to buy the defense.

The Court found that the seniority system had its origin in discrimination and that the discrimination continued despite changes in the Collective Bargaining Agreement. Only the continuation of discrimination could account for a situation in which *98 percent* of high-paying jobs were occupied by whites 30 years after an alleged *change* in the seniority system.

The Court held the company and the union liable.

Adapted from *EEOC v. E. I. duPont de Nemours & Co. et al.,* 60 EPD Section 41,898 (1992).

whole (11 percent of the population). Union membership has been rewarding for African-American workers, who average about 50 percent more income than African-American nonunion workers. In the future, African-Americans are likely to increase their role in union leadership and membership. The labor movement has been an important vehicle in the growth of the African-American middle class and partially explains the proclivity of black Americans to join unions. At the same time, there is a shift away from heavy industry and manufacturing in the American economy, and union workers are losing their jobs and are being left unprepared for the new high-skilled labor market.[8] Whereas blacks in general have shown a greater preference for union membership than whites,[9] women and Hispanics do not exhibit the same preference for union membership, nor has their employment been greater in the union sector.[10]

Women and Unions

To begin to improve women's participation in unions, women within the U.S. labor movement organized the founding conference of the **Coalition of Labor Union Women (CLUW)** in 1974. Recognizing that less than 12 percent of the women in the labor force are unionized, and that most working women are suffering economically, the CLUW was formed to promote unionism. Following is the statement of purpose adopted at the CLUW founding conference:

> It is imperative that within the framework of the union movement the Coalition of Labor Union Women take aggressive steps to more effectively address the critical needs of millions of unorganized sisters and make our unions more responsive to the needs of all women, especially the needs of minority women who have traditionally been singled out for particularly blatant oppression.
>
> Union women work in almost every industry, in almost every part of the country. Despite their geographical, industrial and occupational separations, union women share common concerns and goals.
>
> Full equality of opportunities and rights in the labor force require the full attention of the labor movement . . . and especially, the full attention of women who are part of the labor movement.
>
> The primary purpose of this National Coalition is to unify all union women in a viable organization to determine our common problems and concerns and to develop action programs within the framework of our unions to deal effectively with our objectives. This struggle goes beyond the borders of this Nation and we urge our working sisters throughout the world to join us in accomplishing these objectives through their labor organizations.[11]

Women will provide almost two-thirds of the new entrants into the job market by the year 2000. The two major areas of potential growth for unionization is in the health industry and among clerical workers. Both of these industries are made up mostly of women workers.

The reluctance of unions to include women fully and women's reluctance to unionize may have the same basis. During the post–Civil War period, women who had entered the workforce during the war continued to work. The National Labor Union found itself in the center of controversy for recognizing representatives of women's unions into its congress. Because unions did not welcome women into their organizations, protective unions and trade associations for women were formed. Sometimes women and men working right next to each other had separate unions. Most men workers viewed women as competition, so they decried their employment. The NLU allowed representatives of a number of the women's protective unions to join their 1868 congress, including Susan B. Anthony, the most famous suffragette. When Anthony admitted that her protective union was used as a strikebreaking organization because the women's movement needed to do so, the NLU dispelled her. After that, protective unions for women lost support from their fellow male workers and by 1872 most had died out.[12]

In the years between 1903 and World War I, new women's labor unions emerged, mostly founded by middle-class reformers and working-class women. The reformers had gathered and organized around settlement houses in major urban areas. These settlement house reformers and active working women met with male union leaders in 1903 to form the Women's National Trade Union League, later changed to the National Women's Trade Union League.[13] The league's first convention in 1907 adopted the following six-point platform:

1. Equal pay for equal work
2. Full citizenship for women
3. An eight-hour workday
4. A minimum wage

5. Organization of all workers into unions
6. The economic programs of the AFL

During the early 1900s, the league supported unionization of women workers in many industries, but it had its major successes in the garment industry. Unfortunately, the AFL, led by Samuel Gompers, gave no more than lip service to support of the league's activities.

During World War I, women entered industries in huge numbers to support the men at war. The working men left in those factories resented the influx of women because it caused them to have to compete and because they believed it lowered wage rates.

The Great Depression, which started in 1929, caused unemployment to rise from 3 million in 1930 to nearly 15 million in 1933 and wages to drop 45 percent. Among the casualties of the depression were working women, especially married working women. In response to such high unemployment, they were targeted for discharge because they were taking jobs away from men. Laws were passed or policies instituted to lay off women in favor of men, the false assumption being that married women did not *have* to work, whereas married and single men did.

The depression greatly damaged the Women's Trade Union League, which had no convention from 1929 to 1936. Following the passage of the Wagner Act and the strong growth of the CIO, women's auxiliaries to CIO unions became a major factor in the success of CIO's organization. The famous and effective sit-down strikes of that period in the auto, steel, and mine industries were possible because of the support that wives, mothers, and sisters gave to the strikers. These women were rewarded by a promise from the CIO that women should be taught about unionism as "an effective means of mobilizing support for unionism among the families of union members."[14] Although the CIO *never overtly* denied admission of women into unions as had the AFL, neither had it ever encouraged women to organize.

During World War II, women continued to invade the man's working place—first of necessity and then by choice. When the war ended, men expected women to go back home and give the jobs to men, just as had occurred previously. Many women tried not to do that, but the pattern of layoff was such that twice as many women as men lost their jobs during the spring and summer of 1945. The CIO's Reemployment Plan, adopted at its 1944 convention, failed to mention women workers. Despite layoffs, women did not leave the job market, although to a large extent they did leave the factories. The real expansion in women's employment took place in clerical and service operations such as education and the health fields. As those workers were not targets of union organizing, the history of the women's movement for equality and their interest in labor unions began to branch off into different directions.

As the women's movement focused on improving the position of women in the United States, including women in the workforce, the goal was legislation to ensure equal treatment, equal pay, and equal rights. The success of that movement can be seen in the passage of Title VII to the Civil Rights Act of 1964, which prohibited job discrimination on the basis of gender (among other things).

With that law theoretically protecting women in the workforce from employers, women had the ability to turn to unionization again to increase their power in the workforce. The Coalition of Labor Union Women, formed in 1974, was the manifestation of this renewed interest among women to unionize.

Immigrants and Unions

Except for American Indians and their descendants, all of the people of the United States are immigrants or descendants of immigrants. Despite this fact, the history of the American labor movement chronicles both the inclusion and exclusion of immigrants from the ranks of organized labor.

Skilled laborers of whatever background were included in trade unions in the earliest days of organization. But as the industrial revolution converted many trade industries to industrial factories, competition with immigrant labor was keenly felt. When trade unionism first experienced the challenge of industrial unionism, the organizing of immigrants, who had largely migrated from England, Iceland, and northern Europe, swelled the ranks of those unions. It was not until after World War I that industrial labor unions took a negative stand on immigration, especially regarding people from Italy and southern Europe. The Immigration Acts of 1921 and 1924 that restricted immigration were supported by unionists because they reduced the nation's labor supply. Union members believed that they would reap the benefit of these policies with higher wages and job security.

The rise of industrial unionism after World War II signaled a more open time for immigrants and unions, as it had for women and African-Americans. Many CIO unions established ethnic locals and targeted various Catholic immigrants to disregard their ethnic differences in joining industrial unions.[15]

In the 1980s and 1990s, the United States has solved its problem of a shrinking workforce base just as it did in the last century: by an influx of immigrants, which represent 39 percent of the total U.S. population growth.[16]

Today's immigrants come primarily from Asia and Latin America. By the year 2000 it is projected that Hispanics will account for 10 percent of the American workforce and Asian-Americans will account for most of the 4 percent attributed to people of color. Together these people of color will outnumber by 2 percent African-Americans in the workforce. Add them to the number of African-Americans, and over one-quarter of the American workforce will be people of color by the year 2000.

A fourth of the new immigrants coming into the United States are college graduates; a third are high school dropouts. The immigrant workforce in that respect is like the American workforce—split between the highly skilled and well educated and those with minimal skills and little education. U.S. business is taking advantage of both groups.

For the skilled immigrant, the United States is seen as a place of opportunity. As immigrants gravitate to America's urban centers, some cities have seen a rebirth in older sections and suburbs, where immigrants start businesses, buy homes, and pay taxes. In Dallas, Texas, Hispanics turned around Jefferson Boulevard, which had been a dying inner-city business district.

At the other end of the immigrant scale, however, unskilled workers face problems similar to, but perhaps more severe than, the unskilled American worker. These workers fill the low-paid jobs that make our modern service economy operate—hotel and restaurant and domestic and child-care work. Any downturn in the economy puts these laborers out of work. Most of these jobs have no health benefits, no retirement program, and no educational opportunities. Many immigrants do not qualify for or will not take welfare benefits.

Unskilled immigrants compete with unskilled Americans for low-paying jobs. Such competition threatens some African-Americans and causes racial tension in urban America. The reports of the destruction to Asian businesses in Los Angeles

Figure 14-1 — Harris Poll on Immigration

Do you think more or fewer immigrants are coming into the U.S.? (All surveyed)

More	64%
Fewer	11%
Same	21%
Not sure	4%

Has immigration been good or bad for the U.S.? (All surveyed)

Good	59%
Bad	35%
Neither	3%
Not sure	3%

Is it good or bad now?

	African-Americans	Non-Blacks
Good	40%	26%
Bad	53%	69%

Should the U.S. admit more, fewer, or the same number of immigrants in the 1990s as in 1980s?

	African-Americans	Non-Blacks
More	12%	3%
Fewer	47%	62%
Same	34%	31%

Does business prefer to hire immigrants or African-Americans?

	African-Americans	Non-Blacks
Immigrants	73%	49%
African-Americans	15%	30%

Is the "American dream" still realistic for new immigrants? (All surveyed)

Yes	56%
No	39%
Not sure	5%

Source: Adapted from Christopher Power, "America's Welcome Mat Is Wearing Thin," *Business Week*, July 13, 1993, p. 119.

in May 1992 after the Rodney King court decision alerted many people to the resentment brewing among the disfranchised of that city.

A survey by Louis Harris and Associates found that 73 percent of African-Americans surveyed thought that business was more likely to hire immigrants than African-Americans. Nevertheless, African-Americans were more positive than whites about the impact of immigration on the United States. Some of the results of the Harris Poll are summarized in Figure 14-1. The challenge facing the United States and labor unions is to allow these first and second generations of immigrants full participation in the workforce.

Unions' Response to Diversity

The overall downward trend in union membership is a major concern to labor leaders. The percentage of union membership has continued to decline gradually from its peak in the 1950s. Even though there have been significant membership increases in the public and professional sectors, the overall figures are still greatly disappointing to labor leaders. Public sentiment, once strongly behind unions and the collective bargaining process, has waned in recent years. For example, AT&T and PATCO strikers found that the public support so necessary to the success of their walkouts never materialized. The lack of strength in numbers and general public support will have a long-term impact on the collective bargaining process. Public sympathy for strikes, boycotts, and other union activities is often in the minds of labor and management as they consider the tools available in their arsenals.

In a long-term effort to attract a new generation of union supporters, the AFL-CIO at its 1985 convention broke historic ground. Led by its president, Lane Kirkland, the union federation voted to offer associate membership to former union members and nonunion members. The large volume of people the union hopes to include (starting with their 13.5 million members) will enable the AFL-CIO to offer low-cost group life, auto, and health insurance, dental insurance, prescription drugs, legal services, retirement accounts, and even low-interest credit cards. Union strategists hope the associate members will develop strong ties to the union movement and that someday they will strongly demand union representation through collective bargaining. The success of this new approach can be seen in Table 14-1, which outlines some of the **worker associations** being formed.

A Sampling of Worker Associations

Table 14-1

Association	No. of Years in Existence	No. of Members	Union Affiliation	Services
Montana Family Union	3	1,400	AFL-CIO	Union credit cards, group-rate health insurance, legal consultation
9 to 5: The Association for Working Women (Cleveland)	20	15,000	Service Employees Int'l Union	Toll-free hotline, courses on sexual harassment and VDT injuries, lobbying on workplace issues
Nat'l Association for Working Americans (Cincinnati)	2	1,700	AFL-CIO	Hotline rallies and petitions to legislation, dislocated-worker support group
California Immigrant Workers Association	3	6,000	AFL-CIO	Help processing immigration papers, legal representation and enforcement of minimum wage and overtime rules
AIM (Associate ILGWU Members), New York	5	2,500	Int'l Ladies Garment Workers Union	English classes, graduate-equivalency diploma courses, computer courses, skills training; legal help with immigration, minimum wage, OSHA, sexual harassment, disability, and pensions

Source: Dana Milbank, "Labor Broadens Its Appeal by Setting Up Associations to Lobby and Offer Services," *Wall Street Journal*, January 13, 1993, pp. B1, 6. Reprinted by permission of *Wall Street Journal*, Dow Jones & Company, Inc. All rights reserved worldwide.

THE DIVERSITY ISSUE

"Workforce 2000"

In 1987, the Hudson Institute, funded by the U.S. Department of Labor, released the study *Workforce 2000: Work and Workers for the 21st Century*. The predictions of that study grabbed the attention of corporate America. Although probably not the first indication of a changing American workforce, the study certainly brought the future of America's workforce changes into clear and dramatic focus.

The study predicted that the homogeneous workforce, long composed of and led by white males born in the United States, would soon begin to change. Only 15 percent of the new entrants into the labor force by the year 2000 would be white males. Women (both white and women of color) would make up 61 percent of new workers, and people of color (including women of color) would provide 29 percent of the new century's beginning workforce. Coupled with the changing faces of the workforce will be a reduction of the number of new entrants into the workforce. In the 1970s, the labor force grew by 2.9 percent a year. A growth of only 1 percent a year has been recorded in the 1990s.[17] A new wave of immigrants into the U.S. workforce will be the solution to the shrinking labor pool just as it was at the turn of the twentieth century.

Following the *Workforce 2000* study, the U.S. Bureau of Labor Statistics projected in detail the U.S. labor force and occupational employment that will most likely exist in the year 2000. The projected labor force will contain a larger percentage of minority and female workers and a smaller percentage of white male workers than the current workforce contains. From 1985 to 2000, the white labor force is expected to grow by 15 percent, the African-American labor force by 29 percent (3.7 million), and the Hispanic labor force by 74 percent (6 million). Other groups combined (American Indians, Alaskan Inuit, Asians, and Pacific Islanders) will grow by 70 percent (2.4 million). All minorities combined will likely represent 57 percent of the labor force growth during the 15-year period. When white females are added to the total of all minorities, the combined share of labor force growth is estimated to be 90 percent! Thus, only one of 10 new workers in the year 2000 will be a white male.[18] Table 14-2 shows the projected labor force statistics for the year 2000.

The labor force for the year 2000 is growing slowly (the baby-boom generation is already part of the labor force), is becoming older each year (median age of 38.9), and is becoming increasingly female and minority. Changes in the unemployment rate for specific segments of the labor force (the 16 to 19 age group, the 20 to 24 age group, and blacks and Hispanics) are also projected. The decline of job seekers ages 16 to 24, combined with the expected continued growth in service industries, which traditionally hire younger workers, should significantly lower the unemployment rate for them. African-Americans and Hispanics, however, may experience increasing unemployment problems because they will represent a larger share of the labor force, unless past problems such as the location of jobs and educational training requirements can be resolved. College-educated job seekers should find a lower unemployment rate in 2000. Occupations requiring the most education are expected to have the most rapid growth rates, while the demand for new college graduates will strengthen because of the shrinkage of the college-age population.[19]

Between 1986 and 2000, about 21 million new jobs will have been created in the United States, bringing total employment to 133 million. Some industries, such as electronic computing equipment, transportation, recreation, child care, communications, and the medical field, will expand while others, such as manu-

Composition of the Civilian Labor Force Age 16 and Over, by Year (in millions)   Table 14-2

	1979		1986		2000	
	Labor Force	Percentage	Labor Force	Percentage	Labor Force	Percentage
Total	104.9	100	117.8	100	138.8	100
Gender						
Men	60.7	57.9	65.4	55.5	73.1	52.7
Women	40.2	42.1	52.4	44.5	65.6	47.3
Race						
White	91.9	87.6	101.8	86.4	116.7	74.1
Black	10.7	10.2	12.7	10.8	16.3	11.8
Hispanic	5.2	5.0	8.1	6.9	14.1	10.2
Asian and others	2.3	2.3	3.4	2.8	5.7	4.1
Age						
16–24	25.4	24.2	23.3	19.8	22.6	16.3
25–54	64.5	61.4	69.5	67.5	100.9	72.6
55 and over	15.0	14.3	14.9	12.6	15.4	11.1

Note: Some groups do not match totals because of double counting, rounding.
Source: Adapted from Howard N. Fullerton, "Labor Force Projections: 1986 to 2000," *Monthly Labor Review* 110, no. 9 (September 1987), p. 20.

facturing, mining, and petroleum, will diminish. Virtually all of the net increase of 21 million jobs is in the service sector. Most of the goods-producing industries will shrink, with the exception of home construction and defense-related contracts such as aircraft, missiles, and communication equipment.[20] Table 14-3 shows the projected employment by section for the year 2000.

These statistics and projections should be of critical importance to today's labor leaders. The labor movement must appeal to the increasingly diverse workforce. It is important to understand the historical relationship unions have had with these diverse groups as well as the unique challenges these groups bring to the workplace.

Employment by Section by the Year 2000 (in thousands)   Table 14-3

Sector	By 2000	Growth per Year 1986–2000
Goods producing	24,678	3
Mining	724	59
Construction	5,794	890
Manufacturing	18,160	834
Service producing	94,478	20,115
Transportation and public utilities	5,719	475
Retail and wholesale trade	29,968	6,338
Finance, insurance, and real estate	7,917	1,620
Services	32,545	10,014
Government	18,329	1,618
Agriculture	2,917	335

Source: Adapted from Valerie A. Persavich, "Industry Output and Employment through the End of the Century," *Monthly Labor Review* 110, no. 9 (September 1987), p. 32.

MAJOR FEDERAL LAWS AFFECTING DIVERSE WORKERS

The major federal laws that regulate fair and equal rights in employment forbid union and employer discrimination against certain categories of individuals. They apply not only to the hiring process but also to pay, promotion, and other employment opportunities. These laws are set in chronological order in Table 14-4.

As the profile of America's workforce changes and labor becomes scarce, neither unions nor employers can afford to ignore the need for these "protected" individuals. Not discriminating against these employees—women, African-Americans, older workers, people with disabilities, and immigrants—will be not only a matter of legal compliance but a necessity.

Since the civil rights movement of the 1960s and the creation of legally enforceable work rules protecting individuals from society's prejudices, U.S. society is changing. The changes are not a complete reformation of attitudes, but advances have been made. With laws against discrimination underpinning the increased need for a diverse workforce, the workplace will change. Understanding the laws will give unions and employers a better chance to proceed through the coming changes with little or no disruption in the workplace.

CIVIL RIGHTS LEGISLATION

The Civil Rights Act of 1964

The primary federal law in the field of fair employment practice is the **Civil Rights Act of 1964**, passed only months after the assassination of President John F. Kennedy, its major supporter and author. The act requires employment and compensation of employees without discrimination based on race, color, religion, sex, or national origin.[21]

Both employer and union are responsible for fair treatment under Title VII of the Civil Rights Act. The employer may not blame failure to comply with the act on barriers in the union contract or threat of a suit if such action is taken. Courts have held that compliance with such contract provisions is not a justifiable necessity.[22]

Title VII requires the removal of artificial, arbitrary, and unnecessary barriers to employment when the barriers discriminate on the basis of racial or other nonpermissible classifications.[23] Such barriers identified by the Supreme Court and other federal courts include practices and policies of recruitment, selection, placement, testing, transfer, promotion, and seniority as well as other basic terms and conditions of employment.

Equal Employment Opportunity Commission. The 1964 act established the federal Equal Employment Opportunity Commission (EEOC). The EEOC was given the authority to investigate employee complaints of discrimination arising under the provisions of the act. The EEOC can bring suit in federal court against employers and unions if it finds such action justified. A court procedure in a discrimination case requires that the aggrieved employee must generally prove that he or she is a minority or female, was qualified for the position and available, and was not hired for the position.[24] The employee must also prove that the employer continued to seek others for the job or hired a nonprotected individual. This proof establishes a prima facie case of discrimination.

As a defense, the employer may choose to claim that the employee did not have the required bona fide occupational qualifications (BFOQ). Or the employer may prove it was a business necessity not to hire the complainant. This defense requires proof that the individual could not have performed the job successfully be-

Table 14-4

1938	*Fair Labor Standards Act (FLSA).* Established minimum wage, 40-hour week, end of child labor.
1963	*Equal Pay Act.* Amended FLSA to provide equal pay for women.
1964	*Civil Rights Act.* Prohibited discrimination based on race, sex, religion, or national origin. Established EEOC.
1965	*Executive Order 11246.* Required federal contractors to have affirmative action plans. Created Office of Federal Contract Compliance.
1967	*Age Discrimination in Employment Act (ADEA).* Prohibited discrimination against older workers.
1972	*Equal Employment Opportunities Act.* Increased EEOC authority to enforce Civil Rights Act. Included more employers for coverage.
1973	*Rehabilitation Act.* Required federal contractors to have affirmative action plans for handicapped.
1974	*Vietnam Era Veterans Readjustment Act.* Required federal contractors to have affirmative action plans for Vietnam veterans.
	Amended FLSA. Included public employees in coverage of FLSA and Equal Pay Act.
1978	*Pregnancy Discrimination Act.* Prohibited treating pregnancy different from other medical conditions.
	Age Discrimination in Employment Act (ADEA). Amended to prohibit forced retirement for anyone under age 70.
1986	*Age Discrimination in Employment Act (ADEA).* Amended to prohibit forced retirement for anyone.
	Immigration Reform and Control Act. Gave amnesty to undocumented workers and imposed penalties for employer hiring them in the future.
1988	*Civil Rights Restoration Act.* Expanded scope of coverage of act to more private institutions.
	Employee Polygraph Protection Act. Limited use by employers of polygraph tests.
1989	*Whistleblower Protection Act.* Protected federal employees from retaliation when "blowing the whistle" in certain circumstances.
1990	*Immigration Act.* Raised numbers of allowable immigrants.
	Older Workers Benefit Protection Act (WBPA). Prohibit offering older workers different benefits than younger workers.
	Americans with Disabilities Act. Extended coverage of Civil Rights Act to disabled.
1991	*Civil Rights Act.* Amended 1964 act to correct unfavorable Supreme Court decisions.
	Glass Ceiling Act. Recognized need to allow women and minorities to reach top management positions.
1993	*Family and Medical Leave Act.* Gave workers job protection when faced with illness or family crisis.

cause of an inability to work the required hours or to relate to specific clientele. Or the person hired is, in fact, better qualified for the job than the complainant. The last is the most common defense of employers with professional personnel systems.

In 1972, Congress amended the 1964 Civil Rights Act to require labor unions and employers to provide survey information to the EEOC (see Figure 14-2). This information is used to compile workforce analysis and labor market information.

Prior to the Supreme Court decision in *Griggs v. Duke Power Co.*, discrimination in employment was usually in the context of an individual worker rather than a

Figure 14-2   Equal Employment Opportunity Local Union Report (EEO-3)

Union Reporting Program
Washington, DC 20507

EQUAL EMPLOYMENT OPPORTUNITY
LOCAL UNION REPORT (EEO-3)

Approved by OMB
No. 3046-0006
Expires 12/31/93

Part A.   LOCAL UNION IDENTIFICATION

1. Full name of local union for which this report is filed. (include local number, if any.)

2. Mailing address.

   a. Where official mail should be sent to the union.

   _____
   Number and street

   _____
   City

   _____
   County

   _____
   State

   _____
   Zip Code

b. Union office, if different from 2a.

_____
Number and street

_____
City

_____
County

_____
State   Zip Code

3. Indicate type of local union report by a check in applicable box:

   a. ☐ Report filed by local union in its own behalf
   b. ☐ Other (explain)

4a. Are you affiliated with or chartered by a national or international union or national federation? Yes ☐   No ☐

   b. If "Yes" to item 4a, give name and address of such national or international organization.

5. Are you affiliated with the AFL-CIO?   Yes ☐   No ☐

Part B. LOCAL UNION PRACTICES

1. To the best of your knowledge, does your membership include any:

a. Blacks (Non-Hispanic)?................................ Yes ☐   No ☐

b. Hispanics?.. Yes ☐   No ☐

c. Women?.. Yes ☐   No ☐

3. To the best of your knowledge, has your international union chartered a separate local within the same work and/or area jurisdiction which consists only of:

a. Persons of the same race/ethnic identity... Yes ☐   No ☐

b. Persons of the same sex?.............................. Yes ☐   No ☐

2. If "No" to any items 1a, 1b, or 1c, is this because the group or groups not represented:	(Check All Applicable Boxes)		
	Black, Non-Hispanic 1 (a)	Hispanic 1 (b)	Women 1 (c)
a. Are not in the local community?			
b. Are not in the bargaining unit?			
c. Are excluded by provision in constitution or bylaws?.............			
d. Have not applied for membership?......			
e. Have applied, but did not have a sponsor?...................................			
f. Have applied, but did not meet qualifications other than sponsorship?...............................			

g. Other reason(s) (Explain) _____

Part C. LOCAL UNIONS REQUIRED TO FILE

1. Has the local union had 100 or more members at any time since December 31 of the preceding year?   Yes ☐   No ☐

2. Does the local union, or any unit, division, or agent of the local union, or any labor organization which performs, within a specific jurisdiction, the functions ordinarily performed by a local union, whether or not it is so designated:

   a. Operate a hiring hall or hiring office?   Yes ☐   No ☐

   b. Have an arrangement under which one or more employers are required to consider or hire persons referred by the local union or an agent of the local union?   Yes ☐   No ☐

   c. Have 10 percent or more of its members employed by employers which customarily and regularly look to the union, or any agent of the union, for employees to be hired on a casual or temporary basis, for a specified period of time, or for the duration of a specified job?   Yes ☐   No ☐

The union must complete the entire report if it answered "YES" to Item 1, *AND* the answer is "YES" to any of the three questions in Item 2.

The union is not required to complete the entire report if it answered "NO" to Item 1, *OR* "NO" to all three questions in Item 2. If that is the case, the union must complete Parts A, B, C and E and return this form to the specified address.

EEOC Form 274, JUN 88   Previous Editions Are Obsolete

group of employees.[25] Under Title VII of the Civil Rights Act of 1964, an individual who could show intentional discrimination was entitled to protection under a **disparate treatment** theory. The *Griggs* decision shifted the focus of employment discrimination from individuals to groups subjected to adverse impact by employers. This adverse impact theory opened up a new area of industrial relations to include the equal employment, compensation, and mobility of minorities and females.[26] To gain the protection of Title VII, employees or job seekers needed to show that an otherwise neutral employment practice resulted in a racially or sexually imbalanced workforce. The employer then had to justify the practice as a **business necessity**.

Court-Ordered Remedies. When the courts have found discrimination under Title VII, a variety of remedies may be applied, including the reinstatement or hiring of employees, the awarding of back pay and seniority rights, and the payment of the cost of litigation. The courts have ruled that remedies must not only open the doors to equal employment for all persons but also must "make whole" and restore the rightful economic status of those affected.

The make whole concept refers to a concept of providing back pay, position, and lost seniority as a remedy to people who have suffered discrimination. The phrase refers to the practice of providing remedies that place the person in the position he or she would have been in had he or she not been discriminated against originally.

The awarding of remedies can lead to conflict among employees within a collective bargaining unit. If a group of employees is awarded back pay or additional seniority, or both, from a court case, resentment from other employees can lead to internal conflict within the union as well as with the employer.

Affirmative Action Programs. Affirmative action programs require employers or unions to increase the employment and promotion of certain people or groups of individuals. These programs go a step beyond equal employment opportunity laws that require mere obedience and not discrimination against minorities and women. Affirmative action programs require that employers and unions take specific steps to be nondiscriminatory in their employment opportunities and to improve their record of minority employment.

An affirmative action plan may be implemented under a labor agreement by three basic steps:

1. The plan should focus on the recruitment and selection of minority employees rather than attempt to change employees' attitudes toward minorities and females.
2. The agreement should encourage participation in the design and implementation of the program from all levels within the union and the organization.
3. The agreement should relate the organization's overall affirmative action goals to each department's specific goals and timetables.

The conflict between a desire to promote affirmative action and a call for "race-neutral" decision making continues. In 1995, the Supreme Court invalidated an affirmative action program authorized by Congress in which federal agency contracts gave additional compensation to contractors who hired minority subcontractors. The court said a "compelling state interest" must be demonstrated and the program was narrowly designed only to address that interest. In this instance, the Court said the federal government had failed to demonstrate such a compelling interest to justify the program.[27]

Seniority and Title VII.   In the late 1970s, a number of Supreme Court cases attempted to resolve the critical conflict between Title VII and the collective bargaining process in the area of employee seniority. In collective bargaining, a seniority system usually provides an individual with certain rights related to his or her date of employment. In general, seniority is used to determine employment decisions on the basis of the first hired receiving first preference; for example, when two qualified employees bid for a job opening, the one with the greater seniority receives the promotion. Another common example occurs when the last employee hired is the first to be laid off.

The Civil Rights Act of 1964 provides that differences in employment conditions resulting from a bona fide seniority system are permitted as long as the system was not developed with discriminatory intentions. Congress also provided that employees with longer service can be given greater rewards by the employer solely on the basis of seniority, and, even if an employer had discriminated, those employees should not be held responsible.

With the passage of the Civil Rights Act, a common scenario occurs. An employer for many years has not hired minorities or females and then—due to an active equal employment opportunity program or court order—begins to include a larger percentage of these groups in the workforce. Because of past hiring practices, white males have far greater seniority than minorities or females. In terms of promotion or necessary layoffs, white males as a group fare better due to their greater seniority. This can represent a no-win situation for all parties concerned and can result in litigation.

In a landmark decision, the Supreme Court ruled that the routine operation of a seniority system is not an unlawful employment practice under Title VII, even if the seniority system has some discriminatory consequences. Only if the seniority system was designed with an intention to discriminate—a rare occurrence—could it be considered a violation of the act.[28]

Reverse Discrimination.   In a 1979 case, *United Steelworkers v. Weber*, the Supreme Court ruled on what is considered a landmark decision on **reverse discrimination**.[29] In the suit, Weber alleged that the Kaiser Aluminum Voluntary Affirmative Action Program, in reserving 50 percent of the craft training openings for blacks, had discriminated against white employees with more seniority by giving preference to blacks with less time on the job. The Court noted that, although the argument made by Weber had some merit, it did not consider the spirit of the 1964 Civil Rights Act. The act was primarily concerned with the plight of blacks in the U.S. economy. Congress intended to open employment opportunities for them in previously closed occupations; the Court contended that Congress did not want to prohibit the private sector from accomplishing the goal of the act. The *Weber* decision permitted employers to establish affirmative action plans voluntarily that can include quotas or require that a certain number or percentage of positions can be reserved for minorities or women.

Another Supreme Court decision, *Bakke v. University of California*, came shortly before the *Weber* case.[30] In the *Bakke* case, a white male claimed reverse discrimination when denied admission to the University of California Medical School, even though he had scored higher on entrance exams than some minority students. The school had reserved a certain number of positions for minority candidates. The Supreme Court, in a 5–4 decision, ruled that Bakke should be admitted even though race could be considered in a school's admission plan.[31]

Civil Rights Act of 1991

The Civil Rights Act of 1991 was largely the result of Congress's desire to undo Supreme Court decisions of the 1980s that eroded the effectiveness of previous civil rights laws.[32] The Supreme Court had made the following rulings in a series of cases:

1. Racial harassment in the workplace was not the same as racial discrimination.[33]
2. An employment decision motivated by a discriminatory reason was all right if the employer would have made the same decision without a discriminative motive.[34]
3. Coverage by the act to overseas employees of American companies operating abroad was denied.[35]
4. An injured party can object to a discriminatory seniority system only within a year of its effective date.[36]
5. White employees could object to a consent decree a long time after its implementation.[37]
6. An employer could continue a discriminatory employment practice as long as there was some legitimate reason for the practice, regardless of the effect on protected employees.[38]

The goal of the Civil Rights Act amendments of 1991 was to undo the previous rulings on these cases and restore some of the rights of the protected employees. But the effectiveness of the act in this and other areas was immediately brought into question by a 1993 Supreme Court decision on the burden of proof necessary in an individual case of discrimination. Before the *St. Mary's Honor Center et al. v. Melvin Hicks*[39] decision, some lower federal courts had ruled that when the employer's "legitimate reason" for the action taken was not true, the employer had automatically discriminated. In *St. Mary* the Supreme Court ruled that even if an employer's legitimate reason for the action was found to be untrue, the complaining party has the burden of proving discrimination by some active, demonstrable fact.

Nondiscrimination Clauses

Many collective bargaining agreements today include a nondiscrimination clause to avoid both civil rights violations and pay inequities. The following nondiscrimination clause appears in the agreement between the Kentucky State District Council of Carpenters, Local 2501 and Anderson Wood Products Co., Inc. (1996–1999):

ARTICLE VI
No Discrimination

The Company and the Union agree that no employee shall be discriminated against because of race, color, religion, national origin, physical handicap, age or sex.

The EEOC suggests that such clauses be extended to four key areas of the union-employer relationship:

1. Open membership to all employees regardless of race, national origin, or sex
2. Job referrals by a union to management without discrimination
3. Design or redesign of department or plantwide seniority systems so past discriminatory effects are eliminated

4. Grievance arbitration procedures in the collective bargaining agreement that provide for discrimination grievances along with other types of union member grievances

WOMEN AND EQUAL EMPLOYMENT OPPORTUNITY

Title VII of the Civil Rights Act prohibits discrimination whether it is because of race, color, religion, sex, or national origin. Women, however, have found that some areas of discrimination are predominantly geared toward them. In areas of sexual harassment, pay equity, and issues surrounding pregnancy, women in the workforce struggle against an undercurrent of discrimination often obscured by a concern for their welfare or by the "old boy network."

Sexual Harassment

On the basis of the Civil Rights Act, the EEOC developed guidelines that declared **sexual harassment** a form of illegal sex discrimination. Sexual harassment constitutes a form of behavior directed toward an employee specifically because of his or her sex.

The EEOC has issued guidelines that describe types of harassment known as *quid pro quo*: sex in exchange for favors such as a job or promotion or to avoid adverse actions such as being fired, and a "hostile work environment," which may include verbal abuse, sexist remarks, patting, pinching, leering, or ogling.[40] Figure 14-3 is an example of a sexual harassment policy in a labor agreement that includes all these acts and the process of investigation. Notice the list of people covered by the policy.

Regardless of which type of harassment is involved, the same criteria are involved. The conduct, whether physical or verbal, must be both unwelcome and of a sexual nature.[41]

Unwelcome Sexual Advances.   Such advances mean the conduct was unsolicited. The victim viewed the conduct as undesirable or offensive and did nothing to initiate it even if the victim acquiesced, as in Case 14-2.

In 1986 the Supreme Court issued its first ruling on sexual harassment. The historic decision, *Meritor Savings Bank v. Vinson*, clarified the duty of employers and unions in instances involving possible sexual harassment. The Court stated that businesses may be held liable for sexual harassment by their employees even if they are unaware of illegal actions. Furthermore, the Court decided that "without question, when a supervisor sexually harasses a subordinate because of the subordinate's sex, that supervisor discriminates on the basis of sex."[42]

In the *Meritor* case, the Supreme Court focused on whether the sexual conduct was unwelcome and concluded that a person may be the victim of illegal sexual harassment even though he or she voluntarily participated in sexual acts.[43] The harassment may occur at a later date when the employee no longer wishes to be participating in sexual activities or finds such participation a requirement for favorable employment decisions. The Court also criticized the employer's harassment policy, which required employees to report incidents to their immediate supervisor, who may be the harasser.

Since the *Meritor* decision, the issue of sexual harassment was brought into dramatic, nationwide focus when college professor Anita Hill accused Supreme Court Justice nominee Clarence Thomas of sexual harassment. In a politically charged,

POLICY STATEMENT:

Sexual harassment violates Chrysler Corporation's long-standing policy against discrimination on the basis of sex. Sexual harassment in the workplace is also illegal. It violates Title VII of the 1964 Civil Rights Act, the Civil Rights Act of 1991 and various state fair employment laws in locations in which the Corporation does business. Chrysler's policy to prohibit the occurrence of sexual harassment is based on concern for the individual as well as good business judgement.

DEFINITION:

For the purpose of determining whether a particular act or course of conduct constitutes sexual harassment under this policy, the following definition will be used:

Unlawful sexual advances, requests for sexual favors, and other verbal or physical conduct of a sexual nature constitutes sexual harassment when:

1. submission to such conduct is made either explicitly or implicitly a term or condition of an individual's employment,
2. submission to or rejection of such conduct by an individual is used as the basis for employment decisions affecting such individual, or
3. such conduct has the purpose or effect of unreasonably interfering with an individual's work performance or creating an intimidating, hostile, or offensive working environment.

PROCEDURE:

Employees, applicants, suppliers, independent contractors, customers, business invitees, and other outsiders who come in contact with Chrysler employees who in good faith believe they have been subjected to or witnessed unlawful sexual harassment activity or behavior in the workplace by other Chrysler employees (including managers, supervisors and co-workers), applicants, suppliers, independent contractors, customers, business invitees or outsiders are encouraged to promptly report this occurrence. For the purposes of this policy, the Chrysler workplace will be defined as any place where Chrysler work is being performed. Individuals wishing to make the Corporation aware of unlawful conduct may use any or all of the following methods:

notify immediate management,
notify the Personnel Office,
notify the Corporate Workforce Diversity and Economic Equity Office.

Employees covered by a Collective Bargaining Agreement may utilize mechanisms provided under the terms and conditions of their applicable contracts. Further, Chrysler employees who are included under the provisions of the UAW-Chrysler Equal Application Program may also report occurrences of unlawful sexual harassment as noted above to their Local Plant Equal Application Committee.

All sexual harassment complaints will be investigated in a lawful, timely and impartial manner. Maximum confidentiality will be maintained throughout the investigation process and information process and information will be shared only on a need-to-know basis. Because of the sensitivity of sexual harassment issues, all investigations will be designed to protect the privacy and reputation of all individuals concerned. Chrysler will take appropriate steps to assure that a person who in good faith reports, complains about, or participates in the investigation of a sexual harassment allegation will not be subjected to retaliation. Chrysler will also take appropriate steps to assure that a person against whom such an allegation is made is treated fairly.

(continued)

Chrysler is firmly committed to providing a work environment free of hostility and will not tolerate sexual harassment in the workplace. Violations of this policy will result in immediate corrective action. Appropriate discipline, up to and including discharge, may be imposed.

Chrysler and the UAW are in agreement that complaints of sexual harassment should be dealt with promptly and fairly under existing internal procedures as provided under Section (4) of the National Agreement and Letter (116).

Further, the parties have agreed to provide training for Civil Rights and Equal Application Committees as specified under a separate Letter (158) of this Agreement.

Source: Agreement between Chrysler Corporation and the UAW, 1993–1996, pp. 253–255.

media-magnified hearing, Hill brought forward for the U.S. Senate's consideration her allegation that Thomas had sexually harassed her 10 years earlier when he was chairman of the Federal EEOC and she was an attorney on his staff.

Millions of Americans watched days of testimony as they learned firsthand how difficult and complex the issues of sexual harassment in the workplace could be. The burden placed on a woman who alleges sexual harassment to prove that it happened in the absence of any third-party witness was no heavier than the burden placed on a man accused of sexual harassment to prove a negative—that something did not happen.

The Thomas-Hill hearings pointed to the most difficult problem in sexual harassment—to report or not to report. Surveys done after the hearings turned up amazing statistics regarding women's unwillingness to report sexual harassment. In one phone survey of women executives, 65 percent who said they had been harassed admitted they never reported it. A *New York Times* poll found that only one in 10 women reported harassment. And a poll taken by the Federal Merit System's Protection Board reported only 5 percent of the people harassed (men and women) reported the harassment.[44]

Equal Pay for Equal Work

In 1963, Congress amended the 1938 Fair Labor Standards Act with what is often termed the *Equal Pay Act*. This act contains the principle of **equal pay for equal work**, regardless of gender.

Equal pay for equal work does *not*, in fact, require that jobs be identical to receive equal wages, nor does it require that jobs that are not exactly identical be placed in separate wage categories. Instead, the act as prescribed by Congress requires that organizations pay men and women approximately the same wages for substantially equal work. The concept of **substantially equal** refers to jobs containing similar skill, effort, responsibility, and working conditions.[45]

The Equal Pay Act does provide for legal variances in wages paid to individuals performing identical jobs. Employees may receive different wage rates while performing the same work if such differences are based on seniority, merit, quantity or quality of production, or factors other than gender.[46] These important exceptions provide the basis on which organizations and unions can defend the fact that men performing the same work as women receive, on the average, higher levels of pay.

SEXUAL HARASSMENT

The grievant was discharged as a result of his alleged sexual harassment of a female coworker. The grievant had been employed by the company for eight years and had no record of prior disciplinary offenses. The grievant's job required him to perform tasks on a large open site at the power plant. Because of the large geographic size of the area, it was necessary for him to be transported to various locations by a company van driven by another employee. The woman bringing the charges was a female employee who was married and had five children. She was employed as a laborer and was assigned to drive the grievant and other employees to the various locations. During one early morning drive, when the female employee and the grievant were alone, the grievant asked the employee if she would go driving with him off the premises. The employee responded no, and when the grievant described very detailed sexual fantasies that he had regarding her, the employee became frightened and asked him to quit talking and not to talk to her anymore. After driving the grievant to his work location, the employee went to her supervisor and reported the incident. She also asked that it not be repeated. Later that day, the employee discussed the incident with two fellow employees, who had both received obscene phone calls in which the caller used language similar to that the grievant had allegedly used with the female employee. The three female employees took their problem to their supervisor, who, after further investigation, called in the grievant. When he was asked to explain the incident of the alleged sexual harassment, the grievant totally denied that the incident had taken place. The grievant was suspended pending further investigation. After further investigation, the company decided to dismiss the grievant.

The company's decision to discharge the grievant was based on the following:

1. There was no reason for the female employee to fabricate the charges.
2. The remarks allegedly made by the grievant were cruel.
3. Although the grievant denied the incident, he seemed to recognize the identity of the accuser.
4. The grievant appeared to be untruthful to the supervisor.
5. The employee was visibly frightened by the incident.
6. The incident adversely affected the ability of the three female employees to work with the grievant.

The company made the decision despite the fact that the grievant was an eight-year employee with no other problems on his record.

The union grieved the issue on the basis of the premise that there was no just cause for the discharge. During the grievance process, the grievant continued to deny the incident, and only after a voice stress test in which the tester contended that the grievant was lying, did the grievant acknowledge that the incident had taken place. The union proceeded with the grievance on the issue that, although the incident had in fact happened, the discipline imposed was unnecessarily severe. The grievant's conduct was admittedly abusive, but it was the union's position that on the basis of the grievant's record, firing the grievant was not reasonable.

Decision

The arbitrator found that the company was not arbitrary in firing the grievant for the sexual harassment charge. The arbitrator found that when viewed in totality, the facts of the case warranted management's decision to dismiss the grievant.

Adapted from *Tampa Electric Company*, 88 LA 791 (1986)

Many employers and labor unions have developed new wage and salary systems based on formal job analysis and job evaluation programs to comply with the Equal Pay Act. Such programs ensure that employees are paid according to the content of their jobs and not according to other factors such as sex, supervisory bias, or job titles. Despite efforts to the contrary, the thirtieth anniversary of the Equal Pay Act found women's pay scales still substantially below those of men for the *same* job (70 percent in 1993 versus 60 percent in 1963). The data from a Bureau of Labor Statistics report, by job category, are shown in Table 14-5.

Comparable Worth

According to Winn Newman of the General Council of the Coalition of Labor Union Women, the leading women's labor economic issue of today is pay equity or comparable worth.[47] The Equal Pay Act does not always protect women from discrimination; it only guarantees women equal pay on jobs with the same job classification.

At the heart of the issue is the concept of **comparable worth**, which the U.S. Supreme Court acknowledged as a valid legal doctrine in a 1981 decision.[48] The *comparable worth doctrine* requires that pay be equal not just for men and women performing the same job but for all jobs requiring comparable skills, effort, responsibility, and working conditions. According to supporters, the doctrine represents the spirit and the letter of the Equal Pay Act. Opponents of the comparable worth doctrine argue that the large percentage of women in lower-paying jobs such as secretary, nurse, and elementary school teacher is a result of women's attraction to those jobs. The pay levels are a result of the external marketplace, as verified by wage surveys. Furthermore, opponents argue that comparable worth is not a demand for equal opportunity but a demand to be protected against one's career choice.[49]

Glass Ceiling

The **glass ceiling** is often discussed as limiting the advancement of women to top management of American corporations.

Identifying the Problem. The U.S. Department of Labor conducted a study between 1988 and 1990 of 94 Fortune 1000 companies. The study showed that, although women represented 37.2 percent of the total workforce of the companies,

Table 14-5	Women's Salaries as a Percentage of Men's Salaries in 1991
Data-entry keyers	95.0
Secretaries	91.6
Pharmacists	90.1
Engineers	85.6
Computer programmers	84.1
Lawyers	78.0
Doctors	72.2
Marketing managers	68.5
Machine operators	67.7
Financial managers	62.4

Source: Bureau of Labor Statistics (Washington, DC: GPO, 1992).

only 16.9 percent were in any level of management, and only 6.6 percent were managers at the executive level.[50]

In a follow-up to this study, the Department of Labor undertook a pilot project to try to identify systematic barriers to the career advancement of minorities and women. The project made the following points.

1. *Equal opportunity principles not embraced by the corporation.* Almost none of the corporations studied viewed the development of management staff in conjunction with equal opportunity policies. Internal and external training and development opportunities, corporate outreach through civic involvement, or special projects or assignments were not monitored to ensure that *all* qualified employees were given equal access.

2. *Compensation and appraisal systems not monitored.* Not one of the companies surveyed reviewed its *total* compensation packages to ensure nondiscrimination in those packages.

3. *Women placed in staff positions more often than in line positions.* Staff positions, such as human resources, research, administration, and public relations, are less likely to lead to top management positions. Line functions, such as sales or production, affect the corporation's bottom line, and experience in these areas is critical for promotion.

4. *Inadequate record keeping.* The lack of records in regard to their EEO/Affirmative Action responsibilities turned out to be another common trait among the companies surveyed. The Department of Labor attributed this lack of documentation to an overall lack of awareness that the EEO/Affirmative Action principles applied *across the board* to *all* employment practices, not just hiring of entry-level employees.

Just as the companies surveyed exhibited common traits, the survey found common barriers to the career advancement of women in each of the companies.

Americans with Disabilities Act

OTHER PROTECTED CLASSES

With the passage of the **Americans with Disabilities Act (ADA)** in 1990, people with disabilities have legal protection from discrimination.

The U.S. Department of Health and Human Services estimates that 43 million people in the United States have one or more disabilities. A 1986 Lou Harris poll found that 66 percent, or slightly over 28 million, were unemployed. The poll also found that two-thirds or over 18 million who are unemployed *want to work*.[51]

The ADA bars discrimination in both the public and private sector in areas of public services, such as bus and rail transportation; in public accommodations, such as restaurants and hotels; and in telecommunications. Following is a study of the ADA provisions affecting the workplace.

Employers Affected. All public and private employers of more than 15 employees are subject to the ADA employment provisions, which prohibit discrimination against qualified individuals with disabilities in regard to all activities affecting employment. A person is considered disabled under the ADA if he or she:

- Has a physical or mental impairment limiting substantially one or more of the major life activities of the person.
- Has a record of such an impairment
- Is regarded as having such an impairment

Major life activities include such functions as caring for one's self, performing manual tasks, walking, seeing, hearing, speaking, breathing, learning, or working. The following is a brief list of impairments covered by the ADA:

Alcoholism	Mental retardation
Cancer	Multiple sclerosis
Cerebral palsy	Muscular dystrophy
Diabetes	Orthopedic, visual, speech, or hearing
Emotional illness	impairments
Epilepsy	*Past* drug addiction
Heart disease	Specific learning disabilities
HIV disease (symptomatic or asymptomatic)	Tuberculosis

A "disabled" person, however, is covered by the ADA only if a qualified individual. A "qualified individual" is one who can carry out the *essential functions* of the job, with or without *reasonable accommodation*.

Hiring under the ADA.   The first compliance step for an employer subject to the ADA is to make certain that people with disabilities have access to the application process and that the selection process is nondiscriminatory. One area of concern is how far an employer can go in determining whether an applicant has or had a problem with alcoholism or drug addiction. Certain questions regarding past drug and alcohol use are off limits, although drug tests for the current use of illegal drugs are not prohibited.

Essential Functions.   The act provides guidance on the conditions that will prove that a particular function is essential to the job. These conditions include a written job description and the terms of a collective bargaining agreement. Many collective bargaining agreements have established the respective duties of the union members. Their duties are reflected by their job classification and pay rates.

Reasonable Accommodation.   If a person can perform the essential functions of a job without the need of any accommodation, the employer is bound by the ADA not to discriminate against that person because of his or her disability. If accommodation is needed, then the ADA requires such **reasonable accommodation** that does not impose an undue hardship on the employer. An accommodation is a change in a work process or the work environment that enables a person with disabilities to do the job.

The EEOC has suggested that an appropriate process for the employer in determining a reasonable accommodation is to involve the disabled qualified person in the decision.[52] Any architectural changes to the workplace, for example, that could be readily achieved with little or no difficulty or expense would be, by definition, a reasonable accommodation to make.

Undue Hardship.   The accommodation is not required if it requires significant difficulty or expense, an undue hardship. Factors to consider when deciding the difficulty or expense are:

1. Nature and cost of accommodation
2. Size and resources of the facility affected

3. Size and resources of employer overall (financial)
4. Type of operation, composition, and structure of workforce (nonfinancial)
5. Impact of accommodation on operation

Direct Threat. If the employer believes that a person with a disability cannot perform that job without creating a *direct threat* to him- or herself or others, the employer is not required to hire the individual. It is in the area of "reasonable accommodation" that compliance with ADA may conflict with a collective bargaining relationship. The ADA does not include compliance with an existing collective bargaining agreement as a bar to making accommodations. In fact, allowing the employer to deal directly with a disabled employee who might be represented by a union is a conflict with NLRA and union bargaining rights.[53]

AIDS

AIDS, acquired immune deficiency syndrome, is a disability protected under ADA. Prior to the passage of the ADA, the issue arose under the Rehabilitation Act of 1973, a forerunner of the ADA, of whether a person with a "contagious disease" was handicapped under the act and therefore protected. The Supreme Court, in a ruling involving a teacher with tuberculosis,[54] found that a person with a contagious disease is "handicapped" or "disabled" because one or more of that person's physical or mental capacities were impaired by the disease. Certainly a contagious disease that has a long or recurring life span, like tuberculosis or AIDS, has given the person a "record of impairment."

Having determined that the person was subject to protection under the act, the Court had to determine if the individual was otherwise "qualified" for the job and if the employer could make reasonable accommodations to meet that individual's condition. The employer, a school in this case, was reluctant to put the person in contact with children because of the contagious nature of the tuberculosis. The Court held that because *some* people with *some* types of contagious diseases may pose a threat to others in the workplace, *all* people with contagious diseases cannot be discriminated against. The Court acknowledged that a person who poses a significant risk to others in the workplace will not be qualified for employment if reasonable accommodation does not eliminate the risk.

In what is certainly going to be a controversial decision, the Washington, D.C., fire department was ordered by a lower court to reinstate a newly hired firefighter who informed the department he was HIV-positive after receiving an offer of employment. The department had adopted a policy of not hiring HIV-infected people. However, the medical officer for the fire department had to admit that an individual who passes the physical exam administered by the fire department is capable of performing the job. The court noted that his HIV-positive status did not present a "measurable risk" of transmission in the workplace if the usual and appropriate precautions that all firefighters take on the job to avoid blood-to-blood contact were taken. The court decided this case under the Rehabilitation Act but referenced the ADA in its decision.

Coworkers and AIDS. A difficult employment issue concerns the rights of coworkers of a person with AIDS. OSHA requires every employer to provide a safe and healthy workplace. The secretary of labor may take action against employers who fail to provide a safe working environment. Coworkers of a person with AIDS who might seek such action, however, would need to prove that they are at risk of contracting the disease, a difficult task given current medical evidence.

Federal OSHA regulations do provide that an employee may refuse to work if "a reasonable person would conclude [that] he faced an immediate risk of death or serious injury." Such action may not be considered reasonable by the Labor Department unless direct contact with blood or other body fluids were required by the job.[55]

Age Discrimination in Employment Act

The **Age Discrimination in Employment Act (ADEA)** makes it illegal for employers to discriminate against individuals over the age of 40. Employers cannot refuse to hire or discriminate in terms of compensation, promotion, or other conditions solely on the basis of an individual's age. Employers are also prohibited from using age as a preference in their recruiting practices.

In 1996, the Supreme Court reviewed a lower court decision that a claimant who was fired at age 56 and replaced by a 40-year-old worker could not claim age discrimination. The lower court said that, because the replacement worker was also a member of the class protected by ADEA, the claimant could not prevail in a claim for discrimination. The Supreme Court reversed, saying that the status of the replacement worker as a member of the protected class was immaterial. The issue, rather, was whether the claimant was replaced because of his age. All other things being equal, what is relevant is the age difference between the two workers. Replacing a 56-year-old worker with a 55-year-old worker may not indicate age discrimination, but going from a 56-year-old to a 40-year-old, may.[56]

A 1986 ADEA amendment prohibits *any mandatory retirement age* for workers. One area of controversy is whether incentive plans to gain voluntary retirement of older workers are legal under the act. In the early 1980s, restructuring, downsizing, and reorganization occurred in many businesses. That pressure, along with a continued need to respond to the promotion desires of baby boomers, caused employers to try to offer incentives for "voluntary" retirements. Some older workers who had felt pressured to accept these packages later complained of age discrimination. In a number of court cases, guidelines for acceptable voluntary agreements that legally waived the older person's rights under the ADEA were outlined by the courts.

Older Workers Benefit Protection Act. The Older Workers Benefit Protection Act (OWBPA) provided additional protection for workers by instituting the "equal benefit–equal cost" test, which meant that employers could not deny older workers the same benefits that younger workers received if (any) such benefits cost the same.

The OWBPA also incorporated guidelines for early retirement incentive plans. The act notes that early retirement incentive packages should be made available to older workers in a nondiscriminatory way. For example, offering incentives to workers 50 to 55 years of age but not to those over 55 would be unacceptable.

Finally, numerous states have begun to address the prohibition of discrimination based on employees' off-duty conduct. Either through state laws or state court decisions, protections have been granted in three areas: smoker's rights, the right to use lawful substances (most often thought of as tobacco and alcohol), and the right to engage in lawful activities (use of tobacco and alcohol, personal relationships between coworkers, and homosexuality). The goal of this legislation and court decisions is to protect workers from job actions based on their engaging in any lawful activity off of the work premises and during nonworking hours unless the prohibited activity is related to a bona fide occupational requirement or the job action is necessary to avoid a conflict of interest.[57]

LIFESTYLE PROTECTION STATUTES

With the Environmental Protection Agency's declaration that "passive smoke" can cause health problems, smoking in the workplace has become a very controversial issue. Prior to this EPA release in January 1993, many employers had attacked smoking as a health issue for the smoking employee. In order to curb health-care costs, an employer would refuse to hire a smoker or would require an employee to quit smoking. The legislatures of 29 states and the District of Columbia reacted to this trend by passing laws *protecting* smokers from such employer actions, noting that employers had no right to regulate the private life of employees.[58]

Employers had also instituted restrictions on smoking in the workplace as anti-smoking advocates become more vocal. One survey suggests that the percentage of companies that have restrictions on smoking went from 16 percent in 1980 to 60 percent in 1991. Unions seldom enter into the debate over workplace smoking policies despite the obvious "working conditions" connection to collective bargaining because their members are generally split on the issue.[59]

Gay men and lesbians constitute one group of employees not covered by any comprehensive federal legislation that protects them from job discrimination based on their sexual orientation and affection. In the early 1980s, the crisis of the AIDS epidemic brought the issue of homosexuality to the attention of the American people in an alarmingly new way. The spread of AIDS initially in large urban homosexual populations caused many people to view AIDS as a homosexual disease. Fear of the AIDS disease and ignorance as to its contagion caused increased discrimination for gay men and lesbians in the workplace. The response from the gay community, which had long advocated equal protection, was to push for a more aggressive national policy to combat AIDS with significant research moneys and humane and affordable health care for people living with AIDS. In addition, the gay community increased its advocacy for federal, state, and local legislation that would put equal protection for people regardless of their sexual orientation or affection into the civil rights laws.

Activism for legislation on the state level has met with mixed results. Eight states and the District of Columbia include a prohibition against discrimination on the basis of sexual orientation in their fair employment practices laws. One state has a separate law specifically prohibiting discrimination for sexual orientation, and eight states protect public employees from such discrimination by executive orders.[60]

The relationship between U.S. labor unions and African-Americans began shortly after the Civil War. African-Americans and women workers often viewed the union movement as a means to achieve economic equality. Today unions recognize that all members of the diverse workforce are critical to their survival.

SUMMARY

The courts have used the remedies of awarding back pay, cost of litigation, and reinstatement of position in discrimination cases since the 1960s. These court-ordered remedies are similar to those used in labor relations cases involving unfair labor practices.

The comparable worth or wage equity issue is an area in which collective bargaining principles and equal employment principles are quite similar. Although unions historically have demanded equal pay for jobs comparable in the areas of skills, effort, responsibility, and working conditions, they have also recognized in practice the use of wage surveys to determine wage rates. Union efforts on the comparable worth issue have attracted some largely nonunion professions such as clerical and nursing, and if successful, more will likely follow.

With passage of the ADA, the potential for conflicts between compliance with the law and compliance with a collective bargaining agreement again arises. An employer who has to accommodate a disabled worker might violate a labor agreement. Unions have become aware of the ADA requirements and how they affect their members.

Age discrimination and discrimination against smokers or homosexuals may present problems to the employer and the union. Familiarity with the legal requirements of applicable laws can help both organizations avoid discrimination.

CASE STUDY 14-1

REVERSE RACIAL DISCRIMINATION

Facts

The claimant was a white female social worker for the public school system. Because of a reduction in funding, the school board decided to cancel all nurses' and social workers' contracts with the school system. The claimant and five other social workers were informed that their contracts were canceled, and they were offered a hearing to see if the determination was arbitrary, capricious, or otherwise unjustified. One of the other social workers whose contract was canceled was a black male. The black male social worker complained that his dismissal was discriminatory because he was one of the few black administrators of the system, and he was being laid off with the other social workers.

An internal investigation by the school system's affirmative action officer found no discrimination, although she did note that it was unfortunate they would be losing their only black administrator by the layoff.

However, upon hearing the case of all six social workers who were dismissed, the hearing officer recommended to the board of education that the black social worker be retained by the system. The school board agreed and reinstated the black male social worker. The claimant filed suit charging racial discrimination under Title VII of the Civil Rights Act of 1964. The claimant demonstrated that race was the only reason the black administrator had been retained by the system and that, had they decided to retain only one social worker, she should have been the one retained because of her seniority. The position of the school board was that canceling the black administrator's contract was contrary to the spirit of the board's affirmative action plan.

Questions

1. The purpose of Title VII of the Civil Rights Act of 1964 was to remove barriers to em-

ployment based on racial classifications. Guided by recent Supreme Court decisions, what would you decide in this case?

2. How can employers protect themselves from reverse discrimination suits and still enforce an affirmative action plan?

Adapted from *Cunico v. Pueblo School District No. 60*, 47 FEP Cases 1346 (1988).

SAME-SEX SEXUAL HARASSMENT

Facts

Two fact situations have been placed before the court for a ruling on whether these victims were subject to sexual harassment in the workplace.

Victim 1 was a heterosexual male employed at a pizza shop. His immediate supervisor and five coworkers were openly homosexual males. Victim 1 also had three heterosexual male coworkers who did not join in this complaint. According to Victim 1, his supervisor and the homosexual employees attempted to find out the sexual orientation of new employees and, having discovered he was a heterosexual, began pressuring him to engage in homosexual activity. The harassment suffered by Victim 1 included graphic descriptions of homosexual sex; sexual advances; vulgar homosexual remarks, innuendoes, and suggestions; and touching in sexually provocative ways. There were specific examples of physical advances made by the homosexual employees to the heterosexual employees. It was established that the pizza shop manager knew of the harassment and took no disciplinary action although she did direct the homosexual employees to stop the complained of activities.

Victim 2 was a male heterosexual with a learning disability that caused him to be noticeably slow. He was hired as an auto mechanic and began working with coworkers collectively known as the "lube boys." These coworkers subjected Victim 2 to a wide variety of harassing behavior. The conduct included graphic de-

scriptions of sexual activities, taunts regarding his lack of sexual relations with women, and physical assaults on at least three occasions. One such assault involved tying the victim up, blindfolding him, and placing a finger in his mouth to simulate an oral sexual act. There was no allegation that the lube boys were homosexual or considered Victim 2 to be a homosexual. Victim 2 complained of some of these actions to his supervisors but did not reveal all of what had happened until the filing of the lawsuit.

Victim 1 and Victim 2 claimed that their employers violated Title VII of the Civil Rights Act in that they were subjected to harassment of a sexual nature on the job. Both claimed that a "hostile work environment" was created by the actions of the employees; that the employer knew of the actions and failed to stop them; and that "but for" their gender, the harassment would not have taken place. The court must determine if the harassment was based upon the victims' gender in order to find a violation of Title VII.

Questions

1. How do you think the court ruled in the case with Victim 1? Why?
2. How do you think the court ruled in the case for Victim 2? Why?
3. Would you expect the same decision if Victim 1 had been a female and all other facts stayed the same? If Victim 2 had been a female and all other facts remained the same?

Adapted from *Wrightson v. Pizza Hut*, 72 FEP Cases 186 (1996) and *McWilliams v. Fairfax County Board*, 69 FEP Cases 1085 (1996).

Age Discrimination in Employment Act (ADEA)
Americans with Disabilities Act (ADA)
business necessity
Civil Rights Act of 1964
Coalition of Labor Union Women (CLUW)
comparable worth
disparate treatment
Equal Employment Opportunity Commission (EEOC)

equal pay for equal work
glass ceiling
National Colored Labor Union (NCLU)
reasonable accommodation
reverse discrimination
sexual harassment
substantially equal
Title VII of Civil Rights Act
Womens Trade Union League
Workforce 2000

REVIEW QUESTIONS

1. Why was the relationship between unions and African-Americans one of advances and defeats?
2. Why does the collective bargaining process fall under Title VII? Does Title VII affect negotiated contracts?
3. In which industry did women enjoy the most organizing success in the early 1900s?
4. According to the Hudson study, in the year 2000 what percent of new entrants into the labor force will be white males?
5. How do affirmative action programs differ from federal employment laws?
6. What does the principle of equal pay for equal work entail?
7. Explain the comparable worth concept. Why is it critical to women's issues?
8. What items should appear in a nondiscrimination contract clause? In what other areas can unions and employers help promote nondiscrimination?
9. Discuss the key elements to a sexual harassment charge.
10. What must an employee do to ensure compliance with the ADA when hiring?

TAKE IT TO THE NET

We invite you to visit the Carrell/Heavrin page on the Prentice Hall Web site at:

http://www.prenhall.com/carrellr

for this chapter's World Wide Web exercise.

EXERCISE 14-1 Diversity Awareness

Purpose:
To sample the kinds of diversity training actually being used in the workforce.
Task:

Step 1: Divide the class into pairs and assign each pair an organization to approach regarding their "diversity" training. Organizations should include large and small companies, locally owned and subsidiaries of larger companies, government, the university, and franchised operations.

Step 2: Each pair should do a synopsis of the diversity training programs, if any, going on at their assigned organization. Report back to the class.

Step 3: If available, each pair should bring back a "diversity awareness" training exercise for the class to experience and to evaluate its usefulness in changing attitudes and behaviors.

Source: Michael R. Carrell, Daniel F. Jennings, and Christina Heavrin, *Fundamentals of Organizational Behavior* (Prentice Hall, 1997), pp. 310–311.

Diversity and Unions   EXERCISE 14-2

Purpose:

For students to recognize how the changes in the makeup of the workforce affect the management-labor relationship.

Task:

Divide the class into teams and have each team suggest new solutions to old problems.

1. The typical collective bargaining agreement provides that the "last hired, first fired" rule applies to layoffs. How can a union attract women and minorities to its membership and still preserve jobs for its longtime union members?

2. The union is asked to pursue a member's grievance when the member is fired for sexually harassing a fellow employee who is also a union member. What should the union do to preserve its relationship with both members?

3. An agreement has contained a two-tier pay system for several years. Recently, women union members have complained because they have a larger proportion of their members on the lower tier (70 percent) than the men do (25 percent). New employees move to the higher tier after 10 years of service. How can the union fairly represent both groups? Management claims that the cost savings due to the two-tier system are significant. About 33 percent of all union workers are on the lower tier.

If you are using Smith/Carrell/Golden *Collective Bargaining Simulated, 4E,* with this text, please refer to the following:

p. 14, Article III, which includes the nondiscrimination clause.

Labor Relations in a Global Context

Movie strike, Japanese style. Japanese movie studio workers and stars strike for higher wages to meet the inflation of the yen.

The First NAFTA Labor Cases

The NAO is the new agency created by the United States Department of Labor to review and report on public communications concerning labor law matters under the NAFTA labor side agreement. Each NAFTA country established its own NAO to treat labor law matters in another NAFTA country. As a national entity that takes up labor rights issues outside the national territory, the NAO is a unique institution. The most established and best-known forum for labor rights treatment is the International Labor Organization (ILO), a United Nations-related 160-member body that fashions labor rights and labor standards adopted by government, business, and labor delegates to its annual conference.

On February 14, 1994, the International Brotherhood of Teamsters (IBT) and the United Electrical, Radio and Machine Workers of America (UE) filed the first submissions to the U.S. National Administrative Office under the North American Agreement on Labor Cooperation. The cases are similar in their timing and in their allegations and were processed jointly by the U.S. NAO. Both labor submissions alleged dismissals of groups of employees in late 1993 because of their attempts to form a union affiliated with the Frente Autentico del Trabajo (Authentic Labor Front), F.A.T. The IBT submission concerned events at a Honeywell factory in Chihuahua; the UE submission involved events at a General Electric plant in Ciudad Juarez. Both submissions were accompanied by sworn affidavits from Mexican workers alleging that they were discharged for union activity. Such anti-union discrimination is unlawful under the Mexican constitution, the Mexican Federal Labor Law, and ILO Convention 87, ratified by Mexico and thus part of its law.

The U.S. NAO's hearing on the IBT and UE submissions under the NAALC took place on September 12, 1994, in a large conference room at the United States Department of Labor headquarters in Washington, D.C. The only witnesses that appeared were trade union representatives. Officials of Honeywell and General Electric did not testify at the hearing, choosing instead to file written statements.

The F.A.T. union official described his work attempting to organize at the Honeywell and General Electric plants. He alleged discrimination by the Mexican government against his independent union federation, contrasting it to the favorable treatment received by the government-affiliated C.T.M. federation. He also alleged widespread use of blank forms, which workers are required to sign as a condition of employment and that are later presented as signed resignation statements if workers contest their dismissal, and widespread use of a blacklist by maquiladora employers.

On October 12, 1994, the U.S. NAO issued its public report on the IBT and UE submissions. The report summarized or cited information received from submitting unions from the Honeywell and General Electric companies, from the NAO of Mexico, from outside experts, and from other sources.

In its key last section on findings and recommendations, the U.S. NAO first repeated its admonition that its review "has not been aimed primarily at determining whether or not the two companies named in the submissions may have acted in violation of Mexican labor law," but rather "to gather as much information as possible to allow the NAO to better understand and publicly report on the government of Mexico's promotion of compliance with, and effective enforcement of, its labor law. . . ."

During the review, a number of other relevant issues regarding enforcement of labor law in Mexico, were brought to the attention of the NAO. They include the difficulties in establishing unions in Mexico, the hurdles faced by independent unions in attaining legal recognition, company blacklisting of union activists, the use of blank sheets, and government preference for and support of official unions.

Most press accounts portrayed the NAO Report as a victory for the corporations and the Mexican government. "Reich Supports Mexico on Union Organizing," said the headline in the *New York Times*. According to the *Wall Street Journal*, "In its findings, the Labor Department said that the Mexican government protected worker rights." Submitting unions reacted with anger to the NAO's final report, terming the process that led to it a "grand fiasco" and a "false promise," while Honeywell and General Electric officials commended it.

Union advocates suggested that the NAO decision gives U.S. companies and the Mexican government carte blanche to violate worker rights. This may be too dire a conclusion. The easy access for trade union and worker complaints to a public review and a public hearing on the types of issues raised in the first NAO cases might, on the other hand, make companies more careful in their employment policies where union organizing is underway.

Source: Adapted from Lance A. Compa, "The First NAFTA Labor Cases: A New International Labor Rights Regime Takes Shape," *United States-Mexico Law Journal*, University of New Mexico School of Law, 1995.

As the last decade of the twentieth century began to unfold, the world watched the disintegration of the Soviet Union, the economic union of Europe, and the continued growth of Japan as an economic giant.

As discussed in the first three chapters, labor-management relations in the United States are profoundly affected by the global marketplace. No U.S. company or union can avoid this influence.

In this chapter we look at labor relations in other countries that are playing a major part in the new global economy. We examine how their labor-management relations developed, how they differ from or resemble labor-management relations in the United States, and how one influences the other.

PATTERNS OF LABOR-MANAGEMENT RELATIONS

In the beginning chapters of this text, we studied the growth of unions in the United States as representatives of workers and the reaction of both employers and the government to that growth. In studies of union-employer-government relations in other countries, similar patterns have been observed.

There are three distinct attitudes that governments have displayed in reaction to unionization of workers: suppression, tolerance, and encouragement. Although there is some support for the view that governments tend to move through those three attitudes linearly, other evidence supports a more complicated relationship.[1]

Suppression

Early in the development of their industrial economy most countries worked to suppress unions and the notion of collective bargaining. In Great Britain at the beginning of the industrial revolution, the Combination Acts, passed in 1799 and 1800, made a union of employees illegal as a conspiracy to restrain trade. In France, a 1791 law that forbade employee *combinations*—ostensibly to prevent any organization from coming between the government and the workers—was actually used to suppress unions. In the United States in the early 1800s government reaction to the labor movement through the court system was similar. "Combinations of laborers" were considered illegal.

In the late nineteenth and early twentieth centuries, when industrialization reached Germany, Russia, and Japan, these nations passed laws suppressing or banning unions. Some Third World countries just emerging into the industrial world have not directly banned unions but have attempted to suppress collective bargaining. The governments of Ghana, Nigeria, and Singapore, for example, supported unions legislatively but limited their authority. The job of unions was seen as a support role to employees, not as a representative of employees to their employers.

This suppression early in the industrialization process seems to be generated by a sense of fear—fear that workers will destroy what is being created. Many labor leaders feared that the downturn in the economies of developed nations in the 1970s would result in renewed suppression of unions by government. In the United States, President Reagan's actions toward the air traffic controllers union (PATCO) realized those fears. In Great Britain, Margaret Thatcher's actions to limit unions and discourage collective bargaining also supported those fears. The governmental inclination to suppress unions seems to be most prevalent during a low level of economic development when there is concern that workers' demands will threaten the nation. Totalitarian governments, market-oriented governments, or governments controlled by business interests, as well as any government fearing rebellion, are also likely to suppress unions as a way to control the masses.

Toleration

The history of the union movement in most countries shows a period when government, after attempts at suppression, begins to tolerate unions. Such action was usually made of necessity because unions continued to function despite anti-union attitudes. In countries with economic growth, the ability or desire to keep workers from organizing just lost support.

As representatives of the working masses, unions became powerful political forces that could not be ignored. Some nations, such as the United States in the 1930s, went from mere tolerance to protecting unions legally and to collective bargaining.

Protection and Encouragement

Industrial nations fighting World War I and World War II found it necessary to marshal capital and labor for the war effort. Governments found that what "capital" wanted in exchange was money and what labor wanted was collective bargaining. Collective bargaining was mandated by law or policy in the United States and Britain largely as a result of this need.

As developed economies strove for stability, the desire for industrial peace encouraged collective bargaining. Such stability allowed for growth, which strengthened the economy.

Just as the national economy fluctuates, so will a nation's attitude toward unions and collective bargaining. Governments encourage collective bargaining when it is perceived as having a positive effect on the economy. Naturally, when labor-based political parties come into power, collective bargaining is encouraged.

The ability of governments to actually influence the growth or demise of union membership can be seen in Table 15-1. The selected country-by-country profiles later in this chapter reflect the current labor management attitudes around the world.

			Union	Collective
Country	Years	Attitude	Membership	Bargaining
United States	1806–1942	Discouraged	Erratic	Sporadic
	1917–1920	Encouraged	Grew	Grew
	1932–1947	Encouraged	Grew	Grew
	1980–1990	Discouraged	Decreased	Decreased
United Kingdom	1799–1824	Discouraged	Erratic	Sporadic
	1940–1945	Encouraged	Grew	Grew
	1973–1979	Encouraged	Grew	Grew
	1980–1990	Discouraged	Decreased	Probably decreased
Japan	1901–1925	Discouraged	Flat	Little
	1938–1945	Discouraged	None	None
	1945–1948	Encouraged	Grew	Grew
Germany	1878–1990	Discouraged	Submerged	Little
	1915–1921	Encouraged	Grew	Grew
	1933–1945	Discouraged	None	None

Source: Roy J. Adams, "Regulating Unions and Collective Bargaining: A Global, Historical Analysis of Determinants and Consequences," *Comparative Labor Law Journal* 14, no. 3 (Spring 1993), pp. 272–300.

INTER-NATIONAL LABOR RELATIONS

American labor law and labor relations are unique. Although wages, benefits, working conditions, and job security are important issues to workers everywhere, the American *process* of collective bargaining was largely shaped by historical events and entities in this country.

The primary tool in the resolution of American labor disputes—private arbitration—is hard for many foreign observers to grasp. The decentralized bargaining process, which is a cornerstone of American collective bargaining, is rarely found elsewhere. In Europe, the pattern is multiemployer or industrywide, and the issues are broader in nature. In Germany, the primary function of unions has been to bargain regional tariffs or geographic minimum wage rates. In the United States, worker disciplinary actions are addressed by collective bargaining and not through legislation, which is more common in other countries. The number of subjects resolved by collective bargaining is considerably greater in the United States than in Europe or Japan, where negotiations are more likely to be centralized on a few national issues.[2]

These basic differences are outlined in the following summaries of labor relations in other parts of the world. Table 15-2 compares union membership within some of these key nations.

The European Union

The European Single Act, adopted in 1987, decreed that, in 1992, border restrictions regarding goods, services, labor, and capital between 12 European countries would be lifted, and uniform standards affecting trade would be established. The term that was given to this event was *Europe 1992*, now called the European Union.

**Selected Data of Union Membership in Five Countries, 1955–1990
(in thousands and in percentage of total wage and salary employees)**

Table 15-2

	1955	1960	1970	1980	1985	1990
United States	16,802	17,049	21,248	22,228	16,996	16,740
	33%	31%	30%	25%	17%	16%
Canada	1,268	1,459	2,178	3,397	3,666	4,031
	31%	30%	31%	35%	36%	36%
Japan	6,286	7,662	11,605	12,369	12,418	12,265
	36%	33%	35%	31%	29%	25%
Germany	7,499	7,687	7,958	9,261	9,324	9,400
	44%	40%	37%	40%	40%	40%
United Kingdom	9,738	9,835	11,187	12,947	10,821	10,600
	46%	45%	50%	56%	51%	44%

Source: Adapted from Clara Change and Constance Sorrentino, "Union Membership Statistics in 12 Countries," *Monthly Labor Review* (December 1991), pp. 46–53.

The 1987 agreement created four steps of economic and political integration of the European Community. The first step, which is farthest away from the realization of a unified European Community, includes 12 countries: Bulgaria, Cyprus, Czech Republic, Estonia, Hungary, Latvia, Lithuania, Malta, Poland, Romania, Slovakia, and Slovenia, and is built around various types of trade and financial cooperation.

The next step, in 1995, included the countries of Sweden, Finland, and Austria.

The third step included the six countries that are full members of the former European Community but were not the initiators of Europe 1992: Spain, United Kingdom, Portugal, Greece, Denmark, and Ireland. These countries have participated in past economic European unions but not necessarily as the major players.

Finally, the last step, and the one the other countries are heading for, includes the six countries credited with establishing the European Community: Belgium, France, Germany, Italy, Luxembourg, and The Netherlands.[3]

The ability of European nations to overcome cultural and historical differences and cooperate in the global marketplace remains to be seen.[4] In the meantime, industrial relations practices vary from country to country.

European Corporatism

During the period from World War II through the early 1970s, industrial relations in Western Europe developed into what has been termed **corporatism**. Corporatism generally refers to a nationally centralized system of collective bargaining in which business corporations, mass unions, employers' associations, and the government play a major role. The government ensured organized labor a representational monopoly within their industry. Bargaining occurred at the national level among employers, government, and unions. Since the early 1980s, however, the European economic downswing, financial crises, high unemployment, and the growth of deregulation have led to a decline in corporatism. The trend in recent years among many European countries has been away from centralized collective

ITALY'S UNION RELATIONS:
FIAT AND ALFA ROMEO

In the 1980s, Italy's two most recognizable auto makers, Fiat and Alfa Romeo, faced financial crisis. Their response to the crisis resulted in one company's eliminating its union and the other company's establishing an ongoing relationship with its union.

Fiat was founded in 1899 and modeled itself after Henry Ford's auto business. Fiat used an assembly line to mass produce its autos. It paid high wages to attract good employees. The employees were unionized, and the union had become very powerful over the years, negotiating not only wages but many day-to-day organizational conditions.

The same crisis that hit U.S. auto makers hit Fiat in the late 1970s. Fiat proposed a reorganization to stave off a bankruptcy that would have involved laying off 18 percent of its employees. The union objected and cut off talks with management. Fiat used the union's refusal to bargain as legal justification for dismissing 15,000 employees. A strike called by the union never materialized because a majority of the union workers kept working. The union agreed to Fiat's conditions just a week after the strike started. The union was essentially busted by this time, and the subsequent reorganization of Fiat completely bypassed the union.

Fiat modernized its plants, created modular design, and used computer-assisted technology and industrial robots. It compressed or eliminated job duties and titles and trained workers for multiple roles. By and large, it did all of these things without consulting the union. It went directly to employees, who were happy to participate.

In contrast, Alfa Romeo, founded in 1906, was not a mass-production auto company. It concentrated on high-quality automobiles. It stressed workers' skills, cooperation, and loyalty to the firm. In the 1960s, Alfa Romeo decided to enter the mass-production market to manufacture *Alfasud.* By getting into the mass-market field not long before the financial crisis in the auto industry, Alfa Romeo was doomed to problems. Although union relations became strained as a result of the financial crisis, the subsequent developments between Alfa Romeo and its unions led to very different results from those of Fiat.

Before the crisis hit, Alfa Romeo had negotiated a series of agreements with the union concerning productivity and worker training. Alfa Romeo had already redesigned its assembly plant into "team" operations and compressed its hierarchy of management and quality control.

Although Alfa Romeo's financial difficulties led to another reorganization in the mid-1980s, the union continued to participate in the planning. Layoffs were reduced, and by 1988 virtually all laid-off workers had been called back.

Experts compare the labor-management approaches of the parties in the Fiat and Alfa Romeo situations to emphasize how necessary cooperation is to the life of both companies and unions.

Richard M. Locke, "The Demise of the National Union in Italy: Lessons for Comparative Industrial Relations Theory," *Industrial and Labor Relations Review* 45, no. 2 (January 1992), pp. 229–249.

agreements to agreements negotiated at the corporate level. The shift toward decentralization has also caused the weakening of central unions, an increase in the number of cooperative alliances between groups of workers and management, and an increase in the direct participation of workers in managerial decision making. These changes have occurred most notably in Sweden, Austria, Germany, and Italy.[5] Profile 15-1 examines how Italy has changed some of its labor-management relations as a reaction to economic realities.

Germany. In Germany, for example, industrial agreements are negotiated regionally or nationally, but the enforcement of the agreements is left to **work councils**. Work councils do not bargain and are not part of a union organization, although most council members are members of the union. These work councils are a part of the daily management of the industry.[6]

Since the European depression of the mid-1970s, unions have lost a great many jobs, members, and thus, influence. The weakened European economy brought high unemployment, low growth, and meager wage increases. The traditional European union strongholds—steel, automobiles, and the chemical industry—lost many jobs and union members. Unions replaced higher wages as their top negotiating priority with job security in the form of guaranteed hours of work. Employers have responded with demands for flexible work schedules, which would help them increase productivity without adding new workers. A critical turning point in the then West German labor relations occurred in 1978–1979 when West German steel workers struck six weeks for a 35-hour work-week. The employers' association refused any reduction in hours and demanded flexibility in work scheduling. The striking workers lost and went back to work, although they have continued to push for shorter hours. In 1987, the Metal Workers Union and the employers' association negotiated the same issues. The union achieved a reduced standard 37.5-hour week, but the employers maintained flexibility in scheduling between 37 and 39.5 hours.[7]

Great Britain.　Britain's trade unionism is clearly akin to that of the United States. But in 1996 trade union density in Great Britain was 38 percent, whereas in the United States the rate was 15 percent. In recent years, studies of Britain's trade union movement have tried to pinpoint what influences cause a rise or a decline in union membership.

These studies have resulted in two opinions, both supported by significant research: first, that union growth is determined by outside forces such as the economy and government action, and second, that union growth is determined by a union's recruitment efforts and attitudes.

People who believe that outside forces control union growth point to periods of high inflation and high unemployment as growth periods for British unions. They also point to both post–World War periods, when the government fostered union growth. People who believe that a union's policies foster growth point to periods when in one union aggressive union leadership led to growth whereas during the same periods other unions that failed to recruit did not grow.[8]

During Prime Minister Thatcher's term in office, a number of changes occurred in labor-management relations in Britain. These "new-style" agreements typically include the union as the sole bargaining representative in each company (most British plants in the past have had multiple unions), a no-strike–no-lockout clause, and final-offer arbitration.

The underlying theme of the new-style British agreements is the recognition by both sides of the necessity for new, cooperative approaches to problem solving and long-term measures of productivity.[9]

Japan

Contrary to most aspects of Japanese society, the system of labor relations is not the product of years of tradition or the closed nature of that society. Instead, it is the conscious choice of contemporary decision makers. The Japanese system of labor relations can be summarized as having **five pillars**, or foundations, starting with the first pillar, the concept of lifetime employment. The *regular employee* is a

Japanese term that applies to workers in large companies who often enjoy lifetime employment with the same employer. A common American misconception is that all Japanese employees achieve such lifetime job security, but in fact only about one-third of the nonagricultural workforce enjoys this advantage.[10] The regular employee in Japan is not given a lifetime employment contract by the employer but instead is part of "a way of thinking on both sides by the employee and by the employer."[11]

The second pillar of the Japanese system is a wage system based on seniority. The Japanese correlate pay with length of service and age more than is common in the West.

Enterprise unionism is the third pillar. In typical Japanese unions, almost all employees, including supervisors and white-collar workers, are members. Bargaining is primarily conducted at the local level, but general issues may be conducted at the industry level.

The fourth pillar of the system is harmony between Japanese labor and management. However, though Japan's number of workdays lost because of strikes is far lower than in the United States, it is higher than in several European countries.

Since the early 1950s, local union leaders have annually mounted a "spring offensive" for higher wages. However, they recognize that most Japanese workers have a strong loyalty to their employer and thus are not likely to support any collective action. When strikes do occur, they often last for less than four hours. Slowdowns and employee refusal to work overtime are more typical means that Japanese unions use to express their dissatisfaction with management.

Unions in Japan have been very successful in building labor-management consultation methods including quality control (QC) groups and zero defects (ZD) movements. This fifth pillar of labor-management relations was modeled on similar American programs with one distinct difference. American programs often focus the responsibility for quality control on managers and engineers whereas Japanese programs focus on the individual employee and preventive efforts, not corrective methods.

Together, these five pillars have produced a labor climate in Japan that might be described as one of sharing information and obtaining consensus, and thus results in little conflict.[12] The Japanese Golden Rules (see Table 15-3) grew out of these five pillars.

Understanding the five pillars of Japanese labor relations lets foreigners have a better grasp of the attitudes of the typical Japanese worker, "Mr. Suziki." He rides 90 minutes one way to work each day in a sardine-packed train, works marathon hours, lives in a tiny rental apartment with a family he almost never sees, and pays three times what Americans pay for a hamburger. By world standards he is comparatively rich, yet he appears to be an overworked, poorly fed and housed, angry consumer. Why doesn't he demand that his union bargain for more money, shorter hours, or early retirement? Why doesn't he just walk out and move to greener pastures? Foreign managers and union leaders ask these questions because they are puzzled by his acceptance of this lifestyle. The answer, mostly invisible to outsiders but a way of life in Japan, is **gaman**. Loosely translated, gaman is perseverance and self-denial for the greater cause. Gaman is a way of life, taught from birth by parents, grandparents, and teachers.

A new generation of Japanese workers and consumers is slowly challenging gaman. Midcareer job transfers, once taboo for workers, are becoming common. Japanese consumers are beginning to demand imports in order to improve their

1. Teamwork.	10. Job security.
2. No craft unions.	11. Few status differentials between workers and managers.
3. One company union for all employees—workers and managers.	12. Layoffs are a last resort.
4. Union bargainers are aware of the company's real situation.	13. Frequent job rotation.
5. No seniority rules.	14. Peer group competition in-house for top management positions.
6. In-house labor markets so employees stay.	
7. In-house training.	15. Large biannual bonuses.
8. No midcareer recruiting.	16. Diffusion of individual accountability and responsibility.
9. The *ringi* system: proposals for changes can come from anywhere and reach top management.	

Source: Thomas Nevins, "How the Game Is Played in Japan," *Cornell Enterprise* (Summer–Fall 1990), pp. 25–31.

lifestyle. The reason for these changes may be that Japan has become affluent enough so that the old ways of austerity and sacrifice for national purpose appear to be no longer necessary to young workers. One American corporate executive, T. Boone Pickens Jr., commenting on Japan noted, "The workers of this country are carrying the load on their backs . . . and one of these days they're going to get tired of putting up with it." Even though workers and consumers may demand "indulgences" such as central heating in offices and homes, many believe that the decline of gaman will be slow.[13]

Japanese Collective Bargaining. The Japanese style of collective bargaining includes a *joint consultation* system that provides a mechanism for continual information sharing and communication. **Joint consultation committees (JCCs)** are made up of both senior corporate executives and high-level union officials. Wage negotiations are *not* done by these committees, but the practice of sharing confidential business and financial information with the union through these committees before wage negotiations is common. A study was conducted on the influence of joint consultation committees on collective bargaining with 97 bargaining pairs in Japan. Evidence from that study suggests that more information sharing is related to a *lower* probability of long and difficult negotiation. In addition, both the initial demands of a union and the final wage settlement were lower in cases in which financial information was shared. The approach of Japanese employers and unions to a cooperative collective bargaining process through information sharing has resulted in more employment security but more moderate wage increases.[14]

Two related developments have altered Japanese labor policy and politics in recent years. One was the transformation of the structure of the labor union movement: the emergence of the moderate, pragmatic union, Rengô, with a membership of about 8 million (in 1995, 62 percent of organized labor). This transformation followed the gradual dissolution of the former national union centers (Sôhyô, Dômei, Chûritsu Rôren, and Shinsanbetsu). The formation of Rengô in 1989 was heralded by its founders as the conclusion of a long, bumpy process of reunification of the labor movement and the beginning of a new era in organized labor's internal relations and its relations with employers' associations, political parties, and the state bureaucracies. The second development was the increasing participation of labor leaders in formal, semiformal, and informal forums of public policy making and policy implementation. This trend was closely related to increasingly cooperative labor relations at the enterprise level since the mid-1970s. It also marked the confluence of, on the one hand, state bureaucracies' readiness to give a large, though selective, part of organized labor access to policy processes and, on the other hand, labor's choice to increase its participation in public policy processes.[15]

Rengô expanded its Research Institute for the Advancement of Living Standards (Sôgô Seikatsu Kaihatsu Kenkyûjo, Sôken) and the research units of some of its affiliates and has contracted out research to organizations and individual scholars outside the labor movement. It has also established forums and study groups whose members include not only members of Rengô and its affiliates but also Diet members, leaders of employers' associations, scholars, and journalists. These forums and study groups resemble in their membership composition statutory and nonstatutory advisory bodies established by the government. The largest national center of organized labor, Rengô behaves as if it were the sole representative of organized labor. This behavior is reinforced by the tendency of the Ministry of Labor (MOL) and other state bureaucracies to exclude the smaller national centers and most unaffiliated industrial unions from participation in policy processes. Contacts between MOL bureaucrats and non-Rengô unions are generally limited to the presentation of petitions by the latter to the former. There has been a marked increase in Rengô's participation in statutory and nonstatutory advisory councils—most notably, but not only, in those formed by the MOL—and in informal contacts between Rengô officials and bureaucrats. Rengô has four publicly stated policy goals:[16]

1. To acquire new rights and benefits of direct concern to its members
2. To defend acquired rights and benefits
3. To promote macroeconomic policies with direct and indirect effects on its members
4. To increase benefits to the unorganized and underprivileged

China

Labor relations in the People's Republic of China began to change after the breakup of the Soviet Union and the dissolution of the Communist governments in Eastern Europe. Traditionally, trade unions in China were part of the Communist government. They viewed their role as helping the government raise productivity and defuse potential conflicts rather than representing the workers to management. In general, the 100 million workers who made up the trade unions were peasants for whom the socialist system has brought a slightly better life. China's move from a communist economic system to a market economy system, although still dominated by state enterprises, is causing unrest. The restructuring eliminated state support for unprofitable enterprises. Unemployment has begun to rise. There is also an influx of nonunionized foreign ventures.

Labor unions are being formed independently from the unions sanctioned by the Chinese government. In 1993, over 8,000 strikes were recorded in a country where strikes are illegal. In response to this growing unrest, the Chinese government passed a labor law that prohibited the use of child labor (under 16); established an eight-hour workday and a 44-hour workweek; prohibited discrimination based on race, sex, nationality, or religion; established a maternity leave of at least 90 days; required that each province set a minimum wage; and required foreign enterprises to establish unions within their organizations. In addition, the government instituted a job-training program and a national unemployment insurance plan.[17]

Taiwan

In Taiwan, a positive economic climate has meant a growth in union membership. Taiwan, along with South Korea, Brazil, Mexico, Singapore, and Hong Kong, is considered a *newly industrialized country (NIC)*.

Taiwan's economic growth since the mid-1950s has been accompanied by a growth in union membership. In 1955, 104,000 workers, or 3.8 percent of the total labor force, were union members. In 1987, 1,874,000 workers, or 22.9 percent of the total workforce (27.6 percent of nonagricultural workers), were union members.

As in other developing nations, however, trade unionism in Taiwan does not resemble the U.S. system. When Taiwan was a Japanese colony from the end of the Sino-Japanese War (1894–1895) to the end of World War II (1945), trade unionism was banned. As part of China in 1945, trade unionism was allowed, although, because of labor strikes, it was again banned in 1947. When Taiwan separated from mainland China in 1949 as a reaction to the Communist Chinese government, trade unions were seen as a positive force to help the government mobilize workers behind it. Since that time, unionism has been encouraged by the Taiwanese government.

Labor unions in Taiwan are politically and socially oriented. By active political participation, labor union members serve in the Taiwanese National Assembly and participate in the passage of laws that protect the workers. In addition, many welfare programs are administered by the trade unions. In 1981, for example, 307 different social services were offered to workers by over 1,800 unions.

The traditional role of U.S. unions in negotiating collective bargaining agreements is not shared by Taiwan's trade unionists. Formal collective bargaining agreements are rare. Strikes by workers are prohibited. Labor unions are able to represent their members through their political positions and through informal agreements with employers.[18]

The Former Soviet Union and Eastern Europe

In 1989, more than 300,000 Soviet coal miners conducted a week-long strike. The striking workers demanded more food, safer working conditions, and better housing. For the first time since the Communist revolution in 1917, union leaders dared to force a showdown with the Soviet government. The strikers demanded that President Mikhail S. Gorbachev deliver on the promises he had made during the previous four years—promises of better working conditions and living conditions. However, the major demand by the strikers was even more critical—local control of the mines with worker participation. Such demands may very well have been met with military resistance only a few years earlier. However, President Gorbachev had openly promised revolutionary changes in Soviet labor relations. He had promised workers all over the Soviet Union that they would have direct input in management decisions, such as setting work schedules and production goals, and they would share locally in increased revenues, similar to American profit-sharing plans. One Soviet newspaper underscored the significance of the miners' strike. "Until recently, *perestroika* had been a revolution from above, but now it is getting strong support from below."[19]

As the world watched in stunned silence, perestroika evolved into a breakup of the Soviet Union. In an analysis of the economic goals of perestroika we can see the inevitability of that breakup.

Perestroika was based on four principles:

1. There was a need to disengage the Communist Party from the state.
2. Production of some goods and services needed to be commercialized.
3. Production standards needed to focus on the value of the goods produced in place of the numbers produced.
4. Capital had to become available to motivate production and innovation.

Principles 2, 3, and 4 above could not be achieved unless the Communist Party lost its hold on the state because the economic principles it fostered were in direct opposition. Now that the breakup has been accomplished, the economies of the countries that made up the former Soviet Union (FSU) need to change. It is anticipated that the following conditions need to be met to change the nations of the FSU into a market economy:

1. Private ownership rights must be established.
2. Bureaucratic and governmental supervision of business and industry must be suspended.
3. Enterprises must be free to hire and fire labor and to go bankrupt, and subsidies to unprofitable concerns must stop.
4. Government ownership of enterprises must be restricted.

Russia.   In Russia, full employment was a reality. Full employment was achieved through a centralized labor regulation system that firmly attached a worker to an enterprise. Movement of workers between jobs, much less careers, was discouraged if not banned outright.

Because most of Russia's enterprises were concentrated in manufacturing and old-line industries, such as fuel and power, metallurgy, building materials, and nonpetrochemicals, 70 percent of the workers were in material or goods-producing industries. Roughly two-thirds of Russia's workers were manual workers, compared with one-half the workers in the United States and Japan.

Retooling industries in Russia means retraining the workers. The risks of creating open labor markets there includes increased unemployment. It has also led to substantial labor unrest and strikes in Russia's vital energy, chemicals, pulp and paper, and mining industries. The widespread nonpayment of wages in these industries mounted to six months' pay in 1996.[20]

The transformation of the labor relations system in Russia is proceeding very slowly. The privatization program has created employee-owned enterprises, but the control of them remains in the hands of the same managers who directed the work under the Communist system. The Federation of Independent Trade Unions of Russia still dominates as a workers' organization, but, to some extent, it is still controlled by the senior managers. Management makes most decisions on wages unilaterally and, by charging for benefits previously provided, has kept living standards low.[21]

Eastern Europe.   When the labor union movement in Eastern European countries is examined, a decline is easily seen. In Poland, where worker revolts led the way to the overthrow of the Communist government, the union movement known as Solidarity, which had numbered as many as 9 million in 1989 fell to 2 million in 1991. Solidarity, itself, is torn between its political arm, which is trying to convert Poland into a market economy, and its trade unionist arm, which is trying to protect the workers.

The Czech Republic trade unions supported the revolution against the Communist party, but now their influence is weakening. The government, by law, must discuss labor issues with the unions but need not agree with them before enacting changes to the Labor Code. The government is taking the role of arbitrator between unions and private employers as private enterprise grows.

In Hungary there are competing unions, but without a procedure for collective bargaining they have little influence on the changes taking place. Unemployment figures continue to rise. Foreign investment is coming into Hungary through joint ventures with local businesses, but the high wage rates available in these ventures have kept employees from unionizing. The Confederation of Trade Unions with 3.5 million members, the League for Democratic Trade Unions with 80,000 members, and the smaller Worker Solidarity Trade Union have not been able to find common ground in order to unite in their efforts. As unemployment and inflation rise, they may find such unity impossible to achieve.[22]

Hungary, Slovakia, and the Czech Republic are scheduled to begin formal negotiations with the European Union in hopes of joining by the year 2000.[23]

Labor Relations "Down Under"

Australia and New Zealand offer another example of the influence of government policies on trade unionism and the dynamics that decide policies. The Australian and New Zealand system of labor relations was founded on an industrial relations policy in which centralized arbitration—as opposed to collective bargaining—determined the conditions of a worker's employment. Through national labor laws both countries had in place a compulsory arbitration process for deciding labor disputes. The decision, called "an award," would govern *not only* the parties asking for the decision *but all* employers and employees involved in the same work as that which was arbitrated. Thus, an Australian judge deciding a wage dispute between an auto manufacturer and its assembly-line workers would determine the wage rate for *all line* workers in all the auto-manufacturing workplaces.

Originally, this centralized system was supported both by employers, who believed the award system would equalize wages and, thereby, eliminate them as a competitor factor, and by unions, which were in favor of the award system because decisions tended to support wage equity for their members. Support for the system began to erode, however, as Australia and New Zealand experienced competition from the Pacific Rim nations. Industries, citing their inability to remain competitive, pointed to the central system of wage fixation, arbitration, and awards as stifling their ability to respond to new economic realities.

Because union organization in Australia is occupational- or craft-based, as opposed to industry- or enterprise-based, the resolution of traditional labor-management issues has cut across industries to affect multiple employers. Employers complain that such a system prevents cooperation between one employer and its union employees, who should share an interest in the success of the enterprise.

In 1991, labor, management, and government in Australia began implementing a profound transition in industrial relations by shifting from the tribunal and central award system to enterprise-based agreements. The Industrial Relations Reform Act of 1993 streamlined collective bargaining and microeconomic labor market reform.[24]

In New Zealand, under a 1987 act, there were four ways to conduct the wage-fixing process. The first two were **awards** and **composite awards**, which are the result of a conciliation process. *Awards* involve multiemployers but single unions; *composite awards* involve multiemployers and multiunions. Both awards and composite awards could bind not only the parties to the settlement but also others in the same work.

Agreements and **composite agreements** were the second two ways to decide wages. These ways involved single-employer settlements and affected only the employer or employers who agreed to the settlement.

The Employment Contract Bill, passed in 1991, radically changed the industrial relations system in New Zealand. The system for compulsory arbitration of unsettled interest disputes, which resulted in an award's affecting the entire industry, was gone. Along with it was much of the incentive for multiemployer, industrywide agreement.

After 1991, when an award or an agreement expired, a negotiated contract took its place. Such negotiated contracts could be with individual employees as well as with a union. Until a negotiated contract was entered into, the workplace was governed by the expired award or agreement.[25]

This shift in government support from a compulsory system to a voluntary system resulted in an almost immediate decrease in the number of employees covered by collective bargaining agreements. The drop from 1990 to 1991 is reflected in Table 15-4.

| Table 15-4 | Decrease of Collective Bargaining Coverage by Settlement Type in New Zealand, 1990–1991 (in thousands of workers) |

	1990	1991	Percentage Decrease
Multiemployer settlement awards	484.2	340.4	
Composite awards	68.0	105.3	
Subtotal	552.2	445.7	19
Single-employer settlement agreements	149.9	134.8	
Composite agreements	19.3	29.7	
Subtotal	169.2	164.5	2.7
Total	721.4	610.2	15

Source: Adapted from Raymond Harbridge, "Collective Bargaining Coverage in New Zealand: The Impact of the Employment Contracts Bill," *Australian Bulletin of Labor* 17, no. 4 (April 1991), p. 318.

The Third World

Many Third World trade unions can trace their origins to 1947 when the Labour government gained power in Great Britain. The government sent labor organizers to many African countries to organize workers into trade unions. Although Africans were for the first time permitted to organize labor unions, they were still not permitted to be involved in politics. As a result, the African Mineworkers Union (AMU) was formed in 1947—the culmination of a long struggle by African miners to have their own union. The Third World has only recently taken interest in industrial democracy. In countries such as India, Pakistan, Peru, and Bangladesh, the movement for workers' participation in decision making came originally from the government and not from a trade union movement. The governments in developing countries often view codetermination as a method of reducing conflict between labor and management. In Zambia, for example, new government legislation created work councils to guarantee worker participation in decision making, improve working conditions, and promote industrial peace. Tradition in many African cultures makes it difficult to gain acceptance of such innovations in the workplace. In most communities, the chief and elders make all decisions; hence greater involvement by workers is not easily accomplished.[26]

Canada

Traditionally, labor relations in Canada followed that of the United States. In fact, in 1966, the percentage of workers in unions in the two countries was almost identical. In recent years, however, that has not been the case. In Canada, for example, approximately 33 percent of the nonagricultural workforce is unionized compared with about 15 percent in the United States. As the percentage steadily declined in the United States since the 1940s, the pattern was reversed in Canada, where more-collectivist traditions led to more-favorable political attitudes toward unions and thus a growth in the union movement. Another contributing factor is Canada's governmental and legal environment. For example, Canadian labor boards have the authority to (1) certify unions without formal elections; (2) make quick, final decisions on unfair labor practice cases; and (3) impose first contracts when employers refuse to bargain with a new union. Canadian labor laws have also provided public sector unions a stronger position by giving them the right to strike (in most instances) and the right to compulsory arbitration.

These stronger Canadian labor laws have resulted largely from the rise and success of a political party endorsed by organized labor—the Cooperative Commonwealth Federation, renamed the New Democratic Party in 1961. Although general public attitudes toward unions have declined similarly in Canada and the United States, Canadian unions have been more successful in passing favorable labor laws and are likely to continue to be a much stronger presence in their country in the future.[27] Figure 15-1 demonstrates the different growth pattern between U.S. and Canadian union membership. Three provinces of Canada have passed labor law reforms that ban the hiring of replacement workers on either a temporary or a permanent basis.[28] In fact, the Canada Labor Code maps out explicit support for trade unions for collective bargaining and compulsory conciliation as a dispute resolution method.[29]

Figure 15-1   Union Density in the United States and Canada, 1935–1995

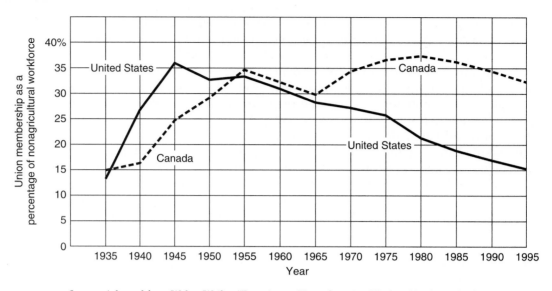

Source: Adapted from Walter Weiler, "Promises to Keep: Securing Workers' Rights to Self-Organization under the NLRA," *Harvard Law Review* 96 (1983), p. 1818. Copyright © 1983 by the Harvard Law Review Association, and the U.S. Dept. of Labor, 1997.

Mexico

Examination of labor relations in Mexico confirms the opinions cited previously that government encourages labor in times of crisis and when the economy is good and that developing nations encourage unions but limit their authority. At the time of the Mexican Revolution in 1917, the support of the laboring classes was essential to the success of the conflict. The Mexican constitution, therefore, expressly recognized the basic, inalienable rights of workers. Again, in 1968, the Mexican government called upon the workers' organizations to resist joining the "student movement," which was protesting the policies of the party in power. As a result of this support during a crisis, the 1970 Federal Labor Law was passed.

Unlike labor relations in the United States, however, the Mexican federal law gives rights to the individual employee not to the organization of employees. Mexico rejects the U.S. doctrine of "employee-at-will," and gives *every* worker the right to keep a job for a specified term unless terminated *for cause*.

The 1970 Federal Labor Law requires an individual employment contract for each worker, or presumes one if a document is never executed. The contract governs the employee's terms of employment, the services to be performed, the salary and benefits, and termination for cause only. What constitutes cause is spelled out in the law as well. A worker can be dismissed for such things as using false documents to get a job, being dishonest or violent on the job, negligently or intentionally damaging the employer's property, immoral or impaired behavior on the job, or three unexcused absences.

The law even spells out the worker's remedy if unjustly dismissed. The worker may request either to be reinstated or to be paid three months' salary in addition to any back pay owed. The Mexican Federal Labor Law mandates a year-end bonus, paid vacations and holidays, a profit-sharing plan for employees, and protection when businesses change ownership.[30]

Collective bargaining agreements are allowed under the law, but workers' rights cannot be *diminished* by any agreement. Such agreements are generally used for nationwide bargaining. Strikes are also allowed, although extensive regulation by the **Mexican Conciliation and Arbitration Board** severely limits their use.

In recent years, as a reaction to Mexico's economic crisis, national collective bargaining agreements have been used by labor, management, and the government to further the national goal of controlling inflation. With the economic recovery Mexico experienced in the early 1990s, and the possibility of positive results from the North American Free Trade Agreement, Mexican government leaders are anticipating changes in their nation's labor laws. Mexico's president, Dr. Carlos Salinas de Gortari, has acknowledged a need to modernize the labor relations process and has recognized that a healthy economy gives Mexico the opportunity to support workers' rights.[31]

North American Free Trade Agreement. The **North American Free Trade Agreement (NAFTA)** enacted by Congress in December 1993 created a "free trade zone" between the United States, Mexico, and Canada. The reason this zone was created is in large part an American reaction to Europe 1992. The implication for the United States if Europe 1992 is a success is one of opportunity and threat. U.S. companies need to take advantage of the new markets and growth opportunities in Europe or risk losing their competitiveness in the global economy.

The U.S. response to the consolidation of Europe's markets has been an increased effort to create a free-trade zone throughout North America. The U.S.–Canada Free Trade Agreement signed in 1988 and the passage of NAFTA in 1993 signaled the commitment of North American countries to remove artificial impediments to trade and investment on the continent.[32]

NAFTA, however, was not without critics. Unlike Europe 1992, NAFTA does not create a common market. A common market has a common external tariff, allows for labor mobility across borders, and coordinates the participating countries' economic policies. NAFTA deals only with the flow of goods, services, and investments among the three member nations.

As a matter of national priorities, NAFTA may have fallen short. In a nationwide *New York Times*–CBS poll conducted in late June 1993, just months before the expected vote on the agreement, 49 percent of Americans had never heard of the agreement.[33] Unfortunately, as information on NAFTA increased during the summer of 1993, support weakened. A heated debate began regarding the expected and anticipated effects of NAFTA, and labor unions led the organized opposition to U.S. participation in NAFTA.

Labor unions regarded NAFTA as a threat to union jobs in the United States. This threat could materialize in two ways. U.S. employers could move their operations to Mexico, where labor costs are cheaper, and U.S. wage earners could feel a drop in their wages as imports from Mexico increase in the U.S. market. On the issue of moving operations, however, supporters of NAFTA pointed out that relocations have already taken place. NAFTA's favorable trade policies should increase the exportation of U.S. goods and thereby help U.S. companies stay competitive. A healthy U.S. economy will increase jobs in the United States.

Some environmentalists and some church groups united against NAFTA. Environmentalists feared that weak environmental laws and their lax enforcement in Mexico would increase the pollution currently experienced on the U.S.–Mexican border. Church groups decried the human rights record of the Mexican government and considered the U.S. support of NAFTA as tacit support of these policies.[34] In response to the opposition of environmentalists, President Clinton dedicated $5 billion to fund an environmental cleanup along the U.S.–Mexican border. Despite the organized opposition and the heated exchanges during the Congressional debates about NAFTA, it passed the House of Representatives by a vote of 234 to 200, and the Senate by a vote of 61 to 38.[35]

MULTI-NATIONAL CORPORA-TIONS

U.S. companies, and therefore U.S. unions, interact in the global marketplace in a number of ways. Companies that have established offices or subsidiary companies abroad are the most noticeably *global*. They might be called **multinationals** or **transnationals**. These names indicate that the organization's activities are in more than one nation and culture. Partnerships, joint business ventures, and licensing agreements between U.S. companies and other national or international companies are also common ways that U.S. companies operate in the world economy.

U.S. companies are also in the world economy by competing in the United States with "foreign" businesses located here. The revolution in the U.S. auto industry caused by the growing number of Japanese auto companies locating in California, Indiana, Tennessee, and Kentucky cannot be ignored. Some of the issues Japanese companies have raised through their business practices in this country were discussed in previous chapters and can be seen in Case 15-1. U.S. companies find themselves competing in the worldwide economy through competition for a quality labor base.

Workers are no longer limited to their immediate surroundings. Travel and communication have increased so rapidly that there are no untappable labor pools. U.S. companies will need to have a large immigrant labor influx if they are to have a large enough worker base. With a more culturally diverse workforce, U.S. companies and unions will need to prepare to compete in the global economy in their own backyard.

U.S. labor unions are intimately affected by operation of U.S. companies internationally. A multinational or transnational corporation operates in one or more countries in addition to the country of its origin—its home country. The extent to which having multiple operations in different nations affects its identity depends on such things as how much of its operation is here or there, who owns and controls the operation, how it is "legally" organized, and who are its employees and managers.

Geography and Scope

Multinational corporation (MNC), *transnational organization*, and *global enterprise* are all terms used to describe businesses that operate in the international arenas. These are businesses that do more than just buy or sell abroad. Some significant portion of their operation is carried on across national borders. Case 15-2 gives an example of how complicated some business relationships can become in the global market.

Every business is housed at some specific location or locations within the boundaries of a nation. Typically, an organization identifies itself by that nation—a U.S. business, a German company, or a Japanese corporation. Multinational corporations are said to be "stateless." For an MNC to be stateless, either the coun-

APPLYING U.S. LAW ON FOREIGN EMPLOYERS

Quasar, located in the United States, is a division of a U.S. corporation wholly owned by a Japanese corporation. In 1986, 10 Japanese citizens, executives of Quasar, were in the United States on temporary visas. They were on loan, in effect, because they retained their status as employees of the Japanese corporation that owned Quasar.

The Japanese executive in charge of the Quasar company reorganized and discharged three American executives. Two Japanese executives were sent back to Japan but still had a job with the Japanese corporation. The Japanese executives who remained at Quasar received pay increases, but the American executives who were not discharged did not. Two of three Japanese-Americans who worked at Quasar were also dismissed.

The discharged American executives brought suit against Quasar for discrimination based on national origin. They contended they were fired because they were not Japanese. A lower court agreed and awarded a $3 million judgment against Quasar. The decision and the judgment were appealed.

Decision

The appeals court disagreed that the American executives were discharged because they were not Japanese as a *national origin* designation. It found that they were discharged because they were not *citizens* of Japan, a totally different basis and a discrimination that is *allowed* under a U.S. treaty with Japan.

The court noted that having Japanese ancestry did not help the Japanese-American workers who were discharged. The only actions that Quasar took regarding its employees were based on their being citizens of Japan.

Adapted from *Fortino v. Quasar Co.*, 950 F.2d 389 (7th Cir. 1991).

AN APPEAL OF AN INTERNATIONAL CASE

A contract dispute arose between Oriental Commercial, a Saudi Arabian corporation, and Rossell, a Belgian corporation. The parties agreed to submit the issue to arbitration and also agreed that an appeal to "confirm or vacate" the arbitration award would take place in the U.S. District Court, the Southern District of New York.

Despite that agreement, after Rossell won the arbitration, it sought to *enforce* the award in London, England. Oriental objected.

Decision

The court relied on an interpretation of the U.N. Convention to decide in Rossell's favor. Confirming or vacating an arbitration award is questioning the validity of the decision the arbitrator reached. Enforcement of an award is purely ministerial and can be done in *any* jurisdiction in which the parties can be found.

Adapted from *Oriental Commercial & Shipping Co., (U.K.), Ltd. v. Rossell, N.V.*, 769 F.Supp. 514 (S.D.N.Y. 1991).

Table 15-5   Examples of Multinational's International Presence

Company	Percentage of Assets *Outside* Home Country	Percentage of Total Number of Employees *Outside* Home Country
IBM (1989)	46	44
General Motors (1989)	24	31
duPont (1989)	35	24
General Electric (1989)	9	17

Source: Adapted from Yao-Su Hu, "Global or Stateless Corporations Are National Firms with International Operations," *California Management Review* 34, no. 2 (Winter 1992), p. 109. Copyright 1992 by the Regents of the University of California. Reprinted by permission.

try in which it operates has no influence on its operation, or *each* country in which it operates has an *equal* influence on its operation. One study disputes the likelihood that each country in which it operates has an equal influence on it by comparing a company's assets and number of employees in its *home country* with assets and employees outside its home country. Table 15-5 demonstrates that more than 50 percent of a company's assets and employees usually reside in the home country. As likely as not, outside-of-home-country operations will be distributed through many different countries so that the home country is still a *major influence* on the company's business.

Ownership and Control

Most multinational corporations operate as parent companies, located in the home country, with subsidiaries in one or more foreign countries. Under this structure the influence of the home country on the MNC is significant because it is most likely that the controlling shareholders of the parent corporation are citizens of the home country. Certainly with 100 percent ownership of the subsidiaries by the parent company, the home country exerts a significant influence on subsidiaries.

Ownership of subsidiaries by the parent company means that all profits of the subsidiaries belong to the parent company. The parent company can trade and deal in its home currency, which probably influences the MNC to keep investment in its home nation. Because subsidiaries are wholly owned by the parent corporation, the people of the foreign country in which it is located could not have any ownership interest in that company. Their control would be limited to what they might exert as employees.

Employees.   For most MNCs, more of its workers are citizens of the home country rather than of any other one country. Collectively, employees of its foreign operations may represent more than the home country employees, but no other one nationality will exceed its home base employees. Typically, the top management of an MNC's subsidiaries are home country nationals or host country nationals who have been proven compatible by working for the parent corporation in the home country. The laws concerning management-labor relations in the home country of a multinational corporation will have a major impact on the relationship throughout the corporation's activities.

Legal Site

A company is chartered or formed under a nation's laws. There is no "international" charter. Therefore, from a purely legal perspective, an MNC has to have a home country. In addition to labor-management laws, the home country of the MNC may raise questions about such things as which tax and environment laws apply to the subsidiaries, how security is to be managed, and to whom diplomatic allegiance is given. To the degree that the various components above exist within an MNC, its corporate culture will be influenced by the national culture of its home country.

SUMMARY

In the United States the future of labor unions and the collective bargaining process is uncertain. Union membership, public support, and political clout have diminished in recent years in the face of nonunion and foreign competition. Around the world, however, the collective rights of workers appear to be growing stronger. In the former Soviet Union, for example, there are opportunities for unions to participate in the enormous changes taking place. In Western Europe, the traditional highly centralized bargaining process is giving way to new-style agreements negotiated at the company level. Japanese workers are beginning to demand improved working conditions and lifestyles, while Third World workers are beginning to take an interest in labor relations. In Australia and New Zealand, unions are being challenged to undertake more collective bargaining duties.

The United States has begun a new relationship with Canada and Mexico as a result of the North American Free Trade Agreement. Whether that relationship encourages or discourages improvement in U.S. labor relations remains to be seen.

CASE STUDY 15-1

NLRB JURISDICTION OVER U.S. COMPANIES LOCATED ABROAD

Facts

The employer is headquartered in Louisiana and operates an oceangoing, U.S. flag vessel in Hong Kong's territorial waters. The employer has a million dollar dredging contract with the Hong Kong government and employs 12 Hong Kong crew members and 14 American crew members. Hong Kong labor laws require the hiring of a certain percentage of Hong Kong nationals, and the work permits issued to the American crew members were conditioned upon an agreement by the employer to lay off the American workers before the Hong Kong workers in case of a reduction in force. The employer had sought and received permission from the U.S. Coast Guard, which has laws mandating that U.S. flag vessels employ only Americans, to allow it to employ the Hong Kong workers in order to secure the dredging contract.

The union had filed a representation petition to allow for a union vote of the members of the crew before the vessel left American territory for Hong Kong. The NLRB ordered the election to be held by mail after the vessel was at its Hong Kong work site. The union won the election and tried to begin the collective

(continued)

bargaining negotiations. The employer refused and challenged the jurisdiction of the NLRB in federal court.

The employer's position was that the NLRB lacked jurisdiction because the vessel was being operated in Hong Kong territorial waters under a contract with the Hong Kong government and the employer had no plans to return the vessel to U.S. territory. The vessel, therefore, was not engaged "in commerce" as that term is used in the NLRA. In addition, because of the conflict between Hong Kong and U.S. labor laws, the NLRB should decline to assert any jurisdiction over the vessel because there are limitations over what the employer and the union would be allowed to negotiate.

The NLRB disagreed noting that it is a recognized tenet of international law that the law of the flag state ordinarily governs the internal affairs of the ship. In this instance, because the ship was an American owned and operated U.S. flag vessel, the NLRB considered it to be U.S. territory. It would not matter if the ship ever returned to the United States. The million dollar contract between the vessel and the

Hong Kong government or the employer (headquartered in Louisiana) and the Hong Kong government is sufficient to establish "commerce" under the act. The NLRB noted, as to the employer's second argument, that, although it might choose not to exert jurisdiction in situations in which the employees are subject to the laws of a foreign country, the majority of the employees in this case are American. The union and employer would have to arrive at a collective bargaining agreement that recognized the appropriate application of Hong Kong labor laws.

Questions

1. As the judge in this case, would you rule that the ship was covered by the NLRA? Why or why not?
2. How would the arguments and the decision change if the majority of the employees aboard the vessel were Hong Kong nationals instead of Americans?
3. Would you expect the union to be representing the Hong Kong workers as well as the American workers?

Adapted from *NLRB v. Dredge Operators*, 146 LRRM 2217 (1994).

CASE STUDY 15-2

NLRB JURISDICTION OVER FOREIGN CORPORATIONS

Facts

The State Bank of India operates branch offices in the United States and furnishes a full range of commercial banking services to the public. The local branches employ American residents in furtherance of these commercial ventures. Over 92 percent of the stock of the State Bank of India is owned by the Indian government.

In 1982, a union representing employees of the bank petitioned for a representation election. The bank objected to the election on the

basis that the NLRB had no authority over the bank. The bank used the following reasoning:

1. As an "instrumentality" of the Indian government, the bank is exempt from the definition of "employer" under the NLRB. The language relied on is ". . . but shall not include the United States or any wholly owned Government corporation. . . ." Previous Supreme Court decisions had interpreted that language to deny NLRB jurisdiction over foreign

ships with foreign employees docked temporarily in a U.S. port.

2. The Foreign Sovereign Immunities Act insulates a foreign nation from court actions against it in the United States.

The NLRB response to these two defenses was:

1. The employees of the bank were American residents and the bank's operation was not temporary.
2. The Foreign Sovereign Immunities Act exempts suits against foreign countries based on their "commercial objections."

Adapted from *State Bank of India v. NLRB*, 808 F.2d 526 (1987).

Questions

1. The top management of the State Bank of India would be located in India and be unfamiliar with U.S. labor relations. Is it fair to subject the bank to NLRA?
2. A U.S. bank has branches in India and operates under Indian labor laws. To what extent should the U.S. bank use NLRA to guide its actions?

KEY TERMS AND CONCEPTS

agreements and composite agreements
awards and composite awards
Canadian labor boards combinations
corporatism
The European Union
five pillars of Japanese labor relations
gaman
joint consultation committee (JCC)
Mexican Conciliation and Arbitration Board

multinationals
New Zealand Employment Contract Bill
North American Free Trade Agreement (NAFTA)
perestroika
Rengô
transnationals
work councils

REVIEW QUESTIONS

1. Describe the three stages of governmental reaction to unionization. Give reasons and examples for each stage.
2. What impact might the European Union have on labor relations in Western Europe?
3. Describe the five pillars of Japan's system of labor relations.
4. What new trends in Japan threaten its current labor relations process?
5. How do labor unions in newly industrialized and developing nations have the greatest impact?
6. What are the problems facing trade unionism in the former Soviet Union?
7. Explain why New Zealand has decentralized its labor relations process. Will Australia follow suit?
8. Why have Canadian unions continued to increase in membership while U.S. unions have decreased?
9. Explain the issues that were raised in support of and in opposition to the U.S. ratification of the North American Free Trade Agreement.
10. How might U.S. labor unions influence the attitudes of multinational corporations toward employees' rights?

We invite you to visit the Carrell/Heavrin page on the Prentice Hall Web site at:

http://www.prenhall.com/carrellr

for this chapter's World Wide Web exercise.

EXERCISE 15-1 | Other Nations' Labor Laws

Purpose:
For students to understand the differences between unions in the United States and in foreign countries.

Task:
Choose a nation *not* described in this chapter and using electronic and library resources research the labor-management relations in that country. Provide a written summary of its labor relations, history of unionization, and similarities and differences with U.S. labor relations.

EXERCISE 15-2 | Adapting U.S. Labor Relations

Purpose:
To demonstrate to students how U.S. labor relations might benefit by adopting laws or practices of other nations.

Task:
Divide the class into nine groups and assign each group one of the countries discussed in this chapter. Each group should borrow *one* idea from its country's labor relations approach and explain how it might improve U.S. labor-management relations. Share each group's suggestions with the class.

Texts of Statutes

National Labor Relations Act

Also cited NLRA or the Act; 29 U.S.C. §§151–169

[Title 29, Chapter 7, Subchapter II, United States Code]

FINDINGS AND POLICIES

Section 1. [§151.] The denial by some employers of the right of employees to organize and the refusal by some employers to accept the procedure of collective bargaining lead to strikes and other forms of industrial strife or unrest, which have the intent or the necessary effect of burdening or obstructing commerce by (a) impairing the efficiency, safety, or operation of the instrumentalities of commerce; (b) occurring in the current of commerce; (c) materially affecting, restraining, or controlling the flow of raw materials or manufactured or processed goods from or into the channels of commerce, or the prices of such materials or goods in commerce; or (d) causing diminution of employment and wages in such volume as substantially to impair or disrupt the market for goods flowing from or into the channels of commerce.

The inequality of bargaining power between employees who do not possess full freedom of association or actual liberty of contract and employers who are organized in the corporate or other forms of ownership association substantially burdens and affects the flow of commerce, and tends to aggravate recurrent business depressions, by depressing wage rates and the purchasing power of wage earners in industry and by preventing the stabilization of competitive wage rates and working conditions within and between industries.

Experience has proved that protection by law of the right of employees to organize and bargain collectively safeguards commerce from injury, impairment, or interruption, and promotes the flow of commerce by removing certain recognized sources of industrial strife and unrest, by encouraging practices fundamental to the friendly adjustment of industrial disputes arising out of differences as to wages, hours, or other working conditions, and by restoring equality of bargaining power between employers and employees.

Experience has further demonstrated that certain practices by some labor organizations, their officers, and members have the intent or the necessary effect of burdening or obstructing commerce by preventing the free flow of goods in such commerce through strikes and other forms of industrial unrest or through concerted activities which impair the interest of the public in the free flow of such commerce. The elimination of such practices is a necessary condition to the assurance of the rights herein guaranteed.

It is declared to be the policy of the United States to eliminate the causes of certain substantial obstructions to the free flow of commerce and to mitigate and eliminate these obstructions when they have occurred by encouraging the practice and procedure of collective bargaining and by protecting the exercise by workers of full freedom of association, self-organization, and designation of representatives of their own choosing, for the purpose of negotiating the terms and conditions of their employment or other mutual aid or protection.

DEFINITIONS

Sec. 2. [§152.] When used in this Act [subchapter]—

(1) The term "person" includes one or more individuals, labor organizations, partnerships, associations, corporations, legal representatives, trustees, trustees in cases under title 11 of the United States Code [under title 11], or receivers.

(2) The term "employer" includes any person acting as an agent of an employer, directly or indirectly, but shall not include the United States or any wholly owned Government corporation, or any Federal Reserve Bank, or any State or political subdivision thereof, or any person subject to the Railway Labor Act [45 U.S.C. §151 et seq.], as amended from time to time, or any labor organization (other than when acting as an employer), or anyone acting in the capacity of officer or agent of such labor organization.

[Pub. L. 93–360, §1(a), July 26, 1974, 88 Stat. 395, deleted the phrase "or any corporation or association operating a hospital, if no part of the net earnings inures to the benefit of any private shareholder or individual" from the definition of "employer."]

(3) The term "employee" shall include any employee, and shall not be limited to the employees of a particular employer, unless the Act [this subchapter] explicitly states otherwise, and shall include any individual whose work has ceased as a consequence of, or in connection with, any current labor dispute or because of any unfair labor practice, and who has not obtained any other regular and substantially equivalent employment, but shall not include any individual employed as an agricultural laborer, or in the domestic service of any family or person at his home, or any individual employed by his parent or spouse, or any individual having the status of an independent contractor, or any individual employed as a supervisor, or any individual employed by an employer subject to the Railway Labor Act [45 U.S.C. §151 et seq.], as amended from time to time, or by any other person who is not an employer as herein defined.

(4) The term "representatives" includes any individual or labor organization.

(5) The term "labor organization" means any organization of any kind, or any agency or employee representation committee or plan, in which employees participate and which exists for the purpose, in whole or in part, of dealing with

employers concerning grievances, labor disputes, wages, rates of pay, hours of employment, or conditions of work.

(6) The term "commerce" means trade, traffic, commerce, transportation or communication among the several States, or between the District of Columbia or any Territory of the United States and any State or other Territory, or between any foreign country and any State, Territory, or the District of Columbia, or within the District of Columbia or any Territory, or between points in the same State but through any other State or any Territory or the District of Columbia or any foreign country.

(7) The term "affecting commerce" means in commerce, or burdening or obstructing commerce or the free flow of commerce, or having led or tending to lead to a labor dispute burdening or obstructing commerce or the free flow of commerce.

(8) The term "unfair labor practice" means any unfair labor practice listed in section 8 [section 158 of this title].

(9) The term "labor dispute" includes any controversy concerning term, tenure or conditions of employment, or concerning the association or representation of persons in negotiating, fixing, maintaining, changing, or seeking to arrange terms or conditions of employment, regardless of whether the disputants stand in the proximate relation of employer and employee.

(10) The term "National Labor Relations Board" means the National Labor Relations Board provided for in section 3 of this Act [section 153 of this title].

(11) The term "supervisor" means any individual having authority, in the interest of the employer, to hire, transfer, suspend, lay off, recall, promote, discharge, assign, reward, or discipline other employees, or responsibly to direct them, or to adjust their grievances, or effectively to recommend such action, if in connection with the foregoing the exercise of such authority is not of a merely routine or clerical nature, but requires the use of independent judgment.

(12) The term "professional employee" means—

(a) any employee engaged in work (i) predominantly intellectual and varied in character as opposed to routine mental, manual, mechanical, or physical work; (ii) involving the consistent exercise of discretion and judgment in its performance; (iii) of such a character that the output produced or the result accomplished cannot be standardized in relation to a given period of time; (iv) requiring knowledge of an advanced type in a field of science or learning customarily acquired by a prolonged course of specialized intellectual instruction and study in an institution of higher learning or a hospital, as distinguished from a general academic education or from an apprenticeship or from training in the performance of routine mental, manual, or physical processes; or

(b) any employee, who (i) has completed the courses of specialized intellectual instruction and study described in clause (iv) of paragraph (a), and (ii) is performing related work under the supervision of a professional person to qualify himself to become a professional employee as defined in paragraph (a).

(13) In determining whether any person is acting as an "agent" of another person so as to make such other person responsible for his acts, the question of whether the specific acts performed were actually authorized or subsequently ratified shall not be controlling.

(14) The term "health care institution" shall include any hospital, convalescent hospital, health maintenance organization, health clinic, nursing home, extended care facility, or other institution devoted to the care of sick, infirm, or aged person.

[Pub. L. 93–360, §1(b), July 26, 1974, 88 Stat. 395, added par. (14).]

NATIONAL LABOR RELATIONS BOARD

Sec. 3. [§153.] (a) [Creation, composition, appointment, and tenure; Chairman; removal of members] The National Labor Relations Board (hereinafter called the "Board") created by this Act [subchapter] prior to its amendment by the Labor Management Relations Act, 1947 [29 U.S.C. §141 et seq.], is continued as an agency of the United States, except that the Board shall consist of five instead of three members, appointed by the President by and with the advice and consent of the Senate. Of the two additional members so provided for, one shall be appointed for a term of five years and the other for a term of two years. Their successors, and the successors of the other members, shall be appointed for terms of five years each, excepting that any individual chosen to fill a vacancy shall be appointed only for the unexpired term of the member whom he shall succeed. The President shall designate one member to serve as Chairman of the Board. Any member of the Board may be removed by the President, upon notice and hearing, for neglect of duty or malfeasance in office, but for no other cause.

(b) [Delegation of powers to members and regional directors; review and stay of actions of regional directors; quorum; seal] The Board is authorized to delegate to any group of three or more members any or all of the powers which it may itself exercise. The Board is also authorized to delegate to its regional directors its powers under section 9 [section 159 of this title] to determine the unit appropriate for the purpose of collective bargaining, to investigate and provide for hearings, and determine whether a question of representation exists, and to direct an election or take a secret ballot under subsection (c) or (e) of section 9 [section 159 of this title] and certify the results thereof, except that upon the filling of a request therefor with the Board by any interested person, the Board may review any action of a regional director delegated to him under this paragraph, but such a review shall not, unless specifically ordered by the Board, operate as a stay of any action taken by the regional director. A vacancy in the Board shall not impair the right of the remaining members to exercise all of the powers of the Board, and three members of the Board shall, at all times, constitute a quorum of the Board, except that two members shall constitute a quorum of any group designated pursuant to the first sentence hereof. The Board shall have an official seal which shall be judicially noticed.

(c) [Annual reports to Congress and the President] The Board shall at the close of each fiscal year make a report in writing to Congress and to the President summarizing significant case activities and operations for that fiscal year.

(d) [General Counsel; appointment and tenure; powers and duties; vacancy] There shall be a General Counsel of the Board who shall be appointed by the President, by and with the advice and consent of the Senate, for a term of four years. The General Counsel of the Board shall exercise general supervision over all attorneys employed by the Board (other than administrative law judges and legal assistants to Board members) and over the officers and employees in the regional offices. He shall have final authority, on behalf of the Board, in respect of the investigation of charges and issuance of complaints under section 10 [section

160 of this title], and in respect of the prosecution of such complaints before the Board, and shall have such other duties as the Board may prescribe or as may be provided by law. In case of vacancy in the office of the General Counsel the President is authorized to designate the officer or employee who shall act as General Counsel during such vacancy, but no person or persons so designated shall so act (1) for more than forty days when the Congress is in session unless a nomination to fill such vacancy shall have been submitted to the Senate, or (2) after the adjournment sine die of the session of the Senate in which such nomination was submitted.

[The title "administrative law judge" was adopted in 5 U.S.C. §3105.]

Sec. 4. [§154. Eligibility for reappointment; officers and employees; payment of expenses] (a) Each member of the Board and the General Counsel of the Board shall be eligible for reappointment, and shall not engage in any other business, vocation, or employment. The Board shall appoint an executive secretary, and such attorneys, examiners, and regional directors, and such other employees as it may from time to time find necessary for the proper performance of its duties. The Board may not employ any attorneys for the purpose of reviewing transcripts of hearings or preparing drafts of opinions except that any attorney employed for assignment as a legal assistant to any Board member may for such Board member review such transcripts and prepare such drafts. No administrative law judge's report shall be reviewed, either before or after its publication, by any person other than a member of the Board or his legal assistant, and no administrative law judge shall advise or consult with the Board with respect to exceptions taken to his findings, rulings, or recommendations. The Board may establish or utilize such regional, local, or other agencies, and utilize such voluntary and uncompensated services, as may from time to time be needed. Attorneys appointed under this section may, at the direction of the Board, appear for and represent the Board in any case in court. Nothing in this Act [subchapter] shall be construed to authorize the Board to appoint individuals for the purpose of conciliation or mediation, or for economic analysis.

[The title "administrative law judge" was adopted in 5 U.S.C. §3105.]

(b) All of the expenses of the Board, including all necessary traveling and subsistence expenses outside the District of Columbia incurred by the members or employees of the Board under its orders, shall be allowed and paid on the presentation of itemized vouchers therefore approved by the Board or by any individual it designates for that purpose.

Sec. 5. [§155. Principal office, conducting inquiries throughout country; participation in decisions or inquiries conducted by member] The principal office of the Board shall be in the District of Columbia, but it may meet and exercise any or all of its powers at any other place. The Board may, by one or more of its members or by such agents or agencies as it may designate, prosecute any inquiry necessary to its functions in any part of the United States. A member who participates in such an inquiry shall not be disqualified from subsequently participating in a decision of the Board in the same case.

Sec. 6. [§156. Rules and regulations] The Board shall have authority from time to time to make, amend, and rescind, in the manner prescribed by the Administrative Procedure Act [by subchapter II of chapter 5 of title 5], such rules and regulations as may be necessary to carry out the provisions of this Act [subchapter].

Sec. 7. [§157.] Employees shall have the right to self-organization, to form, join, or assist labor organizations, to bargain collectively through representatives of their own choosing, and to engage in other concerted activities for the purpose of collective bargaining or other mutual aid or protection, and shall also have the right to refrain from any or all such activities except to the extent that such right may be affected by an agreement requiring membership in a labor organization as a condition of employment as authorized in section 8(a)(3) [section 158(a)(3) of this title].

UNFAIR LABOR PRACTICES

Sec. 8. [§158.] (a) [Unfair labor practices by employer] It shall be an unfair labor practice for an employer—

(1) to interfere with, restrain, or coerce employees in the exercise of the rights guaranteed in section 7 [section 157 of this title];

(2) to dominate or interfere with the formation or administration of any labor organization or contribute financial or other support to it: Provided, That subject to rules and regulations made and published by the Board pursuant to section 6 [section 156 of this title], an employer shall not be prohibited from permitting employees to confer with him during working hours without loss of time or pay;

(3) by discrimination in regard to hire or tenure of employment or any term or condition of employment to encourage or discourage membership in any labor organization: Provided, That nothing in this Act [subchapter], or in any other statute of the United States, shall preclude an employer from making an agreement with a labor organization (not established, maintained, or assisted by any action defined in section 8(a) of this Act [in this subsection] as an unfair labor practice) to require as a condition of employment membership therein on or after the thirtieth day following the beginning of such employment or the effective date of such agreement, whichever is the later, (i) if such labor organization is the representative of the employees as provided in section 9(a) [section 159(a) of this title], in the appropriate collective-bargaining unit covered by such agreement when made, and (ii) unless following an election held as provided in section 9(e) [section 159(e) of this title] within one year preceding the effective date of such agreement, the Board shall have certified that at least a majority of the employees eligible to vote in such election have voted to rescind the authority of such labor organization to make such an agreement: Provided further, That no employer shall justify any discrimination against an employee for nonmembership in a labor organization (A) if he has reasonable grounds for believing that such membership was not available to the employee on the same terms and conditions generally applicable to other members, or (B) if he has reasonable grounds for believing that membership was denied or terminated for reasons other than the failure of the employee to tender the periodic dues and the initiation fees uniformly required as a condition of acquiring or retaining membership;

(4) to discharge or otherwise discriminate against an employee because he has filed charges or given testimony under this Act [subchapter];

(5) to refuse to bargain collectively with the representatives of his employees, subject to the provisions of section 9(a) [section 159(a) of this title].

(b) [Unfair labor practices by labor organization] It shall be an unfair labor practice for a labor organization or its agents—

---

(1) to restrain or coerce (A) employees in the exercise of the rights guaranteed in section 7 [section 157 of this title]: Provided, That this paragraph shall not impair the right of a labor organization to prescribe its own rules with respect to the acquisition or retention of membership therein; or (B) an employer in the selection of his representatives for the purposes of collective bargaining or the adjustment of grievances;

(2) to cause or attempt to cause an employer to discriminate against an employee in violation of subsection (a)(3) [of subsection (a)(3) of this section] or to discriminate against an employee with respect to whom membership in such organization has been denied or terminated on some ground other than his failure to tender the periodic dues and the initiation fees uniformly required as a condition of acquiring or retaining membership;

(3) to refuse to bargain collectively with an employer, provided it is the representative of his employees subject to the provisions of section 9(a) [section 159(a) of this title];

(4)(i) to engage in, or to induce or encourage any individual employed by any person engaged in commerce or in an industry affecting commerce to engage in, a strike or a refusal in the course of his employment to use, manufacture, process, transport, or otherwise handle or work on any goods, articles, materials, or commodities or to perform any services; or (ii) to threaten, coerce, or restrain any person engaged in commerce or in an industry affecting commerce, where in either case an object thereof is—

(A) forcing or requiring any employer or self-employed person to join any labor or employer organization or to enter into any agreement which is prohibited by section 8(e) [subsection (e) of this section];

(B) forcing or requiring any person to cease using, selling, handling, transporting, or otherwise dealing in the products of any other producer, processor, or manufacturer, or to cease doing business with any other person, or forcing or requiring any other employer to recognize or bargain with a labor organization as the representative of his employees unless such labor organization has been certified as the representative of such employees under the provisions of section 9 [section 159 of this title]: Provided, That nothing contained in this clause (B) shall be construed to make unlawful, where not otherwise unlawful, any primary strike or primary picketing;

(C) forcing or requiring any employer to recognize or bargain with a particular labor organization as the representative of his employees if another labor organization has been certified as the representative of such employees under the provisions of section 9 [section 159 of this title];

(D) forcing or requiring any employer to assign particular work to employees in a particular labor organization or in a particular trade, craft, or class rather than to employees in another labor organization or in another trade, craft, or class, unless such employer is failing to conform to an order or certification of the Board determining the bargaining representative for employees performing such work:

Provided, That nothing contained in this subsection (b) [this subsection] shall be construed to make unlawful a refusal by any person to enter upon the premises of any employer (other than his own employer), if the employees of such employer are engaged in a strike ratified or approved by a representative of such employees whom such employer is required to recognize under this Act [subchapter]: Provided further, That for the purposes of this paragraph (4) only, nothing contained in such paragraph shall be construed to prohibit publicity, other than picketing, for the purpose of truthfully advising the public, including consumers and members of a labor organization, that a product or products are produced by an employer with whom the labor organization has a primary dispute and are distributed by another employer, as long as such publicity does not have an effect of inducing any individual employed by any person other than the primary employer in the course of his employment to refuse to pick up, deliver, or transport any goods, or not to perform any services, at the establishment of the employer engaged in such distribution;

(5) to require of employees covered by an agreement authorized under subsection (a)(3) [of this section] the payment, as a condition precedent to becoming a member of such organization, of a fee in an amount which the Board finds excessive or discriminatory under all the circumstances. In making such a finding, the Board shall consider, among other relevant factors, the practices and customs of labor organizations in the particular industry, and the wages currently paid to the employees affected;

(6) to cause or attempt to cause an employer to pay or deliver or agree to pay or deliver any money or other thing of value, in the nature of an exaction, for services which are not performed or not to be performed; and

(7) to picket or cause to be picketed, or threaten to picket or cause to be picketed, any employer where an object thereof is forcing or requiring an employer to recognize or bargain with a labor organization as the representative of his employees, or forcing or requiring the employees of an employer to accept or select such labor organization as their collective-bargaining representative, unless such labor organization is currently certified as the representative of such employees:

(A) where the employer has lawfully recognized in accordance with this Act [subchapter] any other labor organization and a question concerning representation may not appropriately be raised under section 9(c) of this Act [section 159(c) of this title],

(B) where within the preceding twelve months a valid election under section 9(c) of this Act [section 159(c) of this title] has been conducted, or

(C) where such picketing has been conducted without a petition under section 9(c) [section 159(c) of this title] being filed within a reasonable period of time not to exceed thirty days from the commencement of such picketing: Provided, That when such a petition has been filed the Board shall forthwith, without regard to the provisions of section 9(c)(1) [section 159(c)(1) of this title] or the absence of a showing of a substantial interest on the part of the labor organization, direct an election in such unit as the Board finds to be appropriate and shall certify the results thereof: Provided further, That nothing in this subparagraph (C) shall be construed to prohibit any picketing or other publicity for the purpose of truthfully advising the public (including consumers) that an employer does not employ members of, or have a contract with, a labor organization, unless an effect of such picketing is to induce any individual employed by any other person in the course of his employment, not to pick up, deliver or transport any goods or not to perform any services.

Nothing in this paragraph (7) shall be construed to permit any act which would otherwise be an unfair labor practice under this section 8(b) [this subsection].

(c) [Expression of views without threat of reprisal or force or promise of benefit] The expressing of any views, argument, or opinion, or the dissemination thereof, whether in written, printed, graphic, or visual form, shall not constitute or be evidence of an unfair labor practice under any of the provisions of this Act [subchapter], if such expression contains no threat of reprisal or force or promise of benefit.

(d) [Obligation to bargain collectively] For the purposes of this section, to bargain collectively is the performance of the mutual obligation of the employer and the representative of the employees to meet at reasonable times and confer in good faith with respect to wages, hours, and other terms and conditions of employment, or the negotiation of an agreement or any question arising thereunder, and the execution of a written contract incorporating any agreement reached if requested by either party, but such obligation does not compel either party to agree to a proposal or require the making of a concession: Provided, That where there is in effect a collective-bargaining contract covering employees in an industry affecting commerce, the duty to bargain collectively shall also mean that no party to such contract shall terminate or modify such contract, unless the party desiring such termination or modification—

(1) serves a written notice upon the other party to the contract of the proposed termination or modification sixty days prior to the expiration date thereof, or in the event such contract contains no expiration date, sixty days prior to the time it is proposed to make such termination or modification;

(2) offers to meet and confer with the other party for the purpose of negotiating a new contract or a contract containing the proposed modifications;

(3) notifies the Federal Mediation and Conciliation Service within thirty days after such notice of the existence of a dispute, and simultaneously therewith notifies any State or Territorial agency established to mediate and conciliate disputes within the State or Territory where the dispute occurred, provided no agreement has been reached by that time; and

(4) continues in full force and effect, without resorting to strike or lockout, all the terms and conditions of the existing contract for a period of sixty days after such notice is given or until the expiration date of such contract, whichever occurs later:

The duties imposed upon employers, employees, and labor organizations by paragraphs (2), (3), and (4) [paragraphs (2) to (4) of this subsection] shall become inapplicable upon an intervening certification of the Board, under which the labor organization or individual, which is a party to the contract, has been superseded as or ceased to be the representative of the employees subject to the provisions of section 9(a) [section 159(a) of this title], and the duties so imposed shall not be construed as requiring either party to discuss or agree to any modification of the terms and conditions contained in a contract for a fixed period, if such modification is to become effective before such terms and conditions can be reopened under the provisions of the contract. Any employee who engages in a strike within any notice period specified in this subsection, or who engages in any strike within the appropriate period specified in subsection (g) of this section, shall lose his status as an employee of the employer engaged in the particular labor dispute, for the purposes of sections 8, 9, and 10 of this Act [sections 158, 159, and 160 of this title], but such loss of status for such employee shall terminate if and when he is reemployed by such employer. Whenever the collective bargaining involves employees of a health care institution, the provisions of this section 8(d) [this subsection] shall be modified as follows:

(A) The notice of section 8(d)(1) [paragraph (1) of this subsection] shall be ninety days; the notice of section 8(d)(3) [paragraph (3) of this subsection] shall be sixty days; and the contract period of section 8(d)(4) [paragraph (4) of this subsection] shall be ninety days.

(B) Where the bargaining is for an initial agreement following certification or recognition, at least thirty days' notice of the existence of a dispute shall be given by the labor organization to the agencies set forth in section 8(d)(3) [in paragraph (3) of this subsection].

(C) After notice is given to the Federal Mediation and Conciliation Service under either clause (A) or (B) of this sentence, the Service shall promptly communicate with the parties and use its best efforts, by mediation and conciliation, to bring them to agreement. The parties shall participate fully and promptly in such meetings as may be undertaken by the Service for the purpose of aiding in a settlement of the dispute.

[Pub. L. 93–360, July 26, 1974, 88 Stat. 395, amended the last sentence of Sec. 8(d) by striking the words "the sixty-day" and inserting the words "any notice" and by inserting before the words "shall lose" the phrase ", or who engages in any strike within the appropriate period specified in subsection (g) of this section." It also amended the end of paragraph Sec. 8(d) by adding a new sentence "Whenever the collective bargaining ... aiding in a settlement of the dispute."]

(e) [Enforceability of contract or agreement to boycott any other employer; exception] It shall be an unfair labor practice for any labor organization and any employer to enter into any contract or agreement, express or implied, whereby such employer ceases or refrains or agrees to cease or refrain from handling, using, selling, transporting or otherwise dealing in any of the products of any other employer, or cease doing business with any other person, and any contract or agreement entered into heretofore or hereafter containing such an agreement shall be to such extent unenforceable and void: Provided, That nothing in this subsection (e) [this subsection] shall apply to an agreement between a labor organization and an employer in the construction industry relating to the contracting or subcontracting of work to be done at the site of the construction, alteration, painting, or repair of a building, structure, or other work: Provided further, That for the purposes of this subsection (e) and section 8(b)(4)(B) [this subsection and subsection (b)(4)(B) of this section] the terms "any employer," "any person engaged in commerce or an industry affecting commerce," and "any person" when used in relation to the terms "any other producer, processor, or manufacturer," "any other employer," or "any other person" shall not include persons in the relation of a jobber, manufacturer, contractor, or subcontractor working on the goods or premises of the jobber or manufacturer or performing parts of an integrated process of production in the apparel and clothing industry: Provided further, That nothing in this Act [subchapter] shall prohibit the enforcement of any agreement which is within the foregoing exception.

(f) [Agreements covering employees in the building and construction industry] It shall not be an unfair labor practice under subsections (a) and (b) of this section for an employer engaged primarily in the building and construction industry to make an agreement covering employees engaged (or who, upon their employment, will be engaged) in the building and construction industry with a labor organization of which building and construction employees are members (not established, maintained, or assisted by any action defined in section 8(a) of this Act [subsection (a) of this section] as an unfair labor practice) because (1) the majority status of such labor organization has not been established under the provisions of section 9 of this Act [section 159 of this title] prior to the making of such agreement, or (2) such agreement requires as a condition of employment, membership in such labor organization after the seventh day following the beginning of such employment or the effective date of the agreement, whichever is later, or (3) such agreement requires the employer to notify such labor organization of opportunities for employment with such employer, or gives such labor organization an opportunity to refer qualified applicants for such employment, or (4) such agreement specifies minimum training or experience qualifications for employment or provides for priority in opportunities for employment based upon length of service with such employer, in the industry or in the particular geographical area: Provided, That nothing in this subsection shall set aside the final proviso to section 8(a)(3) of this Act [subsection (a)(3) of this section]: Provided further, That any agreement which would be invalid, but for clause (1) of this subsection, shall not be a bar to a petition filed pursuant to section 9(c) or 9(e) [section 159(c) or 159(e) of this title].

(g) [Notification of intention to strike or picket at any health care institution] A labor organization before engaging in any strike, picketing, or other concerted refusal to work at any health care institution shall, not less than ten days prior to such action, notify the institution in writing and the Federal Mediation and Conciliation Service of that intention, except that in the case of bargaining for an initial agreement following certification or recognition the notice required by this subsection shall not be given until the expiration of the period specified in clause (B) of the last sentence of section 8(d) of this Act [subsection (d) of this section]. The notice shall state the date and time that such action will commence. The notice, once given, may be extended by the written agreement of both parties.

[Pub. L. 93–360, July 26, 1974, 88 Stat. 396, added subsec. (g).]

REPRESENTATIVES AND ELECTIONS

Sec. 9 [§159.] (a) [Exclusive representatives; employees' adjustment of grievances directly with employer] Representatives designated or selected for the purposes of collective bargaining by the majority of the employees in a unit appropriate for such purposes, shall be the exclusive representatives of all the employees in such unit for the purposes of collective bargaining in respect to rates of pay, wages, hours of employment, or other conditions of employment: Provided, That any individual employee or a group of employees shall have the right at any time to present grievances to their employer and to have such grievances adjusted, without the intervention of the bargaining representative, as long as the adjustment is not inconsistent with the terms of a collective-bargaining contract or agreement then in effect: Provided further, That the bargaining representative has been given opportunity to be present at such adjustment.

(b) [Determination of bargaining unit by Board] The Board shall decide in each case whether, in order to assure to employees the fullest freedom in exercising the rights guaranteed by this Act [subchapter], the unit appropriate for the purposes of collective bargaining shall be the employer unit, craft unit, plant unit, or subdivision thereof: Provided, That the Board shall not (1) decide that any unit is appropriate for such purposes if such unit includes both professional employees and employees who are not professional employees unless a majority of such professional employees vote for inclusion in such unit; or (2) decide that any craft unit is inappropriate for such purposes on the ground that a different unit has been established by a prior Board determination, unless a majority of the employees in the proposed craft unit votes against separate representation or (3) decide that any unit is appropriate for such purposes if it includes, together with other employees, any individual employed as a guard to enforce against employees and other persons rules to protect property of the employer or to protect the safety of persons on the employer's premises; but no labor organization shall be certified as the representative of employees in a bargaining unit of guards if such organization admits to membership, or is affiliated directly or indirectly with an organization which admits to membership, employees other than guards.

(c) [Hearing on questions affecting commerce; rules and regulations] (1) Whenever a petition shall have been filed, in accordance with such regulations as may be prescribed by the Board—

(A) by an employee or group of employees or any individual or labor organization acting in their behalf alleging that a substantial number of employees (i) wish to be represented for collective bargaining and that their employer declines to recognize their representative as the representative defined in section 9(a) [subsection (a) of this section], or (ii) assert that the individual or labor organization, which has been certified or is being currently recognized by their employer as the bargaining representative, is no longer a representative as defined in section 9(a) [subsection (a) of this section]; or

(B) by an employer, alleging that one or more individuals or labor organizations have presented to him a claim to be recognized as the representative defined in section 9(a) [subsection (a) of this section]; the Board shall investigate such petition and if it has reasonable cause to believe that a question of representation affecting commerce exists shall provide for an appropriate hearing upon due notice. Such hearing may be conducted by an officer or employee of the regional office, who shall not make any recommendations with respect thereto. If the Board finds upon the record of such hearing that such a question of representation exists, it shall direct an election by secret ballot and shall certify the results thereof.

(2) In determining whether or not a question of representation affecting commerce exists, the same regulations and rules of decision shall apply irrespective of the identity of the persons filing the petition or the kind of relief sought and in no case shall the Board deny a labor organization a place on the ballot by reason of an order with respect to such labor organization or its predecessor not issued in conformity with section 10(c) [section 160(c) of this title].

(3) No election shall be directed in any bargaining unit or any subdivision within which, in the preceding twelve-month period, a valid election shall have been held. Employees engaged in an economic strike who are not entitled to reinstatement shall be eligible to vote under such regulations as the Board shall find are consistent with the purposes and provisions of this Act [subchapter] in any election conducted within twelve months after the commencement of the strike. In any election where none of the choices on the ballot receives a majority, a run-off shall be conducted, the ballot providing for a selection between the two choices receiving the largest and second largest number of valid votes cast in the election.

(4) Nothing in this section shall be construed to prohibit the waiving of hearings by stipulation for the purpose of a consent election in conformity with regulations and rules of decision of the Board.

(5) In determining whether a unit is appropriate for the purposes specified

in subsection (b) [of this section] the extent to which the employees have organized shall not be controlling.

(d) [Petition for enforcement or review; transcript] Whenever an order of the Board made pursuant to section 10(c) [section 160(c) of this title] is based in whole or in part upon facts certified following an investigation pursuant to subsection (c) of this section and there is a petition for the enforcement or review of such order, such certification and the record of such investigation shall be included in the transcript of the entire record required to be filed under section 10(e) or 10(f) [subsection (e) or (f) of section 160 of this title], and thereupon the decree of the court enforcing, modifying, or setting aside in whole or in part the order of the Board shall be made and entered upon the pleadings, testimony, and proceedings set forth in such transcript.

(e) [Secret ballot; limitation of elections] (1) Upon the filing with the Board, by 30 per centum or more of the employees in a bargaining unit covered by an agreement between their employer and labor organization made pursuant to section 8(a)(3) [section 158(a)(3) of this title], of a petition alleging they desire that such authorization be rescinded, the Board shall take a secret ballot of the employees in such unit and certify the results thereof to such labor organization and to the employer.

(2) No election shall be conducted pursuant to this subsection in any bargaining unit or any subdivision within which, in the preceding twelve-month period, a valid election shall have been held.

PREVENTION OF UNFAIR LABOR PRACTICES

Sec. 10. [§160.] (a) [Powers of Board generally] The Board is empowered, as hereinafter provided, to prevent any person from engaging in any unfair labor practice (listed in section 8 [section 158 of this title]) affecting commerce. This power shall not be affected by any other means of adjustment or prevention that has been or may be established by agreement, law or otherwise: Provided, That the Board is empowered by agreement with any agency of any State or Territory to cede to such agency jurisdiction over any cases in any industry (other than mining, manufacturing, communications, and transportation except where predominately local in character) even though such cases may involve labor disputes affecting commerce, unless the provision of the State or Territorial statute applicable to the determination of such cases by such agency is inconsistent with the corresponding provision of this Act [subchapter] or has received a construction inconsistent therewith.

(b) [Complaint and notice of hearing; six-month limitation; answer; court rules of evidence inapplicable] Whenever it is charged that any person has engaged in or is engaging in any such unfair labor practice, the Board, or any agent or agency designated by the Board for such purposes, shall have power to issue and cause to be served upon such person a complaint stating the charges in that respect, and containing a notice of hearing before the Board or a member thereof, or before a designated agent or agency, at a place therein fixed, not less than five days after the serving of said complaint: Provided, That no complaint shall issue based upon any unfair labor practice occurring more than six months prior to the filing of the charge with the Board and the service of a copy thereof upon the person against whom such charge is made, unless the person aggrieved thereby was prevented from filing such charge by reason of service in the armed forces, in which event the six-month period shall be computed from the day of his discharge. Any such complaint may be amended by the member, agent, or agency conducting the hearing or the Board in its discretion at any time prior to the issuance of an order based thereon. The person so complained of shall have the right to file an answer to the original or amended complaint and to appear in person or otherwise and give testimony at the place and time fixed in the complaint. In the discretion of the member, agent, or agency conducting the hearing or the Board, any other person may be allowed to intervene in the said proceeding and to present testimony. Any such proceeding shall, so far as practicable, be conducted in accordance with the rules of evidence applicable in the district courts of the United States under the rules of civil procedure for the district courts of the United States, adopted by the Supreme Court of the United States pursuant to section 2072 of title 28, United States Code [section 2072 of title 28].

(c) [Reduction of testimony to writing; findings and orders of Board] The testimony taken by such member, agent, or agency or the Board shall be reduced to writing and filed with the Board. Thereafter, in its discretion, the Board upon notice may take further testimony or hear argument. If upon the preponderance of the testimony taken the Board shall be of the opinion that any person named in the complaint has engaged in or is engaging in any such unfair labor practice, then the Board shall state its findings of fact and shall issue and cause to be served on such person an order requiring such person to cease and desist from such unfair labor practice, and to take such affirmative action including reinstatement of employees with or without back pay, as will effectuate the policies of this Act [subchapter]: Provided, That where an order directs reinstatement of an employee, back pay may be required of the employer or labor organization, as the case may be, responsible for the discrimination suffered by him: And provided further, That in determining whether a complaint shall issue alleging a violation of section 8(a)(1) or section 8(a)(2) [subsection (a)(1) or (a)(2) of section 158 of this title], and in deciding such cases, the same regulations and rules of decision shall apply irrespective of whether or not the labor organization affected is affiliated with a labor organization national or international in scope. Such order may further require such person to make reports from time to time showing the extent to which it has complied with the order. If upon the preponderance of the testimony taken the Board shall not be of the opinion that the person named in the complaint has engaged in or is engaging in any such unfair labor practice, then the Board shall state its findings of fact and shall issue an order dismissing the said complaint. No order of the Board shall require the reinstatement of any individual as an employee who has been suspended or discharged, or the payment to him of any back pay, if such individual was suspended or discharged for cause. In case the evidence is presented before a member of the Board, or before an administrative law judge or judges thereof, such member, or such judge or judges, as the case may be, shall issue and cause to be served on the parties to the proceeding a proposed report, together with a recommended order, which shall be filed with the Board, and if no exceptions are filed within twenty days after service thereof upon such parties, or within such further period as the Board may authorize, such recommended order shall become the order of the Board and become affective as therein prescribed.

[The title "administrative law judge" was adopted in 5 U.S.C. §3105.]

(d) [Modification of findings or orders prior to filing record in court] Until the record in a case shall have been filed in a court, as hereinafter provided, the

Board may at any time, upon reasonable notice and in such manner as it shall deem proper, modify or set aside, in whole or in part, any finding or order made or issued by it.

(e) [Petition to court for enforcement of order; proceedings; review of judgment] The Board shall have power to petition any court of appeals of the United States, or if all the courts of appeals to which application may be made are in vacation, any district court of the United States, within any circuit or district, respectively, wherein the unfair labor practice in question occurred or wherein such person resides or transacts business, for the enforcement of such order and for appropriate temporary relief or restraining order, and shall file in the court the record in the proceeding, as provided in section 2112 of title 28, United States Code [section 2112 of title 28]. Upon the filing of such petition, the court shall cause notice thereof to be served upon such person, and thereupon shall have jurisdiction of the proceeding and of the question determined therein, and shall have power to grant such temporary relief or restraining order as it deems just and proper, and to make and enter a decree enforcing, modifying and enforcing as so modified, or setting aside in whole or in part the order of the Board. No objection that has not been urged before the Board, its member, agent, or agency, shall be considered by the court, unless the failure or neglect to urge such objection shall be excused because of extraordinary circumstances. The findings of the Board with respect to questions of fact if supported by substantial evidence on the record considered as a whole shall be conclusive. If either party shall apply to the court for leave to adduce additional evidence and shall show to the satisfaction of the court that such additional evidence is material and that there were reasonable grounds for the failure to adduce such evidence in the hearing before the Board, its member, agent, or agency, the court may order such additional evidence to be taken before the Board, its member, agent, or agency, and to be made a part of the record. The Board may modify its findings as to the facts, or make new findings, by reason of additional evidence so taken and filed, and it shall file such modified or new findings, which findings with respect to question of fact if supported by substantial evidence on the record considered as a whole shall be conclusive, and shall file its recommendations, if any, for the modification or setting aside of its original order. Upon the filing of the record with it the jurisdiction of the court shall be exclusive and its judgment and decree shall be final, except that the same shall be subject to review by the appropriate United States court of appeals if application was made to the district court as hereinabove provided, and by the Supreme Court of the United States upon writ of certiorari or certification as provided in section 1254 of title 28.

(f) [Review of final order of Board on petition to court] Any person aggrieved by a final order of the Board granting or denying in whole or in part the relief sought may obtain a review of such order in any United States court of appeals in the circuit wherein the unfair labor practice in question was alleged to have been engaged in or wherein such person resides or transacts business, or in the United States Court of Appeals for the District of Columbia, by filing in such court a written petition praying that the order of the Board be modified or set aside. A copy of such petition shall be forthwith transmitted by the clerk of the court to the Board, and thereupon the aggrieved party shall file in the court the record in the proceeding, certified by the Board, as provided in section 2112 of title 28, United States Code [section 2112 of title 28]. Upon the filing of such petition, the court shall proceed in the same manner as in the case of an application by the

Board under subsection (e) of this section, and shall have the same jurisdiction to grant to the Board such temporary relief or restraining order as it deems just and proper, and in like manner to make and enter a decree enforcing, modifying and enforcing as so modified, or setting aside in whole or in part the order of the Board; the findings of the Board with respect to questions of fact if supported by substantial evidence on the record considered as a whole shall in like manner be conclusive.

(g) [Institution of court proceedings as stay of Board's order] The commencement of proceedings under subsection (e) or (f) of this section shall not, unless specifically ordered by the court, operate as a stay of the Board's order.

(h) [Jurisdiction of courts unaffected by limitations prescribed in chapter 6 of this title] When granting appropriate temporary relief or a restraining order, or making and entering a decree enforcing, modifying and enforcing as so modified, or setting aside in whole or in part an order of the Board, as provided in this section, the jurisdiction of courts sitting in equity shall not be limited by sections 101 to 115 of title 29, United States Code [chapter 6 of this title] [known as the "Norris-LaGuardia Act"].

(i) Repealed.

(j) [Injunctions] The Board shall have power, upon issuance of a complaint as provided in subsection (b) [of this section] charging that any person has engaged in or is engaging in an unfair labor practice, to petition any United States district court, within any district wherein the unfair labor practice in question is alleged to have occurred or wherein such person resides or transacts business, for appropriate temporary relief or restraining order. Upon the filing of any such petition the court shall cause notice thereof to be served upon such person, and thereupon shall have jurisdiction to grant to the Board such temporary relief or restraining order as it deems just and proper.

(k) [Hearings on jurisdictional strikes] Whenever it is charged that any person has engaged in an unfair labor practice within the meaning of paragraph (4)(D) of section 8(b) [section 158(b) of this title], the Board is empowered and directed to hear and determine the dispute out of which such unfair labor practice shall have arisen, unless, within ten days after notice that such charge has been filed, the parties to such dispute submit to the Board satisfactory evidence that they have adjusted, or agreed upon methods for the voluntary adjustment of, the dispute. Upon compliance by the parties to the dispute with the decision of the Board or upon such voluntary adjustment of the dispute, such charge shall be dismissed.

(l) [Boycotts and strikes to force recognition of uncertified labor organizations; injunctions; notice; service of process] Whenever it is charged that any person has engaged in an unfair labor practice within the meaning of paragraph (4)(A), (B), or (C) of section 8(b) [section 158(b) of this title], or section 8(e) [section 158(e) of this title] or section 8(b)(7) [section 158(b)(7) of this title], the preliminary investigation of such charge shall be made forthwith and given priority over all other cases except cases of like character in the office where it is filed or to which it is referred. If, after such investigation, the officer or regional attorney to whom the matter may be referred has reasonable cause to believe such charge is true and that a complaint should issue, he shall, on behalf of the Board, petition any United States district court within any district where the unfair labor practice in question has occurred, is alleged to have occurred, or wherein such person resides or transacts business, for appropriate injunctive relief pending the final adjudication of the Board with respect to such matter. Upon the filing of any such petition the district court shall have jurisdiction to grant such injunctive relief or temporary restraining order as it deems just and proper, notwithstanding any other provision of law: Provided further, That no temporary restraining order shall be issued without notice unless a petition alleges that substantial and irreparable injury to the charging party will be unavoidable and such temporary restraining order shall be effective for no longer than five days and will become void at the expiration of such period: Provided further, That such officer or regional attorney shall not apply for any restraining order under section 8(b)(7) [section 158(b)(7) of this title] if a charge against the employer under section 8(a)(2) [section 158(a)(2) of this title] has been filed and after the preliminary investigation, he has reasonable cause to believe that such charge is true and that a complaint should issue. Upon filing of any such petition the courts shall cause notice thereof to be served upon any person involved in the charge and such person, including the charging party, shall be given an opportunity to appear by counsel and present any relevant testimony: Provided further, That for the purposes of this subsection district courts shall be deemed to have jurisdiction of a labor organization (1) in the district in which such organization maintains its principal office, or (2) in any district in which its duly authorized officers or agents are engaged in promoting or protecting the interests of employee members. The service of legal process upon such officer or agent shall constitute service upon the labor organization and make such organization a party to the suit. In situations where such relief is appropriate the procedure specified herein shall apply to charges with respect to section 8(b)(4)(D) [section 158(b)(4)(D) of this title].

(m) [Priority of cases] Whenever it is charged that any person has engaged in an unfair labor practice within the meaning of subsection (a)(3) or (b)(2) of section 8 [section 158 of this title], such charge shall be given priority over all other cases except cases of like character in the office where it is filed or to which it is referred and cases given priority under subsection (1) [of this section].

INVESTIGATORY POWERS

Sec. 11. [§161.] For the purpose of all hearings and investigations, which, in the opinion of the Board, are necessary and proper for the exercise of the powers vested in it by section 9 and section 10 [sections 159 and 160 of this title]—

(1) [Documentary evidence; summoning witnesses and taking testimony] The Board, or its duly authorized agents or agencies, shall at all reasonable times have access to, for the purpose of examination, and the right to copy any evidence of any person being investigated or proceeded against that relates to any matter under investigation or in question. The Board, or any member thereof, shall upon application of any party to such proceedings, forthwith issue to such party subpoenas requiring the attendance and testimony of witnesses or the production of any evidence in such proceeding or investigation requested in such application. Within five days after the service of a subpoena on any person requiring the production of any evidence in his possession or under his control, such person may petition the Board to revoke, and the Board shall revoke, such subpoena if in its opinion the evidence whose production is required does not relate to any matter under investigation, or any matter in question in such proceedings, or if in its opinion such subpoena does not describe with sufficient particularity the evidence whose production is required. Any member of the Board, or any agent or agency designated by the Board for such purposes, may administer oaths and affirmations, examine witnesses, and receive evidence. Such attendance of witnesses and the production of such evidence may be required from any place in the United States or any Territory or possession thereof, at any designated place of hearing.

(2) [Court aid in compelling production of evidence and attendance of witnesses] In case on contumacy or refusal to obey a subpoena issued to any person, any United States district court or the United States courts of any Territory or possession, within the jurisdiction of which the inquiry is carried on or within the jurisdiction of which said person guilty of contumacy or refusal to obey is found or resides or transacts business, upon application by the Board shall have jurisdiction to issue to such person an order requiring such person to appear before the Board, its member, agent, or agency, there to produce evidence if so ordered, or there to give testimony touching the matter under investigation or in question; and any failure to obey such order of the court may be punished by said court as a contempt thereof.

(3) Repealed

[Immunity of witnesses. See 18 U.S.C. §6001 et seq.]

(4) [Process, service and return; fees of witnesses] Complaints, orders and other process and papers of the Board, its member, agent, or agency, may be served either personally or by registered or certified mail or by telegraph or by leaving a copy thereof at the principal office or place of business of the person required to be served. The verified return by the individual so serving the same setting forth the manner of such service shall be proof of the same, and the return post office receipt or telegraph receipt therefor when registered or certified and mailed or when telegraphed as aforesaid shall be proof of service of the same. Witnesses summoned before the Board, its member, agent, or agency, shall be paid the same fees and mileage that are paid witnesses in the courts of the United States, and witnesses whose depositions are taken and the persons taking the same shall severally be entitled to the same fees as are paid for like services in the courts of the United States.

(5) [Process, where served] All process of any court to which application may be made under this Act [subchapter] may be served in the judicial district wherein the defendant or other person required to be served resides or may be found.

(6) [Information and assistance from departments] The several departments and agencies of the Government, when directed by the President, shall furnish the Board, upon its request, all records, papers, and information in their possession relating to any matter before the Board.

Sec. 12. [§162. Offenses and penalties] Any person who shall willfully resist, prevent, impede, or interfere with any member of the Board or any of its agents or agencies in the performance of duties pursuant to this Act [subchapter] shall be punished by a fine of not more than $5,000 or by imprisonment for not more than one year, or both.

Sec. 13. [§163. Right to strike preserved] Nothing in this Act [subchapter], except as specifically provided for herein, shall be construed so as either to interfere with or impede or diminish in any way the right to strike, or to affect the limitations or qualifications on that right.

Sec. 14. [§164. Construction of provisions] (a) [Supervisors as union members] Nothing herein shall prohibit any individual employed as a supervisor from becoming or remaining a member of a labor organization, but no employer subject to this Act [subchapter] shall be compelled to deem individuals defined herein as supervisors as employees for the purpose of any law, either national or local, relating to collective bargaining.

(b) [Agreements requiring union membership in violation of State law] Nothing in this Act [subchapter] shall be construed as authorizing the execution or application of agreements requiring membership in a labor organization as a condition of employment in any State or Territory in which such execution or application is prohibited by State or Territorial law.

(c) [Power of Board to decline jurisdiction of labor disputes; assertion of jurisdiction by State and Territorial courts] (1) The Board, in its discretion, may, by rule of decision or by published rules adopted pursuant to the Administrative Procedure Act [to subchapter II of chapter 5 of title 5], decline to assert jurisdiction over any labor dispute involving any class or category of employers, where, in the opinion of the Board, the effect of such labor dispute on commerce is not sufficiently substantial to warrant the exercise of its jurisdiction: Provided, That the Board shall not decline to assert jurisdiction over any labor dispute over which it would assert jurisdiction under the standards prevailing upon August 1, 1959.

(2) Nothing in this Act [subchapter] shall be deemed to prevent or bar any agency or the courts of any State or Territory (including the Commonwealth of Puerto Rico, Guam, and the Virgin Islands), from assuming and asserting jurisdiction over labor disputes over which the Board declines, pursuant to paragraph (1) of this subsection, to assert jurisdiction.

Sec. 15. [§165.] Omitted.

[Reference to repealed provisions of bankruptcy statute.]

Sec. 16. [§166. Separability of provisions] If any provision of this Act [subchapter], or the application of such provision to any person or circumstances, shall be held invalid, the remainder of this Act [subchapter], or the application of such provision to persons or circumstances other than those as to which it is held invalid, shall not be affected thereby.

Sec. 17. [§167. Short title] This Act [subchapter] may be cited as the "National Labor Relations Act."

Sec. 18. [§168.] Omitted.

[Reference to former sec. 9(f), (g), and (h).]

INDIVIDUALS WITH RELIGIOUS CONVICTIONS

Sec. 19. [§169.] Any employee who is a member of and adheres to established and traditional tenets or teachings of a bona fide religion, body, or sect which has historically held conscientious objections to joining or financially supporting labor organizations shall not be required to join or financially support any labor organization as a condition of employment; except that such employee may be required in a contract between such employeeÕs employer and a labor organization in lieu of periodic dues and initiation fees, to pay sums equal to such dues and initiation fees to a nonreligious, nonlabor organization charitable fund exempt from taxation under section 501(c)(3) of title 26 of the Internal Revenue Code [section 501(c)(3) of title 26], chosen by such employee from a list of at least three such funds, designated in such contract or if the contract fails to designate such funds, then to any such fund chosen by the employee. If such employee who holds conscientious objections pursuant to this section requests the labor organization to use the grievance-arbitration procedure on the employeeÕs behalf, the labor organization is authorized to charge the employee for the reasonable cost of using such procedure.

[Sec. added, Pub. L. 93–360, July 26, 1974, 88 Stat. 397, and amended, Pub. L. 96–593, Dec. 24, 1980, 94 Stat. 3452.]

Labor-Management Relations Act

Also cited LMRA; 29 U.S.C. §§141–197

[Title 29, Chapter 7, United States Code]

SHORT TITLE AND DECLARATION OF POLICY

Section 1. **[§141.]** (a) This Act [chapter] may be cited as the "Labor Management Relations Act, 1947." [Also known as the "Taft-Hartley Act."]

(b) Industrial strife which interferes with the normal flow of commerce and with the full production of articles and commodities for commerce, can be avoided or substantially minimized if employers, employees, and labor organizations each recognize under law one another's legitimate rights in their relations with each other, and above all recognize under law that neither party has any right in its relations with any other to engage in acts or practices which jeopardize the public health, safety, or interest.

It is the purpose and policy of this Act [chapter], in order to promote the full flow of commerce, to prescribe the legitimate rights of both employees and employers in their relations affecting commerce, to provide orderly and peaceful procedures for preventing the interference by either with the legitimate rights of the other, to protect the rights of individual employees in their relations with labor organizations whose activities affect commerce, to define and proscribe practices on the part of labor and management which affect commerce and are inimical to the general welfare, and to protect the rights of the public in connection with labor disputes affecting commerce.

TITLE I, Amendments to

NATIONAL LABOR RELATIONS ACT

29 U.S.C. §§151–169 (printed above)

TITLE II

[Title 29, Chapter 7, Subchapter III, United States Code]

CONCILIATION OF LABOR DISPUTES IN INDUSTRIES AFFECTING COMMERCE;
NATIONAL EMERGENCIES

Sec. 201. [§171. Declaration of purpose and policy] It is the policy of the United States that—

(a) sound and stable industrial peace and the advancement of the general welfare, health, and safety of the Nation and of the best interest of employers and employees can most satisfactorily be secured by the settlement of issues between employers and employees through the processes of conference and collective bargaining between employers and the representatives of their employees;

(b) the settlement of issues between employers and employees through collective bargaining may be advanced by making available full and adequate governmental facilities for conciliation, mediation, and voluntary arbitration to aid and encourage employers and the representatives of their employees to reach and maintain agreements concerning rates of pay, hours, and working conditions, and to make all reasonable efforts to settle their differences by mutual agreement reached through conferences and collective bargaining or by such methods as may be provided for in any applicable agreement for the settlement of disputes; and

(c) certain controversies which arise between parties to collective-bargaining agreements may be avoided or minimized by making available full and adequate governmental facilities for furnishing assistance to employers and the representatives of their employees in formulating for inclusion within such agreements provision for adequate notice of any proposed changes in the terms of such agreements, for the final adjustment of grievances or questions regarding the application or interpretation of such agreements, and other provisions designed to prevent the subsequent arising of such controversies.

Sec. 202. [§172. Federal Mediation and Conciliation Service]

(a) [Creation; appointment of Director] There is created an independent agency to be known as the Federal Mediation and Conciliation Service (herein referred to as the "Service," except that for sixty days after June 23, 1947, such term shall refer to the Conciliation Service of the Department of Labor). The Service shall be under the direction of a Federal Mediation and Conciliation Director (hereinafter referred to as the "Director"), who shall be appointed by the President by and with the advice and consent of the Senate. The Director shall not engage in any other business, vocation, or employment.

(b) [Appointment of officers and employees; expenditures for supplies, facilities, and services] The Director is authorized, subject to the civil service laws, to appoint such clerical and other personnel as may be necessary for the execution of the functions of the Service, and shall fix their compensation in accordance with sections 5101 to 5115 and sections 5331 to 5338 of title 5, United States Code [chapter 51 and subchapter III of chapter 53 of title 5], and may, without regard to the provisions of the civil service laws, appoint such conciliators and mediators as may be necessary to carry out the functions of the Service. The Director is authorized to make such expenditures for supplies, facilities, and services as he deems necessary. Such expenditures shall be allowed and paid upon presentation of itemized vouchers therefor approved by the Director or by any employee designated by him for that purpose.

(c) [Principal and regional offices; delegation of authority by Director; annual report to Congress] The principal office of the Service shall be in the District of Columbia, but the Director may establish regional offices convenient to localities in which labor controversies are likely to arise. The Director may by order, subject to revocation at any time, delegate any authority and discretion conferred upon him by this Act [chapter] to any regional director, or other officer or employee of the Service. The Director may establish suitable procedures for cooperation with State and local mediation agencies. The Director shall make an annual report in writing to Congress at the end of the fiscal year.

(d) [Transfer of all mediation and conciliation services to Service; effective date; pending proceedings unaffected] All mediation and conciliation functions of the Secretary of Labor or the United States Conciliation Service under section 51 [repealed] of title 29, United States Code [this title], and all functions of the United States Conciliation Service under any other law are transferred to the Federal Mediation and Conciliation Service, together with the personnel and records of the United States Conciliation Service. Such transfer shall take effect upon the sixtieth day after June 23, 1947. Such transfer shall not affect any proceedings pending before the United States Conciliation Service or any certification, order, rule, or regulation theretofore made by it or by the Secretary of Labor. The Director and the Service shall not be subject in any way to the jurisdiction or authority of the Secretary of Labor or any official or division of the Department of Labor.

FUNCTIONS OF THE SERVICE

Sec. 203. [§173. Functions of Service] (a) [Settlement of disputes through conciliation and mediation] It shall be the duty of the Service, in order to prevent or minimize interruptions of the free flow of commerce growing out of labor disputes, to assist parties to labor disputes in industries affecting commerce to settle such disputes through conciliation and mediation.

(b) [Intervention on motion of Service or request of parties; avoidance of mediation of minor disputes] The Service may proffer its services in any labor dispute in any industry affecting commerce, either upon its own motion or upon the request of one or more of the parties to the dispute, whenever in its judgment such dispute threatens to cause a substantial interruption of commerce. The Director and the Service are directed to avoid attempting to mediate disputes which would have only a minor effect on interstate commerce if State or other conciliation services are available to the parties. Whenever the Service does proffer its services in any dispute, it shall be the duty of the Service promptly to put itself in communication with the parties and to use its best efforts, by mediation and conciliation, to bring them to agreement.

(c) [Settlement of disputes by other means upon failure of conciliation] If the Director is not able to bring the parties to agreement by conciliation within a reasonable time, he shall seek to induce the parties voluntarily to seek other means of settling the dispute without resort to strike, lockout, or other coercion, including submission to the employees in the bargaining unit of the employer's last offer of settlement for approval or rejection in a secret ballot. The failure or refusal of either party to agree to any procedure suggested by the Director shall not be deemed a violation of any duty or obligation imposed by this Act [chapter].

(d) [Use of conciliation and mediation services as last resort] Final adjustment by a method agreed upon by the parties is declared to be the desirable method for settlement of grievance disputes arising over the application or interpretation of an existing collective-bargaining agreement. The Service is directed to make its conciliation and mediation services available in the settlement of such grievance disputes only as a last resort and in exceptional cases.

(e) [Encouragement and support of establishment and operation of joint labor management activities conducted by committees] The Service is authorized and directed to encourage and support the establishment and operation of joint labor management activities conducted by plant, area, and industrywide committees designed to improve labor management relationships, job security and organizational effectiveness, in accordance with the provisions of section 205A [section 175a of this title].

[Pub. L. 95-524, §6(c)(1), Oct. 27, 1978, 92 Stat. 2020, added subsec. (e).]

Sec. 204. [§174. Co-equal obligations of employees, their representatives, and management to minimize labor disputes]

(a) In order to prevent or minimize interruptions of the free flow of commerce growing out of labor disputes, employers and employees and their representatives, in any industry affecting commerce, shall—

(1) exert every reasonable effort to make and maintain agreements concerning rates of pay, hours, and working conditions, including provision for adequate notice of any proposed change in the terms of such agreements;

(2) whenever a dispute arises over the terms or application of a collective-bargaining agreement and a conference is requested by a party or prospective party thereto, arrange promptly for such a conference to be held and endeavor in such conference to settle such dispute expeditiously; and

(3) in case such dispute is not settled by conference, participate fully and promptly in such meetings as may be undertaken by the Service under this Act [chapter] for the purpose of aiding in a settlement of the dispute.

Sec. 205. [§175. National Labor-Management Panel; creation and composition; appointment, tenure, and compensation; duties]

(a) There is created a National Labor-Management Panel which shall be composed of twelve members appointed by the President, six of whom shall be selected from among persons outstanding in the field of management and six of whom shall be selected from among persons outstanding in the field of labor. Each member shall hold office for a term of three years, except that any member appointed to fill a vacancy occurring prior to the expiration of the term for which his predecessor was appointed shall be appointed for the remainder of such term, and the terms of office of the members first taking office shall expire, as designated by the President at the time of appointment, four at the end of the first year, four at the end of the second year, and four at the end of the third year after the date of appointment. Members of the panel, when serving on business of the panel, shall be paid compensation at the rate of $25 per day, and shall also be entitled to receive an allowance for actual and necessary travel and subsistence expenses while so serving away from their places of residence.

(b) It shall be the duty of the panel, at the request of the Director, to advise in the avoidance of industrial controversies and the manner in which mediation and voluntary adjustment shall be administered, particularly with reference to controversies affecting the general welfare of the country.

Sec. 205A. [§175a. Assistance to plant, area, and industrywide labor management committees]

(a) [Establishment and operation of plant, area, and industrywide committees] (1) The Service is authorized and directed to provide assistance in the establishment and operation of plant, area and industrywide labor management committees which—

(A) have been organized jointly by employers and labor organizations representing employees in that plant, area, or industry; and

(B) are established for the purpose of improving labor management relationships, job security, organizational effectiveness, enhancing economic development or involving workers in decisions affecting their jobs including improving communication with respect to subjects of mutual interest and concern.

(2) The Service is authorized and directed to enter into contracts and to make grants, where necessary or appropriate, to fulfill its responsibilities under this section.

(b) [Restrictions on grants, contracts, or other assistance] (1) No grant may be made, no contract may be entered into and no other assistance may be provided under the provisions of this section to a plant labor management committee unless the employees in that plant are represented by a labor organization and there is in effect at that plant a collective bargaining agreement.

(2) No grant may be made, no contract may be entered into and no other assistance may be provided under the provisions of this section to an area or industrywide labor management committee unless its participants include any labor organizations certified or recognized as the representative of the employees of an employer participating in such committee. Nothing in this clause shall prohibit participation in an area or industrywide committee by an employer whose employees are not represented by a labor organization.

(3) No grant may be made under the provisions of this section to any labor management committee which the Service finds to have as one of its purposes the discouragement of the exercise of rights contained in section 7 of the National Labor Relations Act (29 U.S.C. §157) [section 157 of this title], or the interference with collective bargaining in any plant, or industry.

(c) [Establishment of office] The Service shall carry out the provisions of this section through an office established for that purpose.

(d) [Authorization of appropriations] There are authorized to be appropriated to carry out the provisions of this section $10,000,000 for the fiscal year 1979, and such sums as may be necessary thereafter.

[Pub. L. 95-524, §6(c)(2), Oct. 27, 1978, 92 Stat. 2020, added Sec. 205A.]

NATIONAL EMERGENCIES

Sec. 206. [§176. Appointment of board of inquiry by President; report; contents; filing with Service] Whenever in the opinion of the President of the United States, a threatened or actual strike or lockout affecting an entire industry or a substantial part thereof engaged in trade, commerce, transportation, transmission, or communication among the several States or with foreign nations, or engaged in the production of goods for commerce, will, if permitted to occur or to continue, imperil the national health or safety, he may appoint a board of inquiry to inquire into the issues involved in the dispute and to make a written report to him within such time as he shall prescribe. Such report shall include a statement of the facts with respect to the dispute, including each party's statement of its position but shall not contain any recommendations. The President shall file a copy of such report with the Service and shall make its contents available to the public.

Sec. 207. [§177. **Board of inquiry**] (a) [Composition] A board of inquiry shall be composed of a chairman and such other members as the President shall determine, and shall have power to sit and act in any place within the United States and to conduct such hearings either in public or in private, as it may deem necessary or proper, to ascertain the facts with respect to the causes and circumstances of the dispute.

(b) [Compensation] Members of a board of inquiry shall receive compensation at the rate of $50 for each day actually spent by them in the work of the board, together with necessary travel and subsistence expenses.

(c) [Powers of discovery] For the purpose of any hearing or inquiry conducted by any board appointed under this title, the provisions of sections 49 and 50 of title 15, United States Code [sections 49 and 50 of title 15] (relating to the attendance of witnesses and the production of books, papers, and documents) are made applicable to the powers and duties of such board.

Sec. 208. [§178. **Injunctions during national emergency**]

(a) [Petition to district court by Attorney General on direction of President] Upon receiving a report from a board of inquiry the President may direct the Attorney General to petition any district court of the United States having jurisdiction of the parties to enjoin such strike or lockout or the continuing thereof, and if the court finds that such threatened or actual strike or lockout—

(i) affects an entire industry or a substantial part thereof engaged in trade, commerce, transportation, transmission, or communication among the several States or with foreign nations, or engaged in the production of goods for commerce; and

(ii) if permitted to occur or to continue, will imperil the national health or safety, it shall have jurisdiction to enjoin any such strike or lockout, or the continuing thereof, and to make such other orders as may be appropriate.

(b) [Inapplicability of chapter 6] In any case, the provisions of sections 101 to 115 of title 29, United States Code [chapter 6 of this title] [known as the "Norris-LaGuardia Act"] shall not be applicable.

(c) [Review of orders] The order or orders of the court shall be subject to review by the appropriate United States court of appeals and by the Supreme Court upon writ of certiorari or certification as provided in section 1254 of title 28, United States Code [section 1254 of title 28].

Sec. 209. [§179. **Injunctions during national emergency; adjustment efforts by parties during injunction period**]

(a) [Assistance of Service; acceptance of Service's proposed settlement] Whenever a district court has issued an order under section 208 [section 178 of this title] enjoining acts or practices which imperil or threaten to imperil the national health or safety, it shall be the duty of the parties to the labor dispute giving rise to such order to make every effort to adjust and settle their differences, with the assistance of the Service created by this Act [chapter]. Neither party shall be under any duty to accept, in whole or in part, any proposal of settlement made by the Service.

(b) [Reconvening of board of inquiry; report by board; contents; secret ballot of employees by National Labor Relations Board; certification of results

to Attorney General] Upon the issuance of such order, the President shall reconvene the board of inquiry which has previously reported with respect to the dispute. At the end of a sixty-day period (unless the dispute has been settled by that time), the board of inquiry shall report to the President the current position of the parties and the efforts which have been made for settlement, and shall include a statement by each party of its position and a statement of the employer's last offer of settlement. The President shall make such report available to the public. The National Labor Relations Board, within the succeeding fifteen days, shall take a secret ballot of the employees of each employer involved in the dispute on the question of whether they wish to accept the final offer of settlement made by their employer as stated by him and shall certify the results thereof to the Attorney General within five days thereafter.

Sec. 210. [§180. Discharge of injunction upon certification of results of election or settlement; report to Congress] Upon the certification of the results of such ballot or upon a settlement being reached, whichever happens sooner, the Attorney General shall move the court to discharge the injunction, which motion shall then be granted and the injunction discharged. When such motion is granted, the President shall submit to the Congress a full and comprehensive report of the proceedings, including the findings of the board of inquiry and the ballot taken by the National Labor Relations Board, together with such recommendations as he may see fit to make for consideration and appropriate action.

COMPILATION OF COLLECTIVE-BARGAINING AGREEMENTS, ETC.

Sec. 211. [§181.] (a) For the guidance and information of interested representatives of employers, employees and the general public, the Bureau of Labor Statistics of the Department of Labor shall maintain a file of copies of all available collective bargaining agreements and other available agreements and actions thereunder settling or adjusting labor disputes. Such file shall be open to inspection under appropriate conditions prescribed by the Secretary of Labor, except that no specific information submitted in confidence shall be disclosed.

(b) The Bureau of Labor Statistics in the Department of Labor is authorized to furnish upon request of the Service, or employers, employees, or their representatives, all available data and factual information which may aid in the settlement of any labor dispute, except that no specific information submitted in confidence shall be disclosed.

EXEMPTION OF RAILWAY LABOR ACT

Sec. 212. [§182.] The provisions of this title [subchapter] shall not be applicable with respect to any matter which is subject to the provisions of the Railway Labor Act [45 U.S.C. §151 et seq.], as amended from time to time.

CONCILIATION OF LABOR DISPUTES IN THE HEALTH CARE INDUSTRY

Sec. 213. [§183.] (a) [Establishment of Boards of Inquiry; membership] If, in the opinion of the Director of the Federal Mediation and Conciliation Service, a threatened or actual strike or lockout affecting a health care institution will, if permitted to occur or to continue, substantially interrupt the delivery of health care in the locality concerned, the Director may further assist in the resolution of the impasse by establishing within 30 days after the notice to the Federal Mediation and Conciliation Service under clause (A) of the last sentence of section 8(d) [section 158(d) of this title] (which is required by clause (3) of such section 8(d) [section 158(d) of this title]), or within 10 days after the notice under clause (B), an impartial Board of Inquiry to investigate the issues involved in the dispute and to make a written report thereon to the parties within fifteen (15) days after the establishment of such a Board. The written report shall contain the findings of fact together with the Board's recommendations for settling the dispute, with the objective of achieving a prompt, peaceful and just settlement of the dispute. Each such Board shall be composed of such number of individuals as the Director may deem desirable. No member appointed under this section shall have any interest or involvement in the health care institutions or the employee organizations involved in the dispute.

(b) [Compensation of members of Boards of Inquiry] (1) Members of any board established under this section who are otherwise employed by the Federal Government shall serve without compensation but shall be reimbursed for travel, subsistence, and other necessary expenses incurred by them in carrying out its duties under this section.

(2) Members of any board established under this section who are not subject to paragraph (1) shall receive compensation at a rate prescribed by the Director but not to exceed the daily rate prescribed for GS-18 of the General Schedule under section 5332 of title 5, United States Code [section 5332 of title 5], including travel for each day they are engaged in the performance of their duties under this section and shall be entitled to reimbursement for travel, subsistence, and other necessary expenses incurred by them in carrying out their duties under this section.

(c) [Maintenance of status quo] After the establishment of a board under subsection (a) of this section and for 15 days after any such board has issued its report, no change in the status quo in effect prior to the expiration of the contract in the case of negotiations for a contract renewal, or in effect prior to the time of the impasse in the case of an initial bargaining negotiation, except by agreement, shall be made by the parties to the controversy.

(d) [Authorization of appropriations] There are authorized to be appropriated such sums as may be necessary to carry out the provisions of this section.

TITLE III

[Title 29, Chapter 7, Subchapter IV, United States Code]

SUITS BY AND AGAINST LABOR ORGANIZATIONS

Sec. 301. [§185.] (a) [Venue, amount, and citizenship] Suits for violation of contracts between an employer and a labor organization representing employees in an industry affecting commerce as defined in this Act [chapter], or between any such labor organization, may be brought in any district court of the United States having jurisdiction of the parties, without respect to the amount in controversy or without regard to the citizenship of the parties.

(b) [Responsibility for acts of agent; entity for purposes of suit; enforcement of money judgments] Any labor organization which represents employees in an industry affecting commerce as defined in this Act [chapter] and any employer whose activities affect commerce as defined in this Act [chapter] shall be bound by the acts of its agents. Any such labor organization may sue or be sued as an entity and in behalf of the employees whom it represents in the courts of the United States. Any money judgment against a labor organization in a district court of the United States shall be enforceable only against the organization as an entity and against its assets, and shall not be enforceable against any individual member or his assets.

(c) [Jurisdiction] For the purposes of actions and proceedings by or against labor organizations in the district courts of the United States, district courts shall be deemed to have jurisdiction of a labor organization (1) in the district in which such organization maintains its principal offices, or (2) in any district in which its duly authorized officers or agents are engaged in representing or acting for employee members.

(d) [Service of process] The service of summons, subpoena, or other legal process of any court of the United States upon an officer or agent of a labor organization, in his capacity as such, shall constitute service upon the labor organization.

(e) [Determination of question of agency] For the purposes of this section, in determining whether any person is acting as an "agent" of another person so as to make such other person responsible for his acts, the question of whether the specific acts performed were actually authorized or subsequently ratified shall not be controlling.

RESTRICTIONS ON PAYMENTS TO EMPLOYEE REPRESENTATIVES

Sec. 302. [§186.] (a) [Payment or lending, etc., of money by employer or agent to employees, representatives, or labor organizations] It shall be unlawful for any employer or association of employers or any person who acts as a labor relations expert, adviser, or consultant to an employer or who acts in the interest of an employer to pay, lend, or deliver, or agree to pay, lend, or deliver, any money or other thing of value—

(1) to any representative of any of his employees who are employed in an industry affecting commerce; or

(2) to any labor organization, or any officer or employee thereof, which represents, seeks to represent, or would admit to membership, any of the employees of such employer who are employed in an industry affecting commerce;

(3) to any employee or group or committee of employees of such employer employed in an industry affecting commerce in excess of their normal compensation for the purpose of causing such employee or group or committee directly or indirectly to influence any other employees in the exercise of the right to organize and bargain collectively through representatives of their own choosing; or

(4) to any officer or employee of a labor organization engaged in an industry affecting commerce with intent to influence him in respect to any of his actions, decisions, or duties as a representative of employees or as such officer or employee of such labor organization.

(b) [Request, demand, etc., for money or other thing of value] (1) It shall be unlawful for any person to request, demand, receive, or accept, or agree to receive or accept, any payment, loan, or delivery of any money or other thing of value prohibited by subsection (a) [of this section].

(2) It shall be unlawful for any labor organization, or for any person acting as an officer, agent, representative, or employee of such labor organization, to de-

mand or accept from the operator of any motor vehicle (as defined in part II of the Interstate Commerce Act [49 U.S.C. §301 et seq.]) employed in the transportation of property in commerce, or the employer of any such operator, any money or other thing of value payable to such organization or to an officer, agent, representative or employee thereof as a fee or charge for the unloading, or in connection with the unloading, of the cargo of such vehicle: Provided, That nothing in this paragraph shall be construed to make unlawful any payment by an employer to any of his employees as compensation for their services as employees.

(c) [Exceptions] The provisions of this section shall not be applicable (1) in respect to any money or other thing of value payable by an employer to any of his employees whose established duties include acting openly for such employer in matters of labor relations or personnel administration or to any representative of his employees, or to any officer or employee of a labor organization, who is also an employee or former employee of such employer, as compensation for, or by reason of, his service as an employee of such employer; (2) with respect to the payment or delivery of any money or other thing of value in satisfaction of a judgment of any court or a decision or award of an arbitrator or impartial chairman or in compromise, adjustment, settlement, or release of any claim, complaint, grievance, or dispute in the absence of fraud or duress; (3) with respect to the sale or purchase of an article or commodity at the prevailing market price in the regular course of business; (4) with respect to money deducted from the wages of employees in payment of membership dues in a labor organization: Provided, That the employer has received from each employee, on whose account such deductions are made, a written assignment which shall not be irrevocable for a period of more than one year, or beyond the termination date of the applicable collective agreement, whichever occurs sooner; (5) with respect to money or other thing of value paid to a trust fund established by such representative, for the sole and exclusive benefit of the employees of such employer, and their families and dependents (or of such employees, families, and dependents jointly with the employees of other employers making similar payments, and their families and dependents): Provided, That (A) such payments are held in trust for the purpose of paying, either from principal or income or both, for the benefit of employees, their families and dependents, for medical or hospital care, pensions on retirement or death of employees, compensation for injuries or illness resulting from occupational activity or insurance to provide any of the foregoing, or unemployment benefits or life insurance, disability and sickness insurance, or accident insurance; (B) the detailed basis on which such payments are to be made is specified in a written agreement with the employer, and employees and employers are equally represented in the administration of such fund, together with such neutral persons as the representatives of the employers and the representatives of employees may agree upon and in the event the employer and employee groups deadlock on the administration of such fund and there are no neutral persons empowered to break such deadlock, such agreement provides that the two groups shall agree on an impartial umpire to decide such dispute, or in event of their failure to agree within a reasonable length of time, an impartial umpire to decide such dispute shall, on petition of either group, be appointed by the district court of the United States for the district where the trust fund has its principal office, and shall also contain provisions for an annual audit of the trust fund, a statement of the results of which shall be available for inspection by interested persons at the principal office of the trust fund and at such other places as may be designated in such written agreement; and (C) such payments as are intended to be used for the purpose of providing pensions or annuities for employees are made to a separate trust which provides that the funds held therein cannot be used for any purpose other than paying such pensions or annuities; (6) with respect to money or other thing of value paid by any employer to a trust fund established by such representative for the purpose of pooled vacation, holiday, severance or similar benefits, or defraying costs of apprenticeship or other training programs: Provided, That the requirements of clause (B) of the proviso to clause (5) of this subsection shall apply to such trust funds; (7) with respect to money or other thing of value paid by any employer to a pooled or individual trust fund established by such representative for the purpose of (A) scholarships for the benefit of employees, their families, and dependents for study at educational institutions, or (B) child care centers for preschool and school age dependents of employees: Provided, That no labor organization or employer shall be required to bargain on the establishment of any such trust fund, and refusal to do so shall not constitute an unfair labor practice: Provided further, That the requirements of clause (B) of the proviso to clause (5) of this subsection shall apply to such trust funds; (8) with respect to money or any other thing of value paid by any employer to a trust fund established by such representative for the purpose of defraying the costs of legal services for employees, their families, and dependents for counsel or plan of their choice: Provided, That the requirements of clause (B) of the proviso to clause (5) of this subsection shall apply to such trust funds: Provided further, That no such legal services shall be furnished: (A) to initiate any proceeding directed (i) against any such employer or its officers or agents except in workman's compensation cases; or (ii) against such labor organization, or its parent or subordinate bodies, or their officers or agents, or (iii)against any other employer or labor organization, or their officers or agents, in any matter arising under the National Labor Relations Act, or this Act [under subchapter II of this chapter or this chapter]; and (B) in any proceeding where a labor organization would be prohibited from defraying the costs of legal services by the provisions of the Labor-Management Reporting and Disclosure Act of 1959 [29 U.S.C. §401 et seq.]; or (9) with respect to money or other things of value paid by an employer to a plant, area or industrywide labor management committee established for one or more of the purposes set forth in section 5(b) of the Labor Management Cooperation Act of 1978.

[Sec. 302(c)(7) was added by Pub. L. 91-86, Oct. 14, 1969, 83 Stat. 133; Sec. 302(c)(8) by Pub. L. 93-95, Aug. 15, 1973, 87 Stat. 314; and Sec. 302(c)(9) by Pub. L. 95-524, Oct. 27, 1978, 92 Stat. 2021.]

(d) [Penalty for violations] Any person who willfully violates any of the provisions of this section shall, upon conviction thereof, be guilty of a misdemeanor and be subject to a fine of not more than $10,000 or to imprisonment for not more than one year, or both.

(e) [Jurisdiction of courts] The district courts of the United States and the United States courts of the Territories and possessions shall have jurisdiction, for cause shown, and subject to the provisions of rule 65 of the Federal Rules of Civil Procedure [section 381 (repealed) of title 28] (relating to notice to opposite party) to restrain violations of this section, without regard to the provisions of section 17 of title 15 and section 52 of title 29, United States Code [of this title] [known as the "Clayton Act"], and the provisions of sections 101 to 115 of title 29, United States Code [chapter 6 of this title] [known as the "Norris-LaGuardia Act"].

(f) [Effective date of provisions] This section shall not apply to any contract in force on June 23, 1947, until the expiration of such contract, or until July 1, 1948, whichever first occurs.

(g) [Contributions to trust funds] Compliance with the restrictions contained in subsection (c)(5)(B) [of this section] upon contributions to trust funds, otherwise lawful, shall not be applicable to contributions to such trust funds established by collective agreement prior to January 1, 1946, nor shall subsection (c)(5)(A) [of this section] be construed as prohibiting contributions to such trust funds if prior to January 1, 1947, such funds contained provisions for pooled vacation benefits.

BOYCOTTS AND OTHER UNLAWFUL COMBINATIONS

Sec. 303. [§187.] (a) It shall be unlawful, for the purpose of this section only, in an industry or activity affecting commerce, for any labor organization to engage in any activity or conduct defined as an unfair labor practice in section 8(b)(4) of the National Labor Relations Act [section 158(b)(4) of this title].

(b) Whoever shall be injured in his business or property by reason of any violation of subsection (a) [of this section] may sue therefor in any district court of the United States subject to the limitation and provisions of section 301 hereof [section 185 of this title] without respect to the amount in controversy, or in any other court having jurisdiction of the parties, and shall recover the damages by him sustained and the cost of the suit.

RESTRICTION ON POLITICAL CONTRIBUTIONS

Sec. 304. Repealed.

[See sec. 316 of the Federal Election Campaign Act of 1972, 2 U.S.C. §441b.]

Sec. 305. [§188.] Strikes by Government employees. Repealed.

[See 5 U.S.C. §7311 and 18 U.S.C. §1918.]

TITLE IV

[Title 29, Chapter 7, Subchapter V, United States Code]

CREATION OF JOINT COMMITTEE TO STUDY AND REPORT ON BASIC PROBLEMS AFFECTING FRIENDLY LABOR RELATIONS AND PRODUCTIVITY

Secs. 401–407. [§§191–197.] Omitted.

TITLE V

[Title 29, Chapter 7, Subchapter I, United States Code]

DEFINITIONS

Sec. 501. [§142.] When used in this Act [chapter]—

(1) The term "industry affecting commerce" means any industry or activity in commerce or in which a labor dispute would burden or obstruct commerce or tend to burden or obstruct commerce or the free flow of commerce.

(2) The term "strike" includes any strike or other concerted stoppage of work by employees (including a stoppage by reason of the expiration of a collective-bargaining agreement) and any concerted slowdown or other concerted interruption of operations by employees.

(3) The terms "commerce", "labor disputes", "employer", "employee", "labor organization", "representative", "person", and "supervisor" shall have the same meaning as when used in the National Labor Relations Act as amended by this Act [in subchapter II of this chapter].

SAVING PROVISION

Sec. 502. [§143.] [Abnormally dangerous conditions] Nothing in this Act [chapter] shall be construed to require an individual employee to render labor or service without his consent, nor shall anything in this Act [chapter] be construed to make the quitting of his labor by an individual employee an illegal act; nor shall any court issue any process to compel the performance by an individual employee of such labor or service, without his consent; nor shall the quitting of labor by an employee or employees in good faith because of abnormally dangerous conditions for work at the place of employment of such employee or employees be deemed a strike under this Act [chapter].

SEPARABILITY

Sec. 503. [§144.] If any provision of this Act [chapter], or the application of such provision to any person or circumstance, shall be held invalid, the remainder of this Act [chapter], or the application of such provision to persons or circumstances other than those as to which it is held invalid, shall not be affected thereby.

ENDNOTES

1. Gerald G. Somers, ed., *Collective Bargaining*: *Contemporary American Experience* (Madison, WI: Industrial Relations Research Assoc., 1980), pp. 553–556.

CHAPTER 1

2. Ibid.
3. Scott A. Kruse, "Giveback Bargaining: One Answer to Current Labor Problems?" *Personnel Journal* 62, no. 4 (April 1983), p. 286.
4. "This Is the AFL-CIO," American Federation of Labor and Congress of Industrial Organizations, pamphlet (Washington, DC: AFL-CIO, 1987).
5. "Major Union Strikes a Real Low Point," *Courier-Journal*, February 27, 1986; see also U.S. Bureau of Census, *Statistical Abstract of the United States*: *1992*, 112th ed. (Washington, DC, 1992), p. 420.
6. Glenn Barkins and Glenn Simpson, "As Democrats Meet, the Teachers' Unions Will Show Their Clout," *Wall Street Journal*, August 23, 1996, pp. A1, 2.
7. Foster Rhea Dulles and Melvyn Dubofsky, *Labor in America, A History*, 4th ed. (Arlington Heights, IL: Harlan Davidson, 1984), p. 1.
8. Ibid., pp. 32, 70–73.
9. Robert Asher and Charles Stephens, eds., *Labor Dividend*: *Race and Ethnicity in United States Labor Struggles 1835–1960* (Albany, NY: State University of New York Press, 1990), pp. 154–158.
10. Maurice F. Neufeld, "The Persistence of Ideas in the American Labor Movement: The Heritage of the 1830s," *Industrial and Labor Relations Review* 35, no. 2 (January 1982), p. 212.
11. John R. Commons, *History of Labor in the United States*, vol. 2 (New York, Macmillan, 1946), pp. 7–8.
12. Joseph G. Rayback, *A History of American Labor* (New York: The Free Press, 1966), pp. 120–122.
13. Dulles and Dubofsky, *Labor in America*, pp. 111–112; Rayback, *A History of American Labor*, 1966, pp. 131–133.
14. Samuel Yellen, *American Labor Struggles* (New York: Harcourt, Brace, 1936), pp. 3–38.
15. Joseph Rayback, *A History of American Labor* (New York: Macmillan, 1959), p. 135.
16. Yellen, *American Labor Struggles*, pp. 39–71.
17. Richard O. Bayer and Herbert M. Morris, *Labor's Untold Story* (New York: United Electrical Radio and Machine Workers of America, 1955), pp. 98–99, by permission of United Electrical and Radio Machine Workers.
18. Richard O. Bayer and Herbert M. Morris, *Labor's Untold Story* (New York: United Electrical, Radio and Machine Workers of America, 1955), p. 99; and see Dulles and Dubofsky, *Labor in America*, pp. 116–118.
19. Dulles and Dubofsky, *Labor in America*, p. 135.
20. Sherman Anti-Trust Act, 15 U.S.C. sec. 1 (1892).
21. Bayer and Morris, *Labor's Untold Story*, p. 131.

22. Ibid., p. 119.

23. J. Robert Constantine, "Eugene V. Debs: An American Paradox," *Monthly Labor Review* 114, no. 8 (August 1991), pp. 30–33.

24. Stuart Bruce Kaufman, "Birth of a Federation: Mr. Gompers Endeavors Not to Build a Bubble," *Monthly Labor Review* 104, no. 11 (November 1981), p. 24.

25. Rayback, *A History of American Labor*, 1966, pp. 194–226.

26. Alice Kessler-Harris, "Trade Unions Mirror Society in Conflict between Collectivism and Individualism," *Monthly Labor Review* 110, no. 8 (August 1989), pp. 34–35.

27. Rayback, *A History of American Labor*, 1966, pp. 238–239.

28. Dulles and Dubofsky, *Labor in America*, p. 214.

29. Richard Feldman and Michael Betzold, *End of the Line: Autoworkers and the American Dream* (New York: Weidenfeld & Nicolson, 1988), p. 6.

30. Albert Rees, *The Economics of Trade Unions* (Chicago: University of Chicago Press, 1977), p. 30.

31. Jack Fiorito, "Unionism and Altruism," *Labor Studies Journal* (Fall 1992), pp. 19–34.

32. Michael H. LeRoy, "State of the Unions: Assessment by Elite American Labor Leaders," *Journal of Labor Research* XIII, no. 4 (Fall 1992), pp. 371–379.

33. Carol Keegan, "How Union Members and Nonunion View the Role of Unions," *Monthly Labor Review* 110, no. 8 (August 1987), pp. 50–51.

34. Daniel J. B. Mitchell, *Unions, Wage and Inflation* (Washington, DC: The Brookings Institution, 1980), pp. 1–22, 77–112.

35. James F. Rand, "Preventive-Maintenance Techniques for Staying Union-Free," *Personnel Journal* 59 (June 1980), pp. 497–499.

36. Russell Heavrin, "Thoughts on Labor Unions by a Rank-and-File Member, Circa 1993." Unpublished paper, by permission of Russell Heavrin.

37. Thomas A. Kochan, "How American Workers View Labor Unions," *Monthly Labor Review* 102, no. 4 (April 1979), pp. 23–31. See also George W. Bohlander, "How the Rank and File Views Local Union Administration—A Survey," *Employee Relations Law Journal* 8 (Autumn 1983), pp. 217–235.

38. Kochan, "American Workers," pp. 23–24.

39. Kessler-Harris, "Trade Unions Mirror Society," pp. 34–35.

40. John P. Bucalo Jr. "Successful Employee Relations," *Personnel Administrator* 31, no. 4 (April 1986), pp. 63–84.

41. Aaron Bernstein, "The Difference Japanese Management Makes," *Business Week*, July 14, 1986, pp. 47–50.

42. Bucalo, "Successful Employee Relations," pp. 63–84.

43. Amos N. Okafor, "White-Collar Unionization: Why and What to Do," *Personnel* 62, no. 8 (August 1985), pp. 17–21.

44. William T. Dickens and Jonathan S. Leonard, "Accounting for the Decline in Union Membership, 1950–1980," *Industrial and Labor Relations Review* 38, no. 3 (April 1985), pp. 323–334.

45. Philip M. Doyle, "Area Wage Surveys Shed Light on Declines in Unionization," *Monthly Labor Review* 108, no. 9 (September 1985), pp. 13–20.

46. Steven G. Allen, "Declining Unionization in Construction: The Facts and the Reasons," *Industrial and Labor Relations Review* 41, no. 3 (April 1988), pp. 343–359.

47. Larry T. Adams, "Labor Organization Mergers 1979–84: Adapting to Change," *Monthly Labor Review* 107, no. 9 (September 1984), pp. 21–27.

48. Ethel B. Jones, "Private Sector Union Decline and Structural Employment Change, 1970–1988," *Journal of Labor Research* XIII, no. 3 (Summer 1992), pp. 257–272.

49. Daniel C. Stove Jr., "Can Unions Pick Up the Pieces?" *Personnel Journal* 65, no. 2 (February 1986), pp. 37–40.

50. Okafor, "White Collar Unionization," pp. 17–21.

51. "Paid Union Organizers," 107 *Labor Law Reports* no. 468 (August 1995).

52. Robert J. Grossman, "Employers Brace for 'Salting' after High Court Ruling," *HR News*, January 1996, pp. 1–5.

53. Ronald L. Seeber and William N. Cooke, "The Decline in Union Success in NLRB Representation Elections," *Industrial Relations* 22, no. 1 (Winter 1983), pp. 34–44.

54. John C. Anderson, Charles A. O'Reilly III, and Gloria Busman, "Union Decertification in the U.S.: 1947–1977," *Industrial Relations* 19, no. 1 (Winter 1980), pp. 100–107; and "The Decertification Process: Evidence from California," *Industrial Relations* 21, no. 2 (Spring 1982), pp. 178–195.

55. "Huge 4-Year Losses Renew Union Campaign to Spur Membership," *Resource* (American Society for Personnel Administration), April 1985, p. 5.

56. Monty L. Lynn and Jazell Brister, "Trends in Union Organizing Issues and Tactics," *Industrial Relations* 28, no. 1 (Winter 1989), pp. 104–113.

57. "Labor Letter," *Wall Street Journal*, February 22, 1994, p. A1.

58. Robert L. Aronson, "Unionism among Professional Employees in the Private Sector," *Industrial and Labor Relations Review* 38, no. 3 (April 1985), pp. 352–364.

59. "New Data on Contingent and Alternate Employment Arrangements," 746 *Labor Law Reports* no. 468 (August 30, 1995), p. 4.

60. J. S. Lubin, "Health Care Workers Are Target of Big Union Organizing Drive," *Wall Street Journal*, February 24, 1984, p. 26.

61. Ibid.

62. *NLRB v. Health Care & Retirement Corporation*, 114 S.Ct. 1778 (1994).

63. Richard N. Hind and Adriene McElwain, "Organizing Clerical Workers: Determinants of Success," *Industrial and Labor Relations Review* 41, no. 3 (April 1988), pp. 360–373.

64. P. Pagans, "Labor Women Get Together for 925," *Louisville Courier-Journal*, March 4, 1981, p. 36.

65. C. Trost, "The Labor Activists Lead a Growing Drive to Sign Up Women," *Wall Street Journal*, January 29, 1985, p. 1.

66. Ibid.

67. D. D. Buss, "Japanese Owned Auto Plants in the U.S. Present a Tough Challenge for the UAW," *Wall Street Journal*, March 24, 1983, p. 1.

68. Ibid.

69. M. Kanabayashi, "How a Japanese Firm Is Faring in Its Dealings with Workers in U.S.," *Wall Street Journal*, October 2, 1981, p. 1.

70. Buss. "Japanese Owned Auto Plants."

71. James Risen, "UAW Rejected at Nissan Plant in Major Defeat," *Los Angeles Times*, July 28, 1989, pp. 1, 15.

72. Bob Baker, "Unions Try Bilingual Recruiting," *Los Angeles Times*, March 25, 1991, pp. A1, A22, A24.

CHAPTER 2

1. Paul Kennedy, *Preparing for the Twenty-First Century* (New York: Random House, 1993), p. 4.

2. Ralph K. Andrist, ed. *The American Heritage History of the Confident Years* (New York: American Heritage Publishing, 1969), p. 306.

3. Alistair Cooke, *America* (New York: Alfred A. Knopf, 1973), pp. 273–288.

4. Robert B. Reich, *The Work of Nations* (New York: Vintage Books, 1992), p. 35.

5. Foster Rhea Dulles and Melvyn Dubofsky, *Labor in America, A History*, 4th ed. (Arlington Heights, IL: Harlan Davidson, 1984), pp. 343–354.

6. Charles R. Morris, *The Coming Global Boom* (New York: Bantam Books, 1990), pp. 10–54.

7. Wayne F. Cascio and Manuel G. Serapino Jr. "Human Resources Systems in an International Alliance: The Undoing of a Done Deal," *Organizational Dynamics* (February 21, 1991), pp. 63–74.

8. Reich, *The Work of Nations*, p. 70.

9. Kennedy, *Preparing for the Twenty-First Century*, pp. 47–81.

10. Anthony P. Carnevale, *America and the New Economy* (Washington, DC: GPO, 1990), unpaged.

11. Reich, *The Work of Nations*, p. 84.

12. Neil Gross, "This Is What the U.S. Must Do to Stay Competitive," *Business Week*, December 1991, pp. 92–96.

13. William B. Johnston, "Global Workforce 2000: The New World Labor Market," *Harvard Business Review* (March–April 1991), pp. 115–127.

14. Michael M. Robert, "Attack Competitors by Changing the Game Rules," *Journal of Business Strategy* (September–October 1991), pp. 53–56.

15. Carnevale, *America and the New Economy*, unpaged.

16. S. M. Jameel Hason, "Human Resource Management in a New Era of Globalism," *Business Forum* (Winter 1992), pp. 56–59.

17. "Year after NAFTA: U.S. Looks Like a Winner," *Louisville Courier-Journal*, November 26, 1994, p. 148.

18. Paul D. Staudohar, "Labor-Management Cooperation at NUMMI," *Labor Law Journal* (January 1991), pp. 57–63. Martha Groves, "Rolling On: GM-Toyota Plant Prospers Amid Auto Industry Slump," *Los Angeles Times*, December 12, 1991, pp. D1–D2.

19. Robert Schrank, "Are Unions an Anachronism?" *Harvard Business Review* 57, no. 5 (September–October 1979), pp. 56–59.

20. William Winpisinger, "Job Satisfaction," *AFL-CIO American Federationist* 80, no. 2 (1973), pp. 9–10.

21. Gary B. Hansen, "Innovative Approach to Plant Closings: The UAW-Ford Experience at San Jose," *Monthly Labor Review* 108, no. 7 (July 1985), pp. 56–59.

22. George L. Whaley, "The Impact of Robotics Technology upon Human Resources Management," *Personnel Administrator* 27, no. 9 (September 1982), p. 61.

23. Sar A. Levitan and Clifford M. Johnson, "The Future of Work: Does It Belong to Us or to the Robots?" *Monthly Labor Review* 105, no. 9 (September 1982), p. 10.

24. Carl Renick, "Robots: New Faces on the Production Line," *Management Review* 68 (May 1979), p. 26.

25. Levitan and Johnson, "The Future of Work," pp. 11–12.

26. Whaley, "The Impact of Robotics," p. 61.

27. Levitan and Johnson, "The Future of Work," p. 12.

28. "Some Lessons Learned for the Decade Ahead," *U.S. News and World Report*, December 31, 1979, pp. 73–74.

29. Robert R. Blake and Jane S. Mouton, "Developing a Positive Union-Management Relationship," *Personnel Administrator* 28, no. 6 (June 1983), pp. 23–31.

30. Louis Harris, *Daily Labor Report* (Washington, DC: Bureau of National Affairs, June 3, 1981), pp. A14–A16.

31. D. Quinn Mills, "Reforming the U.S. System of Collective Bargaining," *Monthly Labor Review* 106, no. 3 (March 1983), pp. 21–22.

32. Shaun G. Clark, "Rethinking the Adversarial Model in Labor Relations: An Argument for Repeal of Section 8(a)(2)," *Yale Law Review* 96 (1987), pp. 2021–2050.

33. Leonardo Rico, "The New Industrial Relations: British Electricians' New-Style Agreements," *Industrial and Labor Relations Review* 41, no. 1 (October 1987), pp. 75–77.

34. Ibid. See also Scott Kafker, "Exploring Saturn: An Examination of 'Total' Labor-Management Cooperation and the Limitations Presented by the NLRA," *Labor Lawyer* 5, no. 4 (Fall 1989), pp. 703–738.

35. Dana Milbank, "Labor Broadens Its Appeal by Setting Up Associations to Lobby and Offer Services," *Wall Street Journal*, January 13, 1993, pp. B1, 6.

36. Charles C. Heckscher, *The New Unionism* (New York: Basic Books, 1988), pp. 188–190.

37. Lee M. Oyley and Judith S. Ball, "Quality of Work Life: Initiating Success in Labor-Management Organizations," *Personnel Administrator* 27, no. 5 (May 1982), pp. 27–29.

38. Harry C. Katz, Thomas A. Kochan, and Kenneth R. Gobelle, "Industrial Relations Performance and QWL Programs: An Interplant Analysis," *Industrial and Labor Relations Review* 37, no. 1 (October 1983), pp. 3–17.

39. William G. Ouchi, *Theory Z* (Reading, MA: Addison-Wesley, 1981), chap. 11, pp. 1–7.

40. Sandra R. McCandless, "Avoiding Workplace Violence—The Employer's Legal Dilemma," *American Bar Association's 1996 Mid-Winter Meeting Program Materials*, January 25–28, 1996.

41. Marvin E. Shaw, *Group Dynamics: The Psychology of Small Group Behavior*, 2nd ed. (New York: McGraw-Hill, 1976).

42. S. Dillingham, "Topeka Revisited," *Human Resource Executive* 4, no. 5 (May 1990): pp. 55–58.

43. Steve Jordan, "Union Defies U.P. Quality Concept," *Omaha World Herald*, April 6, 1993, p. M1.

44. Ken Murphy, "Venture Teams Help Companies Create New Products," *Personnel Journal* 70, no. 3 (March 1991), pp. 60–67.

45. Richard Wellins and Jill George, "The Key to Self-Directed Teams," *Training and Development Journal* 45 (April 1991), pp. 26–29.

46. Frank Shipper and Charles C. Manz, "Employee Self-Management without Formally Designed Teams: An Alternative Road to Empowerment," *Organizational Dynamics* 20 (Winter 1992), pp. 48–61.

47. Wellins and George, "The Key to Self-Directed Teams," p. 27.

48. Richard S. Wellins, William C. Byham, and Jeanne M. Wilson, *Empowered Teams* (San Francisco: Jossey-Bass, 1991), pp. 3–5.

49. Clay Carr, "Managing Self-Managed Workers," *Training and Development Journal* 45 (September 1991), pp. 36–42.

50. Shipper and Manz, "Employee Self-Management," p. 48.

51. Wellins, Byham, and Wilson, *Empowered Teams*, pp. 10–13.

52. Wellins and George, "The Key to Self-Directed Teams," p. 28.

53. Jana Schilder, "Work Teams Boost Productivity," *Personnel Journal* 71, no. (February 1992), pp. 67–71.

54. Wellins, Byham, and Wilson, *Empowered Teams*, pp. 13–15.

55. Schilder, "Work Teams Boost Productivity," p. 68.

56. Dick Richardson, "Teams Not Always the Best Way to Get Work Done," *HR News*, August 1996, p. 11.

57. Joe Ward, "It's a New Day on the Assembly Line," *Courier Journal*, February 7, 1993, p. J4.

58. Jordan, "Union Defies U.P. Quality Concept," p. M1.

59. Harold J. Datz, "Employee Participation Programs and the National Labor Relations Act—A Guide for the Perplexed," presented at the Ninth Annual Labor and Employment Law Institute (1992) at the University of Louisville.

60. *Electromation*, NLRB Case No. 25-CA-19818 (1991).

61. *E. I. duPont de Nemours Company v. Chemical Workers Association, Inc.*, 311 N.L.R.B. 88 (1993), 143 LRRM 1121 (1993) (corrected at 143 LRRM (268)).

62. *General Foods Corp.*, 231 NLRB 1232, 1235 (1977).

63. Earl F. Mellor, "Shift Work and Flextime: How Prevalent Are They?" *Monthly Labor Review* 109, no. 11 (November 1986), pp. 14–21.

64. Charlene Marmer Soloman, "24-Hour Employee," 70, no. 8 *Personnel Journal* (August 1991), pp. 56–63.

65. "Flexible Work Schedules," *Small Business Report*, October 1978, pp. 24–25.

66. John R. Turney, "Alternative Work Schedules Increase Employee Satisfaction," *Personnel Journal* 62, no. 3 (March 1983), pp. 202–207.

67. Randall B. Durham and John L. Pierce, "The Design and Evaluation of Alternative Work Schedules," *Personnel Administrator* 28 (April 1983), pp. 67–75.

68. Bernhard Teriet, "Flexiyear Schedules in Germany," *Personnel Journal* 61, no. 6 (June 1982), pp. 428–429.

69. Marcia M. Kelley, "Exploring the Potentials of Decentralized Work Settings," *Personnel Administrator* 29, no. 2 (February 1984), pp. 48–49.

70. Toby Kahn, "Vermont Home Knitters," *People Weekly* 21 (March 19, 1984), p. 64.

71. Thomas J. Nardone, "Part-Time Workers: Who Are They?" *Monthly Labor Review* 109, no. 2 (February 1986), pp. 13–19.

72. Heywood Klein, "Interest Grows in Worksharing, Which Lets Concerns Cut Workweeks to Avoid Layoffs," *Wall Street Journal*, April 7, 1983, p. 27.

CHAPTER 3

1. Joseph Rayback, *A History of American Labor* (New York: Macmillan, 1959), pp. 54–57.

2. David P. Twomey, *Labor Law and Legislation* (Cincinnati: South-Western, 1980), pp. 7–8.

3. *Commonwealth v. Hunt*, 45 Mass. (4 Met.) III (1842).

4. Richard O. Bayer and Herbert M. Morris, *Labor's Untold Story* (New York: United Electrical, Radio, and Machine Workers of America, 1955), p. 131.

5. Erdman Act, 30 Stat. 424 (1898), amended by Pub.L. 6, 38 Stat. 103 (1913); referenced in 45 U.S.C. sec. 101 (1976).

6. Rayback, *A History of American Labor*, p. 212.

7. Clayton Act, ch. 323, sec. 1, 6, and 7, 38 Stat. 730 (1914); referenced in 15 U.S.C. sec. 12, 17, and 18 (1982).

8. Theodore Kheel, *Labor Law* (New York: Matthew Bender, 1988), chap. 5, p. 24.

9. *Duplex Printing Press Co. v. Deering*, 254 U.S. 443, 41 S.Ct. 172, 65 L.Ed. 349 (1921); and *Redford Cut Stone Co. v. Journeymen Stone Cutters' Association*, 274 U.S. 37, 47 S.Ct. 522, 71 L.Ed. 916 (1927).

10. Railway Labor Act, 45 U.S.C. sec. 151 (1976).

11. *Texas and New Orleans Railroad Co. v. Brotherhood of Railway & Steamship Clerks*, 281 U.S. 548 (1930).

12. Ibid., 570.

13. Davis-Bacon Act, Title 40 U.S.C.A. sec. 276a (1931).

14. Norris–La Guardia Act, 29 U.S.C. sec. 101 (1982).

15. National Industrial Recovery Act, Pub.L. 67, 48 Stat. 195 (1933); referenced in 7 U.S.C. sec. 601 (1982).

16. *Schechter Poultry Corp. v. United States*, 295 U.S. 495, 55 S.Ct. 837, 79 L.Ed. 893 (1937).

17. Patrick Hardin, ed., *The Developing Labor Law*, 3rd ed. (Washington, DC: Bureau of National Affairs, 1992), pp. 12–13.

18. Ibid., p. 28.

19. National Labor Relations Act, 29 U.S.C. sec. 151 et seq. (1982).

20. *Associated Press v. National Labor Relations Board*, 301 U.S. 103 (1937); and *National Labor Relations Board v. Jones & Laughlin Steel Corporation*, 301 U.S. 1, 57 S.Ct. 615, 81 L.Ed. 893 (1937).

21. Walsh-Healy Act, Title 29 U.S.C.A. sec. 557 and Title 41 U.S.C.A. sec. 35–45.

22. Fair Labor Standards Act, 29 U.S.C. sec. 201 (1982).

23. War Labor Disputes Act, Pub.L. 89, 57 Stat. 163 (1943).

24. *Thornhill v. Alabama*, 310 U.S. 88 (1940); and *Milk Drivers Local 753 v. Meadowmoore Dairies, Inc.*, 312 U.S. 287 (1941).

25. Small Business Protection Act, H.R. 3448 (August 2, 1996).

26. James S. Ray and Barbara Berish Brown, "Federal Leg. Update April–Aug. 1990," *Labor Lawyer* 6, no. 4 (Fall 1990), pp. 1029–1030.

27. Hardin, *The Developing Labor Law*, p. 35.

28. Labor-Management Relations (Taft-Hartley) Act, 29 U.S.C. sec. 141 et seq. (1982).

29. Neil W. Chamberlain, *Sourcebook on Labor* (New York: McGraw-Hill, 1964), pp. 26–29.

30. Labor-Management Reporting and Disclosure (Landrum-Griffin) Act, 29 U.S.C. sec. 401 et seq. (1982).

31. *Transportation Workers Local 525*, 317 N.L.R.B. 62, 149 L.R.R.M. 1222 (1995).

32. James W. Robinson, "Structural Characteristics of the Independent Union in America Revisited," *Labor Law Journal* (September 1992), pp. 567–578.

33. Paul D. Staudohar, *The Sports Industry and Collective Bargaining* (New York: ICR Press, 1986), pp. 1–7.

34. Ibid.

35. See *Curtis C. Flood v. Bowie K. Kuhn, et al.*, 407 U.S. 258, 32 L.Ed. 2d 728, 92 S.Ct. 2099 (1972).

36. Staudohar, *The Sports Industry*, pp. 20–29.

37. "Flawed Diamonds," *Economist*, May 1, 1993, p. 98.

38. Timothy K. Smith and Erle Nortus, "One Baseball Statistic Remains a Mystery: The Real Bottom Line," *Wall Street Journal*, April 2, 1993, pp. A1, 4.

39. John Helzer, "The Fat Lady Sings," *Wall Street Journal*, September 15, 1994, p. A6.

40. Staudohar, *The Sports Industry*, pp. 55–86.

41. Harris Collingwood, "Did the NFL Owners Gain Yardage?" *Business Week*, February 8, 1993, p. 118.

42. *Brown v. Pro Football*, 152 L.R.R.M. 2513 (1995).

43. *Robertson v. National Basketball Association*, 389 F. Supp. 867 (1975).

44. Staudohar, *The Sports Industry*, pp. 87–118.

45. *Caldwell v. ABA, Inc.*, 66 F.3d 523 (2d Cir. 1995).

46. Ronald Blum, "NBA Union Survives Player Vote," Associated Press and *Lexington Herald-Leader*, September 13, 1995, pp. C1, 3.

47. Elizabeth Comte and Sabrata Chakravarty, "How High Can David Stern Jump?" *Forbes*, June 7, 1993, pp. 42–44.

48. Staudohar, *The Sports Industry*, pp. 119–144.

49. Elizabeth Comte, "Is Hockey the Next Baseball?" *Forbes*, June 7, 1993, p. 44.

CHAPTER 4

1. 29 U.S.C. sec. 151 et seq. (1982); and 29 U.S.C. sec. 141 et seq. (1982).

2. U.S. Constitution, art. I sec. 8.

3. 29 U.S.C. sec. 151 (1982).

4. Ludwig Teller, *Labor Disputes and Collective Bargaining*, vol. 2 (New York: Baker, Voorhis & Co., 1940), p. 688.

5. 29 U.S.C. sec. 152 (1) (1982).

6. *Plumbers & Steamfitters Local 298 v. County of Door*, 359 U.S. 354, 79 S.Ct. 844, 3 L.Ed. 2d 872 (1959).

7. 29 U.S.C. sec. 152 (9) (1982).

8. Ibid.

9. Ibid.

10. *Cincinnati Association for the Blind v. National Labor Relations Board*, 672 F.2d 567 (1982), discussed in *University of Detroit Urban Law Journal* 60 (Winter 1983), pp. 324–337.

11. Theodore Kheel, *Labor Law* (New York: Matthew Bender, 1988), chap. 8, p. 122.

12. *Res-Care, Inc.*, 280 NLRB 670, 122 LRRM 1265 (1986).

13. *Management Training*, 317 NLRB 190, 149 LRRM 1313 (1995).

14. U.S. Congress, 39 U.S.C. sec. 1209 (1982).

15. *National Labor Relations Board v. Cabot Carbon Co.*, 360 U.S. 203, 79 S.Ct. 1015, 3 L.Ed. 2d 1175 (1959).

16. *San Diego Building Trades Council v. Garmon*, 359 U.S. 236, 76 S.Ct. 773, 3 L.Ed. 2d 775 (1959); *Amalgamated Association of Street, Electric Railway & Motor Coach Employees v. Lockridge*, 403 U.S. 224, 91 S.Ct. 1909, 29 L.Ed. 2d 473 (1971); *Sears, Roebuck & Co. v. San Diego District Council of Carpenters*, 98 S.Ct. 1745, 56 L.Ed. 2d 209 (1978); and *Tamburelli v. Comm-Tract Corporation*, 67 F.3d 973 (1st Cir. 1995).

17. *Smith v. Evening News Association*, 371 U.S. 195, 51 LRRM 2646 (1962); and *Local 174, Teamsters v. Lucas Flour Co.*, 369 U.S. 95, 49 LRRM 2717 (1962).

18. *Lingle v. Norge Division of Magic Chef, Inc.*, 486 U.S. 399 (1988); Patrick Hardin, ed., *The Developing Labor Law*, 3rd ed. (Washington, DC: Bureau of National Affairs, 1992), pp. 1698–1706; and *Jimeno v. Mobil Oil Corporation*, 66 F.3d 1514 (1995).

19. Jane Byeff Korn, "Collective Rights and Individual Remedies: Rebalancing the Balance after *Lingle v. Norge Division of Magic Chef, Inc.*," *Hastings Law Journal* 1149 (July 1990), pp. 1149–1196.

20. *May Department Stores Co. v. National Labor Relations Board*, 326 U.S. 376, 66 S.Ct. 203, 90 L.Ed. 145 (1945).

21. *Labor Relations Reporter* (Washington, DC: Bureau of National Affairs, 1976), p. 4106.

22. Stephen I. Schlossberg and Judith A. Scott, *Organizing and the Law*, 4th ed. (Washington, DC: Bureau of National Affairs, 1991), p. 216.

23. Ibid., p. 217.

24. James L. Perry and Harold L. Angle, "Bargaining Unit Structure and Organizational Outcomes," *Industrial Relations* 20, no. 1 (Winter 1981), pp. 47–59.

25. *Short Stop Inc.*, 192 NLRB 184, 78 LRRM 1087 (1971); *Mock Road Super Duper Inc.*, 156 NLRB 82, 61 LRRM 1173 (1966); *Wil-Kil Pest Control*, 440 F.2d 371 (7th Cir. 1971); and *National Labor Relations Board v. Saint Francis College*, 562 F.2d 246 (3rd Cir. 1977); *National Labor Relations Board v. Action Automotive*, 469 U.S. 490, 118 LRRM 2577 (1985).

26. Cases cited, in order of listing are: *General Electric*, 107 NLRB 21, 33 LRRM 1058 (1953); *T.C. Wheaton Co.*, NLRB 14 LRRM 142 (1944); *Safety Cabs, Inc.*, 173 NLRB 4, 69 LRRM 1199 (1968); and *Land Title Guarantee & Trust Co.*, 194 NLRB 29, 78 LRRM 1500 (1971).

27. *Globe Machinery & Stamping Co.*, 3 NLRB 294, 1-A LRRM 1122 (1937); and *Short Stores, Inc.*, 192 NLRB 184, 78 LRRM 1087 (1971).

28. Harold S. Roberts, *Roberts' Dictionary of Industrial Relations*, 3rd ed. (Washington, DC: Bureau of National Affairs, 1986), p. 243.

29. *Bendix Products Corporation*, 3 NLRB 682 (1937).

30. *National Labor Relations Board v. Delaware-New Jersey, Ferry Co.*, 128 F.2d 130 (3rd Cir. 1941).

31. Schlossberg and Scott, *Organizing and the Law*, p. 219.

32. *Tidewater Oil Co. v. National Labor Relations Board*, 358 F.2d 363 (2d Cir. 1966).

33. Labor-Management Relations Act, sec. 9(b)(1)(2)(3); 29 U.S.C. sec. 159 b(1)(2)(3).

34. *National Labor Relations Board v. Textion, Inc.*, 85 LRRM 2945 (1975); and *Palace Laundry Dry Clean Corp.*, NLRB, 21 LRRM 1039 (1947).

35. *National Labor Relations Board v. Hendricks City Rural Electric Mem. Cor.*, 108 LRRM 3105 (1981).

36. 444 U.S. 672 (1980).

37. Clarence R. Dietsch and David A. Dilts, "*NLRB v. Yeshiva University*: A Positive Perspective," *Monthly Labor Review* 106, no. 7 (July 1983), pp. 34–37; and Marsha Huie Ashlock, "The Bargaining Status of College and University Professors under the National Labor Relations Laws," *Labor Law Journal* 35, no. 2 (February 1984), pp. 103–111.

38. 64 USLW 4269 (1996), decided April 23, 1996.

39. 64 USLW 4022 (1995), decided November 28, 1995.

40. Hardin, *The Developing Labor Law*, pp. 463–464.

41. 162 NLRB 387, 64 LRRM 1011 (1967); see also *Airco, Inc.*, 273 NLRB 53, 118 LRRM 1053 (1984).

42. Hardin, *The Developing Labor Law*, pp. 464–466.

43. *Stephens Produce*, 515 F.2d 1373, 89 LRRM 2311 (8th Cir. 1975); Hardin, *The Developing Labor Law*, pp. 467–468.

44. Schlossberg and Scott, *Organizing and the Law*, pp. 226–228.

45. Clifford Oviatt, "Bargaining Unit Proposal Has Far-Reaching Impact," *HR News*, November 1995, p. 11.

46. Richard R. Carlson, "The Origin and Future of Exclusive Representation in American Labor Law," *Duquesne Law Review* 30, no. 4 (Summer 1992), pp. 779–867.

47. *National Labor Relations Board v. Beck Engraving Co.*, 522 F.2d 475 (3d Cir. 1975).

48. Hardin, *The Developing Labor Law*, pp. 473–489.

49. Ibid., pp. 476–477.

50. Joe Ward, "Unions, Nurses Mutually Attracted," *Courier-Journal*, April 16, 1989, pp. E1, E3; Joe Ward, "Hospitals Boost Pay Benefits of Nurses, Other Workers," *Courier-Journal*, April 20, 1989, p. B10; and Associated Press, "Board Issues Final Rules That Unions Say Will Help Hospital Organizing," *Courier Journal*, April 21, 1989, p. F1. See also, John Thomas Delaney and Donna Sockell, "Hospital Unit Determination and the Preservation of Employee Free Choice," *Labor Law Journal* 39, no. 5 (May 1988), pp. 259–272; and Cynthia A. Shaw, "Appropriate Bargaining Units in the Health Care Industry," *The Labor Lawyer* 5, no. 4 (Fall 1989), pp. 787–823.

51. 111 S.Ct. 1539 (1991).

52. Hardin, *The Developing Labor Law*, pp. 483–485 and 1811–1812. See also Stephen A. Mayunk, "The Status of the Employment Relationship: The 1990–91 Supreme Court Term," *The Labor Lawyer* 7, no. 849 (1991), p. 872.

53. 114 S.Ct. 1778 (1994).

54. Jonathan A. Segal, "Keeping Norma Rae at Bay," *HR Magazine*, August 1996, pp. 111–119.

55. *Organizing for Change, Challenging to Organize*. A report from the AFL-CIO Leadership Task Force on Organizing (Washington, DC, 1996), pp. 6–26.

56. Roberts, *Dictionary of Industrial Relations*, p. 668.

57. Kheel, *Labor Law*, chap. 7A, p. 20.

58. Ibid., chap. 13, pp. 3–4.

59. *Sunrise Rehabilitation Hospital*, 320 NLRB 28, 151 LRRM 1234 (1996); and *Perdue Farms*, 320 NLRB 64, 151 LRRM 1267 (1996), respectively.

60. *YMCA of San Francisco*, 286 NLRB 98, 126 LRRM 1329 (1987).

61. *Good Shepherd Home*, 321 NLRB 56, 152 LRRM 1137 (1996).

62. *Mailing Service, Inc.*, 293 NLRB 53 (1989).

63. *Midland National Life Ins. Co. v. National Labor Relations Board*, 263 NLRB 24, 110 LRRM 1489 (1982).

64. Herbert G. Heneman III and Marcus H. Sandver, "Predicting the Outcome of Union Certification Elections: A Review of the Literature," *Industrial and Labor Relations Review* 36, no. 4 (July 1983), p. 555.

65. Richard N. Block and Myron Roomkin, "Determinants of Voter Participation in Union Certification Elections," *Monthly Labor Review* 105, no. 4 (April 1982), pp. 45–47.

66. Roberts, *Dictionary of Industrial Relations*, p. 101.

67. 227 NLRB 326, 94 LRRM 1135 (1976).

68. Muriel H. Cooper, "Out in the Open: The Richmark Story," *America at Work*, November/December 1996, pp. 10–11.

69. *National Labor Relations Board v. Gissel Packing Co.*, 395 U.S. 575, 71 LRRM 2481 (1969).

70. *Gourmet Foods*, 270 NLRB 578, 116 LRRM 1105 (1984), overruling *United Dairy Farmers* 257 NLRB 772, 107 LRRM 1577 (1981), and *Conair Corp.* 261 NLRB 1189, 110 LRRM 1161 (1982).

71. Timothy P. Summers, John H. Betton, and Thomas A. Decatus, "Voting for and against Unions: A Decision Model," *Academy of Management Review* 11, no. 3 (July 1986), pp. 643–655.

72. George S. Rorkis and Mandouh Farid, "Balancing Partisan Bargaining Interests Requires More Than Labor Law Reform," *Labor Law Journal* 42, no. 2 (February 1991), pp. 67–80.

73. "Union Elections Decreased in 1995, BNA Data Show," 152 *Labor Relations Reporter* 275 (July 1, 1996).

74. Harold L. Angle and James L. Perry, "Dual Commitment and Labor-Management Relationship Climates," *Academy of Management Journal* 29, no. 1 (March 1986), pp. 31–50.

75. James B. Dworkin and Marian Extejt, "Why Do Workers Decertify Their Unions? A Preliminary Investigation," *Academy of Management—Proceedings of the 39th Annual Meeting* (August 7–11, 1979), p. 244.

76. Marvin T. Levine, "Double-Digit Decertification Election Activity: Union Organizational Weakness in the 1980's," *Labor Law Journal* (May 1989), pp. 311–319.

77. "Union Elections Decreased in 1995, BNA Data Show," 152 *Labor Relations Reporter* 275 (July 1, 1996).

78. Bob Baker, "Nordstrom's Employees in Seattle Cashier Union," *Los Angeles Times*, July 21, 1991, pp. B1, 3.

79. Carlson, "Exclusive Representation in American Labor Law."

80. Shaun G. Clark, "Rethinking the Adversarial Model in Labor Relations: An Argument for Repeal of Section 8(a)(2)," *Yale Law Journal* 96 (1987), pp. 2021–2050.

81. Hardin, *The Developing Labor Law*, p. 1496.

82. Elena Matsis, "Procedural Rights of Fair Share Objectors after *Hudson* and *Beck*," *Labor Lawyers* 6, no. 2 (Spring 1990), pp. 251–294.

83. *California Saw & Knife Works*, 320 NLRB 11, 151 LRRM 1121 (1995).

84. *Collective Bargaining Negotiations and Contracts* (Washington, DC: Bureau of National Affairs, 1981), pp. 87.1, 87.3.

85. *National Labor Relations Board v. Niagara Machine & Tool Works*, 117 LRRM 2689 (2d Cir. 1984); *Local 900, International Union of Electrical, Radio and Machine Workers v. National Labor Relations Board*, 727 F.2d 1184 (D.C. Cir. 1984).

86. *Ellis v. Railway Clerk*, 466 U.S. 435, 104 S.Ct. 1883, 80 L.Ed. 2d 428 (1984); *Communication Workers of America v. Beck*, 56 USLW 4857 (1988); *Teachers Local 1* (Chicago, American Federation of Teachers) *v. Hudson*, 121 LRRM 2793 (1986). See also James T. Bennett and John Thomas Delaney, "Research on Unions: Some Subjects in Need of Scholars," *Journal of Labor Research* XIV, no. 2 (Spring 1993), pp. 95–110.

87. States with right-to-work laws include

Alabama	Nevada
Arizona	North Carolina
Arkansas	North Dakota
Florida	South Carolina
Georgia	South Dakota
Idaho	Tennessee
Iowa	Texas
Kansas	Utah
Louisiana	Virginia
Mississippi	Wyoming
Nebraska	

88. Kheel, *Labor Law*, chap. 42, p. 2; Norman Hill, "The Double-Speak of Right-to-Work," *AFL-CIO American Federationist* 87 (October 1980), pp. 13–16.

89. Barry T. Hirsch, "The Determinants of Unionization: An Analysis of Interarea Differences," *Industrial and Labor Relations Review* 33, no. 2 (January 1980), pp. 147–161.

90. Kenneth A. Kovach, "National Right-to-Work Law: An Affirmative Position," *Labor Law Journal* (May 1977), pp. 305–314.

91. Robert Swidinsky, "Bargaining Power under Compulsory Unionism," *Industrial Relations* 21, no. 1 (Winter 1982), pp. 62–72.

92. William A. Wines, "An Analysis of the 1986 'Right-to-Work Referendum in Idaho,'" *Labor Law Journal* (September 1988), pp. 622–628.

93. Thomas M. Carroll, "Right to Work Laws Do Matter," *Southern Economic Journal* 5, no. 2 (October 1983), pp. 494–509.

94. Wines, "An Analysis of the 1986 'Right-to-Work Referendum in Idaho,'" pp. 622–628.

95. Gary N. Chaison and Dileep G. Dhavale, "The Choice between Union Membership and Free-Rider Status," *Journal of Labor Research* XIII, no. 4 (Fall 1992), pp. 355–369.

96. 323 U.S. 192, 15 LRRM 708 (1944).

97. *Airline Pilots Association v. O'Neill*, 59 USLW 4175, 136 LRRM 2721 (U.S. 1991).

98. 386 U.S. 171, 64 LRRM 2369 (1967).

99. 112 LRRM 2281 (1983).

CHAPTER 5

1. 29 U.S.C. sec. 157 (1982).

2. 29 U.S.C. sec. 158(a) (1982).

3. Donald L. Dotson, "Processing Cases at the NLRB," *Labor Law Journal* (January 1984), pp. 3–9.

4. Matthew M. Franckiewicz, "How to Win NLRB Cases: Tips from a Former Insider," *Labor Law Journal* (January 1993), pp. 40–47.

5. William N. Cooke and Frederick H. Gautschi III, "Political Bias in NLRB Unfair Labor Practice Decisions," *Industrial and Labor Relations Review* 35, no. 4 (July 1982), pp. 539–549. See also Myron Roomkin, "A Quantitative Study of Unfair Labor Practice Cases," *Industrial and Labor Relations Review* 34, no. 2 (January 1981), p. 256.

6. Thomas F. Phalen Jr., "The Destabilization of Federal Labor Policy under the Reagan Board," *Labor Lawyer* 2, no. 1 (Winter 1986), pp. 1–31.

7. Fred W. Batten, "Recent Decisions of the Reagan Board: A Management Perspective," *Labor Lawyer* 2, no. 1 (Winter 1986), pp. 33–46.

8. Thomas F. Phalen Jr., "The Return to the Center of the National Labor Relations Board," delivered at the Tenth Annual Meeting of the Labor & Employment Law Institute, May 20–21, 1993, University of Louisville, Louisville, KY.

9. Clifford M. Coen, Sandra J. Hartman, Dinah M. Payne, "NLRB Wields a Rejuvenated Weapon," *Personnel Journal*, December 1996, pp. 85–87.

10. *Cooper Thermometer Co.*, 154 NLRB 502, 59 LRRM 1767 (1965); and *American Freightways Co.*, 124 NLRB 646, 44 LRRM 1202 (1959).

11. *National Labor Relations Board v. Preston Feed Corp.*, 309 F.2d 346 (4th Cir. 1962).

12. 107 NLRB 427, 33 LRRM 1151 (1953); and *Rodac Corp.*, 231 NLRB 261, 95 LRRM 1608 (1977).

13. Stephen I. Schlossberg and Judith A. Scott, *Organizing and the Law*, 4th ed., (Washington, DC: Bureau of National Affairs, 1991), pp. 298–300.

14. *Republic Aviation*, 324 U.S. 793, 16 LRRM 620 (1945).

15. *Lechmere, Inc. v. NLRB*, 112 S.Ct. 841 (1992). See also Roger C. Hartley, "The Supreme Court's 1991–92 Labor & Employment Law Term," *Labor Lawyer* 8, no. 4 (Fall 1992), p. 757.

16. *UFCW Local No. 880 v. NLRB*, 151 LRRM 2289 (1996).

17. *Malta Co.*, 276 NLRB 171 (1985).

18. *The Cincinnati Enquirer*, 279 NLRB 149 (1986).

19. *Midland National Life Ins. Co. v. National Labor Relations Board*, 263 NLRB 24, 110 LRRM 1489 (1982).

20. *Houston Chronicle Publishing Co.*, 293 NLRB 38 (1989).

21. James P. Swann Jr., "Misrepresentation in Labor Union Elections," *Personnel Journal* 59, no. 11 (November 1980), pp. 925–926.

22. *National Labor Relations Board v. Gissel Packing Co.*, 395 U.S. 575, 71 LRRM 2481 (1969).

23. Gary L. Tidwell, "The Supervisor's Role in a Union Election," *Personnel Journal* 62, no. 8 (August 1983), pp. 640–645.

24. *Kalin Construction Co.*, 321 NLRB 94 (1996).

25. James H. Hopkins and Robert D. Binderup, "Employee Relations and Union Organizing Campaigns," *Personnel Administrator* 25, no. 3 (March 1980), pp. 57–61.

26. *Automated Products, Inc.*, 242 NLRB 424, 101 LRRM 1208 (1979).

27. Schlossberg and Scott, *Organizing and the Law*, pp. 316–318.

28. *Struksnes Construction Co.*, 165 NLRB 1062, 1063, 65 LRRM 1385 (1967).

29. *Rossmore House*, 269 NLRB 1176, 116 LRRM 1025 (1984).
30. Patrick Hardin, ed., *The Developing Labor Law*, 3rd ed. (Washington, DC: Bureau of National Affairs, 1992), pp. 125–126.
31. Schlossberg and Scott, *Organizing and the Law*, p. 301.
32. *Federal-Magul Corp., Coldwater Distributors Center Division v. National Labor Relations Board*, 394 F.2d 915 (Mich. Cir. 1968).
33. *RCA del Caribe, Inc.*, 262 NLRB 963, 110 LRRM 1369 (1982), and *Bruckner Nursing Home*, 262 NLRB 955, 110 LRRM 1374 (1982).
34. *Electromation, Inc.*, 309 NLRB 163, 142 LRRM 1001 (December 16, 1992); see also Bennet D. Zurofsky, "Everything Old Is New Again: Company Unions in the Era of Employee Involvement Programs," *Labor Lawyer* 8, no. 381 (Spring 1992); and Melvin Hutson, "Electromation: Employee Involvement or Employee Domination," *Labor Lawyer* 8, no. 389 (Spring 1992).
35. *E. I. duPont de Nemours & Company v. Chemical Workers Association Inc.*, 311 NLRB 88 (1993), 143 LRRM 1121 (1993) (corrected 143 LRRM 1268).
36. Barbara Presley Noble, "A Worker-Involvement Program Violates Labor Law, U.S. Rules" *New York Times*, June 8, 1993, p. A11.
37. Lawrence Woods, "Review of NLRB Decisions," delivered at the Thirteenth Annual Meeting of the Carl Warns Labor & Employment Law Institute, Louisville, KY, June 6–7, 1996, p. 10.
38. David Vaughn, "Mixed Motives in Unfair Labor Practices." *New York University, 35th Annual National Conference on Labor* (New York: Matthew Bender, 1983), pp. 169–194.
39. *Meyers Industries v. Prill*, 268 NLRB 493 (1984); *Meyers Industries, Inc. II*, 281 NLRB 118 (1986).
40. Hardin, *The Developing Labor Law*, pp. 137–146.
41. Ibid., pp. 148–161.
42. *National Labor Relations Board v. Weingarten, Inc.*, 420 U.S. 251, 88 LRRM 2689 (1975).
43. *Sears, Roebuck and Co.*, 274 NLRB 230 (1985); and *E. I. duPont de Nemours & Co.*, 289 NLRB 81 (1988).
44. *Roadway Express, Inc.*, 246 NLRB 1127 (1979); and Neil N. Bernstein, "*Weingarten*: Time for Reconsideration," *Labor Lawyer* 6, no. 4 (Fall 1990), pp. 1005–1027.
45. *New Jersey Bell Telephone Co.*, 308 NLRB 32 (August 18, 1992); and Christopher J. Martin, "Some Reflections on Weingarten and the Free Speech Rights of Union Stewards," *Employee Relations Law Journal*, 18, no. 4 (Spring 1993), pp. 647–653.
46. Hardin, *The Developing Labor Law*, pp. 161–168.
47. 473 U.S. 95, 119 LRRM 2928 (1985). For analysis see Beverly A. Williams, "*Pattern Makers' League v. National Labor Relations Board*: Individual Autonomy v. Union Solidarity," *Rutgers Law Review* 39 (Fall 1986), pp. 197–216.
48. Hardin, *The Developing Labor Law*, pp. 178–184.
49. Schlossberg and Scott, *Organizing and the Law*, pp. 322–324.
50. *United Broadcasting Co.* 248 NLRB 403, 103 LRRM 1421 (1980).
51. 29 U.S.C. sec. 158(a)(5) (1982).
52. *National Labor Relations Board v. Montgomery Ward & Co.*, 133 F.2d 676, 686 (9th Cir. 1943), 12 LRRM 508.
53. Ludwig Teller, *Labor Disputes and Collective Bargaining*, vol. 2 (New York: Baker, Voorhis, 1940), p. 884.
54. 29 U.S.C. sec. 158(d) (1982).
55. *National Labor Relations Board v. General Electric Co.*, 418 F.2d 736, 72 LRRM 2530 (2d Cir. 1969) cert. denied, 397 U.S. 965, 73 LRRM 2600 (1970).
56. *Utility Workers (Ohio Power Co.)*, 203 NLRB 230, 83 LRRM 1099 (1973).
57. *U.S. Gypsum Co.*, 200 NLRB 132, 82 LRRM 1064 (1972).
58. Theodore Kheel, *Labor Law* (New York: Matthew Bender, 1988), chap. 16, pp. 26–31.
59. *National Labor Relations Board v. Gellan Iron Works, Inc.*, 377 F.2d 894 (2d Cir. 1967).
60. Hardin, *The Developing Labor Law*, p. 635, n. 317.

61. *National Labor Relations Board v. Katz*, 369 U.S. 736, 82 S.Ct. 1107, 8 L.Ed. 762 (1962).

62. Jeffrey P. Chicoine, "The Business Necessity Defense to Unilateral Changes in Working Conditions under the Duty to Bargain in Good Faith," *Labor Lawyer* 8, no. 2 (Spring 1992), pp. 297–312.

63. *JI Case v. National Labor Relations Board*, 321 U.S. 332, 64 S.Ct. 576, 88 L.Ed. 762 (1944).

64. *National Labor Relations Board v. Truitt Manufacturing Co.*, 351 U.S. 149, 38 LRRM 2024 (1955).

65. Robert E. Block, "The Disclosure of Profits in the Normal Course of Collective Bargaining: All Relevant Information Should Be on the Table," *Labor Lawyer* 2, no. 1 (Winter 1986), pp. 47–74.

66. *Nielsen Lithographing Co.*, 305 NLRB 90, 138 LRRM 1444 (1988); and Reid Canon and Kathryn Ernst Noecker, "The Employer's Duty to Supply Financial Information to the Union: When Has the Employer Asserted an Inability to Pay?" *Labor Lawyer* 8, no. 4 (Fall 1992), p. 815.

67. *Efrain Rivera-Vego, et al. v. Conagra, Inc.*, 70 F.3d 153 (1st Cir. 1995).

CHAPTER 6

1. Bureau of National Affairs, *Basic Patterns in Union Contracts*, 14th ed. (Washington, DC: Bureau of National Affairs, 1995), p. 3.

2. Irving Paster, "Collective Bargaining: Warnings for the Novice Negotiator," *Personnel Journal* 60, no. 3 (March 1981), pp. 203–207.

3. Reed C. Richardson, *Collective Bargaining by Objectives* (Englewood Cliffs, NJ: Prentice Hall, 1977), p. 150; and Johanna S. Hunsaker, Philip L. Hunsaker, and Nancy Chase, "Guidelines for Productive Negotiating Relationships," *Personnel Administrator* 26 (March 1981), pp. 37–40.

4. 29 U.S.C. sec. 159(a) (1982).

5. *National Labor Relations Board v. Wooster Division of the Borg-Warner Corp.*, 356 U.S. 342, 78 S.Ct. 718, 1 L.Ed. 2d 823 (1958).

6. E. J. Dannin, "Statutory Subjects and the Duty to Bargain," *Labor Law Journal* (January 1988), pp. 44–45.

7. *Allied Chemical & Alkali Workers Local Union No. 1 v. Pittsburgh Plate Glass Company*, 404 U.S. 157 (1971).

8. Mairead E. Connor, "The Dubuque Packing Decision: New Test for Bargaining Over Decision to Relocate," *Labor Lawyer* 8, no. 2 (Spring 1992), pp. 289–295; see also Jay E. Grenig, "The Removal of Work from Bargaining Unit Employees: The Supreme Court, the Board and Arbitrators," *Willamette Law Review* 27 (1991), p. 595.

9. Donna Sockell, "The Scope of Mandatory Bargaining: A Critique and a Proposal," *Industrial and Labor Relations Review* 40, no. 1 (October 1986), pp. 19–34.

10. *Fibreboard Paper Products Corp v. National Labor Relations Board*, 379 U.S. 203 (1964), pp. 210–223; *First National Maintenance Corp. v. National Labor Relations Board*, 452 U.S. 666 (1981), pp. 677–689. Also *Otis Elevator Company*, 269 NLRB 891 (1984).

11. *W. W. Cross & Co. v. National Labor Relations Board*, 174 F.2d 875 (1st Cir. 1949).

12. Bureau of National Affairs, *Basic Patterns in Union Contracts*, p. 49.

13. Kevin B. Zeese, *Drug Testing Legal Manual* (New York: Clark Boardman Company, 1988), chap. 4, pp. 14–15; *Johnson Bateman Company*, 295 NLRB 26 (1989).

14. Bureau of National Affairs, *Basic Patterns in Union Contracts*, p. 4.

15. Roy J. Lewicki and Joseph A. Litterer, *Negotiation* (Homewood, IL: Irwin, 1985), pp. 7–9.

16. Ibid.

17. Frederick Rose, "Longshoremen Are Expected to Reject Contract," *Wall Street Journal*, August 28, 1996, p. A2.

18. David A. Dilts and Clarence R. Deitsch, *Labor Relations* (New York: Macmillan, 1983), p. 131.

19. Roy J. Lewicki, David M. Saunders, and John W. Minton, *Essentials of Negotiation* (Chicago: Irwin, 1997), pp. 30–36.

20. Ibid.
21. Roger Fisher and William Ury, *Getting to Yes* (Boston: Houghton-Mifflin, 1981), p. xii.
22. David A. Bender and William P. Curington, "Interaction Analysis: A Tool for Understanding Negotiations," *Industrial and Labor Relations Review* 36, no. 3 (April 1983), pp. 389–401.
23. Richardson, *Collective Bargaining*, p. xi.
24. Ibid., p. 151.
25. Ibid., p. 137.
26. Lewicki, Saunders, and Minton, *Essentials of Negotiation*, pp. 55–60.
27. Ibid.
28. Bruce E. Kaufman, "Bargaining Theory, Inflation, and Cyclical Strike Activity in Manufacturing," *Industrial and Labor Relations Review* 34, no. 3 (April 1981), pp. 333–355; and Bruce E. Kaufman, "Inter-Industry Trends in Strike Activity," *Industrial Relations* 22, no. 1 (Winter 1983), pp. 45–57.
29. Angelo B. Henderson and Carl Quintanilla, "UAW Members Aren't Geared Up for a Strike," *Wall Street Journal*, September 6, 1996, p. B1.
30. *Lyng v. Automobile Workers*, 27 LRRM 2977 (March 23, 1988); *Pattern Makers League v. National Labor Relations Board*, 53 USLW 4928 (June 25, 1985).
31. *Noel Corp. v. National Labor Relations Board*, 82 F.3d 1113 (D.C. Cir. 1996).
32. "Breakthrough at Bridgestone," *America at Work*, November/December 1996, p. 5.
33. B. E. Kaufman, J. W. Skeels, M. Paldam, and P.J. Pedersen, "Replies," *Industrial and Labor Relations Review* 39, no. 2 (January 1986), pp. 269–278.
34. Hoyt N. Wheeler, "Comment: Determinants of Strikes," *Industrial and Labor Relations Review* 37, no. 2 (January 1984), pp. 263–269.
35. Martin J. Mauro, "Strikes as a Result of Imperfect Information," *Industrial and Labor Relations Review* 35, no. 4 (July 1982), pp. 522–538.
36. Dennis R. Make, "The Effect of the Cost of Strikes on the Volume of Strike Activity," *Industrial and Labor Relations Review* 39, no. 4 (July 1986), pp. 552–553.
37. Cynthia L. Gramm, "The Determinants of Strike Incidence and Severity: A Microlevel Study," *Industrial and Labor Relations Review* 39, no. 3 (April 1986), pp. 361–376.
38. *North Carolina Fuel Company v. National Labor Relations Board*, 645 F.2d 177 (3d Cir. 1981).
39. Frederick J. Bosch and Paul A. Tufano, "Establishing a Uniform Standard for Striker Misconduct in Arbitration Cases," *Labor Law Journal* (September 1988), pp. 629–633.
40. 268 NLRB 173, 115 LRRM 1113 (1984).
41. Bosch and Tufano, "Establishing a Uniform Standard," pp. 629–633.
42. Brenda Paik Sunoo, "Managing Strikes, Minimizing Loss," *Personnel Journal*, January 1995, pp. 50–60.
43. John P. Kohl and David B. Stephens. "Labor Relations, Replacement Workers during Strikes. Strategic Options for Managers," *Personnel Journal* 65, no. 4 (April 1986), pp. 93–98.
44. "Labor Letter," *Wall Street Journal*, June 8, 1993, p. A1.
45. Linda Stockman Vines, "High Court Upholds NLRB Strike Replacement Policy," *HR News*, June 1993, p. 10.
46. *NLRB v. Mackay Radio and Telegraph Co.*, 304 U.S. 333 (1938).
47. George S. Roukis and Mamdouhj I. Farid, "An Alternative Approach to the Permanent Striker Replacement Strategy," *Labor Law Journal* (February 1993), pp. 80–91.
48. David Westfall, "Striker Replacements and Employee Freedom of Choice," *Labor Lawyer* 7 (1991), pp. 137–158.
49. William A. Stone, "Striker Replacement Law Isn't Needed," *Business First*, June 21, 1993, p. 7.
50. Larry Reynolds, "Business and Labor Ready to Battle Over Striker Bill," *HR Focus* 70, no. 4 (April 1993), pp. 1, 8.
51. *Chamber of Commerce v. Reich*, 152 LRRM 2199 (1996).

52. Patrick Hardin, ed., *The Developing Labor Law*, 3rd ed. (Washington, DC: Bureau of National Affairs, 1992), p. 1112.
53. Ibid., pp. 1115–1120.
54. David S. Bradshaw, "Labor Relations, How to Put Teeth into a Labor Injunction," *Personnel Journal* 64, no. 10 (October 1985), pp. 80–85.
55. Stephanie N. Mehta, "Declining Power of Picket Lines Blunts New York Maintenance Worker's Strike," *Wall Street Journal*, January 17, 1996, p. B1.
56. Joann S. Lublin, "AT&T Walkout Could End by Weekend: Optimism Buoyed by Job-Security Talks," *Wall Street Journal*, August 18, 1983, p. 3.
57. John Breeher and Alexander Still, "Telescabbing: The New Union Buster," *Newsweek* 102 (August 29, 1983), pp. 53–54.
58. Ibid.
59. Peter Perl, "Steel Firms Start Crucial Labor Talks," *Washington Post*, March 9, 1986, p. K1.
60. Rebecca Blumenstein, Nichole Christian, Oscar Suris, "GM Local Labor Dispute Spins Out of Control," *Wall Street Journal*, March 13, 1996, p. B1.
61. *American Shipbuilders*, 380 U.S. 300, 58 LRRM 2672 (1965).
62. George S. Roukis and Mamdoah Farid, "Balancing Partisan Bargaining Interests Requires More Than Labor Law Reform," *Labor Law Journal* (February 1991), pp. 67–80.
63. *International Paper*, 319 NLRB 150, 151 LRRM 1033 (1995).
64. Bureau of National Affairs, *Basic Patterns in Union Contracts*, pp. 91–93.
65. Ibid., p. 94.
66. Peter Perl, "Steel Firms Start Crucial Labor Talks," *Washington Post*, March 19, 1986, pp. K1, 7.
67. John R. Stepp, Robert P. Baker, and Jerome T. Barrett, "Helping Labor and Management See and Solve Problems," *Monthly Labor Review* 105, no. 9 (September 1982), pp. 15–20.
68. Ahmad Karim and Richard Pegnetter, "Mediator Strategies and Qualities and Mediation Effectiveness," *Industrial Relations* 22, no. 1 (Winter 1983), pp. 105–113.
69. Fritz Ihrig, "Labor Contract Negotiations: Behind the Scenes," *Personnel Administrator* 31, no. 4 (April 1986), pp. 55–60.

1. Mitchell Marks and Philip Mirvis, "Wage Guidelines: Impact on Job Attitudes and Behavior," *Industrial Relations* 20, no. 3 (Fall 1981), p. 296.
2. Chris Berger and Donald Schwab, "Pay Incentives and Pay Satisfaction," *Industrial Relations* 19, no. 2 (Spring 1980), p. 206.
3. *UAW-Chrysler Newsgram*, October 1996, pp. 2–3.
4. Michael R. Carrell, "A Longitudinal Field Assessment of Employee Perceptions of Equitable Treatment," *Organizational Behavior and Human Performance* 21 (1978), pp. 108–118.
5. Lawrence Mishel, "The Structural Determinants of Union Bargaining Power," *Industrial and Labor Relations Review* 40, no. 1 (October 1986), pp. 90–104.
6. Dale L. Belman and Paul B. Voos, "Wage Effects of Increased Union Coverage: Methodological Considerations and New Evidence," *Industrial and Labor Relations Review* 46, no. 2 (January 1993), pp. 368–379.
7. Stephenie Overman, "Caterpillar and UAW Agree to Mediation," *HR News*, May 1992, pp. A1, 7.
8. Lawrence F. Katz and Alan B. Krueger, "The Effect of the Minimum Wage on the Fast Food Industry"; David Card, "Using Regional Variation in Wages to Measure the Effects of the Federal Minimum Wage"; David Card, "Do Minimum Wages Reduce Employment? A Case Study of California 1987–89," *Industrial and Labor Relations Review* 46, no. 1 (October 1992), pp. 6–54.
9. G. P. Zachary, "Many Firms Refuse to Pay Overtime, Employees Complain," *Wall Street Journal*, June, 1996, p. A1.

CHAPTER 7

10. Gina Ameci, "Bonuses and Commissions: Is Your Overtime Pay Legal?" *Personnel Journal* 66, no. 1 (January 1987), pp. 107–110.

11. Bureau of National Affairs, *Basic Patterns in Union Contracts* (Washington, DC: BNA Books, 1995), pp. 50–53.

12. Robert A. Zaldivar, "Bills Would End 40-Hour Work Week," Knight-Ridder Bureau, as reported in *The Herald-Leader*, January 29, 1997, pp. A1, 5.

13. John C. Richardson, "Prevailing Wage Laws a Boon, Not a Threat," *L.A. Times*, March 10, 1991, p. D1.

14. Charles Hughes, *Making Unions Unnecessary* (New York: Executive Enterprises, 1976), pp. 105–106.

15. Leonard R. Burgess, *Wage and Salary Administration* (Columbus, OH: Merrill, 1984), p. 242.

16. Agreement between UAW and Chrysler Corporation, 1997–1999.

17. Sanford M. Jacoby, "Cost-of-Living Escalators Became Prevalent in the 1950's," *Monthly Labor Review* 108, no. 5 (May 1985), pp. 32–33.

18. Bureau of National Affairs, *Basic Patterns in Union Contracts*, p. 111.

19. Michael R. Carrell and William A. Hailey, "COLAs: An Analysis of Their Past and Their Relationship with Other Factors," *Labor Law Journal* (October 1989), pp. 658–662.

20. Lisa M. Williamson, "Collective Bargaining in 1993: Jobs Are the Issue," *Monthly Labor Review* 116, no. 1 (January 1993), pp. 7, 11.

21. Bureau of National Affairs, *Basic Patterns in Union Contracts* p. 119.

22. "Pay Day: Typical Ford Worker Gets $1,200 for Profit-Sharing," *Courier-Journal*, March 13, 1986, p. B8; "Auto Workers Will Feel Pinch of Lower or No Profits," *Bakersfield Californian*, February 20, 1990, p. 87.

23. Douglas Frasier, speech at the University of Louisville, April 22, 1986.

24. Harold S. Roberts, *Roberts' Dictionary of Industrial Relations*, 3rd ed. (Washington, DC: Bureau of National Affairs, 1986), p. 645.

25. Robert J. Schulhof, "Five Years with a Scanlon Plan," *Personnel Administrator* 24 (June 1979), pp. 55–62; see also Shaun G. Clark, "Rethinking the Adversarial Model in Labor Relations: An Argument for Repeal of Section 8(a)(2)," *Yale Law Review* 96 (1987), pp. 2021–2050.

26. John Savage, "Incentive Programs at Nucor Corporation Boost Productivity," *Personnel Administrator* 22 (August 1981), pp. 33–36.

27. "The Revolutionary Wage Deal at G.M.'s Packard Electric," *Business Week*, August 29, 1983, p. 54.

28. Bureau of National Affairs, *Basic Patterns in Union Contracts*, p. 113.

29. "The Double Standard That's Setting Worker against Worker," *Business Week*, April 8, 1983, p. 70.

30. Ivan Ross, "Employers Win Big in the Move to Two-Tier Contracts," *Fortune*, April 29, 1985, pp. 82–92; Robert J. Harris Jr., "More Firms Set Two-Tier Pacts with Unions, Hurting Future Hires," *Wall Street Journal*, December 12, 1983, p. 34; Dan Wessel, "Two-Tier Pay Spreads, But the Pioneer Firms Encounter Problems," *Wall Street Journal*, October 14, 1985, p. 1; Ken Jennings and Earle Trajuham, "The Wages of Two-Tier Pay Plans," *Personnel Journal* 67, no. 3 (March 1988), p. 58.

31. James E. Martin and Melanie M. Peterson, "Two-Tier Wage Structures: Implications for Equity Theory," *Academy of Management Journal* 30, no. 2 (June 1987), pp. 297–315.

32. Thomas D. Heetderks and James E. Martin, "Employee Perceptions of the Effects of a Two-Tier Wage Structure," *Journal of Labor Research* 7, no. 3 (Summer 1991), pp. 279–295.

33. Bureau of National Affairs, *Basic Patterns in Union Contracts*, p. 113.

34. Julia Laulor, "Auto Talks Revive Two-Tier Wage Concept, Concerns" *USA Today*, September 17, 1993, p. 5B.

35. Susan Carey and Scott McCartney, "Airlines Big Profits Raise Unions' Expectations," *Wall Street Journal*, January 10, 1997, p. A2.

36. Reid Carron and Kathlyn Ernst Noecker, "The Employer's Duty to Supply Financial Information to the Union: When Has the Employer Asserted an *Inability* to Pay?" *Labor Lawyer* 8, no. 4 (Fall 1992), p. 815.

37. David W. Belcher, *Wage and Salary Administration* (Englewood Cliffs, NJ: Prentice Hall, 1982), pp. 106–113.

38. *Agreement*, The Lockheed-Georgia Company and the International Association of Machinists and Aerospace Workers, AFL-CIO, 1968–1971, pp. 86–87.

39. Bureau of National Affairs, *Grievance Guide*, 9th ed. (Washington, DC: BNA Books, 1995), pp. 433–435.

40. Belcher, *Wage and Salary Administration*, pp. 106–113.

41. Ibid., pp. 236–243.

42. Gordon S. Skinner and E. Edward Herman, "The Importance of Costing Labor Contracts," *Labor Law Journal* (August 1981), pp. 497–504.

43. Wayne F. Cascio, *Costing Human Resources: The Financial Impact of Behavior in Organizations* (Boston: Kent Publishing, 1982), p. 99.

44. Michael H. Granof, *How to Cost Your Labor Contract* (Washington, DC: Bureau of National Affairs, 1973), pp. 4–5.

45. Ibid., p. 33.

46. Skinner and Herman, "Costing Labor Law Contracts," pp. 500–501.

47. Cascio, *Costing Human Resources*, p. 102.

48. Granof, *Cost Your Labor Contract*, p. 34.

49. Frederick L. Sullivan, *How to Calculate the Manufacturer's Costs in Collective Bargaining* (New York: AMACOM, 1980), pp. 23–26.

50. Michael R. Carrell and Lynn Hampton, "Computer Enhanced Labor Negotiations," *Labor Law Journal* (October 1985), pp. 795–800.

51. U.S. Department of Labor, Bureau of Labor Statistics, *Handbook of Labor Statistics* (Washington, DC: GPO, 1980), p. 56.

52. Michael Podgursky, "Unions, Establishment Size and Intra-Industry Threat Effects," *Industrial and Labor Relation Review* 39, no. 2 (January 1986), pp. 277–294.

CHAPTER 8

1. Olivia S. Mitchell, "Fringe Benefits and the Cost of Changing Jobs," *Industrial and Labor Relations Review* 37, no. 1 (October 1983), pp. 70–78.

2. James R. Morris, "Those Burgeoning Worker Benefits," *Nation's Business*, February 1987, pp. 53–54.

3. Bureau of National Affairs, "Give-backs Highlight Three Major Bargaining Agreements," *Personnel Administrator* 28, no. 1 (January 1983), pp. 33–35.

4. Bureau of National Affairs, *Report on Labor Relations in an Economic Recession: Job Losses and Concession Bargaining* (Washington, DC: Bureau of National Affairs, 1982), pp. 56–59.

5. George Ruben, "Collective Bargaining in 1982: Results Dictated by Economy," *Monthly Labor Review* 106 (January 1983), pp. 30–33.

6. Bureau of National Affairs, *Collective Bargaining and Labor Relations Database* (Washington, DC: Bureau of National Affairs, 1984), p. 21.

7. Dana Milbank, "Inland Steel Sets Accord with Steelworkers," *Wall Street Journal*, May 28, 1993, p. A2.

8. Robert L. Rose, "Northwest Wins Pay Concessions from Two Unions," *Wall Street Journal*, May 28, 1993, p. A2.

9. Amy Harmon, "Auto Workers War Crosses Union Hires," *Los Angeles Times*, March 15, 1992, pp. D1, 8.

10. Dave Kansas, "Pratt & Whitney, Union Pact to Save Connecticut Jobs," *Wall Street Journal*, June 8, 1993, p. A8.

11. Mark Schuster, "The Impact of Union-Management Cooperation on Productivity and Employment, *Industrial and Labor Relations Review* 36, no. 4 (1983), pp. 415–430.

12. Mark Plovnick and Gary Chaison, "Relationships between Concession Bargaining and Labor-Management Cooperation," *Academy of Management Journal* 28, no. 3 (September 1985), pp. 697–704.

13. Gary N. Chaison and Mark S. Plovnick, "Is There a New Collective Bargaining?" *California Management Review* 28, no. 4 (Summer 1986), pp. 54–61.

14. Judy L. Ward, "Firms Forcing Employees to Repay Some Costs If They Quit Too Soon," *Wall Street Journal*, July 16, 1985, p. 30.

15. "Auto Workers Will Feel Pinch of Lower or No Profits," *Bakersfield Californian*, February 20, 1990, p. B7; Scott A. Kruse, "Giveback Bargaining: One Answer to Current Labor Problems?" *Personnel Journal* 62 no. 4 (April 1983), pp. 286–289; Douglas Lavin, "Chrysler Aides to Get Bonuses Equal to Salaries," *Wall Street Journal*, February 22, 1994, p. A3.

16. James M. Rosbrow, "Unemployment Insurance System Marks Its 50th Anniversary," *Monthly Labor Review* 108, no. 9 (September 1985), pp. 21–28.

17. Jerry Flint, "The Old Folks," *Forbes* 125, no. 4 (February 18, 1980), pp. 51–56.

18. Dale Detlefs, *1984 Guide to Social Security* (Louisville, KY: Meidinger and Associates, 1984), pp. 6–9.

19. Bureau of National Affairs, *Basic Patterns in Union Contracts*, 14th ed. (Washington, DC: BNA Books, 1995), p. 27.

20. Lawrence Meyer, "Many Workers Lose Retirement Benefits Despite Reform Laws," *Washington Post*, September 7, 1982.

21. William Alpert, "Unions and Private Wage Supplements," *Journal of Labor Research* 3, no. 2 (Spring 1982), pp. 179–199.

22. Augustin Fosu, "Impact of Unionism on Pension Fringes," *Industrial Relations* 22, no. 3 (Fall 1983), pp. 419–425.

23. Steven G. Allen and Robert L. Clark, "Unions, Pension Wealth, and Age—Compensation Profits," *Industrial and Labor Relations Review* 39, no. 4 (July 1986), pp. 502–512. Also Steven G. Allen, Robert Clark, and Dan Summer, "Post-Retirement Adjustments of Pension Benefits," *Journal of Human Resources* 21, no. 1 (1986), pp. 118–137.

24. Kenneth H. Anderson, Robert V. Burkhauser, and Jane F. Quinn, "Do Retirement Dreams Come True? The Effect of Unanticipated Events on Retirement Plans," *Industrial and Labor Relations Review* 39, no. 4 (July 1986), pp. 518–526.

25. Vicky Cahan, "Mandatory Retirement Gets Put Out to Pasture," *Business Week*, November 3, 1986, p. 31.

26. "Pension Landscape Being Transformed," *Sunday World-Herald*, June 6, 1993, p. G1.

27. The Retirement Equity Act of 1984.

28. "When Pension Liabilities Dampen Profits," *Business Week*, June 16, 1983, pp. 80–81.

29. Marilyn Schaefer, "Continental Can to Pay $415 Million," *HR Executive* 5, no. 2 (February 1991), p. 10.

30. Michael H. Granof, *How to Cost Your Labor Contract* (Washington, DC: BNA, 1973), p. 61.

31. Bureau of National Affairs, *Basic Patterns in Union Contracts*, p. 41.

32. Ibid., p. 44.

33. D. Quinn Mills, "When Employers Make Concessions," *Harvard Business Review* (May–June 1983), pp. 103–113.

34. Peter Cappelli, "Auto Industry Experiments with the Guaranteed Income Stream," *Monthly Labor Review* 107, no. 7 (July 1984), pp. 37–39.

35. Cristina Pita, "Advance Notice and Severance Pay Provisions in Contracts," *Monthly Labor Review* (July 1996), pp. 43–50.

36. Martin Joy Galvin and Michael Robert Lied, "Severance: A Liability in Waiting?" *Personnel Journal* 65, no. 6 (June 1986), pp. 126–131.

37. *UAW v. Roblin Industries*, 114 LRRM 2428 (Mich. Cir. 1984).

38. *Agreement* between Anaconda Aluminum Co. and Aluminum Workers Local No. 130 and the Aluminum Workers International Union, AFL-CIO, 1980–1983, pp. 26–27. Used with permission.

39. Bureau of National Affairs, *Basic Patterns in Union Contracts*, pp. 13–14.

40. Allan P. Blostin, "Is Employer-Sponsored Life Insurance Declining Relative to Other Benefits?" *Monthly Labor Review* 104, no. 7 (September 1981), pp. 31–33.

41. Bureau of National Affairs, *Basic Patterns in Union Contracts*, p. 21.

42. Ibid.

43. *Agreement* between Anaconda Aluminum Co. and Aluminum Workers Local No. 130 and the Aluminum Workers International Union, AFL-CIO, 1980–1983, pp. 27–30. Used with permission.

44. Melissa Praffitt Reese, "Strikes and the Obligation to Continue Group Health Care Coverage under COBRA," *Labor Law Journal* 39, no. 11 (November 1988), pp. 766–770.

45. Bureau of National Affairs, *Basic Patterns in Union Contracts*, pp. 23–25.

46. Ibid.

47. Bureau of National Affairs, *Grievance Guide*, 9th ed. (Washington, DC: Bureau of National Affairs, 1995), p. 135.

48. Health Maintenance Organization Act.

49. Michael R. Carrell, "Employer Provided Health Care—What Are the Alternatives?" *Business Forum*, 13, no. 2 (Spring 1988), pp. 4–7.

50. Bureau of National Affairs, 1995, *Basic Patterns in Union Contracts*, pp. 11–21.

51. Robert N. Frumkin, "Health Insurance Trends in Cost Control and Coverage," *Monthly Labor Review* 109, no. 9 (September 1986), pp. 3–8.

52. "Reduced Costs, Increased Worker Production Are Rationale for Tax-Favored Corporate Fitness Plans," *Employee Benefit Plan Review*, November 1983, p. 21.

53. Charles A. Berry, *An Approach to Good Health for Employees and Reduced Health Care Costs for Industry*, Washington, DC: Health Insurance Association of America, (1981), p. 9.

54. Jane Daniel, "An Offer Your Doctor Can't Refuse," *American Health*, November/December 1982, p. 82.

55. Berry, *Approach to Good Health*, p. 15.

56. Jack N. Kondrasuk, "Corporate Physical Fitness Programs: The Role of the Personnel Department," *Personnel Administrators* 29, no. 12 (December 1984), pp. 75–80.

57. Richard Feldman and Michael Betzold, *End of the Line: Autoworkers and the American Dream* (New York: Weidenfeld & Nicolson Publishers, 1988), p. 21.

58. Diane Kirrane, "EAPS: Dawning of a New Age," *HR Magazine* 35, no. 1 (January 1990), pp. 30–34.

59. Ibid.

60. Roger K. Good, "What Bechtel Learned Creating an Employee Assistance Program," *Personnel Journal* 63, no. 9 (September 1984), pp. 80–86.

61. "Employees Join Efforts to Trim Health Care Costs," *Resource* (Alexandria, VA: American Society for Personnel Administration, January 1986), pp. 1, 6.

62. "Cutting Costs with Unions," *Resource* (Alexandria, VA: American Society for Personnel Administration, November 1986), p. 6.

63. Bureau of National Affairs, *Grievance Guide* p. 111.

64. Bureau of National Affairs, *Basic Patterns in Union Contracts*, p. 57.

65. Ibid., p. 101.

66. *Agreement* between Anaconda Aluminum Co. and Aluminum Workers Local No. 130 and the Aluminum Workers International Union, AFL-CIO, 1980–1983, pp. 9–11. Used with permission.

67. Granof, *How to Cost Your Labor Contract*, pp. 45–51.

68. Ibid., pp. 50–51.

69. Bureau of National Affairs, *Basic Patterns in Union Contracts*, pp. 71–77.

70. Ibid., p. 52.

71. Ibid., pp. 50–53.

72. Sandra L. King and Harry B. Williams, "Shift Work Pay Differentials and Practices in Manufacturing," *Monthly Labor Review* 198, no. 12 (December 1985), pp. 26–33.

73. Peter Fritsch, "Bilingual Employees Are Seeking More Pay, and Many Now Get It," *Wall Street Journal*, November 13, 1996, pp. A1, 6.

74. Betty A. Iseri and Robert R. Cangemi, "Flexible Benefits: A Growing Option," *Personnel* 3 (March 1990), pp. 30–32.

75. "Flex Plans Lower Health Care Costs: Hewitt Study," *Employee Benefit Plan Review* 44, no. 1 (July 1989), pp. 19–20.

76. Michael R. Carrell, Norbert F. Elbert, and Robert Hatfield, *Resource Management*, 5th ed. (Englewood Cliffs, NJ: Prentice Hall, 1995), pp. 472–475.

77. Carol Ann Diktaban, "Employer Supported Child Care as a Mandatory Subject of Collective Bargaining," *Hofstra Labor Law Journal* 8, no. 2 (1991), p. 385.

78. *Agreement* between Ziniz, Inc. and Kentucky State District Council of Carpenters, Millwrights, Conveyors, and Machinery Erectors, 1995–1999, p. 23.

79. *Agreement* between Ford Motor Company and the UAW, 1996, p. 241.

CHAPTER 9

1. Sumner H. Slichter, *Union Policies and Industrial Management* (Washington, DC: Brooklyn Institute, 1941), pp. 1–5.

2. *Agreement* between Chrysler Corp. and UAW, 1997–1999.

3. Daniel Cornfield, "Seniority, Human Capital, and Layoffs: A Case Study," *Industrial Relations* 21, no. 3 (Fall 1982), pp. 352–364.

4. William Cooke, "Permanent Layoffs: What's Implicit in the Contract?" *Industrial Relations* 20, no. 2 (Spring 1981), pp. 186–192.

5. Francine Blau and Lawrence Kahn, "Unionism, Seniority, and Turnover," *Industrial Relations* 22, no. 3 (Fall 1983), pp. 362–373.

6. Maryellen Kelley, "Discrimination in Seniority Systems: A Case Study," *Industrial and Labor Relations Review* 36, no. 1 (October 1982), pp. 40–41.

7. Bureau of National Affairs, *Basic Patterns in Union Contracts*, 14th ed. (Washington, DC: BNA Books, 1995), p. 85.

8. Stephen Cabot, *Labor Management Relations Manual*, 1981 Supplement (Boston: Warren, Gorham, Lamont, 1981), chap. 15, p. 1.

9. *Agreement* between Anaconda Aluminum Co. and Aluminum Workers Trades Council of Columbia Falls, AFL-CIO, 1980, p. 6.

10. *Agreement* between E. I. duPont Co. and the Affiliated Chemical Workers of Kentucky, 1943.

11. Cabot, *Labor Management Relations Manual*, chap. 15, p. 4.

12. Bureau of National Affairs, *Basic Patterns in Union Contracts*, p. 69.

13. *Gulton Electro-Voice, Inc.*, 266 NLRB 406, 112 LRRM 1361 (1983).

14. Bureau of National Affairs, *Basic Patterns in Union Contracts*, p. 86.

15. Bureau of National Affairs, *Grievance Guide*, 9th ed. (Washington, DC: Bureau of National Affairs, 1995), pp. 278–285.

16. Katherine G. Abraham and James L. Medoff, "Length of Service and Promotions in Union and Nonunion Work Groups," *Industrial and Labor Relations Review* 38, no. 3 (April 1985), pp. 408–420. Also D. Quinn Mills, "Seniority versus Ability in Promotion Decisions," *Industrial and Labor Relations Review* 38, no. 3 (April 1985), pp. 421–425.

17. Adapted from *Agreement* between Anaconda Aluminum Co. and Aluminum Workers Local No. 130 and the Aluminum Workers International Union, AFL-CIO, 1980–1983, pp. 16–17. Used with permission.

18. Bureau of National Affairs, *Grievance Guide*, p. 201.

19. Ibid.

20. *Bethlehem Steel Co.*, 1924 LA 820 (1955).

21. *Copeo Steel & Engineering Co.*, 12 LA 6 (1979).

22. *Metallab, Inc.*, 65 LA 1191 (1975).

23. Bureau of National Affairs, *Grievance Guide*, pp. 207–208.

24. *Agreement* between Anaconda Aluminum Co. and Aluminum Workers Local No. 130 and the Aluminum Workers International Union, AFL-CIO, 1980–1983, pp. 14–16. Used with permission.

25. Valerie Frazel, "Striking a Balance: Temps and Union Workers," *Personnel Journal* 75, no. 1 (January 1996), pp. 103–105.

26. Public Law 100-379. 102 Stat. 895, August 14, 1988.

27. "Reagan Succumbing to Politics, Decides against Vetoing Plant Closings Measure," *Wall Street Journal*, August 3, 1988, p. 3.

28. Wilson McLeod, "Judicial Devitalization of the WARN," *Labor Law Journal* 44, no. 4 (April 1993), pp. 220–229.

29. Paul D. Staudohar, "New Plant Closing Laws Aids Workers in Transition," *Personnel Journal* 68, no. 1 (January 1989), pp. 87–90, and comments by Conte Silvio, *Congressional Record* no. 105, July 13, 1988, p. H5507.

30. Dale Yoden and Paul D. Staudohar, "Management and Public Policy in Plant Closure," *Sloan Management Review* 26, no. 4 (Summer 1985), p. 52.

31. Kevin G. Salwen, "Clinton Mulls Requiring More Notice of Layoffs," *Wall Street Journal*, September 14, 1993, p. A2.

32. Gillian Flynn, "The Unions' Power to Sue Is Growing," *Personnel Journal* (September 1996), pp. 135–141; and *United Food and Commercial Workers Union Local 751 v. Brown Group Inc.*, 116 S.Ct. 1529 (1996).

33. *North Star Steel Co.* and *Thomas et al. v. USWA*, 115 S.Ct. 1927 (1995).

34. John Zalusky, "Short-Time Compensation: The AFL-CIO Perspective." *Monthly Labor Review* 109, no. 5 (May 1986), pp. 33–34.

35. Frank Elkouri and Edna Asper Elkouri, *How Arbitration Works*, 4th ed., 1985–87 Supp. (Washington, DC: Bureau of National Affairs, 1988), pp. 614–616.

36. Bureau of National Affairs, *Grievance Guide*, pp. 278–285.

37. Adapted with permission from Frank Elkouri and Edna Asper Elkouri, *How Arbitration Works*, 4th ed. (Washington, DC: Bureau of National Affairs, 1988), pp. 621–656. Copyright © 1988 by the Bureau of National Affairs, Inc., Washington, D.C.

38. Thomas Kennedy, *Labor Arbitration and Industrial Change* (Washington, DC: Bureau of National Affairs, 1963), pp. 1–34.

39. Elkouri and Elkouri, *How Arbitration Works*, pp. 607–609.

40. Walter Baer, *Winning in Labor Arbitration* (Columbus, OH: Crain, 1982), p. 20.

41. "Union Wins $6 Million Settlement with AT&T," *Louisville Courier-Journal*, January 10, 1987, p. B1.

42. *Fibreboard Paper Products Corp. v. NLRB*, 130 NLRB 1558 (1961).

43. *Agreement* between UAW and Ford Motor Company, 1996, pp. 236–240.

44. Reprinted by permission from Bureau of National Affairs, *Grievance Guide*, 9th ed. (Washington, DC: Bureau of National Affairs, 1995), pp. 376–380. Copyright © 1995 by the Bureau of National Affairs, Inc., Washington, D.C.

45. *First National Maintenance Corp.*, 452 U.S. 666 (1981).

46. *Milwaukee Spring Division of Illinois Coil Spring Co. (I)*, 718 F.2d 1102 (7th Cir. 1983); *(II)*, 268 NLRB 601 (1984).

47. *Otis Elevator*, 269 NLRB 891, 115 LRRM 1281 (1984).

48. Patrick Hardin, ed., *The Developing Labor Law*, 3rd ed. (Washington, DC: Bureau of National Affairs, 1992), pp. 916–918.

49. *Dubuque Packing Co. v. NLRB*, 303 NLRB 66, 137 LRRM 1185 (1991).

50. Bureau of National Affairs, *Grievance Guide*, p. 376.

51. Dawn Gunsch, "Training Prepares Workers for Drug Testing," *Personnel Journal* 72, no. 5 (May 1993), pp. 52–59.

52. "Drug Testing Has Joined Mainstream," *Sunday World-Herald*, May 23, 1993, pp. G1, 4 (Omaha, Nebraska).

53. *Johnson-Bateman Co.*, 295 NLRB 26 (1989).

54. *Minneapolis Star Tribune*, 295 NLRB 63 (1989).

55. *New York City Transit Authority v. Beazer*, 440 U.S. 568, 99 S.Ct. 1355, 59 L.Ed. 2d 587 (1979).

56. David D. Schein, "How to Prepare a Company Policy Abuse Control," *Personnel Journal*, 65, no. 7 (July 1986), pp. 30–38.

57. *International Brotherhood of Teamsters no. 878 v. Commercial Warehouse*, 84 F.3d 299 (8th Cir. 1996).

58. *Skinner v. Railway Labor Executives Association*, Supreme Court Report, vol. 109 (1989), p. 1402.

59. *Pacific Motor Trucking*, 86 LA 497 (1986); *Amalgamated Transit Union, Local 1433 and Phoenix Transit System*, 87-2 ARB Paragraph 8510 (1987).

60. *Shelby County Health Care Center*, 90 LA 1225 (1988).

61. *Boise Cascade Corp.*, 90 LA 105 (1987).

62. *Warehouse Distribution Centers*, 90 LA 979 (1987).

63. *Gem City Chemicals*, 86 LA 1023 (1986).

64. *Signal Delivery Services, Inc.*, 86 LA 7S (1986).

65. *Consolidated Coal Co.*, 87 LA 111 (1986).

66. Michael H. LeRoy, "The Presence of Drug Testing in the Workplace and Union Member Attitudes," *Labor Studies Journal* 16, no. 4 (Fall 1991), pp. 33–42.

67. *Fall River Dyeing v. National Labor Relations Board*, U.S. 107, S.Ct. 2225 (1987).

68. Robert F. Mace, "The Supreme Court's Labor Law Successorship Doctrine after Fall River Dyeing," *Labor Law Journal* 39, no. 2 (February 1988), pp. 102–109.

69. Hardin, *The Developing Labor Law*, pp. 779–780.

70. Steven B. Goldstein, "Protecting Employee Rights in Successorship," *Labor Law Journal* 44, no. 1 (January 1993), pp. 18–29.

71. Celestine J. Richards, "The Efficacy of Successorship Clauses in Collective Bargaining Agreements," *Georgetown Law Journal* 79 (1991), p. 1549.

72. *317 NLRB v. Canteen Company*, 1052 (1995).

CHAPTER 10

1. *H. J. Heinz Co. v. National Labor Relations Board*, 311 U.S. 514, 51 S.Ct. 320, 85 L.Ed. 309 (1941).

2. 29 U.S.C. sec. 158(b)(1982).

3. David A. Dilts and Clarence Deitsch, *Labor Relations* (New York: Macmillan, 1983), p. 152.

4. Bureau of National Affairs, *Grievance Guide*, 9th ed. (Washington, DC: Bureau of National Affairs, 1995), pp. 411–413.

5. Bureau of National Affairs, *Basic Patterns in Union Contracts*, 14th ed. (Washington, DC: BNA Books, 1995), pp. 1–3.

6. Harold S. Roberts, *Roberts' Dictionary of Industrial Relations*, 3rd ed. (Washington, DC: Bureau of National Affairs, 1986), p. 396.

7. Kevin J. Murphy, "Determinants of Contract Duration in Collective Bargaining Agreements," *Industrial and Labor Relations Review* 45, no. 2 (January 1992), pp. 352–365.

8. Marvin Hill Jr. and Anthony V. Sinicrope, *Management Rights* (Washington, DC: Bureau of National Affairs, 1986), p. 3.

9. Bureau of National Affairs, *Basic Patterns in Union Contracts*, pp. 79–81.

10. Hill and Sinicrope, *Management Rights*, pp. 4–5.

11. Arthur J. Goldberg, "Management's Reserved Rights: A Labor View," *Proceedings of the 9th Annual Meeting of The National Arbitration Association*, 118 (1956), pp. 120–121.

12. *Agreement* between the Anaconda Company and United Steel Workers of America. AFL-CIO Local Union No. 4612.

13. Hill and Sinicrope, *Management Rights*, pp. 6–7.

14. Paul Prasow and Edward Peters, *Arbitration and Collective Bargaining: Conflict Resolution in Labor Relations*, 2nd ed. (New York: McGraw-Hill, 1983), pp. 33–34.

15. *Fibreboard Corp.*, 379 U.S. 203, 57 LRRM 2609 (1964).

16. *First National Maintenance*, 452 U.S. 666, 107 LRRM 2705 (1981).

17. *Otis Elevator Co.*, 269 NLRB 891, 115 LRRM 1281 (1984).

18. *Dubuque Packing Co.*, 303 NLRB 66, 137 LRRM 1185 (1991).

19. Mairead E. Connor, "The Dubuque Packing Decision: New Test for Bargaining Over Decision to Relocate," *Labor Lawyer* 8, no. 2 (1992), pp. 289–295.

20. Bureau of National Affairs, *Basic Patterns in Union Contracts*, pp. 79–82.

21. *Labor Relations Bulletin* 667, no. 56 (October 1996), p. 1.

22. Stephen I. Schlossberg and Judith A. Scott, *Organizing and the Law*, 4th ed. (Washington, DC: BNA Books, 1991), p. 285.

23. Patrick Hardin, ed., *The Developing Labor Law*, 3rd ed. (Washington, DC: Bureau of National Affairs, 1992), pp. 699–701; also see *Bonnell/Tredegar Industries, Incorporated v. NLRB*, 46 F.3d 339 (4th Cir. 1995); *NLRB v. Unbelievable, Inc. (dba Frontier Hotel & Casino)*, 71 F. 3d 1434 (9th Cir. 1995).

24. 29 U.S.C. sec. 158(d) (1982).

25. U.S. Senate, Committee on Labor and Public Welfare, *Committee Report*, S. Rep. 105, 80th Cong., 1st sess., 1947, pp. 16–18.

26. Benjamin Aaron et al., *The Future of Labor Arbitration in America* (New York: American Arbitration Association, 1976), p. 87.

27. *Textile Workers Union v. Lincoln Mills*, 353 U.S. 448, 40 LRRM 2113 (1957).

28. *United Steelworkers v. American Mfg. Co.*, 363 U.S. 564, 46 LRRM 2414 (1960); *United Steelworkers v. Warrior & Gulf Navigation Co.*, 363 U.S. 574, 46 LRRM 2416 (1960); *United Steelworkers v. Enterprise Wheel & Car Corp.*, 363 U.S. 593, 46 LRRM 2423 (1960).

29. Aaron et al., *Future of Labor Arbitration in America*, p. 56.

30. *Collyer Insulated Wire*, 192 NLRB 837, 77 LRRM 1931 (1971).

31. *Spielberg Manufacturing Company*, 112 NLRB 1080, 36 LRRM 1152 (1955); see also Frank Elkouri and Edna Asper Elkouri. *How Arbitration Works*, 4th ed., 1985–1987 Supp. (Washington, DC: Bureau of National Affairs, 1988), pp. 6–7.

32. *Paperworkers International v. Misco*, 484 U.S. 29, 108 S.Ct. 364, 98 L.Ed. 2d 286 (1987); Marlin M. Volz et al., "Labor Arbitration and the Law of Collective Bargaining Agreements," *Labor Lawyer* 5, no. 3 (Summer 1989), pp. 599–606.

33. Michael H. LeRoy and Peter Feuille, "The *Steelworkers Trilogy* and Grievance Arbitration Appeals: How the Federal Courts Respond," *Industrial Relations Law Journal* 13, no. 1 (1992), pp. 78–120; see also *American Postal Workers Union, AFL-CIO v. U.S. Postal Service*, 52 F.3d 359 (1995).

34. *Olin Corp.* 268 NLRB 573 (1984), *Combustions Engineering, Inc.*, 272 NLRB 32 (1984); *Badger Meter, Inc.* 272 NLRB 123 (1984).

35. Benjamin W. Wolkinson, "The Impact of the *Collyer* Policy of Deferral: An Empirical Study," *Industrial and Labor Relations Review* 38, no. 3 (April 1985), pp. 377–391.

36. *Boys Market, Inc. v. Retail Clerks Union Local 770*, 398 U.S. 235, 90 S.Ct. 1583, 26 L.Ed. 2d 199 (1970).

37. *Sinclair Refining Company v. Atchison*, 370 U.S. 195, 82 S.Ct. 1328, 8 L.Ed. 440 (1962).

38. *Buffalo Forge Company v. United Steelworkers of America*, 428 U.S. 397, 96 S.Ct. 3141, 49 L.Ed. 2d 1022 (1976).

39. *Indianapolis Power and Light Company*, 276 NLRB 211 (1985).

40. *IBEW Local 387 v. NLRB*, No. 85-7129 (9th Cir., May 6, 1986).

41. *Vaca v. Sipes*, 386 U.S. 171, 64 LRRM 2369 (1967); *Hines v. Anchor Motor Co., Inc.*, 424 U.S. 554, 91 LRRM 2481 (1976); and *Bowen v. U.S. Postal Service*, 112 LRRM 2281 (1983).

42. See George W. Bohlander, "Fair Representation: Not Just a Union Problem," *The Personnel Administrator* 25, no. 3 (March 1980), pp. 36–40, 82.

43. Roberts, *Roberts' Dictionary of Industrial Relations*, p. 285.

44. Bureau of National Affairs, *Basic Patterns in Union Contracts*, pp. 2–3.

45. *Agreement* between E. I. duPont de Nemours and Company and the Neoprene Craftsmen Union, 1994, p. 28.

46. *Jacobs Manufacturing Company*, 94 NLRB 1214 (1951).

47. Daniel D. Cook, "Boycott! Labor's Last Resort," *Industry Week* 189 (June 18, 1976), pp. 23–32.

48. *De Bartola Corp. v. Florida Gulf Coast Trades Council*, 56 USLW 4328 (1988).

49. Samuel A. DiLullo, "Secondary Boycotts: Has the Court Gone Too Far or Maybe Not Far Enough?" *Labor Law Journal* 40, no. 6 (June 1989), pp. 376–381.

50. *Delta Airlines, Inc.*, 293 NLRB 67 (1989).

51. *Johnston Development Group v. Local 1578*, 131 LRRM 2417 (N.J. Cir. 1989).

52. Gerard Morales, "Labor Unions' Rights to Handbill Neutral Employers and to Picket on Private Property," *Labor Lawyer* 6, no. 2 (1990) pp. 295–300.

53. *Pye v. Teamsters Local 122*, 149 LRRM 3089 (1st Cir. 1995).

54. *D'Amico v. Painters District Council 51 (Manganaro Corp. of Md.)*, 120 LRRM 3473 (Md. Cir. 1985).

55. Hardin, *The Developing Labor Law*, p. 1385.

56. National Labor Relations Act, Section 8(b)(6).

57. Schlossberg and Scott, *Organizing and the Law*, p. 110.

CHAPTER 11

1. Vice President Al Gore, *From Red Tape to Results: Creating a Government That Works Better and Costs Less*, text of a speech delivered to the National League of Cities in Washington, D.C., September 7, 1993, p. 87.

2. William H. Holley and Kenneth M. Jennings, *The Labor Relations Process*, 5th ed. (Chicago: Dryden Press, 1991), pp. 156–164.

3. Harry H. Wellington and Ralph K. Winter, *Unions and Cities*, 2nd ed. (Washington, DC: Brookings Institute, 1988), pp. 1–18.

4. Richard B. Freeman and Carey Ichniowski, "Introduction: The Public Sector Look of Unionism," in *When Public Sector Workers Unionize*, ed. Richard B. Freeman and Carey Ichniowski (Chicago: University of Chicago Press, 1988), pp. 50–97.

5. David Lewin and Richard B. Peterson, "A Model for Measuring Effectiveness of the Grievance Process," *Monthly Labor Review* 106, no. 4 (April 1983), pp. 47–49.

6. Dan R. Dalton and William D. Tudor, "Grievance Arbitration May Be Expensive, But What of the Alternative?" *Personnel Administrator* 26, no. 3 (March 1981), pp. 25–29.

7. Frank Elkouri and Edna Asper Elkouri, *How Arbitration Works*, 4th ed. (Washington, DC: Bureau of National Affairs, 1985), pp. 153–154.

8. *Cudahy Packing Co.*, 7 LA G45, G46 (1947).

9. Elkouri and Elkouri, *How Arbitration Works*, pp. 155–156; and *E. I. duPont de Nemours and Co.*, 29 LA 646, 650 (1957).

10. *Diamond Shamrock Corp.*, 55 LA 827 (1946).

11. Bureau of National Affairs, *Grievance Guide*, 6th ed. (Washington, DC: Bureau of National Affairs, 1978), p. 306.

12. *Alexander's Personnel Providers, Inc.*, 68 LA 249 (1947).

13. Thomas B. Knight, "Feedback and Grievance Resolution," *Industrial and Labor Relations Review* 39, no. 4 (July 1986), pp. 585–598.

14. Harold Davey, Mario Bognanno, and David Estenson, *Contemporary Collective Bargaining*, 4th ed. (Englewood Cliffs, NJ: Prentice Hall, 1982), p. 169.

15. Bureau of National Affairs, *Basic Patterns in Union Contracts*, 14th ed. (Washington, DC: BNA Books, 1995), p. 35.

16. See the *Steelworkers Trilogy Cases: United Steelworkers of America v. Enterprise Wheel & Car Corp.*, 80 S.Ct. 1358, 34 LA 569 (1960); *United Steelworkers of America v. American Mfg. Co.*, 363 U.S. 566–567 (1960); and *United Steelworkers of America v. Warrior & Gulf Navigation Company*, 363 U.S. 582 (1960).

17. Steven Briggs, "The Grievance Procedure," *Personnel Journal* 60, no. 6 (June 1981), pp. 471–474.

18. Dalton and Tudor, "Grievance Arbitration May Be Expensive," pp. 25–27. Reprinted with permission of *HR Magazine* (formerly *Personnel Administrator*) published by the Society for Human Resource Management, Alexandria, VA.

19. Stephen Cabot, *Labor-Management Relations Manual* (Boston: Warren, Gorham, Lamont, 1979), chap. 16, pp. 1–2.

20. Bureau of National Affairs, *Grievance Guide*, pp. 4–5.

21. Cabot, *Labor-Management Relations Manual*, chap. 16, pp. 3–5.
22. Maurice S. Trotta, *Arbitration of Labor-Management Disputes* (New York: American Management Association, 1974), p. 218.
23. David W. Ewing, "What Business Thinks about Employee Rights," *Harvard Business Review* 55, no. 5 (September–October 1977), pp. 81–94.
24. *Norton-Children's Hospitals Employee Handbook* (Louisville, KY: Norton-Children's Hospitals, undated), pp. 17–18, by permission of Norton-Children's Hospitals, Inc.
25. James P. Swann, "Formal Grievance Procedures in Non-union Plants," *Personnel Administrator* 26, no. 8 (August 1981), pp. 66–70.
26. Beber I. Helburn and Robert Rodgers, "Hesitancy of Arbitrators to Accept Interest Arbitration Cases: A Test of Conventional Wisdom." *Public Administration Review* 45 (1985), pp. 398–402.
27. Arnold M. Zack, "The Arbitration of Interest Disputes: A Process in Peril," *Arbitration Journal* 45 (1985) and 55 (1994).
28. Elkouri and Elkouri, *How Arbitration Works*, p. 97.
29. *Harrell Alexander, Sr. v. Gardner-Denver Co.*, 415 U.S. 36, 944 S.Ct. 101 (1974). *W.R. Grace and Co., v. Local Union 759, International Union of the United Rubber Cork, Linoleum and Plastic Workers of America*, 461 U.S. 757, 103, S.Ct. 2177 (1963).
30. *Newsday, Inc. v. Long Island Typographical Union, Local 915, CWA, AFL-CIO*, 915 F.2d 840 (2d Cir. 1990), *Stroehman Bakeries, Inc. v. Local 776, International Brotherhood of Teamsters*, 969 F.2d 1436 (3rd Cir. 1992). *Chrysler Motors Corp. v. International Union, Allied Industrial Workers of America, AFL-CIO*, 959 F.2d 685 (7th Cir. 1992).
31. Mollie H. Bowers, "Grievance Mediation: Another Route to Resolution," *Personnel Journal* 61, no. 2 (February 1982), pp. 132–133.
32. William E. Simkin, *Mediation and the Dynamics of Collective Bargaining* (Washington, DC: Bureau of National Affairs, 1971), p. 300.
33. Bowers, "Grievance Mediation," p. 131.
34. Jeanne M. Brett and Steven B. Goldberg, "Wildcat Strikes in Bituminous Coal Mining," *Industrial and Labor Relations Review* 32, no. 4 (July 1979), pp. 467–483.
35. Jeanne M. Brett and Steven B. Goldberg, "Grievance Mediation in the Coal Industry: A Field Experiment," *Industrial and Labor Relations Review* 37, no. 1 (October 1983), pp. 49–68.
36. Ibid., pp. 67–68.
37. Bowers, "Grievance Mediation," pp. 134–136.
38. Matthew T. Roberts, Roger S. Walters, William H. Holley Jr., and Hubert S. Field, "Grievance Mediation: A Management Perspective," *Arbitration Journal* 45, no. 3 (September 1990), pp. 15–23.

CHAPTER 12

1. Edwin Witte, *Historical Survey of Labor Arbitration* (Ithaca, NY: Cornell University Press, 1952), pp. 29–33.
2. Ibid.
3. Robban W. Fleming, *The Labor Arbitration Process* (Urbana, IL: University of Illinois Press, 1965), pp. 2–8.
4. Jean T. McKelvey, *The Profession of Labor Arbitration: Selected Papers from the First Seven Annual Meetings of the National Academy of Arbitrators* (Washington, DC: Bureau of National Affairs, 1957), pp. 42–46.
5. *Textile Workers Union of America v. Lincoln Mills of Alabama*, 353 U.S. 448, 77 S.Ct. 912 (1957); *United Steelworkers of America v. American Mfg. Co.*, 363 U.S. 564, 80 S.Ct. 1343 (1960); *United Steelworkers of America v. Warrior & Gulf Navigation Co.*, 363 U.S. 574, 80 S.Ct. 1347 (1960); *United Steelworkers of America v. Enterprise Wheel & Car Corp.*, 363 U.S. 593, 80 S.Ct. 1358 (1960).
6. Charles J. Coleman and Theodora T. Haynes, *Labor Arbitration: An Annotated Bibliography* (Ithaca, NY: ILR Press, 1994), pp. 10–22.
7. Arnold M. Zack, *Handbook for Grievance Arbitration: Procedural and Ethical Issues* (New York: Lexington Books, 1992), pp. 76–93.

8. *United Steelworkers of America v. Warrior & Gulf Navigation Co.*, 363 U.S. 574, 80 S.Ct. 1347 (1960).

9. *E. I. duPont de Nemours & Co. v. Grasselli Employees Independent Association of East Chicago, Inc.* No. 85-1577 (7th Cir. May 9, 1986.)

10. Frank Elkouri and Edna Asper Elkouri, *How Arbitration Works*, 4th ed. (Washington, DC: Bureau of National Affairs, 1985), pp. 8–9.

11. Ibid., p. 125.

12. *Labor Arbitration Procedures and Techniques* (New York: American Arbitration Association, 1978), pp. 12–13.

13. Stephen Cabot, *Labor-Management Relations Manual* (Boston: Warren, Gorham, Lamont, 1979), chap. 18, pp. 4–6.

14. Steven B. Goldberg, "The Mediation of Grievances under a Collective Bargaining Contract: An Alternative to Arbitration," *Northwestern University Law Review* 77, no. 3 (October 1982), pp. 270–273.

15. Nels Nelson and Earl Curry, "Arbitrator Characteristics and Arbitral Decisions," *Industrial Relations* 20, no. 3 (Fall 1981), pp. 312–317.

16. Steven Briggs and John Anderson, "An Empirical Investigation of Arbitrator Acceptability," *Industrial Relations* 19, no. 2 (Spring 1980), pp. 163–173.

17. Elkouri and Elkouri, *How Arbitration Works*, pp. 138–143.

18. Ibid., pp. 129–132.

19. *Agreement* between the Mechanical Contractors Association and Plumbers and Gas Fitters Local Union No. 107, 1979–1982, p. 21.

20. Elkouri and Elkouri, *How Arbitration Works*, p. 213.

21. *United Steelworkers of America v. Warrior & Gulf Navigation Co.*, 80 S.Ct. 1347, 1352–1353 (1960).

22. *AT&T Technologies v. Communication Workers of America*, 475 S.Ct. 11-758 (1986).

23. Judd H. Lees, "To Arbitrate or Not to Arbitrate: Who Decides?" *Labor Law Journal* 39, no. 7 (July 1988), pp. 418–422.

24. Theodore Kheel, *Labor Law* (New York: Matthew Bender, 1988), chap. 24, p. 41.

25. *Labor Arbitration Procedures and Techniques*, pp. 17–20.

26. Ibid.

27. *Instrument Workers v. Minneapolis Honeywell Co.*, 54 LRRM 2660, 2661 (1963).

28. Cabot, *Labor-Management Relations Manual*, chap. 18, p. 6.

29. Margaret A. Lareau and Howard R. Sacks, "Assessing Credibility in Labor Arbitration," *Labor Lawyer* 5, no. 3 (Spring 1989), pp. 151–193.

30. Kheel, *Labor Law*, chap. 24, p. 55.

31. Cabot, *Labor-Management Relations Manual*, chap. 18, pp. 7–8.

32. Kheel, *Labor Law*, chap. 24, p. 56.

33. Roger I. Abrams and Dennis R. Nolan, "Arbitral Craftsmanship and Opinion Writing," *Labor Lawyer* 5, no. 2 (Spring 1989), pp. 195–222.

34. Kheel, *Labor Law*, chap. 24, pp. 50–51.

35. Reprinted with permission from Frank Elkouri and Edna Asper Elkouri, *How Arbitration Works*, 4th ed. (Washington, DC: Bureau of National Affairs, 1985), p. 293. Copyright © 1985 by the Bureau of National Affairs, Inc., Washington, DC 20037.

36. Daniel F. Jennings and A. Dale Allen Jr., "How Arbitrators View the Process of Labor Arbitration: A Longitudinal Analysis," *Labor Studies Journal* 18, no. 1 (Winter 1993), pp. 41–50.

37. Howard Stiefel, "The Labor Arbitration Process: Survey of the New York State Bar Association Labor and Employment Law Section," *Labor Lawyer* 8, no. 4 (Fall 1992), pp. 971–983.

38. Wallace B. Nelson, "The Role of Common Law in Just Cause Disputes," *Personnel Journal* 58, no. 8 (August 1979), pp. 541–543.

39. Bureau of National Affairs, *Grievance Guide* (Washington, DC: Bureau of National Affairs, 1978), pp. 1–3.

40. Elkouri and Elkouri, *How Arbitration Works*, p. 688.
41. Nelson, "The Role of Common Law in Just Cause Disputes," pp. 541–543.
42. Kevin B. Zeese, *Drug Testing Legal Manual* (New York: Clark Boardman Company, 1988), chap. 4, p. 18.
43. *NTEU v. Von Raab*, 649 F.Supp. 380 (ED La 1986), 57 LW 4338 (March 21, 1989).
44. *Johnson Bateman Company*, 295 NLRB 26 (1989).
45. Zeese, *Drug Testing Legal Manual* chap. 4, pp. 18–19.
46. *N.L.R.B. GC 87-5; Brotherhood of Locomotive Engineers v. Burlington Northern RR. Co.*, 620 F.Supp. 163 (Mont. Cir. 1985).
47. *Maple Meadow Mining*, 90 LA 873 (1988).
48. *Vulcan Materials Co.*, 90 LA 1161 (1988).
49. *Pacific Motor Trucking*, 86 LA 497 (1986); *Amalgamated Transit Union, Local 1433, and Phoenix Transit System*, 87-2 ARB 8510.
50. *Shelby County Health Care Center*, 90 LA 1225 (1988).
51. *Boise Cascade Corp.*, 90 LA 105 (1987); see also Elkouri and Elkouri, eds., *How Arbitration Works*, 4th ed. 1985–1987 Supp. (Washington, DC: Bureau of National Affairs, 1988), p. 131.
52. *Warehouse Distribution Centers*, 90 LA 979 (1987).
53. *Gem City Chemicals*, 86 LA 1023 (1986).
54. *Signal Delivery Service, Inc.*, 86 LA 75 (1986).
55. Nelson, "The Role of Common Law in Just Cause Disputes," p. 551.
56. *Agreement*, General Motors Corporations and the United Auto Workers, 1970, p. 43.
57. *Bethlehem Steel Co.*, 24 LA 699, 702 (1955).
58. Steve Markham and Dow Scott, "Controlling Absenteeism: Union and Nonunion Differences," *Personnel Administrator* 30, no. 2 (February 1985), pp. 87–102.
59. Ibid.
60. Frank E. Kuzmits, "What to Do about Long-Term Absenteeism," *Personnel Administrator* 31, no. 10 (October 1986), pp. 93–100. See also Elkouri and Elkouri, *How Arbitration Works*, p. 545.
61. Bureau of National Affairs, *Grievance Guide*, p. 87.
62. Gail Schur White, "Past and Current Trends in Negligence and Incompetence Arbitration," *Personnel Journal* 58, no. 11 (November 1979), pp. 795–801.
63. *Agreement* National Conference of Brewery and Soft Drink Workers and Teamsters Local No. 745 and Jos. Schlitz Brewing Co., Longview, Texas, 1979, p. 24.
64. 9 LA 20 (1947).
65. Bureau of National Affairs, *Grievance Guide*, p. 204.
66. 11 LA 33 (1949).
67. *Agreement*, Mechanical Contractors Association of Kentucky, Inc. and Plumbers and Gas Fitters Local Union No. 107, 1979–1982, p. 6.
68. Bureau of National Affairs, *Grievance Guide*, pp. 226–227.
69. Ibid., p. 225.

CHAPTER 13

1. http://www.schoolreport.com/epi/files/neaftbk/book0000.htm, February 28, 1997.
2. Pub. L. 91-375, 84 Stat. 737, 39 U.S.C. sec. 1209 (1970).
3. Benjamin Aaron et al., *Public-Sector Bargaining* (Washington, DC: Bureau of National Affairs, 1979), p. 46.
4. David Lewin and Shirley B. Goldenberg, "Public Sector Unionism in the U.S. and Canada," *Industrial Relations* 19, no. 3 (Fall 1980), pp. 239–256.
5. Jerry Wurf, "Establishing the Legal Right of Public Employees to Bargain," *Monthly Labor Review* 92, no. 7 (July 1969), p. 66.
6. Henry Campbell Black, *Black's Law Dictionary*, 4th ed. (St. Paul, MN: West Publishing, 1968), p. 1568.
7. Robert Wechsler, "The Birth of Modern Public Employees Unions," *New York Labor History Association News Service*, 1995.

8. 5 U.S.C. sec. 7116(a)(1982).

9. Ibid.

10. Ibid.

11. 58 Fed. Reg. 52,201 (1993); "Federal Service Labor and Employment Law," *Labor Lawyer* 10, no. 3 (Summer 1994), p. 336.

12. For an overview of state and local legislation see Aaron et al., *Public-Sector Bargaining*, pp. 191–223; and Nels E. Nelson, "Public Policy and Union Security in the Public Sector," *Journal of Collective Negotiations in the Public Sector* 7, no. 2 (1978), pp. 87–117.

13. *National League of Cities v. Usery*, 426 U.S. 833 (1976).

14. Gregory M. Saltzman, "Bargaining Laws as a Cause and Consequence of the Growth of Teacher Unionism," *Industrial and Labor Relations Review* 38, no. 3 (April 1985), pp. 335–351.

15. Lewin and Goldenberg, "Public Sector Unionism," p. 245.

16. Aaron et al., *Public-Sector Bargaining*, pp. 80–117.

17. E. Edward Herman and Alfred Kuhn, *Collective Bargaining and Labor Relations* (Englewood Cliffs, NJ: Prentice Hall, 1981), p. 101.

18. James E. Martin, "Employee Characteristics and Representation Election Outcomes," *Industrial and Labor Relations Review* 38, no. 3 (April 1985), pp. 365–376.

19. *Rhode Island State Labor Relations Bd. of City of Woonsocket*, 3 Public Employee Bargaining (CCH) 43,730 (R.I., 1984).

20. Douglas E. Ray, Jennifer Gallagher, and Nancy A. Butler, "Regulating Union Representation Election Campaign Tactics: A Comparative Study of Private and Public Sector Approaches," *Nebraska Law Review* 66 (1987), pp. 532–561.

21. *Ellis v. Brotherhood of Railway, Airline and Steamship Clerks*, 446 U.S. 435, 104 S.Ct. 1883, 80 L.Ed. 2d 428 (1984). See also *Abood v. Detroit Board of Education*, 230 N.W.2d 322, 90 LRRM 2152 (1975). Charles M. Rehmus and Benjamin A. Kerner, "The Agency Shop after *ABOOD*: No Free Ride, But What's the Fare?" *Industrial and Labor Relations Review* 34, no. 1 (October 1980), pp. 90–100.

22. *Elrod v. Burns*, 427 U.S. 347 (1976).

23. "Compulsory Unionism in Government Employment," Public Service Research Council, reprinted in *Should the Federal Government Significantly Curtail the Powers of Labor Unions in the United States?* (Washington, DC: GPO, 1981), pp. 473–482.

24. G. Pascal Zachary, "Two-Edged Sword: Some Public Workers Lose Jobs as Agencies Outsource, *Wall Street Journal*, August 6, 1996, pp. A1, 6.

25. Ibid.

26. Javed Ashraf, "Union Wage Effects in the Public Sector: An Examination of the Impact across Alternative Governmental Structures," *Journal of Collective Negotiations in the Public Sector* 21, no. 4 (1992), pp. 287–297.

27. Greg Hundley, "Collective Bargaining Coverage of Union Members and Nonmembers in the Public Sector," *Industrial Relations* 32, no. 1 (Winter 1993), pp. 72–93.

28. Benjamin Aaron et al., *The Future of Labor Arbitration in America* (New York: American Arbitration Association, 1976), p. 18.

29. *National Treasury Employees Union (NTEU) et al. v. Von Raab*, 57 LA 4338 (3-21-89) and *Skinner v. Railway Labor Executive's Association*, 57 LA 4324 (3-21-89).

30. *Consolidated Rail Corporation v. Railway Labor Executives' Association et al.*, 57 LA 4742 (6-20-89).

31. *Dykes v. Southeastern Pennsylvania Transportation Authority*, 68 F.3d 1564 (1995).

32. *Vernonia School District, 47 J v. Acton*, 115 S.Ct. 2386 (1995).

33. Charles R. Orms, "Police Officers' Need for Collective Bargaining," unpublished. Used with permission of Charles R. Orms, President, Kentucky State Lodge, Fraternal Order of Police.

34. Lewin and Goldenberg, "Public Sector Unionism," p. 249.

35. Peter Feuille and John C. Anderson, "Public Sector Bargaining: Policy and Practice," *Industrial Relations* 19, no. 3 (Fall 1980), pp. 309–324.

36. Roger L. Bowlby and William R. Shriver, "The Behavioral Interpretation of Bluffing: A Public Sector Case," *Labor Law Journal* 32, no. 8 (August 1981), pp. 469–473.

37. Eugene H. Becker, "Analysis of Work Stoppages in the Federal Sector, 1962–81," *Monthly Labor Review* 105, no. 8 (August 1982), pp. 49–53.

38. Theodore W. Kheel, "Resolving Deadlocks without Banning Strikes," *Monthly Labor Review* 92, no. 7 (July 1969), p. 62.

39. John M. Capozzola, "Public Employee Strikes: Myths and Realities," *National Civic Review* 68, no. 4 (April 1979), pp. 178–188.

40. Aaron et al., *Public-Sector Bargaining*, p. 151.

41. Bernard F. Ashe, "Current Trends in Public Employment," *Labor Lawyer* 2, no. 2 (Spring 1986), pp. 277–298.

42. Randy Steele, "The Rise of PATCO," *Flying* 109 (March 1982), p. 35.

43. Ibid.

44. Michael Doan, "When Workers Took On Uncle Sam," *U.S. News and World Report*, August 1981, pp. 17–20.

45. Steele, "The Rise of PATCO," p. 35.

46. Herbert R. Northrup, "The Rise and Demise of PATCO," *Industrial and Labor Relations Review* 37, no. 2 (January 1984), pp. 167–184.

47. David Westfall, "Striker Replacements and Employee Freedom of Choice," *Labor Lawyer* 7, no. 1 (Winter 1991), p. 138.

48. Kenneth P. Swan, "Public Bargaining in Canada and the U.S.: A Legal View," *Industrial Relations* 19, no. 3 (Fall 1980), pp. 272–291.

49. David E. Bloom, "Is Arbitration Really Compatible with Bargaining?" *Industrial Relations* 20, no. 3 (Fall 1981), pp. 233–244. See also Patricia Compton-Forbes, "Interest Arbitration Hasn't Worked Well in the Public Sector," *Personnel Administrator* 29, no. 2 (February 1984), pp. 99–104.

50. Angelo S. DeNisi and James B. Dworkin, "Final-Offer Arbitration and the Naive Negotiator," *Industrial and Labor Relations Review* 35, no. 1 (October 1981), pp. 78–87; and John C. Anderson, "The Impact of Arbitration: A Methodological Assessment," *Industrial Relations* 20, no. 2 (Spring 1981), pp. 129–148.

51. J. Joseph Loewenberg, "The 1984 Postal Arbitration: Issues Surrounding the Award," *Monthly Labor Review* 109, no. 6 (June 1986), pp. 31–32.

52. 5 U.S.C. sec. 7103(a)(12) (1982).

53. 5 U.S.C. sec. 7106 (1982).

54. 5 U.S.C. sec. 7122 (1982).

55. Henry Graham and Virginia Wallace, "Trends in Public Sector Arbitration," *Personnel Administrator* 27, no. 4 (April 1982), pp. 73–77.

56. Michael J. Duane, "To Grieve or Not to Grieve: Why Reduce It to Writing?" *Public Personnel Management* 20, no. 1 (Spring 1991), pp. 83–90.

57. David L. Dilts and Clarence K. Deitsch, "Arbitration Lost: The Public Sector Assault on Arbitration," *Labor Law Journal* 35, no. 3 (March 1984), pp. 182–188.

CHAPTER 14

1. Foster Rhea Dulles and Melvyn Dubofsky, *Labor in America, A History* 4th ed. (Arlington Heights, IL: Harlan Davidson, 1984), p. 86.

2. Ibid., p. 96.

3. Joseph G. Rayback, *A History of American Labor* (New York: The Free Press, 1966), pp. 122–123; and Norman Hill, "Forging a Partnership between Blacks and Unions," *Monthly Labor Review* 100, no. 8 (August 1987), pp. 38–39.

4. Daniel Guerin, *100 Years of Labor in the USA* (London, England: Ink Links, 1979), pp. 144–160.

5. Michael Honey, "Fighting on Two Fronts: Black Trade Unionists in Memphis in the Jim Crow Era," *Labor's Heritage* 4, no. 1 (Spring 1992), p. 55.

6. Ibid., p. 59.

7. Michael Flug, "Organized Labor and the Civil Rights Movement of the 1960s: The Case of the Maryland Freedom Union," *Labor History* 31, no. 3 (Summer 1990), pp. 322–346.
8. Hill, pp. 38–39.
9. Henry Farber, "The Determination of the Union Status of Workers," *Econometrica* S1, no. 5 (September 1983), pp. 1417–1438.
10. Jonathan S. Leonard, "The Effect of Unions on the Employment of Blacks, Hispanics, and Women," *Industrial and Labor Relations Review* 39, no. 1 (October 1985), pp. 115–132.
11. The Coalition of Labor Union Women, *Forging Change for a New Generation of Families, Workers, and Unions* (New York: CLUW, March 1974).
12. Rayback, pp. 120–122.
13. Philip S. Foner, *Women and the American Labor Movement*, vol. 1 (New York: Free Press, 1979), pp. 290–300.
14. Philip S. Foner, *Women and the American Labor Movement*, vol. 2 (New York: Free Press, 1980), p. 327.
15. Robert Asher and Charles Stephenson, eds. *Labor Divided: Race and Ethnicity in U.S. Labor Struggles 1835–1960* (Albany, NY: State University of New York Press, 1990), pp. 22–23.
16. Michael J. Mandel and Christopher Farrell, "The Immigrants," *Business Week*, July 13, 1992, pp. 114–122.
17. Beverly Geber, "Managing Diversity," *Training* 27 (July 1990), pp. 23–30.
18. Ronald E. Kutscher, "Overview and Implications of the Projections to 2000," *Monthly Labor Review* 110, no. 8 (September 1987), pp. 3–9.
19. Ibid.
20. Valerie A. Persavich, "Industry Output and Employment through the End of the Century," *Monthly Labor Review* 110, no. 9 (September 1987), pp. 30–45.
21. Civil Rights Act of 1964, Title VII, 42 U.S.C. sec. 2000e.
22. U.S. Equal Employment Opportunity Commission, *Affirmative Action and Equal Employment: A Guidebook for Employers* (Washington, DC: GPO, 1974), pp. 57–58.
23. *Griggs v. Duke Power Co.*, 401 U.S. 424 (1971).
24. *McDonnell-Douglas Corp. v. Green*, 411 U.S. 792 (1973).
25. *Griggs v. Duke Power Co.*, 401 U.S. 424 (1971).
26. Marc Rosenblum, "Evolving EEO Decision Law and Applied Research," *Industrial Relations* 21, no. 3 (Fall 1982), pp. 340–351.
27. *Adarand Construction, Inc. v. Pena*, 115 S.Ct. 2097, 132 L.Ed. 2d 158 (1995).
28. *Franks v. Bowman Transportation Co.*, 424 U.S. 747 (1976).
29. *United Steelworkers v. Weber*, 443 U.S. 193 (1979).
30. *Bakke v. University of California*, 443 U.S. 187 (1978).
31. David Brookmirl, "Designing and Implementing Your Company's Affirmative Action Program," *Personnel Journal* 58, no. 4 (April 1979), pp. 232–237.
32. Thomas J. Piskorski and Michael A. Warner, "The Civil Rights Act of 1991: Overview and Analysis" *Labor Lawyer* 8, no. 1 (Winter 1992), pp. 9–17.
33. *Patterson v. McLean Credit Union*, 491 U.S. 164 (1989).
34. *Price Waterhouse v. Hopkins*, 490 U.S. 228 (1989).
35. *EEOC v. Arabian Am Oil Co.*, 111 S.Ct. 1227 (1991).
36. *Lorance v. AT&T*, 109 S.Ct. 2261 (1989).
37. *Martin v. Wilks*, 109 S.Ct. 2180 (1989).
38. *Ward's Cove Packing Co. v. Atonia*, 109 S.Ct. 2115 (1989).
39. *St. Mary's Honor Center v. Hicks*, 92-602 S.Ct. (1993).
40. Hope A. Cominsky, " 'Prompt and Effective Remedial Action?' What Must an Employer Do to Avoid Liability for 'Hostile Work Environment' Sexual Harassment?" *Labor Lawyer* 8, no. 2 (Spring 1992), pp. 181–201.
41. Paul S. Greenlaw and John P. Kohn, "Proving Title VII Sexual Harassment: The Court's View," *Labor Law Journal* 43, no. 3 (March 1992), pp. 164–171.

42. *Meritor Savings Bank v. Vinson*, 477 U.S. (1986).

43. David S. Bradshaw, "Sexual Harassment: Confronting the Troublesome Issues," *Personnel Administrator* 32, no. 1 (January 1987), pp. 51–53.

44. Donald J. Petersen and Douglas Massengill, "Sexual Harassment Cases Five Years after *Meritor Savings Bank v. Vinson*," *Employee Relation Law Journal* 18, no. 3 (Winter 1992–93), pp. 489–515.

45. *Schultz v. Wheaton Glass Co.*, 421 F.2d 259 (3d Cir. 1970).

46. 29 U.S.C. sec. 206(d)(1)(1977).

47. Winn Newman, "Pay Equity Emerges as a Top Labor Issue in the 1980s," *Monthly Labor Review* 105, no. 4 (April 1982), pp. 49–50.

48. Editorial Staff, American Society for Personnel Administration, *Resource*, pamphlet (Alexandria, VA: American Society for Personnel Administration, October 1983), pp. 1, 8.

49. Robert D. Hershey, "The Wage Gap between Men and Women Faces a New Assault," *Louisville Courier-Journal*, November 6, 1983, pp. 1, 4.

50. "A Report on the Glass Ceiling Initiative," U.S. Department of Labor, Lynn Martin, Secretary, 1991. See also Jeffery Greenhaus, Sarjob Parasuramon, and Wayne Wromley, "Effects of Race on Organizational Experience, Job Performance Evaluations and Career Outcomes," *Academy of Management Journal* 33, no. 1 (1990), pp. 64–86.

51. Adrienne Ward, "No More Excuses," *Advertising Age* 62 (November 25, 1991), p. 18.

52. Wayne E. Barlow, "Act to Accommodate the Disabled," *Personnel Journal* 70, no. 11 (November 1991), pp. 119–124.

53. Eric H. J. Stahlhut, "Playing the Trump Card: May an Employer Refuse to Reasonably Accommodate under the ADA by Claiming a Collective Bargaining Obligation?" *Labor Lawyer* 9, no. 1 (Winter 1993), pp. 71–96.

54. *School Board of Nassau County, Fl. v. Arline*, 107 S.Ct. 1123, 480 U.S. 273 (1987).

55. Lawrence Z. Lorber and J. Robert Kirk, *Fear Itself: A Legal and Personnel Analysis of Drug Testing, AIDS, Secondary Smoke, VDTs* (Washington, DC: ASPA Foundation, 1987), pp. 25–33.

56. *O'Connor v. Consolidated Coin Caterers Corporation*, 64 USLW 4243 (decided April 1, 1996).

57. "State Labor Law Developments," *The Labor Lawyer* 10, no. 3 (Summer 1994), p. 557.

58. "State Smokers' Rights Laws Comparison Chart," 8A *Labor Relations Reporter* sec. 451.111 (August 1996).

59. Jeffrey S. Harris, "Clearing the Air," *HR Magazine* 38, no. 2 (February 1993), pp. 72–79.

60. "State Sexual Orientation Bias Laws/Orders," 8A *Labor Relations Reporter* sec. 451.115 (August 1996).

CHAPTER 15

1. Roy J. Adams, "Regulating Unions and Collective Bargaining: A Global, Historical Analysis of Determinants and Consequences," *Comparative Labor Law Journal* 14, no. 3 (Spring 1993), pp. 272–300.

2. William B. Gould IV, *A Primer on American Labor Law*, 2nd ed. (Cambridge, MA: MIT Press, 1986), pp. 1–8.

3. James L. Cerruti and Joseph Holtzman, "Business Strategy in the New European Landscape," *Journal of Business Strategy* 11, no. 6 (November–December 1990), pp. 18–23.

4. Ibid.

5. Paul Windolf, "Productivity Coalitions and the Future of European Corporations," *Industrial Relations* 28, no. 1 (Winter 1989), pp. 1–20.

6. Clause Schnabel and Joachim Wagner, "Unions and Innovative Activity in Germany," *Journal of Labor Research*, 13, no. 4 (Fall 1992), pp. 393–406.

7. Windolf, "Productivity Coalitions."

8. Bob Mason and Peter Bain, "The Determinants of Trade Union Membership in Britain: A Survey of the Literature," *Industrial and Labor Relations Review* 46, no. 2 (January 1993), pp. 332–351.

9. Leonard Rico, "The New Industrial Relations: British Electricians' New-Style Agreements," *Industrial and Labor Relations Review* 41, no. 1 (October 1987), pp. 63–73.

10. Joseph Krislov, "How Does the Japanese Industrial Relations System Differ?" *Labor Law Journal* 40, no. 6 (June 1989), pp. 338–339.

11. T. Kane, *Strategy and Structure of Japanese Enterprises* (Armonk, NY: M.E. Sharpe, 1984), p. 319.

12. Krislov, "How Does the Japanese Industrial Relations System Differ?" pp. 338–346.

13. Karl Schoenberger, "Self-Denial Wears Thin for Japanese," *Los Angeles Times*, July 7, 1989, pp. 1, 10.

14. Motohiro Morishma, "Information Sharing and Collective Bargaining in Japan: Effects on Wage Negotiations," *Industrial and Labor Relations Review* 44, no. 3 (April 1991), pp. 469–485.

15. Ehud Hararí, "Japanese Labor Organizations and Public Policy," *Social Science Japan* no. 6 (February 1996), as reported on the homepage, Institute of Social Science, University of Tokyo <www.iss.u-tokyo.ac.jp./center/SSJ/SSJ6/Hararí.html>

16. Ibid.

17. Ruth Wang and Michael Ballot, "Chinese Labor Relations in Transition: Where Will All the Workers Go?" *Labor Law Journal* 46, no. 6 (June 1995), pp. 376–379.

18. Basu Sharma and Peter Sephton, "The Determinants of Union Membership Growth in Taiwan," *Journal of Labor Research* 12, no. 4 (Fall 1991), pp. 429–437.

19. Michael Parks, "Soviet Miners' Strike Grows: 100,000 Join In," *Los Angeles Times*, July 17, 1989, pp. A1, 2.

20. "Russia Faces General Strike as Wages Arrears Mount," *ICEM Info* 1, no. 4 (1996), p. 1.

21. Michael Ballot, "Labor Relations in Russia and Eastern Europe," *Labor Law Journal* 46, no. 3 (March 1995), pp. 169–174.

22. Horst Brand, "Perestroika and Its Impact on the Soviet Labor Market," *Monthly Labor Review* 114, no. 12 (December 1991), pp. 38–45; and "The State of Union Activity in Central Eastern Europe," *International Executive* 32, no. 5 (March–April 1991), pp. 39–41.

23. Ballot, "Labor Relations in Russia and Eastern Europe."

24. Bahman Bahrami, "Australian Labor Relations: The Recent Developments," *Labor Law Journal* 47, no. 5 (May 1996), pp. 327–341.

25. Raymond Harbridge, "Collective Bargaining Coverage in New Zealand: The Impact of the Employment Contracts Bill," *Australian Bulletin of Labor* 17, no. 4 (April 1991), pp. 310–324.

26. Harold L. Gilmore, "Industrial Democracy in Zambia: Is It Working?" *Labor Law Journal* 39, no. 4 (April 1988), pp. 199–207.

27. Peter G. Bruce, "Political Parties and Labor Legislation in Canada and the U.S.," *Industrial Relations* 28, no. 2 (Spring 1989), pp. 115–141.

28. Joseph B. Rose and Gary N. Chaison, "Canadian Labor Policy as a Model for Legislative Reform in the United States," *Labor Law Journal* 46, no. 5 (May 1995), pp. 259–272.

29. Harbridge, pp. 310–324.

30. Charles J. Hollon, "Employee Profit Sharing under the Mexican Federal Labor Law," *Labor Law Journal* 47, no. 5 (May 1996), pp. 323–326.

31. Mark E. Zelek and Oscar de la Vega, "An Outline of Mexican Labor Law," *Labor Law Journal* 43, no. 7 (July 1992), pp. 466–470.

32. "North American Free Trade Agreement," *HR Magazine* 36, no. 12 (December 1991), p. 85.

33. "Poll Finds Free-Trade Pact Faces a Big 'Huh?' " *Louisville Courier-Journal*, July 12, 1993, p. A3.

34. Peter Behr, "NAFTA, Bringing Old Enemies Together," *Washington Post National Weekly Edition* 10, no. 46 (September 13–19, 1993), p. 12.

35. David Espo, "Tough Win on Trade Pact a Big Victory for Clinton," *Louisville Courier-Journal*, November 18, 1993, p. A1. Also, Mike Brown, "Ford Line Prompts End-of-Session Laughter," *Louisville Courier-Journal*, November 21, 1993, p. 12B.

Ability to pay. The financial position of a company and its ability to change its wage rates are general factors involved in negotiations. They are usually a reflection of company profits and will be a basis of a negotiator's wage proposal.

Absenteeism (no-fault). An innovative absenteeism policy, negotiated by management and the union, in which an employer may take action against an employee whose excessive absences from work significantly reduce service to the company.

Absolute Rank Principle. The seniority principle giving employees on merging seniority lists the same ranking that they held on the prior seniority lists, resulting in two employees being ranked first, two employees ranked second, and so on.

Accretion doctrine. The practice of allowing the addition of new employees and jobs to existing bargaining units, provided their work satisfies the same criteria of the original unit.

Acquired Immune Deficiency Syndrome (AIDS). A disease caused by the human immunodeficiency virus that attacks the immunity system, rendering it unable to fight off other diseases. With no current effective treatment, the mortality rate of this disease is extremely high.

Affirmative action programs. A selection policy employers use to analyze their workforce for underuse of certain persons or groups of individuals considered to have been deprived of opportunities because of illegal discrimination, and to develop a plan of action to correct that problem.

Age Discrimination in Employment Act of 1967 (ADEA). Passed by Congress in 1967, and amended in 1978 and 1986. The ADEA makes it illegal for government agencies, labor unions, and employers with 20 or more employees to discriminate against individuals over age 40. The 1986 amendment prohibits any mandatory retirement age and requires employers to provide the same health benefits to workers of all ages.

Agency shop. A labor contract provision that requires employees to contribute a sum of money equal to union membership dues, but does not require the employee to join the union. The employee benefits from collective bargaining by the union and in turn gives financial support to the union for negotiations, contract administration, and other actions.

Agreements and composite agreements. In New Zealand, arbitrators decide wage and other disputes between an employer and employee and bind the parties by agreement. This is a substitute for collective bargaining.

Albermarle Paper Co. v. Moody. The Supreme Court ruling that set standards for back pay awards granted for discrimination, as protected by Title VII of the Civil Rights Act. The Court also ruled that the reliability of employment tests must fall within the EEOC guidelines.

Alcohol testing. (*See* Drug and alcohol testing.)

Alexander v. Gardner-Denver, Co. A landmark case in which the Supreme Court ruled that arbitration of a discrimination claim does not bar an employee from filing a Title VII (Civil Rights Act) suit of the same claim. The Court also ruled that great weight would be given to the arbitrator's decision.

Americans with Disabilities Act (ADA). Passed in 1990, this act gave civil rights act protections to people with disabilities. Prohibits discrimination in jobs, housing, public buildings and services, and transportation.

Anthropomorphic robots. Industrial robots that approximate the appearance and functions of humans.

Appropriate unit. The number of employees and jobs in an organization determined by the National Labor Relations Board to comprise a bargaining unit for purposes of collective bargaining.

Arbitrability. The challenge of whether or not a disputed issue is subject to arbitration under the terms of the contract.

Arbitration. A process in which the parties involved agree to submit an unresolved dispute to a neutral third party, whose decision is final and binding.

Arbitrator's award. The arbitrator's decision in a grievance case, presented in written format and signed by the arbitrator. Examples of awards include back pay and reinstatement of job or benefits.

Arbitrator's opinion. An arbitrator's written statement discussing the reasons for the decision in the case.

Associated unionism. A new type of worker organization that combines employee associations with the traditional union. Tends to focus on support of the members rather than collective bargaining.

Auction bargaining. The willingness to make concessions during negotiations, demonstrated by both parties stating their positions, presenting their proposals, then trading off the proposals to arrive at agreeable terms.

Awards and composite awards. In New Zealand, arbitrators fix wages by deciding disputes between employers and employees that bind all of the industry. This is a centralized system of labor-management relations and is a substitute for collective bargaining.

Back-loaded contracts. A multiyear contract that provides a lower wage adjustment in the first year, with higher wage increases in the later years.

Bargaining items. The issue previously determined to be negotiable in a collective bargaining session. Items are generally either economic or noneconomic in nature.

Base. An employee's general rate of pay per unit or hour, disregarding payments for items such as overtime, pension benefits, and bonuses.

Borg-Warner doctrine. The 1958 case that outlined three categories of bargaining subjects and the rules governing each. They are (1) *mandatory subjects*, such as wages and hours; (2) *permissive subjects*, such as pension benefits of retired employees; and (3) *illegal subjects*, such as a proposal for a closed shop or discriminatory treatment.

Boulwarism. A collective bargaining approach in which management presents its entire proposal as its final offer, holding nothing back for further negotiations. This approach lacks any "give-and-take" in bargaining.

Boys Market **case.** A case in which the Supreme Court upheld an injunction against a union that struck an employer despite a no-strike clause in its contract. The Court also ruled that an employer is ordered to arbitrate while seeking a court injunction against a union striking in violation of a no-strike clause.

Bumping. A procedure commonly used during layoffs, in which employees with greater seniority whose jobs are eliminated displace employees with lesser seniority. Bumping is more often used in companies with plantwide seniority in unskilled jobs.

Business agent. The full-time administrator of a local union paid to handle the negotiation and administration of the union contract as well as the daily operation of the union hiring hall.

Cafeteria plans. Refers to flexible benefit plans that offer employees a decision on what benefits they want from the employer.

Call-in pay. A supplemental payment given to employees called back to work before they are normally scheduled to return.

Certification. The determination by the National Labor Relations Board that a union represents the employee's free choice, and therefore the union can become the official bargaining agent for a bargaining unit.

Cheap riders. Employees within a bargaining unit who choose not to join the union which bargains for an agreement, but they are required to pay a fee to the union to provide their share of the costs associated with negotiations (usually 20%–85% of regular unions' dues).

Check-off provision. A contract provision requiring that the employer deduct union dues directly from union employee paychecks. The collected dues are then deposited in the union treasury.

Civil Rights Act of 1964. A federal law designed to eliminate racial and sexual discrimination. Title VII of the law makes it unlawful for an organization of 15 or more employees to discriminate against an individual because of race, color, religion, sex, or national origin. The act received major amendments in 1972 (Equal Employment Opportunity Act) and 1978 (Pregnancy Discrimination Act).

Civil Service Reform Act of 1978. Signed into law in October 1978, the act was designed to reform the outdated federal civil service structure and was modeled after the National Labor Relations Act. One of the major provisions is a three-member panel, the Federal Labor Relations Authority, whose purpose is to oversee labor-management relations within the federal government, thus acting in a manner similar to that of the National Labor Relations Board in the private sector.

Civil service system. A governmental system of employment based on merit. Employee selection is based on examination scores or an assessment of experience and abilities. Promotion, advancement, and discipline are based on job performance.

Clayton Act. Passed by Congress in 1914, this law was designed to limit the use of the Sherman Anti-Trust Act in labor disputes and to limit the court's injunctive powers against labor organizations, stating that labor was not a commodity and union members were not restrained from lawful activities. Strict interpretation by the courts limited the effectiveness of the act.

Closed shop. A union security arrangement that requires employers to hire only union members. Closed shops were made illegal under the Taft-Hartley Act.

Coalition of Labor Union Women. Founded in 1974, this union was to promote the unionization of women in the workforce.

Collective bargaining by objectives (CBO). A method of collective bargaining developed by Reed C. Richardson, in which the negotiating parties list the bargaining items, evaluate them according to feasibility and priority, and list their initial position on each. This method of collective bargaining allows each party to see objectively its range of compromise prior to the negotiations.

Collyer case. A 1971 ruling in which the National Labor Relations Board deferred its jurisdiction, ordering the concerned parties to resolve an unfair labor practice dispute through arbitration. The board ruled that cases involving unfair labor practices can be ordered to arbitration if the dispute centers on conditions negotiated in the collective bargaining agreement.

Combinations. Original organizations of employees who banded together for better wages and working conditions. They were outlawed in most countries as a threat to private property rights of employers and a restraint on trade.

Community of interest doctrine. Descriptive criteria used by the National Labor Relations Board to evaluate a group of employees and determine whether they constitute an appropriate bargaining unit.

Company unions. An employee organization formed by and recognized within a company, initiating reforms such as health benefits and better living conditions. This type of union usually does not meet the requirements of the National Labor Relations Act and thus is not considered a true union.

Comparable worth. The doctrine requires that pay be equal not only for men and women performing the same job, but for all jobs requiring similar skills, effort, responsibility, and working conditions, regardless of the external labor market.

Compressed workweek. Any workweek in which the scheduled working days are fewer than the traditional five workdays per week.

Concerted activities. Any legitimate action taken by employees to further their common but not individual interests, such as wages, hours, and working conditions.

Concession bargaining. Collectively bargained reductions in previously negotiated wages, benefits, or work rules, usually in exchange for management guaranteed employment levels during the term of a contract.

Consolidated Omnibus Budget Reconciliation Act (COBRA). A law passed by Congress in 1986 that provides for the continuation of medical and dental insurance for employees, spouses, and dependents in the event of an employee's death, termination, divorce, or other loss of health-care eligibility. Employees may elect to continue health care coverage for up to 18 or 36 months, if they pay 100 percent of the cost.

Contract bar. The general rule followed by the National Labor Relations Board, stating that a current and valid labor contract can prevent another union from petitioning for an election and being certified as the exclusive representative for the term of the existing contract.

Contributory plans. A pension plan in which the employer contributes a portion of the funding and the employee contributes the other portion.

Coordinated bargaining. The joint bargaining with several unions and/or employers being represented by one negotiating team. The various unions of employers agree to one overall contract.

Cordwainers conspiracy cases. A series of court cases that challenged the association of cordwainers and their wage agreement, ruling their action to be an illegal conspiracy and a conspiracy to impoverish others. The 1806 Supreme Court ruling that found the mere combination of workers to conspire to raise their wages to be illegal was later overturned.

Corporatism. A nationally centralized system of collective bargaining between business corporations, mass unions, employee associations, and government.

Costing wage provisions. The methods of determining the financial impact of a contract change such as (1) annual cost; (2) cost per employee per year; (3) percent of payroll; and (4) cents-per-hour.

Cost-of-living adjustment (COLA). The negotiated compensation increase given an employee based on the percentage by which the cost of living has risen, usually measured by a change in the consumer price index (CPI).

Craft severance. The desire of a group of craft employees to break away from an existing union or one that has traditionally represented them.

Craft unions. Workers who have been organized in accordance with their craft or skills.

Craft units. A bargaining unit composed exclusively of workers with a specific and recognized skill, such as electricians or plumbers.

Current expenditure pension plan. A pension plan in which pensions paid to retired employees are funded from a company's current operating income and are treated as a current expense. This type of pension plan cannot guarantee that its current employees will have retirement pensions.

Decertification. The process of removing a union as the certified representative of employees within a bargaining unit.

Deferred wage rate increases. Wage rate increases that become effective at later dates as specified in the collective bargaining agreement.

Delaying tactics. The methods used by either negotiating party to impair the negotiation process, such as the cancellation of meetings, lengthy speeches, or the infrequent scheduling of meetings.

Departmental seniority. A seniority system in which employees accrue seniority according to the time that they work within a specific department, with the seniority credit being valid only in that department.

Disciplinary procedures. The program of actions that an employer may take, as outlined in a collective bargaining agreement, against an employee who has violated work rules or policies.

Discretionary workweek. A workweek designed to offer employees greater freedom in regulating their lives by allowing them to choose their daily starting and stopping times within certain restrictions.

Drug and alcohol testing. The practice of requiring applicants and/or employees to submit to a screening test for chemical substances that can adversely affect their job performance.

Dual employer. A situation involving a unionized employer which establishes a separate, similar operation that is nonunion. Such employers are most often found in the construction industry.

Duty of fair representation. The Taft-Hartley requirement that a union must fairly represent all of the members of the bargaining unit. This includes the negotiation of the collective bargaining agreement, and its enforcement without discrimination or hostility. The requirement includes the pursuit of grievances.

Duty to sign a contract. The obligation of both parties to reduce to writing and sign any agreement reached through the collective bargaining process. Refusal to sign can be declared an unfair labor practice.

Economic strike. An employee strike over the failure to negotiate economic issues such as wages, benefits, or other conditions of employment. During an economic strike, the employer is entitled to replace strikers permanently, and need only reinstate those for whom it has vacant positions.

Employee Assistance Programs (EAPs). Company-sponsored programs designed to assist employees in resolving personal problems, such as stress, finances, and alcoholism, that may adversely affect job performance and attendance.

Employee Retirement Income Security Act (ERISA). The first comprehensive reform law, passed by Congress in 1974, to protect employee pensions. Additionally, it places strict regulations on private pension plans and protects the vested rights of employees' beneficiaries. The act also created the Pension Benefit Guarantee Corporation.

Employee stock ownership plan (ESOP). An employee benefits plan in which the employees are given shares of stock or are allowed to purchase discounted stock. Through this program, the company hopes to develop a pride of ownership among the employees that will result in increased efficiency and production, low turnover, and possibly opposition to outside unionization.

Employer unfair labor practices. Activities by an employer that interfere with an employee's rights as protected by the National Labor Relations Act. Examples include the interference of the formation of a union, discrimination against union member employees, and refusal to bargain with employee representatives.

Equal Employment Opportunity Commission (EEOC). A federal commission created by the 1972 amendment of the Civil Rights Act of 1964. The EEOC was appointed to investigate employee complaints of job discrimination and to file suit in federal district court if it is unable to obtain a conciliation agreement between the parties involved.

Equal pay for equal work. The principle that job pay rates should be dependent on relevant factors, such as quantity or quality of work, and independent of irrelevant factors, such as sex or race.

Escape clause. A contract provision that allows either negotiating party to be released from a previously agreed-to provision.

Exclusive bargaining agent/representative (exclusivity rule). Having been certified as the collective bargaining agent for a particular unit, the union has the legal right to bargain for all the employees within the unit, nonunion as well as union.

Executive Order (E.O.) 10988. The executive order signed by President John F. Kennedy in 1962 allowing federal employees bargaining representation, forms of employee recognition, and the right to collective bargaining.

Fact-finding. A dispute resolution procedure in which a neutral third party reviews both sides of a dispute and then publicly recommends a reasonable solution.

Family and Medical Leave Act (FMLA). Passed in 1993, it gives employees up to 12 weeks of job-protected, unpaid leave for illness or family emergencies.

Featherbedding. A labor practice that unions use to create work for their members; e.g., by limiting production, using more workers than a job requires, or paying for work not performed. The practice is prohibited by the Taft-Hartley Act.

Federation of unions. The uniting of many national unions to increase union power and recognition. The federation serves as a national spokesperson for its members while it itself is not a union. The only existing federation of unions in the United States is the AFL-CIO.

Firefighters v. Stotts. The precedent Supreme Court decision that ruled that the affirmative action goals of a consent decree requiring the hiring of minorities cannot be given greater protection than a seniority system established by a collective bargaining agreement, in the event of unanticipated layoffs.

Flexible benefit plans. Negotiated in lieu of fixed benefits, employees can choose the benefits that fit their needs among a designated list and within a price established by the contract. Usually includes medical insurance, vacation, pensions, life insurance.

Flextime. An alternative work schedule that allows employees to determine their starting and stopping times each day, provided that they work a set number of hours per day or week, and work their scheduled core hours.

Floating holiday. A paid holiday that may be used at the employee's discretion or when mutually agreed to by the employee and management.

Follow the Work Principle. A seniority principle, used in the merger of two companies, which allows employees to continue previously earned seniority on separate seniority lists when their work with the merged company can be separately identified.

Formal grievance. The step in a grievance procedure at which the grievance is reduced to writing, usually on a grievance form.

Franks v. Bowman Transportation Co. A 1977 Supreme Court ruling that the normal operation of a seniority system is not an illegal employment practice, as outlined in Title VII, even if it may have some discriminatory results, unless the system was deliberately established for discriminatory purposes.

Free riders. Employees within a bargaining unit who choose to not join the union which bargains for an agreement for the unit. While the employees receive all negotiated benefits, they pay no costs associated with the union.

Front-end loading. A deferred wage increase in which a larger proportion of the total increase occurs in the first year of a multiyear contract.

Gaman. The Japanese tradition of individuals practicing self-denial and perseverance for the greater national cause.

Gissel **doctrine.** The Supreme Court decision that allows the use of authorization cards as a substitute for a certification election when an employer shows unfair labor practices and that the results of an election may be unreliable. The ruling allows an employer both to reject authorization cards as proof of a majority vote and to request a representation election.

Givebacks. Collectively bargained reductions in previously negotiated wages, benefits, or work rules, usually in exchange for management-guaranteed employment levels during the term of the contract.

Glass ceiling. Refers to the artificial and often invisible barriers for women and minorities keeping them from reaching top management positions.

Globe doctrine. The policy set by the National Labor Relations Board to help it determine the representation wishes of employees when establishing an appropriate bargaining unit. The board may use the secret ballot election process as a means of giving weight to the desires of a group of employees, such as a smaller craft group within a larger industrial group.

Good faith bargaining. Refers to the reasonable efforts demonstrated by both management and labor during labor negotiations. Generally, it requires both sides to meet, confer, and make written offers. It does not require either side to concede or agree, but rather to show reasonable intent to set the terms of employment in a collective bargaining agreement.

Grievance. Any formal complaint filed by an employee or union concerning any aspect of the employment relationship. A grievance is generally a perceived violation of a contract provision.

Grievance mediation. The use of a neutral third party as one step in a grievance procedure to interpret the provisions of a contract in an effort to resolve a dispute and avoid arbitration.

Ground rules. The general procedures and policies that each party agrees to adhere to during negotiations. These are usually agreed to in writing prior to the negotiations and may include such items as the time, date, and location for the negotiating session.

Guaranteed Income Stream (GIS). An alternative plan to the traditional supplemental unemployment plans, the GIS plan has three major differences: (1) it furnishes benefits to eligible workers until they retire; (2) worker qualification is based on earnings, rather than employment; and (3) benefits are only partially offset by outside earnings.

Haymarket Square Riot. A meeting held in Chicago in 1886 to protest the police shooting of striking workers that ended with the bombing of police officers and the subsequent trial and conviction of eight defendants. The Knights of Labor did not participate, but because of their previous violence, they were associated with the riot and began to lose public support.

Health-care units. Eight basic units identified by the NLRB for the health-care industry under the 1974 Health Care Amendment to the NLRA.

Health Maintenance Organizations (HMO). Organizations of physicians and other health-care professionals that provide a wide range of health services to employees and their families for a fixed, prepaid fee instead of a fee-for-service basis. HMOs strive to emphasize preventing care, lower total health-care cost, and total health care at one location.

Holiday pay. Contract provision requiring an employer to pay for time not worked on a holiday.

Homestead Strike. An 1892 strike at a steel plant owned by Andrew Carnegie. Plant operator responded with paid police and strikebreakers. The strike ended when martial law was declared and state militia were sent in by the governor.

Hot cargo agreements. A negotiated contract provision stating that union members of one employer have the right to refuse to handle nonunion or struck goods of other employers.

Illegal bargaining subjects. Items termed illegal and nonnegotiable by the Borg-Warner case ruling or the National Labor Relations Board. These items cannot be negotiated even if both parties are in agreement. Examples of illegal subjects are a closed shop, racial separation of employees, or discrimination against nonunion members.

Immigration Reform and Control Act (IRCA). A federal law passed in 1986 that requires employers to verify the identity and work eligibility of each new employee. In addition, the act makes it illegal for an employer to hire, recruit, refer, or continue to employ an illegal alien. The act also makes it illegal for employers to discriminate against "foreign-looking" applicants.

Impasse. A stalemate that occurs in negotiations between union and management over the terms and conditions of employment. Impasses are often resolved through mediation or arbitration.

Industrial jurisprudence. The system of rules and regulations that labor and management fashion to define their specific rights and obligations in the workplace.

Industrial union. A labor union whose membership is composed primarily of semiskilled or unskilled workers such as automobile workers and steelworkers, who are organized on the basis of the product they produce. Usually all production and maintenance (not management) workers within an organization will belong to the same industrial union.

Interest arbitration. A process used to resolve an impasse in negotiations where the parties submit the unresolved items to a neutral third party to render a binding decision.

Intermediate organizational units. A level of union organization consisting of regional or district offices that serves to bring the national and local union offices closer together.

International Workers of the World (IWW). Founded in 1905, this federation hoped to organize all the workers of the world into one union. Its political agenda included the overthrow of capitalism.

Job bidding (up, down, lateral). The process of a company posting notices of new job positions in order to give permanent employees the opportunity to apply. Bids are based on plant seniority and competency and fall into three categories: (1) *up-bid*, a bid from a lower to a higher pay grade; (2) *down-bid*, a bid from a higher to a lower pay grade; and (3) *lateral-bid*, a bid from one classification to another classification in the same pay grade.

Job evaluation. A systematic method of determining the worth of a job to an organization. This is usually accomplished by analysis of the internal job factors and comparison to the external job market.

Job sharing. Generally refers to the division of hours worked in a full-time job into two part-time positions. It often refers to the holding of one full-time position by two employees who are friends or relatives.

Job splitting. A method of creating part-time work, in which the tasks of a single full-time job are divided into two separate part-time jobs, each having separate duties.

Joint committees. Cooperative labor-management committees formed to analyze and solve organizational problems.

Jurisdictional strike. A strike called as the result of a dispute between two competing unions over who has the legal authority (jurisdiction) in a specific situation.

Just cause. Sufficient or proper reasons for which management has the right to discipline or discharge employees.

Knights of Labor. An organization open to skilled and unskilled laborers, formed in 1869 as The Noble Order of the Knights of Labor (KOL). It sought economic and social reform through political action rather than strikes.

Labor agreement. A phrase referring to a collective bargaining agreement between a union and management.

Labor injunction. A court order that prohibits any individual or group from performing any act that violates the rights of other individuals concerned. Until 1932, injunctions were primarily used by employers to end boycotts or strikes.

Labor-Management Reporting and Disclosure Act (Landrum-Griffin Act). Passed in 1959 to help regulate internal union operations, the act amended the Wagner Act and Taft-Hartley Act and resulted in the limitation of boycotts and picketing, the creation of safeguards for union elections, and the establishment of controls for the handling of union funds.

Labor organization unfair labor practices. Any action taken by a union that does not demonstrate the union's desire to negotiate in good faith, such as refusing to sign an agreement previously agreed to by negotiators for the union and management.

Length of Service Principle. A method used to establish seniority during the merger of two companies, in which an employee's length of service is considered regardless of the company for which he or she worked; therefore, the two seniority lists are merged into one with no loss of any previous seniority to any employee.

Lincoln Mills case. In a landmark decision, the Supreme Court ordered an employer to arbitrate grievances as provided for in a collective bargaining agreement, stating that an employer's agreement to arbitrate grievance disputes was a tradeoff for the union's agreement not to strike.

Local union. The union that represents a specific unit or geographic area of unionized workers and is usually affiliated with a national union. One main function of the local union is to negotiate and administer contracts with employers.

Lockout. An employer's refusal to allow employees to return to work until an agreement is signed. It is considered the employer's equivalent of an economic strike and is intended to bring pressure on workers to accept management's terms.

Maintenance of membership. A union security provision which requires that those who are union members when a contract is entered into, or those who subsequently join the union, must remain union members until the contract expires.

Make-whole concept. The concept of providing back pay, position, and lost seniority in an attempt to return to the employee those things that he or she may have been deprived of because of discrimination.

Management rights. The rights of management to govern the workplace in areas not subject to discussion with the union or to collective bargaining. Included in these rights are production control, price setting, supervision of the workforce, scheduling, and sales.

Mandatory bargaining subjects. Those items that must be bargained in good faith, if either party so requests, such as wages, hours, and benefits.

Maryland Freedom Union. A union organized by African-Americans after the civil rights movement of the 1960s to respond to their union needs.

Master agreement. The collective bargaining agreement negotiated between a national union and an industry. The terms and conditions of the contract serve as employment guidelines for the entire industry. Local terms and conditions may be negotiated in addition to the master agreement.

Mediation. The introduction of a neutral third party into collective bargaining when the union and management are unable to reach an agreement. While mediators have no decision-making powers, they can make recommendations, suggest new proposals to either or both parties, and actively work to develop compromises.

Molly Maguires. A group of union organizers who were prosecuted and either executed or imprisoned after a 1875 strike against anthracite mine owners failed.

Multiemployer units. Collective bargaining conducted between a group of related employers and a single representative union.

Multinationals. A corporation that operates in more than one nation for a significant portion of its business. Also called transnationals.

Multiplant units. Bargaining which occurs between a single employer and a union or unions that represent workers in two or more plants of the employer.

National Colored Labor Union. Organized in 1870, this union was in response to the segregated National Labor Union and the American Federation of Laborers.

National Labor Relations Act (Wagner Act). Passed in 1935, this act was created to recognize employee rights to organize and bargain collectively through representatives of their own choosing. The act required employers to meet with the certified representatives of a majority of their employees. The act made several unfair labor practices illegal and created the National Labor Relations Board to hold employee elections and to enforce the act.

National Labor Relations Board (NLRB). An independent agency of the federal government that serves to investigate unfair labor practices, determine appropriate bargaining units, certify unions that legally represent a majority of employees, and administer the provisions of the National Labor Relations Act.

National Labor Union. Founded in 1866, this was the first union to allow skilled and unskilled workers to join in one union. It pursued a political as well as a workplace agenda.

National (or international) union. A union formed by regionally organizing local unions. Its powers, determined by the charter drawn between itself and the local unions it represents, may range from advising the local unions to collective bargaining.

National War Labor Board. An agency formed in 1918 (during World War I) to prevent labor disputes from disrupting the war efforts by providing mediation for labor-management disputes and establishing wage stabilization.

Norris-La Guardia Act. Passed in 1932, this act restricts the federal courts from issuing injunctions in labor disputes, except to maintain law and order. The act also made yellow-dog contracts illegal.

Office of Federal Contract Compliance (OFCC). Created by Executive Order 11246, this office implements equal employment opportunity in the federal procurement process and specifies the regulations applying to all federal organizations, contractors, and subcontractors.

On-call pay. Additional employee compensation given to workers who must remain available to be called in to work if needed.

Open shop. A form of union security in which the workers within a bargaining unit may decide whether or not to join a union. Those who choose not to join are not required to pay union dues or fees, or amounts equal to dues or fees.

Opener clause. A clause in a collective bargaining agreement that allows negotiations to take place during the term of the contract on certain mandatory items, such as wages or insurance coverage.

Organizing drive. A movement initiated by dissatisfied employees or a union organizer to submit a representation petition to the NLRB and win a representation election, thus providing union certification and collective bargaining.

Outsourcing. When work which could be performed within a bargaining unit is given by management to outside, nonunion providers. The purpose of such action is to lower costs and/or reduce the number of bargaining unit employees. A similar practice is called privatization in the public sector.

Pattern bargaining. A collective bargaining practice in which a national union strives to establish equal wages and benefits from several employers in the same industry. The union uses the negotiated contract of one company to serve as a model contract for the entire industry.

Pay-back agreements. A signed agreement that requires an employee who voluntarily quits before a specified time, usually one year, to pay back to the employer the cost of certain benefits.

Pay equity. A historic union doctrine of "equal pay for equal work" that provides for one standard pay rate for each job and all employees who perform it.

Pay for time not worked. Wages paid to an employee for time away from the job, such as breaks, lunch, vacations, maternity leave, sick leave, jury duty, and personal leave.

Pendleton Act. Also known as the Civil Service Act of 1883, the Pendleton Act created the federal merit system. The act was responsible for (1) the creation of a Civil Service Commission to administer open competitive examinations for selecting federal employees; (2) the right of Congress to regulate the wages, hours, and working conditions of public employees; (3) the merit principle; and (4) the protection of employees from being fired for failure to make campaign contributions, and even forbidding some classes of employees from making such contributions.

Permanent striker replacements. Under NLRB, when workers are engaged in an economic strike, management can hire permanent replacements. After the strike, the striking workers cannot claim their jobs back.

Permissive bargaining subjects. Those items not related to wages, benefits, working conditions, or other mandatory subjects, which may be negotiated in collective bargaining if both parties agree. However, if one party refuses to negotiate a permissive item, the other party cannot claim bad faith bargaining or declare an impasse in negotiations over the item.

Personal day. A paid employee holiday (sometimes called a floating holiday) that can usually be selected at the employee's discretion. Personal days often are given in place of sick days, which are more limited in use.

Piece-rate systems. A wage system in which employees receive a standard rate of pay per unit of output. The rate of pay is usually based on the average level of production, with bonus rates given on output units exceeding the average level.

Plantwide seniority. An employee's length of continuous service with the employer. The employee's accrued seniority in the plant allows for competition for the same position with any other employee within the same unit.

Posturing. The pattern established during the initial bargaining session in which each negotiating party demonstrates its willingness to negotiate, identifies its basic bargaining positions, and generally sets the tone of the negotiations.

Premium pay. Wages that exceed the standard or regular pay rate given an employee for work performed under undesirable circumstances, such as overtime hours, weekend work, holiday work, or dangerous and hazardous circumstances.

Pressure bargaining. A negotiating technique in which one side that believes it holds a superior position pressures the other side to accept its position on each issue. As an example, if the union believes the employer cannot withstand even a short strike, it may use its position of strength by threatening to strike over many issues.

Primary strike. A strike called by a union for economic reasons to achieve its bargaining objectives.

Principled negotiations. A negotiating process developed by the Harvard Negotiations Project, in which attention is focused on the merits of the negotiating items, rather than on the attitudes of the negotiating parties.

Probable cause. A general term referring to the reasonable possibility that a certain condition exists, such as employer wrongdoing in a discrimination case.

Productivity theory. The negotiating position that employees should share in increased profits gained by the greater productivity achieved because of their efforts.

Professional Air Traffic Controllers (PATCO) Strike (1981). The first declared national strike against the federal government resulted not only in the firing of all striking PATCO workers, but also the prohibition of any PATCO striking worker from ever working again as an air traffic controller.

Profit sharing. A pay incentive system in which employees receive a share of the employer's profits in addition to their regular wages. A precise formula specifying how profits will be distributed to employees is the heart of a profit-sharing plan.

Prohibited conduct. Activities used to interfere with union organizational efforts, such as the threat of loss of benefits, misrepresentation of campaign materials, and interrogation of employees.

Public-sector union security. The ability of a public-sector union to grow and to perform its collective bargaining role without interference from management or other unions. Automatic dues deduction is the most commonly allowed public-sector union security provision.

Pullman Strike. The strike in 1894 by Pullman Car Company employees, who were demanding higher wages and lower rents. The strike was honored by other groups of railroad workers, who shut down railroads from Illinois to Colorado until the strike was broken by a federal court injunction and the use of federal troops.

Pyramiding of overtime. The payment of overtime on overtime, which occurs if the same hours of work qualify for both daily and weekly overtime payment. Most contracts prohibit this type of payment.

Qualifications of an arbitrator. The attributes or characteristics generally desired in an arbitrator, such as neutrality, honesty, experience, and legal training.

Quality circles (QC). The voluntary meeting of groups of workers with common work interests for the purpose of identification, analysis, and development of solutions to work problems.

Quality of working life (QWL). The process used by the union, the employees, and management to determine how the work environment may be changed to create a better quality of life, with the desired result being increased efficiency and employee job satisfaction.

Railway Strike. The railroads' former policies of cutting wages and increasing living costs to their employees resulted in the first general strike in the United States. The bitter and violent strike of 1877 involved railroad workers from Maryland to Missouri, who protested 10 percent wage cuts after a 35-percent cut three years earlier.

Ratio-Rank Principle. The seniority principle that combines seniority lists according to the ratio established by comparing the total number of employees in the merging groups. If Group A has one hundred employees, and Group B has fifty employees, the ratio is 2:1. The new seniority list will then give positions one and two to the highest employees from Group A, and position three to the highest employee from Group B.

RC petition. The petition filed with the National Labor Relations Board by a group of employees or a union representing employees seeking certification of an appropriate unit for purposes of collective bargaining.

Reasonable accommodation. Under the ADA and the Rehabilitation Act, employers must make changes in the workplace to enable disabled Americans to work. The ADA spells out what accommodation is considered reasonable.

Remaining units. Employee groups that are separate from the primary production and maintenance units in their job duties, such as professional, technical, guard, and clerical units.

Reporting pay. The minimum payment guaranteed for employees who report for work, even if work is not available, provided they have not been given adequate notice not to report to work.

Representation cases. Cases in which the National Labor Relations Board determines the appropriate unit of employees for purposes of collective bargaining.

Republic Aviation case. A 1945 court case in which the Supreme Court upheld an employee's legal right to seek union support during personal time. The Court ruled that union solicitation by employees outside of their work time, even on company property, was legal.

Reserve clause. A practice in professional sports whereby only one team is given the right (by the league) to negotiate a contract with a player. Thus the player is not free to negotiate a better contract with another team.

Reserved rights. The theory generally contending that all rights not specified in an agreement, or shared with a union, remain the unwritten or implied rights of management.

Residual units. Employees who do not fit into the major job units except by their common working situations, such as janitors and salespeople, may be grouped together to form a unit. Employees left unrepresented after the bulk of the employees are organized may be entitled to separate representation by a residual unit.

Restricted rights. The union's use of contract clauses to impose specific restrictions on management's decision-making rights, such as plant relocation or subcontracting.

Reverse discrimination. A general, nonlegal term referring to preferential treatment given to minorities in excess of affirmative action requirements, resulting in the discrimination of nonminority individuals.

Rights arbitration. The submission to arbitration for the interpretation or application of current contract terms. In grievance cases, the arbitration involves the rights of the parties involved under the terms of the contract.

Right-to-work laws. The laws permitting states to prohibit agreements requiring membership in a labor organization as a condition of employment.

Robotics. The operation of programmable robots (computer controlled machines) to perform routine operations such as assembly, painting, welding, and inventory.

Rolling strike. A strike technique used by unions that moves a strike against an employer from location to location so that hiring replacement workers becomes more difficult.

Roll-up. The direct increase in the cost of benefits that results from a negotiated increase in wage rates, such as social security, overtime pay, and pensions.

Rules of evidence. An arbitrator's determination of how a hearing will be conducted, how evidence will be presented, and how much weight or credibility will be given to the evidence presented.

Runoff election. The successive election held when a representation election involving three or more choices results in no one choice receiving the majority vote. The choices receiving the most votes are again voted on, until one receives the majority of the votes cast.

Salting. Members are encouraged by their union to seek employment at a nonunion company. Once hired they promote unionization. The union may supplement their regular pay with a supplement to provide equity with a "union" wage.

Saturn agreement. The agreement between the UAW and the General Motors Corporation that included several innovative joint labor-management practices and was arrived at before the new Saturn plant in Tennessee began production.

Scanlon plans. A group incentive plan designed by Joseph Scanlon, in which greater production is achieved through increased efficiency, with the accrued savings being distributed among the workers and the employer.

Secondary boycotts. Union pressure exerted on a neutral party indirectly related to the primary employer. The neutral party then exerts pressure against the primary employer.

Self-managed teams. A small group of employees given responsibility for an entire segment of a work process.

Seniority. The length of service an individual employee has with an employer or unit.

Seniority list. A company list used to identify employees in a bargaining unit according to their length of continuous employment.

Separability clause. A contract clause stating that any portion of a contract declared invalid by state or federal law shall be declared null and void, while still holding the remainder of the contract valid.

Severance pay. A lump-sum or a dispersal of payments given to employees who are permanently separated from the company through no fault of their own.

Sexual harassment. Unwelcome sexual advances, requests for sexual favors, and other verbal or physical conduct having the purpose or effect of unreasonably interfering with an individual's work performance, or creating an intimidating, hostile, or offensive working environment.

Shared work. The reduction by management of employee work time, and consequently wages, in an effort to reduce personnel costs without reducing personnel.

Shop-In. Slang term referring to a union method of conducting a secondary boycott. Several union members converge on retail establishments, which sell a boycotted product and cause disruptions in service by overcrowding the stores and parking lots and thus a loss of regular customers. The result desired by the union is to pressure the retailers into not stocking the boycotted product.

Showing of interest. The demonstration of employee support, usually in the form of petitions or authorization cards, that a union is required to compile before a representation election can be considered.

Sick leave. Time off allowed an employee because of illness or injury, with the provision of continued employment when the employee is able to report back to work.

Sovereignty doctrine. The unrestricted and paramount power of the people to govern. In the public sector, this is presented as a basic reason for not allowing employees to have collective bargaining rights or the right to strike their public employers.

Spillover. The duplication of wage and benefit increases for nonunion and management personnel that an employer provides as a result of negotiated union increases.

Staggered start. An example of the discretionary workweek system in which the employee chooses one of several alternative starting times and works an eight-hour day.

Standard rate. The flat or hourly rate of pay established for each job classification or occupation within a plant or industry, effective for the duration of the collective bargaining agreement.

Steelworkers Trilogy **cases.** Three 1960 Supreme Court rulings that upheld the grievance arbitration process and limited judicial intervention.

Steps of a grievance procedure. The detailed procedure an employee must follow when filing a grievance. The grievance must be (1) discussed with the supervisor; (2) put in writing; (3) taken to the union-management level; (4) reviewed by a plantwide grievance committee; and (5) taken to arbitration.

Steward. An on-the-job union representative who carries out the responsibilities of the union in the plant at the departmental level.

Stipulated units. A bargaining unit agreed to by an employer and a union that cannot be altered by the National Labor Relations Board.

Subcontracting. The arrangement by a company to have another firm make goods or perform work that could be accomplished by the company's own employees, usually because the work can be done more efficiently or for less cost.

Substantially equal. The conclusion that two jobs, although not identical, may be considered generally equal and thus require equal pay. Evaluations of effort, skills, working conditions, and responsibility are necessary to compare the jobs.

Successorship. The status of the collective bargaining relationship between an employer and the union when a change in the ownership of the organization or a change in a union occurs.

Sunshine laws. Statutes requiring that public sector collective bargaining sessions be open to the public.

Superseniority. The special seniority rights granted to union officers and committee personnel that override ordinary seniority during layoffs and recall situations in order to maintain active union representation within the company.

Surface bargaining. The act by either negotiating party of simply going through the motions without any real intention of arriving at an agreement.

Surviving Group Principle. A principle used for the determination of seniority in merging companies, in which seniority lists are merged by adding the names of the acquired company employees to the bottom of the list of names of employees of the acquiring company.

Taft-Hartley Amendments. Also known as the Labor Management Relations Act of 1947, it generally was created to counterbalance the provisions of the National Labor Relations Act of 1935. The law declared closed shops and automatic check-offs illegal, cited unfair labor union practices, and protected the rights of employees who chose not to unionize. The law also created the Federal Mediation and Conciliation

Service, restricted secondary boycotts and strikes, and gave states the right to outlaw union shops.

Technological change and retraining. A company's need to increase productivity through the use of new machinery and equipment often results in employee reduction or termination. Many companies have developed employee assistance programs that provide testing, vocational training, and job placement assistance in a conscientious effort to help employees affected by technological change to reenter the labor market.

Telecommuting. Work scheduling that allows employees to do some or all of their work at home, usually involving the use of computers.

Telescabbing. The use of modern technology, such as automated equipment, as a substitute for labor during a strike instead of hiring scab labor. The term was first applied to the 1983 AT&T strike when management relied on automated equipment to process 97 percent of all telephone calls.

Termination-at-will. The termination or discharge of an employee by an employer for any reason or no reason.

Terms of employment. Those items generally negotiated between union and management, including wages, benefits, work rules, job classifications, work practices, seniority, promotions, and management and union rights.

Title VII. A section of the Civil Rights Act of 1964 that prohibits an employer from discriminating against an individual because of the individual's race, color, sex, religion, or nationality, and delegates authority to the Equal Employment Opportunity Commission to investigate an employee's complaints and act as his or her attorney.

Totality of conduct doctrine. A test or review of the total bargaining process used to determine if a negotiating party has acted in good faith, as opposed to isolated acts that may have occurred during negotiations. Generally requires some "give-and-take" by a negotiating party to warrant good faith.

Transnational. A corporation that operates in more than one nation for a significant portion of its business. Also called multinationals.

Tripartite arbitration board. An arbitration board composed of one or more members representing management, an equal number representing labor, and a neutral member who serves as chairperson.

Two-tier wage systems. A wage system that pays newly hired workers less than current employees performing the same or similar jobs.

Undue hardship. Under the ADA, an employer can refuse to accommodate a disabled person if it will be too expensive or will change the operation significantly.

Unemployment insurance. Established under the Social Security Act of 1935 and funded through payroll taxes paid by employers, the program is designed to provide compensation, after a brief waiting period, to those employees who have been laid off from employment. Recipients are expected to seek employment actively.

Unfair labor practice strike. A strike called over an employer's action determined by law to be an unfair labor practice, such as employee discrimination because of union activity.

Unilaterally changing conditions. Any method an employer may use during contract negotiations, such as changing wages or hours of employment, in an effort to bypass the union and deal directly with the employees.

Union hiring hall. A local union office that coordinates workers seeking employment with available jobs. Since closed shops are illegal under the Taft-Hartley Act, hiring halls today must serve both union and nonunion members.

Union security. The provisions of collective bargaining agreements that directly protect and benefit the union, such as dues check-off and union shops.

Union shop. A union security provision that all new employees must join the union and pay dues within a specified time.

United Steelworkers v. Weber. A landmark reverse discrimination case in which the Supreme Court upheld the discrimination provisions of the Civil Rights Act, concluding that Congress's intent to eliminate discrimination must be considered along with the literal interpretation of the laws, and that employers have the right to establish affirmative action plans in an effort to eliminate racial imbalance.

Value added concept. The theory that wages should equal the contribution of labor to the final product.

Variable hours. A method of employment in which the employee contracts to work for a specified time each day, week, and so on, with the option of varying the schedule daily if both parties agree.

Vested rights. The time required for employees to accrue an irrevocable right to pension contributions made by their employer.

Vietnam Era Veterans Readjustment Act of 1974. An act passed to help Vietnam War veterans secure jobs, requiring that all organizations holding government contracts of $10,000 or more hire and promote these veterans.

Vocational Rehabilitation Act of 1973. A federal law requiring any employer with federal contracts of

$2,500 or more to establish an affirmative action program for the handicapped. This program must include recruitment efforts, advancement, and environmental changes within the organization.

Wage employment guarantees. A contract negotiation assuring employees a minimum amount of work or compensation during a specified amount of time.

Wage reopener. A collective bargaining provision, effective for the term of the contract, that allows contract talks to be reopened only for the renegotiation of wage rates.

Wage survey. The collection and appraisal of data from various sources used to determine the average salary for specified positions in the job market.

Wellness program. Any of a variety of company-sponsored programs designed to enhance the employee's well-being, such as stress management, cancer detection, exercise programs, and complete physical fitness centers.

Whistleblowers. Employees or other individuals who make public allegations of alleged employer wrongdoing.

Wildcat strike. Any work stoppage not authorized by the union.

Wobblies. Nickname for members of the Industrial Workers of the World (IWW) organization.

Workforce 2000. A study of the demographics of the workforce in the United States in the year 2000. Shows an increase in women, minorities, and immigrants and a decrease in native-born white males.

Work sharing. A method of reducing the number of employees to be laid off by asking all employees to work fewer hours.

Workers Adjustment and Retraining Notification Act (WARN). Commonly known as the Plant Closing Act, WARN became effective in 1989 and generally requires employers to provide 60 days advance written notice to employees and communities of either a plant closing or mass layoffs.

Worker's compensation. A program designed to provide employees with assured payment for medical expenses or lost income due to injury on the job.

Zipper clause. A provision of a collective bargaining agreement that restricts either party from requiring the other party to bargain on any issue that was not previously negotiated in the agreement for the term of the contract.

INDEX

9194310715SS

For additional information, visit the Web sites of these **companies** featured in this text.

American Airlines
http://www.amrcorp.com/amr/amr_home.htm

Anheuser–Busch, Inc.
http://www.budweiser.com/index.htm

AT&T
http://www.att.com/

Beverly Enterprises
http:www.beverlynet.com/

Caterpillar
http://www.cat.com/

Chrysler Corporation
http:www.chryslercars.com

6490
9194

DuPont
http://www.dupont.com

Electronic Data Systems
http://www.eds.com:80/home.html

Ford Motor Company
http://www.ford.com/global/

91943555
92 85

General Electric Company
http://www.ge.com/

General Foods/Kraft
http://www.kraftfoods.com/

General Mills
http://jobs.genmills.com/index.htm

General Motors
http://www.gm.com/index.cgi

Honda
http://www.honda.com

IBM
http://www.ibm.com/

Lockheed Martin Corporation
http://www.lmco.com/

McDonald's Corporation
http://www.mcdonalds.com/

Nissan Motor Company, Ltd.
http://www.nissan.co.jp

PepsiCo, Inc.
http://www.pepsico.pcy.mci.net/web_pages/
pepsicohome.html

Pizza Hut
http://pizzahut.com/

Southwest Airlines
http://www.iflyswa.com/

Union Pacific Railroad
http://www.uprr.com/

UPS
http://www.ups.com

USX U.S. Steel
http://www.usx.com/ or go to
http://www.usx.com/uss.htm